INTRODUCTION TO LAW IN CANADA

Ontario Edition

Volume 1

Laurence M. Olivo
B.A., M.A., J.D. of the Ontario Bar

Captus Press

INTRODUCTION TO LAW IN CANADA (Ontario Edition, Volume 1)
Laurence M. Olivo

ISBN 978-1-55322-304-7

The publisher and the editor gratefully acknowledge the authors, publishers and organizations for their permission to reproduce their work in this book. Care has been taken to trace ownership of copyright material contained in this book. The publisher will gladly take any information that will enable the rectification of any reference or credit in subsequent editions and apologizes for any errors or omissions.

Captus Press Inc.
Mail: Units 14 & 15
        1600 Steeles Avenue West
        Concord, Ontario
        Canada   L4K 4M2
Telephone: (416) 736–5537
Fax: (416) 736–5793
Email: info@captus.com
Internet: http://www.captus.com

Canada   We acknowledge the financial support of the Government of Canada through the Canada Book Fund for our publishing activities.

0 9 8 7 6 5 4 3 2
Printed in Canada

Volume 1
Contents

Preface

This book emerged twenty years ago out of the need to provide a suitable text on the law for non-lawyers studying legal topics and issues in a variety of college and university programs. What started as a 5-module text for law clerks at Seneca College of Applied Arts and Technology in Toronto is now a 2-volume work used across Canada with modules on many facets and areas of law, including province-specific versions of some of the modules.

Many authors from across the country with expertise in various areas of law have contributed to or updated modules. Some have been involved from the beginning; others are more recent arrivals — but all are dedicated to presenting often complex material in a well-written style that meets our students' needs. It is our contributors' efforts that have made this book a unique and valuable text.

In bringing out this new edition, we are cognizant that law texts, unlike fine wines, do not get better with age. The law changes constantly, and it is important that our students have a text that is up to date and cover recent legal developments.

This new, updated edition would not have been possible without the Pauline Lai and her staff at Captus Press. As ever, they have met the challenge to produce a high quality text on time.

L.M. Olivo
Toronto, Ontario
August 2014

Introduction to Legal Studies —
Law as a Concept and System

Laurence M. Olivo
SENECA COLLEGE

Learning Objectives

After reading this chapter, the reader should be able to:

➣ appreciate that law is more than simply a set of rules
➣ understand that law is a flexible concept that varies in accordance with the social needs it must meet
➣ understand the various explanations about why we obey rules
➣ understand the limits of law
➣ understand the arguments in favour of different schools of legal interpretation
➣ understand the dynamics of the relationship between law and morality
➣ understand issues involving law and social change
➣ understand the societal functions performed by a legal system
➣ identify the characteristics of a valid legal system in a democratic society

TABLE OF CONTENTS

INTRODUCTION

In this chapter, we will first discuss the concept of law in general, and then examine it as a component of a democratic society. While there are certain basic elements that are common to all legal systems, we will see that there are a number of perennial "open" questions about law to which there is no one "right" answer on which everyone can or does agree. Instead, we will see that the answers to questions about law depend in part on the nature of a particular society, and in part on the values and expectations of members of that society. We will see that there are various reasons given for why we obey laws, how we should interpret them, whether they should reflect morality and what the limits of law are. We won't necessarily tell you the "right" answer, because there is not necessarily a right answer to all of these questions. There is often simply a range of answers that depend on legitimate, but different, points of view. We hope you will gain an appreciation for the complexity and flexibility of law as a concept and as a system, and you will feel that you are equipped to intelligently weigh and judge competing points of view. This is not simply an abstract, academic exercise — in a democratic society it is a necessary one. As a responsible citizen, you have to consider points of view, examine your own values and assumptions, analyze, and decide. We hope that this chapter will help you to do that and help you to appreciate the social context that lies behind the specific areas of law that are discussed in subsequent chapters of this text.

THE CONCEPT OF LAW

What Is Law?

Consider the various definitions of law set out in Exhibit 1.1.

These definitions of law are not all the same; some leave out aspects that seem to be important in others. The first definition focuses on law as having a function of regulating behaviour, and instilling tolerance and forbearance. It says nothing about where law comes from, or about what happens if you do

---

Definitions of Law   **EXHIBIT 1.1**

"[A] set of rules that enable people to live together and respect each other's rights."[1]

"[A] body of rules for the guidance of human conduct which are imposed upon and enforced among the members of a given state."[2]

"[A] statement of circumstances in which the public force will be brought to bear through the courts."[3]

"That which is laid down, ordained or established."[4]

Notes
1. Statement by Irwin Dorfman, President, Canadian Bar Association, 1975, cited in John A. Willes, *Contemporary Canadian Business Law*, 4th ed. (Toronto: McGraw-Hill Ryerson, 1994) at 3.
2. William Blackstone, *Commentaries on the Laws of England*, cited in Willes, *ibid.* at 3.
3. Oliver Wendell Holmes, cited in Willes, *supra* note 1, at 3.
4. *Black's Law Dictionary*, Revised 4th ed. (St. Paul, MN: West Publishing Company, 1968).

not obey it. The second definition also refers to ordering behaviour, but it introduces the further ideas of legal rules as being imposed externally, applying within a state and being enforced if disobeyed. The third definition merely says that in some situations you will be compelled by state force to obey the law, but the definition does not identify the situations in which obedience will be compelled. The fourth definition also focuses on regulating and ordering behaviour, and again talks about imposing rules externally and enforcing them against those who disobey.

Several themes emerge:

- Laws are rules imposed on us by an external body.
- Laws enable us to live together by controlling conflict.
- Laws teach us to tolerate and respect others (and perhaps the rules themselves — telling us what is "right" or "moral").
- Laws compel us to behave in certain ways because sanctions are applied if we behave improperly.
- Laws indicate when the force of the state will be used to compel you to behave in certain ways.

While these definitions help us to define what law is as a social structure, they leave us with a variety of questions about law and how it functions. The answers to these questions, as we will see, depend in part on the political, philosophical, religious and social views of the individuals asking the questions.

What Is a Legal Rule?

It should be clear from the definitions at the head of this section that not all rules are legal rules. So, how do we distinguish legal from non-legal rules? Consider the following rules of conduct:

- If someone opens a door for you, you say, "Thank you."
- You may not kill another person.

If someone opens a door for you and you walk through it and say nothing, you have broken a rule by being rude, but all would recognize that the rule you have violated is a social **norm**, based on a social value (courteousness). People may avoid you or shun you or say unpleasant things about you because your behaviour is unpleasant to them. But no one will arrest you, find you guilty of an offence, or bring down state-supported sanctions on you. If you kill another person, however, you may also be violating a norm based on the high value placed on human life, but all would recognize that the negative reactions would include detention and a formal determination that a legal rule had been broken, followed by legal punishment.

What makes some societal rules "legal" rules and others not? The short answer is that we can identify legal rules because they have certain features other rules do not: they are backed or enforced by the authority and power of the state. But why are some rules singled out for this kind of treatment and not others? Legal rules are those that are deemed to be very important in preventing a society from becoming dysfunctional and breaking down into anarchy and chaos. In most societies, legal rules help to create order and certainty, and control the use of force and fraud by individuals to get what they want. For example, most societies will have rules about ownership of property, exchange of property rights, and methods to resolve conflicts and disputes. These rules are so central that all in a society must agree to be bound by them and must accept the consequences of not obeying those rules.

How Do Individuals Recognize Some Rules as "Legal" Rules?

In every society, there are clues or indicators to tell members of the society that some rules are legal and must be obeyed. One commentator refers to such clues or indicators as the "rule of recognition",[1] and they will vary from society to society. In traditional societies, the rule of recognition will often involve magic, either alone or mixed with religion, to identify certain basic rules. Supernatural origins for rules go a long way towards getting people's attention.

Consider the Ten Commandments. These are 10 basic rules to govern a simple, tribal society. To get everyone's attention, they are revealed by Moses, a recognized leader, in a dramatic way as a revelation directly from God. It must have been quite clear to all but the most dense that these rules were a serious business; this was not just risking others' displeasure for not holding open a door. Look at the nature of the rules: they are not trivial — honouring parents and the deity, no murdering, no stealing, no lying, and so on.

In our society, appeals to magic or the supernatural are not entirely absent. Consider the formal court procedures, the judges' robes, and the ritual recitation for the opening of courts calling upon the deity to protect the sovereign, and the use of oaths to ensure that witnesses tell the truth.

In Canada, we have a variety of rules of recognition, based on our political and social values. We recognize sanctions for rule breaking backed by the force of the state as identifying legal rules, and we recognize certain acts — the passage of rules by a legislature, or the pronouncements of judges — as ways of creating legal rules. We also have some rules about rule making and enforcement — constitutional law — that define valid law and valid legal procedure and tell us whether a rule is a valid legal rule or something else.

Why Do We Obey Legal Rules?

The first reaction of many would be to say that we obey because we fear we will be punished if we do not. While this is probably true in part, it is not a wholly satisfactory explanation. If fear of punishment were the only reason for obedience, we would need to have, as one English Court of Appeal Judge said, "a policeman at everyone's elbow". But clearly, most of us obey most legal rules most of the time, even when the threat of enforcement is not immediate. Most people do not use force and fraud to get their way. Why is this?

There are a number of reasons: one legal commentator, H.L.A. Hart, has said that we obey in part because we have "a habit of obedience".[2] What Hart means here is that through a **socialization** process we learn and internalize norms and values that help us to recognize legal institutions, laws and the requirement of obeying them. Think of how children are socialized in our society. From birth, children are taught to follow rules; schools and other institutions further enforce this. Often, we discover there are negative and unpleasant consequences for not following rules. A desire to be accepted, "to fit in", may also contribute to following rules. So may the fact that there are positive benefits for those who obey.

While Hart's approach explains *how* people learn to obey, it does not explain their motivation for doing so. Explaining motivation requires an examination of human nature. There are two generally competing views on the relationship between human nature and obedience to law. They are associated

---

[1] H.L.A. Hart, *The Concept of Law* (Oxford: Clarendon Press, 1961) chs. 1 and 2.
[2] *Ibid.*

with two English political writers. The more pessimistic view of human nature is that of the 16th-century clergyman and academic, Thomas Hobbes. The more optimistic view is that of the 17th-century writer, John Locke.

The Hobbesian View of Human Nature

Hobbes sees human beings as selfish, violent, and predisposed to use force and fraud to get what they want.[3] The society in which they lived was anarchic, where life was, as Hobbes described it, "nasty, brutish and short". It was only when individuals realized that they could improve their lives by entering into civil society that they were prepared to give up their freedom to resort to force and fraud, which they had while in the state of nature. Hobbes described individuals as entering into a covenant with a sovereign, in which they gave up their individual rights to act as they wished, by permitting the sovereign to have a monopoly on law making and enforcement and the use of force. A covenant without the sovereign having the power to compel obedience would be worthless: as Hobbes put it, "a covenant without the sword is but words." A just and fair sovereign would ensure that individuals lived according to the rule of law and would punish those who did not. But there was no assumption that individuals would behave co-operatively just because it was to their material advantage. Nor was there any notion that individuals had any input into the law, or that their consent to its continued operation was required. The threat of state violence beyond their control was still needed to keep individuals in line and to give them a sense of security. In the end, for Hobbes, we obey the sovereign's rules because we fear the disorder that will arise if we do not, and because we will certainly be punished if we do not.

The Lockean View

Locke, writing in the late 17th century, took quite a different view of human nature and of individuals in the state of nature. His view was that in the state of nature individuals were given to living peacefully with each other and co-operating to assist one another. They were not automatically disposed to engaging in force and fraud. And their lives were not seen as being "nasty, brutish and short". To make their lives easier yet, Locke argued that individuals consented to enter into a civil society by way of a compact, where a ruler ruled and made laws only with the consent of the governed, and where the ruler respected certain basic individual rights: chief among them, the right to own property. For Locke, the purpose of law was not to suppress a violent human nature, but to regulate human activity in the interest of preserving and enhancing property and individual rights. For Locke, individuals obeyed law only so long as they consented to rule by the sovereign, and only so long as the sovereign kept his part of the deal by respecting their political and legal rights, and their right to property. Individuals did not obey out of fear of either the sovereign or each other. Rather, they obeyed because they saw the law as serving their interests, and because they had consented to its creation — it was "their" law: they had some control over what the rules were and how they were enforced.

Locke's approach underlies the view of law we have in a democratic state: we obey only so long as a majority of us consent to the law-making process and to the laws made under that process. Mere fear of disorder and of punishment for breaking the law is no longer the only reason for obedience.

---

[3] The work in which this viewpoint was first set out by Hobbes was his principal work, *The Leviathan*. For a summary of his work, see G. Sabine, *A History of Political Thought*, 3d ed. (New York: Holt Rinehart and Winston, 1965) at 455–76.

What Are the Limits of Law?

The legal system can bring order and certainty to the law, and control force and fraud, but only so long as the whole of the society is prepared to be governed by the **rule of law**. We cannot have a situation in a democratic society where the law applies only to some but not to others. Another way of putting this is to say that no one is above the law. If we are all subject to the law equally, we are more likely to accept our obligations under law, knowing that we have lots of company.

Living under the rule of law has another important consequence. Those elected to govern us must obey the same law that we do, and not use their power to ignore laws they don't like. It also means that they must follow the rules for governing and running the state. For example, in Canada political power is exercised by elected representatives. If an army general, unhappy with the civil government, decides to call out his troops and seize power by a *coup d'état*, there is no question that he is putting himself above the law. Here, we have rule by physical force rather than by law. At this point, the most elegant and inspiring national constitution is no more than wastepaper.

If the law fails to deal with or contemplate situations of serious evil, we may have to recognize that the law will not assist us in dealing with evil. We cannot expect law to solve every problem, and some matters may have to be left to non-legal means. For example, after World War II, leading Nazis were tried for crimes against humanity that did not exist when the offences were committed. Crimes against humanity were not part of international law until after the war, and they were not acts contrary to the valid law of the German state. In such a situation, there may be solutions, but they may not come from the law.[4] To deal with these issues in the legal system, we would have to do a number of things that would violate fundamental principles about how the rule of law should operate. For example, we would punish people for offences that were not known legal offences at the time they were committed.

The law is also limited in its reach when it simply is not respected or accepted by a majority or large minority of the population. The laws about the consumption of alcohol and drugs furnish very clear examples. The attempt to outlaw the sale of alcohol in the United States in the early 20th century was largely judged to be a failure. Prohibition simply did not have any support in urban areas or among those parts of the population who did not see alcohol as the devil's mousetrap but, instead, saw it as part of the expression of their culture. No matter what the law said, and no matter how much effort the government made to enforce it, the law was simply ineffective because large numbers of people were prepared to disobey it. In the end, the law was repealed.

The same can be said for the various attempts to prevent the use of controlled drugs, especially cannabis. Some police departments, and even the Canadian Senate, have suggested that the time and effort and money spent in trying to control cannabis use are largely wasted. In the United States, a "war on drugs" has been raging since the 1980s, with little to indicate that the "war" is being won. Again, many people simply do not accept the idea that using some types of drugs does any significant social harm that requires the law's intervention.

---

4 This is taken up in Discussion Question #2 at the end of this chapter.

When individuals decide that the law is wrong, or evil, or even silly, they may engage in civil disobedience, either as an individual act or together with others in a group. The early challenges by Blacks in the 1950s and 1960s to state laws requiring segregation on the basis of race were active forms of civil disobedience. They differed from the type of disobedience seen with respect to drug and alcohol consumption laws. The civil rights protesters were not just breaking laws they did not like; they were also making a political statement when they disobeyed segregation laws.

Should Law Reflect Morality? Whose Morality?

Civil rights protesters decided to disobey the law because they believed the law to be wrong and immoral. The perception that law reflects morality, or that it *should* reflect morality, has deep roots in our minds and in our history, going back to Roman law. Today, this view is expressed in a theory of law called **natural law**, which has its origins in Roman law and the religious law of the Middle Ages. Those who favour this approach argue three points:

- Either through a religious or secular perspective, it is possible, through the use of reason, to discover the true morality that the law should reflect. Divine or natural law is superior to human law, and human law should mirror natural or divine law.

- Human law that does not reflect the moral content of natural or divine law is not valid law.

- Last, law that is not valid need not be obeyed.

Thus, civil rights protesters could argue that segregation laws were immoral because they were contrary to natural law principles and, therefore, need not be obeyed.

This works as long as we all agree on what is morally right. The problem arises when we ask the question, "By whose morality do we decide what we should or should not obey?" This problem is illustrated by the polarized positions on the right of a woman to obtain an abortion. On the one hand, those who believe that life begins at the moment of conception regard abortion as unlawful killing. On the other hand, those who believe that a pregnant woman has a paramount right to control her own body regard abortion as a right that should be available to every woman without having strangers dictate what happens to her. At present, the Supreme Court of Canada has ruled that the last attempt by Parliament to regulate abortion as part of the criminal law violated the *Charter of Rights and Freedoms* and was, therefore, unlawful. This left Canada with no law at all regulating abortion, a condition that has prevailed for several decades, as Parliament has been disinclined to tackle this difficult and divisive issue again, in part because there are polarized views as to which moral principles apply.

The abortion debate illustrates the problems with respect to the relationship between law and morals. It is simply not possible to "prove" that one side or the other is morally correct in the way that scientific truths are proved. When you ask a scientist how she knows she is correct, she can point to her experiment and observations, which others can repeat. If others obtain the same result, we then know a scientific finding is valid or true. If you ask a natural law theorist how he knows he is right, in the end his answer depends on "right reason" or "divine revelation". But his assumptions cannot be tested or proven to be true. For those who require empirical evidence, the natural law theorist can provide none.

An answer to this problem of morality and law has been proposed in another legal theory called **legal positivism**. The positivists say that natural law is "nonsense on stilts",[5] and argue that it is ridiculous to suppose that morality is anything more than the assumptions, beliefs and prejudices of those that hold them. This is not to say that moral views are not important or that the law should not reflect them. But it is nonsense to say that we can know for certain which of several competing moral views might be correct and, on that basis, decide what law is valid and what law is not. The positivist answer is to say the following:

- The law is no more than the language that expresses it.
- The law should accurately express the intent of the lawmakers, and we should accurately interpret the language of the law without distorting the meaning of the language used.
- We should not be concerned with the moral content of the law as a test for validity.

For the positivist, the law simply is: it may be morally obnoxious, but the answer is not to deny that it is law but to recognize it as law that needs to be altered. In the meantime, the duty of the positivist is to apply the law as he or she finds it.

The positivist is also concerned with procedure. Once you have determined what the proper procedure is for making, interpreting, administering and enforcing the law, the positivist is content if the law meets those procedural requirements. Behind this lies the positivist concern that the law is made according to the rules for rule making in a given society, and operates with order, certainty and regularity — if it does, then the law is valid. If it does not, then it is not valid. But its validity will not turn on whether its content is morally correct.

Judicial Realism

Positivism and natural law identify two opposed philosophical positions on the role of law as a social institution, and on how legal rules should be interpreted. But they do not explain how individuals in the legal system actually engage in judicial decision making. The school of **judicial realism** that developed in the 1920s and 1930s claims to provide this explanation. This is a behavioural theory that holds the psychosocial makeup of judges as the most important factor in understanding how they interpret and apply law. Judicial realism provides a way of predicting and explaining judicial behaviour that realists claim more accurately describes the interpretative process than simply trying to determine if a judge is a positivist or natural law adherent. Realism goes further by trying to explain why a particular judge might take a positivist or natural law position, and why a particular judge might be a positivist on some issues and a naturalist on others. From this view came the idea that judicial theories or legal reasons given in case decisions aren't the "real" reasons for judicial decisions, but merely a smokescreen for the real reasons, which are a judge's political, social or moral values, or personality type.

For example, realists argued in the 1930s that the U.S. Supreme Court, in opposing the Roosevelt New Deal legislation, wasn't just applying the common law to strike down these statutes, but was using it as a cover for its conservative social and economic values. Similarly, a realist might argue today that the Supreme Court of Canada, in striking down Parliament's attempts to legislate on abortion, was not just applying the rules in the *Charter of Rights and Freedoms*, but was using its own values to decide the outcome. Realism does have its detractors, some of whom refer to it as the "what the judge had for breakfast" school of jurisprudence. By this they mean that to focus on a

---

[5] The English 19th-century legal positivist, Jeremy Bentham, first used the phrase.

judge's personality and values as the source of a judicial decision overstates the case and ignores the extent to which judicial values of objectivity, rationality and fairness may minimize the role of a judge's personal views.

What Is Justice?

We can sum up the argument about law and morality by asking the question, "What is justice?" A natural law advocate would argue that justice is providing a morally acceptable outcome. A positivist would argue that justice is applying legal rules literally, without injecting morality or values, so that like cases are treated alike. A realist might argue that asking what justice is is the wrong question. Instead, justice is a legal outcome dependent on the psychosocial makeup of those who decide and interpret the law.

Does Law Lead or Follow Social Change?

The rule maker, be it a king, dictator, legislature or judge, may make rules that may change societal institutions and forms of conduct or behaviour. For example, when Parliament passed the first Canada-wide *Divorce Act* in 1968, it made no-fault divorce possible for the first time, and a divorce, in general, became easier and less expensive to obtain. While attitudes towards divorce were changing anyway, the law brought about an increase in the number of divorces in the country, with various cultural and social changes following the change in the law. Suddenly, there were more single-parent families, divorce was not seen as a social stigma or disgrace, and a new phenomenon — the "blended family" — made its appearance, composed of two remarried spouses, and the children of both their previous marriages.

On the other hand, when the rule maker makes or changes law to accommodate changes already occurring in society, then the law is responding to social change that has already occurred in society. When, for example, the first legislation giving trade unions the right to bargain collectively was passed in Canada in the late 19th century, the law was merely regulating economic and social changes in labour relations that were already well underway.

These examples are fairly straightforward, but the reality is a bit more complex. In many cases, it is hard to say whether the law is bringing about social change or social change is transforming the law. The process of law making is a dynamic one. Lawmakers may be responding to the perceived views of the electorate on some issues, to inputs and ideas from the civil service on others, or to inputs from interest groups and lobbyists. These inputs may represent views and values that are already held by individuals and groups. To the extent that these views become reflected in the law, they, in turn, may bring about further social change.

Consider the complex relationship between legal and social change. In 1990, the Ontario government attempted to change the laws governing employment benefits by extending the definition of who qualified for these benefits. The definition had included married or unmarried spouses of heterosexual employees. It was now proposed to extend these benefits to "same-sex" spouses. The initial impetus was a lawsuit by a government employee who argued that denial of benefits to his same-sex spouse amounted to discrimination on the basis of sex and sexual orientation. But there were also inputs — pros and cons — from various lobby groups, and a lengthy public consultation process, indicating same-sex family benefits had some support, as well as some opposition, in society. At that time, the law was not changed by the legislature. The legislation was introduced but failed to pass. However, the law did change as the result of a series of court decisions, taken over a 10-year period, where judges held that denial of benefits to same-sex spouses was a violation of the equality rights under section 15 of the *Charter of Rights and Freedoms*. The change in the law then attracted little attention as it came incrementally. In the same period, the government had quietly extended such benefits to its employees, as had a number of private employers.

How one views the relationship between law and social change depends on what one expects of the law. If law is seen as a means of regulating and controlling individual behaviour, creating order and certainty, and resolving conflicts, then law's purpose may be to conserve the status quo, not introduce social change. On the other hand, law may be seen as a way of bringing about significant social change. Laws eliminating the consumption of alcohol were designed to make the world a kinder, gentler place. Increasing penalties for drunk driving have brought about a huge change in public attitude and behaviour concerning the use of alcohol and motor vehicles. In these cases, law is seen as an agent for a transformation of society, not just for regulating existing patterns of behaviour.

"Vehicles Are Not Allowed in the Park": How Should We Interpret Legal Rules?

As you can now appreciate, how one approaches the law can determine how one will interpret it. By way of a summary of our discussion of concepts of law, consider how the natural law adherents, positivists, and realists might approach the problem presented in Exhibit 1.2.

How might different approaches to the purpose of law determine the outcome? A positivist might say that interpretation means finding and applying the meaning of ordinary English, and interpreting the law according to the meaning of the language used, without going beyond that to draw on external sources as aids to interpretation. This might result in an interpretation that finds the word "vehicle" modified by the word "toy", so as to take the object out of the reach of the law. It might equally well find that a vehicle is a vehicle, and the law has been broken. In either case, the answer is a technical analysis of language rather than content. It may result in an absurdity, but it is for judges to interpret and apply the law, not question the purpose or intent of the lawmakers. If the law is absurd, then it is up to the democratically elected legislature, not judges, to make the necessary changes. Here, the law is seen as limited to what it says — the interpretation is limited to the actual language, is narrow, and is somewhat mechanical. But following this approach, we get the same answer every time — the "right" answer, in the sense that we maintain order, certainty and predictability in the law, so we can all easily know the consequences. Like cases are treated alike.

A "natural" lawyer might see this differently. She would note the absurdity of arresting a child with a toy truck, and note that it would be immoral to give the law such effect and purpose. She would draw on principles and values

---

Interpreting Legal Rules: A Discussion	EXHIBIT 1.2

A three-year-old child is walking with his parents into a park, along the path. The child is pulling a toy car behind him on a string. At the entrance to the park there is a sign that says, "Vehicles are not allowed in the park." A police officer sees the family and issues a ticket to the parents for permitting their child, under their control, to bring a vehicle, albeit a toy, into the park where this is prohibited by law. The parents argue that this is ridiculous. The officer's reply is that it is her job to enforce the law, not to question its wisdom.

Source: The example is developed from one used by H.L.A. Hart in *The Concept of Law* (Oxford: Clarendon Press, 1961). See chs. 1–2.

— perhaps on a moral code that supports a child's imaginative play — to give the words a context, rather than interpret them abstractly and without regard for the results. Here, the law would be interpreted according to a morally proper result.

A realist might look at a case like this in terms of his or her own social and political values, and interpret the law to advance particular political principles. What values and principles the judge might choose would not come from an external moral code, but would be influenced by the judge's personality, political or moral views, life experiences and psychological makeup.

This discussion of approaches to interpreting legal rules can seem to be very academic, based on competing legal philosophies. And for this reason one might be tempted to dismiss the importance of these approaches. But in modern legal systems on some issues, judges can be described in practical terms as being on a continuum running from judicial activist to strict constructionist.

Interestingly, some judges may be strict constructionists on some issues and activists on others. A **judicial activist** is one who sees interpretation as a quasi-legislative function where law is interpreted in a way that is consistent with identifiable principles, values and views of society. A **strict constructionist** takes a narrower view, looking to the plain or literal meaning found in the language of the law, and ignoring social policy or values. These approaches are particularly true of, and particularly important in, constitutional law. Political values and principles come to the fore in constitutional law, where courts deal with fundamental issues about rights and the uses of political power. Further, the Constitution requires the courts to decide how fundamental legal principles in the Constitution and in the *Charter of Rights and Freedoms* are to be interpreted and applied. Judges spend much time trying to fathom the extent of rights identified in the Constitution. For example, section 15 of the *Charter* sets out certain equality rights by prohibiting discrimination based on a list of grounds, such as race, religion, colour, ethnicity. Activists have said that you must look to the spirit, nature, and purpose of section 15, and be ready to expand the list to include discrimination that is not specifically mentioned but is based on things that are related to items on the list: e.g., not just discrimination on the basis of sex, but also discrimination based on sexual orientation. A strict constructionist, on the other hand, would restrict equality rights to the categories listed, arguing that if the framers of the Constitution wanted to be more expansive, they would have been. They would say that if sexual orientation is not an already protected category explicitly set out in the *Charter*, it is not the job of judges to put it there — to do so would be to **usurp** the job of the legislature as supreme lawmaker.

Judicial activists are often seen as social engineers trying to implement their own view of the world despite the clear intention of Parliament. In contrast, strict constructionists are often portrayed as narrow and conservative, using narrow interpretations of law to advance a conservative, if not reactionary, agenda. But this probably overstates the case. In reality, most judges bring some activist and some self-restraint approaches to bear on legal interpretation, and their approach may vary depending on the legal issues or questions before them.

CONCLUSION: THE HALLMARKS OF A FUNCTIONAL AND EFFECTIVE LEGAL SYSTEM

So far we have been discussing different concepts of law in terms of the law's function in society. The concern here has been a political one: what is the role of law in a democratic society? What rules are valid legal rules, and what rules are something else? Most commentators agree that in a democratic society the rule of law should prevail — that is, no one should be above the law. But beyond that, are there minimal requirements of a legal system that will be generally accepted in a democratic society? What is necessary to get members of a society to prefer legal solutions to non-legal ones? Lon Fuller, a legal theorist, argues that the reliance on law, rather than on brute force, is a reliance on a rational, consensual approach to problem solving where people defer to norms associated with peaceful conflict resolution.[6] To put it another way, people must have an expectation that the system will work rationally, that like cases will be treated alike, and that outcomes of conflict resolution, and action in general, will be predictable and certain.

Although Fuller does not say so, the expectation of rationality requires a certain type of society: at a minimum, most members of the society must have access to social and economic resources; they must be free of fear for their own survival and safety. The state apparatus of this society must be seen to be rational and reasonably transparent in its operation, and to have a monopoly over the use of force, which is used with restraint and in accordance with established rules. Examples of political societies that would meet these criteria include Canada, the United States, the European Union countries, and many Asian countries. Examples of states that would not meet these criteria would include Afghanistan and some of the states of sub-Saharan Africa. These latter are sometimes referred to as "failed states": politically unstable, where many societal institutions are in disarray, where the rule of law is not present, and where life is chaotic or, to use Hobbes's phrase, "nasty, brutish and short".

The Characteristics of a Functional Legal System in a Democratic State

Where the rule of law operates, legal systems usually have the following characteristics:

1. Laws Are General in Their Application

Legal rules should exist for most of the requirements and prohibitions in a given society. These rules should also be general in nature, and directed at everyone in a specific situation. For example, the rule prohibiting drivers from exceeding a speed limit applies to all persons driving on a particular section of highway governed by that speed limit. An example of a law that fails to meet this requirement is one actually passed in the English Parliament in the reign of Henry VII: "Richard Rose shall be detained, and boiled in oil." Whoever Rose was, he certainly had powerful enemies: powerful enough to get a law proclaimed just to "get" him. This would be regarded as a perversion of the law.

2. Laws Must Be Promulgated

In a rational system of law, we would expect that if we are to obey laws, they must be proclaimed in such a way that we know what they are. In a society like ours, there are specific rules about rule making and rule proclaiming that must be followed; otherwise, the rules are deemed to be invalid and of no effect. If the rules for making and proclaiming law are followed, it is presumed that we can all find the law and know what obedience is required. In a society like ours, we are presumed to know the law because it is publicly available. The reality is that the mechanisms for finding the law

---

[6] See Lon Fuller, *The Morality of Law* (New Haven: Yale University Press, 1969).

are so technical that most people will need the help of a lawyer to locate the law and determine how it applies to them. There are some who argue that the legal profession and the judiciary contribute to obscuring the process of finding the law by perpetuating the mystery and complexity that surrounds the law.

It follows from this discussion that "secret" law is no law at all. An example arose some years ago when prison reform activists discovered that prison authorities had, and applied, some internal regulations that they refused to promulgate. Prison reformers succeeded in striking down these "secret" regulations on the grounds that no one could obey or know that they were disobeying a law that was kept a secret. Nor could anyone know if the rules were being applied properly, if only those who made them knew what they were.

Because law making is complicated in Canada, the courts also require laws to be proclaimed according to the proper procedures. For example, a regulation that is drafted, but inadvertently not posted to the official provincial or federal **gazette**, is no law at all. In order for the regulation to be valid and in effect, it must be properly proclaimed, or "gazetted".

3. Laws Should Be Prospective Rather Than Retroactive

If a law is passed and proclaimed today, then the expectation is that it takes effect as of today, and governs behaviour from today. Past behaviour should not be made illegal today if, at the time the behaviour occurred, it was legal. Also, no penalty should attach for behaviour that was legal when it occurred. For example, if we pass a law today that says, "All persons who let their cell phone go off in class shall be shot", you would all reach for the button that turns off the ringer on your cell phone. You would know what is expected of you, and you would be able to take the necessary steps to avoid punishment. However, if we pass a law today that says, "As of last Thursday, anyone who let their cell phone ring in class shall be shot", it would be seen as very unfair because persons who let their cell phones ring in class before it was outlawed would be punished for doing something that was perfectly lawful and not subject to penalties when they did it.

There are some situations where the law may permit retroactive application or impact. Under the **doctrine of foreshadowing**, where a proposed law has had much publicity and been much discussed, it may apply before it is proclaimed. As its content is well known, it is presumed that people would have already taken steps to obey. Similarly, when a budget is passed, it often is deemed to take effect at some time before its passage. For example, a budget passed in March may be given effect as of January 1, as that is the beginning of the taxation year for many taxpayers, although the budget is usually not ready for a month or two later.

There is one other situation where there is retroactive impact. Where a statute is proclaimed in force, we often will not know how the statute is to be interpreted until someone brings a court case challenging the interpretation of language in the statute. It may take the courts months or years to determine the outcome, and the decision will apply back in time to when the dispute first arose for the parties that were involved in the dispute. For others, the decision should take effect only from the time it is made.

4. Laws Should Be Clear

This means that the law should not be so obscure or confusing or contradictory that no rational sense can be made of it. It does not mean that the law cannot be complex, or that it cannot be subject to interpretation. The courts have developed various interpretative techniques by which we should be able to clarify and interpret law so that we know what is required.

5. Laws Should Not Be Contradictory

A given behaviour or course of conduct should not be legal under one law and illegal under another. In a federal state like Canada, it is possible to have the two levels of government passing contradictory laws. However, the Constitution contains a mechanism that permits the courts to determine which law is valid and should be obeyed, and which is invalid and can be ignored. It does this using constitutional rules to determine which level of government has jurisdiction to enact a particular rule, which in turn resolves the conflict over which law to obey. The problem of contradictory law also looms large in international trade, where in a contract dispute two sets of national laws may apply. Usually these disputes can be resolved by **conflict of laws** rules to determine which of two conflicting rules applies. Similarly, free trade agreements, such as the North American Free Trade Agreement (NAFTA), contain rules for resolving conflicts between domestic rules and rules agreed to by the parties under the trade agreement.

6. Laws Should Not Make Impossible Demands

The law should not make rules that are impossible to apply on any rational or logical basis.

7. Laws Should Be Reasonably Constant and Durable

While the law needs to change to adapt to changing circumstances, it should not be constantly amended and changed so that there is confusion over what law actually is in operation. In order for people to plan complex, long-term undertakings, there must be some assurance that the laws relevant to that undertaking remain certain and predictable.

There are some laws that are amended frequently, however. Tax law is often amended, sometimes annually, in accordance with the requirements of the government's budget.

8. Laws Should Be Capable of Enforcement

There is an expectation in society that when behavioural requirements have been set out in the law, those requirements will be enforced. Where the rules are breached, sanctions or negative consequences should follow reasonably quickly. This is not only true for criminal law, with its prescribed penalties, but also true for civil disputes where breach of one person's rights by another gives rise to negative consequences for the transgressor in the form of a requirement to pay for the harm done to another.

Without penalties or sanctions, the law would be no more than a statement of principle about what we *ought* to do. It would not be a statement of what we *have* to do. For the most part, the expectation that sanctions will be applied is enough to ensure compliance without having a policeman at everyone's elbow. But as we noted earlier, there may be circumstances where the failure of government to effectively enforce the law may result in increased disregard of the law. For example, if we know the highway speed limits are not going to be enforced because the government decided not to hire more police, we may disregard them because we know we run little risk of being caught and penalized.

But there are other circumstances where vigorous enforcement does not seem to compel obedience. The American "War on Drugs" has gone on for years, with serious penalties for transgressors. But there seems to be little indication that the non-medical use of drugs is subsiding. Similarly, attempts to enforce prohibition and suppress the liquor trade were largely unsuccessful. These examples indicate that where a law is not accepted as legitimate or valid, harsh penalties will not bring about compliance or deter people from breaking said law.

CHAPTER SUMMARY

In this chapter, we examined the concept of law, exploring some of its facets and components. We focused particularly on some open questions about the purpose of law in a democratic society and the minimal requirements for a valid legal system. We began with a discussion of what law is, distinguishing it from other social institutions, and noted that different commentators focus on different aspects of law as being important. We went on to distinguish legal rules from other kinds of rules, noting that there are different consequences for breaching legal rules and non-legal ones. We also discussed how, in any society, people learn to recognize some rules as legal ones. Having learned to recognize legal rules, we turned to a discussion of why we obey, exploring some contrasting views of human nature that purport to explain why we obey, why we accept the rule of law, and what we expect law to do for us. In this context we also tried to identify law's limitations. Are there things it cannot achieve? Are there circumstances where it will not meet our expectations? We then looked at the relationship between law and morality, asking whether valid law requires a "right" moral content, or whether law should simply promote order and certainty by treating like cases alike. In this context we examined the competing theories of natural law, positivism and judicial realism, and then examined less theoretical approaches to these issues in the context of judicial activism and judicial self-restraint. We next turned to an examination of the relationship between social and legal change, noting the complex interactions that bring about legal change in society. We concluded with a discussion of the characteristics of a legal system in a democratic state by identifying what we think are the minimal requirements that a valid legal system must meet.

GLOSSARY OF NEW TERMS AND KEY CONCEPTS

conflict of laws
An area of law concerned with determining which law applies when there is a conflict between the laws of two national systems that could apply to the situation.

coup d'état
A French expression used to describe the seizure of state power by force or by the threat of force.

doctrine of foreshadowing
Where the requirements of a new law are well known in advance of its final proclamation; it may be considered in a case prior to its actual proclamation.

gazette
An official government publication in which official notices are published, such as the promulgation of government regulations or the proclamation that a statute is in force. Publication in a gazette is deemed to be notice to the public of the item published; at that point members of the public are deemed to be aware of the contents of the notice, whether they have read it or not. The Government of Canada publishes the *Canada Gazette*; provinces publish them as well. Ontario, for example, publishes the *Ontario Gazette*.

judicial activist
One who draws on social value and principles in interpreting law, and who is likely to see the law as a way of implanting key principles and policies.

judicial realism
A behavioural theory that holds that the psychosocial makeup of judges directly affects how they interpret and apply law. It provides a way to both predict and explain judicial behaviour.

legal positivism	A legal theory that argues that valid law is law that is made in accordance with accepted procedure, and is interpreted by giving accurate meaning to what a law actually says, without trying to fit it to our own moral or value preferences.
natural law	A theory of law that presupposes the existence of a divine or natural law external to and superior to human law. Human law, to be valid, must conform to the moral requirements of natural law, or it is invalid and need not be obeyed.
norm	An identifiable behaviour pattern that is expected and appropriate in a given set of circumstances in a particular society.
rule of law	The idea that no one, including rule makers and enforcers, is above the law or exempt from it.
socialization	A process that describes how we learn the norms and values of our society through interaction in various social institutions: families, schools, and peer groups, for example.
strict constructionist	A judge who interprets the law in terms of what it says literally, and who does not try to change the law by interpreting it to adapt to new principles, values or policies.
usurp	To wrongfully seize control of a legal and political system, and administer it in a way that is contrary to what the law requires.

REVIEW QUESTIONS

1. What are some of the key functions of a legal system?

2. How are legal rules distinguished from other kinds of rules?

3. How do we recognize legal rules so as to differentiate them from others?

4. Why do we obey legal rules?

5. What is Hobbes's explanation for why we obey?

6. How does Locke explain why we obey law?

7. What are some of the things the law cannot be expected to do?

8. How does civil disobedience differ from other forms of disobedience?

9. What does natural law tell us about obedience to law?

10. What does a positivist define as valid law that we must obey?

11. What is judicial realism?

12. Does social change result in legal change?

13. How does a judicial activist differ from a strict constructionist?

14. What are the minimal requirements of a legal system in a democratic system?

15. What is the doctrine of foreshadowing?

16. In what circumstances might we come across contradictory law in Canada?

17. After 9/11, Canadian anti-terrorism legislation permitted the government to apprehend immigrants as terrorism suspects and hold them indefinitely on security certificates, and deport them if a federal court judge found the evidence used to support the certificate reasonable. The detainee was not allowed to see or question the evidence. What might Fuller have to say about this law?

18. Albert went fishing in the Northern Ontario wilderness. A Game and Fish officer fined him for taking certain fish out of season. Before he left for the trip, Albert had checked to see which fish were in season. As it happened, the regulations were amended and proclaimed after he left home and while he was in the wilderness. Should Albert have been fined?

19. Suppose you were asked to set up a legal system. Describe three methods that you could use to get people to obey legal rules.

20. Describe what you consider to be a shortcoming for the following legal theories:
    (a) natural law
    (b) positivism

DISCUSSION QUESTIONS

1. If a general conducts a *coup d'état* and takes over political power, we have descended into the world of Thomas Hobbes. Discuss.

2. Consider the following facts:

   At the end of World War II, the Allies decided that they needed to punish the leading Nazis for the acts of the German state designed to eliminate whole populations based on ethnic, political or religious grounds. The Allies established a court, sitting in Nuremberg, Germany, with judges from each of the major Allied nations. Leading Nazis were indicted for certain war crimes: genocide (the destruction of an entire ethnic or religious group) and crimes against humanity. They were allowed counsel and the right to present a defence. A number were found guilty of these offences, and were sentenced to hang or to long terms of imprisonment. Many of the accused raised a number of defences. Among them were these:

   (i) They were following orders and obeying laws made in accordance with rules and procedures for making and enforcing law in the state in which those laws were valid and legitimate.

   (ii) The laws creating the offences they were charged with did not exist at the time the offences were committed; the laws are, therefore, retroactive.

   How would natural law and positivism deal with these defences?

3. In the October 5, 2002 edition of *The Globe and Mail*, columnist Doug Saunders reported in his article entitled "What do you do with a problem like Noelle?" that Noelle Bush, the daughter of then Florida Governor Jeb Bush (and niece of then President George W. Bush), had been arrested for a drug offence — using a forged prescription to obtain a tranquillizer used by cocaine addicts. Although she had a long record of drug offences and a serious problem with cocaine, she had been in treatment rather than in jail. Her father Jeb Bush had campaigned for governor on a platform that advocated jailing drug offenders. He had described drug use as a moral problem requiring stiff jail sentences, asserting that it was not a health problem requiring medical treatment but a criminal offence requiring jail. When questioned by reporters, Jeb Bush replied, "This is a private issue, as it relates to my daughter and

myself and my wife. ... The road to recovery is a rocky one for a lot of people who have this kind of problem."

    (a) Discuss Jeb Bush's response in the context of the principle that no one is above the law. Does Jeb Bush appear to believe that like cases should be treated alike?

    (b) Is Bush's publicly advocated approach to punish drug users likely to succeed?

4. In 2012–2013, the federal government introduced legislation to amend the criminal law of Canada to limit the discretion of judges to impose a range of possible sentences for criminal acts. Instead, new minimum jail sentences were attached to various criminal acts, preventing judges from using probation, house arrest, or other penalties, and requiring them to impose prison sentences in all cases that did not fall below the prescribed minimum. The intended result is that convicted criminals would serve jail sentences, and longer sentences than previously served for an offence.

    Is this approach based on a Hobbesian view of the law? Lockean? A mix of both?

SUGGESTED READING AND OTHER RESOURCES

Finch, J.D. *Introduction to Legal Theory*, 3d ed. (London: Sweet and Maxwell, 1979).

Gall, G.R. *The Canadian Legal System*, 5th ed. (Toronto: Carswell, 2004).

Hart, H.L.A. *The Concept of Law*, 2d ed. (Oxford: Clarendon Press, 1997).

Shears, P., & J. Stephenson, *Introduction to English Law* (London: Butterworths, 2005).

Lloyd, D. *The Idea of Law*. Reprinted with revisions (Baltimore: Penguin, 1976).

M.D.A. Freeman. *Lloyd's Introduction to Jurisprudence*, 7th ed. (London: Sweet & Maxwell, 2001).

Sabine, G., & W. Thorson, *A History of Political Theory*, 4th ed. (New York: Holt, Rinehart and Winston, 1973).

VIDEOS AND DVDS

Kramer, Stanley, prod. & dir. *Judgment at Nuremberg*. With Spencer Tracy, Maximilian Schell. 1961. [Video release, 1989; b and w; approximately 190 minutes.] Also available on DVD.

Brook, Peter, dir. *Lord of the Flies*. 1963. [Video release, 1993; colour; approximately 90 minutes.] Also available on DVD.

Lumet, Sidney, dir. & Henry Fonda and Reginald Rose, prod. *12 Angry Men*. [Video release, 1995; b and w; approximately 92 minutes.] Also available on DVD. Remade for TV in colour in 1997 with Ossie Davis, James Gandolfini et al. Available on DVD.

Zimmerman, Fred, dir. *A Man for All Seasons*. With Paul Schofield, Wendy Hiller. 1961. Original Play by Robert Bolt [1954]. [DVD release, 1999; technicolour film, 120 minutes.] Also available on Blu-ray.

WEBSITES

Amnesty International Canada:

Canadian Bar Association: <http://www.cba.org/CBA/Links/Main/>

Canadian Civil Liberties Association:

LawCentral Alberta (formerly known as *Access to Justice*):
    <www.acjnet.org/splash/default.aspx>

The Law Dictionray: <http://thelawdictionary.org/>

Systems of Law in Canada

Laurence M. Olivo
SENECA COLLEGE

Learning Objectives

After reading this chapter, the reader should be able to:

➢ identify and understand the distinctive features of the common law system

➢ identify and understand the distinctive features of the civil law system of Quebec

➢ understand how the two legal systems developed

➢ understand the system of legal reasoning used to reach legal decisions in each system

➢ compare and differentiate the key elements in each system

➢ identify the ways in which the two systems have affected each other

TABLE OF CONTENTS

SYSTEMS OF LAW IN CANADA

National Legal Systems

Nation states usually have one legal system. A **legal system** consists of legal rules, principles, institutions, and procedures that operate in a distinctive way. Modern nation states, such as Canada, that are **federal states** may subdivide their legal system into local and national systems, but the two systems usually operate in the same way, according to the same principles. Such systems have simply divided **jurisdictions** on a territorial basis, between local and national political units.

Origins of Canada's Legal Systems

The development of legal systems in Canada has been different from that of most nation states. As a federal state, Canada has divided its legal system into national and local components on a territorial basis: there are provincial and federal laws and courts. There is another division as well: the common law system used at the federal level, including the federal northern territories, and in nine of the provinces; and the civil law system used in the province of Quebec for matters that fall within Quebec's jurisdiction.

This peculiar arrangement is a result of Canada's colonial experience. When France was defeated in the Seven Years' War, sovereignty over Quebec (then called New France) passed from the French to the British in 1760. The British found themselves ruling a colony composed primarily of French-speaking Roman Catholics. The British colonial administrators had to decide how to rule this new colony with its non-British, non-Protestant majority population. British North American colonies up to that time had simply adopted British political institutions and laws when a colony was established. At first, the British followed this policy in Quebec by imposing British political rules and laws on the inhabitants. The latter were unhappy with this arrangement, as social and political institutions were well established, and the intrusion of alien British institutions was disruptive. By the 1770s, as the 13 British colonies on the Atlantic coast inched closer to rebellion, it occurred to subtler minds among British colonial administrators that it might make sense to try to win over the Francophone inhabitants of Quebec by tolerating their religion and accepting their institutions.

Through passage of the *Quebec Act* in 1774, and by some adroit politicking with local elites who were won over and who publicly endorsed British rule, Quebeckers were given the freedom to practise the Roman Catholic religion and exercise other freedoms. Among these was the right to keep the province's **private law**, the law governing legal relations, rights, and liabilities between individual persons. This law was based on the laws of France in the late 18th century, as well as on local laws and customs. Laws governing relations between the subject and the state (often referred to as **public law**) were based on British common law.

Subsequently, the Maritime colonies and Upper Canada were established with legal systems based on the British common law, as were all of the later western additions to the Canadian state. In this way, Canada developed with two quite different legal systems: the civil law system in Quebec, governing private law matters, and the common law system everywhere else.

THE COMMON LAW SYSTEM

Legal Rules Based on Previously Decided Cases

In the common law system, decisions in previously decided cases provide the basis for legal rules. Consequently, much of the law in this system is referred to as **case law**. Lawyers also refer to case law as **common law** to distinguish it from **statutory law**, which is law passed by Parliament or a legislature. There are, in fact, different meanings for the term "common law", depending on the context in which the term is used. This is discussed at the end of this chapter.

How Common Law Developed

The Norman Kings Centralize Law Making

The common law legal system had its origins in feudal England. When the Duke of Normandy invaded England and seized the Crown in the 11th century, his successors faced the political task of consolidating their rule over local populations and over the local feudal lords. The Norman kings sought to do this by establishing a strong, effective central government as a counter to the power of local feudal lords.

Judges Develop a Law Common to All England

As part of this strategy, the king travelled about the country dispensing justice personally by resolving disputes that were brought to him. In time, responsibility for dispensing the king's justice fell to the king's advisors, from whose ranks there eventually emerged full-time judges. These judges would travel out from London to major towns in the realm to hear cases. The judges, when travelling, were said to be **on circuit**. To this day, in many common law jurisdictions, judges of some courts still go on circuit to hear cases.

Judges, in the course of solving disputes before them, gradually departed from local custom and developed rules that were common to the realm. These rules, derived from cases and applied as precedents to later disputes, formed the basis for the common law of England. This did not happen quickly or by design. Certain other things had to happen first. Persons who appeared as advocates for disputants began to write down the decisions of judges and, more important, the judges' reasons for these decisions. Once this was done, it was possible to circulate these reasons among judges and advocates (from whose ranks the legal profession later developed). Advocates would then argue that a judge in a previous case had decided the issue in a particular way, and that the decision, being sensible and wise, should then be followed. Of course, the advocate for the other party would argue that the facts of the case currently before the court, or the issue before the court, were different from the facts in the previous case, so the previous case was not really a precedent for deciding the present case. Lawyers refer to this latter type of argument as distinguishing a precedent case from the **case at bar** (the case currently before the judge).

Distinguishing cases, and otherwise avoiding the application of an alleged precedent case, are discussed later in this chapter.

Significantly, there was no concerted attempt to attack the common law system of precedent as the basis for developing a system of legal rules. The approach used was practical. Judges saw their role as resolving disputes in a national arena that had little in the way of national law. They developed this law — not consciously or intentionally, but over time — on a case-by-case basis, in reaction to whatever disputes litigants brought before them. It was not elegant; no one sat down and decided to create a body of national law as a conscious, coherent, related whole, as was the case with Roman law and, later, civil law. Instead, the common law evolved, in bits and pieces over time, slowly growing into a body of law covering most of the problems of life in society.

Precedent and *Stare Decisis*

Precedent

As noted in the previous section, the common law system is characterized by a particular process of making rules from the decisions of judges in ordinary lawsuits. This form of rule making is based on the use of **precedent cases**. After a judge has given reasons for judgment in a particular case, another judge hearing a similar case may be persuaded to decide his/her case by applying the reasons for judgment in that earlier and similar case. When this happens, the judge in the second case is said to be using the reasons for the decision in the first case as a **precedent** for the decision of his/her case. The first case is then called a precedent case, and other judges are expected to apply its reasons and to **follow the precedent** when the precedent case has ruled on the legal issues raised in the case before them. In time, a series of cases are decided following the original precedent case. Often the later cases refine and expand the rule (reason for decision) in the original precedent case, and the series of cases will develop a number of related legal rules.

It is useful to note in discussing precedent that the precedent value of a case does not lie in the actual decision (who won, who lost), but in the legal reasons for the decision. The reason for the decision, formally referred to as the *ratio decidendi* or, more simply, the **ratio** of the case, is where the precedent value of a case lies.

Stare Decisis

A second important feature of the law-making process in the common law system is the doctrine of *stare decisis*. This term is an abbreviation of a longer Latin phrase that means to "stand by decided matters". It reinforces the operation of the doctrine of precedent by compelling judges to follow precedents, in certain circumstances, even where a judge might otherwise not want to.

This idea of a judge being compelled to follow a precedent case is closely tied to the idea of a **hierarchy of courts**. The idea of a hierarchy of courts involves classifying or ranking courts in terms of their power and authority. Courts can be classified as follows:

- **courts of first instance**, or trial courts, where legal disputes are first heard and decided
- **appellate courts**, which review the decisions of courts of first instance, and correct errors made by the "lower" courts

Courts can also be classified in terms of the subject matter of cases they can hear and remedies they can grant. The area of activity open to a court to exercise is sometimes referred to as its **jurisdiction**. "Higher" courts have jurisdiction over a broader range of subjects and remedies than "lower" courts do. For example, a "higher" court, the Superior Court of Justice, can hear cases with claims for any amount of money, involving any subject matter. Small Claims Court, which is a "lower court", is limited in the types of claims it can hear and the monetary value of those claims.

The operation of *stare decisis* depends on the hierarchy of courts. Generally, courts higher up in the hierarchy of courts can bind judges in the lower courts in the same geographical jurisdiction so that the latter are bound to follow precedent cases from higher courts. Decisions by courts on a particular level are not binding on courts at the same level, but are considered to be **persuasive**. For example, a decision of a Superior Court of Justice judge is not binding on another Superior Court of Justice judge, but that decision should be treated as persuasive by being accorded respect and by being followed, if possible. Decisions by judges in courts from other jurisdictions are also not binding, but may be considered as persuasive if the decisions come from a higher court in the other jurisdiction, or if the decisions come from judges in another jurisdiction who are highly respected for their legal knowledge and expertise.

EXHIBIT 2.1   **Which Decision Is Binding?**

¤   A decision of the Supreme Court of Canada binds all courts in the provincial court systems.

¤   A decision of the provincial court of appeal binds all other courts in the provincial court system, and may be considered persuasive by judges in other provinces.

¤   A decision of the superior trial court binds lower trial courts in the province and should be considered persuasive by other judges at the same level in the jurisdiction.

¤   A decision of the lower trial court is not binding on any other court, but may be considered persuasive by other courts at the same level.

The Role of Precedent and *Stare Decisis* in a Common Law System

To summarize, if the doctrine of precedent sets out the idea that a precedent case *ought* to be followed, *stare decisis* sets out the idea that a precedent case *must* be followed in certain circumstances. While there have been some recent developments that lessen the force of *stare decisis* in Canada, making its application less rigid and mechanical, it is considered to be an important feature of a common law legal system.

The common law system differs dramatically from most other kinds of legal systems. Legal rules in this system are not consciously assembled from a series of carefully developed principles laid out and connected in a logical way, as is the case in many other legal systems. Instead, judges "made up" the rules as they went along, deciding practical problems that were presented in cases by people with disputes and disagreements. Once a judge made a rule to solve the problem before him, his "solution" would be adopted by other judges with a similar case.

In a sense, legal rules in this system result as a reaction to problems. In other systems, notably the civil law system used in Quebec and in many other parts of the world, rules are often derived from abstract principles, which are organized and codified in a systematic way, ready to be applied to resolve disputes. The latter approach seems simpler, more efficient, less haphazard, and more rational. If this is so, why did the common law not follow this pattern? If we consider the ad hoc way in which the common law developed as an extension of the king's personal power to do individual justice, it is clear that the focus was primarily on the need to make decisions and solve problems, not on developing a systematic and integrated body of law.

A Gloss on the Common Law: The Law of Equity

Origins of the Law of Equity

While common law developed slowly without anyone consciously managing the process, its growth was checked, after a couple of centuries, by the power of the nobility. The local nobles had watched as the king used the development of a centralized legal system, operating out of London, as one of many ways of consolidating royal power. Eventually, the nobles extracted some concessions from the king to check the expansion of royal power and, in particular, the power of the Royal Courts of Justice to interfere with the nobles' management of local affairs. They did this by getting the king to "freeze" the expansion of the common law by prohibiting the creation of any further legal rights to sue, or **causes of action**. The common law was thus left for several hundred years with what came to be called the **ancient forms of action**. This step contributed to the common law becoming unable to use precedent to expand or develop the law further. Instead, the law became frozen.

Avoiding Precedent

EXHIBIT 2.2

Whether a previous case is actually a precedent is not always clear. Legal representatives have a variety of techniques they use to find a way around a precedent case, particularly when they wish to avoid, or get around, a precedent that stands in their client's way.

¤ **Distinguishing a case on its facts:** When faced with an apparent precedent, a legal representative may argue that it is not really a precedent because it is different in its material and relevant facts from the **case at bar** (the case that is being argued by the legal representative before the court).

¤ *Obiter dicta:* There is no simple, objective test for identifying the ratio of a case. Because finding the "true" ratio is a subjective exercise, it is open to argument that the judicial opinion in a case is not the ratio, but mere *obiter dicta*, or more simply, *obiter*. *Obiter dicta* is a judicial opinion set out in a case, but it is not the opinion on which the decision in the case rests. Judicial opinions that are *obiter* are thought to have no precedent value in a case, although they may provide insights for deciding other cases, where the judicial observations may be more relevant. However, note that in Canadian case law there is a suggestion that *obiter* in cases from the Supreme Court of Canada may be binding on lower courts, if relevant to cases before them.[1] Previously, *obiter* was thought to be persuasive, but not binding.

¤ *Per incuriam:* A legal representative may argue that a case should not be followed because the judge based her decision and her reasoning on an error of fact or law. For example, the legal representatives arguing a case may have inadvertently failed to cite an important precedent case to the judge, or left out important facts by mistake. In either of these situations, the precedent value of the case is arguably weakened if its true legal or factual base is other than what the judge hearing the case thought it was.

The *per incuriam* problem illustrates the extent to which a judge in the common law system is dependent on the legal representatives presenting a case to define the issues, facts and law to be relied on. When a legal representative makes a mistake and fails to find a relevant case when doing his research, and the other legal representative does not catch the mistake, there is no assurance that a judge, busy with a heavy caseload, will, either. While judges often "check" the cases cited to them, they do not always do so. Further, in the common law system, judges are relatively passive participants in the trial process, reasoning their way to a decision on the basis of legal and evidential information supplied by the legal representatives presenting the case.

¤ **Concurring opinions:** In some proceedings — appeals, for example — the case is heard by a panel of several judges, rather than by one judge sitting alone. When this happens, different judges may come to the same conclusion for different reasons. When two or more judges agree on the result but give different reasons for their decision, their judgments are concurring opinions, but there cannot be said to be a single ratio for the case on which a precedent could be founded. In such a case, the reasons of a particularly eminent judge might carry more weight than the reasons of her colleagues sitting on the same panel, but this does not provide a clear-cut solution to the problem of deciding what the true ratio is.

¤ **Precedent wrongly decided:** In some cases, it is possible for a legal representative to argue that an earlier case may technically and logically be a precedent but that the reasoning should not be followed because it is wrong. A case may be seen as wrong when, for example, the social situations that gave rise to the reasons no longer exist, so the application of the precedent would give rise to ridiculous results. This approach is not used often, as it constitutes a direct attack on the doctrine of *stare decisis*, which lies at the core of the common law system. Legal representatives, being masters of legal subtlety, usually can find a more indirect way of avoiding precedent.

[1] *Sellars v. R.*, [1980] 1 S.C.R. 527.

EXHIBIT 2.3

An Illustration of the Use of Precedent

A owns a house with a flat roof. *B* is planning to build a house on the next lot, right next to *A*'s house. *B*'s house is going to be 10 feet higher than *A*'s. *A* discovers that *B*'s house, if built, will create conditions that will increase the snowload on *A*'s house and cause damage to *A*'s roof. *A* tells this to *B* and asks him to redesign his proposed house. *B* refuses.

A wants to stop *B* from building. *A* sues *B* for a tort called nuisance. The tort of nuisance allows one landowner to sue another for damage done to his land as a result of activity by the other on his own land. However, the definition of nuisance, as stated here, is fairly broad, and *A* has to find some cases that show that the definition of nuisance applies to his circumstances.

A finds a case where the court awarded damages to a person whose basement was flooded, when the defendant built a house that diverted rain runoff towards the plaintiff's house and into his basement. At the time the defendant built the house, neither party knew that flooding would result.

A can argue that this case is a precedent:

¤   Its facts on the relevant issue are similar to the case at bar; damage is caused to the plaintiff's property by an act of the defendant on his own property.

¤   Damage was caused by a natural element being channelled by the defendant where otherwise no damage would have resulted. Whether the element was snow or water and whether the damage was to the roof or basement are irrelevant, given that the issue is physical damage caused by the defendant.

B can argue that this case can be distinguished on its facts:

¤   In this case, the defendant had built his house, and the damage to the plaintiff's house had already occurred. Arguably, this case means that you can't sue until damage has occurred. In the case at bar, *B* hadn't built his house, and no damage had occurred to *A*'s house yet.

¤   This case creates liability for water damage. But the case at bar involves snowload. Snow and water behave differently. Therefore, this case cannot, on its facts, support a claim for liability for snowload, where other causal factors may be involved or where the risk may be too remote to impose liability.

¤   This case concerns damage to basements from water. The case at bar is different on its facts, as it concerns snow damage to a roof where other causal factors may be involved or where the risk may be too remote to impose liability.

Meanwhile, as society and social institutions changed and developed, the law did not. As well, because the law was frozen and rigid, the application of its rules could and did cause obvious injustice and unfairness. When the legal result was obviously unfair, a **suitor** would occasionally complain about this to the king who, unlike his judges, was, as the source of justice in the realm, free to fashion personal justice as he saw fit. If the king was persuaded by a suitor, he would issue a decree overruling the judgment of the courts. As more subjects brought these complaints to the king, he referred these matters to his chief administrative officer, the **Chancellor.** The Chancellor would then issue a Chancellor's decree to overrule the court and correct an obvious injustice. Good news travels quickly: in time, the flow of complaints grew so great that the Chancellor had to designate some of his staff to hear these complaints. Gradually the process became institutionalized: the Chancellor's staff became Chancery judges, operating out of the **Court of Chancery.** The decrees of the Chancellor, through the use of the precedent process, evolved into a separate body of law called the **law of equity.** Thus, a second, parallel system of courts was established. As the Chancery system became institutionalized, however, the justice delivered became less personal and less flexible. In particular, Chancery judges resorted to judicial reasoning using precedent. This tended to inhibit the expansion of equity law. The result was that the law of equity also became rigid and unresponsive.

Features of the Law of Equity

The common law courts continued to administer the common law while the Court of Chancery administered the law of equity. Initially, the law of equity developed a body of legal rules with three main features:

- rules that would "correct" unfair results of following common law rules
- **equitable remedies** that provided fair results when common law remedies were insufficient or inadequate
- preconditions that a suitor had to comply with first in order to invoke the law of equity

As a corrective for the common law, equity was sometimes referred to as "a gloss on the common law". For example, at common law, if one party broke a contractual arrangement, the only remedy the common law recognized was money damages. If the breaking of a contract would cause some injury that could not be compensated for in damages, there was nothing the common law could do. The law of equity, however, could be invoked, and an **injunction** obtained to order a stop to the wrongful behaviour.

Before a suitor could resort to the Court of Chancery and the law of equity, she had to satisfy certain preconditions. Originally, before a suitor could get the Chancellor to interfere with a court decision, the suitor had to show that she had been wronged, that a common law remedy was inadequate or non-existent, and that she had behaved properly in her dealings with her opponent. In time, this meant that a suitor in Chancery had to show the court that she had behaved properly in the lawsuit, and she had not acted underhandedly or oppressively against the other side. If the suitor could not **come into court with clean hands**, Chancery would refuse to hear her or grant the equitable remedies requested.

For example, if a suitor had tried to hide evidence in a case, then it was unlikely that the suitor would meet the preconditions required to invoke the law of equity.

Merger of the Common Law and Equity Jurisdiction

In time, the two parallel court systems and systems of legal rules became cumbersome and rigid, and problems arose:

- It was often difficult for even a highly experienced lawyer to decide whether to start a lawsuit in Chancery or in a common law court. If an error was made, a case would be thrown out and would have to start from the beginning in the other court.

- Decrees from the Chancery Court might conflict with, or be inconsistent with, the orders of the common law courts.

These kinds of problems caused uncertainty in the law, delayed proceedings, and made them more expensive. In the late 19th century, a major court reform movement in the common law world, including Canada, resulted in the merger of the two court systems into one superior court with the power to administer the common law and the law of equity together.

While the separate courts administering the law of equity have passed into history, the law of equity is still relevant today. It continues to be administered by superior court judges who have the power to administer the common law and the law of equity together. Courts today still have available and, where relevant, use powerful equitable remedies, such as injunctions, and orders for specific performance of contracts. These remedies achieve results that cannot otherwise be achieved by traditional common law remedies, which are generally limited to the payment of money for damages sustained.

The Modern Common Law System: Case Law, Equity, and Statutes

The Modern Common Law System as a "Mixed" System of Law

While the common law originated out of a process where the law developed on a case-by-case basis, modern common law systems are more complex and have more sources of legal rules than previously decided precedent cases.[1]

Modern common law systems are mixed systems in terms of the sources of law. In Canada, the principal sources of written law are case law, including both common law rules and equitable rules, and statutory law, which also includes regulations made under the authority of statutes. The development of the law of equity alongside common law has been examined; we now turn to the development of statutory law in the common law system.

How Common Law Developed into a Mixed System of Law

When the common law began to develop, it was the principal source of legal rules. Statutes, which are laws passed by Parliament or a legislature, were not yet a significant factor in legal rule making. In the 11th and 12th centuries, when the common law began to take form, Parliament as we know it did not exist. Over the next several centuries, however, Parliament began to take both the form and function we would recognize today. At first, composed of the Lords (clergy and nobility) and the Commons (representatives of wealthy towns), Parliament was summoned by the king when he needed to raise large sums of money by taxation, usually to finance a war. In time, in exchange for consenting to taxation, Parliament extracted concessions from the king, which resulted in Parliament's increasing its participation in government by passing laws or statutes dealing with matters other than taxation.

Parliamentary Supremacy

As this expansion of parliamentary power represented an erosion of royal power, the king sometimes resisted, and from the 17th century on, there was considerable tension between king and Parliament over the exercise of power by the latter.

All this came to a "head", literally, in 1649, when Charles I lost his head, after trying to dismiss Parliament to rule alone. The result was a civil war between the king's adherents and those of Parliament, after which the king was beheaded and Parliament ruled alone. What emerged from the English Civil War was a new legal doctrine, **the Doctrine of Parliamentary Supremacy** (also called Parliamentary Sovereignty), under which Parliament was declared to be the supreme lawmaker. This meant that when Parliament passed a law, it negated any other law or rule made outside of Parliament that conflicted with an Act of Parliament. Further, not only did ordinary citizens have to obey the law, but so did royal officials, so that those who governed had to do so according to the law passed by Parliament. Another way of looking at this

---

[1] The sources of law in the common law system are discussed in another chapter, "Sources of Law", offered in the complete edition of this modular textbook. In this chapter, the relationship and development of the main written sources of law are explored.

is to say that no one is above the law. With respect to judge-made law, a statute passed by Parliament would cancel out any conflicting law developed from previously decided cases.

Advantages of Statutory Law over Case Law

Once Parliament had a relatively free hand to legislate, it increased its output of statutes and, from the 17th century onward, it gradually became the source of a growing proportion of legal rules in the common law system. The reason for this growth of statutory law was not simply that Parliament now had the power to act. For example, Parliament could use statutes to respond to particular problems relatively quickly and in a comprehensive way. As society became more complex, statutes provided a more effective way to make rules than the slow and cumbersome common law process of developing judge-made law on a case-by-case basis.

Sorting Out Conflicts between Sources of Law

It is apparent from this chapter that both statutory law and equity developed, at least in part, because of perceived shortcomings of the common law case law precedent system, which was seen as too rigid, too slow and too unresponsive to the needs of a complex society. However, these later additions to the common law system created potential for conflict. If, for example, a rule developed from case law conflicted with a statute, which would prevail? Gradually, over time, the answers to these questions were worked out:

- If there is a conflict between a case law rule and an equitable rule, the equitable rule shall prevail.
- If there is a conflict between a statutory rule and an equitable or common law rule, the statutory rule shall prevail.

While statutory law prevails over case law, note that there is a continuing relationship between statute law and case law. Disputes about the meaning of all or part of a statute are resolved by court cases. Where a case has interpreted part of a statute and expanded or refined previous understandings of what the statute meant, then that case becomes an important determinant of a statute's meaning.

THE CIVIL LAW SYSTEM

In a civil law system, principles and rules of law are found in a set of clearly articulated and connected principles set out in a coherent system of law, in contrast to the common law system, where they are found, if at all, in case law. The system of law usually has a base in a legal theory that has an integrated worldview and that determines the content, focus, and direction of legal rules and principles. For example, modern European (and Quebec) civil law systems owe a great deal to theories of law found in Roman law and in natural law. In addition, the rules and principles are organized in a systematic and logical way. This organizing process, usually called **codification**, results in the codes that are a feature of modern civil law systems.

Key features of a civil law system are

- a coherent, theoretically interrelated system of law, and
- a codified system of law.

In Quebec, private law is based on modern European civil law, organized and codified in the Quebec Civil Code.

**The Origins of
the Quebec Civil
Code**

The Law of New France at the Time of the Conquest

When the British took over the governance of New France, now to be called Quebec, they found a French-speaking society that had been established on the shores of the St. Lawrence for over a century. While the colony was governed by French officials, its institutions had evolved in response to local conditions. The legal system in use fit this pattern. It was based originally on the customary law of the Paris region. In its origins, it was a mixture of local custom — some of which was rooted in the feudal system of the Middle Ages — and civil law derived from Roman law. It had been codified before being introduced to New France, and was overhauled afterwards. Thus, the French customary law base, by the time the British arrived, had been further customized to suit local conditions, and had been systematized and codified.

The Impact of British Rule on Quebec's Legal Institutions

As noted, the British experimented with several models of government, as they tried to decide how to treat the French-speaking population of their recently acquired colony. With the *Quebec Act* of 1774 the British opted for leaving the Quebec legal system intact, with respect to the private law. This was not popular with the recently arrived British merchant class, and the Quebec legal institutions did not really become secure until the British, in 1791, separated their colony into Upper Canada (now Ontario), which was primarily English speaking, and Lower Canada (now Quebec), which was primarily French speaking.

In the early British period, the civil law system in Quebec fell into decline. Based as it was on a civil law base, affecting only private law, in an English colony undergoing rapid change, it was not particularly well-suited to solving private law problems. It was also not clear how the civil law system could work alongside the rest of the Quebec system of public law, which ran on common law principles. It also did not help that there was no system for legal education in the civil law in Quebec. The civil law system recovered from this decline, however, in part because of a renewal and modernization of civil law in Europe.

The Impact of the Modernization of European Civil Law on Quebec's Legal Institutions

The European systems, while different in substance from each other, shared a systematic codification of legal rules. This was part of a well-established tradition of codification that extended back to codified Roman law. While the influence of Roman law had waned after the collapse of the Roman Empire, it continued to have an impact on European law. The tradition had new life breathed into it during the Renaissance and the **Enlightenment**, with the development of rationally based theories of natural law. Interestingly, none of the intellectual ferment in the civil law reached Britain in any significant way. British law had been largely unaffected by Roman law, and the results of changes in the civil law in the early modern period had no effect, either.

In the early 19th century, following political changes brought about by the French Revolution and the reforms to the legal system by Napoleon, law reformers in France and elsewhere in Europe sought to modernize the civil law and to recodify it.

Codification was, and is, more than merely collecting all existing law between the covers of a code book. The process also involves a close review of legal rules and principles, to ensure that they form a consistent, coherent, interrelated system, based on clearly identified principles. In some respects this is a philosophical exercise, in which legal scholars attempt to

---

Avoiding Confusion:
Different Uses of "Common Law" and "Civil Law"

EXHIBIT 2.4

By now it should be apparent that both "common law" and "civil law" can have different meanings depending on the situations where they are used.

Common Law

◻ The body of common custom, or law common to all England, which was an early product of the justice system created by the Norman kings. This usage is now only of historical interest and does not have a contemporary meaning.

◻ The body of case law, from which legal precedents are drawn, is called common law to distinguish it from law from other sources, such as statutory law.

◻ The legal system that developed in England and that features the use of precedent cases as a major source of law is called a common law legal system.

Civil Law

◻ Civil law describes a system of law derived from Roman law and natural law, which is usually codified.

◻ Civil law in the common law system describes private law, consisting primarily of the law of torts and contract.

---

develop a theory of law that underlies and illuminates the rules and principles in a code.

In Quebec, the reformers, influenced by law reforms in France in the 19th century, recodified private law, abandoning the earlier French customary law base and replacing it with a system of principles adapted from the Napoleonic Code, or the French Civil Code. This code covered both substantive private law (similar to the common law of torts and contracts) and civil procedure. Since the mid-19th century when the Quebec Civil Code was formally adopted, Quebec has periodically reviewed and overhauled the code. The latest extensive revisions were completed in 1993. So extensive were these revisions that members of the Quebec Bar were expected to take continuing education courses in the new code if they expected to continue to practise law in Quebec.

Features of a Civil Law Code System Compared with a Common Law System

Codified Principles vs. Case Ratios as the Basis for Legal Rules

Codification is a process whereby legal rules and principles are developed and organized into a coherent, interrelated system. The rules or principles, compared to common law rules, are much more general in nature, and are not developed as a narrow answer to a specific case. Instead, the civil law principles are developed as general abstract statements. The general statement of principle or law in the code can then be applied to make a legal decision, with the same principle being applied to many different fact situations.

This is quite different from the common law, where general principles of law are developed as a result of problem solving in specific cases; in other words, judges in the common law system develop legal rules as a result of a search for remedies to practical problems. They reason, **inductively**, from the particular to the general. In the civil law system, judges start with a general principle, clearly identified and defined, and apply it to particular facts in an attempt to define competing rights. They reason, **deductively**, from the general to the particular.

The Function of Precedent in a Civil Code System

In reasoning their way to legal decisions, judges using code systems do not rely on precedent cases. The primary source of law is the code itself, which the judge is expected to interpret and apply without resort to secondary sources, such as cases. Judges are not seen as lawmakers in a code system; they do not make binding rules from cases that can be applied to later cases or used as alternatives to the code itself. It is not necessary for a judge in this system to find a case that supports his position: finding a principle in the code to solve a legal problem is sufficient. More particularly, in contrast to the common law system, in the civil code system, the doctrine of *stare decisis* is non-existent: a previously decided case is not binding authority for deciding the case at bar.

At the same time, precedent has some function in the Quebec system. One of the weaknesses of a code system is that the principles and rules in the code are based on philosophical and other assumptions about the way society works or should work. Occasionally, a situation arises that is not specifically covered by an **article** in the code. In such a case, it is generally permissible for a judge in coming to a decision to reason by analogy with a previously decided case that is in some way similar to the case at bar.

Precedent cases may also be used in other, more common situations. First, civil code jurisdictions, like common law jurisdictions, have a hierarchy or ranking of courts, where, for example, trial courts are seen as subordinate to appeal courts. In this context, the decision in an appeal court, on a case similar to the case at bar in a trial court, may be persuasive for the lower court because of the added authority carried by a decision of a higher court. Note, however, that in the civil code system, a higher court does not automatically bind a lower court as it is presumed to do in the common law system. In a code system, the lower court can ignore a similar decision of a higher court. This is not without a potential cost: a judge in a lower court who ignores a decision of a higher court may find her decision reversed by an appeal court. To put it succinctly, precedent may operate, but the doctrine of *stare decisis* does not.

Sources of Law in a Civil Law System

The primary source of law is the Civil Code itself, which contains relatively general rules and principles that are grouped together by subject matter. Another primary source is other statutes. A secondary source is **doctrine**, which is a term that describes commentary by legal scholars on the meaning of various provisions of the code. Note that case law is not a formal source of law in civil code systems. As well, there is no concept of a separate law of equity, as there is in the common law system. The principles in the code are general, rather than narrow or rigid, so that the circumstances that gave rise to the law of equity in the common law system never arose in the civil code systems. However, illustrating Quebec's ability to borrow from the common law, some equitable remedies, such as injunctions, have found their way into Quebec law.

The System of Law in Quebec: A Mixed Common Law and Civil Law System

We can see that the private law in Quebec is based on the civil law system, using the Quebec Civil Code. To go on from there, to state that Quebec is a civil law and civil code jurisdiction would be to overstate the situation. In fact, the civil law system and the common law system have cohabited in Quebec for over 200 years. As a result of this contact, each has affected the other in a variety of ways. Further, as the result of Quebec's legal system operating in a federal system, large areas of law affecting life in Quebec are based on

	COMMON LAW	CIVIL LAW
Avoiding Confusion: Key Differences between "Common Law" and "Civil Law" **EXHIBIT 2.5**		
Use of precedent	yes	rarely
Codified rules	sometimes (statutes)	yes
Defers to higher court	yes	sometimes

federal common law. The effects in Quebec of the mingling of the two systems are as follows:

- The private law, affecting the relations between private citizens in their dealings with each other, is primarily codified civil law.

- Commercial law is based on common law, or on statutes.

- Public law, which governs the relations between the individual and the state (including criminal law), is common law, based on statutes and case law.

- There is a general acknowledgement that Quebec judges tend to resort to precedents more than judges in other civil code jurisdictions. In particular, attention is paid and deference given to the decisions of the Supreme Court of Canada on issues involving the Quebec Civil Code. As well, ignoring decisions of higher courts within the Quebec legal system is unusual, although more frequent than in other provinces. Much of this judicial behaviour can be attributed to the influence of common law and of common law judges in the rest of Canada.

CHAPTER SUMMARY

In this chapter, the reader is introduced to the two systems of law in Canada: the civil law in Quebec, and the common law in every other part of Canada. The main characteristics of the common law system are discussed, including the use of previously decided cases as the basis for developing legal rules (the doctrine of precedent), the tendency of precedents to become binding (the doctrine of *stare decisis*), and the development of equity to avoid the rigid application of precedents where unfairness resulted. The chapter also explored a number of analytic devices to avoid the application of precedents. As much modern law is now based on statutes rather than on case law, the relationship between the two sources of law is discussed in terms of the supremacy of the legislature, which results in statute law being able to override case law.

The chapter then identified the main features of the civil law system in Quebec and traced its origins back to French and European law. In contrast to common law, legal rules and principles in the civil law system are found in code books, not cases. One applies the principles in the code to the facts of a case to come to a decision. The chapter concluded by noting that, as a result of Quebec's history in Canada, it is not a "pure" civil law system, as some of the law applied in Quebec is based on English law, and common law methods of legal reasoning have had some influence on legal reasoning in the civil code system.

GLOSSARY OF NEW TERMS AND KEY CONCEPTS

ancient forms of action During the early development of the common law, by royal order, no new causes of action could be added to the law; this resulted in the existing causes of action becoming frozen and rigid over a long period. These "frozen" causes of action are referred to as ancient forms of action.

appellate court A court that reviews the decisions of lower courts or courts of first instance for errors of fact or law. *See* "courts of first instance", below.

article In civil code systems, specific rules or groups of rules.

case at bar The case currently being tried before the court.

case law Legal rules derived from decided cases.

causes of action Facts that give rise to a right to sue based on a legal rule or legal right.

Chancellor The royal official who originally administered the law of equity. Later, the title was also used by judges appointed to the Court of Chancery, which dealt with equity matters. In England today, the Lord Chancellor is the chief official responsible for the administration of justice in the realm.

codification A process that results in a coherent, theoretically related and logically consistent system of rules.

Court of Chancery The court that administered the law of equity.

"come into court with clean hands" A principle of the law of equity that requires someone seeking to invoke equitable rules to have conducted himself or herself fairly and honourably in the events leading up to the lawsuit, and in the lawsuit itself.

common law The Anglo-Canadian system of law that features decided cases as a principal source of law. Also used as a synonym for **case law**, as distinguished from law based on statutes.

court of first instance The court in which a dispute is first heard and a decision is made. Also called a trial court.

distinguishing cases Showing how the facts of a case are significantly different from the facts of a case that has been cited as a precedent case.

deductive reasoning A reasoning process where one draws specific, narrow conclusions based on an analysis of general principles. *See also* inductive reasoning.

doctrine In civil code systems, secondary sources of law that explain and expand on the articles in the codes that are the primary sources of law.

Doctrine of Parliamentary Supremacy In a parliamentary system of government like Canada's, the legislative bodies at the federal and provincial levels are free to make whatever laws they wish within their own spheres: the courts cannot overrule them, and are limited to interpreting what the legislature intended. The doctrine has been weakened somewhat by the *Charter of Rights and Freedoms*, which is discussed in another chapter.

Enlightenment, the An 18th-century European intellectual movement characterized by an interest in rationalism and scientific inquiry.

equitable remedies A class of remedies that supplement and expand the principal remedies available at common law.

federal state A state in which the power to govern is divided between two or more levels of government. Each level of government usually has supreme governing power within its own sphere; the other level of government cannot interfere with the exercise of jurisdiction.

hierarchy of courts	An idea that in any judicial system the courts can be ranked in terms of their power and jurisdiction.
inductive reasoning	A reasoning process where one makes general conclusions based on an analysis of particular facts. *See also* deductive reasoning.
injunction	A court remedy, developed under the law of equity, where the court can order someone to do something or to refrain from doing it.
jurisdiction	The power or authority of a court to decide matters before it. Often used to refer to the boundary or limits of judicial power, in which case one refers to matters "outside" or "beyond" the court's jurisdiction.
law of equity	Developed in the early common law period as an administrative response to the rigidity and occasional unfairness of the common law courts; the law of equity prevails over the common law, where there is a conflict between the two.
legal system	Includes all of the structures, functions, values, rules, and procedures that are involved in the making and application of legal rules in society.
obiter dicta, obiter	An opinion or principle of law stated in reasons for judgment, which is not the principle that decides the case; for this reason, an *obiter* opinion has little precedent value.
on circuit	A method of administering justice originally used in England to make sure that judges were available in all parts of the realm and not just in the capital. Superior Court judges not only hear cases in the capital city, but also **go on circuit**, hearing cases in county towns on a regular basis. It has also been used in parts of Canada.
persuasive	In the context of *stare decisis*, a case is to be considered persuasive if it should be accorded respect and should be followed, but is not binding.
precedent case, following precedent	An earlier case that is similar in facts to the case at bar so that it can determine the legal result in the case at bar. To **follow the precedent** means that the judge, having found a case to be a precedent, applies the rule from that case to the case at bar.
private law	The law governing legal relationships between individuals.
public law	The law relating to the operation of government, covering relations between the citizen and the state.
ratio, or *ratio decidendi*	The reason for decision, or principle on which the legal outcome of the case can be determined.
stare decisis	A legal doctrine that says that a case determined to be a precedent must be followed, even if a judge does not favour the results that must come from application of the precedent.
statutory law	Law based on a statute; can be contrasted with law derived from cases, called **case law**.
suitor	A person who is suing someone else.

REVIEW QUESTIONS

1. How did Canada come to have two legal systems?

2. What is the doctrine of precedent?

3. What is the difference between the doctrine of precedent and the doctrine of *stare decisis*?

4. (a) What does it mean to "distinguish a case"?
   (b) What is "*obiter dicta*"?
   (c) What is a "*per incuriam*" decision?
   (d) What is the effect of concurring opinions in a case on its value as a precedent?

5. How did the common law method of deciding cases develop?

6. Why did the law of equity develop?

7. What are some of the features that distinguish the law of equity from the common law?

8. What is the relationship between the law of equity and the common law?

9. What problems arose in administering the common law and the law of equity, and how were they resolved?

10. What is statute law? How is it different from case law?

11. What advantages does statute law have over common law? Common law over statute law?

12. Describe ways in which the civil law system differs significantly from the common law system.

13. Describe the process for making judicial decisions in the civil law system. How does this process differ from the decision-making process in the common law system?

14. In what ways has the common law system had an impact on the civil law system of Quebec?

15. Describe three different meanings of "common law" and two different meanings of "civil law".

16. In what circumstances can you invoke the law of equity?

17. What is the relationship today between the law of equity, the common law (case law) and statutes?

18. What role, if any, does precedent play in the civil law system of Quebec?

19. Cite two features of the common law system and the civil code system that introduce flexibility into the rule-making and rule-application process.

DISCUSSION QUESTIONS

1. The civil law system in Canada was the result of an experiment in British colonial administration. Discuss and explain.

2. Legal reasoning in the common law system has been described as an ad hoc exercise in solving practical problems. Does this describe the process? How is the legal reasoning process in the common law system different from the legal reasoning process used in the civil law system?

3. In legal argument, one lawyer says that the decision in the case at bar can be determined by referring to the case of *Blogett v. Snogg*, which is a clear precedent. If the other lawyer wishes to avoid this conclusion, what techniques might be used to argue that *Blogett* is not a precedent?

4. All legal systems tend to become rigid and inflexible. Discuss this proposition as it might apply to the common law.

5. If you were a member of the British Colonial authorities in Quebec in 1774, and you were considering letting Quebec keep some of its laws,

what areas might you let Quebec keep, and what areas might you want to terminate in favour of British Law?

6. The law of equity is a "gloss on the common law". Discuss the meaning of this statement.

SUGGESTED READING AND OTHER RESOURCES

Baker, J. *An Introduction to English Legal History*, 4th ed. (London: Butterworths, 2002).

David, R. *Major Legal Systems in the World Today: An Introduction to the Comparative Study of Law*, 4th ed., translated and adapted by J.E.C. Brierley (London: Sweet & Maxwell, 1993).

Gall, Gerald L. *The Canadian Legal System*, 5th ed. (Toronto: Carswell, 2004).

Glenn, H.P. *Legal Traditions of the World*, 4th ed. (Oxford, Ont.: Oxford University Press, 2010).

Keir, D.L. *The Constitutional History of Modern Britain Since 1485*, 9th ed. (Princeton, N.J.: Van Nostrand, 1966).

Kelly, J.M. *A Short History of Western Legal Theory* (Oxford: Oxford University Press, 1994).

Kiralfy, A.K.R. *The English Legal System*, 8th ed. (London: Sweet & Maxwell, 1990).

Plucknett, T.F.T. *A Concise History of the Common Law*, 5th ed. (London: Butterworths, 1956).

———. *Studies in English Legal History*. (London: Hambleton, 1983).

Stychin, Carl, & Mulcahy, Linda. *Legal Method and Systems: Text and Materials* (London: Sweet & Maxwell, 2007).

Waddams, S.M. *Introduction to the Study of Law*, 7th ed. (Toronto: Carswell, 2010).

WEBSITES

Canada, Ministry of Justice: <http://www.justice.gc.ca/eng/csj-sjc/just/>

Canadian Judicial Council's Resource Centre:
<http://www.cjc-ccm.gc.ca/english/resource_en.asp?selMenu=resource_main_en.asp>

Canadian Superior Courts Judges Association:
<http://www.cscja-acjcs.ca/rule_of_law-en.asp?l=4>

The Law Dictionray: <http://thelawdictionary.org/>

Sources of Law

Laurence M. Olivo
SENECA COLLEGE

Learning Objectives

After reading this chapter, the reader should be able to:

➢ understand the concept of legal relevance in determining sources of law

➢ identify the major sources of law in Canada

➢ know how statutory and case law sources are organized and accessed

➢ understand the relationship between statutes and subordinate legislation

➢ become familiar with basic rules of statutory interpretation

➢ understand the relationship between, and the importance of, the various sources of law

TABLE OF CONTENTS

INTRODUCTION: DETERMINING WHAT INFORMATION CONSTITUTES A SOURCE OF LAW

The Concept of a Valid Source of Law

In any legal system, the process of solving a legal dispute involves the reasoned application of "law" to the facts of a dispute. However, how do we know what "law" is? To put it another way, what rules or principles that might solve a dispute are acceptable as legal rules or principles? In answering this question, we are really deciding, by choosing from among the possibilities, what rules or principles are legally relevant and can be accepted by the users of a legal system as a valid source of law.

For example, if you are supposed to clear your sidewalk of snow and ice, and you forget to do it, and someone slips and falls, what is legally relevant to determining whether you are responsible?

- A statute?
- A by-law?
- Case law?
- Moral duty not to cause injury to others?
- Your standing in the community?
- A revelation from God telling you what to do?

In this example, we have to decide which of the above sources of a rule might be legally relevant as the source of a rule in our legal system. Once we have done this, we may describe a source of information that is relevant for inclusion in a legal system as a valid source of law. Then, from among the valid sources of legal rules and principles, we have to choose the rule or principle that is relevant to the problem at hand. In this chapter, we are primarily concerned with the first problem: deciding what are valid sources of law so that we know where to find rules that are legitimate for use in the legal system.

Determining a Valid Source of Law

There is no automatic, objective formula that can be applied to determine what will be considered a valid source of law in a legal system. In each legal system, what is considered a valid source of law depends on many factors, including historical development, customs, and traditions.

For example, because the common law system developed as a means of enhancing royal power, it was important that the king's judges quickly developed some rules that were distinct from local ones and common to the country as a whole. From that need developed the case law system with which we are now familiar, and which we accept as a major source of law. In other systems, historical forces led to the government's convening a conference to set up a code of law, as happened in Napoleon's France and in Quebec.

MAJOR SOURCES OF LAW IN CANADA

In Canada, in the common law system, the major sources of law, in the order of their importance to the system, are statute law and case law or common law. There are also some other miscellaneous sources of law that are discussed at the end of this chapter. Another feature discussed here is how the major sources of law are organized so that legal rules can be found, retrieved from their organizational system, and used.[1]

---

[1] This topic will be explored in more detail in another chapter, "Legal Research", which deals with basic legal research skills, offered in the complete edition of this modular textbook.

EXHIBIT 3.1

The process of enacting a statute is fairly cumbersome and time consuming. While on the surface the process looks inefficient, it does provide time and opportunity for members of a legislature to scrutinize and criticize proposed legislation.

Most bills that are introduced are **public bills**, brought in to implement government policy. There are also **private bills,** in which the legislature is asked to implement legislation for some private or purely local purpose. For example, municipalities often request legislation to amend their powers to allow them to exercise some minor power that they feel they need. Last, there are **private member's bills**, introduced by individual legislators, which deal with subjects that are not taken up by the government as part of its programs. Because most of a legislature's time is taken up with the government's business, private member's bills are rarely enacted. The enactment process set out below is based on the process in Ontario. Other provinces have similar procedures. For the federal government, note that after passage in the House of Commons, the bill must go through the same process in the Senate before it can receive Royal Assent.

The Enactment Process

1. **Idea for legislative proposal.** This may come from a minister's initiative, advocacy or lobby group proposal, or other source.

2. **Ministry review of proposal.** Staff advise on proposal, and make recommendations to the minister.

3. **Minister's approval.** A policy submission is prepared by staff and approved by the minister.

4. **Cabinet submission by minister.** A detailed Cabinet submission on the legislative proposal is prepared, reviewed, and commented on by other ministries.

5. **Cabinet submission reviewed by Management Board of Cabinet.** Cabinet reviews amended Cabinet submission and approves, amends, or rejects submission.

6. **Approved Cabinet submission sent to Legislative Drafting Office.** Ministry staff and drafting office staff develop the first draft of the bill. The drafting office will continue to make changes resulting from amendments during the legislative process.

7. **First reading of the bill.** The bill is introduced by the minister, and background information is given to the legislature. The bill is put on the legislative agenda, printed and distributed to legislators and the public, in both a paper version and in an electronic version on the government website.

8. **Second reading.** The bill is debated in general terms. The minister makes opening and closing speeches. All members may speak once on the bill. There are no amendments at this stage. The Speaker calls a vote. If there is unanimous consent, the bill goes directly to third reading; if not, it goes to a standing or select committee of the House, as determined by the minister.

9. **Select or standing committee.** Members of the committee can comment on the bill, hold public hearings, allow public input, and call and question witnesses. The committee then does a clause-by-clause examination, and may amend the bill. The bill is then reported back to the whole House, and, if amended, is reprinted in a second reading version. If there is unanimous consent in the House, the bill may go directly to third reading; otherwise, it is referred to the committee of the whole House.

10. **Committee of the whole House.** Members debate the bill with less formality than is usual in the House; there is no public participation. Members may pass amendments. If so, the bill is reprinted in a third reading version.

11. **Third reading.** The bill is formally debated in general terms; no further amendments are permitted. Any member may move that the final vote be held on the bill.

12. **Royal assent.** If the bill passes, it is presented to the lieutenant governor for his signature or assent to the bill's passage. When the bill receives Royal Assent, it becomes an Act of the legislature and is given a statute number and reprinted.

13. **Proclamation of Act in force.** A section of the Act itself will determine whether it is proclaimed in force upon receiving Royal Assent or on a day fixed by the lieutenant governor or on a specified date.

The discussion of sources at the provincial level uses Ontario as a primary example, although the sources in other provinces are organized in a similar way.

Major Sources: Statute Law

Statutes, or Acts of legislatures ("legislature" as used here includes both provincial legislatures and the federal Parliament), are perhaps the most important sources of law because of the vast quantity of statutory rules, and because they overrule the common law where they conflict with it.

Statutes in a Federal System

In a federal system, the constitution divides the power to govern between the national and provincial governments. The subject matter of a statute determines whether it should be passed by Parliament or by a provincial legislature. To be a valid law, the subject matter of legislation must come within the heads of power granted by section 92 to the provinces or by section 91 to the federal government, under the *Constitution Act, 1867*. If a level of government passes legislation on a subject for which that level has no legislative authority in the *Constitution Act, 1867*, then that legislation is ***ultra vires***, or beyond the power of the legislature to enact. In such a situation, once a court declares the legislation is invalid, it is of no force or effect and need not be obeyed.

Relationship between Statutes and Case Law

As noted earlier in this chapter, when a statute is inconsistent with previous case law, the statute overrules the case law. However, it is also important to remember that a large body of case law is case law that interprets statutes, giving depth and meaning to statutory provisions. In some circumstances, case law develops new directions, giving additional meaning to statutory provisions that they may not have had when the statute was originally passed.

Finding Statute Law

On each of the three readings of a bill, a printed version is available through either the clerk of the legislative body or from the Internet statute-search website that each province and the federal government maintains. Use of anything other than the third-reading version is not advisable, as the bill is usually amended to some extent between first and third reading.

Bills are numbered sequentially in the order in which they are introduced during a session, and are referenced and accessed by their bill number. Federal bills have the alphabetical prefix "C" before the sequential number, but are otherwise referenced in the same way as provincial bills.[2]

To look up a bill, go to the current bill service on the Internet statute search site, and click on the bill number. The site will show each stage of the bill until it receives Royal Assent and becomes a statute.

When a bill is passed and becomes a statute, it will be listed on the Internet statute search site alphabetically by title as source law for a period before it is moved and listed alphabetically by title as consolidated law with other statutes passed previously. Numbers are given sequentially to each bill that becomes a statute. The reference to the annual volume of statutes is "S.O.", for Statutes of Ontario, followed by the year and the chapter number.

Example: *Civil Remedies Act*, 2001, S.O. 2001, c. 28

The key to finding statute law, whether newly passed or consolidated with other statutes previously passed, is the name of the Act, as the Internet

---

[2] See "Suggested Reading and Other Resources" at the end of the chapter for sources of law databases.

EXHIBIT 3.2

The Outline of a Statute

The way a statute is organized will vary with its subject matter. Knowing how a statute is organized, generally, will make it easier for someone reading a particular statute for the first time to find information. The basic organizational scheme for modern statutes is as follows:

1. Long title and chapter number.
2. Preamble. (Usually begins with "Whereas" and sets out the main principles and purposes of the Act; the preamble is a useful and legitimate aid to interpreting the statute. Not all statutes have preambles.)
3. Introductory sections containing definitions used in the Act, the scope or application of the Act, powers of officials administering the Act, and other administrative matters.
4. Body of the Act.
5. Housekeeping sections — proclamation date, regulation-making powers, short title of the Act, as required.

Following is a reproduction of an Ontario Act, as it appears in the Ontario government website: e-Laws <http://www.e-laws.gov.on.ca/index.html>.

Absentees Act
R.S.O. 1990, CHAPTER A.3

Last amendment: 2006, c. 19, Sched. C, s. 1(1).

Definition

1. An absentee within the meaning of this Act means a person who, having had his or her usual place of residence or domicile in Ontario, has disappeared, whose whereabouts is unknown and as to whom there is no knowledge as to whether he or she is alive or dead. R.S.O. 1990, c. A.3, s. 1.

Declaration by court

2. (1) The Superior Court of Justice may by order declare a person to be an absentee if it is shown that due and satisfactory inquiry has been made, or may direct such further inquiry to be made and proceedings to be taken as the court considers expedient before making any order. R.S.O. 1990, c. A.3, s. 2 (1); 2006, c. 19, Sched. C, s. 1 (1).

Application, who may make

(2) The application for the order may be made by,
    (a)   the Attorney General;
    (b)   any one or more of the next of kin of the alleged absentee;
    (c)   the person to whom the alleged absentee is married;
    (d)   the person with whom the alleged absentee was living in a conjugal relationship outside marriage immediately before the absentee's disappearance;
    (e)   a creditor; or
    (f)   any other person. R.S.O. 1990, c. A.3, s. 2 (2); 1999, c. 6, s. 1; 2005, c. 5, s. 1.

Appeal

(3) Any person aggrieved or affected by the order has the right to appeal therefrom. R.S.O. 1990, c. A.3, s. 2 (3).

Order declaring person no longer absentee

3. Upon application at any time, the court, if satisfied that such person has ceased to be an absentee, may make an order so declaring and superseding, vacating and setting aside the order declaring the person an absentee for all purposes except as to acts or things done in respect of the estate of the absentee while such order was in force. R.S.O. 1990, c. A.3, s. 3.

Administration of estate

4. The court may make an order for the custody, due care and management of the property of an absentee, and a committee may be appointed for that purpose. R.S.O. 1990, c. A.3, s. 4.

The Outline of a Statute

EXHIBIT 3.2 (continued)

Who may be appointed committee

5. A trust corporation with or without one or more persons may be appointed such committee. R.S.O. 1990, c. A.3, s. 5.

Powers and duties of court and committee

6. Where a committee of the estate of an absentee has been appointed, the powers and duties of the court and committee are the same, with necessary modifications, as the powers and duties of the court and of a guardian of property under the *Substitute Decisions Act*, 1992. 1992, c. 32, s. 1.

Powers of committee to expend money out of estate

7. The committee, subject to the direction of the court, has authority to expend moneys out of the estate of an absentee for the purpose of endeavouring to trace the absentee and in endeavouring to ascertain whether he or she is alive or dead. R.S.O. 1990, c. A.3, s. 7.

Lands in Ontario of foreign absentee

8. Where a person who has had his or her usual place of residence or domicile out of Ontario and who has an interest in land in Ontario has been declared to be an absentee by a court of competent jurisdiction, the Superior Court of Justice may by order, upon being satisfied that the person has disappeared, that his or her whereabouts is unknown and that there is no knowledge as to whether the person is alive or dead, appoint a committee with such authority to manage, sell or otherwise deal with the interest in land as in the opinion of the court is in his or her best interests and those of his or her family. R.S.O. 1990, c. A.3, s. 8; 2006, c. 19, Sched. C, s. 1 (1).

---

sites, such as Ontario's E-laws, list all statutes alphabetically and not by chapter number or year of passage. In the example above, you would find the Act listed under "C" in both source law and consolidated law.

At one time, at both the provincial and federal level, legislative bodies consolidated all of the statutes and their amendments for the preceding period in a series of volumes called **revised statutes**. These volumes included all of the public statutes of the legislature in the form they were in at the revision date. The statutes were set out in alphabetical order and numbered sequentially in the revision volumes, using both the letter of the first word of the Act and a number. The volume in which it appeared, the *Revised Statutes of Ontario*, is also cited by its initials, R.S.O., followed by the year of revision and an alphanumeric chapter number.

Example: The *Courts of Justice Act*, R.S.O. 1990, c. C.43

When the only sources for statutes were in paper format only, the consolidation process made finding statutes a lot easier. But with statutory materials now being available online, the revised statute consolidation system is now obsolete. The last time consolidation was done in Ontario was in 1990. Previously, it had been done every ten years. The last federal revision was in 1985, and there has been none since. Nor will there be. If a statute existed in the last statutory revision, it keeps the R.S.O. citation format even today. (See the example above for the *Courts of Justice Act*.)

Now that all available statutes are online, when new laws are passed, or existing ones amended by an amending Act, they can easily be edited into the

---

| EXHIBIT 3.3 | Finding Statutes Using E-Laws |

E-laws (http://www.e-laws.gov.on.ca) is the Government of Ontario statute law database that has generally replaced the annual statutes of Ontario, the Revised Statutes of Ontario and other print versions of statutes and regulations. You may also search for provincial and federal statutes using private legal research databases such as LexisNexis, Quicklaw or CanLII.

- Current Bills service — click on the bill number to find a bill for any session and track its progress as it becomes a statute.

- New Laws — any statute passed in the previous 60 days is listed as new law alphabetically by the title of the statute.

- Current Consolidated Law — contains all recently passed statutes as well as any consolidated statute in existence at the time of the last revision in 1990 but in its current form, up to date including all amendments and updates. (An amendment to a statute is passed as a separate statute and is listed as a new law, after which it will then be incorporated into the statute it amends — the updated amended statute will be set out in consolidated law, listed alphabetically.)

  Example: The Courts of Justice Amendment Act, S.O. 2009, amends the *Courts of Justice Act*, R.S.O. 1990. The *Court of Justice Amendment Act* was found in source law when it was passed in 2009, and was then incorporated into the *Courts of Justice Act*, which is found in current consolidated law under "C".

- Source Law — archives statutes as they read when they were first enacted, and shows regulations as they read when first filed.

- Period in Time Law — shows the form and content of consolidated law at any point in time in the past.

- Repealed, Revoked, and Spent Law — shows consolidated statutes and regulations as they read immediately before repeal, revocation, or expiry if they ceased to be in force after a certain date.

- Legislative Tables — lists alphabetically all statutes and regulations in a variety of tables; shows legislative history; shows which Ministry is responsible for administering a statute; lists of statutes enacted in a given year; and so on.

- Ontario Gazette — an E-version of the *Gazette* containing government announcements, proclamations, statutory notices and regulations. (No longer available in print format).

---

electronic statute database so that they are always in their most up-to-date version. The cumbersome periodic paper process has been replaced by a much simpler, easier to use statutory search process.

Primary and Subordinate Legislation

The legislatures of the 10 provinces, those of the territories, and the federal Parliament all enact legislation by the process described above (with some minor variations). However, the statutes, or **primary legislation**, passed by the legislature may be only the tip of the legislative iceberg on the particular subject covered by the legislation. Many statutes contain provisions, usually found at the end of the statute, in a part dealing with "housekeeping", where either the Cabinet (formally called the Lieutenant Governor in Council for a province and the Governor General in Council for the federal government) or a minister has the power to make regulations under the Act with respect to subject matter that is set out in the section authorizing the making of regulations. Regulations made by this process are called **subordinate legislation**. In practice, the actual creation and drafting of regulations is left to civil servants in the ministry responsible. The subject matter of regulations usually deals with administrative details and procedures for carrying out the statute's general purposes.

For example, procedural rules used in the courts of Ontario could have been included in the *Courts of Justice Act*. However, if that had been done, the act would have been many times longer than it is now, and the legislature could not have adequately addressed all the technical issues involved in keeping the rules up-to-date. Moreover, as the rules are amended frequently, the legislature would have to be in constant session to deal with the amendments and would have little time for other government business. Instead, the much more responsive and faster regulation-making process is used. In the case of the rules of civil procedure, the regulations establish a rules committee, composed of persons with specialized knowledge who have the power to make the necessary rule amendments by regulation.

Finding Regulations

A torrent of regulations are passed every year. Initially, before they take effect, they must appear in the government's official publication for public notices, called a **gazette** (the *Canada Gazette* is at the federal level, and there are gazettes at the provincial level). When a regulation is gazetted, it is assigned a number in sequence for the year in which it is made. The regulation can then be referenced as, for example, Ontario Regulation 45/12. This means it was the 45th regulation to be gazetted for 2012. The abbreviation of the citation is: O. Reg. 45/12.

In Ontario, as in many jurisdictions, the gazette is now available in electronic format. In Ontario, current and past issues are listed in sequence and are available on e-laws. However, they are often posted just as quickly under the statute that authorized them. For example, on e-laws, if you know that the O. Reg. 45/12 was made under the authority of the *Courts of Justice Act*, you can find that regulation listed under that statute in consolidated law, along with all the other regulations under that Act, listed in alphabetical order.

As is the case with statutes, regulations traditionally have gone through a revision process about once a decade in most Canadian jurisdictions. However, as with statutes, that is no longer the case. In Ontario, the last consolidation of regulations, the *Revised Regulations of Ontario*, took place in 1990. Regulations included in that revision are cited by the citation they had at the time of revision. For example, the Rules of Civil Procedure, a regulation under the *Courts of Justice Act*, is cited as R.R.O. 1990, Reg. 194. As with statutes, if you look up any regulation on the database, you will see the current version of the regulation, updated with the latest amendments.

Finding Regulations Using E-Laws	EXHIBIT 3.4

Click on Ontario Gazette — you can search by regulation number and year: for example, O. Reg. 45/12 for the edition of the *Gazette* with the posting of this regulation.

If you know the name of the statute under which the regulation was made, click on Consolidated Law, and click on the plus sign next to the name of the statute. A list will appear of all of the current regulations made under that Act in their amended and current format, listed alphabetically. Click on the title of the regulation to open it to see the text.

"The Plain Intention of the Legislature" — Interpreting Statutes

Judges often use the phrase "the plain intention of the legislature" (or one like it) when interpreting statutes. When they use it, they are saying that the meaning of a section of a statute is clear to them. Yet there are few statutes that have not been the subject of litigation, where one lawyer or another has argued that a section of a statute is ambiguous or unclear. This is why case law is sometimes said to give further depth and meaning to statutory rules.

Modern statutes are often very clearly drafted, although the same cannot be said for statutes drafted before 1900. But no statute drafter can foresee every possible situation or contingency that the statute may deal with. Nor does the drafter wish, in every case, to be overly precise, as by so doing the scope of the statute may become too narrow and inflexible.

The Basic Rule: Determine the Intent of the Legislature

If parliamentary supremacy is to mean anything, it must mean that legislation takes on the meaning that was intended by the members of the legislative body that created the statute. Judges are not free to recreate their own idea of what the statute means.

However, the intention of the legislature is really a fiction. Not all the members of the legislature would necessarily agree on the meaning of the statute; even legislators who are members of the governing party might not agree on the meaning or, even, be aware of what the Act is about. But the approach to interpreting an Act begins and ends with finding the legislative intent.

Rules of Construction

A judge begins the search for legislative intent by applying logical and grammatical rules to the language of the statute. Here a judge relies on one or more of the rules of statutory construction. If a judge chooses one rule over another to interpret the language of a specific statute, the result may be very different from what it might have been had another rule been chosen. There is no automatic "right" rule, and some might argue that a judge simply chooses the rule to justify where he or she wants to go, obscuring the real basis for interpretation. Five of the more common interpretative rules are discussed below:

1. **The plain meaning rule:** If the words of the statute are clear and precise in their meaning, then that is the meaning the words are to be given, even if the judge thinks the outcome leads to absurdity or unfairness. If Parliament is supreme, then it may be unfair or absurd if it chooses to be, subject to limits on legislative action imposed by the *Charter of Rights and Freedoms*.[3]

    Example: Consider this excerpt from the *Dog Owners' Liability Act*. "The owner of a dog is liable for damages resulting from a bite or attack by the dog on another person or domestic animal." If the dog bit your pet boa constrictor, a judge, applying the plain meaning rule, might hold that the Act did not apply in this situation because a boa constrictor, though your pet, is a wild animal and not a domestic animal, as domestic animals are considered to be tamed. Here, a plain, obvious and usual meaning is given to the keywords, "domestic animal".

---

[3] The relationship between the supremacy of the legislature and the *Charter* is explored in the discussion of the role of the judges and the courts in other chapters — "The Court System", "The Constitution", and "The *Canadian Charter of Rights and Freedoms*" — which are offered in the complete edition of this modular textbook.

2. **The golden rule:** The words of the statute are to be given their clear meaning unless this would result in an absurdity, in which case it is permissible to examine the ambiguous part of the statute to see if it is inconsistent with the meaning and purpose of the rest of the statute. This rule expands the first rule by inviting a judge to give meaning to ambiguous language in part of the statute by reading it in the context of the whole statute.

   Example: Consider again the statutory language used for the preceding rule. "The owner of a dog is liable for damages resulting from a bite or attack by the dog on another person or domestic animal." If the golden rule is applied, the judge might look for the purpose of the statute and might conclude that it is intended to protect humans and animals with which humans choose to live from being harmed. In this case, the judge might interpret the language more broadly; the judge might reason that because the boa constrictor is a pet, given the Act's purpose, the snake should come within the category of "domestic animal".

3. **The mischief rule:** This rule is restricted in use to statutes that change the common law, rather than codify the common law. With such statutes, the ambiguity might be resolved by asking three questions:
   (i)   What was the common law before the Act changed it?
   (ii) What was the mischief or problem that the common law did not adequately address?
   (iii) What remedy did the legislature create to prevent the mischief?

   With the answers to these questions in hand, judges are then supposed to have true insight into the nature and purpose of the Act so that they can interpret the ambiguous language to give effect to the remedy sought and to prevent the mischief from occurring.

   Example: Assuming the section of the *Dog Owners' Liability Act* that is discussed here is not a codification of the common law, a judge might use the mischief rule to determine the true purpose of the statute. Here, the steps for doing that are spelled out. First, the judge asks what the common law was: it might have only afforded protection to humans who were seriously hurt. If so, the judge might ask the second question, as to what mischief arose under the common law; here, the judge might find that domestic animals and pets were not protected. Last, the judge would ask what remedy was created by the legislature; the answer was protection for humans and domestic animals and pets, with penalties for dog owners.

4. *Ejusdem generis*: This Latin term means that the meaning of a general word or phrase comes from the more specific words that precede it in a sentence or clause. For example, in the clause "no cats, dogs, or other animals shall be permitted in residences", the word "animals" arguably includes domestic pets, but not barnyard animals or wild animals.

5. *Expressio unius, exclusio alterius*: Under this rule, the specific use of one word or phrase, by logic, implies the exclusion of another word or phrase. Often this means that an ordinary dictionary-defined antonym (a word with an opposite meaning) is excluded. At other times, an appreciation of a particular context is required to use this rule. Where the context itself is ambiguous, the rule may provide more problems than solutions.

Example: Consider the phrase "domestic animal" in the section of the *Dog Owners' Liability Act* previously referred to. "The owner of a dog is liable for damages resulting from a bite or attack by the dog on another person or domestic animal." Here, if the issue was about a dog attack on a wild animal, the judge might cite the *expressio unius alterius rule*, holding that the qualification of "animal" by the word "domestic" excluded wild animals from the statute's protection.

External Aids to Statutory Interpretation

In addition to the linguistic interpretive rules noted above, there are other sources a judge can use to interpret statutes:

1. **Scholarly and academic writing:** There are a number of articles and texts that deal with major legislation, which judges may cite when interpreting a statute, often as a way of confirming their approach to an issue of interpretation. As well, there are texts, such as *Maxwell on Interpretation of Statutes* or E.A. Driedger's *The Construction of Statutes*, that are virtual encyclopedias for statutory interpretation in Canada.

2. **Interpretation statutes:** These statutes exist at both the federal and provincial levels, and attempt to systematically set out some basic rules of interpretation and construction governing all other statutes in their jurisdiction. Such statutes often contain definition sections that give a meaning for words to be used in all other statutes. An interpretation statute will also set out general canons, or rules of interpretation, to be used in all statutes. An example is the rule that all statutes are remedial and should be given a broad and expansive interpretation.

3. **Legislative history:** In the search for legislative intent, it has long been traditional in Canada and Britain to ignore *Hansard* (the official record of debates in a legislature), committee reports, royal commission reports, ministers' speeches, press releases, and other such documents. The assumption in Canada has always been that the intent of the legislature is summed up in the words of the statute itself, and one need go no further than the words of the statute to find the meaning.

   The American experience is somewhat different, and much of what one might call historical documentation from the legislative process may be used as an aid to interpretation, particularly in constitutional cases.

   However, in *Charter of Rights* cases, and also in native treaty rights cases, there is some indication that legislative history may have a legitimate interpretive role. There is a growing use of the technique in constitutional cases as a way of gaining insight into the meaning of legislation under the constitutional challenge.

4. **Statutory presumptions:** Over time, as a result of custom, convention, historical events and interpretative case law, a number of presumptions have attached like barnacles to statutes dealing with specific subject matter. For example, there is a presumption in criminal law statutes that all crimes shall be interpreted strictly and narrowly rather than broadly. Another is a presumption that no statute is to be read **retroactively.** This means the statute does not apply to situations that existed prior to the statute's enactment but applies only to situations arising after its passage.

Major Sources: Common Law

Common Law or Case Law

The use of decided cases as a source of law has been a distinctive feature of the common law system. The importance of cases as a source of law was due in part to the doctrine of precedent, which requires that cases decided in the past that are similar to the case at bar be followed. The doctrine of *stare decisis* took the doctrine of precedent a step further by making precedent cases of higher courts binding on lower courts within the same jurisdiction.

Case law is not followed if a statute contradicts the ratio of the case, or if the case can be distinguished. It is noted that when a court considers a precedent to be binding, it needs to first determine whether the court that decided the precedent is a "higher court".

Also to be considered is whether a precedent, though not binding, should be seen as **persuasive**. This is determined by a number of possible subjective factors — the reputation of the judge and the reputation of the court. If the case comes from a high-level court in another jurisdiction that is respected by judges in Canada, deference may be given to its decisions. For example, cases from British superior courts are often deferred to, while cases from American superior courts often are not. Also, on rare occasions, a judge will reject a precedent altogether, and take the law from a line of cases in a new direction entirely. These observations are a reminder that common law can be more flexible than it at first appears to be.

Finding Case Law

Case law developed as an integral part of the common law system at an early stage because it was written down so that it was accessible. No one had to try and remember all of the rules. Its continued importance owes much to the fact that it continues to be written down and made accessible through **law reports**, which are published reports of decided cases, traditionally published and available as hard copy, but also published in electronic format on the Internet from a variety of sources.

There is no particular system to law report publishing, and much of it, both in paper and in electronic format, is in private hands. There are "official reports" published by some courts, such as the *Supreme Court Reports*, which report the decisions of the Supreme Court of Canada; there are provincial reporting series, which report a medley of cases from a particular province; and there are Canada-wide reporting services, which report decisions of note from across the country. There are also reports that focus on specialized areas of law, such as the *Canadian Practice Cases* that report cases dealing with procedural law. Some cases are reported in only one reporting series, while others may be reported in several. Some, however, are not reported at all. The decision to report is a subjective one, made by the editorial boards of the various law reports, and by electronic case report providers.

An unreported case, though not easily accessed as hard copy, still has precedent value. In recent years, particularly with the establishment of computer case databases, it has become possible to list and easily summarize many of these unreported cases. Cases can easily be added to a case law database, and the technology puts few restrictions on the size of the database. On the other hand, printed books come with a comparatively greater cost — printing — and libraries have only so much room for volumes of case books.

Finding case law is made even easier with electronic databases as there are computerized indices of legal issues that allow relatively quick and thorough searches to be done that will identify reported and unreported cases. Because the case reporting process is unco-ordinated and unsystematic, the process of finding an appropriate precedent case can still be a time-consuming exercise, particularly compared to the search for a principle in the civil law

EXHIBIT 3.5	What Judgments, Reasons for Decision, and Reported Reasons for Decision Look Like

1. A **judgment** or **order** is a command from the court; it tells parties what they must do, but not why the judge decided the way he did. Page 1 of a judgment is produced below:

Court file no. 2987/90

SUPERIOR COURT OF JUSTICE

THE HONOURABLE MR. JUSTICE SNORK

TUESDAY, THE 16 DAY OF APRIL 1992

BETWEEN:

HENRY SNOOT

and   Plaintiff

MICHAEL SNIT

Defendant

Judgment

THIS ACTION was heard on the 2nd, 3rd, and 16th day of April, 1992, without a jury at Brampton, in the presence of counsel for both parties,

ON READING THE PLEADINGS AND HEARING THE EVIDENCE and submissions of counsel for the parties,

1. THIS COURT ORDERS AND ADJUDGES that the plaintiff recover from the defendant the sum of $102,000.00.
2. THIS COURT ORDERS AND ADJUDGES that the defendant do pay to the plaintiff his costs of this action, forthwith after assessment.

THIS judgment BEARS INTEREST at the rate of 3 per cent per year, commencing on April 16, 1992.

J.R. Snerg,
Local Registrar

2. A judge's written **reasons for decision** is like an essay, explaining in writing the basis for his decision. Page 1 of a sample reasons for decision is set out below:

SUPERIOR COURT OF JUSTICE

BETWEEN:

ANNA ADAMANT   ]   J.W. Tough, Esq.
                                           ]   for the Plaintiff
        Plaintiff   ]
                                           ]
and   ]
                                           ]
                                           ]
EDWARD ADAMANT   ]   Sandra Sharp,
                                           ]   for the Defendant
        Defendant   ]
                                           ]   Heard: July 2,3, 1994

What Judgments, Reasons for Decision, and Reported Reasons for Decision Look Like

EXHIBIT 3.5 (continued)

TRAINOR, J.

The single issue in this proceeding, is the custody of the child, Adam Adamant, born February 1, 1991.

The resolution of that issue is often one of the most difficult problems that judges encounter. It is particularly so where both parents have demonstrated concern over the welfare of their child. The fact that both parents are well educated, sophisticated, professional people having considered and firm opinions about the proper way in which a child ought to....

3. In a **reported reasons for decision** the typed essay in the preceding example is set out in printed form in a law report, and contains additional information. A sample law report version of Reasons for Decision is set out below.

RE GILL AND REGISTRAR OF MOTOR VEHICLES ET AL.
RE HEFFREN AND REGISTRAR OF MOTOR VEHICLES

Ontario Court of Appeal, Houlden, Goodman and Finlayson JJ.A.

Sentence — Driving offences — Provincial suspension of driver's licence — Legislation providing for increased periods of suspension depending on number of convictions for Criminal Code driving offences — Motorist liable for increased period of suspension only where offence for which increased penalty sought occurred after prior conviction — Highway Traffic Act, R.S.O. 1980, c. 198, s. 26.

Section 26(1) of the *Highway Traffic Act*, R.S.O. 1980, c. 198, which provides that the driver's licence of a motorist who is convicted of a *Criminal Code* driving offence is thereupon suspended for a period of "(a) upon the first conviction, three months; (b) upon the first subsequent conviction, six months; and (c) upon an additional subsequent conviction, three years" imposes a penalty and should be construed in the same way as criminal legislation which imposes an increased penalty by reason of previous convictions. Accordingly, the rule of statutory interpretation applies that where a statute imposes an increased penalty for a subsequent conviction, the offence for which the increased penalty is sought must have occurred after the prior conviction, before the increased penalty can be imposed. The fact that section 26(1) refers to a "conviction" rather than "offence" is not a significant distinction. An occurrence does not become an offence until there is a conviction but once there is a conviction, the terms "conviction" and "offence" are used interchangeably for the purpose of applying the rule of interpretation.

Benn v. Registrar of Motor Vehicles et al. (1981), 59 C.C.C. (2d) 421, 10 M.V.R. 214, **overd**

R. v. Cheetham (1980), 53 C.C.C. (2d) 109, 17 C.R. (3d) 1; *R. v. Skolnick*, [1982] 2 S.C.R. 47, 68 C.C.C. (2d) 385, 138 D.L.R. (3d) 193, 29 C.R. (3d) 143, 16 M.V.R. 35, 42 N.R. 460, **apld**

R. v. Joslin (1981), 59 C.C.C. (2d) 512, 10 M.V.R. 29; *R. v. Negridge* (1980), 54 C.C.C. (2d) 304, 17 C.R. (3d) 14, 6 M.V.R. 14, **consd**

Other cases referred to

Christie v. Britnell (1895), 21 V.L.R. 71; *Farrington v. Thomson and Bridgeland*, [1959] V.R. 286; *R. v. O'Brien, Ex. p. Chamberlain* (1908), 38 N.B.R. 381; *O'Hara v. Harrington*, [1962] Tas. S.R. 165

Statutes referred to

Criminal Code, ss. 234, 234.1, 235, 236

Highway Traffic Act, R.S.O. 1980, c. 198, s. 26(1) (am. 1983, c. 63, s. 11), (2) (rep. & sub. 1984, c. 61, s. 1)

EXHIBIT 3.5 (continued)	What Judgments, Reasons for Decision, and Reported Reasons for Decision Look Like

Rules and regulations referred to

(Ont.) Rules of Civil Procedure (Ont.), rule 21.01
(Ont.) Rules of Practice (Ont.), Rule 124
(Ont.)

APPEALS by the registrar from a judgment of Smith J., 12 C.C.C. (3d) 23, and of McKinley J. on applications pursuant to Rule 124 (Ont.) to determine points of law.

Leslie M. McIntosh, for appellants.
Alan D. Gold, for respondent, Sukhpal-Singh Gill.
Robert J. Upsdell, for respondent, Louis Arnold Heffren.

The judgment of the court was delivered by

FINLAYSON J.A.:—Both these appeals are by the Registrar of Motor Vehicles (hereinafter Registrar) with respect to licence suspensions under s. 26(1) of the *Highway Traffic Act*, R.S.O. 1980, c. 198, as amended, by reason of convictions by the two respondents for certain automobile related offences under the *Criminal Code*....

Source: *Re Gill and Registrar of Motor Vehicles et al., Ontario Court of Appeal, Houlden, Goodman and Finlayson JJ. A., September 3, 1985,* 21 C.C.C. (3d) 1986, pp. 234–35. Reproduced with the permission of Canada Law Book, a division of The Thomson Reuters Canada Limited.

---

system, where an article in the code that provides the answer can be quickly located. But as more lawyers use indexed electronic databases of unreported cases, such as CanLII, which is available free of charge, and Quicklaw and LexisNexis, which are not, the distinction between reported and unreported cases may diminish.[4] If you have access to an electronic case report database, submission of the case name, with or without the citation, will often bring the case report up quickly, including cross references if the case was appealed and the appeal also reported. You can also quickly find out, on electronic databases, if a case was cited as an authority, or distinguished, or otherwise referred to in another reported case.

MISCELLANEOUS SOURCES OF LAW

While statute and case law are the most common and most important sources of law in the common law system, there are other sources of law that crop up occasionally.

Practice and Usage These two terms loosely describe ways in which things may be done that may achieve legal recognition. These forms of behaviour, which have no formal authorization or sanction, will generally be accepted as a source of law if

---

[4] The subject of finding law and dealing with basic legal research techniques is explored in another chapter, "Legal Research", which is offered in the complete edition of this modular textbook.

How Reasons for Decision Are Set Out in Published Law Reports   EXHIBIT 3.6

Case reports usually follow a generic format, which is set out below:

1. case name
2. court and judge(s)
3. date of decision
4. catch lines — phrases in bold print that can be scanned quickly to identify key facts and issues in the case, and that are also used as index headings and subheadings in the index to the law report series
5. headnote: a summary of the facts, the decision, and the reasons for the decision, including a list of cases, statutes, and other authorities referred to
6. a brief description of the form or purpose of proceeding (Appeal from ... Motion for....)
7. names of lawyers for the parties
8. full text of the judgment
9. final disposition

---

they go unchallenged, and other conduct or consequences that rest upon them will also be seen as legitimate. However, if a practice is challenged, the fact that it occurs is not sufficient to justify it as a source of law.

Custom and Convention

A practice or usage that has been in existence and in use for long enough (whatever "long enough" may mean), at some point can become enshrined in law as a custom or convention, at which time it is a source of law. Determining when the threshold is reached is a subjective process, with different results in different jurisdictions. There are, however, two key factors:

- The activity has gone on for a long time.
- There has been no interruption of or interference with the activity.

In Canada, custom and convention has been a very important source of constitutional law. In 1981, the Supreme Court of Canada decided that the Trudeau government could **repatriate** the Canadian Constitution by taking over control of constitutional change from the Parliament of the United Kingdom. The court's decision turned on a lengthy and detailed analysis of custom and convention with respect to the amount of provincial support required before the federal government could seek an amendment to the Constitution.[5]

Scholarly Legal Writing

On rare occasions, the musings of legal scholars may be a source of legal rules, where no other authority speaks to an issue. More often, however, such works are commentaries on existing law, useful in interpreting the law, rather than being a source of it.

Morality

Ever the delight of natural law theorists, morality has had a rough ride in modern common law. In the 19th and 20th centuries, where the issue was

---

[5] *Reference re Amendment of the Constitution of Canada*, [1981] 1 S.C.R. 753.

raised, the court would often deflect it by stating that "the court is not a court of morals." While morality might underlie a particular legal rule or principle, it is rarely the source of law, and operates only when no other source of law provides a solution to a particular legal problem.

The Crown or Royal Prerogative

This describes the power of the sovereign or, in Canada, the sovereign's representative (the Governor General, federally, and the Lieutenant Governor, provincially) to act in certain ways. Historically, the power is derived from the pre-democratic era when the King had power to rule personally and use his personal power as a royal right. As the relationship between the King and Parliament evolved, so did the prerogative. Parliaments have steadily taken away parts of the prerogative power by legislating it away; once a prerogative power is lost, by custom and convention, it cannot be revived. Further, the sovereign or his or her representatives rarely exercise a prerogative power without advice from the government.

Some examples of the use of the prerogative are the dissolution of a legislature prior to calling an election and the pardoning of criminals. To the extent that the prerogative can be exercised without having to take or follow advice of elected representatives, the prerogative can be viewed as a source of law.

CHAPTER SUMMARY

This chapter was about the sources of law used for legal problem solving in the common law system. There are two principal sources of law: statute law, including subordinate legislation, and case law. There are also some miscellaneous secondary sources: practice and usage, custom, convention, scholarly legal writing, morality, and the Crown prerogative. The secondary sources are used only when statute and case law do not provide answers. As between statute and case law, where a statute contradicts case law, the statute prevails.

The chapter also went beyond a description of the sources of law: it showed how statutes are made, in terms of how statutes are developed from a policy making and refining process, then formally prepared according to modern drafting conventions, and then formally enacted. The chapter went on to make the point that a statute is like a skeleton, and that it is fleshed out with regulations and with case law interpreting the sections of the Act.

Attention then turned to the interpretation of statutes by the courts. The major interpretive purpose is to discover the intent of the legislature, but the rules for doing this are sufficiently flexible to allow for quite different conclusions to be drawn, in a particular case, as to what the intent was. The chapter then identified other, more technical, rules for interpreting statutes.

The chapter then turned to case law, including a discussion of how one finds appropriate case law.[6]

Last, the miscellaneous or secondary sources of law (practice and usage, custom and convention, scholarly legal writing, morality, the Crown prerogative) were identified and discussed in terms of when they can be used and what their range or utility is.

---

[6] This issue is canvassed in more detail in another chapter, "Legal Research", which is offered in the complete edition of this modular textbook.

GLOSSARY OF NEW TERMS AND KEY CONCEPTS

bill	What a statute is called when it is introduced in a legislature. If it passes, it is then called an **Act**.
Cabinet submission	A document used to circulate a policy proposal for comment, or other government action, among the various ministries of the government. It then goes to Cabinet, where Cabinet ministers decide how to deal with the matter.
committee of the whole House	While a bill is normally scrutinized by a **standing committee** of the legislature that deals with the subject matter covered by the bill, a bill may be considered by a committee consisting of all of the members of the legislature for the clause-by-clause discussion usually done in standing committee.
first reading	The first stage of the legislative process in which a bill is introduced by the minister, and background information is given to the legislature. The bill is put on the legislative agenda, printed and distributed to legislators and the public, in both a paper version and in an electronic version on the government website.
gazette	The name of a publication issued by governments in Canada on a regular basis, usually weekly, containing official notices and announcements, and in which regulations made under the authority of a statute are first published. A regulation usually takes effect at publication; consequently, the **gazetting** of a regulation is an important step in its becoming enforceable.
judgment or **order**	A command from the court that must be followed.
law reports	Cases in which judges give reasons for judgment explaining a legal decision are gathered up and published in case reporting books called **law reports**. Law reports may be officially published by the government, law societies, or private publishers. They are no longer necessarily only in book form, as many law report series are available from online computer services.
Legislative Drafting Office	Most legislative bodies have a group of lawyers who are specialists in the art of drafting statutes. This office does not determine the content of legislation but does determine the form that legislation takes.
Management Board of Cabinet	A Cabinet committee that acts as a gatekeeper, determining which matters come before Cabinet.
persuasive	With respect to case law, a case decided by a respected judge from another jurisdiction, which is not binding on the court in the case at bar, is said to be persuasive if it otherwise influences the court.
primary legislation	Statutes are primary legislation; the term is used to distinguish statutes from regulations passed under the authority of statutes. Regulations are sometimes referred to as **subordinate legislation**.
private bill	A bill usually passed at the request of a specific person and that affects a particular person or body. For example, municipalities often ask to have a private bill passed in order to amend that municipality's powers.
private member's bill	A bill introduced by an individual MP or legislator that is not part of the government's legislative program. As the government controls the agenda of a legislature in order to get **government bills** passed, there is rarely time to consider private member's bills, and these usually do not come to a final vote.
proclaim in force	A bill does not come into force automatically when it is passed; it must first be proclaimed in force. This may be on a specific date, or when the government is ready, or upon passage of the bill, if the bill so provides.
public bill	A bill that affects the general law of the jurisdiction and concerns matters of a general or public nature.
repatriate	One repatriates something when one recovers its nationality. Canada repatriated its Constitution when it recovered from the United Kingdom the right as a nation to amend its own Constitution.

reasons for decision, reported	A judge's written reasons for making a judgment or an order. A reported reasons for decision is a judgment set out in printed form in a law report.
retroactive	A legal rule that takes effect in the period before the rule was created. Law is not supposed to be retroactive, and it is presumed that a law, when passed, takes effect only from and after the time of its passage.
revised statutes	In Canada, the federal government and the provinces consolidate and revise all statutes at regular intervals, deleting parts that have been repealed, and adding amendments since the date of the last revision.
Royal Assent	The final stage that a bill must complete before officially becoming an Act of Parliament. If a bill passes, it is presented to the lieutenant governor for his signature or assent to the bill's passage. When the bill receives Royal Assent, it becomes an Act of the legislature and is given a statute number and reprinted.
second reading	A stage of the process that results in a bill becoming a law. At this stage, the bill is debated in the legislature at length, the basic principles are discussed, and the bill is defended by the minister responsible for it. A vote to approve at this stage is a vote of approval in principle.
select or **standing committee**	A select or standing committee is a committee established by the legislature to examine legislation in detail prior to enactment. Members of the committee can comment on the bill, hold public hearings, allow public input, and call and question witnesses. The committee then does a clause-by-clause examination, and may amend the bill. The bill is then reported back to the whole House, and, if amended, is reprinted in a second reading version. If there is unanimous consent in the House, the bill may go directly to third reading; otherwise, it is referred to the committee of the whole House.
subordinate legislation	A law made by a body subordinate to the Parliament or a legislature under the authority of a parliamentary statute.
third reading	When the bill comes before the legislature after the committee stage has been completed, it receives its third and final reading and is voted on in its third reading form.
ultra vires	A Latin maxim that describes action that is unlawful because there is no authority to take that action; in a federal system, the maxim describes a statute passed by a legislative body that had no authority to pass the statute. The statute is, therefore, invalid and unlawful.

REVIEW QUESTIONS

1. How do we decide what a "valid source of law" is in a particular society?

2. What are the primary and miscellaneous sources of law in a common law system?

3. What steps have to be taken to make a political policy proposal into law?

4. Suppose the federal government and a provincial government both pass the exact same legislation. Does this create a problem? If so, what rules do we have for resolving the problem?

5. Suppose there is a common law rule that requires you to do something, and a statute that requires you to do the exact opposite. Which law do you obey? Why?

6. Does the Internet make searching for statute law easier than it used to be?

7. If a provincial statute was passed last year, describe the process to be used to locate it so you can read it.

8. You are told to look for a provincial statute called the *Road Servicing Act*. You have no idea whether it is a new statute, an amended statute, an old statute that has not been amended, or a bill. Describe, in sequential order, the sources you would examine to find the statute.

9. What are revised statutes? What problem did they solve? Are they necessary?

10. What is subordinate legislation? Why is it necessary?

11. Suppose you came across a reference to Regulation 4/12. Describe what you would do to find the regulation so you could read it.

12. What has been the impact of electronic databases on finding legal sources?

13. What is the main difference between government law databases and private databases?

14. Describe the following rules of statutory interpretation:
    (i) the plain meaning rule
    (ii) the golden rule
    (iii) the mischief rule

15. Are there real distinctions between the rules in Question 11, or are they really the same rule?

16. Using examples, explain how the following grammatical interpretive rules operate:
    (i) *ejusdem generis*
    (ii) *expressio unius, exclusio alterius*

17. Is it permissible to delve into the history of legislation to determine the meaning of the statute?

18. What are statutory presumptions? Give two examples, and illustrate how the presumptions work.

19. What is an "unreported case"?

20. What is the difference between a "judgment", "reasons for judgment", and "reported reasons for judgment"?

21. Are electronic case law searches easier to do than paper ones?

22. A legal practice has been going on for 700 years; it was challenged once in court 10 years ago. Can we rely on the practice and cite it as a source of law?

23. In what circumstances could one cite the writings of a very learned, erudite, and respected legal scholar as a source of law?

24. Suppose a law was passed this year that criminalized a conduct that occurred in 1988, when that conduct was lawful. What do we call this kind of law? Is it a valid law?

25. The last revision of Ontario statutes and regulations took place in 1990. Is it time for another?

DISCUSSION QUESTIONS ─────────────────────────────────

1. Anna signed an apartment lease that contained the following clause: "A tenant may keep a dog, cat or other domestic pet on the premises." Anna doesn't own a cat or a dog, but she caught a young aardvark on a trip to Africa, tamed it, and brought it home. The aardvark is an anteater that lives in southern Africa. It is small, quiet, and well-behaved. The landlord found out about the aardvark. He saw it looking out of Anna's window and knew it wasn't a cat or a dog. The landlord argued that Anna is violating the lease by keeping the aardvark. Anna argues that her keeping an aardvark does not violate the lease.

   Using rules of statutory construction, and statutory presumptions, where relevant, argue both Anna's case and the landlord's.

2. If you have access to the Internet, use the free Web search service e-Laws to find a section of an Ontario statute, the *Family Law Act*, that indicates how the Act applies to polygamous marriages. See "Suggested Reading and Other Resources" for the appropriate website address.

3. If you have access to the Internet, use the free case and statute law service CanLII to find the following case. See the list of websites under suggested readings for the appropriate website address.

   Your instructions from a lawyer were to find a case on natural justice involving someone named Spiegel and some college or other. That was all you were given. Try to find the case.

SUGGESTED READING AND OTHER RESOURCES ─────────────────

Attorney General of Canada v. Attorney General of Manitoba et al., [1981] 1 S.C.R. 72; originally called *A Reference re the Amendment of the Constitution of Canada*, this case contains a discussion of the nature of convention as a source of law.

Derbyshire, P. *Derbyshire on the English Legal System*, 10th ed. (London: Maxwell & Sweet, 2011).

Driedger, E. *The Interpretation of Statutes*, 4th ed. (Toronto: Butterworths, 1983).

Fitzgerald, M.F. *Legal Problem Solving: Reasoning, Research and Writing*, 5th ed. (Toronto: Lexis-Nexis, 2010).

Sullivan, R. *Driedger on the Construction of Statutes*, 4th ed. (Toronto: Butterworths, 2003).

WEBSITES

CanLII: <http://www.canlii.org/en/>
  (provincial and federal cases and statutes — public website)
e-Laws: <http://www.e-laws.gov.on.ca/index.html>
  (Ontario statutes, regulations and current bills — free access)
Federal laws: <http://laws.justice.gc.ca/en/index.html>
  (federal government consolidated statutes and regulations)
The Law Dictionray: <http://thelawdictionary.org/>
LexisNexis Canada: <http://www.butterworths.ca> for information
  (all U.S., provincial and federal cases and statutes — private subscription service)
Quicklaw: <http://ql.quicklaw.com>
  (all provincial and federal statutes and Canadian case law — private subscription service)

Types of Law

Laurence M. Olivo
SENECA COLLEGE

Learning Objectives

After reading this chapter, the reader should be able to:

➢ understand the distinction between public and private law

➢ understand the distinction between substantive and procedural law

➢ know the principles underlying private law

➢ know the principles underlying procedural law

➢ have an overview of the subject areas of public and private law

TABLE OF CONTENTS

INTRODUCTION: A LAW BESTIARY

In the Middle Ages, a bestiary was a book that described the animal kingdom. It was full of fabulous beasts, some of which had not ever been seen by the authors, and some of which, like the unicorn, did not actually exist.

A formal categorization of different types of law could take the form of a "law bestiary", full of distinctions that, while interesting, are not particularly helpful in giving students an idea of the breadth and reach of the law. Instead, this typology will define its organizing principles in terms of the way legal practitioners look at the law, and then define types of law in light of the principles identified.

Principles to Consider in Organizing a Typology of Law

Artificial and Real Distinctions

It is quite possible to build a largely theoretical typology of law that is both logical and elegant. But to be useful, a typology of law must define law in terms of concepts and areas of law that will help a student to understand the operation of the Canadian legal system. For example, to simply define law by subject matter alone is to really do no more than give dictionary definitions. Instead we need to identify important elements of law, and then see how they relate to each other.

Organizing Concepts

In developing a typology, the following concepts are of some importance:

1. **Positive law:** We need to focus on positive law — that is, the law of the state system. One of the features of a positive law system is that legal rules are in the command mode: *A* shall pay *B*, which means that there was implied an element of compulsion with penalties if *A* did not pay *B*. These are essential parts of any state legal system or positive law system. Contrasted to this are other conceptions of law: norms, values, morality, and religious beliefs, in which obedience does not depend on physical force. Some very interesting typologies of law can be built from norms, values, etc., but a non-positive law's impact on legal systems in operation in the world is, at best, indirect. Consequently, non-positive law is omitted from our typology.

2. **Domestic and international law:** To some extent, international law has some impact that requires our attention. However, when it has impact, it is usually because it has been incorporated within the domestic system of law of the Canadian state or influenced the content of that law. For example, the *Hague Convention* governing international child abduction is a piece of international law. But its rules might as well be yelled out in a desert for all the importance that law has. What makes the *Hague Convention* important is that it has been incorporated into the Ontario *Children's Law Reform Act* and has become part of Ontario's domestic law and part of the domestic law of other provinces as well. Another example is the International Tribunal dealing with war crimes and crimes against humanity. This international court has detained, tried, and sentenced a number of individuals involved in war crimes and crimes against humanity in the Balkans and Africa. But the tribunal's power requires co-operation by nation states to apprehend accused persons and send them to the tribunal for trial. In both examples of effective public international law, the distinctive feature is that nation states, in these very limited situations, are prepared to act within their own domestic jurisdictions to make the international public law system

work. But this is still fairly unusual. Because public international law usually lacks independent enforcement mechanisms and because states often ignore such a law when it suits a state's interests to do so, public international law will be excluded from our typology.

There is a sphere of international law, however, that is of great practical importance, and that is private international law. Private international law concerns private disputes between individuals that involve more than one national jurisdiction. There are two principal questions that usually have to be considered in the private international law arena:

- In which jurisdiction shall the issues be determined? This involves deciding which court system of which nation has the right to try the matter.
- Under the law of which jurisdiction shall the issues be determined? This involves deciding which national legal system shall be used as a source of legal rules. Even where one national system is determined to have jurisdiction, the law that is applied to the problem may be the national law of a country other than the one that has jurisdiction to try the matter.

For example, a manufacturer of communication systems in Canada may contract to supply products to a German company making components for a shipbuilding company in Korea. If there are problems with the components and those problems lead to a lawsuit, where would one sue? In Canada? Germany? Korea? Which nation's laws would apply? The international aspects of these transactions make this an international private law problem, but what actually happens is that private international law, in sorting this out, really converts the problem into a domestic legal matter.

This area of law is of growing importance with globalization and the increase in various kinds of transnational commercial and other transactions.

3. **Private and public law:** Within a system of positive domestic law, there are usually significant differences between private law, which regulates the conduct of individuals as between themselves over private matters, and public law. In private law, the focus is on facilitating and regulating interaction rather than punishing it. Public law regulates the operation of the state and the interaction between the citizen and the state. Here the law is more likely to take the form of commands, spelling out rights and obligations, and visiting sanctions on those who disobey.

4. **Procedural and substantive law:** Procedural law concerns itself with the process of the law, the route one takes to justice. Substantive law concerns rights, obligations and rules of conduct that regulate activity. If substantive law is about the content of rules, procedural law is about how those rules are to be used.

To summarize, our concern is to explore the divisions and elements of the domestic or national state system of law in Canada in terms of the way that law is organized.

SUBSTANTIVE LAW OF THE CANADIAN LEGAL SYSTEM

Public Law

Generally, public law is law that concerns public matters rather than purely private ones. There are four principal substantive areas of public law:

Criminal Law

While crime often has a private dimension in terms of injuries done to victims, it almost always is seen in terms of its public dimension. The theory is that crime tatters the social fabric and threatens social stability. Originally, in common law, criminal acts were those that were socially disruptive and were seen as a personal affront to the sovereign, who had primary responsibility for maintaining social peace. At the same time, crime was also seen in terms of the harm to individual victims, so criminal law had some private law aspects. For example, until this century, it was possible and, in some common law jurisdictions, common for crimes to be privately prosecuted by the victim rather than by the state. Today, however, criminal law rules and procedures are quite distinct, and the investigation, prosecution, and punishment of crime is a virtual state monopoly.

Constitutional Law

This area of law is concerned about rules by which the state operates. If the functions of the state were a sort of game, constitutional law would describe the rules by which the game is played. Constitutional law usually takes the form of a statutory document but may also consist of custom, convention and practices. For example, in Canada, such law defines what powers each level of government has, determines how the state apparatus is to be operated, and sets out certain areas of individual freedom upon which the state may not trespass. Constitutional law is sometimes described as fundamental law, without which the political and legal system cannot operate. One characteristic of constitutional law is that it is more difficult to repeal or amend than ordinary law. Another is that when there is a conflict between ordinary law and constitutional law, ordinary law is subordinate to constitutional law.

Administrative Law

This is a very broad and pervasive area of law, generally concerned with the regulation of activity — often private activity where there is a perceived public interest. For example, if you own land in a residential neighbourhood, you cannot build whatever you wish on that land, as the land may be zoned for certain types of buildings. If you seek permission to exceed what the zoning allows, you will have to get permission from an administrative board that balances your private right against the public interest.

Taxation Law

This was one of the earliest areas of public law to develop as the sovereign took a personal interest in collecting public revenue, which, in many respects, was the sovereign's own money. Over time, the state's interest in revenue raising has not diminished, and neither has the citizen's desire to avoid paying taxes. Part of the public law of taxation is concerned with adjudicating disputes between taxpayers and the state. However, where a taxpayer's conduct amounts to fraud, the matter is dealt with as a criminal law matter.

Private Law

Private law is the law concerned with regulating the interactions between individuals as private persons.

Key Private Law Principles

While private law can be characterized in a variety of ways, there is a collection of principles and rules that provides most of the substantive law for almost all private law. These groups of principles are as follows:

- **Tort law:** This area of law can be described as civil wrongs by one individual against another. It includes intentional harm, harm resulting from carelessness (negligence), and some harmful acts where intention is entirely absent. Many torts — assault, for example — are also crimes. This is not surprising, as criminal law developed from tort law. Where a tort has been committed, the remedy granted is usually money damages to compensate the person harmed for the injury sustained.

- **Contract law:** This area developed from the tort of breaking one's word, to become an independent cause of action based on the idea that promises could not be given and broken at will, but were enforceable. Contract law, then, concerns the enforcement of promises, under various conditions. The remedy for breach of contract is usually monetary compensation. Sometimes, however, the courts will order performance of the contract.

- **Property law:** This area of law is concerned with rules for establishing what is capable of ownership, how things are to be owned, how we are to determine who owns something and the definition of types of property: real property (land) and personal property, both tangible (chattels or things) and intangible (rights).

Subject Matter of Private Law

The subject matter of private law is capable of almost endless division, which would result in an indigestible law bestiary. The areas that are set out below are principal areas of law in the Canadian system. For each of the areas listed, bear in mind that all of them will rely to some extent on tort, contract, and property law as the source of their rules.

- **Family law:** This area of law was once part of the now vanished ecclesiastical or church law. It was originally seen as involving moral and religious matters. The religious and moral aspects are now largely absent from the law. Today, the law in this area borrows heavily from the contractual concept of partnership, so the law concerns itself largely with the dissolution of marriage partnerships and things incidental to that dissolution: property, support, custody, and divorce. There are other areas that are included in family law: adoption, child welfare (dealing with children whose basic family needs are not being met), and, in some instances, law dealing with the crimes of children.

- **Estates, wills, and trusts:** This area of law is closely related to family law and property law, as it concerns itself with the distribution of property, often within a family, on the death of an individual. The law of trusts is closely connected to estate law, since it facilitates a person's (called a trustee) holding and controlling property for the benefit of someone else (called a beneficiary). However, the law of trusts is also a major part of commercial law.

- **Real estate law:** This area of law is concerned with the highly technical area of transferring and otherwise dealing with interests in land. An important subset also concerns itself with the process of land-use planning, although this may properly be considered part of administrative law.

- **Corporate and commercial law:** Sometimes this area is simply called business law. Closely involved with contract law, it is concerned with the various forms of business organization, banking, insurance and financial law and, generally, the law governing commercial operations.

- **Patents and intellectual property:** This growing area of law, similar in its basics to business law, is concerned with the law surrounding the protection and marketing of ideas in various forms, whether the substance is patents on things or processes, or copyrights on ideas.

- **Agency:** This area of law concerns itself with the relations of principals and agents among themselves and between themselves and others. The focus is on legal rights and obligations that arise when someone acts on your behalf as an agent. This can also be seen as a proper part of corporate and commercial law, or of contract law.

PROCEDURAL LAW

Procedural law is concerned with the legal process by which rights and liabilities are **adjudicated**. Its focus is on the **adversarial** aspect of the law in the context of legal dispute resolution.

Procedural Norms

While we can describe a system of procedural rules as steps to be taken to settle a dispute, procedural law is about more than what steps to take. It is also about attitudes and values concerning how those steps should be taken.

Generally, procedural rules are structured to deal with the three perennial problems of legal systems: fairness, cost and delay. Procedural rules are designed to deliver justice as inexpensively and quickly as possible without sacrificing a just result.

Second, there is also a concern that, whatever procedural rules are, they be uniformly and evenly applied so that similar cases are treated in the same way. Another way of putting this is to say that the rules of the system should be applied objectively and without bias: justice should not only be done, but be seen to be done.

Closely related to consistency in applying procedural rules is the concern that the rules themselves be fair. Procedures that are inherently one-sided or arbitrary, or cause delay, or raise costs, might be seen to be inherently unfair.

Law of Procedure

Incorporating the norms discussed in the preceding paragraph, this area of law concerns the process of settling disputes. It is characterized by detailed, complex, and technical rules of civil procedure to govern private law disputes, and rules of criminal procedure that are tailored to the criminal law process.

The law of procedure is also looked to for the provision of fair and transparent rules for regulating activities and resolving disputes in administrative law.

Law of Evidence

This area of law is often considered in the context of procedural rules, both civil and criminal. It concerns the legal rules that determine what kind of information can be used to prove facts that are in issue. The law of evidence is concerned with reliability, **probative value**, and the relevance of information to be considered by the court in deciding a dispute.

CONCLUSION

The purpose of this chapter is to provide a panoramic view of the Canadian legal system in terms of some of its major components. By talking about divisions of law, it is easy to assume that the law operates in clear and distinct divisions, and that the divisions here are the only important ones. It is important to remember that the borders between the divisions are not all that distinct and sharp, and that there can be considerable overlap among them.

CHAPTER SUMMARY

This chapter set out a typology that allows the reader to conceptually organize law into categories. The context for this categorization is the positive law of the Canadian legal system. Positive law is the law actually in use, and is distinguished from morality and from religious law, which are omitted from the typology. Also omitted is public international law, except where it has been incorporated into the Canadian legal system.

The chapter then set out the relevant categories of law: public substantive law, private substantive law, and procedural law. Public substantive law consists of rules of law governing conduct that focus on the relationship between the individual and the state. Private substantive law is focused on the legal relationships between individuals. Procedural law concerns itself with rules and processes within a legal system that facilitate the operation of, and use of, substantive legal rules. Throughout the chapter, the reader was reminded that the categories are more than repositories for lists of rules; the contents of the categories are often determined by overarching principles that are grounded in societal norms and values.

GLOSSARY OF NEW TERMS AND KEY CONCEPTS

adjudicate	The process of hearing and deciding a case.
adversarial system	The trial process in the common law system, where the parties attempt to present their case in the best light possible, and to defeat the case of the opposite party.
domestic and international law	The positive law of a nation state. International law is concerned with the law that governs relations between nations and between individuals in an international context.
positive law	The law of nation states that controls and regulates social interaction.
private and public law	Private law concerns legal relationships between private persons; public law concerns legal relationships between private persons and the state.
probative value	The extent to which specific evidence proves a fact alleged by the party presenting it. Evidence of high probative value is evidence that strongly supports a party's case.
procedural and substantive law	Procedural law concerns rules and procedures under which a legal system operates. Substantive law is concerned with legal rights and remedies.

REVIEW QUESTIONS

1. What principles or concepts are used in organizing the typology of law as discussed in this chapter?

2. What is positive law? Give an example of law that is *not* positive law.

3. What impact does international law have on the positive domestic law system?

4. What are the main characteristics of public law? Of private law?

5. What are the main characteristics of procedural law?

6. How is substantive law distinguished from procedural law?

7. In what way is constitutional law distinct from other forms of public law?

8. From the legal situations set out below, identify the categories of law that are relevant to resolving the issues:

   (i) Abraham got into an argument with Isaac in a bar. He punched Isaac in the face and broke several of Isaac's front teeth so that Isaac spent a lot of time and money at his dentist's.
   (ii) Delbert didn't declare some cash he received for a carpentry job as part of his earned income on his tax return.
   (iii) Jo-Ann promised to sell her car to Linda, but later refused to go through with the deal.
   (iv) Armgard, in giving testimony in court, started to say what Juan had told her. The judge stopped her testimony.
   (v) Beryllium wished to have Tungsten appear at trial to give evidence, and to ensure that Tungsten shows up, she issued a summons to a witness.
   (vi) Kate copied friends' CDs, which she then downloaded on her iPod.
   (vii) Graufus was a bloodthirsty tyrant who ruled Doofusonia with an iron hand. He regularly slaughtered opponents and ate small children for dinner.

9. What are the main differences between public and private international law?

10. What is the difference between procedural and substantive law?

DISCUSSION QUESTIONS

1. Private substantive law can be seen as composed of a number of areas of law, but it really all comes down to being aspects of tort, contract, and property law. Discuss this statement.

2. Public international law has sometimes been described as more wishful thinking than law. Discuss.

3. The only reason private international law has real impact is because it is not really international law. Discuss.

4. International law is often described as "not really law" because it lacks an effective enforcement mechanism. But is effective enforcement the only reason the law is obeyed? Discuss.

5. Ox is a car manufacturer in Spain. Many of the components are designed and built elsewhere and then shipped to Ox's assembly plant. McCart, an Australian living in China, bought an Ox. While driving it, the brakes failed. The brakes were designed and manufactured in Argentina. There is evidence that the brakes were defective in design and construction.

   Using your knowledge of types of law, identify issues and problems that might confront McCart in suing for damages.

6. While public international law is said to lack teeth because it does not have enforcement mechanisms, it may not be so much longer. Examine the case of the former president of Serbia, Slobodan Milosevic, who was subjected to international prosecution for crimes against humanity.

In examining the issues, you may wish to use websites such as <www.theglobeandmail.com> to find articles on Milosevic and the International War Crimes Tribunal in The Hague. You may also wish to check the websites maintained by those who criticize the process and the prosecution as simply revenge by the winners, or you may conduct conventional library research.

Does international law have teeth now? Why or why not? Discuss.

7. In 2012, The International Criminal Court (ICC) sentenced Thomas Lubanga, a former militia leader in the Democratic Republic of Congo, to 14 years in prison. The sentence, which was the first imposed by the ICC since it was launched in The Hague 10 years ago, established the use of children in war as an international crime. Read a more detailed account in *World Politics Review* <www.worldpoliticsreview.com/trend-lines/12156/lubanga-sentence-a-victory-for-accountability-icc-legitimacy>. What factors can you identify in the Lubanga case that indicate that the international war crimes tribunal process is not particularly effective?

SUGGESTED READING AND OTHER RESOURCES

David, R. *Major Legal Systems in the World Today: An Introduction to the Comparative Study of Law*, 3rd ed., translated and adapted by J.E.C. Brierley (London: Sweet & Maxwell, 1985).

Derrett, J.D.M. *An Introduction to Legal Systems* (New York: Praeger, 1968).

Gall, Gerald L. *The Canadian Legal System*, 5th ed. (Toronto: Carswell, 2004).

WEBSITES
CanLII: <http://www.canlii.org/en/>
　(provincial and federal cases and statutes — public website)
e-Laws: <http://www.e-laws.gov.on.ca/index.html>
　(Ontario statutes, regulations and current bills — free access)
Federal laws: <http://laws.justice.gc.ca/en/index.html>
　(federal government consolidated statutes and regulations)
The Law Dictionray: <http://thelawdictionary.org/>
Legal Systems Around the World:
　<https://lib.law.washington.edu/content/guides/worldsys>

Structure of
the Canadian Government

Irv Ash
SENECA COLLEGE

Learning Objectives

After reading this chapter, the reader should be able to:

➢ describe and understand the theory of parliamentary democracy and the party system and how it applies to Canada

➢ differentiate between the various levels of government in Canada

➢ understand how the Canadian government operates in each level

➢ understand the concepts of *intra vires* and *ultra vires* as they relate to the validity of a statute passed by a level of government

➢ differentiate between the three branches of government — the executive branch, the legislative (parliamentary) branch, and the judicial branch — recognizing their key components

➢ recognize and apply the theory of parliamentary supremacy in the Canadian context

➢ distinguish between the Canadian theory of parliamentary supremacy and the American theories of separation of powers and checks and balances

➢ recognize how the structure of the Canadian government affects the Canadian legal system

TABLE OF CONTENTS

INTRODUCTION

Constitutional law partly deals with the exercise of power by various parts of government. It explains which parts exercise legislative power (making new laws), executive power (implementing the laws) and judicial power (interpreting the law and deciding disputes). Constitutional law also explains the limitations imposed on those powers. In a federal state, there is constant tension between the levels of government as each level tries to enhance its powers.

This chapter intends to examine basic concepts of the Canadian government in the context of constitutional law. The structure of the Canadian government is based on the Constitution, both written in legislation and also developed in case law, as well as on agreements reached between levels of government. To fully understand the structure, one could initially study the history of English government since the 13th century, as well as the history of Canadian colonial policies, followed by post-Confederation political practice. Such an historical study is not covered in this chapter. It is appropriate, however, to discuss the following concepts in the Canadian context based on both constitutional law and political science:

- *parliamentary democracy* as a theory
- levels of government
- branches of government
- parliamentary supremacy

In dealing with these items, we will occasionally refer to the more well-known American system by way of comparison.

PARLIAMENTARY DEMOCRACY

The theory of government by parliamentary democracy involves a number of basic elements. To understand the theory, it is necessary to look at each element separately and then as a whole. This chapter will compare competing elements and theories in use in other countries with those in Canada. We will also discuss proposals to change the system.

Democracy

The first key element is **democracy**. One definition states: "Democracy in itself is simply a technique, a way of making certain decisions by accepting the will of the majority."[1] Another definition, by Jackson and Jackson, elaborates: "An essential characteristic of democracy, therefore, is the reconciliation of the need for order and certainty with a degree of influence for competing political interests."[2] These and other definitions indicate that democracy can be seen as a system of governance whereby the majority rules but with certain restrictions, such as the recognition of minority rights or universal rights and political interests. Almost every state in the world calls itself democratic, but in order to be democratic, the state must have limitations on the power of the majority to govern. These limitations include a fixed time in power (that is, fixed dates or amount of time in power before elections) and protection of certain rights (usually in constitutional documents or theory).

---

[1] Mark O. Dickerson & Thomas Flanagan, *An Introduction to Government and Politics: A Conceptual Approach*, 5th ed. (Toronto: ITP Nelson, 1998) at 217.

[2] Robert J. Jackson & Doreen Jackson, *An Introduction to Political Science: Comparative and World Politics*, 3d ed. (Scarborough, Ont.: Prentice Hall Allyn and Bacon Canada, 2000) at 92.

Totalitarianism

Contrast the concept of democracy with the concept of **totalitarianism**, which is another common type of governance used in the world today. Jackson and Jackson define the term as "those states in which leaders impose their objectives or goals upon their people to an unlimited degree ... [E]fforts are made to control all aspects of society; to subordinate individuals and groups to the dominant leadership."[3] Some writers[4] have quoted with approval Friedrich and Brzezinski's definition of totalitarianism[5] as including the following elements:

- an official ideology
- a single party typically led by one man
- a terroristic police
- a communications monopoly
- a weapons monopoly
- a centrally directed economy

It could be stated that democracy is the rule of the majority within certain limits, whereas totalitarianism is the rule of one or few with no limits. Although minorities in a democracy may see no practical differences between the systems, it could be argued that the minorities in a democracy have protections inherent in their system, even when the majority exercises power not approved by the minority. Note also that the definitions used above describe the extremes. As each system moves closer to the other, it may be difficult to clearly recognize the differences.

The Athenian Model of Direct Democracy

If democracy means rule of the majority within certain limits, what does the "parliamentary" part of the phrase "parliamentary democracy" mean? "Parliamentary" relates to the method used to allow the majority to rule. The first methodology to use democracy was a "**direct democracy**" employed by the Athenians over 2400 years ago. Decisions were made on the basis of one citizen, one vote, where the majority carried the day. Furthermore, leaders of the state were selected by lot for short terms. This type of democracy had many problems. First, in Athens only male citizens could vote, thereby excluding a large majority of the people in Athens, including slaves and women (children were also excluded, but they have always been excluded in every system), although such exclusions could be eradicated. Second, there was the practical physical difficulty of assembling more than a few thousand people to hear and participate (although this problem can be alleviated somewhat with current and future technology allowing for teleconferencing and electronic voting). Third, it was difficult to have a calm and fruitful discussion on complex political issues that arise in the modern world (especially when the matter was urgent). Fourth, the leaders were not necessarily experienced or, likely, in office long enough to gain experience. A newer expression of direct democracy has developed in the past 300 years, and it will be discussed next.

Representative Democracy

Since the Athenian model of direct democracy was generally ineffective in most circumstances, the next form of democracy to develop was "**representative democracy**", whereby the citizens of a state elected persons who would govern the citizens through laws. Regular elections would allow the majority to somehow control those elected, who would not be in power for life but,

---

[3] *Ibid.* at 99.
[4] *Supra* note 2 and note 1.
[5] Carl J. Friedrich & Zbigniew Brzezinski, *Totalitarian Dictatorship and Autocracy*, 2d ed. rev. (Cambridge, MA: Harvard University Press, 1965).

instead, would have to justify their policies and themselves at some intervals. This system remedied problems of getting participants together, engaging in rational discussions based on experience. This became the broad model for democracies in the past three centuries.

Brief History of the English Parliamentary System

The English parliamentary system was the initial model of representative democracy. Here is a quick overview of how it developed. Initially, when England was united in the 11th century, the style of government it had would now be classified as totalitarianism. The king (or queen) was the government and ruled through ministers appointed by and serving at the pleasure of the monarch. The Parliament, which was elected by a select group of landowners, first convened in 1295 and was strictly an advisory body. Throughout the centuries, the monarch and Parliament argued over power, which led to the English Civil War in the 17th century, with the monarch relinquishing certain powers to Parliament. Eventually, the monarch relinquished more power to Parliament, leading to the system called a **constitutional monarchy**, where, theoretically, all power resides in Parliament. This concept of a monopoly of power being vested in Parliament is called parliamentary supremacy, which will be dealt with at the end of the chapter.

The Canadian Parliamentary System versus the U.S. Presidential System

The Canadian parliamentary system versus the U.S. presidential system of representative democracy is a comparison of two main models: the **parliamentary system** (originally and still in use in England, as well as in Canada and in other countries) and the **presidential system** (originally and still American, and in use in many other countries). Again, comparisons between these two systems can throw light on both and allow for a more detailed discussion of the Canadian system. Both systems depend on three branches of government: the executive branch, which enforces the law; the legislative (parliamentary) branch, which makes the law; and the judicial branch, which interprets and applies the law to settle disputes. However, in the parliamentary system, the theory holds that the legislative (parliamentary) branch is supreme. This means that the laws passed by the legislative branch override what the other two branches do. The presidential system, on the other hand, believes in both "separation of powers" among the three branches and in a concept of "checks and balances" to ensure that no one branch is supreme.

The parliamentary system developed through the election of individuals who were members of parties. Each political party would have a member of its party stand for election in a riding (or district) against members of other parties. Whoever won the election for that riding would be part of the legislative branch representing the people of that riding in Parliament. The leader of the political party who had the majority (or plurality if a minority government) would become the prime minister (or premier) and leader of the executive branch. The leader would appoint individuals from within the elected members of the party to be ministers in the Cabinet, who would be in charge of various ministries, such as health, justice, environment, and so on. The leader and the Cabinet ministers are, therefore, both in the legislative and executive branches in the parliamentary system.

In contrast, the presidential system has an election for a leader in a "presidential election", which is separate from the election for members of the legislative branch (the House of Representatives and the Senate). Remember, in the parliamentary system, the leader of the party stands for election only in a single riding. In contrast, in the presidential system, the president stands for election throughout the country and is elected when he or she receives sufficient votes, even though his or her party does not win the most seats (ridings or districts) in the legislature. This means that the president is not part of the legislative branch. Furthermore, the people the president appoints to Cabinet are also not members of the legislative branch; they are not elected in elections at all and are considered separate from the legislative branch.

Also, in the parliamentary system the executive branch (usually in consultation with other groups) appoints the judiciary. By contrast, in the presidential system some judges can be elected, in some instances, in their districts. Other, more senior judges are appointed by the executive branch and, in some cases, confirmed by the legislative branch.

There is both a clearer separation of powers among the three branches, as well as a system of checks and balances of power of government, in the presidential system than in the parliamentary system. These concepts shall be developed later in the section on "Branches of Government". They are mentioned here simply to allow for some comparison between the two systems.

Elections in Both Systems

Election practices are somewhat similar, although different in key components, in the parliamentary system in Canada and the presidential system in the United States. In both countries, members of parties stand for election in ridings or districts or seats against members of another party or parties. Whoever wins the vote, commonly in Canada by a **plurality** (that is, the most votes cast, even if not more than 50 percent), wins the riding, district, or seat. Neither in Canada nor in the United States is the voter required by law to cast a vote. However, there are other countries that do require all voters to vote. Generally speaking, voter turnout has been shrinking in both Canada and the United States in the past few elections. Commentators have suggested reasons for the decrease in voter turnout, especially voters' apathy caused by distrust of most politicians due to perceived corruption arising from campaign contributions from wealthy persons or by lobbyists. Campaign finance reform and the effect of lobbyists on government are important issues recently discussed in both countries, especially in the United States.

The Party System in Canada

The party system is essential in Canada, even more so than in the United States, because the political party that wins the election wins at least a plurality, if not a majority, of the ridings. By winning a plurality or majority of seats, the party retains control of the legislative branch, with its members also in charge of the executive branch. In the United States, however, due to a separate election of the president, who appoints his Cabinet from people who are not part of the legislative branch, the executive and the legislative branches are not as closely connected. Moreover, even if the party of the president controls the Senate and the House of Representatives, the president does not have most of the controls that the leader of the Canadian executive branch has in controlling the legislative branch. In the United States, the president runs for a fixed term of four years; senators, six years; and members of the House of Representatives, two years.

When referring to the "Government of Canada", the term includes both the leader of the party in power and the party itself because of the close relation between the executive branch and the majority of the legislative branch. The members of the government — federal in the House of Commons and provincial in the provincial legislature — are all elected and consist of the following:

*   **leader (prime minister, premier)**
*   **Cabinet ministers and secretaries** (members of the legislature who head ministries)

- **backbenchers** (members of the government in power who vote with the government)
- **leader of the opposition** (the leader of the party with, usually, the second most seats after the legislature)
- **members in opposition to the government** (members of other parties, independent members or members of the ruling party who have been thrown out of the party caucus)

Municipal governments are very different and will be discussed later in this chapter.

In Canada, there is no fixed term for any member of Parliament or provincial legislature. The constitutional restriction requires that an election must occur no later than five years after the previous election. (However, there is a recent trend in Canada towards fixed-term elections. The federal government, British Columbia, and Ontario all now have four-year fixed terms.) As a matter of convention, there will be an election any time that the government loses a majority vote in the House of Commons or provincial legislature (called "losing confidence"). If the government never loses such a confidence vote, the government can remain in power up to the five-year limit, but it normally chooses an election date that is favourable for its re-election. It is, therefore, essential to the government in power that it never loses such a vote. This is achieved by enforcing party discipline. Each party has a **party whip**, who will talk to party members to ensure that they vote the party's way. Rebel members are "threatened" with removal from caucus or expulsion from the party. A good example of the kind of issues that arise when party discipline fails is seen in the Canadian Alliance Party's problems in the years 2000 to 2002, where various members refused to follow the direction of the party's leaders. Party discipline usually means that all party members vote the way the leader of the party wants; however, sometimes the leader allows party members to vote as they see fit in a **free vote**. The deficiencies, real or perceived, in the current party system in place in Canada have led to calls for possible changes in terms of both direct democracy and **single-member majoritarian** or even **multi-member proportional representation**.

Modern Model of Direct Democracy

Party discipline forces members to vote according to what the party wants even if the member's constituents want the member to vote differently. Party discipline leads to consistency and order, but it is seen as a barrier to "true" representation of constituents. One response is giving constituents more say in governing through various forms of direct democracy. The Canadian Alliance Party[6] led this movement in the past by advocating such proposals as **referendum** (and/or **plebiscite**), **initiative (or proposition)**, and **recall**. Although referenda have been used in the past in Canada to "decide" major issues, such as conscription during World War II, Quebec "separation" in 1980 and 1995, and the Charlottetown Accord to re-arrange federal–provincial powers in 1992, enthusiasts intend to advocate a binding referendum for many more decisions of the government. It would allow voters more control over many areas normally voted on by the legislators. Arguments against referenda centre on the cost, delays, and the complexity of allowing all voters to vote on issues. On the other hand, referenda are seen as a way of controlling the influence of lobbyists, financial supporters, and other organized special interests on the members.

---

[6] The Canadian Alliance Party dissolved in 2003 after merging with the Progressive Conservative Party to form the Conservative Party.

Initiatives or propositions are mechanisms that allow voters to raise issues themselves to be voted upon, unlike referenda, which are proposed by the politicians. The same arguments in favour of or against referenda apply here.

A recall is proposed to make members of government aware that if they do not "make the constituents happy", their constituents can remove them from office. A recall vote is usually authorized when a certain number of voters sign a recall petition. Critics of recall cite costs as well as pressure on members to curry favour with their constituents and support their impulsive whims, making it difficult to make well-thought-out, hard decisions. Of course, direct democracy flies in the face of the theory of representative democracy, which is based on voters' selecting an experienced and/or wise person to represent their interests and the society as a whole. These calls for direct democracy probably occur because a growing number of people do not believe that members represent voters' interests since they are subject to too much influence by lobbyists or are even corrupted by outside sources.

Single-Member Majoritarian and Multi-Member Proportional Representation

During an election in Canada, members of various parties stand for election in a specific riding, and the candidate who gets the most votes, even if not more than 50 percent, wins the seat. Political scientists[7] refer to this as the **single-member plurality system** because one person gets the plurality of the votes. Using the language of horse racing, it is sometimes referred to as the "first past the post" system. In a strong two-party system, such as in the United States, this system almost invariably produces a winner who gets the majority of the votes. However, in Canada, where there are at least four and sometimes more parties fielding candidates in some ridings, the winner often only has a plurality, sometimes as low as 35 percent of the votes cast. In that case, almost two-thirds of the voters who cast their vote wanted someone other than the winner to represent them. This can lead to voter frustration and disaffection. One suggestion is to use the **single-member majoritarian system** to have a runoff election a short time after the first election, with only the top two finishers in the previous election standing in the runoff. This would ensure a majority winner. This system is used in major elections in many countries, for example, in the French election for president. There are extra costs involved, and the difficulty in doing it in all elections makes it unwieldy, but it may be useful in major elections, such as in the presidential races, where voters want to make a clear choice. Such a system might have prevented certain problems arising from the election of U.S. President George Bush in 2000. Green Party backers of Ralph Nader, a well-known consumer advocate and presidential candidate in 2000, would have seen their candidate eliminated in the first round, and their votes would then likely have gravitated to Al Gore, giving him a clear victory over Bush.

As discussed, this single-member majoritarian system does not address concerns in a parliamentary system, where party members are elected by pluralities, and even the party that wins power may have only a plurality of votes. The general concept proposed to make our parliamentary elections more responsive to the views of voters is **proportional representation**. It is used in other countries to deal with this problem. Such a system is described by Jackson and Jackson as being "designed to ensure that parties, or groups of

---

[7] See *supra* note 2 and note 1; and Gregory S. Mahler, *Comparative Politics: An Institutional and Cross-National Approach*, 3d ed. (Upper Saddle River, N.J.: Prentice Hall, 2000).

voters, are represented more fairly and equitably than is often the case under the single-member plurality or majoritarian formulas."[8] Various forms of the system allow for parties to get seats proportionately based on the percentage of votes the party receives, as compared to the number of all votes cast. This can be done either on a national vote or on a riding basis. The major argument against proportional representation is based on the likelihood of a weak minority or a coalition government, such as those in Italy and Israel. This can lead to either numerous elections or a diffusion of power to small parties. In this case, small parties could have the votes to prop up or defeat the government, giving them a power far beyond what is warranted by their actual national support. On the other hand, any party that gains a minimum number of votes will have members in the legislature and, therefore, give its voters some say in governing. Although both direct democracy and proportional representation have been proposed in Canada in recent years, the system has not changed, but readers can expect these or other proposals to continue to be advanced, particularly by those who feel their interests at the political level are not recgonized under the current system.

A number of proposals have been made for variations of proportional representation since 2003 and even put before voters in some provinces. The paper, "Electoral Reform Initiatives in Canadian Provinces", prepared by James R. Robertson and revised in 2006,[9] details the chronology of proposals in British Columbia, New Brunswick, Ontario, Prince Edward Island, and Quebec. In British Columbia, where the proposed system was put to a vote in 2005, it narrowly lost; more recently, in Ontario in 2007, a referendum proposing the system, known as MMP, as noted in the Ontario Referendum site (<http://www.yourbigdecision.ca/en_ca/default.aspx>), lost decisively.[10] Because of the multiplicity of the attempts, the closeness of the vote in British Columbia and the steadily declining popular vote numbers in federal and provincial elections, it is likely that more proportional representation proposals will be made and may even change the structure of some Canadian governments.

FORMS OF GOVERNMENT

Levels of Government in General

A study of the approximately 200 countries in the world shows many forms of government, from the highly centralized to the loosely connected groups within the country. The forms of government depend on the size of the population, the country's traditions in terms of governance, and the complexity of issues facing the country. In addition, for other reasons, countries are governed along a continuum, ranging from one unitary, strong, national government to the loosely confederated regions in a country with a relatively weak national government. The various levels of government that can exist have been broadly described by Dickerson and Flanagan:

> Governments can also be classified according to the degree of centralization they exhibit. The two main types applicable to modern circumstances are the **unitary system**, in which a single sovereign government controls all regions of the country, and **federalism**, in which sovereignty is divided between a central government and several regional or provincial governments. Two other types of less practical significance are **devolution** and **confederation**. The former is a variant of the unitary state in which the central government

---

[8] *Supra* note 2 at 401.

[9] Found at <www.parl.gc.ca/content/LOP/ResearchPublications/prb0417-e.htm> as part of the Library of Parliament.

[10] See Jeff Gray, "Voters roundly reject MMP", *The Globe and Mail* (October 11, 2007). Available online: <http://www.theglobeandmail.com/news/national/voters-roundly-reject-mmp/article695401/>

creates regional governments but can override them as it wishes, even to the point of abolishing them. The latter is an inherently unstable arrangement in which sovereign constituent governments create a central government without sovereign power of its own.[11]

An example of a unitary system was that of Great Britain before the 1990s. They had a national government and municipal governments with no regional governments. Since the referendum of 1997, however, Great Britain would seem to be an example of devolution: a regional government with certain powers allocated to it by the national government has been established in Scotland.

When Canada was formed in 1867, it was called a confederation. In fact, that was, initially, a misnomer, as the country was really a federation of provinces with a central government with paramount power. It could be argued that, over the years, between court rulings and agreements between the federal and provincial governments, Canada has become more of a confederation, with stronger provincial power and a weaker national government. On the other hand, the United States was created in 1776 as, initially, a federation of the original 13 states with a federal government and a shared sovereignty. The American Civil War, starting in 1861, can be looked upon as a dispute where some of the states (the Confederacy) believed that the country was a confederation, thereby allowing any state to secede at will. The northern states believed that there was really a federation, and that states could not easily leave. The North won, and their viewpoint prevailed to the extent that most political scientists would call the United States a federation.

Other examples of countries whose form of government was changed over time are Czechoslovakia and Yugoslavia. From the 1940s on, both were federations. Decades later, they split into separate new countries based on regions: the former by peaceful means, and the latter by a devastating war.

Levels of Government in Canada

As it currently exists, Canada can be classified as a federation, although there are pressures to make it more of a confederation as defined above. A federation is a sovereignty shared between the central and constituent governments. Here the central government, based in Ottawa, is called federal, and the constituent governments are called provincial. Generally, the federal (national) government has **powers** in respect of dealing with other countries (national defence, treaties, income tax, customs, immigration) and with national policies (criminal law, post office, shipping and ports, railways, telecommunication, etc.). The provincial (regional) government is more local in nature (property and civil rights, sales taxes, labour and employment legislation, etc.). Generally, sovereignty is split between the two levels of government on the following bases:

- enumerated (sovereign) powers (each level is given specific and separate powers, allowing each level to legislate exclusively in certain areas)
- concurrent powers (both levels can legislate in the same area, but not on the exact same point)
- overlapping powers (both levels have the same rights to legislate in the same area, and conflicts may arise)
- paramount powers (one level has the final and ultimate right to legislate, and the other level only has a subordinate right or no right to legislate)

[11] *Supra* note 1 at 295.

Municipal Government — Not a Level of Government in Canada

Although we discuss municipal governments, there is no legally separate level of government in Canada called municipal. Municipal government is a creation of the province under the Canadian Constitution and has no independent existence. It can be changed or even abolished by the province that created it. Furthermore, the municipal government derives all of its powers from those handed to it by the province and, therefore, has no greater power than what the province itself has and delegates to it. Although there have been recent discussions about giving extra or new powers to provinces by way of Constitutional status or the granting of certain revenue-raising powers,[12] the current status of municipal government has not changed.

Constitutional Foundations for Levels of Canadian Government

Prior to 1867, there was no national government in what is now Canada. Instead, there were colonies of Great Britain, which were described collectively as British North America in the 1860s. The confederation in 1867 created a national government and turned the colonies into provinces. Under the *British North America Act* (now the *Constitution Act, 1867*) powers were given to both the federal government (s. 91) and the provinces (s. 92).

Outside the Power: Legislation Ruled to Be Invalid

While each level of government has a constitutionally defined area of activity, what happens when one level of government goes outside its own area? The short answer is that if a jurisdictional dispute about the right to legislate in a particular area arises, the courts determine the issue. *Ultra vires* and *intra vires* are terms used by the judicial branch to state that a level of government is either outside (***ultra vires***) or inside (***intra vires***) its power under the Constitution to pass a law; therefore, such law is invalid or valid, respectively.

Mechanics of How Levels Operate

The federal level consists of the House of Commons and Senate, which together comprise the federal legislative branch that makes laws. Members of the House of Commons are elected (with the prime minister and the Cabinet ministers who, with civil servants, form the federal executive branch); senators are appointed by the executive branch. Laws that the federal legislative branch creates are passed pursuant to section 91 of the *Constitution Act, 1867*.

In each province, there is a provincial legislative assembly with all members elected. Also members of the assembly, the premier and the Cabinet ministers, together with civil servants, form the provincial executive branch. Laws that the provincial legislative branch creates are passed pursuant to section 92 of the *Constitution Act, 1867*.

The municipal level usually has a mayor and councillors, all elected with powers given under a municipal Act, a statute passed by each provincial government to allow for the creation of municipalities and to delegate powers to them under section 92 of the *Constitution Act, 1867*.

Municipalities have been amalgamated in Ontario and Quebec over the past few years, even though many in those cities objected. Furthermore, regional governments, which used to be interposed between the provincial and

---

[12] Royson James, "A New Deal for Cities", *Toronto Star* (June 15, 2002).

municipal governments, seem to be disappearing. Both are examples of the provincial government having a free hand to alter part of itself: that is, its creation, the municipal government.

Recent Modifications to the Levels

Over the past 40 years, there have been numerous federal–provincial conferences regarding power-sharing, medicare, funding for education, and so on. These conferences have been attended by the representatives of the executive branches of the federal and provincial governments; the conferences have, to various degrees, successfully exercised power in many areas. It has been argued by Donald V. Smiley, a well-known writer, that this process is an example of **executive federalism**, which is defined as the "relations between elected and appointed officials of the two orders of government in federal–provincial interactions and among the executive in interprovincial interactions."[13] Smiley suggested that the executive branches, both federal and provincial, were gathering more power than possibly should be allowed, both constitutionally and in practice.

OVERVIEW OF THE CANADIAN GOVERNMENT

In Canada, as in most countries, there are three branches of government: one that enforces the laws (executive branch); one that makes the laws (legislative or parliamentary branch); and one that interprets and applies the laws (judicial branch).

The Three Branches of Government

Below is a summary of each branch of government in Canada in respect of (a) its major and associated functions and (b) the people who are part of each branch. (See also Exhibit 5.1.)

Executive Branch

The major function of the executive branch at both the federal and provincial levels is enforcing the laws. Other associated functions the branch is responsible for include

- proposing laws, although laws are voted in by the legislative branch
- passing regulations without going through the legislative branch
- appointing judges, who are in the judicial branch
- helping operate all three branches (through the civil service)

The executive branch includes the prime minister, the federal Cabinet, and the Governor General as the Queen's representative at the federal level. At the provincial level, the executive branch comprises the premier, the provincial Cabinet, and the Lieutenant Governors as the Queen's representatives. Both levels of the executive branch are staffed with civil services, including the police forces.

Legislative Branch

For both federal and provincial governments, the major function of the legislative branch is to make or create laws. And through laws, the legislative branch also creates administrative bodies that have some of the powers of all

---

[13] Donald V. Smiley, *Canada in Question: Federalism in the Eighties*, 3d ed. (Toronto: McGraw-Hill Ryerson Limited, 1980) at 91.

The Branches of Government			EXHIBIT 5.1

	EXECUTIVE BRANCH	LEGISLATIVE BRANCH	JUDICIAL BRANCH
A1. Major Functions	Enforce the laws	Make or create laws	Interpret and apply the laws, and adjudicate and resolve disputes
A2. Associated Functions	¤ Propose laws, although voted in by the legislative branch ¤ Can pass regulations without going through the legislative branch ¤ Appoint judges, who are in the judicial branch ¤ Through the civil service, help operate all three branches.	Through laws, create administrative bodies that have some of the powers of all three branches in a limited setting	¤ Help enforce judgments in civil court ¤ Impose sentences in criminal court
B. People in Branch	1. Federal level ¤ Prime Minister ¤ Federal Cabinet ¤ The Queen's representative: the Governor General ¤ The federal civil service, including the police services 2. Provincial level ¤ Premier ¤ Provincial Cabinet ¤ The Queen's representative: the Lieutenant Governors ¤ The provincial civil service, including the police services	1. Federal level ¤ The federal House of Commons ¤ The Senate 2. Provincial level ¤ The provincial legislatures	The judges, court officials, and associated civil servants
	Please note that the Prime Minister, the federal Cabinet, the premiers, and the provincial Cabinets in the executive branch are also members of their respective parliaments and, as such, are also part of the legislative branch. Note: the terms "parliament" and "legislature" are interchangeable.		
C. Interactions with Other Branches	¤ Note the connections between the people listed in B: 1 to 4 as also being part of the legislative branch; and 1 and 2 also appoint the judges, who form the bulk of the judicial branch. ¤ The executive branch, especially of a majority government, is likely to convince the legislative branch to pass certain laws.	¤ As will be noted, under the theory of parliamentary supremacy, the laws made by the legislatures *are supposed to* override both the decrees of the executive branch and the decisions of the judicial branch.	¤ It is said that judges also make law. ¤ Many people think that, in handing out sentences, judges enforce the law. ¤ As will be discussed, in Canada, judges can somewhat override parliamentary supremacy in three ways.

three branches in a limited setting. The federal legislative branch is made up of members of the House of Commons and members of the Senate, while the provincial branches are composed of members of the provincial legislatures.

Judicial Branch

The judicial branch is made up of judges and court officials and associated civil servants. The branch's major function is to interpret and apply the laws, as well as adjudicate and resolve disputes. Its associated functions include

- helping enforce judgments in civil court
- imposing sentences in criminal court

Interactions between Branches

Because members of the executive branch are also part of the legislative branch, the two branches are connected. The executive branch, especially in a majority government, is likely to persuade the legislative branch to pass specific laws. The fact that part of the executive branch appoints judges, who basically are the judicial branch, implies a connection between the executive branch and the judicial branch.

Under the theory of parliamentary supremacy, the laws made by the legislatures *are supposed to* override both the decrees of the executive branch and the decisions of the judicial branch. But judges can make law as a result of case decisions; and in handing out sentences, they also enforce the law. In Canada, judges can somewhat override parliamentary supremacy in three ways set out below.

PARLIAMENTARY SUPREMACY

The Theory of Parliamentary Supremacy

The theory of parliamentary supremacy states that any law passed by Parliament overrides any decision of a judge or a decree of the executive branch. Traditionally, this theory is reflected in the statement that statute law overrides the law of equity that overrides common law. For example, once the legislature passes a statute, the executive branch cannot, in theory, change it. Furthermore, a statute can be passed to override a decision of the judicial branch that the legislature does not agree with. An example is the fairly recent case where the Supreme Court of Canada held that extreme drunkenness could possibly be a defence to sexual assault. After that case, the legislature amended the *Criminal Code* to state that extreme drunkenness could not be used as a defence in these circumstances. This theory recognizes the supreme power of the legislature, which was first developed in England, where, initially, the Crown possessed political power before ceding it to Parliament. As England at the time was a unitary state, no issue of different levels of government with different areas of power existed.

Parliamentary Supremacy in the Canadian Context

At least one modification to the theory of parliamentary supremacy is necessary since two levels of government exist in Canada. The courts have stated that each level is supreme in its own areas of jurisdiction and that if there is any conflict between the levels, generally the federal level will be supreme. Other modifications based on Canadian reality are noted below, including the concentration of power in the hands of the executive branch, and not in the supremacy of Parliament, under the theory of **responsible government.**

Canadian versus American Theories

In the United States, different theories are subscribed to — namely, the theory of **checks and balances** and the closely associated theory of **separation of powers**. In the American context, the three branches of government discussed above exist, with very specific and separate powers. Following are the branches in the United States:

- the executive branch, which consists of the president and the federal Cabinet, and, at the state level, the governors and the state Cabinet and the civil service
- the legislative branch, which consists of the House of Representatives and the Senate and, in each state, the legislatures
- the judicial branch, made up of the courts at both the state and federal government levels

Furthermore, each branch has the ability to override what the other two branches do: by way of veto for the first two branches, and by judicial decision for the courts. In this way it is hoped that none of the branches will get too powerful but, rather, will be held in "check" by the other branches. Patrick Monahan, a Canadian constitutional law expert, summarized the two competing variations on how the branches of government use power in the following passages:

> [C]ertain constitutions, most notably the United States constitution, embrace the doctrine of the separation of powers. Under this doctrine, there is a strict separation between the executive, legislative, and judicial branches of government, with no single branch being permitted to encroach on the powers or jurisdiction of the others. Thus in the United States, the president (the head of the executive branch, responsible for enforcing and administrating the laws) cannot be a member of the legislative branch, or Congress. ... The United States constitution proceeds from the premise that concentrating power in particular institutions or individuals is dangerous, since those who granted such powers are likely to abuse them at the expense of individual liberty. The solution is to divide the state into mutually exclusive branches so as to preclude this concentration of power and the abuse that will (it is assumed) necessarily flow from it. ... These checks and balances often make it difficult for a president to implement the political program that may have led to his or her election. They reflect (once again) the American suspicion and mistrust of state power, and the preference for limiting government as the best means to protect individual liberty.
>
> The doctrine of the separation of powers has never been a dominant feature of the Canadian or the United Kingdom constitutions. Indeed, far from dividing power, the Canadian and British approach is to concentrate political power in the hands of the executive. This concentration of power is achieved through the doctrine of responsible government, under which both the legislative and executive branch are subject to the control of the prime minister [or premier]. The prime minister controls the executive, since the governor general (the formal head of the executive branch of government) must exercise all of his or her powers on the basis of the prime minister's advice. At the same time, the prime minister controls Parliament — the legislative branch — since the governor general is obliged to appoint as prime minister the leader of the party controlling the greatest number of seats in the elected House of Commons. Thus a Canadian prime minister with a majority in the House of Commons has far greater scope to implement his or her political program than does the American president.[14]

---

14 Patrick J. Monahan, *Constitutional Law* (Concord, Ontario: Irwin Law, 1997) at 22–23.

It appears that the reality of Canadian government is responsible government, which by its nature gives a tremendous concentration of power to the leader of the political party in power. However, certain modifications to parliamentary supremacy allow the judicial branch to limit the power not only of the legislative branch but, also, of the leader of the political party in power.

Modifications to Parliamentary Supremacy

Judicial Interpretation

This is a modification that almost every country in the world theoretically recognizes. A statute is passed and, often, needs to be interpreted in court, either through a case that involves the statute or by **reference**. A reference is a method of getting an issue before the court without needing an actual fact situation affecting real persons to occur before the issue can be decided. The judge is given the right to decide the exact meaning of the words, including the possibility that they mean nothing and, therefore, should be null and void. Thus, even though the statute was legally passed by Parliament, it could, in effect, be overridden by the court. Of course, Parliament can pass a new law to override the decision; but that new statute would come before the courts for interpretation, possibly going through the process again.

Sections 91 and 92 and the Concept of Ultra Vires

Sections 91 and 92 of the *Constitution Act, 1867* create a division of powers between the federal and provincial levels that is specific to Canada. Any federal country, including Canada, with two levels of government that have specific powers gives its courts power to determine if one level of government has inappropriately used power that belongs to the other level of government. Cases have come before the court, either under a fact situation or by reference, where the court must determine whether the level that passed the law operated within its powers or intruded on the other level's powers. If the judge determines that there was an intrusion, it would be decided that the law was *ultra vires* and, therefore, null and void. Thus, the court could determine if the law was valid and, with some finality, override the law made by Parliament.

Infringement of the Rights Set Out in the Charter

As discussed in another chapter, the courts have been given the responsibility under the *Canadian Charter of Rights and Freedoms* (the "*Charter*") of reviewing any law made to determine if that law infringes on anyone's rights or freedoms and, if it does, in certain circumstances to declare the law null and void. There are two exceptions to this right of the court. First, if the court finds that such infringement is "demonstrably justified in a free and democratic society" under section 1 of the *Charter*, the law is saved and declared valid. Second, the legislature can save some laws under the "notwithstanding" provision of section 33 of the *Charter*. There are also other exceptions that protect the rights of separate schools and First Nations. Many people have decried the numerous laws thrown out by the judicial branch, citing this judicial activity as evidence of "judicial activism" that has gone too far from the theory of parliamentary supremacy.

Judicial Activism

The modifications to parliamentary supremacy set out above, especially declaring laws null and void due to infringement of rights set out in the *Charter*, have given power to the judicial branch. Many critics have suggested that this power has led to judicial activism. They denounce this as transferring power from the elected representatives of the people to a non-elected body — the judicial branch. There are many examples where the Supreme Court of Canada has upheld certain principles, which led to disallowing parts of statutes, such as the *Morgentaler* decision in the 1980s regarding abortion and cases in the 1990s regarding mandatory retirement. On one hand, it can be argued that the majority supports one position but, possibly, the courts' decisions sometimes support the minority position. Thus, protecting the minority is served in a democracy by placing more power in the hands of the judicial branch than having complete, uncontrolled parliamentary democracy.

CONCLUSION

By reviewing the representative democratic government that exists in Canada, we have seen how the federal system works within a modified theory of parliamentary supremacy. After this discussion, it can be argued that the whole exercise can be summed up with one question: who has the power in the legal system in Canada? The legislative, executive, or judicial branch? Although parliamentary supremacy states that all power resides in the legislative (parliamentary) branch, the practicalities of political life in Canada suggest that there is a large concentration of power in the hands of the executive branch. Furthermore, it can also be argued that the Constitution of Canada seems to have given more power to the judicial branch. Or that all three branches can be considered more powerful than the other two branches, depending on which theory you approve of, which practicality you find convincing or which constitutional viewpoint you take.

Although there are no clear answers to the question of which branch has the most power, it is important to recognize each branch and how the structure of the Canadian government operates.

CHAPTER SUMMARY

In this chapter, the reader learned that the structure of Canadian government is based initially on parliamentary democracy as both democracy and Parliament are discussed. Features of the competing system of totalitarianism are also summarized to gain a better understanding of democracy.

A parliamentary structure suggests the need for representatives to be elected to a legislative or parliamentary assembly with certain powers. We contrasted this with direct democracy, which either has no representative or one whose powers are circumscribed by electors by various methods. To further understand the parliamentary process, we compared the Canadian parliamentary system and the U.S. presidential system in terms of where the power is in both systems and how they hold elections. Other alternatives to the current electoral system in use in Canada were also examined and discussed.

After the review of parliamentary democracy, we described the levels of government and the federation in place in Canada, with both strong federal and provincial governments. Again, comparisons were made with other types of central-local government structures. It is emphasized that there is no legally separate municipal level of government in Canada, and that municipal government is a creation of the provincial level.

Next were the branches of government: executive, legislative and judicial. Each branch's functions, its members, and the interactions among the branches are outlined. The key point to remember relates to the theory behind the Canadian parliamentary system, the interactions of the branches (parliamentary supremacy) as compared to the theories behind the U.S. presidential system and the interaction among the branches (separation of powers and checks and balances). A comparison of the theories allows for a deeper examination of the Canadian theory of parliamentary supremacy and how it works practically, recognizing three modifications from the classical theory, wherein Parliament has all the power. The three modifications have taken some of Parliament's power (or too much power, if critical thinking about too much judicial activism is accepted) and given it to the judicial branch.

GLOSSARY OF NEW TERMS AND KEY CONCEPTS

backbenchers	Elected members of the legislative branch of the party of the government in power who are not Cabinet ministers or Cabinet secretaries.
Cabinet ministers and secretaries	Elected members of the legislature who head ministries.
checks and balances	The theory that, in combination with separation of powers, supports the presidential system of government, stating that each of the three branches of government has equal power and ensuring that each branch does not allow the other branches to over-step its own powers.
confederation	A loose type of federalism where the strong local governments have sovereign powers over a weak central government.
constitutional monarchy	The government system in countries (such as England and Canada) where the monarch relinquishes his or her power to Parliament to the extent that, theoretically, all power resides in Parliament, and the monarch is a figurehead.
democracy	A type of government where elections allow for making certain decisions by accepting the will of the majority.
devolution	A system where a central government allows some powers to be given to a localized government, with the ultimate power residing with the central government.
direct democracy	A system that allows the electorate more control than other types of democracy and includes at least two types: (i) the **Athenian Model**, where decisions are made on the basis of the one citizen, one vote mechanism, where the majority carried the day and all major decisions were put to a vote of the electorate, and (ii) the **Modern Model**, where representatives are elected, but mechanisms are in place to allow at least some control of the representatives to make them "listen" to the electorate.
executive federalism	A term that describes the relations between elected and appointed officials of the two levels of government in federal–provincial interactions and the relations between the executives of provinces in interprovincial interactions.
federalism	A system of government where sovereignty is divided between a central government and several regional or provincial governments.
free vote	A type of voting by representatives in a party system of government, where the party in power disregards party discipline and allows the members of the party to vote according to their conscience.
initiative (or proposition)	A mechanism of the modern model of direct democracy, where the voters can require that an issue be put on a ballot for a vote by the electorate that will bind the government.
intra vires	A Latin phrase that means "inside the power of the level of government to pass a law".
leader of the opposition	The leader of the party with, usually, the second highest number of seats in the legislature.
members in opposition to the government	Members of parties other than the one in power, independent members, or members of the ruling party who have been thrown out of the party caucus.

multi-member proportional representation	A mechanism to ensure that all parties who receive a minimum number of votes receive a number of seats based on the proportion of that party's vote to all votes cast.
parliamentary system	Originally and still in use in England as well as in Canada and in other countries, where a legislative branch is elected to make laws and where part of the legislative branch is also part of the executive branch.
party whip	A person who talks to party members to ensure that they vote according to the party's way and may even "threaten" removal from caucus or expulsion from the party if the member wishes to rebel.
plurality	The winner in an election who receives the most votes cast, even if it is not more than 50 percent.
powers (types) of federal and provincial governments	The rights given constitutionally to both levels of government in a federation can include the following: (i) **Enumerated (sovereign) powers**, with each level given specific and separate powers, allowing each level to legislate exclusively in certain areas. (ii) **Concurrent powers**, with both levels being able to legislate in the same area but not on the exact same point. (iii) **Overlapping powers**, with both levels having the same rights to legislate in the same area, with conflicts possible as a result. (iv) **Paramount powers**, with one level having the final and ultimate right to legislate, and the other level having only a subordinate or no right at all to legislate.
premier	The leader of a Canadian provincial party in power as the government.
presidential system	A system, originally and still American, but in use in many other countries, where the legislative branch is separate from the executive branch and where the executive branch is headed by a person who is elected in a country-wide election.
prime minister	The leader of a Canadian federal party in power as the government.
proportional representation	A system designed to provide representatives in multi-member constituencies of a number of minorities by calculating the votes for each party and comparing them to the votes cast in an election.
recall	A mechanism of the modern model of direct democracy where the voters can require that an elected representative lose her or his seat if a minimum number of voters sign a recall petition.
reference	A method of getting an issue before the court without requiring an actual fact situation affecting real persons before the issue can be decided.
referendum (and/or plebiscite)	A mechanism of the modern model of direct democracy where the government can require that an issue be put on a ballot for a vote by the electorate, which will bind the government.
representative democracy	A system where the citizens of a state elect candidates who will run the government by laws.
responsible government	A political concept that indicates that the executive (comprised of the elected MPs of one party, who make up the Cabinet) is responsible to all of the elected members of Parliament as a whole.
separation of powers	The theory that, in combination with checks and balances, supports the presidential system of government, stating that each of the three branches of government has separate powers.
single-member majoritarian system	The situation where the candidate in an election who gets the majority of the votes wins the seat.
single-member plurality system	The situation where the candidate who gets the plurality of the votes in an election wins the seat.
totalitarianism	A common type of governance used in the world today, where leaders impose their objectives or goals upon their people to an unlimited degree.

ultra vires   A Latin phrase that means "outside the power of the level of government to pass a law".

unitary system   A political system wherein a single sovereign government controls all regions of the country.

REVIEW QUESTIONS

1. Define democracy and its main characteristics.

2. Compare democracy and totalitarianism.

3. Discuss four problems that arise from the Athenian Model of direct democracy.

4. What is the difference between the parliamentary system and the presidential system?

5. How is a government formed after an election in the parliamentary system?

6. Enumerate the members of the legislative branch by title and function.

7. In the parliamentary system involving parties, define party discipline and how it is used to ensure that members of the governing party vote in a certain way.

8. Discuss three methods proposed under the Modern Model of direct democracy that will give individuals voting for representatives more power over their representatives.

9. Describe and explain by examples the four types of centralization of government currently in use.

10. Discuss the levels of government in Canada. Why is the municipal government not a level of government?

11. Discuss how the branches of government are connected in the parliamentary system and the presidential system, respectively, showing their differences.

12. Define the theory of parliamentary supremacy and the three modifications to that theory in the Canadian context.

13. How does the correction of the infringement of rights under the *Charter of Rights and Freedoms* transfer power away from the legislative branch and give it to the judicial branch?

14. Why are elections for a riding in Canada usually won by a plurality, whereas the elections for a seat in the United States are usually won by a majority?

15. Discuss what mechanism has been suggested to make parliamentary elections more responsive to minorities of voters, and how it works.

16. Which provinces have looked at changing their elections system to include some type of proportional representation?

17. What is judicial activism, and why is it looked upon suspiciously by one group of politicians and approvingly by another group?

18. Discuss the specifics of whether Canada has a constitutional monarchy.

19. Has the federal government attempted to change the maximum term of Parliament as set out in the *Constitution Act, 1867*?

DISCUSSION QUESTIONS

1. Using two issues under the *Charter of Rights and Freedoms*, discuss how the court has exercised too much or appropriate judicial activism to deal with the issue.

2. Based on the need for "effective government, responsive to the needs of all the people", discuss which is better: the parliamentary or presidential system of government.

3. Some of the mechanisms proposed in the Modern Model of direct democracy should be installed in the Canadian system of government. Do you agree with this statement? Why or why not?

4. Do you think Canada should or should not change from a single-member plurality system to either a single-member majoritarian system or a multi-member proportional system, and why or why not?

SUGGESTED READING AND OTHER RESOURCES

Beatty, David. *Constitutional Law in Theory and Practice* (Toronto: University of Toronto Press, 1995).

Carmichael, Don, et al. *Democracy, Rights and Well-Being in Canada*, 2d ed. (Toronto: Harcourt Brace Canada, 2000).

Dickerson, Mark O., & Thomas Flanagan. *An Introduction to Government and Politics: A Conceptual Approach*, 8th ed. (Toronto: ITP Nelson, 2009).

Hogg, Peter W. *Constitutional Law of Canada 2010* (Toronto: Carswell, 2010).

Jackson, Robert J., & Doreen Jackson. *An Introduction to Political Science: Comparative and World Politics*, 3d ed. (Scarborough, Ont.: Prentice Hall Allyn and Bacon Canada, 2000).

Mahler, Gregory S. *Comparative Politics: An Institutional and Cross-National Approach*, 5th ed. (Upper Saddle River, N.J.: Prentice Hall, 2008).

Monahan, Patrick J. *Constitutional Law* (Concord, Ont.: Irwin Law, 1997).

Morrison, Alan B. *Fundamentals of American Law*, 4th ed. (Oxford, U.K.: Oxford University Press, 2013).

Smiley, Donald V. *Canada in Question: Federalism in the Eighties*, 3d ed. (Toronto: McGraw-Hill Ryerson Limited, 1980).

VIDEOS AND DVDS

Churchill, Jane, dir. & Tamara Lynch, prod. 1991. *Government in Canada — Citizen in Action*. 4-part documentary series. Montreal, PQ: National Film Board of Canada.
- *Part 1: Democracy at Work — It's Your Choice*. [Video release, 1990; approximately 25 minutes.] Also available on DVD.
- *Part 2: Our Constitution — The Law of the Land*. [Video release, 1990; approximately 28 minutes.] Also available on DVD.
- *Part 3: Our National Parliament — The Inside Story*. [Video release, 1990; approximately 31 minutes.] Also available on DVD.
- *Part 4: Local & Provincial Governments — Working Together*. [Video release, 1990; approximately 37 minutes.] Also available on DVD.

WEBSITES

Canada, "How Government Works": <http://www.canada.ca/en/gov/system/index.html>

Mapleleafweb: <http://mapleleafweb.com/features/parliamentary-government-canada-basic-organization-and-practices>

Parliament of Canada:
<http://www.parl.gc.ca/marleaumontpetit/DocumentViewer.aspx?Sec=Ch01&Seq=2&Language=E>

The Constitution

Janet I. Mason
BARRISTER AND SOLICITOR

Stanley Gershman
BARRISTER AND SOLICITOR

Learning Objectives

After reading this chapter, the reader should be able to:

➢ understand that Canada's Constitution is based on a series of British statutes, conventions and common law

➢ identify the three main documents that make up Canada's Constitution

➢ understand the division of powers between the provinces and the federal government, distinguishing between matters of a national and local nature

➢ understand the various formulae for amending the Constitution

➢ identify the various methods that may be used where there is a real or potential conflict between laws made by the legislative bodies and the Constitution

➢ understand from the case study the basis upon which each level of government has the power to enact criminal law

➢ identify the formal requirements for valid criminal law from the case study

TABLE OF CONTENTS

INTRODUCTION

Canada's Constitution has evolved as Canada has evolved from being a British colony to a sovereign nation. To appreciate the significance and importance of our Constitution, we have to understand Canada's roots and the history of its development as an independent country. A constitution is an important and fundamental characteristic of a democratic nation and is composed of the rules and practices that provide "a legitimizing framework for the organization and exercise of governmental power in such nation".[1]

Canada began not as an independent nation but as a colony of Great Britain.[2] Prior to our original Constitution, the nation we call Canada was made up of several colonies or provinces, including Upper Canada (later renamed Ontario), Lower Canada (later renamed Quebec), New Brunswick, Nova Scotia, Prince Edward Island, and Newfoundland. These colonies were ruled by governors appointed by, and accountable to, the British government and, to some extent, by elected colonial legislatures. Legislative representatives of all these colonies met in a series of conferences in 1864 in Canada and, finally, in London, England, in 1866, to work out the plans for a new union. These plans were set out as resolutions that were enacted in a statute called the *British North America Act, 1867*,[3] passed by the British Parliament on July 1, 1867. This statute was built upon already existing traditions and colonial constitutions. The preamble to the statute states that the new Dominion of Canada would have "a constitution similar in principle to that of the United Kingdom [Great Britain]".

This Constitution applied at first only to Ontario, Quebec, New Brunswick and Nova Scotia, since Prince Edward Island and Newfoundland refused at this time to join in a new federation.[4] The idea for this union originated from the aspirations of the colonial legislative representatives, who were moved by recent threatening events, such as the bloody American Civil War, the continuing reverberations of the American revolution, the possibility of war between the United States and Great Britain, and the changing feelings of an overextended England as to its relationship with its colonies, especially on the volatile North American continent. The representatives of the four uniting colonies felt the need to bond together to deal more vigorously with these feared potential threats, and to protect and preserve their strongly dependent relationship with Great Britain. In order to unite, the provinces created a new federal level of government and a **Parliament** to deal with matters of interest to the whole country. Provinces with provincial **legislatures** were also established for the four former colonies.

Canada's Constitution serves four main functions:

1. To establish a political and economic union based on federal and democratic principles.

2. To outline a framework for the machinery of government and establish governmental institutions (e.g., Parliament, provincial legislatures, courts).

[1] *Canada (Director of Investigation & Research, Combines Investigation Branch) v. Southam*, [1984] 2 S.C.R. 145 at 155.

[2] The terms "Great Britain" "United Kingdom" and "England" are used interchangeably.

[3] (U.K.), 30 & 31 Vict., c. 3 [*BNA Act, 1867*].

[4] Over the course of time, other provinces joined the federation, creating the Canada we know today. Newfoundland was the last to join in 1949.

3. To distribute legislative, or law-making, powers and executive, or decision-making, powers between the provincial and national levels of government, thereby imposing legal limits on what a particular level of government could or could not do in relation to other governments.[5]

4. To solidify and confirm the colonies' desire to continue to be closely associated with Great Britain and its system of governance, and to reject the influence of the United States of America.

Great Britain's governmental structure had evolved over centuries. The country was first governed by an absolute monarchy and then evolved a constitutional monarchy — i.e., rule by the monarchy and an aristocracy of landowners. Eventually it evolved into a type of liberal representative democracy, where most citizens had the right to vote for representatives to Parliament.[6]

England's constitution in 1867 was not found in a single document. It could be found in separate legal documents, such as the Magna Carta of 1215 and the Bill of Rights of 1689. This constitution was composed mainly of political principles and practices or unwritten rules, known as **conventions**, that had arisen during its evolution into a liberal democracy. But in becoming a democracy, Britain had retained certain formal vestiges of the monarchy and aristocracy in its governmental structure. As a result, Canada's Constitution, which was to be similar in principle to that of the United Kingdom, as formulated in the *BNA Act, 1867*, seemed to express the form of Canada's government as a mixture of democratic institutions and a constitutional monarchy that provided a role for the monarchy and a non-elected "aristocracy" (i.e., the Senate). In practice, the Canadian government also functioned in accordance with British conventions that were not expressed in the *BNA Act, 1867*.

Conventions and Practices

The *BNA Act, 1867* is far from complete in describing the structure and function of our government. Many British constitutional conventions and practices not incorporated in the *BNA Act, 1867* became part of the Canadian "unwritten constitution". These included the following:

* the selection and role of the Prime Minister
* the composition of the executive of the House of Commons or Cabinet
* the existence and role of political parties

These conventions also included various principles, such as the following:

* the rule of law: the concept that no man, not even the monarch, was above the law
* the independence of the judiciary: the concept that judges were independent of the government that appointed them
* parliamentary sovereignty: the concept that Parliament, as the representative of the people, was supreme in making law

In addition to constitutional conventions and practices, case or common law on some subjects is also part of our Constitution, as a result of a series

---

[5] Bernard W. Funston & Eugene Meehan, *Canada's Constitutional Law In a Nutshell*, 2d ed. (Scarborough, Ont.: Carswell, 1998) at 11–12.

[6] In fact, Great Britain did not become a democracy until much later and was an example of what Fareed Zakaria designates as constitutional liberalism. As he points out, in 1867 Great Britain allowed barely 6.4 percent of its population to vote in the parliamentary elections. Fareed Zakaria, *The Future of Freedom: Illiberal Democracy at Home and Abroad* (New York, New York: W.W. Norton & Company, 2003) at 20.

of **precedent** cases that established some constitutional principles. Aboriginal rights were often established in this way. These interpretations of precedent continue to shape constitutional matters today. However, relying on the common law alone as a central source of constitutional matters can be problematic. Ordinary statutes can be used to easily override the common law. This vulnerability to arbitrary change seems to make precedent a poor choice for the protection of constitutional matters.

The Road to Independence

Even though the former colonies were referred to as a "Dominion", Canada in form, if not in practice, remained a colony of Great Britain. Over the years, however, an evolution occurred in which Canada gradually gained independence from Great Britain. An early step in this process was the "Balfour Declaration" of 1926, which gave current and former colonies status equal to Britain.

> [The United Kingdom and the Dominions] are autonomous communities within the British Empire, equal in status, in no way subordinate one to another in any aspect of their domestic or external affairs, although united by a common allegiance to the Crown, and freely associated as members of the British Commonwealth of Nations.[7]

The Balfour Declaration was implemented by the passage of the *Statute of Westminster 1931*[8] in December 1931. Thereafter, no law passed by England could apply to a Dominion unless the Dominion consented: in effect, giving Canada autonomy from the British Parliament. The *BNA Act, 1867* was made an exception to the *Statute of Westminster* so that the British Parliament remained the only legislative body with the power to amend it, since the *BNA Act, 1867* was a British statute. This exemption prevented any Canadian government from making arbitrary changes to our Constitution. It was to be another 50 years before Canada's legal autonomy was fully achieved by the passage of the *Canada Act 1982*,[9] which brought our Constitution under the authority of our Canadian government.

The Privy Council and the Supreme Court of Canada

Until 1949, Canada's final court of appeal was the Privy Council of the United Kingdom. This made the Privy Council, not the Supreme Court of Canada, the final arbiter in the interpretation and application of the *BNA Act, 1867*. On December 23, 1949, a federal bill to abolish the right of appeal to the British Privy Council was proclaimed. For any cases started after that date, the Supreme Court of Canada then became the final arbiter in interpreting the Constitution and also became the final court of appeal.

Canada's Constitutional Independence

The final step to an independent nation and to a constitution that more appropriately reflected the non-colonial liberal democratic nature of our government was taken by Prime Minister Pierre Trudeau in 1982. The prime minister was primarily responsible for promoting the passage of the *Canada Act* by the British Parliament. The *Canada Act* enacted the *Constitution Act, 1982*[10] and did away with the exemption of our Constitution to the *Westminster*

---

[7] M. Ollivier (ed.), *The Colonial and Imperial Conferences from 1887 to 1939*, vol. 3, 137–344 (Ottawa: Edmond Cloutier, Queen's Printer, 1954).

[8] (U.K.), 22 & 23 Geo 5, c. 4 [*Westminster*].

[9] (U.K.), 1982, c. 11 [*Canada Act*].

[10] Being Schedule B of the *Canada Act 1982*, (U.K.), 1982, c. 11, s. 1.

by (i) indicating that no Act of the Parliament of the United Kingdom hence-forth should extend to Canada and (ii) replacing the authority of the British Parliament to amend our Constitution with an amending formula that allows our own government to make such amendments:

> **2.** No Act of the Parliament of the United Kingdom passed after the *Constitution Act, 1982* comes into force shall extend to Canada as part of its law.

The *Constitution Act, 1982* retained the consolidated and amended *BNA Act, 1867* and renamed it the *Constitution Act, 1867.*[11] Most important, the Constitution also included the *Canadian Charter of Rights and Freedoms.*[12] The *Charter* guaranteed certain individual and collective rights and placed limits on the powers of government and legislators to interfere with such rights.

How the Constitution Differs from Statutes

There are two ways in which the Constitution[13] is significant and different from other laws. The first is that the Constitution has **supremacy** over all other laws in Canada. This means that any legislation that contravenes or is inconsistent with the Constitution is invalid and, therefore, of no force or effect (s. 52(1)):

> The Constitution of Canada is the supreme law of Canada, and any law that is inconsistent with the provisions of the Constitution is, to the extent of the inconsistency, of no force or effect.

The second way the Constitution differs from other laws is that it cannot be amended with the relative ease with which other laws are changed (i.e., by repealing or passing new legislation in the traditional manner), but can only be amended in accordance with certain rules and procedures set out in the Constitution itself.

THE DIVISION OF POWERS BETWEEN PARLIAMENT AND THE LEGISLATURES

Interpreting the Constitution

Canada has changed in many ways since the *BNA Act, 1867* was created. For example, the role of government has increased. Publicly funded programs, such as education and health care, have expanded or been introduced, and technological advances have occurred. The drafters of the *BNA Act, 1867* could not have contemplated many of the economic, political and social changes that have occurred. In order to ensure that the Constitution is able to adapt to new events, it is to be interpreted in a flexible manner. Therefore, the heads of powers are not restricted to a narrow definition based on what existed at the time of drafting. For example, the federal power identified as "postal service" is not limited to the postal service available in 1867. To quote Lord Sankey's popular analogy, the Constitution is to be like a "living tree capable of growth and expansion within its natural limits".[14] A progressive understanding of the heads of powers ensures that the Constitution remains relevant and fulfills its function of "provid[ing] the basis for the entire government of a nation over a long period of time".[15]

---

[11] (U.K.), 30 & 31 Vict., c. 3, reprinted in R.S.C. 1985, App. II, No. 5 [*Constitution Act, 1867*].

[12] Part I of the *Constitution Act, 1982*, being Schedule B to the *Canada Act 1982* (U.K.), 1982, c. 11 [*Charter*].

[13] A reference to the Constitution includes the *Constitution Act, 1982* and the *Constitution Act, 1867*.

[14] *Edwards v. Canada (A.G.)*, [1930] AC 124, [1930] 1 D.L.R. 98 (PC).

[15] Peter W. Hogg, *Constitution Law of Canada*, 2002 Student ed. (Scarborough, Ont.: Carswell, 2002) at 398 [*Hogg*].

Federal Powers

The Constitution lists certain matters and allocates them as either federal or provincial responsibilities and leaves any residual power to the federal government. Matters that affect the nation as a whole, such as the military, and those that cross provincial boundaries are referred to as **extraprovincial** matters. For example, railways would be within federal jurisdiction since they extend across provincial borders. Parliament is the legislative body that deals with federal matters, while the legislature of each province has jurisdiction over provincial matters. Jurisdiction under the Constitution empowers Parliament and legislatures to enact laws regarding an area of responsibility. Sections 91 and 92 of the *Constitution Act, 1867* list the specific areas of jurisdiction for each level of government and are reproduced in Exhibits 6.1 and 6.2.

The terms used to describe the heads of power are deliberately broad, and include associated administrative and enforcement functions. For example, "copyright" is an articulated federal head of power that includes the administrative and procedural requirements of registering copyrights within Canada. Parliament would also provide penalties for violations of its statutes.

Peace, Order and Good Government

An exceptional federal power can be found in the "peace, order and good government" ("**POGG**") category. POGG consists of three branches:

1. The gap or residual branch, where power to govern may be found when matters arise that are not specifically allocated in the Constitution to either Parliament or the legislature. (This branch is rarely used as the court prefers to fit the activity being conducted to an existing head of power.)

2. The emergency branch, whereby laws of a *temporary* nature may be implemented that allow Parliament to intrude into matters of provincial jurisdiction (e.g., the *War Measures Act*).

3. The national concern branch, which gives Parliament the power to control matters that are beyond a local or provincial concern, such as aeronautics or atomic energy, which are of concern to the nation as a whole.

Concurrent Jurisdiction

There are also categories where the federal and provincial governments appear to share responsibility. For example, marriage is one head of federal jurisdiction and involves the power to determine what constitutes a legal marriage in Canada (s. 91(26)). However, the province has the authority and responsibility under section 92(12) for the "solemnization of marriage" (i.e., the procedural aspects of getting married). The Constitution also identifies areas where both Parliament and the legislature have **concurrent jurisdiction**. These areas are old age pensions (s. 94(a)), agriculture and immigration (s. 95). Criminal law also has concurrent jurisdiction, and each level of government can pass such laws. However, provincial criminal laws must be grounded under a head of provincial power. Concurrent criminal jurisdiction is how provinces are able to impose fines and other penalties under the *Highway Traffic Act*, since intra-provincial roads would fall under the legislature's power as "local works and undertakings" (s. 92(10)).

Provincial Powers

Provincial heads of power are contained in section 92 of the *Constitution Act, 1867* and are listed in Exhibit 6.2. These matters concern the individual province and are referred to as matters that are **intra-provincial** and, therefore, of local concern.

EXHIBIT 6.1 Section 91 of the *Constitution Act, 1867*
— Parliamentary Heads of Power

91. It shall be lawful for the Queen, by and with the Advice and Consent of the Senate and House of Commons, to make Laws for the Peace, Order, and good Government of Canada, in relation to all Matters not coming within the Classes of Subjects by this Act assigned exclusively to the Legislatures of the Provinces; and for greater Certainty, but not so as to restrict the Generality of the foregoing Terms of this Section, it is hereby declared that (notwithstanding anything in this Act) the exclusive Legislative Authority of the Parliament of Canada extends to all Matters coming within the Classes of Subjects next hereinafter enumerated; that is to say,

1. Repealed.
1A. The Public Debt and Property.
2. The Regulation of Trade and Commerce.
2A. Unemployment insurance.
3. The raising of Money by any Mode or System of Taxation.
4. The borrowing of Money on the Public Credit.
5. Postal Service.
6. The Census and Statistics.
7. Militia, Military and Naval Service, and Defence.
8. The fixing of and providing for the Salaries and Allowances of Civil and other Officers of the Government of Canada.
9. Beacons, Buoys, Lighthouses, and Sable Island.
10. Navigation and Shipping.
11. Quarantine and the Establishment and Maintenance of Marine Hospitals.
12. Sea Coast and Inland Fisheries.
13. Ferries between a Province and any British or Foreign Country or between Two Provinces.
14. Currency and Coinage.
15. Banking, Incorporation of Banks, and the Issue of Paper Money.
16. Savings Banks.
17. Weights and Measures.
18. Bills of Exchange and Promissory Notes.
19. Interest.
20. Legal Tender.
21. Bankruptcy and Insolvency.
22. Patents of Invention and Discovery.
23. Copyrights.
24. Indians and Lands reserved for the Indians.
25. Naturalization and Aliens.
26. Marriage and Divorce.
27. The Criminal Law, except the Constitution of Courts of Criminal Jurisdiction, but including the Procedure in Criminal Matters.
28. The Establishment, Maintenance, and Management of Penitentiaries.
29. Such Classes of Subjects as are expressly excepted in the Enumeration of the Classes of Subjects by this Act assigned exclusively to the Legislatures of the Provinces.

And any Matter coming within any of the Classes of Subjects enumerated in this Section shall not be deemed to come within the Class of Matters of a local or private Nature comprised in the Enumeration of the Classes of Subjects by this Act assigned exclusively to the Legislatures of the Provinces.

Disallowance

While Canada generally considers itself a federal state, in reality it is quasi-federal. In a truly federal state, each level of government enjoys equal status and autonomy under its head of power. However, the *Constitution Act, 1867*, in sections 55, 56 and 90, in effect gives the federal government a veto power

Section 92 of the *Constitution Act, 1867* — Provincial Heads of Power	EXHIBIT 6.2

92. In each Province the Legislature may exclusively make Laws in relation to Matters coming within the Classes of Subjects next hereinafter enumerated; that is to say,

1. Repealed.
2. Direct Taxation within the Province in order to the raising of a Revenue for Provincial Purposes.
3. The borrowing of Money on the sole Credit of the Province.
4. The Establishment and Tenure of Provincial Offices and the Appointment and Payment of Provincial Officers.
5. The Management and Sale of the Public Lands belonging to the Province and of the Timber and Wood thereon.
6. The Establishment, Maintenance, and Management of Public and Reformatory Prisons in and for the Province.
7. The Establishment, Maintenance, and Management of Hospitals, Asylums, Charities, and Eleemosynary Institutions in and for the Province, other than Marine Hospitals.
8. Municipal Institutions in the Province.
9. Shop, Saloon, Tavern, Auctioneer, and other Licences in order to the raising of a Revenue for Provincial, Local, or Municipal Purposes.
10. Local Works and Undertakings other than such as are of the following Classes:
    (a) Lines of Steam or other Ships, Railways, Canals, Telegraphs, and other Works and Undertakings connecting the Province with any other or others of the Provinces, or extending beyond the Limits of the Province:
    (b) Lines of Steam Ships between the Province and any British or Foreign Country:
    (c) Such Works as, although wholly situate within the Province, are before or after their Execution declared by the Parliament of Canada to be for the general Advantage of Canada or for the Advantage of Two or more of the Provinces.
11. The Incorporation of Companies with Provincial Objects.
12. The Solemnization of Marriage in the Province.
13. Property and Civil Rights in the Province.
14. The Administration of Justice in the Province, including the Constitution, Maintenance, and Organization of Provincial Courts, both of Civil and of Criminal Justice, and including Procedure in Civil Matters in those Courts.
15. The Imposition of Punishment by Fine, Penalty, or Imprisonment for enforcing any Law of the Province made in relation to any Matter coming within any of the Classes of Subjects enumerated in this Section.
16. Generally all Matters of a merely local or private Nature in the Province.

over provincial laws, referred to as **disallowance**.[16] Disallowance permits the Governor General or Lieutenant Governor (both positions under federal jurisdiction) the power to set aside objectionable laws. This power is not likely to be exercised often because it tends to undermine the two-tiered approach of our Constitution. The United States, as a point of comparison, is a federal state. Differences include the residual constitutional power being allocated to the individual state and not to the federal government. Only federal powers are articulated in their constitution and receive a broad interpretation.[17] In the

---

[16] Hogg, *ibid.* at 117.
[17] Hogg, *ibid.* at 389.

United States, the issue of paramountcy does not generally arise because of clearly enunciated powers and the equal status of both levels of government. There is nothing in the U.S. Constitution permitting any level of government to disallow legislation validly enacted.

AMENDING THE CONSTITUTION

Sections 38 and 42: The General Amending Formula

The *Constitution Act, 1982* includes specific formulae for amendment, depending on subject matter, and articulates the requirements for general changes (including the identification of certain provincial matters that must use the general formula), specified categories that require unanimity, and federal and provincial unilateral changes.

The general formula (s. 38) requires that seven provinces that make up at least 50 percent of Canada's population agree to the constitutional amendment. Since the population of Ontario and Quebec make up more than 50 percent of Canada's population, at least one of them would have to vote for the amendment for it to be successful.[18] In addition, a province is free to opt out of a proposed change where a majority in the provincial legislature agrees to do so (s. 38(3)).

Section 42 lists matters that must be subject to this formula in order to prevent the federal government from arbitrarily making changes that may affect provincial concerns. These matters include proportionate representation of each province in the House of Commons, powers of the Senate, number of Senators and the establishment of a new province. Any matter not mentioned in sections 41, 43, 44 or 45 must follow the general formula of section 38, as implied in s. 52(3):

> Amendments to the Constitution of Canada shall be made only in accordance with the authority contained in the Constitution of Canada.

Section 41: Amendment by Unanimous Consent; Section 43: Amendments Relating to Some But Not All Provinces

A constitutional amendment for certain matters will require the agreement of Parliament, the legislatures of all provinces, the House of Commons and Senate. These matters are listed in section 41 of the Constitution and include proposed changes to the role of the Governor General or Lieutenant Governor of a province, provincial House of Commons members, and the composition of the Supreme Court of Canada. Alternatively, where a proposed amendment affects only some provinces, those affected by the change are required to agree to it along with federal approval (s. 43).

Sections 44 and 45: Federal and Provincial Unilateral Amendments

For matters that fall completely under federal jurisdiction, Parliament can unilaterally (i.e., without consent of the provinces) amend the Constitution. Provinces have a similar unilateral power to amend where the matter does not concern Parliament in any way. For example, a constitutional change on a provincial matter that directly or indirectly affects the position of Lieutenant Governor (a federal jurisdiction) could not be done under provincial unilateral power. Instead, this type of change would require the unanimity formula found under section 41 of the *Constitution Act, 1982*. The complicated procedure of obtaining consents to amending the Constitution protects it from arbitrary changes by Parliament or the legislatures.

---

[18] Hogg, *ibid.* at 75.

FEDERAL AND PROVINCIAL LEGISLATIVE CONFLICT/INCONSISTENCY

> [F]ederalism was the legal response of the framers of the Constitution to the political and cultural realities that existed at Confederation. It thus represented a legal recognition of the diversity of the original members. The division of powers, one of the basic components of federalism, was designed to uphold this diversity within a single nation. Broad powers were conferred on provincial legislatures, while at the same time Canada's unity was ensured by reserving to Parliament powers better exercised in relation to the country as a whole. Each head of power was assigned to the level of government best placed to exercise the power. The fundamental objectives of federalism were, and still are, to reconcile unity with diversity, promote democratic participation by reserving meaningful powers to the local or regional level and to foster co-operation among governments and legislatures for the common good.[19]

It is reasonable to expect that there will be occasions in our quasi-federal system where a law made by Parliament will or might conflict with a law made by the legislature. There are a number of legal principles that have been developed to sort out constitutional conflicts and legislative inconsistencies:

- the double aspect doctrine
- the paramountcy doctrine
- the colourability doctrine
- the interjurisdictional immunity doctrine
- the necessarily incidental doctrine

> As the final arbiters of the division of powers, the courts have developed certain constitutional doctrines, which, like the interpretations of the powers to which they apply, are based on the guiding principles of our constitutional order. The constitutional doctrines permit an appropriate balance to be struck in the recognition and management of the inevitable overlaps in rules made at the two levels of legislative power, while recognizing the need to preserve sufficient predictability in the operation of the division of powers. The doctrines must also be designed to reconcile the legitimate diversity of regional experimentation with the need for national unity. Finally, they must include a recognition that the task of maintaining the balance of powers in practice falls primarily to governments, and constitutional doctrine must facilitate, not undermine what this Court has called "co-operative federalism"....[20]

When the constitutionality of legislation is challenged based on the division of powers, the analysis always begins with an examination of the "pith and substance" of the legislation. "This initial analysis consists of an inquiry into the true nature of the law in question for the purpose of identifying the 'matter' to which it essentially relates."[21] The purpose of the enacting body and the legal effect of the law will both be examined. If the dominant purpose and effect of the legislation is within the enacting body's jurisdiction, the legislation will be valid even if there are minor intrusions into the other level of government's jurisdiction. In such cases, the double-aspect doctrine or the necessarily incidental doctrine could apply and lead to a finding of validity. Where the enacting body has transgressed into the jurisdiction of the other, the doctrine of colourability (dealt with, as relevant, during the initial "pith and substance" analysis), paramountcy, or interjurisdictional immunity can apply.

---

[19] *Canadian Western Bank v. Alberta*, 2007 SCC 22, at para. 23 [*Western Bank*].
[20] *Ibid.* at para. 24.
[21] *Ibid.* at paras. 25, 26.

What constitutes a "minor intrusion", however, is an issue that even the Supreme Court of Canada cannot agree on. In *Reference re Assisted Human Reproduction Act*, 2010 SCC 61, [2010] 3 SCR 457, four justices declared the challenged provisions to be unconstitutional ("Deschamps"), four declared the provisions to be constitutional ("McLachlin"), and one declared some to be constitutional and some unconstitutional ("Cromwell").

The federal Parliament passed the *Assisted Human Reproduction Act*, S.C. 2004, c. 2 ("Act"), in response to new, and future, developments in human reproduction and associated medical research. Parliament enacted the legislation under its criminal law power of s. 91(27) of the *Constitution Act, 1867*. Certain provisions set up a regulatory scheme, and the issue was whether or not these could be properly enacted under s. 91(27).

The Attorney General of Quebec ("AGQ") had challenged, by way of reference to the Quebec Court of Appeal, the authority of Parliament to enact certain provisions of the Act on the basis that they were beyond its criminal power jurisdiction. The appellate court agreed that certain provisions were unconstitutional because they infringed upon provincial power for hospitals, civil rights, and local matters. The provisions' pith and substance concerned the regulation of medical practice (including doctors and hospitals) and research related to assisted reproduction. As such, it was beyond the scope of federal criminal power.

The Attorney General of Canada ("AGC") appealed that finding by way of a reference to the Supreme Court of Canada. The AGC's position was that the provisions were, in pith and substance, properly constituted criminal law. The purpose of the scheme was to "protect morality, safety and public health in the 'novel' context of the artificial creation of human life. The adoption of prohibitions with exemptions and conditions makes it possible to take a systematic and integrated approach to the problems raised by the various aspects of assisted human reproduction, and the complexity of the issues it raises" (at para. 178). The provisions all pertained to "facets of the same novel reality, the artificial creation of human life", and the Act contemplated "a range of practices that are all related to that activity, and that all pose risks to the fundamental values of public morality and health underlying this mix of concerns ... [M]ost of the provisions ... have nothing to do with the practice of medicine, and none of them solely concern it" (at para. 200). There was little, if any, encroachment on provincial powers as regards the practice of medicine but a connection with the protection of public health. They had nothing to do with medical procedures or the management of hospitals.

The AGQ submitted that Parliament, in pith and substance, was regulating the entire field of medicine related to assisted human reproduction and related research, with the impugned provisions. They concerned activities that were desirable, and therefore could not be based on federal criminal power. The practice of medicine relating to assisted human reproduction was not distinct from the practice of medicine generally, which was under provincial jurisdiction. The AGQ was challenging the provisions that did not impose an absolute prohibition (i.e., improperly constituted criminal law) and those that concerned the application of those provisions. The provisions amounted to the "regulation of an entire area of medicine and research in order to define its evolving framework and ensure safe, accessible, health care ... [A]ll these matters fall indisputably within the provinces' power to make laws in relation to hospitals, education, civil rights and matters of a local or private nature" (at para. 201). In fact, the provisions overlapped or conflicted with provincial laws already in effect in Quebec.

Deschamps identified that the double aspect doctrine and the ancillary powers doctrine could apply. Both doctrines begin their analysis with regard to the "pith and substance" of the legislation, which determines its dominant purpose. The determination of the dominant purpose must be precise, not too general, and also must consider the effect of the legislation. A statute will be invalid where its dominant purpose, when considered as a whole, is connected to the exclusive power of the other level of government. The ancillary powers doctrine will apply where one or more provisions of validly enacted legislation are challenged.[22]

The ancillary powers doctrine permits laws to "validly overflow from the jurisdiction of the government that enacted them so long as the overflow remains ancillary" (at para. 188). However, the extent of the overflow permitted must be assessed by way of a review as to the extent to which they are integrated into the otherwise valid statute. This requires a consideration of rationality, or functionality. If the provision, when viewed in isolation, greatly exceeds the authority of the level of government that enacted it, then the "necessity" of the provision must also be considered. Where a provision is functionally integrated into a valid statute and, when viewed in isolation, its overflow into the other level of government's power is only slight, it will likely be found to be constitutional under the ancillary powers doctrine. The more necessary the provision is to the effectiveness of unchallenged parts of the statute, then the greater the acceptable overflow will be (at para. 193).

In assessing the purpose of the provisions, consideration must be given to the context surrounding the enactment of the statute. This could involve a review of Hansard debates, draft Bills, and government reports. The federal government had, as an example relevant to examining context, established the Baird Commission ("Baird") to report on the issue under a broad mandate, which it did in 1993. The report identified activities that should be prohibited using Parliament's federal criminal power. It also referred to activities that it termed "controlled activities", which should be subject to national standards, and could be grounded on Parliament's peace, order and good government ("POGG") power. The prohibited and controlled activities, according to Baird, required two distinct approaches with different purposes.

The Act's provisions reflected these two distinctions, i.e., prohibited activities and controlled activities. However, based on the two different purposes identified in Baird, the impugned provisions did not share a prohibitory, or criminal law, purpose. "The purpose of the impugned provisions is instead to set up a national scheme to regulate the activities in question" (at para. 217).

Deschamps compared the provisions to Quebec laws, its physician's code of conduct, and federal laws. They determined that some of the provisions conflicted with, or were duplicated in, existing provincial and federal legislation. The Act contained a distinct framework and special rules for assisted human reproduction and impacted those who contributed to such activities, including the professionals involved and associated institutions.

[226] We concluded above that the purpose of the impugned provisions was to establish mandatory national standards for assisted human reproduction. A review of the practical consequences of these provisions shows that they have a significant impact on the practice of medicine. We therefore cannot agree with the Attorney General of Canada that the impugned provisions have nothing to do with the quality of services or the management of health-care institutions.

[227] Rather, the purpose and the effects of the provisions in question relate to the regulation of a specific type of health services provided in health-care institutions by health-care professionals to individuals who for pathological or physiological reasons need help to reproduce. Their pith and substance must

---

[22] See para. 187 for the steps in the ancillary powers analysis.

be characterized as the regulation of assisted human reproduction as a health service. ...

The final step in the pith and substance analysis requires that the dominant purpose of the legislation, or the impugned provisions, be placed under the relevant constitutional head of power. This will determine its constitutionality. It is insufficient, decided Deschamps, for Parliament to simply design legislation with a prohibition, penalty, and exempted prohibitions. The purpose must substantively fall with the criminal law sphere.[23] It cannot be based simply on efficiency or consistency. Otherwise, the division of powers becomes unbalanced and provincial power usurped.

> [246] The principles underlying the balance of Canadian federalism themselves require that rules that relate in pith and substance to the criminal law power be distinguished from those that, although having a regulatory aspect, are intended to govern fields under other — exclusive or concurrent — federal or provincial powers.

Deschamps found that Parliament was, in fact, adopting Baird's recommendation on controlled activities, which was intended to establish national standards for assisted human reproduction. Its purpose was not about suppressing evil or preventing harm. Assisted human reproduction has existed and has been covered by provincial medical insurance for over a decade (in vitro fertilization, as an example). Its development is generally considered to be positive and beneficial.

The impugned provisions clearly fell under a provincial head of power. They concerned the management and standards of hospitals and labs, which are under provincial jurisdiction. The pith and substance of the impugned provisions concerned hospitals, civil rights, and matters of a local or private nature. This was reflected in the context of (i) doctor/patient relationships involving consent; (ii) the donation and use of genetic material for assisted human reproduction; and (iii) management and standards to be applied to hospitals, labs, and medical service providers. These were all local matters under provincial power. The Act clearly overflowed the federal criminal power of Parliament.

There was no double-aspect that provided authority for Parliament to encroach, through the controlled activity provisions, on the province's exclusive jurisdiction to govern local matters. It simply does not have such power in our federal state. The regulatory scheme was dependent on the impugned provisions and automatically, as a result, fell outside Parliament's jurisdiction. There was no need for such a scheme without those activities.

The ancillary powers doctrine could not save the provisions either. This analysis considered the question: "Were the impugned provisions enacted pursuant to a power that is ancillary to Parliament's criminal law power?" (at para. 274). This required consideration of the relationship between the prohibited activity provisions and the controlled activity provisions, and whether they were sufficiently integrated in the constitutionally valid portion of the Act. The extent of the overflow would determine the level of integration needed, which required a functional or necessary relationship. The more significant the overflow, the closer the relationship must be.

It was clear that significant overflow existed and would require a relationship of necessity with the valid provisions. There was no necessary relationship because the prohibitory provisions did not depend on the impugned

---

[23] For example, the gun registry (also referred to below) is proper criminal law despite its regulatory nature of private property. Guns are dangerous weapons, and safeguarding people is a substantive criminal purpose.

provisions or vice versa. Baird had clearly considered the two areas to be independent and distinct. The impugned provisions were unconstitutional.

> [280] Given the legislative history of the ... [A]ct, the significant impact of the impugned provisions on provincial health systems and the fact that the matters they address are clearly connected with provincial heads of power, it must be inferred that in setting up the regulatory scheme, Parliament's intention was to enact legislation in relation to a matter outside its jurisdiction.

In contrast, another four of the nine Supreme Court Justices ("McLachlin") decided that the provisions were constitutional. The provisions, while they infringed provincial power over medical research and practice, only did so incidentally at para. 10:

> [T]he impact is incidental to the legislation's dominant criminal purpose and limited to those ends. Finally, while not criminal law in pith and substance, the administrative, organizational, and enforcement provisions in ss. 14 to 68 are integrated into this prohibition regime, and hence they are valid under the ancillary powers doctrine.

McLachlin also first considered the legislative scheme as a whole to determine its pith and substance, i.e., its dominant purpose, and concluded that it was validly enacted criminal law. Its purposes were morality, public health evils, and security, which served legitimate criminal law purposes. The Act "targets conduct that Parliament has found to be reprehensible. In so doing, it incidentally permits beneficial practices through regulations. But that does not render it unconstitutional" (at para. 30).[24]

McLachlin, after determining the Act's purpose, considered the challenged prohibition provisions and found them to be within the scope of federal criminal power. The ancillary provisions (that concerned access to information, consent, compliance, organizational, administrative, enforcement and regulatory) of the Act constituted only a minor intrusion on provincial jurisdiction, and were rationally connected to the valid criminal law (at para. 147). Therefore they were constitutional pursuant to the ancillary powers doctrine.

Cromwell fell somewhere in the middle of his colleagues Deschamps and McLachlin. He found that only some of the impugned provisions were outside of Parliament's criminal power for the same reason as Deschamps. He posed the relevant question as being "whether the federal criminal law power permits Parliament to regulate virtually all aspects of research and clinical practice in relation to assisted human reproduction" (at para. 283). He concluded that it did not.

The Double Aspect Doctrine

The **double aspect doctrine** applies where both Parliament and the legislature have authority to enact laws on a matter. These powers may be expressly concurrent, such as the power to regulate immigration under section 95 of the *Constitution Act, 1867*, noted earlier, or they may arise from the exercise of the right to legislate the matter under another heading in the Constitution. Assuming that both laws are valid and of equal importance, and that it is possible for each to operate without conflict or inconsistency, they will be upheld as a double-aspect matter. Both laws would be a valid exercise of power for each level of government.

---

[24] Valid criminal law, as stated, requires a prohibition and a penalty, with a public purpose (to suppress evil or safeguard a threatened interest). The Act contained provisions that identified conduct or acts that would not be a prohibition, and were "beneficial practices".

For example, Parliament has the power to regulate the creation and structure of federally incorporated companies (a matter for Parliament since these corporations operate nationally, as opposed to operating within a province and are, therefore, a matter of national or extraprovincial concern). However, the legislature has the power under property and civil rights to regulate commercial activity within the province. This means that Parliament will define the rights, liabilities and internal structure of a federally incorporated company, such as a national retail chain. The legislature will have regulations in place regarding the registration of all corporations within the province and related reporting requirements.

The Paramountcy Doctrine

Where the two valid laws conflict, and an individual cannot comply with both, the federal **paramountcy doctrine** is triggered. Paramountcy results in the provincial statute, to the extent of the conflict or inconsistency, being declared inoperative by the court. The test for paramountcy requires that the party submitting the assertion first demonstrate that the federal and provincial laws were validly enacted in relation to the division of powers under the Constitution. If valid, compliance with both laws simultaneously must be shown to be impossible because of either an operational conflict (it is impossible to comply with both laws) or because compliance with the provincial law frustrates the purpose of the federal law.[25]

The paramountcy doctrine will not necessarily invalidate the whole law, and the provincial law may remain in force despite the inoperable section(s). In the event that the federal law is later repealed and no longer in force, the provincial law will fully operate since the conflict or inconsistency no longer exists. There is no express reciprocal provincial power of paramountcy, though a federal statute can be challenged where it appears that Parliament is attempting to regulate a matter under provincial jurisdiction.

The Colourability Doctrine

The **colourability doctrine** is triggered where a law is enacted with a stated purpose that appears to contradict the actual purpose. *R. v. Morgentaler*[26] concerned provincial legislation that led to the prosecution of Dr. Morgentaler for performing an abortion in his private clinic located outside of a Nova Scotia hospital. Dr. Morgentaler was acquitted at trial after the judge decided that the law the doctor was charged with breaking was beyond the jurisdiction of the province to enact. The Supreme Court, in 1988, had ruled that abortion was not to be regulated by the criminal law and that it was not an offence for a woman to obtain an abortion in a clinic.[27] This judgment determined that a province did not have power to enact criminal legislation regarding the provision of abortion at clinics.

The province appealed the decision to the Supreme Court, submitting that the *Medical Services Act* was a valid exercise of its power under hospitals, property and civil rights, and matters of a local nature, as stated in the Constitution. The stated purpose of the Act was to "prohibit the privatization of the provision of certain medical services in order to maintain a single high-quality health-care delivery system for all Nova Scotians". A regulation passed under the Act listed the medical services to which the Act applied and

[25] *British Columbia (A.G.) v. Lafarge Canada Inc.*, 2007 SCC 23 at para. 77, summarizing *Canadian Western Bank v. Alberta*, 2007 SCC 22 at 75.

[26] [1993] 3 S.C.R. 463, 107 DLR (4th) 537 [*Morgentaler*], aff'g *R. v. Morgentaler* (1991), 83 D.L.R. (4th) 8 (N.S.C.A.) and 99 N.S.R. (2d) 393.

[27] *R. v. Morgentaler*, [1988] 1 S.C.R. 30, 44 D.L.R. (4th) 385 [*Morgentaler 1988*].

Paramountcy Doctrine

EXHIBIT 6.3

Regulations passed under the federal *Food and Drugs Act*, R.S.C. 1970, c. F-27 sought to regulate the minimum and maximum alcohol content for the marketing of "light beer". Labatt was selling a light beer that had an alcohol content above the limit listed in the relevant provisions under the Act. Labatt challenged the provisions of the legislation, alleging the matter was under provincial jurisdiction and, therefore, Parliament had no authority to dictate its alcohol content. The federal government responded by claiming that the power to enact the provisions was valid under its trade and commerce power and, additionally, relied on POGG (national concern branch) and criminal law power.

The Supreme Court examined each source of power and its applicability in the circumstances and determined, in a 6–3 decision, that a federal head of power could not be found to support the validity of the challenged provisions. The Court determined that Parliament's trade and commerce power could not provide the necessary basis by which Parliament enacted the provisions. Labatt had breweries in many provinces, and sales were generally of a local nature (i.e., within the province, as opposed to having one central brewery that distributed the product across provincial boundaries). In addition, Parliament's general trade power is concerned with general trade regulations, as opposed to focusing on the process of a single industry, such as breweries. As a matter concerning intra-provincial trade, breweries appeared to be the responsibility of the legislature.

The national concern branch of POGG also failed to uphold the provision since the alcohol content of light beer was not shown to be of national concern. A criminal law basis was also unsuccessful since the provisions did not serve a public purpose. The provisions did not serve a consumer protection purpose, nor did the law appear concerned with compositional changes in food, or false or misleading advertising or labelling. Justice Estey characterized the provisions as being the detailed regulation of the brewing industry, noting that it did not attempt to protect the health of Canadians.

The Supreme Court held that the relevant provisions were a detailed regulation of the brewing industry regarding the production and sale of its product that infringed on provincial jurisdiction. As such, the provisions could not be constitutionally justified. They were, therefore, found to be outside Parliament's power to legislate, and rendered inoperative.

Source: *Labatt Breweries of Canada Ltd. v. Canada (A.G.)*, [1980] 1 S.C.R. 914, 110 D.L.R. (3d) 594.

---

included abortion where it was performed outside a hospital. The Act also denied health insurance coverage for abortions performed in violation of its provisions, which included those performed at an abortion clinic located outside a hospital.

The Supreme Court examined the Act and found that the province had jurisdiction over hospitals and the medical profession under the *Constitution Act, 1867* (ss. 92(7), (13) and (16), noted above). However, the determinative issue involved a consideration of whether or not the Act's purpose was an attempt to legislate the quality and nature of health care delivery, which would have made it a proper exercise of provincial power, or a criminal law enacted for a public purpose that would have made it improper. The structure of the legislation appeared to be criminal (i.e., a prohibition and penalty for a public purpose). While the province is able to enact criminal laws regarding matters under a provincial head of power, the prohibition of abortion had been held to be a federal criminal matter in the 1988 case. Therefore, the Supreme Court considered whether or not the Act was, in effect, an attempt to prohibit abortions outside of a hospital as a method of suppressing or punishing the "socially undesirable conduct of abortion". The Court was concerned that the *stated* purpose of the Act simply disguised the *intended* purpose of the Act.

In its decision, the Supreme Court decided that the Act, as far as the abortion provision was concerned, had the same legal effect as the federal legislation. This legislation had been struck down in Morgentaler's successful 1988 challenge. It appeared that the intended purpose of the Act was to regulate a matter (e.g., abortion) that had been found to be under Parliament's jurisdiction. In addition, an investigation into the events leading up to the passage of the Act and accompanying legislative debates did not support the purpose as stated in the Act. Therefore, the Court held that the Act was ***ultra vires*** of provincial power by application of the colourability doctrine. The legal effect of the law and accompanying regulations identified a purpose other than that stated in the law.[28]

Interjurisdictional Immunity Doctrine

While a level of overlap is to be expected in our quasi-federal state, the core of the head of power is protected by the **interjurisdictional immunity doctrine**. The core may be understood as a "vital or essential part",[29] and as the "basic, minimal and unassailable content"[30] of a constitutional head of power. To illustrate, Parliament is given authority for federal undertakings under the Constitution. Communication systems that travel across provincial boundaries would be considered a federal undertaking. But federal jurisdiction extends beyond the physical cables and can include associated matters, such as the terms of employment for those employed by the communication provider. Thus, the federal undertaking would be immune from provincial legislation and, for example, minimum wage legislation would not apply to employees. The provincial legislation would not be rendered invalid but may be read down (i.e., interpreted narrowly, thereby reducing applicability) so as to be inoperative regarding the federal undertaking.

> What is "vital" or "essential" is, by definition, not co-extensive with every element of an undertaking incorporated federally or subject to federal regulation. In the case of federal undertakings, [there is] a "general rule" that there is *no* interjurisdictional immunity, provided "the application of [the] provincial laws does not bear upon those [federal] subjects in what makes them specifically of federal jurisdiction."[31]

While the foregoing seems straight forward, consider whether Parliament or the province has jurisdiction over employees of a freight forwarding company that arranges national transport through third party interprovincial carriers. The business that is effectively carried on is extraprovincial, but the company itself does not actually ship the freight; it acts as an intermediary between shipper and various carriers. Is it the service that is provided or the means through which it is carried out that dictates constitutional jurisdiction?

In *Consolidated Fastfrate Inc. v Western Canada Council of Teamsters*, 2009 SCC 53, a majority of the Supreme Court decided that the carrier's employees were under provincial jurisdiction despite the extraprovincial nature of the company:

> I am of the view that an undertaking that performs consolidation and deconsolidation and local pickup and delivery services does not become an interprovincial undertaking simply because it has an integrated national corporate structure and contracts with third party interprovincial carriers. Fastfrate does not perform any interprovincial carriage itself. Absent this, I see no

---

[28] *Ibid.*, defining the colourability doctrine.
[29] *Commission du Salaire Minimum v. Bell Telephone Co.*, [1966] S.C.R. 767.
[30] *Bell Canada v. Quebec (Commission de la santé et de la sécurité du travail du Québec)*, [1988] 1 S.C.R. 749.
[31] *British Columbia (A.G.) v. Lafarge Canada Inc.*, 2007 SCC 23, [2007] S.C.J. No. 23, para. 42.

compelling reason to depart from the general rule that works and undertakings are regulated by the provinces. Accordingly, the labour relations of the employees of Calgary Fastfrate are subject to provincial jurisdiction.... (at para. 3)

The interjurisdictional immunity doctrine may appear to be similar to the paramountcy doctrine, but there exists an important distinction. Paramountcy is triggered only where there are two valid laws, each properly enacted under a level of government's head of power, that conflict or are inconsistent. If the two laws do not conflict, there is no constitutional disagreement. In *Newfoundland (Workplace Health, Safety & Compensation Commission) v Ryan Estate,* 2013 SCC 44 ("*Ryan*"), the Supreme Court overturned the appellate court's decision that found a provision in provincial law (concerning the province's workers' compensation scheme) unconstitutional because it barred a negligence proceeding available under federal legislation. The court of appeal had held that the bar was inapplicable due to interjurisdictional immunity and inoperative by virtue of federal paramountcy. The Supreme Court held that both doctrines did not render the provincial provision inoperative.

Ryan concerned the death of two fishermen after their boat capsized off the coast of Newfoundland and Labrador. The estates had, as a result, obtained compensation under the provincial workers' compensation legislation. It now wanted to bring a tort proceeding in negligence for the design and construction of the boat. The Supreme Court found that workers' compensation schemes, whether provincial or federal, were an insurance regime that protected everyone who participated in it. The ship designer and manufacturer were participants in the provincial scheme. In an interesting turn, the court broadly defined "employer" as any employer participating in the regime and not the specific employer of the injured workers.

The provincial legislation, as regards interjurisdictional immunity, was found to "trench on the core" of the federal legislation because navigation and shipping are under exclusive federal jurisdiction (at para. 59). However, that alone is insufficient to trigger the application of interjurisdictional immunity, which requires that the impugned legislation "impair", and not just "affect", the other level of government's constitutional power (at para. 56).

> [62] Although s 44 of the WHSCA has the effect of regulating a maritime negligence law issue, it neither alters the uniformity of Canadian maritime law nor restricts Parliament's ability to determine who may possess a cause of action under the MLA. Despite their inability to initiate the maritime negligence action provided for by s. 6(2) of the MLA, parties in the positions of the Ryan Estate still receive compensation for the accident in question (albeit through a different mechanism and from a different source). ...

> [64] ... [The section] may affect the exercise of the federal power over navigation and shipping, ... [but] this level of intrusion of s. 44 is not significant or serious when one considers the breadth of the federal power over navigation and shipping, the absence of an impact on the uniformity of Canadian maritime law, and the historical application of workers' compensation schemes in the maritime context. For these reasons, s. 44 of the WHSCA does not impair the federal power over navigation and shipping. Interjurisdictional immunity does not apply here. ...

Paramountcy arises where (i) there is a conflict between a provincial law and a federal law when both laws are valid (i.e., compliance with one law results in violation of the other), or (ii) the provincial law frustrates the purpose of the federal law (at paras. 68 and 69). The court held that the laws were valid, and did not conflict. There was no conflict because there was no express 'right' to bring a claim under the federal legislation. The discretionary nature of the federal provision permitted the provincial provision to operate simultaneously and harmoniously. The absence of a right suggested there could be situations where a claim could not be brought. Having already received compensation from a provincial workers' compensation regime would be such a situation. In addition, the federal purpose was not frustrated because it was, in a broad context, to provide a method of compensation. The purpose of federal and provincial workers' compensation schemes was to take the issue of compensation out of the fault-based tort system, and out of the courts.

Unlike paramountcy, interjurisdictional immunity can be triggered in the absence of any federal law concerning the matter. Where a provincial law intrudes into the core of a federal head of power, despite Parliament's failure to legislate the matter under its relevant head of power, the provincial law would be inapplicable. However, the doctrine should only be considered if there is prior case law favouring its application to the subject matter before the court.[32]

Necessarily Incidental Doctrine

The **necessarily incidental doctrine** allows Parliament or the legislature to infringe on a head of power belonging to the other, provided that it does not go to the power's core. In order to do so, the infringing portion of the legislation must be shown to be "incidental" to the overall purpose and, simply, part of the larger legislative scheme. When applied, the technically invalid part of the legislation is held to be valid because of its close relationship to the larger, valid scheme of the legislation. *General Motors of Canada Ltd. v. City National Leasing*[33] challenged the inclusion of a civil action remedy under the federal legislation. Civil actions (e.g., a tort action) are a provincial head of power, property and civil rights, under the *Constitution Act, 1867*.

The legislation concerned anti-competitive behaviour, and the fact that the option of launching a civil action was under provincial authority was not in dispute. After consideration, the Supreme Court found that the potential civil action infringed on the power of the legislature, and that the remainder was properly enacted under federal jurisdiction. The Court conducted further analysis to see whether the infringement, a relatively minor aspect of the overall valid legislation, could be "constitutionally justified by reason of its connection with valid legislation". The Court held that the provision of the civil action, while encroaching on provincial power, was a remedial one, had been done before and was limited in the Act by restrictions to its application. The option of a civil action was an "integral, well-conceived component" of the legislation, functionally related to the purpose of the Act, and could help the legislation fulfill its objectives. As such, the provision was found to be necessarily incidental to the Act, and constitutionally valid.

DIVISION OF POWER AND CRIMINAL LAW

The criminal law is a concurrent power between Parliament and the legislature. Parliament enjoys a broad power to enact criminal law for the public good, whereas the legislatures must ground their criminal law in an existing head of provincial power. Section 91(27) grants Parliament the broad power to enact criminal legislation, and section 92(15) empowers the legislature to pass criminal laws on matters under their jurisdiction. Parliament's broad power to enact criminal legislation can include economic regulation that includes a

---

[32] *Ryan* at para. 49.
[33] [1989] 1 S.C.R. 641, 58 D.L.R. (4th) 255.

criminal penalty and laws to prevent harm. In addition, criminal law must follow a particular structural format.

The *Criminal Code*[34] is federal legislation and applies on a national level. Regardless of where you reside in Canada, theft and murder, for example, are offences punishable under the *Criminal Code*. Municipal by-laws and provincial offences (e.g., traffic offences) are provincial matters and are applicable only within a particular community or province. This is why, for example, highway speed limits may differ from province to province. Since the province is empowered to deal with local undertakings, they can legislate these areas using their criminal law power. However, should the legislature enact criminal law that concerns a matter outside of its jurisdiction — for example, for a **public purpose** (i.e., to punish or prevent objectionable behaviour) — such a law would be *ultra vires*. Parliament seems to be likewise disallowed from passing criminal legislation that infringes on a head of power of the legislature, such as including a provision in regulatory legislation that provides, as the sole penalty, grounds on which to base a civil action. As discussed, grounds for civil actions are a provincial power under property and civil rights.

> The federal criminal law power is "plenary in nature" and has been broadly construed:
>
>> A crime is an act which the law, with appropriate penal sanctions, forbids; but as prohibitions are not enacted in a vacuum, we can properly look for some evil or injurious or undesirable effect upon the public against which the law is directed. That effect may be in relation to social, economic or political interests; and the legislature has had in mind to suppress the evil or to safeguard the interest threatened. (*Reference re Validity of Section 5(a) of the Dairy Industry Act*, [1949] S.C.R. 1 [the *"Margarine Reference"*], at p. 49)
>
> ...
>
>> For a law to be classified as a criminal law, it must possess three prerequisites: a valid criminal law purpose backed by a prohibition and a penalty (*Reference re Firearms Act (Can.)*, [2000] 1 S.C.R. 783, 2000 SCC 31, at para. 27). The criminal power extends to those laws that are designed to promote public peace, safety, order, health or other legitimate public purpose. In *RJR-MacDonald Inc. v. Canada (Attorney General)*, [1995] 3 S.C.R. 199, it was held that some legitimate public purpose must underlie the prohibition. In *Labatt Breweries [of Canada Ltd. v. Attorney General of Canada*, [1980] 1 S.C.R. 914], in holding that a health hazard may ground a criminal prohibition, Estey J. stated the potential purposes of the criminal law rather broadly as including "public peace, order, security, health and morality" (p. 933). Of course Parliament cannot use its authority improperly, e.g. colourably, to invade areas of provincial competence: *Scowby v. Glendinning*, [1986] 2 S.C.R. 226, at p. 237.
>
> In determining whether the purpose of a law constitutes a valid criminal law purpose, courts also look at whether laws of this type have traditionally been held to be criminal law: *Ward v. Canada (Attorney General)*, [2002] 1 S.C.R. 569, 2002 SCC 17, at para. 51; *Reference re Firearms Act (Can.)*, [2000] 1 S.C.R. 783, 2000 SCC 31, at para. 32; *RJR-MacDonald v. Canada (Attorney General)*, [1995] 3 S.C.R. 199, at para. 204; *R. v. Morgentaler*, [1993] 3 S.C.R. 463, at p. 491.[35]

---

[34] R.S.C. 1985 c. C-46.

[35] *R. v. Demers*, 2004 SCC 46, [2004] S.C.J. No. 43, paras. 16–17.

Parliament may use economic regulations to deal with anti-competitive practices in competitive markets where the efficient use of labour, capital and natural resources is required. Competitive markets include industries such as pulp and paper, cattle farming, and securities. As these markets frequently cross provincial boundaries, making it difficult for a province to regulate anti-competitive practices, Parliament may impose regulatory schemes. These regulatory schemes must fall under federal jurisdiction, such as trade and commerce, and can include a criminal prohibition with a penalty.

In addition to economic regulations and a general power to enact criminal law for a public purpose, Parliament can pass laws designed for the prevention of harm (e.g., gun control legislation).[36] This preventative legislation is in addition to established *Criminal Code* offences regarding firearms. The *Criminal Code* includes penalties for persons who do not comply with the proper use or possession of firearms. The gun control legislation concerns other requirements, such as licensing and the creation of a national registration system. The gun control legislation was seen to maintain the "peaceful character" of Canadian society, and to "help the police fight crime and violence".[37] As such, the Supreme Court upheld the preventative legislation as a valid exercise of Parliament's criminal law power.

Proprietary Articles Trade Assn. v. Canada (A.G.)[38] established that all criminal law must follow a structural formula comprising a prohibition with penal consequences. This translates into the following formula: if you commit "x" act, you may receive "y" consequences, which can be a fine or term of imprisonment. However, this formula alone had the potential to allow Parliament to legislate any matter simply by following the formal structure required for criminal legislation. In an effort to limit federal criminal power, the *Margarine Reference*[39] articulated a third requirement for all criminal legislation: it must serve a public purpose. Where criminal legislation is not concerned with the prevention of harm or fails to provide consequences for public harm or wrongs, it will not fulfill the necessary criteria for a valid criminal law. Parliament would not be able to support such a law under its criminal power, as was the case with *Morgentaler 1988*, discussed earlier under the colourability doctrine.

The public purpose requirement, while placing a boundary on the federal power to enact criminal law, continues to allow Parliament a broad ability to enact criminal legislation. A public purpose may concern the physical protection of a person, such as from an assault, and also extends to cover matters of public concern: for instance, environmental pollution. Additionally, the criminal law should adjust and change in response to evolving cultural values and technological developments. Just as the Constitution is to be interpreted in the context of present-day social values, the criminal law power is to be similarly evolutionary. For example, at one time a married woman was considered to be the possession of her husband and, as a result, he could beat her. Societal values no longer echo this view, and a husband who beats his wife today will be charged with assault. In addition, Parliament has authority to identify new offences and is empowered to deal with emerging social harms. The development and use of the Internet, for example, has given rise to a number of concerns, including misleading advertising, fraud or theft. The criminal law is able

---

[36] *Firearms Act*, S.C. 1995, c. 39.

[37] Joel Bakan et al., *Canadian Constitutional Law*, 3d ed. (Toronto: Emond Montgomery, 2003) at 412–13, quoting the Minister of Justice after the *Firearms Act* 3rd reading in the House of Commons.

[38] [1931] A.C. 310.

[39] *Reference re Validity of Section 5(a) of the Dairy Industry Act (Margarine Reference)*, [1949] S.C.R. 1, [1949] 1 D.L.R. 433.

to respond to these new concerns since its broad power is not frozen in time. As such, the *Criminal Code* contains more than the traditional offences against bodily integrity or theft and includes prohibitions against making, circulating or publishing a false prospectus (s. 400(1)) and forgery of trademarks (s. 406). Thus, as societal values change and technological advances occur, Parliament's power to enact criminal law has the flexibility to deal with concerns about the public good that arise.

CHAPTER SUMMARY

This chapter identified the sources of the Canadian Constitution. The various statutes, conventions and common law developments evolved over time as Canada moved towards autonomy and full independence. The three main documents that make up Canada's Constitution today are the *Constitution Act, 1867*, the *Constitution Act, 1982*, and the *Canadian Charter of Rights and Freedoms*. The Constitution is supreme over all other laws in Canada, and any legislation that contravenes or is inconsistent with it is of no force or effect. In order to protect the Constitution from arbitrary change, a special amending formula determined by subject matter is required.

The Constitution identifies specific matters and allocates them as either federal or provincial responsibility. Matters of national concern are legislated by Parliament, and matters of local concern are legislated by the provincial legislatures. The federal legislative body also has a special power to legislate for the peace, order and good Government of Canada. In addition, there are identified areas where both levels of government can legislate, known as areas of concurrent jurisdiction. The fact that the federal government continues to have the power to veto provincial laws through disallowance supports the proposition that Canada is a quasi-federal state rather than a "true" federal state.

A variety of methods used to resolve conflict or inconsistency between laws enacted by each level of government was examined. The methods explained included the double-aspect doctrine, paramountcy doctrine, colourability doctrine, interjurisdictional immunity doctrine and necessarily incidental doctrine.

The chapter concluded with a discussion of the powers to enact criminal laws. Criminal law is identified as a concurrent power, and both Parliament and the legislature are empowered to enact valid criminal laws. However, only Parliament can enact criminal laws for the public good, and provincial legislatures are restricted to legislating criminal laws grounded under a provincial head of power. It was noted that the criminal law is able to respond to changes in technology and societal values, empowering Parliament and the legislatures to deal with criminal concerns as they evolve.

GLOSSARY OF NEW TERMS AND KEY CONCEPTS

colourability doctrine	Where a law is enacted for a stated purpose that appears to be different from its actual or intended purpose.
concurrent jurisdiction	Where both legislative bodies have power to legislate on the matter.
convention	Political principles and practices or unwritten rules that have become a part of our constitutional order.
disallowance	A power the federal government has that enables it to veto a provincial law.

double aspect doctrine	Applies where both Parliament and the legislature have power to legislate the same matter.
extraprovincial	Matters that cross provincial boundaries.
interjurisdictional immunity doctrine	Protects the core or essential part of a head of power and prevents the other level of government from intruding upon it.
intra-provincial	Matters that concern only a particular province.
legislature	The provincial or local legislative body.
necessarily incidental doctrine	Allows Parliament or the legislature to infringe upon the other's head of power, provided that it does not go to the core of the other's head of power; must be shown to be only incidental to the overall valid legislation.
paramountcy doctrine	Where each level of government has enacted valid legislation on the same matter that results in conflict or inconsistency, paramountcy dictates that the federal law will override the provincial law to the extent of the conflict or inconsistency.
Parliament	The federal or national legislative body.
POGG	A federal head of power with three branches: the gap branch, national concern branch and emergency branch.
precedent	Relevant to the common law: a decided case that provides a basis for later cases involving similar facts; lower courts are required to follow the decisions, or precedents, of higher courts.
public purpose	In the criminal law context, punishes or prevents objectionable behaviour; includes such things as public peace, order, security, health and morality.
supremacy	The position of having the superior or greatest power or authority; the Constitution has legal superiority over any conflicting or inconsistent law.
ultra vires	Beyond the scope of power allowed or granted to the legislative body, thus rendering the legislation of no force or effect.

REVIEW QUESTIONS

1. Identify the three main documents found in the *Canada Act* that make up the Constitution.

2. What are the two most relevant functions of Canada's Constitution today?

3. Canada's Constitution was not exclusively created by legislation. Aside from statutes, in what other ways did the Constitution evolve?

4. Why can Canada be viewed as a quasi-federal state, as opposed to a federal state?

5. Briefly explain the requirements of the five amending formulas.

6. Identify the five doctrines that can be used where there is a real or potential conflict between valid federal and provincial legislation.

7. At the federal level, the criminal law must follow a particular form. How should the legislation be structured at both a federal and provincial level?

8. Identify the important difference between the doctrines of paramountcy and interjurisdictional immunity. In a competition between a federal and provincial law where the doctrines will not apply, what will happen?

9. When will the doctrine of interjurisdictional immunity generally be considered?

DISCUSSION QUESTIONS

1. The provincial government has noticed that people who wear purple shirts cause a serious allergic reaction in the majority of the population. The legislature has decided to pass a law prohibiting the wearing of purple shirts that, when contravened, will result in a fine or imprisonment. Does the province have authority to pass this law? Would such legislation be valid? Why or why not?

2. It is 1940, and you wish to appeal your wrongful conviction to the highest court available. Identify the court you would appeal to. Would you be able to appeal to this court today? Support your answer.

3. Assume that both Parliament and the legislature have the power to pass laws concerning firearms. Each level of government enacts a valid law on the matter. The federal legislation requires that all firearms be registered in a national directory. The provincial legislation requires only that the firearm owner purchase a licence. There is no requirement to register the firearm. How would this inconsistency be resolved?

4. Consider the *Ryan* case and the Supreme Court's decision that a workers' compensation scheme will prohibit a party from suing in tort if they are injured. Workers' compensation is mandatory for employers in all provinces. Discuss whether you think it is fair that employees are not permitted to opt out of such schemes to preserve their right to sue.

5. The federal government has enacted legislation that requires banks to return a portion of their annual profit to each customer. Where the bank fails to return a portion, the customer's only stated recourse is to launch a civil action. Can Parliament enact such a law? Identify the two doctrines that would likely be considered by the court and apply them to the circumstances. Which one is more likely to prevail?

6. A new and potentially valuable mineral has been discovered at the border of a province. Each level of government is claiming a right to legislate regarding the excavation, processing and export of the mineral. Identify and discuss the heads of power under which each level of government can claim authority to legislate the matter. Who do you think would be more likely to have authority should a court be asked to decide? Why?

7. Banking falls within federal jurisdiction pursuant to section 91(15) of the Constitution. Banks are now permitted to sell insurance for various types of loans and general purposes (life and home insurance, for example). Is the insurance component of a bank exclusively within the jurisdiction of Parliament, or will provincial insurance legislation govern?

SUGGESTED READING AND OTHER RESOURCES

Bakan, Joel, et al. *Canadian Constitutional Law*, 3d ed. (Toronto: Emond Montgomery, 2003).

Carcone, Janet, & Stanley Gershman. "The Charter of Rights and Freedoms" in Laurence Olivo, ed., *Introduction to Law in Canada* (Toronto: Captus Press, 2003).

Department of Justice Canada. *A Consolidation of The Constitution Acts 1867 to 1982* (Ottawa, Ont.: Canadian Government, 2001).

Funston, Bernard W., & Eugene Meehan. *Canada's Constitutional Law In a Nutshell*, 2d ed. (Scarborough, Ont.: Carswell, 1998).

Hogg, Peter W. *Constitutional Law of Canada*, 2002 Student ed. (Scarborough, Ont.: Carswell, 2002).

MacIver, R.M. *The Web of Government* (New York: The Free Press, 1965).

Zakaria, Fareed. *The Future of Freedom: Illiberal Democracy at Home and Abroad* (New York: W.W. Norton & Company, 2003).

WEBSITES

CanLII: <http://www.canlii.ca/en/index.html>

Canada, Department of Justice: <http://www.justice.gc.ca/eng/csj-sjc/just/05.html>

Constitutional Law of Canada: <http://www.uottawa.ca/constitutional-law/General.htm>

The Law Dictionray: <http://thelawdictionary.org/>

Mapleleafweb: <http://mapleleafweb.com/features/history-canadian-constitution>

Parliament of Canada:

   <http://www.parl.gc.ca/parlinfo/compilations/Constitution.aspx?Menu=Constitution>

The *Canadian Charter of Rights and Freedoms*

Janet I. Mason
BARRISTER AND SOLICITOR

Stanley Gershman
BARRISTER AND SOLICITOR

Learning Objectives

After reading this chapter, the reader should be able to:

➢ understand that the *Charter* was enacted to protect civil liberties and individual rights

➢ identify the limitations of the *Bill of Rights*

➢ understand how the entrenchment of *Charter* rights and freedoms protects them from arbitrary interference by government

➢ understand that the *Charter* will apply to non-government entities under certain circumstances

➢ distinguish between private and public interest standing

➢ identify the circumstances where government is permitted to infringe on *Charter* rights

➢ comprehend the remedies available for constitutional inconsistency

➢ understand the unique nature of Aboriginal rights under the *Charter*

TABLE OF CONTENTS

INTRODUCTION

Although we live in a representative parliamentary system, the right to elect a legislature to represent us does not fully account for all the positive aspects of our system of governance. Our form of democracy is not characterized simply by governance based on the constitutional exercise of the will of the majority of its citizens. The British political system from which ours is derived has traditionally granted some protections for individual rights against state (i.e., government) interference. These protections evolved through constitutional conventions, practices, and customs. However, the individual rights protected were not guaranteed to be immune from interference. The federal Parliament and provincial legislatures could make laws on any subject matter within their respective constitutional jurisdiction. There was no overarching law that required Parliament or a provincial legislature to take into account individual rights or freedoms when enacting legislation. As a result, elected federal and provincial representatives could enact legislation that took away individual rights and freedoms that had been protected by conventions, practices, and customs. The need thus arose for special legislation that would protect individual rights and freedoms from being arbitrarily infringed upon at the whim of an elected government.

In the latter half of the 20th century, the question for Canadians was whether or not legislative steps should be taken to explicitly define basic individual rights and freedoms. If legislative steps were taken, the next stage would require the implementation of a regime that would protect these rights and freedoms from government interference or from the imposition of the will of the majority on a minority group. This protection would need to have the authority to limit the legislative power of government when the exercise of legislative power infringed on those rights and freedoms. It would also require the power to control inappropriate government actions and systems that negatively affected an individual's rights. Canadians answered the question in the affirmative, and Parliament defined the rights and freedoms to which each citizen is entitled. These rights and freedoms were then protected by their inclusion in the *Constitution Act, 1982* as the *Canadian Charter of Rights and Freedoms*.[1]

While the *Charter* has enjoyed great success and acceptance, a number of policy issues associated with its rights and freedoms have challenged government, the judiciary, and legal theorists:

- Whether or not the rights of an individual (or a minority group) should override the rights of the community (or majority) when the latter rights are also protected by the *Charter*

- Whether or not we should permit unelected judges to override the will of Parliament or provincial legislatures, which are composed of representatives elected by a majority of Canada's citizens

- Whether or not there are circumstances under which the government should be allowed to infringe on a protected right or freedom; and if so, when an infringement is justified

Competing views on rights issues demonstrate the difficulties associated with the balancing of one person's right or freedom against that of another.

---

[1] Part I of the *Constitution Act, 1982*, being Schedule B to the *Canada Act 1982* (U.K.), 1982, c. 11 [*Charter*].

This chapter begins with a discussion of the *Canadian Bill of Rights*,[2] which was enacted as standard federal legislation prior to the *Charter*, and identifies its shortcomings. The protection of the rights and freedoms obtained by the *Charter*'s entrenchment in the Constitution is examined. Attention is then directed towards identifying the entities that are governed by the *Charter* as well as those that are beyond its jurisdiction. Proper **standing** is discussed and is a pre-condition to claiming an infringement of a right or freedom (i.e., initiating a *Charter* challenge in the court). The methods by which the government is permitted to infringe upon *Charter* rights and freedoms are considered. The remedies available when a *Charter* challenge establishes an unjustified infringement of an individual's right are identified. This chapter concludes with a discussion of Aboriginal rights under the *Charter* and recognizes their uniqueness under the law.

THE BILL OF RIGHTS

The route to the creation of the *Charter* began in 1960 with Parliament's enactment of the *Canadian Bill of Rights*. This represented Canada's first attempt to enshrine and protect basic individual rights. The *Bill of Rights* contains many of the rights later included in the *Charter* and remains valid legislation today. However, the *Bill of Rights* was unable to protect the enunciated rights from arbitrary government interference for four reasons: (i) the *Bill of Rights* was limited in its application because it only applied to laws made by the federal government; (ii) the provincial legislature was under no duty to comply with its provisions and was free to infringe on the individual's rights; (iii) as ordinary legislation, the *Bill of Rights* could be easily changed by Parliament through the enactment of new legislation that amended or revoked existing provisions; and (iv) Parliament could pass laws that expressly excluded compliance with the recognized rights.

In practice, the courts came to regard the *Bill of Rights* as "quasi-constitutional" in application if not in form.[3] Federal statutes were expected to comply with the *Bill of Rights* requirements. Federal legislation that infringed on the *Bill of Rights* was held to be either invalid or **inoperative**, although legal opinion on this lacked clarity. The difficulty was that one ordinary piece of legislation (i.e., the *Bill of Rights*) was able to override another ordinary piece of legislation without constitutional authority. To put it another way, if Parliament were supreme in its law-making power, could the Parliament that passed the *Bill of Rights* in 1960 bind or limit the legislative power of future Parliaments to pass laws that contradicted the *Bill of Rights*? The answer to this question divided the judiciary and blunted the effect of the *Bill of Rights*.

The *Charter* deliberately excluded two rights that are contained in the *Bill of Rights*. The first is the right to a fair hearing when a determination concerning an individual's rights and obligations is required. A fair hearing under these circumstances would demand that the individual be allowed to be present at, and generally participate in, such hearing. Determining an individual's right or obligation is a serious matter that should not be decided in the absence of the individual affected by the decision. However, the *Charter* principle of fundamental justice under section 7 can require individual participation. The content of that participation may be limited to written submissions.

---

[2]   S.C. 1960, c. 44, reprinted in R.S.C. 1985, Appendix III [*Bill of Rights*].
[3]   *Hogan v. The Queen*, [1975] 2 S.C.R. 574.

The second omission concerns the protection of property rights through a "due process" clause. This right has a very narrow application under the *Bill of Rights* because property is generally not dealt with under federal legislation. "Property" is a provincial head of power under the Constitution, and the *Bill of Rights* would not protect an individual from provincial interference with property rights. The exclusion of property rights from the *Charter* means that there is no protection of property rights in the provincial context, under the Constitution.

The exclusion of property rights from the *Charter* may be due to concerns that arose as a result of its inclusion in American legislation. The American *Bill of Rights* includes a guarantee of due process of law where a person is to be deprived of property. When federal legislation was passed prohibiting slavery in various states, the guarantee was invoked to protect the property rights of slave owners. In 1857, the U.S. Supreme Court held that all slaves owned prior to the enactment of legislation prohibiting slavery would remain the property of their owners. The U.S. Supreme Court decided that freeing existing slaves would amount to depriving the owners of their property rights in their slaves. The subsequent passage of constitutional amendments resolved the issue and emancipated the slaves.[4] However, the idea that the property rights of one individual might override the basic freedoms of another lingered in the minds of constitutional theorists.

THE *CANADIAN CHARTER OF RIGHTS AND FREEDOMS*

The shortcomings of the *Bill of Rights* led to the *Charter* being included as part of Canada's "supreme" law, the Constitution. Factors that helped identify the need for more extensive legislation included the limited application of the *Bill of Rights*, its questionable authority to demand compliance, and its ability to be easily overridden. Therefore, the new legislation would have to apply to both the federal Parliament and provincial legislatures. It would also have to be powerful enough to protect the rights and freedoms that it contained by demanding compliance with its provisions. To ensure that these requirements were met, the *Charter* was entrenched as part of Canada's Constitution.

The **entrenchment** of the *Charter* in the Constitution means that the courts have been given a clear role in deciding when a *Charter* right has been violated. The result is that, under certain circumstances, the courts have the power to overrule the decision of an elected Parliament. Since 1982, the courts have developed analytical techniques for deciding *Charter* issues. The courts will conduct an analysis that will first consider whether or not the legislation in question is valid under the division of powers in the Constitution. If the legislation is found to be an invalid exercise of legislative power, such as a province passing a law on a federal matter, the courts will decide the matter on this constitutional, division of power basis. Further *Charter* analysis becomes unnecessary. The right that the individual is alleging was infringed does not even have to be considered in such a case. But if the legislation or government action is a valid exercise of constitutional power, the courts must continue with the analysis. The additional analytical stages are discussed later in the chapter.

---

[4] Peter W. Hogg, *Constitutional Law of Canada*, 2002 Student ed. (Toronto: Carswell, 2002) at 696 [Hogg], discussing *Dred Scott v. Sandford* (1857), 60 U.S. (19 How.) 393.

EXHIBIT 7.1

Canadian Charter of Rights and Freedoms

Whereas Canada is founded upon principles that recognize the supremacy of God and the rule of law:

Guarantee of Rights and Freedoms

Rights and freedoms in Canada
1. The Canadian Charter of Rights and Freedoms guarantees the rights and freedoms set out in it subject only to such reasonable limits prescribed by law as can be demonstrably justified in a free and democratic society.

Fundamental Freedoms

Fundamental freedoms
2. Everyone has the following fundamental freedoms:

(a) freedom of conscience and religion;
(b) freedom of thought, belief, opinion and expression, including freedom of the press and other media of communication;
(c) freedom of peaceful assembly; and
(d) freedom of association.

Democratic Rights

Democratic rights of citizens
3. Every citizen of Canada has the right to vote in an election of members of the House of Commons or of a legislative assembly and to be qualified for membership therein.

Maximum duration of legislative bodies
4.(1) No House of Commons and no legislative assembly shall continue for longer than five years from the date fixed for the return of the writs at a general election of its members.

Continuation in special circumstances
(2) In time of real or apprehended war, invasion or insurrection, a House of Commons may be continued by Parliament and a legislative assembly may be continued by the legislature beyond five years if such continuation is not opposed by the votes of more than one-third of the members of the House of Commons or the legislative assembly, as the case may be.

Annual sitting of legislative bodies
5. There shall be a sitting of Parliament and of each legislature at least once every twelve months.

Mobility Rights

Mobility of Citizens
6.(1) Every citizen of Canada has the right to enter, remain in and leave Canada.

Rights to move and gain livelihood
(2) Every citizen of Canada and every person who has the status of a permanent resident of Canada has the right

(a) to move and take up residence in any province; and
(b) to pursue the gaining of a livelihood in any province.

Limitation
(3) The rights specified in subsection (2) are subject to

(a) any laws or practices of general application in force in a province other than those that discriminate among persons primarily on the basis of a province of present or previous residence; and
(b) any laws providing for reasonable residency requirements as a qualification for the receipt of publicly provided social services.

EXHIBIT 7.1 (continued)

Canadian Charter of Rights and Freedoms

Affirmative action programs

(4) Subsections (2) and (3) do not preclude any law, program or activity that has as its object the amelioration in a province of conditions of individuals in that province who are socially or economically disadvantaged if the rate of employment in that province is below the rate of employment in Canada.

Legal Rights

Life, liberty and security of the person

7. Everyone has the right to life, liberty and security of the person and the right not to be deprived thereof except in accordance with the principles of fundamental justice.

Search or seizure

8. Everyone has the right to be secure against unreasonable search or seizure.

Detention or imprisonment

9. Everyone has the right not to be arbitrarily detained or imprisoned.

Arrest or Detention

10. Everyone has the right on arrest or detention

(a) to be informed promptly of the reasons therefore;

(b) to retain and instruct counsel without delay and to be informed of that right; and

(c) to have the validity of the detention determined by way of habeas corpus and to be released if the detention is not lawful.

Proceedings in criminal and penal matters

11. Any person charged with an offence has the right

(a) to be informed without unreasonable delay of the specific offence;

(b) to be tried within a reasonable time;

(c) not to be compelled to be a witness in proceedings against that person in respect of the offence;

(d) to be presumed innocent until proven guilty according to law in a fair and public hearing by an independent and impartial tribunal;

(e) not to be denied reasonable bail without just cause;

(f) except in the case of an offence under military law tried before a military tribunal, to the benefit of trial by jury where the maximum punishment for the offence is imprisonment for five years or a more severe punishment;

(g) not to be found guilty on account of any act or omission unless, at the time of the act or omission, it constituted an offence under Canadian or international law or was criminal according to the general principles of law recognized by the community of nations;

(h) if finally acquitted of the offence, not to be tried for it again and, if finally found guilty and punished for the offence, not to be tried or punished for it again; and

(i) if found guilty of the offence and if the punishment for the offence has been varied between the time of commission and the time of sentencing, to the benefit of the lesser punishment.

Treatment or punishment

12. Everyone has the right not to be subjected to any cruel and unusual treatment or punishment.

Self-incrimination

13. A witness who testifies in any proceedings has the right not to have any incriminating evidence so given used to incriminate that witness in any other proceedings, except in a prosecution for perjury or for the giving of contradictory evidence.

Interpreter

14. A party or witness in any proceedings who does not understand or speak the language in which the proceedings are conducted or who is deaf has the right to the assistance of an interpreter.

EXHIBIT 7.1 (continued)   *Canadian Charter of Rights and Freedoms*

Equality Rights

Equality before and under law and equal protection and benefit of law
15.(1) Every individual is equal before and under the law and has the right to the equal protection and equal benefit of the law without discrimination and, in particular, without discrimination based on race, national or ethnic origin, religion, sex, age or mental or physical disability.

Affirmative action programs
(2) Subsection (1) does not preclude any law, program or activity that has as its object the amelioration of conditions of disadvantaged individuals or groups including those that are disadvantaged because of race, national or ethnic origin, colour, religion, sex, age or mental or physical disability.

OVERVIEW OF THE *CHARTER*

Charter rights and freedoms are not absolute. Section 1 permits government to infringe — i.e., limit — a right or freedom where doing so is "demonstrably justified in a free and democratic society". This ability to infringe is restricted to the *Charter*; therefore, other constitutional provisions, such as the entrenchment of specific Aboriginal rights under section 35, cannot be infringed or limited. The reason that infringements are permitted under section 1 is that circumstances may arise where a limitation of a right or freedom permits the achievement of a benefit to society that is seen to be greater than the detriment that would result from the infringement. In determining whether or not to restrict a *Charter* right, the Supreme Court of Canada has developed a strict test that the government must meet if a right is to be infringed. This is discussed later in this chapter.

Section 2 identifies fundamental freedoms that characterize democratic society. Individuals have the freedom to practise their religion, to think and believe what they choose, express themselves, and associate with others. The freedom of expression contained in section 2(b) can be controversial. The Supreme Court of Canada in *Irwin Toy v. Quebec*[5] held that freedom of expression was important for facilitating the search for truth, participation in social and political decision making, and self-fulfillment. This broad freedom is not concerned with the content of the message contained in the expression. The "truth" of the message is not relevant to its protection unless it runs afoul of a valid criminal law. The form of expression is not limited to art, books, or communications by news agencies. Expression may also be found, for instance, in picketing, handing out pamphlets, or other similar types of physical activity. The only clear exclusion from s. 2(b) protection is violence as a form of expression.[6] However, section 1 can be used to limit freedom of expression. In *Irwin Toy* the Court upheld a Quebec law that banned certain types of advertising geared towards children less than 13 years of age, despite the fact that this form of expression is protected by section 2.

---

[5]   [1989] 1 S.C.R. 927 at 968–71, 58 D.L.R. (4th) 577 [*Irwin Toy* cited to S.C.R.].
[6]   *Ibid.*

Another example of freedom of expression (s. 2(b)) being limited is where it is in tension with another *Charter* right, such as freedom of religion (s. 2(a)). In *Saskatchewan (Human Rights Commission) v. Whatcott*, 2013 SCC 11 ("*Whatcott*"), the Supreme Court of Canada upheld the tribunal's decision, regarding two of four flyers, that found anti-gay flyers to have contravened the provincial human rights act by exposing people to hatred and ridicule based on sexual orientation. The court held that prohibiting distribution of the flyers was a reasonable restriction on Whatcott's right to freedom of religion. The central issue was whether or not the flyers would incite "hatred" in its audience. The court applied an objective test: would the flyer, in the mind of a reasonable person, be seen to expose the protected group to "hatred"? Since the test is objective, the intent of the particular person who has allegedly breached the *Charter* right is irrelevant. It does not matter whether or not the person sincerely believes the expression. The court decided what constituted "hatred" as regards the objective test. It held that merely offensive or repugnant expression would not incite the required level of abhorrence that justified infringing freedom of expression. The expression must generate an extreme reaction of emotion in its audience, such as detestation, vilification, delegitimization or rejection. The analysis should focus on the *effect* of the expression on its audience and whether or not it would expose the targeted group, or person, to hatred by others. The effect, however, does not require proof of actual harm.

Canada enjoys a democratic system of government, and its process should reflect democratic values. This obligation is found in sections 3 to 5. The right is broader than simply a right to vote, mandating the holding of elections every five years (barring "real or apprehended war"), or the minimum time requirement for the sitting of the legislatures. Any procedure or practice that negatively impacts the democratic process may be found unconstitutional under the *Charter*.

Every citizen has "the right to enter, remain in, and leave Canada" under section 6(1). Section 6(2) establishes an individual's right to move across provincial boundaries and to work or gain a livelihood in another province. These mobility rights are derived from the fact that Canada is a federal state. Canadian federalism involves two levels of government authority: the central, or national, federal Parliament; and the regional, i.e., provincial, legislatures.[7] Therefore, a citizen or permanent resident of the national state has the *Charter* right to travel between all provinces. However, that is not to say provinces have no choice about who moves in or out of their jurisdiction. Section 6(3) goes on to state that the mobility right is subject to "any laws or practices of general application in force in a province". In other words, you do not have the right to move to another province and open a business that is not permitted under that province's law. The mobility right should not undermine the autonomy of each provincial authority.

Section 7 contains another broad right: "the right to life, liberty, and security of the person and the right not to be deprived thereof except in accordance with the principles of fundamental justice".[8] While liberty is clearly

---

[7] Hogg, *supra* note 4 at 104.

[8] The meaning of the phrase "principles of fundamental justice" has been judicially discussed in *Charter* challenges brought under the heading of life, liberty and security of the person. Though the term has no precise definition, the principles correspond to established common law principles and the basic tenets of our legal system. These would include such things as procedural fairness (the right to notice and the right to be heard), as well as a substantive component (i.e., that the principles would be considered fundamental to cultural views of justice). See e.g. *Morgentaler 1988, infra* note 11; *Rodriguez v. British Columbia (A.G.)*, [1993] 3 S.C.R. 519, 107 D.L.R. (4th) 342; *New Brunswick (Minister of Health and Community Services) v. G.(J.)*, [1999] 3 S.C.R. 46, 177 D.L.R. (4th) 124.

affected when a person is imprisoned, it can also be infringed outside of the criminal law.[9] For example, laws relating to the involuntary civil commitment of a person with a mental illness also affect a person's liberty because the person is "involuntarily" committed to, and detained in, a psychiatric facility. A s. 7 challenge requires the claimant to prove (i) that there has been or could be a deprivation of a s. 7 right; and (ii) that the deprivation was not, or would not be, in accordance with the principles of **fundamental justice**.[10] If the claimant proves the foregoing, the government bears the burden of justifying the deprivation under section 1.

R. v. Morgentaler (1988)[11] concerned, among other things, the security of the person. Security of the person relates not only to state interference with a person's bodily integrity, it can also include the person's psychological well-being in a criminal context. The *Morgentaler 1988* case concerned criminal legislation that made it a criminal offence for a woman to obtain an abortion when the prescribed procedure was not followed. Where the procedure was complied with, the abortion was legal and the woman obtained the protection of a specific defence contained in the *Criminal Code*. The Court held that the mandatory requirements of a woman to obtain the approval of a committee at an accredited or approved hospital prior to having an abortion, as well as to have the medical procedure at an accredited or approved hospital, breached the s. 7 right to security of the person. Fulfilling the procedural requirements inevitably resulted in delay. The Court found that

> s. 251 of the *Criminal Code* is *prima facie* a violation of the security of the person of thousands of Canadian women who have made the difficult decision that they do not wish to continue with a pregnancy. ... Not only does the removal of the decision-making power threaten women in a physical sense; the indecision of knowing whether an abortion will be granted inflicts emotional stress. ... Forcing a woman, by threat of criminal sanction, to carry a foetus to term unless she meets certain criteria unrelated to her own priorities and aspirations, is a profound interference with a woman's body and thus a violation of security of the person. ... [T]here is yet another infringement of security of the person. It is clear from the evidence that s. 251 harms the psychological integrity of women seeking abortions ... delays ... greatly [increase] the stress levels of patients....[12]

The next issue was whether the infringement was in accord with fundamental justice. Fundamental justice concerns the administrative structures and procedures and their fairness. If the procedures are unfair, the right to fundamental justice may be infringed. The Court in *Morgentaler 1988* found that the structure and procedure imposed were unfair in effect. They contained "so many potential barriers to [legislation's] own operation that the defence it create[d] w[ould] in many circumstances be practically unavailable to women who would *prima facie* qualify for the defence, or at least would force such women to travel great distances at substantial expense and inconvenience in order to benefit from a defence that is held out to be generally available". The law was found to be unconstitutional.

The legal rights contained in sections 8 to 14 include limiting government's power of search and seizure, as well as arbitrary detention or imprisonment; identification of the rights that arise upon arrest or detention and rights

---

[9] *Blencoe v. British Columbia (Human Rights Commission)*, [2000] 2 S.C.R. 307: " 'liberty' is engaged where the state imposes compulsions or prohibitions that 'affect important and fundamental life choices' such as not loitering in a particular place or producing documents or testifying" (para. 49).

[10] *Charkaoui v. Canada (Citizenship and Immigration)*, 2007 SCC 9, [2007] 1 S.C.R. 350.

[11] [1988] 1 S.C.R. 30, 44 D.L.R. (4th) 385 [*Morgentaler 1988* cited to S.C.R.].

[12] *Ibid.* at paras. 23, 24, and 30.

that arise upon being charged with an offence; the right to be free from cruel and unusual punishment; the right of witnesses not to incriminate themselves in a proceeding; and the right of a party or witness to have the assistance of an interpreter. These rights apply to the criminal process and related situations. For example, detention can arise outside of the arrest process and trigger the right to counsel. In *R. v. Therens*[13] the Court held that a demand to accompany a police officer to the station to provide a Breathalyzer sample constituted detention under the *Charter* and that the right to counsel arose.

Sections 2, 7, and 11 were considered in deciding whether a complainant in a sexual assault case could testify at the preliminary inquiry with her face covered by a niqab as her religion dictated.[14] In this case there was tension between the complainant's right to freedom of religion (s. 2(a)) and the accused's fair trial rights (s. 11) and related risk to liberty if convicted (s. 7). The niqab covers everything on a woman's face but her eyes. The credibility of a witness is important at trial. While facial reactions, expressions, and demeanour can undermine or reinforce the oral evidence the witness gives, a clear view of the witness's face is also important in cross-examination for the same reasons (para. 24). Since the face is an important feature of a fair trial (para. 21), the general rule is that witnesses are required to have their faces visible in court (para. 22). The majority of the court decided that fair trial rights will not automatically trump the right to freedom of religion. Determining the risk to a fair trial, and potential wrongful conviction, must be decided on a case-by-case basis.

> [3] For the reasons that follow, I conclude that a witness who for sincere religious reasons wishes to wear the niqab while testifying in a criminal proceeding will be required to remove it if:
>
> (a) requiring the witness to remove the niqab is necessary to prevent a serious risk to the fairness of the trial, because reasonably available alternative measures will not prevent the risk; *and*
> (b) the salutary effects of requiring her to remove the niqab, including the effects on trial fairness, outweigh the deleterious effects of doing so, including the effects on freedom of religion.

The court found that applying that analytical framework required answering four questions (para. 9):

1. Would requiring the witness to remove the niqab while testifying interfere with her religious freedom?

   This requires the witness to "sincerely believe" that her religion requires her to wear the niqab. It does not require a "strong belief".

2. Would permitting the witness to wear the niqab while testifying create a serious risk to trial fairness?

   This involves consideration of the type and importance of the evidence the witness will provide (para. 28). If the evidence is uncontested, there is no issue with trial fairness and the witness may wear the niqab (para. 29).

3. If trial fairness is in issue, is there a way to accommodate both rights and avoid the conflict between them?

   The parties would be required to submit evidence of possible options to accommodate the conflict (para. 33).

---

[13] [1985] 1 S.C.R. 613, 18 D.L.R. (4th) 655 [*Therens* cited to S.C.R.].

[14] *R. v. NS*, 2012 SCC 72 (*NS*).

4. If no accommodation is possible, do the salutary effects requiring the witness to remove the niqab outweigh the deleterious effects of doing so?

> This is a proportional inquiry that considers the effect of requiring the removal of the niqab versus the effect of permitting it to be worn on the stand (para. 35). It can include subjective considerations, such as how important the religious practice is to the witness. It can also include broader societal harms, such as reducing the likelihood of women reporting sexual assault and effectively being denied justice (para. 37). The salutary effects involve consideration of the prevention of harm to a fair trial and protection of the administration of justice (para. 38). Consideration of the importance of the evidence to be provided, where it is contested, would also be relevant, as could the nature of the proceeding. Evidence at trial of a central factual element of the Crown's case might raise more concern than a voir dire where the admissibility of evidence is in issue (paras. 39 and 43). For example, where "the liberty of the accused is at stake, the witness's evidence is central to the case and her credibility vital, the possibility of a wrongful conviction must weigh heavily in the balance, favouring removal of the niqab" (para. 44).

Equality rights are found in section 15. Everyone has the right to be considered equal in the eyes of the law and deserves the protection and benefit of the law without discrimination. This provision relates to enacted or future laws, which must treat all constituents the same. It would similarly apply to government policies that are administered (e.g., a benefit program). The right can be infringed by government action or inaction that explicitly, or by its effect, results in differential treatment. For example, in *Eldridge v. British Columbia (A.G.)*,[15] the Court held that government's failure to provide funding for sign language interpreters in hospitals breached section 15. Communication with health care providers is an indispensable component in the delivery of medical services. The failure to provide an interpreter where necessary to a person with an auditory disability constituted government "inaction". This inaction meant that a disadvantaged group (people with an auditory disability) did not benefit equally from the medical services offered to the general public.

The discriminatory grounds identified in the *Charter* are race, ethnicity, colour, religion, sex, age, and disability. This list is not exhaustive. Analogous grounds of discrimination have been identified by the Court. In *Corbiere v. Canada (Minister of Indian and Northern Affairs)*,[16] the majority noted the following about the identification of analogous grounds:

> It seems to us that what these grounds have in common is the fact that they often serve as the basis for stereotypical decisions made not on the basis of merit but on the basis of a personal characteristic that is immutable or changeable only at unacceptable cost to personal identity. ... s. 15 targets the denial of equal treatment on grounds that are actually immutable, like race, or constructively immutable, like religion.[17]

The Court has held that citizenship, sexual orientation, marital status, and Aboriginal residence are analogous grounds.[18] The test applied in a

---

[15] [1997] 3 S.C.R. 624, 151 D.L.R. (4th) 577 [*Eldridge* cited to S.C.R.].

[16] [1999] 2 S.C.R. 203 [*Corbiere*].

[17] *Ibid.* at para. 13.

[18] See respectively, *Andrews v. Law Society of British Columbia*, [1989] 1 S.C.R. 143; *Egan v. Canada*, [1995] 2 S.C.R. 513; *Miron v. Trudel*, [1995] 2 S.C.R. 418; *M. v. H.*, [1999] 2 S.C.R. 3; and *Corbiere, supra* note 16. In

s. 15(1) challenge requires a finding of "(1) different treatment on the basis of a personal characteristic, (2) that is an enumerated or analogous ground, (3) which is discriminating in purpose or effect."[19]

Section 15(2) permits discrimination where the purpose is to ameliorate disadvantages suffered by an identified group. Government can design programs for the benefit of a specific group despite any discriminatory effect to others outside of that group. Such programs or policies are insulated from *Charter* challenge under section 15(1).

Canada's founding nations are considered to have been the British and the French. Section 16 identifies the official languages of Canada as English and French and gives them equal status. The language rights contained in sections 16 to 23 constitute a limited form of bilingualism.[20] The obligation of government to provide bilingual services is limited to the federal sphere unless there is "significant demand" or it is "reasonable" to have communications and services in both languages (s. 20). New Brunswick is specifically included under both provisions as its provincial government, during negotiations over the *Charter*, agreed to this. Minority language education rights are contained in section 23. Regardless of the language of the majority in a province, and where certain requirements are met, people have the right to have their child educated in the minority language of that province.

The remaining *Charter* provisions, sections 24 to 34, deal succinctly with a variety of issues. Section 24(1) provides for enforcement of the *Charter*, and section 24(2) permits the exclusion of evidence obtained in a manner that infringed a right or freedom. The *Charter* is not to be applied or interpreted in a manner that would limit, reduce, or take away from Aboriginal treaty or other rights and freedoms that attach to First Nations (s. 25). The *Charter* is not the sole source of rights and freedoms and will not override those from another source (s. 26). Common law rights would be an example of a right from another source. The *Charter* is to be interpreted in a manner that upholds and facilitates Canada's multicultural heritage (s. 27). The application of the *Charter* is guaranteed equally to male and female persons (s. 28). The entrenchment of Aboriginal rights is found outside of the *Charter*, in section 35 of the Constitution.

THE APPLICATION OF THE *CHARTER*

The *Charter* applies only to governments, as stated in section 32. Therefore, the *Charter* affects interactions between the government and an individual and does not apply to relationships between private individuals. Individuals are protected from discrimination or harassment in their private dealings by provincial human rights codes. In civil matters and other disputes between individuals, the court renders decisions consistent with *Charter* principles. The court will uphold the fundamental values of Canadian society, which the *Charter* reflects. In addition, section 26 identifies that the *Charter* does not take away from any common law or statutory rights. These rights exist concurrently with the *Charter*.[21]

Corbiere, restricting the voting right in a band election to on-reserve residents (Aboriginal residence) was found to be an analogous ground by the Court.

[19] *Canada (A.G.) v. Hislop*, 2007 SCC 10 (CanLII) at para. 36.

[20] Hogg, *supra* note 4 at 1127.

[21] *Ibid.* at 728.

EXHIBIT 7.2   Application of the *Charter*

32(1) This Charter applies
  (a) to the Parliament and government of Canada in respect of all matters within the authority of
       Parliament ...; and
  (b) to the legislature and government of each province in respect of all matters within the
       authority of the legislature of each province.

GOVERNMENT ACTION AND ACTORS

As discussed, the government must be involved if the *Charter* is to be used
to uphold a right or freedom. A challenge to legislation clearly involves the
application of the *Charter* since government involvement is evident. However,
there are situations where the government may be involved, although not
initially visible in the matter. The *Charter* extends to individuals and entities
exercising governmental responsibility (e.g., ministers and officials) as well as
entities controlled by government. The *Charter* will also apply to entities to
which government responsibilities have been delegated.[22] Government cannot
circumvent *Charter* obligations by privatizing services or delegating responsibility to the private sector. The *Charter* may, therefore, apply in a number of
additional circumstances: where an entity is controlled by government; implementing government programs; exercising government functions; deriving its
powers from the state; or exercising statutory powers of compulsion. The
Charter can also apply to government omissions. There may be situations
where the government's failure to legislate a matter or to legislate it adequately can give rise to a *Charter* infringement.

Entities Controlled
by Government

For an entity to qualify as being "controlled by government", the government
must have significant routine or day-to-day control of the operation of the
entity. This appears to be a straightforward criterion, but the Supreme Court
of Canada has applied it with seemingly conflicting decisions. In *McKinney*,[23]
the mandatory retirement policies of four Ontario universities were challenged.
The allegation was that the retirement policies infringed on *Charter* equality
rights. First, the Court had to determine whether "government" was present
under the circumstances; otherwise, the *Charter* would not apply. The Court
found that universities performed an important public service. However, entities performing a public service *alone* will not automatically trigger the application of the *Charter*. The Court then considered the amount of government
involvement in the agreements negotiated between the universities and their
employees. Evidence showed that the universities negotiated contracts and
collective agreements independently and not at the direction of government.
Therefore, the universities were not controlled by government when they
made the agreements that contained the retirement policies. The Court identified additional factors that supported the independence of the universities. For
example, each university had its own governing body, whose duty "[was] not

---

[22] Joel Bakan et al., *Canadian Constitutional Law*, 3d ed. (Toronto: Emond Montgomery Publications Limited, 2003)
at 787 [Bakan].
[23] *McKinney v. University of Guelph*, [1990] 3 S.C.R. 229, 76 D.L.R. (4th) 545 [*McKinney* cited to S.C.R.].

to act at the direction of the government but in the interests of the university". While the government was seen to regulate and fund universities, it had no legal power to control them, and the *Charter* did not apply.

Douglas/Swantlen Faculty Association v. Douglas College[24] also concerned a challenge to mandatory retirement policies. However, in this case the Court determined that the college was a government entity and the *Charter* applied. The Court noted that the provincial government appointed the governing body of the college. In addition, the minister was also allowed to "issue directions" to the college and was required to approve all by-laws. The government retained the right, at all times, to direct the operation of the college. The college's lack of autonomy distinguished the situation from that of the universities in *McKinney*.[25] The high level of government involvement in the operation and decision-making process at the college meant that it was controlled by government.

Implementing Government Programs

A similar debate surrounded the applicability of the *Charter* to hospitals. In *Stoffman v. Vancouver General Hospital*,[26] the Supreme Court determined that the day-to-day control of a hospital was outside government power. Like *McKinney*, the *Charter* did not apply to the hospital's mandatory retirement policy. However, a successful *Charter* challenge against a hospital was brought in *Eldridge*.[27] Eldridge alleged discrimination because the hospital failed to provide free sign language interpreters for deaf patients. The failure denied deaf patients the same level of medical treatment as able-hearing patients. In providing medical services, the hospital was carrying out a specific government program. Responsibility for identifying the services to be delivered belonged to the government. When providing the services, the hospital was acting as an agent for the government, and the *Charter* applied.

Exercising Government Functions: Power from the State and Statutory Powers of Compulsion

Entities that have the power to implement law, decide a question of law, or force an individual to comply with its ruling are generally subject to the *Charter*. Municipalities are not a level of government specifically recognized in the Constitution. They are created by provincial governments under the power contained in section 92(8) of the Constitution. However, municipalities enact and enforce by-laws and conduct other activities similar to those of government. Since municipalities perform government functions, the *Charter* will apply to the by-laws they enact and other actions. Similarly, statutorily appointed arbitrators (whose powers are derived from the state) and entities exercising powers of compulsion (such as those of the Human Rights Commission, which can compel compliance to decisions) would also fall within the sphere of the *Charter*.

Omissions

The domain of the *Charter* is expansive enough to include not only what the government or government entity *does* but also what it omits to do. An absence of legislation on a matter is unlikely to result in government being forced to legislate on the basis of a *Charter* right. Exceptions do, however, occasionally arise. To illustrate, Alberta's human rights legislation deliberately omitted the grounds of sexual orientation as a basis for discrimination. Therefore, persons discriminated against on the basis of sexual orientation were

---

[24] [1990] 3 S.C.R. 570, 77 D.L.R. (4th) 94.
[25] *McKinney, supra* note 23.
[26] [1990] 3 S.C.R. 451, 77 D.L.R. (4th) 55.
[27] *Supra* note 14.

prevented from filing a human rights complaint. In *Vriend v. Alberta*,[28] the Supreme Court held that sexual orientation was to be included as a ground in the provincial Human Rights Code. Since the Alberta legislature chose to enact a Human Rights Code that was under-inclusive in its application, it was under a positive obligation to ensure that the legislation complied with the *Charter*.

STANDING

Appropriate **standing** is required in order for an individual to bring a *Charter* challenge. Standing can be based on either a private or public interest in the matter. An "individual" includes both a corporation (which is considered to have the same legal rights and responsibilities as a person) and a person. However, a corporation's standing is limited. There is no definitive method of identifying the grounds a corporation may base its challenge on. Each case would be determined by the court in the specific circumstances. Supreme Court decisions have held that corporations can bring a challenge under some s. 2 rights (e.g., freedom of expression in an advertising context[29]), but not others (e.g., freedom of religion has been held inapplicable to corporations, as shown in Exhibit 7.3). The Supreme Court has also limited a corporation's standing in that a corporation cannot bring an "independent civil action" in order to challenge the validity of a law unless it can claim that one of its *Charter* rights has been infringed.[30] A corporation would not have any standing regarding the infringement of rights applicable only to an actual person. For example, a corporation could not complain about a violation of its right not to be arbitrarily detained (s. 9) since that is not physically possible. The type of standing can also affect available remedies.

Private Interest Standing

Private interest standing in a *Charter* challenge may arise in different ways. It can be based solely on a claim of a *Charter* infringement of a right or freedom, or corollary to a proceeding. A challenge can be brought as an independent action that seeks declaratory relief (i.e., the court "declares" that the individual's right or freedom has been infringed) or other remedy. A *Charter* challenge can also be raised as a separate issue in an ongoing criminal or civil proceeding. Where an individual is charged with a criminal offence, standing to bring a *Charter* challenge automatically applies should appropriate circumstances arise. Life, liberty and security of the person, and other legal rights contained in the *Charter* are always relevant to criminal actions.

Public Interest Standing

Where an individual asserts public interest standing, three requirements must be met: (i) the individual must have a genuine interest in the question before the court; (ii) the action must raise a serious legal question; and (iii) there can be no other reasonable or effective way that the issue can be brought before the court.[31] The third requirement is often the most difficult to

---

[28] [1998] 1 S.C.R. 493, 156 D.L.R. (4th) 385.

[29] See e.g. *Irwin Toy*, *supra* note 5; *Rocket v. Royal College of Dental Surgeons*, [1990] 2 S.C.R. 232, 71 D.L.R. (4th) 68; and *RJR MacDonald Inc. v. Canada (A.G.)*, [1995] 3 S.C.R. 199, 127 D.L.R. (4th) 1.

[30] Bakan, *supra* note 22 at 1301.

[31] *Minister of Justice v. Borowski*, [1981] 2 S.C.R. 575, 130 D.L.R. (3d) 588.

Private Interest Standing	**EXHIBIT 7.3**

Big M Drugstore Mart was charged with being open for business on a Sunday in contravention of Alberta's *Lord's Day Act*, R.S.C. 1970, c. L-13 ("*Lord's Day Act*") and brought a challenge asserting that the legislation was unconstitutional. The Attorney General of Alberta claimed that the drugstore was unable to base its challenge on the *Charter* right of freedom of religion since a corporation could not hold religious beliefs. Therefore, Big M Drug Mart Ltd. ("Big M") lacked the required standing by which to bring the challenge. The Court held, however, that any individual charged with a criminal offence could challenge the applicable law on its constitutionality. Big M was asserting that the *Lord's Day Act* was inconsistent with section 2(a) of the *Charter* — i.e., freedom of religion — and, therefore, constitutionally invalid. The drugstore was not asserting that its right to freedom of religion had been infringed.

The Court found that the purpose of the legislation at the time of enactment was to proclaim the "standards of the Christian faith". The standards meant that businesses were closed on Sundays to respect the Christian holy day. As such, it could be seen that the law's purpose was a religious matter that may offend and discriminate against non-Christian Canadians. This would violate section 2(a) of the *Charter*.

> [By this statute] [n]on-Christians are prohibited for religious reasons from carrying out activities which are otherwise lawful, moral and normal. The arm of the state requires all to remember the Lord's Day of the Christians and to keep it holy. The protection of one religion and the concomitant non-protection of others imports disparate impact destructive of the religious freedom of the collectivity.
>
> —Justice Dickson

The Attorney General proposed that the legislation supported a secular day of rest for the benefit of all Canadians. The Court rejected this argument since the legislation's purpose at enactment was clearly religious, and not secular. Legislation should not be construed as having a purpose other than that by which it was enacted. In addition, the *Lord's Day Act* appeared to contradict section 27 of the *Charter*. Section 27 requires that the *Charter* be "interpreted in a manner consistent with the preservation and enhancement of the multicultural heritage of Canadians". The Court held that the Act was constitutionally invalid under section 52(1).

Source: *R. v. Big M Drug Mart Ltd.*, [1985] 1 S.C.R. 295, 18 D.L.R. (4th) 321.

fulfill.[32] The case of the *Canadian Council of Churches v. Canada*[33] was based on public interest standing on behalf of refugees. The Council's concern was that people were being denied refugee status in Canada without their presence at a hearing. Decisions regarding refugee status were generally made on the recommendation of immigration staff without an opportunity for the person to be present or speak to the decision maker. The Council easily met the first two requirements for standing. The Council regularly assisted refugees (genuine interest), and the fact that the hearings did not require the presence of the refugee claimant indicated a violation of the principles of fundamental justice (a serious legal question). However, the Council was unable to fulfill the third requirement. The Court found that people claiming refugees status were able to bring their own claim and had done so in the past. Therefore, there existed a reasonable and effective way for the matter to otherwise come before the court. It was unnecessary for the Council to do so on a refugee's behalf, and standing was not granted.

[32] See also *R. v. Banks* (2007), 84 O.R. (3d) 1, 2007 ONCA 19 at para. 24; known as the "squeegee kids" case.
[33] [1992] 1 S.C.R. 236, 88 D.L.R. (4th) 193.

The Supreme Court of Canada clarified the third requirement for public interest standing in *Canada (Attorney General) v. Downtown Eastside Sex Workers United Against Violence Society*, 2012 SCC 45, 2 S.C.R. 524. It is now unnecessary to show that there is *no* other reasonable or effective way to bring the matter before the court. The party, as concerns the third requirement, now only needs to show that the proceeding is, in all of the circumstances, a reasonable and effective means to bring the matter before the court (para. 52), even if it is not the only way to bring the matter before the court. All requirements for public standing are to be applied in a purposive and flexible manner.

> [20] My view is that the three elements identified in *Borowski* are interrelated factors that must be weighed in exercising judicial discretion to grant or deny standing. These factors, and especially the third one, should not be treated as hard and fast requirements or free-standing, independently operating tests. Rather, they should be assessed and weighed cumulatively, in light of the underlying purposes of limiting standing and applied in a flexible and generous manner that best serves those underlying purposes.

The case concerned a challenge to the prostitution provisions of the *Criminal Code*. The Downtown Eastside Sex Workers United Against Violence Society ("Society") and Ms Kiselbach, who was a sex worker for 30 years, had commenced the proceeding. They had been granted both public and private interest standing by the British Columbia Court of Appeal. The Supreme Court of Canada decided that both the Society and Ms Kiselbach had met the requirements for public interest standing.

The purposive approach to the third requirement instructs the court to consider the following (para. 50):

1. Whether the proceeding is an economical use of judicial resources.
2. Whether the issue(s) are suitable for judicial determination in an adversarial setting.
3. Whether permitting the proceeding to move forward will serve the purpose of upholding the principle of legality.

The lower court had denied standing on the basis that neither the society nor Ms Kiselbach had been charged with any of the impugned provisions, and was not a defendant in a proceeding brought by government that relied on the provisions. It held that anyone charged under those provisions could bring the constitutional challenge. The court had noted that a similar proceeding was already underway in Ontario that could bring the issues before the court (para. 12). The court found that the chambers judge, who had originally denied standing, had not been entitled to give those factors the decisive weight he had given (para. 72). The court found that the relevant considerations supported the granting of public interest standing in this case (para. 73).

> [73] I turn now to other considerations that should be taken into account in considering the reasonable and effective means factor. This case constitutes public interest litigation: the respondents have raised issues of public importance that transcend their immediate interests. Their challenge is comprehensive, relating as it does to nearly the entire legislative scheme. It provides an opportunity to assess through the constitutional lens the overall effect of this scheme on those most directly affected by it. A challenge of this nature may prevent a multiplicity of individual challenges in the context of criminal prosecutions. There is no risk of the rights of others with a more personal or direct stake in the issue being adversely affected by a diffuse or badly advanced claim. It is obvious that the claim is being pursued with thoroughness and skill. There is no suggestion that others who are more directly or personally affected have deliberately chosen not to challenge these

provisions. The presence of the individual respondent, as well as the Society, will ensure that there is both an individual and collective dimension to the litigation.

[74] The record supports the respondents' position that they have the capacity to undertake this litigation. The Society is a well-organized association with considerable expertise with respect to sex workers in the Downtown Eastside, and Ms. Kiselbach, a former sex worker in this neighbourhood, is supported by the resources of the Society. They provide a concrete factual background and represent those most directly affected by the legislation. For instance, the respondents' evidence includes affidavits from more than 90 current or past sex workers from the Downtown Eastside neighbourhood of Vancouver (*R.F.*, at para. 20). Further, the Society is represented by experienced human rights lawyers, as well as by the Pivot Legal Society, a non-profit legal advocacy group working in Vancouver's Downtown Eastside and focusing predominantly on the legal issues that affect this community (Affidavit of Peter Wrinch, January 30, 2011, at para. 3 (A.R., vol. V, at p. 137)). It has conducted research on the subject, generated various reports and presented the evidence it has gathered before government officials and committees (see Wrinch Affidavit, at paras. 6–21 (A.R., vol. V, at pp. 137–44)). This in turn, suggests that the present litigation constitutes an effective means of bringing the issue to court in that it will be presented in a context suitable for adversarial determination.

[75] Finally, other litigation management tools and strategies may be alternatives to a complete denial of standing, and may be used to ensure that the proposed litigation is a reasonable and effective way of getting the issues before the court.

[76] All three factors, applied purposively, favour exercising discretion to grant public interest standing to the respondents to bring their claim. Granting standing will not only serve to enhance the principle of legality with respect to serious issues of direct concern to some of the most marginalized members of society, but it will also promote the economical use of scarce judicial resources: Canadian Council of Churches, at p. 252.

INFRINGING ON *CHARTER* RIGHTS OR FREEDOMS

Charter rights are not absolute, and the government is permitted to infringe upon our civil liberties under certain circumstances. The *Charter* also responds to the special needs of identified groups that have historically been disadvantaged. Ameliorative programs are expressly permitted in the *Charter* (s. 6(4)). These programs aim to protect or improve the position of historically disadvantaged groups, such as Aboriginal peoples or women. Therefore, upholding *Charter* rights may involve balancing competing rights. This balancing can result in one group's rights, such as the more advantaged majority, being infringed by another. Government power to infringe on *Charter* rights can also be found in sections 33 and 1.

Section 33: The "Notwithstanding" Clause

33(1) Parliament or the legislature of a province may expressly declare in an Act of Parliament or of the legislature, as the case may be, that the Act or a provision thereof shall operate notwithstanding a provision included in section 2 or sections 7 to 15 of this Charter.

(2) An Act or a provision of an Act in respect of which a declaration made under this section is in effect shall have such operation as it would have but for the provision of this Charter referred to in the declaration.

(3) A declaration made under subsection (1) shall cease to have effect five years after it comes into force or on such earlier date as may be specified in the declaration.

EXHIBIT 7.4
                                                    General *Charter* Analysis

1. Preliminary Considerations:
    (a) Does the *Charter* apply under the circumstances?
    (b) Is the legislation validly enacted under the Constitution?

2. Stage 1 Analysis: Is the limit prescribed by law?
    (a) Does the law have the required standard of clarity?
    (b) Is the law too vague or overbroad?

3. Stage 2 Analysis: Is the limit "reasonable and justified" in a free and democratic society?
    (a) What is the law's objective?
    (b) What is the law's rational connection to achieving this objective?
    (c) Does the law use the least restrictive means required in order to achieve its objective?
    (d) Is the benefit obtained by the law greater than the level of infringement?

---

(4) Parliament or the legislature of a province may re-enact a declaration made under subsection (1).

(5) Subsection (3) applies in respect of a re-enactment made under subsection (4).

Although it is not often used, section 33 permits Parliament or the legislature to pass legislation that infringes on certain *Charter* rights. Section 33 allows the legislative body to declare the legislation valid notwithstanding the *Charter*. The *Charter* rights that can be limited or overridden are those contained in section 2 and sections 7–15.[34] The notwithstanding clause must follow a set format and automatically expires in five years unless the legislative body re-enacts it. There is no identified limit to the number of re-enactments permitted, and each one will run for an additional five-year period.[35]

Parliament and the majority of the provinces have never used the override provision contained in section 33. This reluctance appears to be due to government's principled commitment to the *Charter*. Furthermore, the use of section 33 may be strongly opposed by "opposition parties, the press, the organized bar and civil liberties groups".[36] It is reasonable to believe that Canadians would not look favourably on a democratic process that regularly and arbitrarily overrides entrenched *Charter* rights. At the same time, section 33 can be seen to leave the legislative "last word" with the elected Parliament or legislature. In effect, section 33 prevents the judiciary from interfering with laws that government, the elected representatives of the people, enact to best serve their constituents.

One province that has used the notwithstanding clause is Quebec. Quebec did not assent to the *Constitution Act, 1982* or to the *Charter* — a position that continues today. When the *Constitution Act, 1982* was proclaimed, the Quebec legislature enacted a statute that added notwithstanding clauses to all existing legislation. In effect, the section 33 override meant that the relevant sections

---

[34] That is, freedom of conscience and religion; freedom of thought, belief, opinion and expression, including freedom of the press and other media of communication; freedom of peaceful assembly; freedom of association; life, liberty and security of the person; legal rights (e.g., unreasonable search and seizure and self-incrimination); and equality rights.

[35] Hogg, *supra* note 4 at 815.

[36] *Ibid.* at 819.

of the *Charter* did not apply to Quebec law. This blanket statute was not renewed after the set term expired.

As a matter of form, the legislation must expressly state that it intends to operate despite one or more of the relevant rights or freedoms being overridden. The specific right or freedom being infringed must be clearly identified in the legislation by section number(s) and can include all of the rights contained in the *Charter*.[37] The law must also contain a declaration that "[the] statute is to operate notwithstanding a Charter right".[38] The declaration makes it clear that the legislative body deliberately intended to override the identified right(s).

Section 1 Justification

1. The *Canadian Charter of Rights and Freedoms* guarantees the rights and freedoms set out in it subject only to such reasonable limits prescribed by law as can be demonstrably justified in a free and democratic society.

The arbitrary use of section 33 to override portions of the *Charter* is not the only method by which government can create or uphold legislation that infringes on *Charter* rights. Section 1 of the *Charter* contains a limitation clause that permits government, where it fulfills necessary requirements, to infringe a right or freedom. This method of infringement often occurs where the legislating body is attempting to balance competing rights between individuals or groups. Section 1 allows an infringement where such a balance is desired. While a particular right or freedom may involve additional analytical and contextual processes for s. 1 justification, the requirements outlined below are generally engaged.

The court must first find that the law was validly enacted under the Constitution and that the *Charter* applies in the circumstances. Validity of the law may be undisputed and, therefore, not considered by the court. (A challenge can be to the application or effect of the law.) The individual alleging the infringement is then required to prove that a *Charter* right has been infringed. Where the infringement is proven, the burden of proof shifts to the government. The government must fulfill two requirements in order for a s. 1 justification to succeed. The first, if disputed, is that the limit must be "**prescribed by law**". The law must be adequately accessible (i.e., published) and must set out the circumstances to which the legal rule applies. Any exceptions to the application of the law must be clearly stated. *Therens*[39] illustrates this point. The accused was required to accompany a police officer and provide a Breathalyzer under [former] section 235 of the *Criminal Code*. However, the Court ruled that Therens's accompaniment of the officer constituted detention. Section 10(b) of the *Charter* states that when detained, the person has the right to be informed of the right to counsel. The officer did not inform Therens of his s. 10(b) right. The Court examined section 235 of the *Criminal Code* and found that the provision did not include an express exemption from the application of section 10(b). Therefore, the officer's failure to inform Therens of his right to counsel was not prescribed by the law and infringed his *Charter* right.

All laws must meet a standard of clarity. They cannot be so vague that individuals cannot understand what is required of them and regulate their conduct accordingly. Additionally, the consequences of non-compliance should be

---

[37] *Ford v. Quebec (A.G.)*, [1988] 2 S.C.R. 712.
[38] Hogg, *supra* note 4 at 815.
[39] *Supra* note 13.

foreseeable to a reasonable degree.[40] The requirements of the first stage of the s. 1 justification are usually fulfilled by government.

The court may also consider, at some point in its analysis, whether the statute suffers from issues of **vagueness** or **overbreadth**. These issues are concerned with the language used in the legislation and whether it is sufficiently detailed so that it can fulfill its objective. The right to freedom of expression may be infringed where a law states that "anyone found with a photograph of a naked child is guilty of possession of child pornography". The objective of such a law would be the protection of children. The protection of children from the harm of child pornography is a pressing and substantial need in our society. However, in an artistic or personal context, there may be material caught by such a broadly worded law that does not put a child at risk of harm. Consider the parents who take a photograph of their baby lying naked on a bearskin rug. The photograph would be caught by the provision, classified as pornography, and the parents charged. The result would be an unnecessary and unjustified infringement of the person's right to freedom of expression. In such a case, the legislation's overbreadth would likely result in a failure of a s. 1 justification.

The second stage is more demanding of government and requires that the limit be justified in a free and democratic society. The court follows a four-step analytical process that examines (i) the law's objective or purpose; (ii) its rational connection to achieving the objective; (iii) whether or not the legislation employs the least drastic means required to achieve the objective; and (iv) whether the level of benefit is proportionate relative to the level of infringement.[41] The burden of justifying the infringement is on the government. Generally, the more severe the infringement, the higher the level of justification required. Social science and/or expert evidence is often used and provides context.

At the first step of the second stage, the court will identify the legislative objective of the infringing statute. In order to support a s. 1 justification, the objective must be considered to be a "pressing and substantial need" within society. This step may require only the assertion of a theoretical objective.[42] The objective can be found in the preamble to the statute, as in *Big M*,[43] and may be characterized either generally or narrowly at the court's discretion.[44] For example, the law may be generalized as protecting a vulnerable group, such as children, which would qualify as a pressing and substantial social objective in support of the infringement.

Rational Connection

Where the first step is met, the next consideration requires that the infringement is rationally connected to achieving the objective. For example, *Oakes* challenged a reverse onus clause in the *Narcotics Act*. The Act stated that any *unauthorized* people who had a narcotic substance in their possession were presumed to be in possession for the purpose of trafficking. The Act did not identify a minimum amount of narcotic. The reverse onus clause meant that the accused had the burden of proving that they were not intending to traffic in narcotics. This burden violated the accused's *Charter* right to be

---

[40] Hogg, *supra* note 4 at 774.

[41] The test was articulated by the Supreme Court of Canada in *R. v. Oakes*, [1986] 1 S.C.R. 103, 26 D.L.R. (4th) 200 [*Oakes* cited to S.C.R.] and further clarified in *Dagenais v. Canadian Broadcasting Corp.*, [1994] 3 S.C.R. 835, 120 D.L.R. (4th) 12.

[42] *R. v. Bryan*, [2007] 1 S.C.R. 527, 2007 SCC 12 at para. 39 [*Bryan* cited to S.C.R.].

[43] *R. v. Big M Drug Mart Ltd.*, [1985] 1 S.C.R. 295, 18 D.L.R. (4th) 321.

[44] Hogg, *supra* note 4 at 783.

presumed innocent (s. 10(d)). The government failed to justify the infringement at this stage of the analysis. The Supreme Court held that there was no rational connection between the basic fact of possession and the presumed fact of possession for the purpose of trafficking. In other words, being in possession of *any* narcotic did not unequivocally translate into trafficking. The *Narcotics Act* was amended to include a minimum amount of narcotic before the reverse onus clause applied:

> The rational connection stage of the test requires the Attorney General to "show a causal connection between the infringement and the benefit sought on the basis of reason or logic": see *RJR-MacDonald*, at para. 153, and *Harper*, at para. 104. It is clear that logic and reason may play a large role in establishing such a causal connection. Such a connection is "often a difficult matter to establish by evidence, and the Supreme Court of Canada has not always insisted on direct proof of the causal relationship": P.W. Hogg, *Constitutional Law of Canada* (loose-leaf ed.), vol. 2, at pp. 35–31, cited with approval in *Thomson Newspapers*, at para. 39.[45]

Minimal Impairment

The minimal impairment, or least drastic or restrictive means, factor requires the government to show that the selected method of achieving the objective results in minimal impairment of the *Charter* right. This tends to be the most onerous hurdle for s. 1 justification. At this step, alternative and potentially fewer infringing means of achieving the objective will be examined. The court may again consider social science and other expert evidence. The government is required to provide evidence that the infringement is virtually the only effective means of achieving the objective. The court may also consider whether or not to defer to the decision of the legislative body that enacted the legislation. Where it is shown that a balancing of the competing interests of various groups has been done to the best of the legislative body's ability, the court can defer to the legislative body's decision. The court is generally sensitive to the boundaries of judicial review and reluctant to be seen as interfering in the democratic process.

> The standard for this stage of the analysis is still best encapsulated by the well-known passage from *RJR-MacDonald*, at para. 160:
>
> > The impairment must be "minimal", that is, the law must be carefully tailored so that rights are impaired no more than necessary. The tailoring process seldom admits of perfection and the courts must accord some leeway to the legislator. If the law falls within a range of reasonable alternatives, the courts will not find it overbroad merely because they can conceive of an alternative which might better tailor objective to infringement...
>
> Of course, as this Court unanimously recognized in *Harper*, the minimal impairment analysis may be the stage of the *Oakes* test in which context is most important: see paras. 33 and 110.[46]

Balancing

The final analytical step reviews the balance between the level of infringement and objective sought — i.e., the *proportionality* of the law. The court considers the effects of the infringement relative to its contribution in achieving the legislative objective. The question can be seen to ask "whether the *Charter* infringement is too high a price to pay for the benefit of the

---

[45] *Bryan, supra* note 42 at para. 39.
[46] *Ibid.* at para. 42.

EXHIBIT 7.5

Application of s. 52(1)

Schachter concerned a challenge to a government benefit program. The challenge was based on constitutional inconsistency because a group had been *excluded* from receiving the benefit. The issue concerned federal employment insurance benefits ("EI") for paternity leave. Only biological mothers were given paid leave under EI, whereas an adoptive mother and father both qualified. A biological father challenged his denial of the benefit as an infringement of his section 15 equality rights. The lower court found that the benefit program did violate the biological father's section 15 equality rights. The court used section 52(1) to extend the benefit program to include EI paid leave for biological fathers. On appeal, the Supreme Court of Canada outlined the additional issues raised by the application of section 52(1).

The application of either section 24 or section 52 requires that the "nature of the violation and the context of the legislation" be considered by the court. The remedies of severance and *reading down* minimize judicial interference with government legislation. *Reading in* allows the law to be "consistent with the basic purposes of the Charter". *Severance* shows respect for the decision of Parliament or the legislature by only removing the offending provision(s). Severance can remove the offending portion with some precision. However, with reading in, the issue of how far to extend the legislation is not so easily defined. Where it is difficult to define the boundary for reading in, it is the role of the legislating body to fill in any omissions or gaps. Under those circumstances, it is not appropriate for the court to read in.

The legislative objective and the implementation process also must be considered by the court. In cases where the objective is furthered by reading in, budgetary repercussions must be considered. Any addition to the benefit group may result in too much interference in the legislative process. Where the process or objective is unclear, or significant budgetary repercussions arise from judicial interference, the matter should be referred back to the legislating body for amendment. The Court determined that both these issues were relevant to the facts in *Schachter*.

The benefit's lack of a clear legislative objective meant that legislative intent may have been to deliberately exclude biological fathers in response to unique circumstances experienced solely by adoptive parents. Furthermore, by expanding the paid leave, the Court applied the benefit to a group much larger than that which the statute expressly covered. This expansion raised significant budgetary issues that potentially denied another benefit to another group due to lack of funds. As such, the lower court was improper in its reading in of biological fathers. The provision should have been declared invalid and temporarily suspended to allow the legislative body time to amend.

However, this was not necessary as the statute had already been amended prior to the hearing of the appeal. The benefit group had been extended to include paternity leave for biological fathers, but the term for which the benefit applied to both groups was for a shorter period.

Source: *Schachter v. Canada*, [1992] 2 S.C.R. 679, 66 D.L.R. (4th) 635.

---

law".[47] A s. 1 justification would fail where the benefit is determined to be less than the level of infringement on a *Charter* right. For example, freedom of expression is a fundamental value of democracy. If Parliament enacted legislation that prohibited news agencies from reporting on criminal trials, freedom of expression would be infringed. The purpose of the legislation may be pressing and substantial: to ensure a fair trial for the accused. Prohibiting news reports prevents influencing potential jurors, which helps achieve the law's purpose and appears rationally connected. But the fairness of most trials would not be compromised by a news report. As a result, many people would experience a significant infringement of a fundamental right, while few would

---

[47] Hogg, *supra* note 4 at 801.

benefit. The degree of infringement would be greatly outweighed by, and disproportionate to, the benefit obtained from the law.

> The final stage of the *Oakes* analysis requires a balancing between the salutary and deleterious effects of the legislation. At this stage, it is important to note that it is inappropriate to require a greater standard of proof for the existence of the salutary effects of the legislation than for the deleterious effects.[48]

REMEDIES

Anyone whose *Charter* right has been infringed can file a claim and seek a remedy under section 52(1) or section 24. The availability of a remedy will depend on the relief requested and the claimant's standing. Constitutional and *Charter* remedies seek to correct constitutional inconsistencies. Constitutional inconsistencies may arise in legislation or through the action or inaction of government. Thus, the *Charter* and Constitution can be said to regulate the conduct of government.

There are two provisions that provide a remedy for a *Charter* infringement. Section 52(1) establishes the supremacy of the Constitution and states that laws that are inconsistent with it are without force or effect. There are a number of ways the court may implement such a remedy. The s. 52(1) remedy is available when legislation is challenged on constitutional or *Charter* grounds.

Section 24(2) empowers the court to exclude evidence obtained in an unconstitutional manner from a proceeding. Section 24(1) contains a remedial remedy that empowers the court to award whatever is appropriate and just in the circumstances. Any court with jurisdiction to hear the matter can use these remedies.[49] However, s. 24 remedies generally apply only to *Charter* infringements.

Canada (A.G.) v. Hislop[50] contains a review of constitutional remedies, commencing at para. 81, that includes identifying when a suspension of a declaration of invalidity, and/or the imposition of a retrospective or prospective remedy, is appropriate.

Section 52(1) Remedy

> 52(1) The Constitution of Canada is the supreme law of Canada, and any law that is inconsistent with the provisions of the Constitution is, to the extent of the inconsistency, of no force or effect.

The applicable remedy for an individual challenging the constitutionality of a law is found in section 52(1). Once the issue of constitutional inconsistency is raised, the analysis shifts from the individual whose right has been infringed to the legislation itself. The issue becomes the constitutionality of the law, rather than a determination of whether or not a *Charter* right has been

---

[48] *Bryan, supra* note 42 at para. 48.

[49] The Superior Court of Justice is always a court of competent jurisdiction to hear a *Charter* matter requesting a s. 24 remedy. However, there are exceptional circumstances where a "court of competent jurisdiction" for a s. 24 remedy may include a tribunal or other court. Where the tribunal has been given statutory powers to settle all differences between the parties (Hogg, *supra* note 4 at 847, referring to *Weber v. Ontario Hydro*, [1995] 2 S.C.R. 929) it may be able to effect a s. 24 remedy. In addition, where a *Charter* issue arises during a trial taking place in a venue other than the Superior Court of Justice, the initial court may be in the best position to decide the matter (Hogg, *supra* note 4 at 846, referring to *R. v. Smith*, [1989] 2 S.C.R. 1120, 1129). It may not be necessary to move the *Charter* issue to the Superior Court of Justice.

[50] [2007] 1 S.C.R. 429; 2007 SCC 10.

infringed. When a court renders a remedy under section 52, it is careful to limit its interference with the legislative process. After all, it is the legislating body, as elected representatives of the people, who draft the law. It is not up to the judiciary to significantly amend or change legislation. Rather, courts limit their interference (i.e., exercise judicial restraint) or order the legislating body to amend.

The court has six options that can be implemented under the s. 52 remedy. The court can strike down, sever, read in, read down, order a constitutional exemption or provide a declaration of invalidity. The remedy chosen will depend on the particular circumstances. After determining that the legislation is inconsistent, the court may **strike down** the offending legislation in its entirety. However, this appears to be an extreme response to a matter that Parliament or the legislature deemed important enough to legislate. Alternatively, the court may choose to **sever** the portion of the law that is inconsistent so long as two requirements are met. First, the remaining legislation must remain coherent and intelligible when the provision(s) is severed. Second, the court must be of the opinion that the legislative body would have intended to enact the legislation without its unconstitutional component.

Where the law is held to be under-inclusive (as in the Alberta Human Rights Code discussed earlier) by excluding a particular group, the court may **read in** the group and thereby include it in the legislation. This would require the legislation to meet the two requirements of intelligibility and intent to legislate, as discussed under severance. If the legislation appears overbroad, the court may **read down** the law so that its application is narrowed to meet constitutional requirements. This remedy may be selected in situations similar to the child pornography example noted prior. On a case-by-case basis, the court may provide a **constitutional exemption**. This means that the law is valid in its application but, under the circumstances, violates a particular claimant's right. The court makes no changes to the law and instead decides that the claimant is entitled to be exempt from the law's application.

The court generally declares a law invalid and then, temporarily, suspends the **declaration of invalidity**. This renders the legislation valid for a limited period of time in order to prevent a more serious outcome. For example, if the theft provisions in the *Criminal Code* were declared to be immediately invalid, theft would not be a crime. This would allow people to loot the local store without consequence. Temporarily suspending the declaration of invalidity avoids such an outcome.

Parliament or the legislature is expected to take the opportunity provided by the suspension to amend the offending legislation. When amending, the enacting legislative body may choose to make the amendment required for constitutional compliance. The legislative body can also choose to exercise a s. 33 exemption (if permitted) or amend to allow for a s. 1 justification. The court will likely intervene in a subsequent challenge to the same legislation where the government has failed to take the opportunity provided to rectify the problem.

Section 24 Remedies

24(1) Anyone whose rights or freedoms, as guaranteed by this Charter, have been infringed or denied may apply to a court of competent jurisdiction to obtain such remedy as the court considers appropriate and just in the circumstances.

(2) Where, in proceedings under subsection (1), a court concludes that evidence was obtained in a manner that infringed or denied any rights or freedoms guaranteed by this Charter, the evidence shall be excluded if it is established that, having regard to all the circumstances, the admission of it in the proceedings would bring the administration of justice into disrepute.

The remedy for a *Charter* infringement on an individual's right may be found in section 24. Claims based on public interest standing cannot use the s. 24 remedies because the claimant has not personally suffered an infringement. The broad power contained in section 24 gives the court full discretion regarding the type of remedy that can be implemented. For example, the court may issue an **injunction** compelling a specific change in the behaviour of the government. If more widespread change is warranted, or there has been a failure of government to meet identified *Charter* requirements, a **structural injunction** may be implemented. Structural injunctions may be used where an institution's process or operations result in the systemic violation of a *Charter* right.[51] For example, a federal law enforcement department may require that all applicants meet a specified fitness standard prior to being hired. The standard chosen is based on a male fitness standard. There is no infringement for having a physical standard that prospective applicants must meet. However, it is likely that most women could not meet the imposed male standard and, as a result, would not be hired. It is the *process* or *system* itself that, when applied, has the *effect* of infringing women's right to equality under the *Charter*. A structural injunction would force the offending institution to stop the infringing behaviour and revise the unconstitutional process or system. The law enforcement department might be required to implement two different fitness standards based on gender to prevent further infringements.

Damages may be awarded under section 24 but would be rare. Constitutional remedies generally seek to correct, rather than punish, constitutional inconsistencies. The goal is to ensure compliance with the *Charter* rather than punish non-compliance. However, circumstances may arise where an award of damages is appropriate. For example, damages may be awarded if the infringing conduct is found to be a blatant violation of the public official's responsibilities (such as acting maliciously or in bad faith). The usual remedy is a declaration that the individual's rights have been violated. The declaration would likely be suspended to give government the opportunity to correct the constitutional inconsistency.

Section 24(2) empowers the court to render evidence inadmissible where it is found to have been obtained by infringing the *Charter*.

ABORIGINAL RIGHTS

35(1) The existing aboriginal and treaty rights of the aboriginal peoples of Canada are hereby recognized and affirmed.

Aboriginal rights are exceptional under the Constitution. When the first Europeans arrived in Canada, the country was already populated by Aboriginal peoples. Aboriginal peoples lived in organized communities, were self-sufficient, had established cultures and exercised their own form of government. The Aboriginal presence in Canada prior to European arrival provides the basis for their unique or *sui generis* rights and subsequent treatment under the Constitution.[52] Constitutional protection of Aboriginal rights extends to those rights and treaties that existed at the time the *Constitution Act, 1982* was enacted. This protection also extends to any treaties signed after that date.

Aboriginal rights concerning Aboriginal title to land only extend to land exclusively occupied by the Aboriginal group. The right attaches to exclu-

---

[51] Bakan, *supra* note 22 at 1299.
[52] *R. v. Van der Peet*, [1996] 2 S.C.R. 507.

Indian Act, s. 88   EXHIBIT 7.6

Subject to the terms of any treaty and any other Act of Parliament, all laws of general application from time to time in force in any province are applicable to and in respect of Indians in the province, except to the extent that those laws are inconsistent with this Act or the *First Nations Fiscal and Statistical Management Act*, or with any order, rule, regulation or law of a band made under those Acts, and except to the extent that those provincial laws make provision for any matter for which provision is made by or under those Acts.

---

sive occupation that occurred prior to sovereignty and that continues today. But Aboriginal rights include more than a right to historically occupied land. Additional rights have been identified and embrace the practices, cultures and traditions of the particular Aboriginal group. These practices, cultures, and traditions must be considered integral and distinctive to the group asserting the right.[53] For example, if the group has traditionally hunted on (but not exclusively occupied) a particular piece of land and continues to do so today, it may be able to establish a present-day Aboriginal right to use that land for hunting. The practice, culture, and tradition must be shown to have existed prior to the Aboriginal group's first contact with European settlers.

The Constitution allocates authority to govern Indian matters to the federal government (s. 91(24)). However, provincial laws of a general nature may be applicable where they do not affect the core of the federal head of power (i.e., "Indianness").[54] Provincial legislatures are able to legislate because the federal *Indian Act*,[55] a statutory instrument, expressly permits it. In effect, the provincial legislation is transformed by section 88 of the *Indian Act* into federal legislation and rendered valid. This is the authority by which the Ontario *Highway Traffic Act*, for example, governs on Indian land — a matter constitutionally under federal jurisdiction. The provincial Act applies to all highway users and does not single out Indians for different treatment. It is a law of "general application" under section 88. The province is not intruding into federal jurisdiction when exercising its authority to legislate highways. But if the Act contained a provision that required Indians to drive at a different speed limit from other road users, issues would arise. The law would be invalid because it specifically deals with Indians and is, therefore, an intrusion into the core of a federal head of power. Such a provision would also infringe on *Charter* rights regarding equality.

Provincial laws of general application and Aboriginal rights can intersect in ways that require adjudication and the application of a constitutional doctrine. In *R. v. Morris*,[56] Tsartlip Indian band members were charged under a provincial wildlife law that prohibited hunting at night with an illuminating device and a firearm. In defence, the accused submitted that they had a right to hunt over the unoccupied lands under an 1852 treaty. At trial, the judge had found that the Tsartlip had indeed hunted at night with illumination since "time immemorial". The trial court ultimately decided, however, that

---

[53] *Ibid.*

[54] "Indianness" is described as "an integral part of primary federal jurisdiction over Indians and lands reserved for the Indians", *Four B Manufacturing v. UGW*, [1980] 1 S.C.R. 1031.

[55] R.S.C. 1985, c. I-5.

[56] [2006] 2 S.C.R. 915, S.C.J. No. 59 [*Morris* cited to S.C.R.].

night hunting was "inherently unsafe" and the provincial legislation applied, effectively trumping the Aboriginal treaty right.

In a 4–3 decision, the majority of the Supreme Court of Canada found that the Tsartlip right to hunt at night with an illuminating device was protected by treaty. The Court also found that the Aboriginal right did not include a right to hunt in a dangerous manner. The prohibition in the provincial law against unsafe hunting would apply to band members. Sections 27(1)(d) and (e) of the provincial wildlife act, however, were held to be overly broad because the prohibition against night hunting with illumination included both safe and unsafe hunting, which infringed the band members' treaty right. The provisions were overly broad in their application, and the law was read down so as not to apply to the Tsartlip band members. The appeal was allowed, and the convictions were set aside and acquittals entered.

The Court decided that the first consideration was whether the impugned provisions of the applicable legislation infringed a treaty right. At this step the character, scope and limit of the Aboriginal right must be identified. This step was dispatched by a historical review of the practices of the band and treaty interpretation. The trial judge's finding that the Tsartlip had hunted at night with illuminating devices since "time immemorial" was significant. The treaty permitted the Tsartlip to hunt and fish in unoccupied lands "as formerly", which included the established practice of night hunting. The Court found that the Tsartlip were not limited to night hunting using only ancestral or historical methods, such as bows and arrows. Hunting practices are permitted to evolve without limiting the right and include 21st century tools and equipment, such as guns, spotlights and motor vehicles. The Court decided that the continuation of existing methods of hunting was the intent of the treaty right:

> This evidence reveals that the weapons, means of transportation and illuminating devices used in hunting have become more modern. But changes in method do not change the essential character of the practice, namely, night hunting with illumination. What was preserved by the Treaty and brought within its protection was hunting at night with illuminating devices, not hunting at night with a particular *kind* of weapon and source of illumination. This conclusion is dictated by the common intentions of the parties to the Treaty, as distilled from the context in which the Treaty was entered into. The purpose of the hunting clause was to preserve the traditional Tsartlip way of life, including methods of gathering food. It was, in addition, designed to benefit the settlers, whose interests at the time lay in friendship with the Indian majority on Vancouver Island.[57]

The evidence did not demonstrate that the Tsartlip hunted in a dangerous manner, and the accused had been acquitted of this charge at trial. Much of the relevant area of the province was uninhabited save for Aboriginal people, who were seen only occasionally:

> Protected methods of hunting cannot, without more, be wholly prohibited simply because in some circumstances they could be dangerous. All hunting, regardless of the time of day, has the potential to be dangerous. ... The blanket prohibition of s. 27(1)(d) and (e) applies ... throughout British Columbia, including the vast regions of the interior. Much of the north of the province is uninhabited except by aboriginal people, and there are areas where even they are seen only occasionally. To conclude that night hunting with illumination is dangerous everywhere in the province does not accord with reality and is not, with respect, a sound basis for limiting the treaty right.[58]

---

[57] *Ibid.*, para. 33.
[58] *Ibid.*, paras. 39–40.

The second consideration examined whether the legislation was valid and applicable under the constitutional division of powers and incorporated under section 88 of the *Indian Act*. There was no dispute regarding provincial authority to enact the law; it concerned property and civil rights, an area under provincial jurisdiction pursuant to section 92(13) of the *Constitution Act, 1982*. Parliament governs Indians, and a provincial law that impairs an "integral part of primary federal jurisdiction over Indians and Lands reserved for Indians ... will be inapplicable to the extent of the impairment ... [P]rovincial laws of general application are precluded from impairing 'Indianness' ".[59] Treaty rights to hunt are squarely within federal jurisdiction. But those facts alone were insufficient to resolve the issue.

The Court found that meeting this test would not automatically result in the Aboriginal right trumping the provincial legislation, which could nevertheless be incorporated under section 88 of the *Indian Act*. While section 88 is expressly subject to treaty rights, the Supreme Court has qualified the "treaty exception" in prior decisions and under certain circumstances. If the provincial law or regulation's interference with the treaty right is *insignificant*, the provincial law can be applicable by incorporation under section 88. Thus, the Court had previously found that the imposition of a small access fee solely for maintenance purposes on land used in the exercise of a treaty right to hunt was "an insignificant interference with a treaty right, and consequently did not infringe that right". However, a licensing scheme that imposed "hunting method, the kind and numbers of game, the season and the permissible hunting area" had been found to infringe a treaty right to hunt. This second type of infringement was referred to as a *prima facie* infringement. The infringement resulted because the provincial legislation "denie[d] to holders of treaty rights ... the very means of exercising those rights ... and was in direct conflict with the treaty right". A *prima facie* infringement will trigger the express protection of treaty rights in section 88 (and the provincial law will not be applicable to the extent it interferes with the right), but an insignificant infringement will not.

The provincial prohibition against night hunting with illumination was "absolute" and applied province-wide, including

> [the] ... most northern regions where hours of daylight are limited in the winter months and populated areas are few and far between. The legislature has made no attempt to prohibit only those specific aspects or geographic areas of night hunting that are unsafe by, for example, banning hunting within a specified distance from a highway or from residences. The impugned provisions are overbroad, inconsistent with the common intention of the parties to the treaties, and completely eliminate a chosen method of exercising their treaty right.[60]

The majority found that the Tsartlip's hunting practice had never resulted in an accident and that it was possible to identify uninhabited areas where night hunting would not "jeopardize safety": "These facts amply demonstrate how something less than an absolute prohibition on night hunting can address concern for safety." The categorical ban on night hunting with illumination was a *prima facie* infringement of the Tsartlip's treaty right and could not be incorporated under section 88 of the *Indian Act*. The impugned provisions were read down so as not to apply to the Tsartlip band.

---

59 *Ibid.*, para. 42.
60 *Ibid.*, para. 58.

EXHIBIT 7.7

Section 25 of the Charter

The guarantee in this Charter of certain rights and freedoms shall not be construed so as to abrogate or derogate from any aboriginal, treaty or other rights or freedoms that pertain to the aboriginal peoples of Canada including

(a) any rights or freedoms that have been recognized by the Royal Proclamation of October 7, 1763; and

(b) any rights or freedoms that now exist by way of land claims agreements or may be so acquired.

Sections 35 and 25 of the Constitution

Aboriginal rights and treaties are protected by section 35 of the *Constitution Act, 1982*. The only reference to Aboriginal rights in the *Charter* is found in section 25. While section 35 does not expressly recognize a right to self-government, any treaties that include such rights, such as a right to make decisions about matters regarding education, would be upheld under this section. The entrenchment of Aboriginal rights outside of the *Charter* means that the s. 33 notwithstanding and the s. 1 justification clauses are not able to support government infringement. In the event that Parliament chooses to infringe on an Aboriginal right, Parliament is required to follow a different process of justification. The process is similar to that already discussed under s. 1 justification. Section 35 also states that where a constitutional amendment is proposed that affects an Aboriginal right, a conference must be held and the matter discussed with Aboriginal representatives.

Section 25 of the *Charter* provides clarity regarding the effect of *Charter* provisions on Aboriginal rights (see Exhibit 7.7). The *Charter* establishes and protects the civil liberties that all individuals are entitled to enjoy. Section 25 ensures that Aboriginal rights are not eliminated or reduced by the application of the *Charter*. Therefore, it is unlikely that a non-Aboriginal Canadian can bring a successful claim based on an infringement of his or her equality right (s. 15). This section appears to prevent *Charter* interference with the *sui generis* nature of the rights belonging to Aboriginal peoples.

The Constitution makes it clear that Aboriginal rights are matters appropriately dealt with in exceptional ways. This also applies to sentencing in criminal matters. Section 718.2(e) of the *Criminal Code* statutorily requires the court to consider appropriate alternative sanctions when sentencing Aboriginal offenders. The Aboriginal community is over-represented in Canada's jails, comprised of around 21 percent of the total federal inmate population. Yet the total population of First Nations, Inuit and Metis constitute only four percent of Canada's total population.[61] Aboriginal women's incarceration rates alone have increased by a shocking 80 percent over the last decade.[62]

> Twenty-one percent of the inmate population is of Aboriginal descent and 9% of inmates are Black Canadians. Incarceration rates for these two groups far exceed their representation rates in Canadian society at large. In the last five years, the number of federally incarcerated women has increased by almost

---

[61] CBC News, "Aboriginal corrections report finds "systemic discrimination"", online: cbc.ca <http://www.cbc.ca/news/canada/story/2013/03/07/canada-aboriginal-prison-population-report.html> (March 7, 2013).

[62] Annual Report of the Correctional Investigator 2011–2012 at page 6, online: <http://www.oci-bec.gc.ca/cnt/rpt/pdf/annrpt/annrpt20112012-eng.pdf>

40% while the number of Aboriginal women has increased by over 80% in the last decade. In fact, if not for these sub-groups, the offender population growth rate would have flat-lined some time ago.[63]

The reader can safely conclude that this over-representation represents a growing shadow over Canada's human rights record that government needs to properly, and promptly, address.

CHAPTER SUMMARY

This chapter began with a discussion of the underlying needs that led to the creation of the *Charter*. The need for legislation to protect civil liberties and limit the behaviour of government was identified. The *Bill of Rights* was an early attempt to limit Parliament's power to interfere with civil liberties. The inclusion of the *Charter* in the *Constitution Act, 1982* entrenched enumerated rights. Entrenchment protects them from arbitrary changes and improper infringements by legislating bodies and government officials.

The *Charter* applies only where government is involved. As discussed, government is not limited to the acts or omissions of Parliament and the legislatures. An entity controlled by government, implementing a government program, exercising government functions, receiving power from the state or statutory powers of compulsion, may be found to qualify as "government" under the specific circumstances. In such cases, the *Charter* will apply. It was seen that the application of the *Charter* may depend on the level of routine control exercised by the government within the entity.

Appropriate standing is required for an individual to bring a *Charter* challenge and can be based on a private or public interest in the matter. The limitations on challenges that can be brought by a corporation were discussed. Public interest standing requires that the individual fulfill three requirements: demonstrate a genuine interest in the matter, raise an important legal question, and demonstrate that there is no other way for the matter to be brought before the court.

It was noted that *Charter* rights and freedoms are not absolute. The implementation of ameliorative programs can mean that, in certain circumstances, government can justify infringing on *Charter* rights. Sections 1 and 33 also allow for government infringement. The steps for s. 1 justification require that the infringement is prescribed by law and "demonstrably justified in a free and democratic society" (s. 1). Alternatively, the government can exercise its right under section 33 to enact legislation despite its infringement on selected sections of the *Charter*.

The discussion of remedies demonstrated that section 52(1) applied to issues concerning the constitutionality of a law. Section 52(1) may apply to any constitutional issue, whether related to the heads of powers under the Constitution, or a *Charter* infringement. Under this section, the court may strike down the offending law in its entirety, sever the offending provision(s), read in an excluded group, read down the legislation and thereby narrow its application, or hold that the matter requires a constitutional exemption. The court can temporarily suspend a declaration of invalidity to give the legislating body the opportunity to amend the law. The remedy available under section 24(1) gives broad discretion to the judiciary to provide any remedy deemed just in the circumstances. However, an award of damages is rare and section

---

[63] *Ibid.*

24 is limited to *Charter* infringements. Section 24(2) permits the exclusion at trial of evidence obtained by a *Charter* infringement.

The chapter concludes with a brief discussion on the *sui generis* nature of Aboriginal rights. Aboriginal rights are predicated on the presence of organized societies of Aboriginal peoples prior to the arrival of the first Europeans. The entrenchment of Aboriginal rights occurs outside of the framework of the *Charter*, and the infringement provisions of sections 1 and 33 do not apply. Section 25 of the *Charter* ensures that Aboriginal rights are not compromised by the civil liberties contained therein.

GLOSSARY OF NEW TERMS AND KEY CONCEPTS

constitutional exemption	In the circumstances, the court holds that the law is valid in its general application but does not apply under the circumstances.
damages	A monetary award to compensate for harm suffered.
declaration of invalidity	Where the court renders a decision striking down a legislation or a portion thereof for unconstitutional inconsistency; usually accompanied by a temporary suspension that makes the law valid for a limited period; the legislating body is expected to amend the legislation during that time in order to achieve constitutional compliance.
entrenchment	Included as part of our Constitution, thereby enjoying constitutional supremacy (i.e., the position of having the superior or greatest power or authority); requires a special procedure to amend; the *Charter* has legal superiority over inconsistent laws, acts or actions of government.
fundamental justice	The principles that correspond to established common law principles and the basic tenets of our legal system, including procedural fairness.
injunction	A court order that compels a specific change in behaviour.
inoperative	The law or portion thereof would be without force or effect, as if it did not exist.
overbreadth	Where the law is so broadly written that it infringes upon a *Charter* right unnecessarily.
prescribed by law	The law must be accessible and clear, with consequences of non-compliance reasonably foreseeable.
read down	Where the court holds that the law is overbroad, it may narrow the law's application so as to ensure constitutional compliance.
read in	Where the court determines that the law is under-inclusive, it may read in the omitted group into the legislation.
sever	Where the court renders invalid the constitutionally inconsistent portion of the law.
standing	Required before a *Charter* challenge can be brought; the individual may have to fulfill certain criteria before achieving standing.
strike down	Where the court rules the whole law is constitutionally invalid and renders it without force or effect.
structural injunction	A court order that compels changes more broadly than that of an injunction; considered where a significant part of an institution is operating unconstitutionally.
sui generis	Unique or of its own kind.
vagueness	An uncertain meaning; the law is unclear and, therefore, persons cannot regulate their behaviour in order to comply with it.

REVIEW QUESTIONS

1. The legislative forerunner to the *Charter* was the *Bill of Rights*. What were its limitations? Is the *Bill of Rights* still relevant legislation today?

2. Can the *Charter* apply to the private sector? Under what conditions will it apply?

3. Identify the three requirements for bringing a public interest challenge for an infringement of a *Charter* right.

4. Are there circumstances under which government is allowed to infringe upon a civil liberty? How could such an infringement be done?

5. List the six options the judiciary can implement under a s. 52(1) remedy.

6. What is the significance of section 35 — Aboriginal rights — being situated outside of the *Charter* provisions? Does this mean that government cannot infringe on Aboriginal rights?

DISCUSSION QUESTIONS

1. A corporation has been charged with violating a provision in the *Criminal Code*. Can the corporation claim that a *Charter* right has been infringed?

2. The Supreme Court of Canada has determined that a provision within a piece of legislation infringes upon a *Charter* right. The remaining portion of the legislation is constitutional. What remedies may the court consider in such circumstances?

3. You are interested in joining a recreational program located in British Columbia. The Musqueam Indian Band runs the program and receives funding from the federal government. Unfortunately, the group declines your application, stating that it accepts only members who are Aboriginal people. You feel that this infringes your equality rights under section 15 of the *Charter*. Would a challenge be successful? Why or why not?

4. The provincial legislature has enacted a new law that states that all female students will receive an education grant of $500.00. Is this legislation constitutional? What might the court determine in such circumstances?

5. Quebec has designed new legislation that requires Canadians to obtain a visa prior to entering the province. Anyone without the visa will be expelled from the province. Included in the legislation is a s. 33 notwithstanding clause. Can the infringement be upheld as constitutionally valid?

6. Obtain a recent Supreme Court of Canada (<http://scc.lexum.org/decisia-scc-csc/scc-csc/en/nav.do>) decision on a constitutional or *Charter* issue. Summarize the analysis of the court, provide your opinion on its findings, and state whether or not you agree.

7. You wear a garment that covers your face for religious reasons. What factors will the court consider in determining whether or not you will be able to wear your religious garment when giving evidence at trial?

SUGGESTED READING AND OTHER RESOURCES

Bakan, Joel, et al. *Canadian Constitutional Law*, 4th ed. (Toronto: Emond Montgomery, 2010).

Department of Justice Canada. *A Consolidation of The Constitution Acts 1867 to 1982* (Ottawa, Ont.: Canadian Government, 2001).

Funston, Bernard W., & Eugene Meehan. *Canada's Constitutional Law In a Nutshell*, 3d ed. (Scarborough, Ont.: Carswell, 2003).

Hogg, Peter W. *Constitutional Law of Canada*, 2012 Student ed. (Scarborough, Ont.: Carswell, 2012).

MacIver, R.M. *The Web of Government* (New York: The Free Press, 1965).

Mason, Janet. "Aboriginal Rights" in Laurence Olivo, ed., *Introduction to Law in Canada* (Toronto: Captus Press, 2013).

Mason, Janet & Stanley Gershman. "The Constitution" in Laurence Olivo, ed., *Introduction to Law in Canada* (Toronto: Captus Press, 2013).

Zakaria, Fareed. *The Future of Freedom: Illiberal Democracy at Home and Abroad* (New York: W.W. Norton & Company, 2003).

WEBSITES

CanLII: <http://www.canlii.ca/en/index.html>

Canada, Department of Justice: <http://www.justice.gc.ca/eng/csj-sjc/just/05.html>

Canada, Canadian Heritage: <http://www.pch.gc.ca/eng/1355260548180/1355260638531>

Fundamental Freedoms: <http://www.charterofrights.ca/en/11_00_01>

The Law Dictionray: <http://thelawdictionary.org/>

Mapleleafweb: <http://mapleleafweb.com/features/history-canadian-constitution>

Parliament of Canada:
<http://www.parl.gc.ca/parlinfo/compilations/Constitution.aspx?Menu=Constitution>

Legal Research

Mary Ann Kelly
BARRISTER AND SOLICITOR

Learning Objectives

After reading this chapter, the reader should be able to:

➢ locate online a federal or provincial statute if given the name of the statute

➢ locate online a federal or provincial regulation if given the name of the regulation

➢ find a case when given the name or citation of the case

➢ find at least one or two cases in point when given a particular legal topic

➢ draft a simple case brief

➢ identify the relevant secondary sources of law, and be able to demonstrate a basic understanding of how they are organized and used

TABLE OF CONTENTS

INTRODUCTION

Legal research is a practical skill and is best learned by carrying out the steps outlined in this chapter. It is difficult to learn much about a practical skill merely by reading about it and imagining the process intellectually. For instance, one can read all about driving a car. The experience, however, does not become real or valuable for the vast majority of people until they have an opportunity to sit behind the wheel of a car and actually set the vehicle in motion.

The chapter is intended to be an introduction to, and an overview of, the process of conducting legal research. Legal research is a complicated skill and requires in-depth study that is beyond the scope of this chapter; but the material here will serve as an introduction to the techniques required to perform some basic research. As with all practical skills, the more opportunity you have to practise, the more familiar you become with the techniques, and the more proficient you become in using them.

The ability to find the current law is an essential skill for anyone working in a legal setting. Legal research is conducted to provide answers to legal problems and questions. The identification of the legal issues involved in any given circumstances provides the framework for researching the question or problem presented. Once you have identified the legal issues, you are ready to begin your search for answers by looking at the appropriate research sources.

However, it is important to remember when doing legal research that the law is a moving target. It is changing and developing all the time. When starting to research a topic, one should always assume that the law has changed and needs to be updated. If it is a statute or a regulation, it may have been amended or repealed by the provincial legislature or by the federal Parliament. If it is a case, a decision by a higher court may have overturned a lower court decision; or there may be a newer case, which deals with a fact situation that is more similar to the facts of the case we are researching and may, therefore, be more directly in point. The first principle of all legal research is "update, update, update". That is the only way to ensure that you are not relying on old law.

SOURCES OF LEGAL RESEARCH

There is a distinction in legal research between **primary** and **secondary sources** of law. Primary sources are the actual statutes, regulations or case law decisions. They are referred to as primary sources because they are law, in and of themselves. They have legal force and effect.

Secondary sources are materials that summarize, analyze or explain the primary sources, such as textbooks, legal encyclopedias, articles, law journals, etc. These secondary sources are not, in themselves, legally binding, but they offer an extremely useful, preliminary method of identifying and defining the legal issue. They provide an excellent starting point for research because they provide us with an overview of an area of law and can help us refine and focus our legal issues and lead us to the most relevant primary sources of law.

For a more detailed examination of the sources of law, refer to the chapter on sources of law in this text.

HOW TO GET STARTED

Do you know the name of the statute, regulation or case for which you are searching? If you do, then your task is to find the legislation or the case. If you do not know the statute or case name, then your search will be much broader, and you will have to approach it in a different way. For instance, you may want to read some legal textbooks or law journal articles that address the area of law you wish to research. These secondary sources of law can be a great help in finding some case law or legislation to use as a starting point in the research.

There are a number of online sites relating to legal research in Canada that can be very helpful. One excellent site is Best Guide to Canadian Legal Research, which can be found at <http://legalresearch.org/>. It is an extensive, free website that provides information on how to conduct every aspect of legal research and gives links to relevant sites to help the researcher complete their task.

Most of the law schools in Canada have information about legal research on their websites. You may want to look at some of the following, for example:

- Bora Laskin Law Library, University of Toronto
  <http://www.law-lib.utoronto.ca/resources/locate/finding.htm>

- Queen's University, Faculty of Law
  <http://library.queensu.ca/law/lederman/index>

- Osgoode Hall Law School Library, York University
  <http://www.osgoode.yorku.ca/library/what-we-have/research-guides>

- University of British Columbia, Faculty of Law
  Best Guide to Legal Research
  <http://guides.library.ubc.ca/friendly.php?s=beginlegal>

Some of the Law Societies in Canada also have libraries that have helpful guides and information pertaining to legal research. One such library is the "Great Library" at Osgoode Hall in Toronto. While the use of the physical library is usually limited to members of the Law Society of Upper Canada, the library's website, <http://rc.lsuc.on.ca/library/research.htm>, can be accessed by anyone.

FINDING THE STATUTE LAW AND CASES WHEN YOU HAVE A GOOD IDEA OF WHAT YOU ARE SEARCHING FOR

Finding Legislation When You know the Statute Name or Topic

Legislation is government-made law. It is important to understand how legislation is made in order to be able to find it when researching.[1] The three types of legislation are statutes, regulations, and bills.

Finding Provincial [Ontario] Statutes and Regulations Online

At one time, in order to find provincial statutes, it was necessary to do an extensive search in hard-copy sources in the library to locate the up-to-date, consolidated versions of the statutes. Today, however, it is possible to locate the statutes online at <http://www.e-laws.gov.on.ca/>. This site is

---

[1] An explanation of the legislation-making process is discussed in another chapter, "Sources of Law", offered in the complete edition of this modular textbook.

operated by the Ontario Ministry of the Attorney General and contains the following:

- current consolidations of most public statutes and their associated regulations
- source law — public and private statutes as enacted and regulations as filed — from January 1, 2000
- historical versions of consolidated statutes and regulations, available for statutes and regulations that were amended or affected by a coming-into-force event after January 1, 2004
- many repealed public statutes
- many revoked or spent regulations

A consolidated version incorporates all the existing amendments to the statute or regulation.

On the e-Laws site, current consolidated statutes can be located by the first letter of the statute's title. The regulations associated with a particular statute are accessed through clicking the plus sign beside the statute name. By clicking on the letter "H" to the right of the statute name, it is possible to obtain a legislative history of each statute.

If you do not know whether there is a statute that relates to your research issue, the site permits a search by keyword. You key in the relevant word or words, and the search engine will list all the Ontario statutes containing those words. The statutes and regulations may be searched together, or each may be searched separately.

The site aims to provide consolidated statutes and regulations within two business days of the enactment of the statute or the filing of the regulation. At the top of each statute there is a notice of e-Laws currency that advises of the currency date of that particular statute.

In addition, you can browse and search for source law from January 1, 2000. There are also a set of legislative tables, a link to current Ontario bills on the Ontario legislature website, and a list of all the source law statutes since January 2001. It is also possible to link to the *Ontario Gazette* online, to the legislation sites for other provinces and to the Justice Canada website, which provides access to federal statutes, regulations, and bills.

Finding Federal Statutes and Regulations Online

The federal government website may be found at <http://laws.justice.gc.ca/en/>. It is operated by the federal Department of Justice. This site functions in much the same manner as the Ontario e-Laws site. It is possible to search for federal statutes by title or by subject matter. When a statute is opened, the related regulations are listed below the index to the statutory provisions. As on the Ontario site, keywords can be used to search the statutes and regulations. The site is generally updated every week. The current — to date — is displayed at the top of every statute or regulation.

The site also gives specific search instructions to help you.

Citation

A legal citation is a method of identifying a case, statute or regulation. It tells the person who knows how to read it a good deal of information about the law to which it relates. The leading authority on legal citation in Canada is the *Canadian Guide to Uniform Legal Citation*. It is published by the McGill Law Journal, at the Faculty of Law at McGill University in Montreal. It is not available for free online, but it is available in any law library and in most major reference libraries.

The citation of a case can tell the person who knows how to read it the names of the parties, the level of court that decided the case, the year the case was decided, and sometimes even the judge who made the decision.

Second, the citation of a case tells the reader where to find the case. The hard copy of case law can be found in books published by private publishers. The citation could lead the researcher to the exact, hard copy volume in which the case was printed and even indicate what page it was on. To illustrate, let's look at the following citation:

R. v. Collins, [1987] 1 S.C.R. 265

This citation tells us that the case is a criminal one, in which the state is indicated by the letter R, which stands for Regina, or Queen. The person prosecuted was named Collins. However, the citation says much more. It tells us that the case was decided in 1987 by the Supreme Court of Canada and that it can be found in the hard copy volume 1 of the Supreme Court Reports for that year, on page 265.

Even though it is not usually necessary to find a hard copy of a case in a library any longer, citation is still important in locating a case and identifying it. For example, a neutral legal citation — one that doesn't lead us directly to a hard copy volume of a legal publisher — will still provide major information about the case and help us find it in the electronic database. The federal courts, including the Supreme Court of Canada, use the neutral case citation format, as do the courts of many provinces.

The neutral case citation for the *Collins* case is as follows:

R. v. Collins, 1987 SCC 11

It tells us that the case was decided by the Supreme Court of Canada, and it was the 11th case decided in that year. We could then go to the Supreme Court of Canada website and find the full case decision.

The electronic databases will often use their own system for citing cases but will normally give the hard copy and/or neutral citation as well.

Finding Case Law When You Know the Name of the Case or the Citation

Finding Case Law Online

There are a number of free websites that provide access to Canadian case law online. The most extensive and helpful is the Canadian Legal Information Institute (usually referred to as CanLII) website, <http://www.canlii.org/>.

The CanLII site contains case law from both federal and provincial/territorial courts and decisions of numerous boards and tribunals at the federal and provincial levels across the country. The site also has links to legal databases in other countries.

Federal and provincial statutes are also available on CanLII, so it can be an extremely valuable database to find Canadian law. You can search by case or statute name, citation, year, or by key words or text to find the material for which you are searching.

In addition, the Supreme Court of Canada has a website on which you can locate judgments from that court, as do the Federal Court and the Courts of Appeals of most provinces.

As noted, the free online websites can be of great assistance in locating case law relevant to the issue being researched, but not all the databases have free access. LexisNexus QuickLaw and Westlaw Canada LawSource are two electronic databases for which one must buy a subscription to gain access.

LawSource from Westlaw Canada provides online access to the contents of Carswell's (a private legal publisher) products, including the *Canadian Encyclopedic Digest*, the *Canadian Abridgment*, and Carswell's law report series, as well as unreported cases, selected legislation, finding and updating tools (*KeyCite Canada, Index to Canadian Legal Literature*), and journals. It also provides access to American case law.

LexisNexis Quicklaw provides the same type of database that is primarily focused on Canadian judgments and Canadian secondary sources of law, such as journal articles and texts, although there is also access to U.S. law and some limited access to U.K. law.

If you want to update a case that you have found in your research, it is most easily done through one of the online subscription databases. Updating involves further research into the case to ensure that it is still good law, e.g., that the case has not been overturned by a higher court. These services are available in all law libraries but are usually only free to persons who have authorization for that library. They may also be available in some larger public resource libraries at no cost to the public.

If you have been given only the name of a case and not the full citation, you may find the full citation by consulting the *Canadian Abridgment*'s *Consolidated Table of Cases*. The *Canadian Abridgment* is a secondary legal source that can be found on LawSource. It provides a number of different components, including the *Consolidated Table of Cases*, that can help the legal researcher in locating and updating cases. If you do not have access to LawSource, all law libraries and most major libraries will have a hard copy set of the *Abridgment* volumes in their reference section.

The *Consolidated Table of Cases* provides an alphabetical list of cases, and the name of either party in the case may be used to find the full case citation. You must then find your case online at CanLII, in the LawSource database, or on the library shelves containing the specific case reporting series. The hardcopies of the law reporting series — e.g., *Canadian Criminal Cases* or the *Supreme Court Reports* — will also have a cumulative index after a certain number of volumes in the series have been published. This cumulative index will list all the cases that have been published over a number of volumes so that you will not need to open each volume in the series to look in each individual index for your case.

Updating Case Law

Once you have found your case by name or by citation, you now must determine whether or not your case has been overturned on appeal. You will also want to determine how other judges have treated the case. For instance, have other judges followed the case, or not? This process is called updating or noting up a case. In order to do this, you must turn to the *Canadian Abridgment*, to the volumes called *Canadian Case Citations*.

The electronic versions of *Canadian Case Citations* can be found in the electronic subscription database in LawSource, KeyCite, and in the LexisNexis Quicklaw database, QuickCite. If you do not have access to the database, you can still update your case in hard copy; it is just more time consuming. You will find hard copies of the *Canadian Case Citations* volumes of the *Canadian Abridgment* in any law library.

There are two parts to *Canadian Case Citations*: a set of hardcover volumes and a set of softcover, supplemental volumes.

If you wish to update a case, go first to the hardcover and then proceed to the update volume in softcover. Cases are listed alphabetically.

The *Case Citations* uses a system of symbols to explain how your case has been dealt with.

F   means that another court has followed the case because it is binding case law.

C   means the case was considered or mentioned in another case.

A   means the case was applied or followed even though it wasn't binding on that court.

D   means the case was distinguished, or not followed, because the facts were found to be different in the other case.

Updating Statute Law

On the official statute sites, such as e-Laws, it is not usually necessary to update a statue since it is automatically updated within a few days. Check the currency date for the statute on the site.

FINDING THE STATUTES AND CASES FOR A GIVEN TOPIC WITHOUT KNOWING WHAT MAY BE RELEVANT

Finding a specific case or statute by name or citation is relatively easy. A more complicated type of research involves locating all the relevant law to answer a particular legal issue or question. A legal research project may seem daunting at first, particularly if you know little about the area of law you are about to research, but starting with some secondary sources will often be of great assistance in developing a focus. For instance, as we noted above, reading a recent textbook or law journal on a particular legal topic may prove very valuable in locating some preliminary primary sources of law on the issue, such as statutes or cases.

Some additional secondary legal sources will also prove helpful.

You can also do a text or keyword search on CanLII to determine whether there are any cases or statutes that apply to your research topic. If you cannot find any at first, you will want to change your keyword organization to see whether you can find relevant material by refining your search. You can also do a keyword search on the government statute websites, such as e-Laws, to find relevant statutes when you do not know if a statute applies to your topic.

Of course, the subscription electronic databases also have internal search engines for locating case or statute law related to a specific topic. If you do not have access to these databases or cannot find what you are looking for on CanLII, or another free online website, you may do a hard copy search in the library by using the *Canadian Abridgment Case Digests* or the *Canadian Encyclopedic Digest*.

The *Canadian Abridgment*: Case Digests

We have already looked at a part of the *Canadian Abridgment*, *The Consolidated Table of Cases*, that will help us find cases when we know the name of the case for which we are searching. *The Canadian Abridgment: Case Digests* is another part of the *Abridgment* that can assist us to find cases when we are presented with a legal issue, topic or problem and don't know if there is relevant case law in that area. The *Consolidated Table of Cases* are online as part of purchased legal research software discussed above. The electronic version may be found in most major libraries for those who have access to the library. The software advises researchers how to use it to conduct searches. The following discusses the hard copy versions for those who do no have access to the software.

The Case Digests, a set of red and black, hardcover volumes, contain summaries or digests of reported Canadian cases covering a period of almost 200 years. The volumes are arranged alphabetically by legal subject. The cut-off date for the cases summarized in each volume is noted on the title page. Each of the hardcover volumes is updated by way of a softcover supplement. The softcover supplements are further updated by another set of softcover supplements that are issued biweekly, and contain the most recent reported cases.

The hardcover volumes are identified by the letter "R" that appears on their cover. For instance, "R14" is volume 14 in the hardcover set, and R14 Supplement would be the supplemental softcover volume relating to that hardcover volume.

Each subject in the *Abridgment* is organized according to a system called the Key Classification System. This means that each subject is broken down into many different, smaller parts made up of specific points related to the main subject area. For instance, "Estates" would be a subject area of law. It is, in fact, located alphabetically in hardcover volume R14.

However, there are numerous subheadings in this major area of law, such as what power the court has to deal with wills and estates, what happens if someone dies without a will, and what does the case law say about changing a will, among many, many others. The Key Classification System identifies each of these subject parts and sub-parts by a series of numbers and letters. All cases related to that specific subject part would have the same Key Classification, starting first with a roman numeral, then Arabic numerals, and then letters.

Using the subject area "Estates", as an example, "Requirements for Validity" is a sub-heading, which is further broken down into various parts, such as "Witnesses", which is then broken down again.

ESTATES
IV. Requirements for Validity
    4. Witnesses
        b. In presence of testator

Therefore, ESTATES IV. 4. b. would contain a summary of all the cases relating to whether a witness had to be present when the testator, or maker of the will, was actually drawing up the will. Each of these cases would have its own individual consecutive number, such as 477, 478.

There are several ways to search using the *Case Digests*.

1. You can go directly to the hardcover volume dealing with the area of law you wish to search. For instance, if you were looking for information on parties to a contract, you could locate the volume dealing with contracts, and search through it until you found all the relevant cases.

2. You can use the *Key and Research Guide*, which provides an alphabetical list of all of the legal subjects and their sub-headings covered in the *Case Digests*. This can be a very helpful way for a novice researcher to start his or her search since the *Key and Research Guide* lays the subject out with all its various parts, which will give you an instant overview of a very complex area of law. The *Key* will direct you to the appropriate hardcover volume, in which you will find the relevant cases summarized under the Key Classification System number.

3. You can use the *General Index*, a separate, loose-leaf part of the *Abridgment*. It is organized alphabetically, by keyword, with citations to the corresponding key numbers in the hardcover volume.

4. If you already have one case on point, you can look that case up by name in the *Abridgment, Consolidated Table of Cases*. The case will be followed in the *Consolidated Table* by its volume and case digest number. It is then possible to go to the appropriate volume and digest number to find other, similar cases.

No matter which method you use, once you have found the cases you are looking for in the hardcover volumes, you must then update the cases by referring to the Supplement for the appropriate volume and then checking each of the most recent monthly issues of the *Canadian Current Law: Case Digests*.

The *Canadian Encyclopedic Digest*

The *Canadian Encyclopedic Digest*, or CED as it is commonly known, is a secondary source of law that can provide information about an area of law and will serve as a reference point for finding relevant primary sources. It is a loose-leaf, multi-volume encyclopedia that can be found in all law libraries and in the reference section of many large public libraries. There are two distinct editions of the CED, although many libraries hold only the edition most relevant to their area. The *Ontario* edition is bound in green, and the *Western* edition, covering the four western provinces, in brown. The service can also be purchased in electronic format. The description below applies to the hard copy version.

There are several hundred legal subject titles that correspond to very broad legal topics. The subject titles are arranged alphabetically in loose-leaf volumes so that librarians can easily update them. Each volume has a volume number. The first pages of each volume provide a table of contents that shows a list of the subject titles located in that volume. (See Exhibit 8.1.)

EXHIBIT 8.1   **The Canadian Encyclopedic Digest**

Table of Cases
Table of Statutes
Table of Rules
Table of Regulations

3   December 2008

Source: *The Canadian Encyclopedic Digest*, Fourth Edition — Ontario Volume 19 Title 46 — Western Volume 21 Title 45 — Table of Contents page (Release Line December 2008). Reproduced by permission of Carswell, a division of Thomson Canada.

Each subject title is broken down into parts. The parts all have separate names and are designated by a Roman numeral. Each part is broken down into sections, each of which has a name and is designated by a number. Finally, each section is broken down into paragraphs that are designated by the typographical symbol § followed by a number. The paragraph contains a short summary of law on a topic, as well as references to the cases and statutes that are relevant to that topic.

Once you have found the applicable subject title, you should check the table of contents at the beginning of the title to ensure that you find all relevant parts, sections and paragraphs.

The main volumes of the CED are updated through the use of yellow supplementary inserts, which are placed at the beginning of each title. If you are looking in a subject title that has a yellow update inserted at the beginning of the title, you must check to see if the paragraphs you are relying on have been updated. You do this by matching the paragraph numbers in the main body of the title with the paragraph numbers in the yellow inserted supplement. If the paragraph numbers you are looking at are not in the supplement, they are current in the main material and have no update.

In addition to the main volumes, the CED has a *Key and Research Guide*. If you are not clear what subject title in the main volume will be most helpful, you may wish to start with the *Index Key*, which is a separate volume of the *Key and Research Guide*. Each subject title in the main volumes contains a subject index related to that title. The *Index Key* combines the individual subject indexes and an extensive system of cross-reference. All phrases or keywords are listed alphabetically. Beside each entry is the volume and title number of the general subject that deals with that keyword or phrase. The volume number appears before the hyphen, and the title number follows the hyphen. For example, 1-1§6 means that the keywords you are looking for are contained in volume 1, title 1, paragraph 6.

BRIEFING A CASE

One of the ways that legal researchers summarize their work is through a **case brief**. Summarizing the research work is important, as it provides a method for the researcher to compare various cases and analyze them without having to read each case in its entirety each time. Case briefs are also necessary if the researcher is conducting the research for someone else. The case brief provides an effective way for the person reading the research to easily access the contents of the relevant cases.

Drafting a case brief is really a matter of style, although each brief should contain certain essential information, such as a concise statement of the facts of the case, an identification of the issue or issues with which the case deals, a statement of the decision, and a summary of the judge's reason for the decision. The brief should also contain the citation for the case so that it can be easily located in the law reports.

The brief should indicate which level of court made the decision, and should also give the name of the judge or judges. The doctrine of *stare decisis*[2] and the importance of precedents in the common law mean that decisions of higher courts, such as appeal courts, are binding on lower courts that are deciding cases on the same facts. In an appellate court case, it is usual that the court sits with a panel of judges, normally three judges in the Ontario

---

[2] Discussed in detail in another chapter, "Sources of Law", offered in the complete edition of this modular textbook.

Court of Appeal, and five, seven or nine judges in the Supreme Court of Canada. One judge will write the reasons for judgment for all the judges or for the majority. Each of the judges involved in the majority decision should be named. If the case involves concurring or dissenting opinions, the names of the judges writing these opinions should also be noted.

The brief should identify the parties. If there are multiple parties involved in the case or if the roles of the parties changed at the various levels of court, the parties' roles should be described: e.g., Smith is the plaintiff at trial, but the respondent on the appeal.

The facts of the case, as found by the court, should be set out or summarized in narrative form and in chronological order. Often the parties will have varying versions of the facts, but it is the facts that the court finds to be true that are essential to the case brief. It is important to identify the type of proceeding before the court: whether it is an action, an application, or an appeal, etc. The remedy being sought should also be noted.

Identifying the issue being determined in the case is a very important part of the case brief. Sometimes, when judges write the case decisions, they will set out the issue in the decision itself. In these cases it is very easy to determine the issue because the court has clearly identified it. In other cases, however, the issue may not be as clearly set out, and the researcher must analyze the case to locate it. The issue is the legal question that the court was asked to decide. For instance, in a torts case, one of the issues might be whether or not the defendant was negligent. Another issue might be the amount of damages.

The judgment may be stated simply — e.g., "the appeal was dismissed", or "the defendant was found liable in negligence", or "the accused was found guilty". It is not necessary to state the judge's reasons for the decision in this part of the brief.

The next section of the brief should deal with the court's reason for the decision. This is referred to as the *ratio decidendi* of the case. This is often the most challenging part of the brief, distilling a lengthy judgment into a concise summary or recognizing the main points in the reasoning of a case report that may not be clearly written. The researcher must analyze the rationale of the judge or judges in applying the law to the facts of a particular case. If there is more than one issue in the case, each issue must be analyzed and the *ratio* set out for each issue the case deals with.

Ratios or reasons for decision are usually supported by legal authorities — i.e., other cases or statutes. The other cases identified in the case the researcher is briefing should be cited. If a judge has distinguished another case, that should also be noted in the case brief.

Finally, the researcher must present a short statement of the principle of law in the case. This involves identifying the precedent value of the case.

CHAPTER SUMMARY

This chapter provided a practical overview of some basic legal research techniques and a summary of some methods of reporting the findings of that research. It reviewed the primary and secondary sources of law and how to find a statute or case law, first online and then in paper format.

The fact that legal research is a practical skill was emphasized, and students were encouraged to read the chapter and use the computer or a law library, where they could access the necessary tools and follow along with the text.

GLOSSARY OF NEW TERMS AND KEY CONCEPTS

case brief	A short summary of a case, provided in a specific format, that a legal researcher prepares to report on and provide future reference of the research results for him or herself, or for the person requesting the research.
primary sources	The actual statutes, regulations or case law decisions that are law and have legal force and effect.
ratio decidendi	Latin phrase that refers to the core legal reason for deciding a case.
secondary sources	Materials that summarize, analyze or explain the primary sources of law, such as textbooks, legal encyclopedias, articles, law journals, etc. These sources are not legally binding but offer an extremely useful, preliminary method of identifying and defining the legal issue.

REVIEW QUESTIONS

1. Is a bicycle a vehicle under the Ontario *Highway Traffic Act*? What section of the statute explains this?

2. You have found the case of *Delaney Boat Lines v. Barrie (City)*. It is a case decided by the Ontario Court of Appeal in 1976 and can be found in two different law reports. It is in the Dominion Law Reports on page 389 of the 128th volume of the third series. It is also in the Ontario Reports, second series, volume 15, on page 675. Give the proper, full citation for this case.

3. Is there a federal statute that tells us who is not eligible to be a member of the National Film Board? Name and give the citation for the statute.

4. Our client is going into the hospital for serious surgery. What statute does she have to follow to make a will?

5. Our client's husband has been ordered to pay child support. He has not paid. What statute applies?

6. The client wants to go moose hunting in Northern Ontario. Does he need a licence?

7. Our client is a landlord who wants to evict the tenant in his downstairs apartment for non-payment of rent. What statute applies?

8. The Ontario *Health Care Consent Act* was passed in 1996. It is chapter 2 for that year. From this information, write the citation for the statute.

DISCUSSION QUESTIONS

1. Read and prepare a case brief for the following case:
   Crocker v. Sundance Northwest Resorts Ltd., [1988] 1 S.C.R. 1186

2. Describe the method you used in locating the following statutes:
   (i) The Ontario *Human Rights Code*
   (ii) The *Canadian Human Rights Act*

3. Using CanLII, answer the following:
   (i) You are looking for a Supreme Court of Canada case. The plaintiff's name is Nelles and the case is about sick children. What is the name of this case?

(ii) You have been given the following citation:

[1980] 2 S.C.R. 834.

What is the name of this case?

SUGGESTED READING AND OTHER RESOURCES

Banks, Cate, & Heather Douglas. *Law on the Internet* (Toronto: Irwin Law, 2006).

Banks, Margaret A., & Karen E.H. Foti. *Banks on Using a Law Library: A Canadian Guide to Legal Research*, 6th ed. (Scarborough, Ont.: Carswell, 1994).

McCormack, N., J. Papadoupoulos & C. Cotter. *The Practical Guide to Canadian Legal Research*, 3d ed. (Scarborough, Ont.: Carswell, 2010).

Kerr, Margaret, JoAnn Kurtz & Arlene Blatt. *Legal Research: Step by Step*, 3d ed. (Toronto: Emond Montgomery, 2009).

McGill Law Journal. *Canadian Guide to Uniform Legal Citation*, 8th ed. (Scarborough, Ont.: Carswell, 2014).

Tjaden, T. *Legal Research and Writing*, 3d ed. (Toronto: Irwin Law, 2010; [Digital edition, 2d ed., 2004]).

Whitehead, P., & A. Anne Matthewman. *Legal Writing and Research Manual*, 7th ed. (Markham, Ont.: LexisNexis Butterworths, 2012).

WEBSITES

CanLII: <http://www.canlii.org>

Catherine P. Best. *Best Guide to Canadian Legal Research*: <http://www.legalresearch.org>

Canadian Bar Association: <http://www.cba.org/cba/national/nov03/feature4.aspx>

The Law Dictionary: <http://thelawdictionary.org/>

Legaltree.ca: <http://www.legaltree.ca/>

LSUC Great Library: <http://www.lsuc.on.ca/greatlibrary.aspx>

Osgoode Hall Law School: <http://www.osgoode.yorku.ca/library/what-we-have/web-links>

The Ontario Court System

Mary Ann Kelly
BARRISTER AND SOLICITOR

Learning Objectives

After reading this chapter, the reader should be able to:

➢ understand the constitutional framework for the court system in Canada and Ontario
➢ describe the hierarchy of courts in Canada and Ontario
➢ understand the impact of court reform in Ontario
➢ describe the issues related to judicial appointments
➢ understand the principal steps in civil and criminal proceedings
➢ identify alternative dispute resolution methods and be aware of the differences

TABLE OF CONTENTS

INTRODUCTION

Generally speaking, the purpose of the court system in Canada is to resolve disputes in a fair and just manner. In the process of examining and resolving the issues put before them, the courts also make law by interpreting and defining and applying both statutes and the common law. Courts, therefore, play a major role in both the structure and operation of government in Canada, as well as affecting Canadian society as a whole.

This chapter will examine the court system in Canada, with particular emphasis on the courts in Ontario.

THE CANADIAN JUDICIAL SYSTEM

Constitutional Framework of the Courts

Canada is a federal state. In a federal state, there is more than one level of government. In Canada, the two levels of government are the federal government and the provincial government. Each level has its own powers and responsibilities, spelled out in the *Constitution Act, 1867*. Since courts are an integral part of the Canadian governmental system, responsibilities for court administration and operation are set out in the Constitution. The system is quite complicated because no single level of government has sole responsibilities for courts, and both levels of government may be involved at the same time in the operation of a particular court or courts.

Power to Create and Administer Courts

Section 92 of the *Constitution Act, 1867* gives the provinces responsibility for the administration of both civil and criminal courts in the province. Therefore, it is primarily the provincial governments that establish the court structure, and operate and administer the courts. The provinces do this by passing statutes and creating regulations that deal with everything from what the courts will be called to what type of robes the judges will wear.

This does not mean that the federal government has no role in the establishment and operation of courts. On the contrary, the *Constitution Act, 1867* gives the federal government some responsibility for the administration of some courts. Section 101 provides the federal government with the power to establish and operate the Supreme Court of Canada, the Federal Court, the Tax Court and military courts that deal with courts martial of people in the Canadian Armed Forces and civilians who accompany units of the Armed Forces while the unit is on active service.

Power to Create Procedural Law

Once courts have been established, there must be procedural rules that dictate how cases will proceed through the court. Each court has its own set of procedural requirements. The Constitution gives the provincial government the power to create procedure for all the civil courts in the province. However, the power to create procedure for the criminal courts is the responsibility of the federal government, since criminal law is a federal responsibility. The federal government also creates the procedural requirements for the courts that it has the power to establish, e.g., the Supreme Court of Canada and the other federally created courts mentioned above.

Power to Appoint Judges

To further complicate the matter, although the province has the responsibility for administering the courts in the province, they do not have the sole power to appoint the judges who sit in those courts. Section 96 of the

The Canadian Judicial System

EXHIBIT 9.1

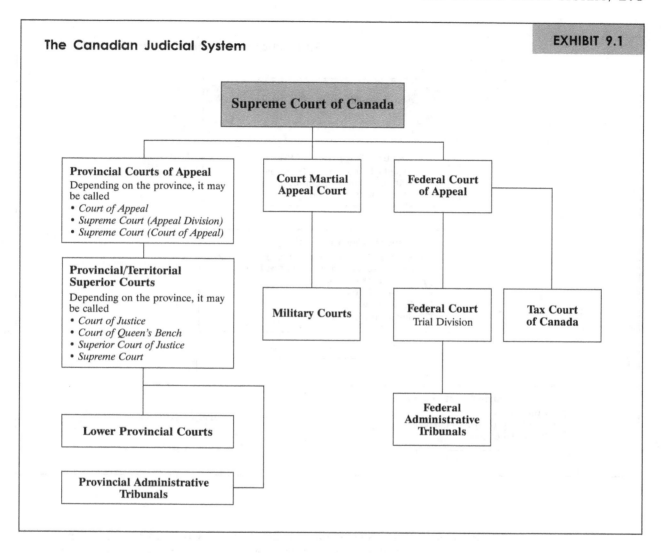

Constitution Act, 1867 gives the federal government the power to appoint judges in the superior courts of each province. The provincial government has the authority only to appoint judges to the lower level of courts in the province. Of course, the federal government has the sole power to appoint judges to the courts that they have the constitutional power to create. For instance, only the federal government has the authority to appoint judges to the Supreme Court of Canada.

Judges who sit in the courts of a province but who are appointed by the federal government are commonly referred to as **federally appointed judges**. Those appointed by the province are referred to as **provincially appointed judges**. In many areas of law, only a federally appointed judge has the legal authority, or jurisdiction, to hear a particular type of case. For example, only a federally appointed judge can deal with a divorce or certain matters in criminal law.

The Organization of Courts

Each province has a statute and a number of regulations that prescribe how the courts in that province will be established, how they will operate, and how they will be administered. Although each statute is distinct, there are

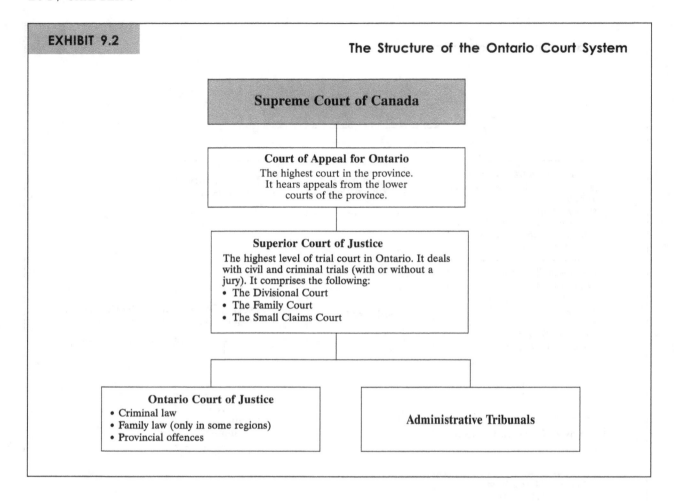

EXHIBIT 9.2

The Structure of the Ontario Court System

Supreme Court of Canada

Court of Appeal for Ontario
The highest court in the province.
It hears appeals from the lower
courts of the province.

Superior Court of Justice
The highest level of trial court in Ontario. It deals
with civil and criminal trials (with or without a
jury). It comprises the following:
• The Divisional Court
• The Family Court
• The Small Claims Court

Ontario Court of Justice
• Criminal law
• Family law (only in some regions)
• Provincial offences

Administrative Tribunals

more similarities among the provincial statutes than there are differences. In Ontario, the statute that governs court creation and administration is called the *Courts of Justice Act*.[1]

There are three levels of court in the present Ontario court system:

1. The Court of Appeal for Ontario, the highest court in the province

2. The Superior Court of Justice, comprising a number of branches:
   (a) The Divisional Court
   (b) The Family Court
   (c) The Small Claims Court

3. The Ontario Court of Justice

The judges of the Court of Appeal and the Superior Court are appointed by the federal government, and those of the Ontario Court of Justice are appointed by the provincial government.

Between 1881 and September 1, 1990, the court structure in Ontario remained essentially the same, and the names of the courts did not vary. However, in 1990 the government undertook a major court reform that drastically altered the framework of the court structure and changed all the names

---

[1] R.S.O. 1990, c. C.43.

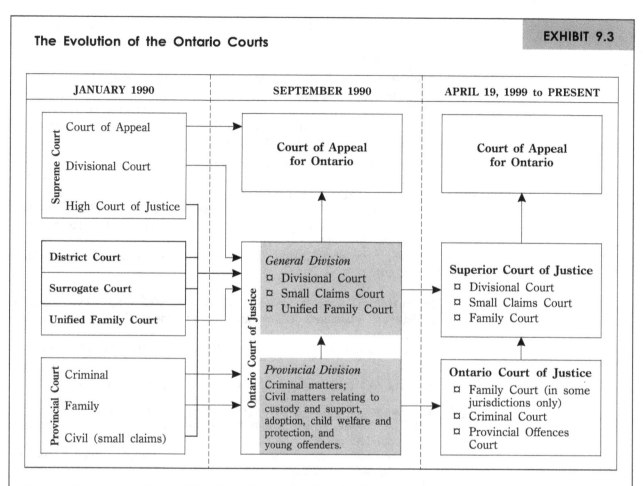

The Evolution of the Ontario Courts   **EXHIBIT 9.3**

| JANUARY 1990 | SEPTEMBER 1990 | APRIL 19, 1999 to PRESENT |

Supreme Court
- Court of Appeal
- Divisional Court
- High Court of Justice

- District Court
- Surrogate Court
- Unified Family Court

Provincial Court
- Criminal
- Family
- Civil (small claims)

Court of Appeal for Ontario

Ontario Court of Justice

General Division
- Divisional Court
- Small Claims Court
- Unified Family Court

Provincial Division
Criminal matters; Civil matters relating to custody and support, adoption, child welfare and protection, and young offenders.

Court of Appeal for Ontario

Superior Court of Justice
- Divisional Court
- Small Claims Court
- Family Court

Ontario Court of Justice
- Family Court (in some jurisdictions only)
- Criminal Court
- Provincial Offences Court

Source: Margaret A. Banks, "The Evolution of the Ontario Courts, 1788–1981", in David H. Flaherty (ed.), *Essays in the History of Canadian Legal History* (Toronto: University of Toronto Press, 1983); Ministry of the Attorney General, "Part I: Background and Vision", *Ontario Civil Justice Review*, online: <http://www.attorneygeneral.jus.gov.on.ca/english/about/pubs/cjr/firstreport/default.asp>.

of the courts. Then, on April 19, 1999, the court names were once again changed, although there was no change, at that time, to the actual structure of the court hierarchy.

The court structure outlined above is the one currently in place in Ontario. It was put into place on April 19, 1999. However, it is necessary to understand the court structure and names prior to that time. The name changes in the court system did not alter a particular level of court's authority to set precedent. Therefore, for the purpose of legal research, it is important to be able to determine whether a court decision is, in fact, binding precedent over another court.

Exhibit 9.3 shows the various changes to the Ontario Court Structure. Prior to September 1, 1990, there were three levels of court in Ontario:

1. The Supreme Court of Ontario, which consisted of three court branches:
   (a) The Court of Appeal, which was the highest court in the province
   (b) The Divisional Court, which heard some types of appeals and some reviews of the decisions made by administrative tribunals

(c) The High Court, which heard trials involving higher claims for money or property, divorce matters, equalization of family property, and more serious criminal offences

2. The intermediate level, which consisted of three courts:
   (a) The District Court
   (b) The Surrogate Court, dealing with wills and estates
   (c) The Unified Family Court, which was a special pilot project begun in 1976 to hear all family law matters

3. The Provincial Court, which had three divisions:
   (a) The Provincial Court (Criminal), which heard bail hearings and less serious criminal matters;
   (b) The Provincial Court (Family), which had the jurisdiction to hear family law matters other than divorce and equalization of family property; and
   (c) The Provincial Court (Civil), which comprised the Small Claims Court.

The Supreme Court of Ontario and the District Court were presided over by federally appointed judges, and the Provincial Court by provincially appointed judges.

Between September 1, 1990, and April 18, 1999, there were two levels of court:

1. The Ontario Court of Appeal, the highest court in the province

2. The Ontario Court of Justice, consisting of two branches:
   (a) The Ontario Court (General Division), presided over by federally appointed judges
   (b) The Ontario Court (Provincial Division), presided over by provincially appointed judges

The Ontario Court (General Division) was equivalent in all but name to the present Superior Court of Justice, and the Ontario Court (Provincial Division) was equivalent to the present Ontario Court of Justice.

THE HIERARCHY OF COURTS

The Supreme Court of Canada

The Supreme Court of Canada is the highest court in the land, and has been since 1949. Before that, decisions made by the court could be further appealed to the Judicial Committee of the Privy Council in England. (Criminal appeals to the Privy Council were ended in 1935.) Once the Court decides an issue and rules, that decision becomes the law of Canada, applicable across the country.

The Supreme Court of Canada hears **appeals** from the provincial or territorial courts of appeal and from the Federal Court of Appeal. In most instances, there is no absolute right to appeal, and the party must first seek **leave of the court** or permission from the Supreme Court to have its case heard. Most often, only cases that involve new interpretations of the law, criminal cases involving serious legal issues, cases involving constitutional issues and cases involving conflicting decisions from different provincial courts of appeal will be granted leave. However, the federal government may refer an important legal matter to the Court for an opinion, and the government does not need to first seek leave. Likewise, in a criminal case, if a judge of the provincial or territorial court of appeal dissents on a point of law, there is an absolute right to appeal the decision to the Supreme Court.

The Supreme Court of Canada consists of nine judges, all appointed by the federal government. By legislation,[2] the Court must have three judges from Quebec. By custom, the balance of the Court is made up of three judges from Ontario, two from the western provinces and one from the Atlantic provinces. The Court sits, whenever possible, as a panel of nine judges. However, if one of the judges is ill, or otherwise unable to hear a case, the panel will often be made up of an uneven number in order to avoid a tie decision. The minimum number of judges required to form a panel is five.

The Court of Appeal

The Ontario Court of Appeal is the highest court in the province. It hears appeals of cases from the Superior Court of Justice. In most instances, the court sits as a panel of three or five judges. An uneven number of judges is required for appeals in order to ensure that there is not a tie decision. There is only one Court of Appeal location for the entire province, and it sits at Osgoode Hall in Toronto. If a party wishes to appeal a decision that was made somewhere else in Ontario, the party must come to Toronto to have the appeal heard.

Court of Appeal judges are appointed by the federal government.

The Superior Court of Justice

The Superior Court of Justice is the highest trial court in the province, and it has "inherent jurisdiction". This means that it can hear any case on any matter except those that are specifically required by statute to be heard in another court. The Superior Court, although it has jurisdiction to deal with any criminal matter, usually hears only the most serious criminal matters. It also has jurisdiction to hear all civil proceedings, such as contract disputes, personal injury matters, most family law proceedings, and wills and estate cases. There is a separate Small Claims Court branch of the Superior Court that hears civil law claims for $25,000 or less. One of the major purposes of the Small Claims Court is to give litigants the opportunity to have claims for lower amounts heard in a less costly and more streamlined manner.

The federal government appoints Superior Court judges. There is a Superior Court in each region of the province.

The Superior Court has the jurisdiction to decide a case on principles of both common law and the law of equity. Although the Small Claims Court branch, historically defined as a court with limited jurisdiction, has had no power to use the law of equity, recent cases give judges in this court the power to apply equitable principles, but not to use equitable remedies.

The court has a number of branches: the Divisional Court, the Family Court, and the Small Claims Court.

The Divisional Court

The Divisional Court is an appellate court, not a trial court. It has jurisdiction to hear judicial reviews related to Ontario government action, appeals from administrative tribunals in the province, appeals from Family Court, appeals from Small Claims Court involving more than $2,500, and certain appeals from civil decisions regarding monetary or property claims. In relation to the latter, the Divisional Court has authority to hear appeals from final orders of judges of the Superior Court involving amounts of not more than $50,000; interlocutory (temporary) orders of judges, with leave; and final orders of masters who are judicial officials who hear some proceedings in the Superior Court.

---

[2] *Supreme Court of Canada Act*, R.S.C. 1985, c. S-26.

All judges appointed to the Superior Court are also judges of the Divisional Court. They sit in the Divisional Court on a rotating basis. In many instances, they hear cases in a panel of three judges, just as does the Court of Appeal, although, in some proceedings, there is jurisdiction for one judge alone to hear a case.

The Family Court

The Family Court is a branch of the Superior Court, and it is a relative newcomer to the Ontario Court system. The court has jurisdiction to hear all family law matters. Prior to the Family Court's forming a specific branch of the Superior Court, family law matters were heard in much the same way that criminal cases and general civil cases were heard. The Superior Court had exclusive jurisdiction to hear divorce cases and those involving equalization of family property, but there were court matters involving the family that this court had no authority to hear, including child protection and adoption cases under the *Child and Family Services Act*. These latter cases were under the exclusive jurisdiction of the Ontario Court of Justice.

There were many family law cases that did not involve a divorce, a division of property or child protection and adoption. A good number of cases involved only issues of family support and custody and access to children. These cases could be heard in either the Superior Court or the Ontario Court of Justice, depending on where the party or his or her lawyer decided to commence the proceeding. This meant that there was no consolidated approach to family law litigation. Different levels of court were dealing with family law matters, and, sometimes, a case would have to change from one level of court to another after it was begun.

Family law matters do not lend themselves easily to an **adversarial system**, particularly one where there is a split jurisdiction between levels of court and the very real possibility of a lack of continuity. To address this situation, in 1977 the Ontario government initiated a pilot project in Hamilton called the Unified Family Court. In 1995, the unified court was extended to four more locations and, in 1998, it was made a branch of the Superior Court of Justice. Since then, the court has expanded into other locations. There is currently a Family Court Branch of the Superior Court in the following locations: Hamilton, Barrie, Napanee, London, Kingston, Ottawa, Newmarket, Oshawa, Peterborough, Lindsay, Cobourg, Bracebridge, St. Catharines, Cornwall, L'Orignal, Brockville and Perth. In all of these locations, only the Superior Court, Family Court, hears family law cases. In all other locations, including Toronto and Brampton, the old system of split jurisdiction remains in place. Some family law matters are heard in the Superior Court, and others in the Ontario Court of Justice.

Small Claims Court

Small Claims Court hears civil cases that involve claims for money or the recovery or possession of property that is valued at no more than $25,000, exclusive of costs and interest. The procedural rules in this court are very simplified, which makes it possible for parties to commence and argue their cases without a lawyer or other legal representation. Licensed paralegals may provide representation in Small Claims Court.

All judges of the Superior Court are judges of the Small Claims Court. However, the *Courts of Justice Act*[3] provides that the senior judge in a region may appoint lawyers as **deputy judges** for a period of three years. In most

---

[3] R.S.O. 1990, c. C.34, s. 32.

regions, it is the deputy judges who sit in Small Claims Court, and not the judges of the Superior Court.

Ontario Court of Justice

Unlike the Superior Court, which has inherent jurisdiction to hear all cases, except those specifically required by statute to be held in another court, the Ontario Court of Justice is a "creature of statute" and, therefore, has a much more limited jurisdiction. For instance, judges of this court cannot decide cases involving equitable principles.

The provincial government appoints the judges of this court. They have jurisdiction to hear some criminal matters and provincial offences, and in regions where there is no specific Family Court branch of the Superior Court, they may also hear family law matters that do not involve divorce or division of matrimonial property.

Cases under the *Youth Criminal Justice Act* are heard in the Ontario Court of Justice. When people refer to "Youth Court", they are actually referring to a courtroom of the Ontario Court of Justice that deals with young people who have been charged with a criminal offence.

Similarly, "Traffic Court" and "Provincial Offences Court" are courtrooms of the Ontario Court of Justice in which proceedings dealing with offences charged under the *Highway Traffic Act* and other provincial statutes and municipal by-laws are heard.

THE ROLE OF COURTS

Courts play an essential role in the Canadian system of government. Certainly, one of their major functions is to resolve disputes, but they also interpret the law, deal with constitutional issues, and have a role in protecting the individual rights and freedoms of Canadians.

Courts and Dispute Resolution

Courts provide a **forum** for resolving disputes between individuals within our society. The dispute will be presented in a formal manner, in which the **litigants** follow prescribed procedural and evidentiary rules. The judge decides the case as a neutral, unbiased figure, after hearing the evidence and the legal submissions of the parties in dispute. The decision will be founded on accepted and established legal principles.

In the event that one or both of the parties are dissatisfied with the result of the court proceeding, they understand that they may be able to pursue their dispute to an **appellate court**. But once the appeal process, if there is one, is complete, there will be an outcome, and the dispute will be resolved, although not always to any party's liking.

Courts and Legislative Interpretation

Another role of the court is to interpret the terms of a statute or a regulation and how the law applies in a particular fact situation. As discussed in the explanation of the development of case law in another chapter, the drafting of statutes is an art that attempts to take into account all the contingencies and all the situations that are to be governed by that particular piece of legislation. This is not an easy task, and oftentimes there are issues that are unclear when a legal dispute arises. Often, the courts are called upon to determine what the legislation really means and how it applies in a specific case. This role of the courts is one of clarifying and finding a just application of the law.

Courts and Constitutional Questions

In much the same way as courts resolve disputes between individuals or between individuals and corporations, our courts resolve disputes between different governments within the Canadian federation. These disputes relate to the distribution of powers between the federal and provincial governments as prescribed by the *Constitution Act*. The Constitution sets out the authority of the federal government and the provinces to make law in specific areas. For example, the federal government has the constitutional authority to make criminal law. Neither the federal government nor the provincial governments have the power to make law in an area not provided by the Constitution.

In this role, the courts provide a check on legislators who may exceed their constitutional limits by passing a statute that is outside their power for making law. We say that a law that exceeds the constitutional power of a level of government is **ultra vires**. Further, where the constitution permits shared or **concurrent** powers at more than one level of government, the courts resolve the questions as to which government is constitutionally paramount, which legislation will prevail and which will be withdrawn.

Courts and Individual Rights and Freedoms

It is through the courts that Canadians have the power to defend their individual rights against the improper exercise of power by government, governmental bodies and agents. This role of the courts has taken on an enhanced importance in more than three decades since the enactment of the *Charter of Rights and Freedoms* and the codification of the former common law remedies for administrative law in the judicial review statutes.

Enforcing the Charter of Rights and Freedoms

It is sometimes said that the *Charter* is a shield, not a sword. What this means is that the *Charter* prescribes rights that an individual may use to defend himself or herself against interference or infringement of that right by the government.

We will discuss the *Charter* in more detail in another chapter in this text, but it is important to note that the Constitution gives the courts two remedial provisions if the court finds that the government has, in fact, infringed on an individual's *Charter* rights.

Section 52 of the *Constitution Act* permits the courts to declare a law that is inconsistent with the provisions of the Constitution to be "of no force and effect". The section of the *Criminal Code* dealing with therapeutic abortions, for example, is a law that the courts have ruled to be inoperative and unenforceable under this section of the Constitution. When the court finds a violation of the *Constitution Act*, or the *Charter*, we say that the court has "struck down" all or part of the offending statute, as the case may be.

Section 24 of the Charter permits an individual to apply to the courts where his rights have been infringed "to obtain such remedy as the court considers appropriate and just in the circumstances." That section has been used in numerous criminal cases to overturn convictions or to stay proceedings when police or the prosecution have violated the rights of an **accused**.

Judicial Review

In the area of administrative law, courts have the authority, on an application for judicial review, to re-examine the exercise of power by a government board, agency or commission. This means that an individual whose rights and privileges are affected by a decision of one of these bodies, or whose eligibility to receive, or continue to receive, a government benefit has been denied, may ask a court to rule whether the agency, board, or commission has properly exercised its power.

The court may grant relief to the individual by ordering the government to do what it is that it should have done, or not to do what it is proposing to do.[4] In this role, the courts apply what are known as the principles of natural justice to both the merits of the agency/board/commission decision and to the process it used to reach its decision.

THE ROLE OF THE JUDICIARY

An Independent Judiciary

Judges, or as they are referred to collectively, the judiciary, form the judicial branch of government. This branch plays an integral part in the justice system since, as we have noted, judges not only make law through the common law system, they also interpret the statute laws made by the legislative branches of government at the federal and provincial levels.

One of the chief characteristics of the judicial branch is that it is to operate independently of the other two governmental branches — the executive branch and the legislative branch — meaning that the judiciary does not answer to the other branches for any decision it makes. This approach is meant to preserve the right of Canadians to have their cases heard by an independent, unbiased court, a court that bases its decisions on the evidence put before it, not on an allegiance to a level of government or to a political party.

However, the fact that judges are not accountable to an elected body is a source of controversy in some circles. Since the entrenchment of the *Charter of Rights and Freedoms* in the Constitution, there are some who take the view that judges have, to a certain extent, usurped or taken over the role of the legislature in the making of law.

The Appointment of Judges

All judges in the Canadian legal system are appointed by one of the levels of government. The power to appoint judges is laid out in the *Constitution Act*. The federal government appoints judges to the Supreme Court of Canada, the Federal Court and the superior court of each of the provinces. This means that in Ontario, the federal government appoints all the judges of the Court of Appeal and the Superior Court of Justice. The provincial government appoints judges of the Ontario Court of Justice.

The actual process for the appointment of judges has, until relatively recent times, been shrouded in mystery. It was generally accepted, up until a couple of decades ago, that affiliation with and financial donation to a political party could result in a judicial appointment once that party came into power and formed the government. Of course, this process put into question the impartiality of judges and made critics of the system wonder about judges' independence.

In the late 1980s, the federal Minister of Justice created new rules and a new process for the appointment of superior court judges in the provinces. There is now an independent committee — made up of lawyers, judges and lay people — that oversees the appointments. Lawyers who have been members of the Bar for a minimum of 10 years may apply to the committee for a consideration for an appointment to the bench. All applications are reviewed, applicants are interviewed, and the committee applies specific criteria in assessing applicants' suitability as judges. The committee then makes recommendations to the minister, and the minister consults further with provincial representatives, judges and people in the community before any appointment takes place. This process has been established with the hope of

---

[4] See *Judicial Review Procedure Act*, R.S.O. 1990, c. J.1 and *Statutory Powers Procedure Act*, R.S.O. 1990, c. S.22.

finding the best candidates — i.e., those who properly reflect the communities they serve rather than the policies of a particular political party.

In Ontario, there is a similar process for the appointment of judges to the Ontario Court of Justice.

Since the advent of the new process, many women and members of various ethnic and cultural groups have been appointed. Slowly, very slowly, the bench is starting to include women and reflect the Canadian multicultural society.

Perhaps the most controversial appointment process involves the selection of the nine judges who sit on the Supreme Court of Canada. A vacancy on the court arises due to the death or retirement of a judge. At that point, the protocol for the selection of a new appointment to the court is put in place. Historically, the vast majority of justices of the Supreme Court have been appointed after serving as judges on the Court of Appeal of their home province; however, two relatively recent appointments have involved the selection of practising lawyers who have never before served as judges on any court.

A list of candidates is prepared subject to certain limitations. The list of possible candidates will be restricted, first, by geography. As we learned earlier in this chapter, by law three of the nine judges must be appointees who are members of the Bar of the province of Quebec. Also by tradition, three judges are from Ontario, two are from the western provinces, and one is from the Atlantic provinces. If an Ontario judge dies or retires, the list of potential appointees will be made up of only eligible members from Ontario.

It is the Governor General who makes the actual appointment of the Supreme Court judges, but the final selection is made by the prime minister in consultation with relevant people. Parliament does not need to approve the appointment. There are those who would argue that the appointment process for the Supreme Court needs revision to have more public input. For instance, in the United States, the Senate must ratify all potential presidential appointments to the U.S. Supreme Court. However, this model has resulted in much political disagreement and what some might argue is an overly detailed examination of the personal history of some candidates. As a result, in the eyes of many Canadians, the American process may not have much to recommend it.

Despite calls for changes to the appointment process in Canada, the court has made strides in presenting a more representative face to Canadians. The first woman justice was appointed in 1982: Madam Justice Bertha Wilson. Justice Wilson retired from the Court in 1991 and passed away in 2007. Since her appointment, a number of women have followed her onto the Court, including the present Chief Justice of the Court, The Right Honourable Beverley McLachlin.

Minorities are still not very well represented on the court, but part of that may change as more Aboriginal people and members of more recent immigrant communities are called to the bar and have an opportunity to establish the necessary credentials to be considered for an appointment to the Supreme Court.

Discipline and Discharge

Once appointed, judges are eligible to remain on the bench until the mandatory retirement age of 70 or 75, depending on the jurisdiction.

Judges are supervised in their roles by the chief justice or the senior judge in a region. Such supervision, however, is normally limited to the assignment of cases and other administrative functions related to court operation. The chief justices or senior judges do not discipline or discharge judges should a complaint arise about the conduct of a judge. Judges are permitted to hold office only during "good behaviour". Complaints that a judge has been deficient or neglectful or has otherwise engaged in inappropriate behaviour or misconduct must be heard by the Canadian Judicial Council if the judge has been federally appointed, and by the provincial judicial council if the appointment has been made by the province (e.g., the Ontario Judicial Council). The federal council is made up of the chief justice of the Supreme Court of Canada and the chief justices of each of the provinces and territories. Provincial judicial councils are made up primarily of judges and lawyers, but some do have members who represent the community at large. In Ontario, for example, a number of positions must be filled by non-lawyer members of the community.

These councils investigate all allegations and complaints made against judges, determine the validity of the complaint and, ultimately, make recommendations to the federal Minister of Justice or the provincial attorney general for disciplinary actions, including removal from the bench by Parliament or the provincial legislature, as the case may be.

COURT PROCEEDINGS

The process followed as a case wends its way through the court system is governed by procedural law. Each step in either a civil or criminal court case is prescribed by a set of rules that dictate the proper procedure to be followed in that court on that type of proceeding. For example, the criminal courts have their own set of rules, and there are separate rules for the Superior Court of Justice, the Small Claims Court, Family Court etc.

The civil law rules of the Superior Court of Justice are called the **Rules of Civil Procedure**. There are also separate rules for various levels of appeal courts. All of these rules are separate regulations to the *Courts of Justice Act*.

There are separate criminal law procedural rules for the Superior Court of Justice, but these rules are not regulations to the Ontario *Courts of Justice Act*. Criminal law can only be created by the federal Parliament, and the criminal law procedural rules for superior courts are a regulation to the *Criminal Code*.

In some areas of law, there are statutes that create procedure for that area. For instance, criminal procedure is found, primarily, in the procedural provisions of the *Criminal Code*, and the Rules of the Criminal Court, which are a regulation to the *Criminal Code*, add more detail to this procedure. Likewise, for provincial offences, procedure is found in the Ontario *Provincial Offences Act*, but there are also Rules of the Ontario Court of Justice in Provincial Offences, a regulation to the Ontario *Courts of Justice Act*.

These rules can be very complicated and may be studied in separate law courses that are specifically related to procedure. For instance, in a course on civil litigation, students would make a very close study of the Rules of Civil Procedure. We will offer only a very brief overview of the major steps in both civil and criminal proceedings. There are two types of civil actions in the Superior Court: an action and an application. The vast majority of cases are actions, not applications, so that is what we will discuss below in relation to civil proceedings.

Civil Proceedings

The Rules of Civil Procedure, used in the Superior Court of Justice, divide a civil lawsuit, or **action**, into four major segments: the pleadings, the pre-trial procedure, the trial and post-trial procedure. These rules govern cases where the claim is in excess of $25,000. Claims for $25,000 or less are heard in the Small Claims Court and governed by separate rules of that court.

Pleadings

In a civil court proceeding, the rules require the parties to exchange certain prescribed documents, setting out the details of the case and their positions on the issues. These documents are referred to collectively as **pleadings**.

The parties in a basic action are the plaintiff and the defendant. The plaintiff commences the court proceeding and seeks a particular remedy from the court. The defendant opposes the plaintiff's claim. In an action, there can be multiple plaintiffs and multiple defendants.

The lawyer for the plaintiff files a **statement of claim** with the clerk or registrar of the particular courthouse. The clerk then opens a court file, places a court seal on the original document, signs it on behalf of the registrar, and returns the original to the plaintiff, keeping a copy in the court file. This process is called **issuing**. Once the pleading has been issued, the court proceeding has been officially commenced.

The statement of claim must then be given to the defendant in a manner set out in the rules so that he can determine the nature of the claim being made against him. The process of giving the document to the other side is called service. Once the defendant has received a copy of the statement of claim in a manner prescribed by the rules, we say that service has been effected. The defendant then has a specified number of days to answer the claim, should he choose to do so. A defendant is not required to file any document in his defence, but if he elects not to do so, it is almost certain that the court will give the plaintiff the relief she is seeking and deliver a judgment against the defendant.

Should the defendant choose to offer a defence to the claim, the pleading he must serve on the plaintiff and file with the court is known as a **statement of defence**. If the defendant delivers the statement of defence within the required time period, then the plaintiff may deliver a reply to any issues the defendant has raised in the statement of defence. Once a reply has been delivered, pleadings — for purposes of this illustration — have been completed, and the action moves on the pre-trial stage.

Pre-trial Procedure

The primary purpose of this stage of proceedings is to permit each party to gather from the other all the available information and evidence to be presented. In this way, they may assess the strength of their own case and determine whether or not a **settlement** of the case, without trial, is possible. The two major steps in pre-trial procedure are discovery and pre-trial conference.

In discovery, the parties may seek disclosure of all the documents that the other is relying upon to support his or her case, and they may also cross-examine the other party, under oath, outside the courtroom. Television and movies sometimes present cases that involve the witness being hit with a major surprise during the trial. This may make for a very exciting television show or film, but it doesn't have much to do with real court practice. In real courts, it is not productive to spend time taking a case all the way to trial when there is information available that, if disclosed to the other party, may result in the case being settled with less time and expense for everyone involved.

If the parties have not been able to arrive at settlement after discovery, the action will be placed on the list for trial. It will not be called for trial, however, until there has been a pre-trial conference. This is an informal meeting of the parties, their lawyers and a judge. The purpose of the conference is to have the judge assist the parties in reaching a possible settlement and, where that is not possible, to narrow the issues for trial. In narrowing the issues, the judge will have the parties focus only on the matters over which there is a real issue. Many facts and legal points in any court case may not be contentious. The parties may agree on these points and will only need to take court time to present the fundamental issues on which they cannot agree.

After the pre-trial conference, if the case is not settled, it will be assigned a trial date.

Trial

The parties must each arrange to have their witnesses served with a sub-poena or a summons requiring them to appear in court to give evidence.

The plaintiff and her witnesses present their side of the case first. Each witness will be **examined in chief** by the plaintiff's lawyer. Then the defendant's lawyer will have an opportunity to **cross-examine** those witnesses.

At the conclusion of the plaintiff's case, the defendant's counsel will then call his witnesses and examine them in chief. The plaintiff's counsel will then cross-examine them. All of the evidence is taken down through a court reporting process, which may involve a live court reporter in the courtroom or the use of tape-recording devices.

Then counsel for both parties will present their final arguments in a last attempt to persuade the judge[5] to accept their witnesses' version of the facts rather than the version of the witnesses for the opposing party. Final argument also involves counsel for each party presenting the points of law that support their client's position. The lawyers will then refer the judge to any supporting case law or statutes that may assist him or her in the decision-making process.

The judge will then decide the case. In some instances, the decision will be delivered orally shortly after the conclusion of the final argument, and the judge may or may not provide reasons or an explanation for the judgment. In other cases, the judge will **reserve judgment** and provide written reasons and the decision at a later date.

The judgment may find for the plaintiff for all or part of his claim, or dismiss the action in favour of the defendant. The judgment may also include an award for **costs**.

In most instances, costs are awarded to the successful party in the action. The unsuccessful party is ordered to pay a portion of the successful party's legal expenses. These costs are awarded on scales that are established and set out in the rules or appendices. The most often applied scale for costs will pay only from a third to a half of the winning party's actual costs, so the winning party will still be significantly out of pocket for a major portion of the expenses related to the litigation.

Occasionally, the higher scale for costs may be used; but even then, the costs awarded usually do not compensate them for the true costs involved in taking the matter to trial.

Post-trial Procedure

In the event that the plaintiff is awarded a money judgment at trial, the judgment is only as good as her ability to enforce it against the defendant and obtain the money. Civil proceedings include a process for enforcing a judgment.

Once the plaintiff has been successful in the action and has been awarded the payment of money, she can now be referred to as the **judgment creditor**.

---

[5] For brevity, this overview does not include a discussion of civil juries.

The judgment creditor has a number of options available if the defendant does not voluntarily pay the money owed under the judgment. The defendant may now be referred to as the **judgment debtor.**

First of all, she can obtain a **writ of seizure and sale** from the court office. This document can then be filed with the sheriff's office. When the document is filed, the debtor is essentially prohibited from selling his assets or disposing of his property. The writ of seizure and sale acts as a lien against his property.

The plaintiff can direct the sheriff to execute the writ and seize and sell the judgment debtor's property or, if she is unclear what property the debtor actually owns for her to seize, she may conduct an **examination in aid of execution.** The judgment debtor will be required to provide sworn evidence about his finances and his property.

The judgment creditor may also rely on a **garnishment**, which provides another avenue of enforcement. A notice of garnishment is obtained from the court office and delivered to any source of income or holdings of the debtor that can be liquidated: that is, converted to money. Upon receipt of the Notice of Garnishment, the source must withhold from the debtor the amount specified in the notice. In this way, the judgment creditor may take a portion of the debtor's wages or salary, a portion of his investments and bank accounts, and any receivables that are payable to him, until the judgment debt is satisfied.

Criminal Proceedings

The term "criminal proceedings" applies to court cases in which a person has been charged with a criminal offence. Most criminal offences are contained in the *Criminal Code.* However, there are other federal statutes that contain criminal law, such as the *Controlled Drugs and Substances Act* and the *Youth Criminal Justice Act.* These are Acts passed by the Parliament of Canada. Under the *Constitution Act*, only the federal government has the authority or jurisdiction to make criminal law.

The provincial governments may, however, create offences under provincial statutes (e.g., speeding or drinking under age). These offences are not criminal in nature, and a conviction for a provincial offence does not ever result in a criminal record. Offences of this nature are usually referred to as provincial offences.

In Canadian law, crimes are dealt with as wrongs against society as a whole, not simply as a wrong against a particular victim. The court procedure is called a prosecution and is normally brought by government lawyers referred to as **Crown prosecutors** or **Crown attorneys**. The person charged with the offence is referred to as the **accused.**

Process

There are several categories of criminal offence in Canadian law. The most serious criminal offences are referred to as **indictable offences.** They are prosecuted in a very formal and complex manner and carry the gravest penalties or sentences. Murder is an example of an indictable offence.

More minor offences under the *Criminal Code* are categorized as **summary conviction offences.** The word "summary" in this case means quick and simple, and the procedure for prosecuting this type of offence is much more condensed and less complicated than the procedure for prosecuting indictable offences. Summary offences carry relatively light penalties. The maximum general punishment for summary offences is a fine of not more than $5,000 and/or a jail term of up to six months.

In addition, there is a category of offence that is neither a summary offence nor an indictable offence. Offences of this type are referred to as hybrid offences and may be prosecuted as either a summary or indictable offence at the preference of the prosecutor. The prosecutor would make this decision based on factors such as the circumstances surrounding the offence and the accused's prior criminal record.

The police lay most criminal charges, although there is provision for an individual to lay a **charge** against another individual. This is called a private prosecution in that it is not a prosecution by the government. When the person is charged with an offence, either by the police or in a private prosecution, he or she is being accused of committing a criminal act. The formal accusation is contained in a formal court document called an **Information**. An Information must be sworn before a **justice of the peace** or a judge, who must be satisfied that there are reasonable and probable grounds for laying the charge.

It is quite likely that the police will arrest the accused if he is being charged with an indictable criminal offence. An arrest involves the police taking the accused person into custody. However, if a person is charged with a less serious summary offence, he or she is not to be arrested unless there is a very good reason for doing so. Instead, the police officer may give an **appearance notice** to the accused, requiring him or her to attend court at a particular time on a specified date in order to answer the charge against him or her. An appearance notice is usually given to the accused when the police officer arrives on the scene and finds the accused at the scene of a less serious criminal offence. If the officer uses an appearance notice, he or she must then lay the Information later.

Another way to bring the accused before the court without an arrest is to lay the Information first before the justice and ask the justice to issue a **summons** to the accused. The summons is a formal order directing the accused to appear in court. The police would use this process when they need time to investigate the situation before charging someone and when, therefore, giving an appearance notice at the scene of the crime would not be appropriate.

An accused who has been arrested may or may not be held in custody until the trial date. Shortly after the arrest, there will be a bail hearing to determine if the accused can be released while awaiting trial. The decision to grant bail will be based on the potential danger to the community and the likelihood that the accused will actually appear for trial if released.

Pre-trial Procedure

If the accused pleads not guilty to the offence, the case will be set for trial. However, before the trial date can be set, there are a number of steps that must be completed. These steps vary according to whether or not the accused has been charged with a summary offence or with an indictable offence.

Summary conviction offences are always tried in the Ontario Court of Justice without a jury. Most indictable offences may be tried either in the Ontario Court or in the Superior Court by a judge alone, or in the Superior Court by a judge and jury. The accused has the right to elect the level of court that he or she wishes to be tried in and, if the Superior Court is chosen, to choose whether the trial will take place before a jury. For hybrid offences, the Crown must first elect whether the matter will proceed summarily or by indictment. Once that choice has been made, the case will proceed in the same manner as a purely summary or indictable offence.

Before trial, the accused is entitled to disclosure from the Crown. In the disclosure process, the prosecution is required to advise the accused of all the evidence in the possession of the police that the Crown intends to present at the trial. This gives the accused and his counsel the opportunity to fully understand the nature of the case against the accused and allows for the preparation of any defence that may be available.

In addition, the case may be "pre-tried" before a trial date is set. A conference will be set up involving the Crown, the counsel for the defence, and a judge. A pre-trial is often used for plea negotiations. It is also used to determine which facts are not in dispute, to narrow trial issues and to assess the time that will be required for trial.

If the accused elects to be tried in the Superior Court of Justice, a **preliminary hearing** will normally be conducted. At the preliminary hearing, the Crown is required to present sufficient evidence to a judge of the Ontario Court of Justice in order to satisfy the judge that there is enough evidence against the accused to necessitate a trial. The defence is not required to present any part of its case, but counsel for the accused has an early opportunity to cross-examine some of the witnesses for the Crown. It is rare for a judge to find that there is not enough evidence to continue the prosecution and proceed to trial. However, a preliminary hearing can be invaluable to the defence in testing the Crown witnesses and in obtaining a picture of the strengths and weaknesses in the prosecution's case.

Trial

In a criminal trial, the Crown presents its case first, and must prove the guilt of the accused beyond a reasonable doubt. Witnesses will be called and examined, in chief, by the Crown prosecutor. The lawyer for the accused will then have an opportunity to cross-examine the Crown's witnesses.

When the Crown has presented all its evidence, then the defence may present its case. Since the accused has a constitutional right to be presumed innocent until proven guilty beyond a reasonable doubt, the accused need not call any evidence at all. At the end of the Crown's case, the defence may take the position that the Crown has not met its burden of proof to prove all the elements of the offence charged, beyond a reasonable doubt, and may ask the trial judge to acquit the accused without the defendant presenting any evidence or any defence. This is called a **directed verdict**.

However, in most cases, the Crown will have presented enough evidence to warrant the accused presenting a defence. If a defence is presented, the Crown will have an opportunity to cross-examine the defence witnesses after the accused's counsel has examined them in chief.

Once each side has concluded its case, the prosecutor and the defence counsel present legal argument. If the case is being heard by a judge and jury, it is the role of the jury to determine which version of the facts it believes. The jury is sometimes referred to as the trier of fact. In a trial by jury, the judge must then instruct the jury on the law and how members of the jury are to apply it. This is called the **charge to the jury**. In a trial by judge alone, it is the judge who determines which version of the facts is more credible.

The accused must be acquitted if there is a reasonable doubt as to guilt. If no reasonable doubt is found, the accused will be convicted, and the judge will impose a sentence. The sentence or the range of sentence for each offence can be found in the *Criminal Code*. If there is a range of sentence, which is the case with most offences, the judge will determine which option is the most appropriate for the offender given the circumstances of the offence, the likelihood of rehabilitation, the need to deter both this particular accused and members of the public who may be tempted to commit a similar offence, and a number of other factors.

In Canadian law, both the accused and the Crown may appeal the decision in a criminal matter. The level of court that hears the appeal will be determined by the level of court that made the decision being appealed.

ADMINISTRATIVE TRIBUNALS

In addition to the court system, there is another major area in which legal disputes are addressed. Governments regulate a great deal of activity under the statute laws that they create. Many of these statutes establish tribunals to administer disputes between the government and private citizens in relation to the application and interpretation of specific regulations. It is the responsibility of these tribunals to resolve complaints and determine remedies for various issues that arise. The Labour Relations Board, the Ontario Human Rights Tribunal and the Workplace Safety and Insurance Board are all examples of provincial agencies that have statutorily created tribunals to resolve disputes. The Immigration and Refugee Board, the RCMP Public Complaints Commission and the National Parole Board are examples of federal administrative tribunals.

Administrative tribunals operate within an area of law called, not surprisingly, administrative law. Certain legal principles must be applied by the tribunals in arriving at their decisions. These principles and rules seek to enforce a standard of fairness. For instance, the tribunal must be unbiased, and the person who will be affected by the tribunal's decision must have an opportunity to be heard.

Usually, if a statute creates an administrative tribunal to deal with a certain issue, a court will not have jurisdiction to deal with the dispute. The role of the courts in relation to administrative tribunals is only to determine that the tribunal decision-making process has been made in accordance with the principles of administrative law.

Administrative tribunals are sometimes referred to as quasi-judicial bodies. That means that although they are less formal than courts, they follow a pattern in their process and procedure similar to that of courts. Tribunals each establish their own forms or pleadings and their own practices. Depending on the statute that creates a tribunal, parties may be able to represent themselves at a hearing, or may be represented by a lawyer or a paralegal.

ALTERNATIVES TO THE COURT SYSTEM

In light of the cost of court proceedings, and the backlog of cases in the court system, more parties and their lawyers are looking for speedier, less adversarial and less costly methods of resolving disputes. As a result, many are relying on approaches to resolving legal conflicts that do not centre on the court system. These methods are collectively referred to as alternate dispute resolution, or ADR.

Alternate dispute resolution has long been used in labour disputes between management and unions. Many business contracts contain provisions for alternate dispute resolution, and it has taken hold in commercial matters. More recently, ADR approaches are also being used in family law and in general disputes involving individuals and between individuals and businesses.

The following comprise the major methods of alternate dispute resolution.

Negotiation

Negotiation is a voluntary process that may be either formal or informal. There is no third person who attempts to resolve the dispute; the parties themselves meet to identify issues of concern, explore options for the resolution of the issues, and search for a mutually acceptable agreement to resolve the issues raised. Lawyers may represent the disputing parties. Any resolution of the dispute is as a result of the parties' agreement between themselves to be bound by the decision that they make together.

Mediation

Mediation is a process where a neutral third person, called a mediator, helps the parties try to resolve the dispute. The parties have the opportunity to describe the issues, discuss their interests, understandings and feelings, provide each other with information, and explore ideas for the resolution of the dispute. The mediator acts as a facilitator assisting the parties in communicating and negotiating more effectively, thereby enhancing their ability to reach a settlement. Parties are not required to come to agreement. The mediator does not have the power to make a decision for the parties but can help the parties find a resolution that is mutually acceptable. The only people who can resolve the dispute in mediation are the parties themselves.

Conciliation

Conciliation and mediation are very much alike in that a neutral third person is involved in attempting to have the parties reach their own resolution to the dispute. There is no universally held view as to what the differences are between mediation and conciliation, but many ADR practitioners in Canada believe that in the process of mediation, the parties meet face-to-face, while in conciliation, each meets only with the conciliator. The conciliator acts as the go-between.

Arbitration

Arbitration is the method of ADR that most resembles a court proceeding. A neutral third person, an arbitrator, is appointed and paid by the parties to make a decision on the dispute. Normally the parties agree that they will be bound by whatever decision is made, although the agreement setting up the arbitration process may provide that the decision may be appealed to a court. The parties also determine the manner in which the issues are presented to the arbitrator. They may decide to present their issues through a formal hearing process, or they may agree to have the arbitrator base the decision on written submissions.

Diversion

This method of ADR is used most often in criminal matters. Diversion removes from the formal criminal justice process people charged with less serious offences who do not have long criminal records. To be eligible for diversion, the accused must admit responsibility for his or her offences and agree to participate in alternative measures programs. This usually entails having to perform acts of contrition or redress, such as writing an essay, writing a letter of apology to the victim, performing community service work, providing restitution or compensation, or making a charitable donation.

Initially, diversion was available only for young persons charged with a criminal offence. Now, however, diversion is more widely available to adults, although it is most often used in Aboriginal communities or in minority communities. The concept involves giving a minor offender the opportunity to take constructive action to remedy the situation that led him to the court system without imposing a conviction and a criminal record.

CHAPTER SUMMARY

This chapter described the constitutional framework for court administration, in which the responsibility for running the courts and appointing judges is split between the provinces and the federal government. The structure and the hierarchy of the courts in the Ontario system were also described.

The reader was introduced to various roles of the court in resolving disputes, interpreting legislation, resolving constitutional disputes, and protecting the rights of individuals. The procedure for appointing judges was introduced, as was the role of the judiciary as a branch of government.

A brief overview of both civil and criminal court proceedings was presented.

Finally, the specialized forums for resolving disputes outside the court system were described. The creation of administrative tribunals was noted as an auxiliary system for dispute resolution related to regulatory government policies and programs. Further, methods of alternate dispute resolution or ADR were surveyed and defined.

GLOSSARY OF NEW TERMS AND KEY CONCEPTS

accused	The person charged with an offence, and the respondent in court as the party opposed to the Crown.
action	A civil proceeding that is not an application and that includes a proceeding commenced by a claim, notice of action, or statement of claim.
adversarial system	A system by which disputes between opposing parties are resolved.
appeal	A review of a decision made at one level in the judicial process by one or more judges at a higher level.
appearance notice	A form in criminal proceedings that requires that an accused appear in court on a specific date to answer charges against him.
appellate court	A court that exercises jurisdiction to hear appeals.
charge	An accused is charged with a criminal offence when a document called an information is sworn before a justice of the peace, alleging that there are reasonable and probable grounds to believe the accused has committed a specifically named criminal offence.
charge to the jury	The jury is the trier of fact but, before jury members enter deliberations, at the conclusion of the case, the judge will instruct them on the necessary law in relation to determining the facts.
concurrent	In constitutional terms, where two or more governments have jurisdiction over the same subject matter.
costs	The allowable fees and disbursements related to the proceedings in an action, usually awarded to the successful party at trial.
cross-examine	The opposite side's examination of a witness following examination-in-chief, used to weaken the effect of that witness's testimony, discredit the witness and elicit favourable evidence for the cross-examining party.
Crown Prosecutor or Crown Attorney	In Canada, the federal government and each of the provincial governments is called the Crown; in criminal proceedings, it is the term used to describe the government as prosecutor.
deputy judge	In Ontario, a barrister and solicitor may be appointed for a three-year term to sit in Small Claims Court as the presiding judge.
directed verdict	When the Crown has been unable to meet the onus to prove all the elements of a criminal offence, at the end of the presentation of the Crown's case the defence has no need to call a defence at all and will ask the court to find the accused not guilty.
examination in aid of execution	In the Rules of Procedure in Ontario, a successful party in an action may question or examine the unsuccessful party to determine the unsuccessful party's ability to pay a judgment and/or an order for costs.
examined in chief	When a witness is questioned in a trial by the counsel who summonsed that witness.
federally appointed judges	Judges appointed by the federal government.
forum	The place where legal remedies can be sought, usually a court.

garnishment

A proceeding whereby a judgment creditor may give notice to a third party that monies owing by that party to the judgment debtor must be paid to the relevant sheriff's office to the credit of the judgment creditor.

indictable offence

A criminal offence that is triable by indictment; the more serious category of criminal offences: equivalent to the American felony.

Information

The legal document, sworn before a justice of the peace, that alleges that the accused has committed a specific offence. It is the document that formally commences all criminal prosecutions.

issuing

The process by which the court office essentially verifies the start of the civil court proceeding by placing a court seal on some documents, which the registrar signs, and then opens a court file.

judgment creditor

The successful party who in an action is owed money by the unsuccessful party, and thereby becomes a creditor for that judgment money.

judgment debtor

The party who owes money as the result of a judgment, and who is subject to certain collection proceedings.

justice of the peace

A judicial official with jurisdiction over minor criminal offences and the initiation of a legal process (e.g., swearing an Information).

leave of the court

Some steps in a court proceeding cannot be taken automatically. Permission from the court must first be obtained.

litigants

The parties to the court proceeding.

pleadings

The documents in a civil lawsuit that set out the factual and legal matters at issue in the case, and that the rules require the parties to exchange prior to the court hearing.

preliminary hearing

A hearing conducted by a provincial judge to determine whether there is sufficient evidence to commit an accused for trial, in relation to an indictable offence charge.

provincial courts

Courts that a provincial legislature establishes and maintains to administer justice in the province, under section 92(14) of the *Constitution Act*.

provincially appointed judges

Judges appointed by the provincial government.

reserve judgment

The judge does not give judgment immediately at the end of a trial but, rather, takes time to consider the matter and write reasons for judgment.

Rules of Civil Procedure

The rules in civil proceedings contained in the relevant regulation passed under the *Courts of Justice Act* for the conduct of civil cases; in criminal proceedings, these are those rules formulated under the authority of the *Criminal Code* for the conduct of criminal prosecutions.

settlement

An agreement by the parties in dispute that resolves the dispute.

statement of claim

The originating process (document) that commences an action and documents the facts relied upon in support of the plaintiff's claim and the remedy or relief sought.

statement of defence

A brief written statement by the defendant that responds to the allegations in a statement of claim.

summary conviction offence

The less serious criminal offences: equivalent to the American misdemeanour.

summons

A legal document, issued by the court, that requires a person to appear in criminal court or suffer certain legal consequences.

ultra vires

Latin, meaning "beyond the powers"; a statute that is determined by the courts to be outside the powers assigned by the Constitution to the legislature that enacted it.

writ of seizure and sale

A document that a judgment creditor obtains from the court office as evidence of an unpaid judgment, and delivers to one or more sheriff's offices in order to enforce the judgment.

REVIEW QUESTIONS

1. What type of cases are heard by the Supreme Court of Canada? *[handwritten: constitutional issues, conflicting decisions from dief. Prov. C. New interpretations of law, serious criminal cases]*

2. Our court system establishes a hierarchy of courts. Name and describe the three major court levels in Ontario.

3. Describe three roles of the courts in our legal system. *[handwritten: interpret law, resolve disputes, protect rights and freedoms]*

4. If a person wishes to sue another in Ontario for non-payment of a loan of $20,000, to which court must the action be brought? *[handwritten: Small claims branch of Superior court]*

5. What have been some of the challenges facing family law court matters in Ontario?

6. What is the role of diversion in the criminal court system?

7. In what circumstances in a criminal proceeding would a preliminary hearing be held?

8. In what sense does the creation of administrative tribunals unclog the court system in Ontario? *[handwritten: Helps to avoid trials.]*

9. What is the primary distinction between arbitration and mediation? *[handwritten: Mediation resolves dispute, arbitration makes decison for dispute]*

10. What legislation dictates the procedure in a court hearing?

11. What do we mean when we say that the judiciary in Canada is independent? *[handwritten: does not answer to executive & legislative branch for any decisions it makes]*

DISCUSSION QUESTIONS

1. Some say that judges are to interpret the law, not to make law. However, from time to time, the Supreme Court of Canada will make findings that do change the law. One example is the case of *Schater v. the Queen*. In this case, the Court found that a federal statute was unconstitutional because it discriminated in the administration of a benefit program. The program was the Unemployment Insurance Program (now called the Employment Insurance Program). The Court was afraid that if it relied on section 52 of the *Charter*, its only remedy was to make the entire statute "of no force and effect". That would basically kill the whole program, cutting millions of unemployed people from benefits, until Parliament could get around to amending the law, which would take some time. So, instead, the Court ordered that the law be read so as to include a segment of the population that it appeared to exclude, and make that segment eligible for those benefits. What is your view? Is the Court making law?

2. Do you think that judges in Canada should be elected rather than appointed? What are the particular advantages or disadvantages to appointment instead of election?

3. What public interest may there be in trying to resolve court cases before they go to trial?

4. Should we have television cameras in our trial courtrooms in Canada?

5. Where an accused person is acquitted after a trial, should the Crown be ordered to compensate the accused in whole or in part for the costs of his defence?

6. Is voluntary mediation likely to be any more successful than mandatory mediation, in which the rules of the court require that the parties hire an independent mediator to attempt to resolve their dispute before they can set a trial date?

SUGGESTED READING AND OTHER RESOURCES

Boyd, Neil. *Canadian Law, an Introduction*, 5th ed. (Toronto: Nelson Education, 2011).

Gulycz, Michael, & Mary Ann Kelly. *Criminal Law for Legal Professionals* (Toronto: Emond Montgomery Publications, 2013).

Olivo, Laurence, & Mary Ann Kelly. *Civil Litigation*, 3d ed. (Toronto: Emond Montgomery Publications, 2013).

Willes, John A. *Contemporary Canadian Business Law, Principles and Cases*, 10th ed. (Toronto: McGraw-Hill Ryerson, 2012).

WEBSITES

Canadian Judicial Council, CJC Resource Centre: <http://www.cjc-ccm.gc.ca/english/resource_en.asp?selMenu=resource_courtsystem_en.asp>

Ontario Courts: <http://www.ontariocourts.ca/>

The Legal Profession in Ontario

Laurence M. Olivo
SENECA COLLEGE

Learning Objectives

After reading this chapter, the reader should be able to:

➢ recognize social, economic, and legal forces that are causing change in the way legal services are offered

➢ know how lawyers are trained

➢ know how lawyers are accredited for specialization

➢ be aware of the general standards of ethics for the legal profession

➢ be aware of the methods used to control lawyers' professional behaviour

➢ understand the role of the legal aid plan and how it operates

➢ appreciate the nature of the lawyer–client relationship, and know the principal responsibilities of both parties in the relationship

➢ understand the roles of the law clerk and the paralegal in the legal services market

➢ know the differences between law clerks and paralegals

➢ be aware of how law clerks and paralegals are trained and regulated

➢ be aware of current changes and developments for law clerks and paralegal-occupational groups

TABLE OF CONTENTS

INTRODUCTION

At one time, the term "legal professional" was used simply to describe lawyers, implying that these were the only legal workers that needed to be described. But much has changed. The legal profession now also includes licensed paralegals who appear as advocates in the lower courts, and this branch of the legal profession will be discussed later in this chapter. We also examine law clerks and court administration staff as specialized legal occupational groups. We will note how these groups have evolved and changed due to economic, attitudinal, and social changes in the society at large.

THE LEGAL PROFESSION — LAWYERS

We begin our examination of lawyers as a professional group by noting major changes as this professional group has evolved over the last century.

The Law Office in 1900 and Today — Changes and Trends

The law is often described as a conservative enterprise, one that is resistant to change. While some things have not changed in 100 years, if one walked into a law office today, there would be some significant differences from what one would have found in Canada in 1900.

Size

Most lawyers in 1900 were sole practitioners, or had a handful of associates or partners. Even established firms in large urban centres would not have had much more than a dozen lawyers. The focus of a legal practice would have been local, with services being provided for local populations.

Today, the size and structure of firms has changed. Elite, establishment firms providing legal services for wealthy individuals and corporations often have hundreds of lawyers on staff, although many of them will be younger associates (employees), rather than partners in the firm. Among the larger firms there has been a trend towards amalgamation so that there are fewer large firms than formerly; but the newly amalgamated firms are quite large indeed, and are sometimes referred to as **mega-firms.** Of these, many will in turn be connected by alliance to other firms in other provinces or countries. Some of these firms have also established branch operations outside their province or country of origin. This is a great departure from former custom, where law firms, even large ones, were local in nature, offering services within one province only. However, the organized Bar is, in fact, structured along provincial lines in Canada. Thus, to be admitted to the Bar in Ontario, for example, does not automatically give a lawyer the right to practise in other provinces or countries. The lawyer must still meet the requirements for practice in other jurisdictions, making the organization of interprovincial firms difficult.

There have been changes in the rules for lawyers who practise in more than one jurisdiction. The Federation of Law Societies of Canada has developed new rules for lawyers who are licensed to practise in one province but also practise occasionally or often in another province. When a lawyer is doing occasional work in a province other than her home province, she will continue to be governed by her home province's law society without having to make formal arrangements with the law society in the other province. On the other hand, if a lawyer is working full-time or continually in a province where he is not a member of the Bar, under the new rules, that lawyer will only have to acknowledge that he has familiarized himself with areas of law that are different from those in his home province, using materials provided by the law society of the province where he wishes to practise. He may then be licensed to practise in that province.[1]

In 2013, the mobility between different common law provinces was extended to Quebec when Ontario and Quebec each agreed to extend mobility rights to each other's lawyers, even though Quebec is a civil law jurisdiction that was previously thought to be too different from common law jurisdictions to permit this kind of recollection, but that is apparently no longer the case.

Lawyers licensed outside of Ontario in a foreign jurisdiction may apply for a licence to provide legal service and advice with respect to the law of a foreign jurisdiction while resident in Ontario. They do not necessarily have to be lawyers licensed in Ontario but must be licensed in their home jurisdiction.[2] In general, the loosening of provincial rules to allow lawyers from outside of Ontario to offer legal services in Ontario is a response to the process of globalization of trade in goods and services that has been ongoing since the 1990s.

Whether an interprovincial firm or not, what would have been a large firm in 1900 (over 20 lawyers) would now be classed as a medium-size firm. Today, medium-size firms in large centres are often quite specialized in what they do (these are sometimes referred to as "law boutiques"), usually operating in Toronto or another large city, or the medium size firm is of the traditional type, or offering full services to small-business clients and the general public. Such firms are often found in smaller cities, providing a full range of services.

Firms with fewer than 20 members would, particularly in urban areas, be classed as small firms. Small firms are the ones that have changed the least: they tend to serve non-elite clients (small businesses and ordinary citizens), and offer a general range of legal services. They are more likely to be found outside the downtown core of major cities, in suburban areas or in the out-lying parts of the province.

Some of the trends towards boutique firms, increased specialization, more internationalization of legal services may be changing the way law firms are organized. The collapse of the Toronto mega-firm Heenan Blaikie in 2014 may have reflected the difficulty large firms have in competing with more efficient and specialized law firms. Notably, other mega firms are no longer growing at the same rate as formerly, and some have shrunk in size.[3]

Demographic Makeup

In 1900, the law was the almost-exclusive preserve of white males of the established Anglo-Celtic or Francophone Quebec ethnic groups. There were few practitioners of "other" ethnic or visible minority origin. There were also a mere handful of women practitioners.

Beginning in the 1950s, however, the demographics began to change. With changes in educational policy following World War II, which made post-secondary education and law school more accessible, a growing number of those of non-British and non-French background began entering the legal

---

[1] The Law Society of Upper Canada, By-Law 4, ss. 9(1) and (2), as amended, January 2011. There are now three classes of lawyer licence: private practitioners, those employed by the Crown, and those who are members of the bars of other provinces who appear occasionally in Ontario. There is also now a licence for paralegals, as a separate branch of the legal profession.

[2] *Law Society Act*, By-Law 14.

[3] Heenan Blaikie was not about to collapse financially, but a number of key lawyers apparently saw a better future elsewhere and left. The collapse has been the subject of considerable comment in legal circles. See <http://www.theglobeandmail.com/report-on-business/industry-news/the-law-page/heenan-blaikie-death-of-a-law-firm/article16759901/?page=all>.

profession. In the early 1970s, the number of women in the profession began to increase as the women's movement helped to redefine occupational choices for women and to insist on rights of access to educational and economic opportunities. At the same time, visible minorities in the legal profession began to increase in numbers, reflecting greater access to educational post-secondary institutions and the increasing proportion of some visible minorities in the general population.

The changes in the ethnic and gender makeup of the legal profession have caused lawyers and their professional governing bodies to examine the experiences of women and minorities in the profession, as there is some evidence of **systemic discrimination**, which may or may not be intentional, within the profession. A number of explanations have been advanced for this pattern — chief among them is the notion that the way in which law has been practised, with long hours, is not compatible with major parenting responsibilities assumed disproportionately in Canada by women, whether they have a career or not.[4] There is also some evidence that suggests that "other" ethnics tend to be proportionately under-represented in large firms serving elite clients. The Law Society of Upper Canada has been in the process of examining accessibility issues within the profession, as have other bodies governing the legal profession in other provinces. It is reasonable to expect that these issues will continue to be of concern for some time to come.

Training

While legal education today is often seen as a theoretical, academic enterprise, training in 1900 was practical. Upon graduation from high school, a student in many parts of Canada could become a lawyer by becoming an **articling clerk** or an apprentice in a law office, "learning the law" from a qualified lawyer. At the end of several years of articling, apprentice lawyers would take the Bar exams and, if successful, would be **called to the bar** and become a full-fledged lawyer, ready to set up on their own. In many respects, this form of training resembled the training programs for skilled tradespersons, such as plumbers or cabinetmakers.

Over time, the program gradually acquired a more academic component. In Ontario, students articled by day and took formal legal subjects at night. No university degree was required prior to commencing legal training, but many students did complete a university course of study before entering formal legal training.

The governing bodies of the profession still saw the training program as one for acquiring practical skills through "hands-on" techniques and played down an academic and analytic approach to legal training.[5] Eventually, those who favoured a more academic approach to law won out. Now, students must complete at least two years of university prior to applying for entry to one of the Canadian law schools offering a three-year law degree, where law and legal reasoning are studied in an academic and theoretical way. There is little

---

[4] The phenomenon of women's not advancing in their profession because of assumptions that they will not have the time or resources to focus on professional life is sometimes referred to as "the glass ceiling".

[5] In Ontario in the late 1940s, the debate between advocates of the academic versus trade-school approach to legal education led to a revolt by the academically inclined teachers at Osgoode Hall Law School (then run directly by the Law Society on a "trade-school" model). Led by Cecil Wright and Bora Laskin, the academically inclined teaching staff resigned from Osgoode Hall and trooped up University Avenue to the University of Toronto, where they established the Faculty of Law at the University of Toronto, Canada's first academic law school. The rebels had tried and failed to persuade the Law Society to modernize its educational system, and went to the University of Toronto only when no option was left. For a highly readable account of these events, see C.I. Kyer & Jerome E. Bickenbach, *The Fiercest Debate* (Toronto: The Osgoode Society, 1987).

practical training in law at law school, although there is pressure now from the legal profession for law schools to offer more.

Upon successful completion of law school, a student must serve as an articling clerk with a practising lawyer for 10 months. Recently, the number of law school graduates appears to have outpaced the number of articling positions made available by law firms. To remedy this situation, the Law Society may permit part-time articling and give credit for legal work done in other jurisdictions, provided applicants can meet the Law Society's requirements. The Law Society, after much contentious discussion, has created an alternative to traditional articling, with online courses and practical text materials, coupled with a short, unpaid internship to gain some practical experience. It is still too early to see how this will pan out: Will there be law firms prepared to take on and supervise unpaid interns? Will the program be perceived as a useful innovation or a second rate form of articling? During or following the articling period, the student must also complete the Bar admission course requirement. Students have some leeway in scheduling when, and in what order, they article and take the Bar exam. The Bar admission course has become a self-paced and self-directed course with exams.

After being called to the bar, lawyers in active practice are required to engage in continuing professional development by attending professional development programs or taking online professional development courses accredited by the Law Society, and by engaging in other forms of professional development and training. This is to ensure that lawyers, once called to the bar, keep their professional knowledge and skills up-to-date. By contrast, in 1900 there were few opportunities to take continuing education subjects, and lawyers were supposed to keep up with changes in the law as best they could.

Specialization

In 1900, all lawyers were trained as "general practitioners", with an assumption that any lawyer could and would provide a whole range of general legal services. While some lawyers had areas of expertise and could be said to specialize in certain areas of law, there was no certification process or formal recognition of specialization among lawyers that would allow the public to identify a specialist.

The situation has changed since 1900. As the law has grown more complex, there has been increasing specialization; in Ontario, this has been recognized by allowing lawyers with specialized practices to apply for certification as specialists and to advertise their specialty to the public. There is still no formal educational process for training specialists, and, on call to the bar, all lawyers have been trained only as generalists, as was the case in 1900.

The situation for lawyers is also mirrored by office staff. In 1900, the other staff would have consisted of a secretary or clerk, often male. Today, a law office is much more likely to have other staff besides a secretary, with the degree of specialization of staff increasing as the size of the law firm increases. In addition to secretaries, one is likely to find law clerks or paralegals, investigators, patent agents, accounting staff, computer systems staff, and law office managers. Some of these staff run the business end of the law firm, while others perform various professional tasks that need not be performed by lawyers and can be performed under a lawyer's supervision.

Marketing

The idea of marketing and advertising a law firm was unknown in 1900. Indeed, lawyers, as professionals, were forbidden to advertise and market themselves in a formal way until the 1980s, when the rules of professional conduct were relaxed to permit "tasteful" advertising. This was seen to benefit smaller firms seeking to tap into the mass market. Large firms with elite clients were thought not to need to advertise, as they marketed themselves discreetly and informally. However, even large firms now do some marketing, often in the form of "newsletters" to clients, advising them on changes and developments in law that affect them. Specialist and boutique firms also advertise their services to other firms to solicit referrals for their specialized services.

Today there are relatively few limits on marketing techniques. In particular, firms that offer legal services to the general public in areas like family law, personal injury, or estate law may advertise in a variety of media and locate offices where they are easily found, such as large shopping malls. As well, rare is the law practice that does not have a website.

Organization of Law Practices

The forms of business organization used by law practices in 1900 were either one lawyer practising as a sole practitioner, perhaps with an employed lawyer as an associate, or several lawyers owning the firm together as partners. The partnership might also employ some lawyers as associates. Lawyers were not permitted to run their businesses as limited liability corporations. The Law Society required lawyers to remain personally liable for professional negligence and defaults. Thus, they could not shelter personal assets by setting up a corporation to insulate themselves from personal liability.

With the growth of firm size and with firms operating in more than one province or country in the 1990s, the Law Society decided to permit lawyers to have limited liability partnerships, thus allowing the law practice to have some of the protections and business efficiencies conferred by the corporate form of business organization. However, lawyers are still held personally liable for negligence arising from the practice of law, even if the firm is a limited liability partnership. A firm using this form of business organization is required[6] to have the letters "LLP" after the firm name.

Also, the Law Society now permits lawyers to form partnerships with other professionals, such as accountants, in order to offer a broader range of services. However, lawyer-partners are required to have control of the firm and to ensure that non-legal professionals do not breach the Law Society's Rules of Professional Conduct.[7]

The Law Society permits firms to incorporate as professional corporations, with the lawyer owners taking shares in the company rather than partnership interests. A corporate form of ownership is considered to be attractive to small firms for tax purposes in some instances.[8] Lawyers will, however, still be personally liable for their own negligence. As well, the lawyers must own all of the shares of the professional corporation. But this may change. In England, as of 2013, it will be possible for outside investors to buy shares in law practices that are incorporated. The reason given in England for this change was to allow for an infusion of outside capital into law firms to make

---

[6] The Law Society of Upper Canada, By-Law 7, as amended, April 2009.

[7] Currently there are some signs that the trend towards larger firms may be changing. This is partly due to high overheads and perceived inefficiencies in these firms, coupled to a trend by large clients to question more closely the high fees these firms are perceived to charge. Large clients, using in-house counsel are better able to demand lower costs. In addition, there has been a trend for specialist lawyers in large firms to break off and start up small, specialized boutique practices, focusing on providing services in a particular area of law with fewer staff. Some work is even outsourced to various subcontractors, including subcontractors for support staff; some subcontracted legal work, such as documentary evidence review formerly done by junior lawyers, is now being sent to lawyers in other common law jurisdictions, such as India, where fees are much lower. Apparently professionals can, like North American industrial workers, experience the effects of globalization.

[8] M. Fitz-James, "Convert Your Law Firm Interest into Corporate Securities" *Law Times* (29 April 2002). Also see, the Ontario *Business Corporations Act*, R.S.O. 1990, c. B.16, s. 3.2.

them more efficient and the cost of their services less expensive for the public, thereby increasing access to legal service and the courts and solve the growing problem of unrepresented litigants in the courts. It is too soon to tell whether this change will indeed make the courts and legal services more accessible. While this kind of change has been discussed in Ontario and in other provinces, there has been little positive response from the Law Society of Upper Canada, at least so far.

Characteristics of the Profession

So far we have been describing how the legal profession and the provision of legal services have changed during this century.

We now turn to a more detailed examination of lawyers as a professional occupational group by examining the characteristics of professionals generally. As we will see later, many of these observations about lawyers as a profession also apply to paralegals.

A profession has the following characteristics:

- A *systematic theory* or *body of knowledge* that is difficult to learn and over which the professional claims a monopoly.

- *Authoritative use of the body of knowledge over which the professional claims a monopoly.* Because the professional has a monopoly over a body of knowledge, the claim is made that the professional is the only one who has authority to use that professional knowledge, as no one else is equipped to do it or to even determine if a professional is using the knowledge properly.

- *Societal approval of the use of the body of knowledge.* Where professionals have persuaded the rest of us that they are the only ones who should be authorized to use a body of knowledge, then the profession has established itself and its monopoly. At this point, the rest of us cease to control what the professional does, and we leave it to the professionals to control themselves.

- *Ethical codes* are important characteristics of professional groups. Because the members of the group have a monopoly over what they do, the rest of us do not have sufficient knowledge to police their activities and prevent them from abusing the power that comes with a monopoly over knowledge. A solution to this has been to permit professionals to form organizations to govern themselves, and to require them to adhere to rules of professional conduct that determine what kind of behaviour is or is not permitted. Many of the regulations contained in these types of ethical codes prohibit and punish behaviour by professionals that would barely raise an eyebrow if the prohibited acts were done by others. For example, a sexual relationship between an employee and customer does not usually attract punishment by co-workers in the same trade, or prevent the employee from ever working in that field again. However, if a doctor has such a relationship with a patient, it is likely to lead to disciplinary actions from the professional regulatory body, possibly with the doctor's licence and right to practise medicine being revoked.

Governance of the Legal Profession

The Law Society — Governance in Whose Interest?

As noted earlier, the legal profession is organized on a provincial, rather than national, basis, reflecting its local origins. This is further reflected in the way in which lawyers, as a professional body, govern themselves. Each province and territory has the right to govern the legal profession within its territorial jurisdiction, and each has, by statute, turned that right over to the profession by allowing it to establish and operate an organization to govern the profession. These organizations, called "law societies", are distinguished from voluntary associations, such as the Canadian Bar Association; the voluntary organizations have no power to regulate the legal profession. The law society, on the other hand,

- determines who can become a lawyer or a paralegal,
- determines educational requirements that must be met to become a lawyer or a paralegal,
- determines admission requirements, and
- disciplines lawyers and paralegals with sanctions up to and including removal from the profession by **disbarment** and revocation of the professional licence.

In the ensuing discussion of how law societies work, the actual example used will be the Law Society of Upper Canada, the governing body of the legal profession in Ontario.

It should be apparent that the Law Society is a very powerful body. It is given its monopoly of control over the legal profession on the assumption that it will act in the public interest, particularly when the public interest and the interest of lawyers as a profession clash.

The governing body of the Law Society is called the **convocation**. It is composed of individual **benchers**, the majority of whom are elected by members of the legal profession itself. The position of bencher is not salaried. Consequently, there is an over-representation of established lawyers from larger firms, whose firms can afford to have them devote considerable time to serving on Law Society committees and otherwise carrying out their duties. Starting in the 1980s, attempts were made to broaden the representative nature of the convocation by ensuring that a certain portion of bencher positions were reserved for lawyers practising outside Toronto. Under paralegal licensing provisions, there are two paralegal benchers elected by paralegals (compared to 40 lawyer benchers). Significantly, public representation is limited to a small number of "lay benchers" (i.e., non-lawyers) who are appointed by the attorney general. One may wonder whether the public interest is represented by this arrangement for choosing the governors of the Law Society or whether the arrangement has more in common with the governance of a private club.

Entry to the Profession — Legal Education

An individual who wishes to become a lawyer must first complete at least two years of a university degree as a prerequisite for applying to law school. Most applicants, however, will have a BA degree prior to making application. Law schools consider applicants on the basis of their academic grade-point averages, together with their scores on a standardized test called the LSAT (Law School Admission Test). Many law schools give no weight to letters of reference, instead relying completely on a formula based on grade-point average and LSAT scores. There are some exceptions: mature students who may lack formal educational requirements may still be admitted. In addition, some law schools have educational-equity policies that purport to keep places available for minorities who are under-represented in the legal profession.

Once admitted to a law school, the law student undergoes three years of instruction leading to a bachelor of laws degree (LLB), or what is now more common, a Juris Doctor (JD). During this period, the student is taught legal rules and principles in an indirect way. Rather than learning rules by rote through lectures and reading, students learn legal principles by reading case law and extracting the rule from the reasoning of the judge in the case. For example, in a contracts course, the students will learn the basic rules governing contract law from reading contract cases. In this way, students learn techniques of legal reasoning and analysis, not just a collection of legal rules (sometimes called "black-letter" law). This method of learning law is very similar to the approach used by judges and lawyers to resolve legal problems through the application of the doctrine of precedent in the common law legal system. This approach, called the case-study method, was pioneered in the United States in the 19th century at Harvard Law School. It did not become a common teaching technique in Canada until after World War II.

With the case-study method as the dominant method of instruction for three years, students are expected to learn enough about the art of legal reasoning to make tolerably good appellate judges. However, there have been criticisms from the profession that the graduates do not have enough practical skills to function as lawyers. Ontario has responded to this criticism in two ways. First, law schools have introduced more clinical programs, where students can work for a term with a practitioner or in a law clinic under a professor's supervision. Second, the Law Society requires and supervises further practical legal education by requiring students to complete one year of articles and to pass Bar admission exams focused on practice skills. And once admitted to the Bar, lawyers are expected to engage in continuing professional development.

Currently, the Law Society is in the process of getting out of the business of educating law students. Instead, students may have the option of taking distance-learning courses prior to taking the Bar exam, or they may take the Bar exam directly after articling. It appears that the Law Society is attempting to shift away from direct responsibility for legal education prior to the call to the bar, expecting the law schools to take up the responsibility for providing practical training. In this writer's view, this is a vain hope. Since the end of World War II, the university-based law schools have been resisting attempts by law societies to get them to do more than approach law as an intellectual exercise. The law schools show minimal signs that they will take responsibility for producing competent practitioners, so the Law Society is likely to be left with the responsibility for practical legal training for the foreseeable future. Furthermore, Canadian law schools show little inclination to offer a law school program on a part-time basis or in the evenings, as is the case in the United States. This creates a significant barrier to becoming a lawyer for students with limited economic resources. As well, the number of seats in Canadian law schools is limited. One result has been that a number of schools in the United Kingdom and Australia have been offering law school studies geared to Canadian students. However, graduates of these schools will have to complete additional certification requirements that graduates of Canadian common law law schools do not have to meet.

Students who have completed law school and have been awarded an LLB or JD degree must decide in which province they wish to be admitted to the Bar. In Ontario, the Law Society recognizes an LLB from any of the law schools in Canada where the common law system is the basis for instruction. Then the students must complete the articling requirement, bar admission course, and testing requirements. Having cleared these last hurdles, the student of law is called to the bar as a **barrister and solicitor**.[9] Once called to the bar, the lawyer may practise in any area of law but will have to meet continuing professional development requirements set by the Law Society.

---

[9] The term "barrister and solicitor" is borrowed from English legal practice. However, in England, unlike Canada, one is either "barrister" or "solicitor", not both. In England, there are two separate and distinct professions. A

Maintenance of Professional Standards —
Specialization and Certification

As noted in the preceding section, once a lawyer has been called to the bar, he or she is loosed upon the public to practise in all areas of law, without further evaluations of competence except in a narrow range of circumstances. However, the Law Society, as well as voluntary organizations such as the Canadian Bar Association, run continuing education programs that many practitioners use in order to keep abreast of changes in the law to meet their continuing professional development requirements, and to specialize. Although the Law Society requires members to participate in continuing education programs or activities, there is no proposal currently to test members or to evaluate them. Further, members are expected to voluntarily report their activities, including "self-conducted" continuing education. However, lawyers who do not engage in activity where they practise or use their professional skills may be required to undertake activities to requalify themselves before being allowed to return to practice.

For those lawyers who wish to specialize in a particular area of law, there is a process for becoming certified as a specialist in an area of law, with the right to advertise that fact to the general public. The certification process requires the applicant to have practised in a particular area of law for a reasonable period of time, to take continuing-education courses in the area, and to undergo a **peer review**. There is, however, no requirement that an applicant for certification work under the supervision of a certified specialist or pass examinations, as there is for medical specialists.

Discipline and Ethical Standards

As a self-governing profession, lawyers claim to have the knowledge to decide when a fellow lawyer has fallen below the standards of appropriate professional behaviour, whether it has to do with incompetence or misbehaviour. When a lawyer has been found to have fallen below professional standards, the Law Society also claims the right to remedy the situation. It does so in three ways. First, it can discipline or punish the lawyer for misbehaviour by taking away a lawyer's right to practise, suspending the lawyer from practice, or requiring the lawyer to practise under conditions imposed by the Law Society. Second, the Law Society can compensate clients for incompetent work through its malpractice insurance fund. Third, it can repay part of a client's loss due to a lawyer's dishonesty through a compensation fund, which is separate from the malpractice insurance fund.

The discipline process begins with a complaint about a lawyer's conduct, either by a member of the public or by another lawyer. The Law Society requires a lawyer who is the subject of a complaint to respond to the complaint. If the response is not satisfactory, or if it is otherwise warranted, the Law Society can carry out further investigations. If misconduct has occurred, the Law Society can charge the lawyer with either of two offences:

---

barrister is an advocate who argues cases in courts; a solicitor deals with all other legal matters we think of as being part of a lawyer's business, except arguing cases in courts. Recently, this split in the English Bar has begun to change, as solicitors have been given the right to argue cases in courts in England. In Ontario and the rest of Canada, we have a unitary Bar — this means that there are no restrictions on the areas in which a lawyer may practise. In Ontario, one is simply a lawyer and is admitted to the legal profession. What is confusing is that we have hung on to English terms that describe forms of professional organization that have not existed in Ontario for more than a century. Now that paralegals are licensed by the Law Society in Ontario, by-laws and the rules of conduct often refer to "licencees" when they affect both lawyers and paralegals.

- **Professional misconduct:** Into this category fall wrongful acts by a lawyer while acting in a lawyer-like capacity. Examples include failing to perform an undertaking given to another lawyer, failing to keep a client's business confidential, and stealing a client's money. Some offences are professional offences only, but some, like stealing a client's money, are criminal acts as well. Interestingly, there are few misconduct proceedings based on mere incompetence. Penalties for professional misconduct range from a reprimand to suspension from practice, to disbarment.

- **Conduct unbecoming to a barrister and solicitor:** This refers to wrongful acts by a lawyer acting outside of her professional capacity that would bring the legal profession into disrepute. An example would include a lawyer who defrauded someone in a non-law-related business transaction, where the victim was led to trust the lawyer because of her professional standing. Penalties are as indicated for professional misconduct.

Any profession that claims to be independent and self-governing must establish publicly accepted high standards of conduct, and enforce those standards rigorously in order to keep its credibility with the public. Specific professional standards of conduct that must be met are set out in Rules of Professional Conduct.[10] (See Exhibit 10.1 for Ontario's Rules of Professional Conduct for lawyers.) The rules prescribe courses of conduct lawyers are expected to follow in certain situations, and describe forms of conduct that are prohibited. In addition, there are also general requirements of integrity and competence to which the practitioner is expected to adhere. There is some variation in ethical rules from province to province.

In addition to the rules of conduct administered by law societies, the Canadian Bar Association, a voluntary association, also has its own code of ethics. The difference between the CBA code of ethics and the rules of professional conduct of the law societies is that the law societies' rules are binding, while the CBA codes are not. There are other differences in the actual rules as well.

Legal Aid

Before the 1960s, in most provinces, a client wishing to retain a lawyer was free to do so, provided he or she could pay for the lawyer's services. There were some exceptions, particularly in serious criminal cases where the death penalty was a possibility, where the court would appoint counsel, at no charge, to serve a client. In other cases, where there was perceived to be a crying need for justice, a lawyer might serve a deserving client *pro bono publico* and charge no fee because the issue before the court was important. However, for most civil lawsuits and less serious criminal matters, a client could either pay a lawyer or represent herself.

Lawyers often say that "a lawyer who represents himself has a fool for a client." The truth behind this is that even a skilled lawyer will have difficulty exercising his judgment coolly, objectively, and dispassionately when the lawyer is personally involved in the case. One might well ask how a layperson, not trained in the law and lacking dispassionate judgment about her own situation, will do when arguing her own case? The answer is that except in minor and simple matters, the skilled help of a lawyer is necessary if justice is to be done.

[10] The Law Society of Upper Canada, *Rules of Professional Conduct*, July 2011, as amended. Other law societies have similar sets of rules. The Canadian Bar Association (CBA) has a code of ethics that is similar in content to the Law Society's rules of professional conduct. However, the CBA code of ethics is not enforceable and consists of mere guidelines. The CBA is a voluntary association of lawyers and has no power over the profession.

EXHIBIT 10.1

Rules of Professional Conduct for Lawyers, The Law Society of Upper Canada
EFFECTIVE OCTOBER 2014

The title of each rule with brief comments is set out below. They have been extensively amended, effective October 2014, to implement the Federation of Law Societies of Canada's *Federal Model Code of Professional Conduct*. A review of the rules will identify the concerns professional bodies have about their members' behaviour. The rules now generally refer to licencees when they refer to rules affecting both lawyers and licensed paralegals.

CHAPTER 1: CITATION AND INTERPRETATION

This rule defines various terms including "conduct unbecoming a barrister and solicitor", "professional misconduct", "independent legal advice", and "limited scope retainer". Some of these terms had not previously been precisely defined. Commentary is provided to aid in interpretation of key terms. As there are now two branches of the legal profession, the generic term "licencee" is used to describe "legal practitioners" who may be either paralegals or lawyers licensed in Ontario. In some circumstances, legal practitioner will include a lawyer who is a member of the bar of another province. The definition of client is broadened to include those who reasonably may think they are clients even where there is no formal retainer.

CHAPTER 2: INTEGRITY

This chapter provides a basic description of the honesty and trustworthiness required of a legal practitioner. In brief, a lawyer must act honourably and with integrity towards clients, opponents, tribunals, and the public and uphold the standards of the profession. In particular, a lawyer is expected to recognize French language rights and the diversity of Ontario's population.

CHAPTER 3: RELATIONSHIP TO CLIENTS

3.1 COMPETENCE: It is now defined with some specificity, and reflects the Law Society's concern that a lawyer have all-around competence in those areas where he or she offers services to the public. Generally, lawyers should not take on work they are not competent to do. It is not expected that generalists or junior lawyers or, even, specialists will be able to provide competent service in every area of law. Lawyers who give business advice should clearly distinguish it from legal advice given to a client. This is particularly important in a multi-disciplinary practice (a firm composed of lawyers and accountants, for example) where a client may assume a lawyer may be able to give more than legal advice.

3.2 QUALITY OF SERVICE: There is a definition of what constitutes quality of service requirements. A lawyer is expected to be honest and objective in his or her advice, and should encourage compromise and settlement where possible; a lawyer should not threaten criminal proceedings in courts or in regulatory tribunals in order to obtain an advantage in civil litigation and, in particular, to collect a debt. A lawyer is obliged to not knowingly assist a client in any dishonesty or crime, or instruct the client on how to violate the law. This includes meeting the requirements of the criminal law to report large cash receipts from clients in order to prevent money laundering by those involved in organized crime. In addition, a lawyer must verify a client's identity and understand the objectives of the retainer. To do this a lawyer may be expected to investigate the background of the client and the matter or transaction for which the lawyer is retained. This is particularly important if the lawyer has any suspicion about the client or the matter for which the lawyer is retained. In particular, fraudulent real estate transactions are singled out for special attention and the rule has identified "Red Flags in Real Estate Transactions" that a lawyer is expected to be on guard for. A lawyer shall not use his or her trust account for any purpose not related to providing legal services. Generally, lawyers are expected to meet very high standards for maintaining vigilance to see that the lawyer is on guard so as not to be a dupe of a client engaged in dishonest or illegal conduct. In this respect, a lawyer may be neither reckless nor willfully blind. Where a lawyer has a personal, intimate or sexual relationship with a client, the lawyer must be especially careful to ensure that he or she can deal objectively and dispassionately with the client's business prior to taking on a retainer. If the client proposes a limited scope retainer where the lawyer is only doing some of the legal work involved, with the client taking responsibility for the rest, the lawyer should fully and frankly discuss and outline what work the lawyer will actually be doing. The lawyer will also advise candidly as to whether such a retainer is advisable and shall be particularly careful in advising clients under disability with respect to limited scope retainers. If a client suffers from a disability that affects decision making, the lawyer shall treat the client as much as possible as he or she would a client in a normal lawyer–client relationship. If a lawyer receives a medical legal report that the doctor has asked not be shown to the client, the report must be returned to the doctor, unless the lawyer has instructions to receive the report on those terms. However, if a report contains information that might cause harm to the client, the lawyer shall attempt to persuade the client not to read the report, and if the client insists, he or she should be persuaded to receive the report at the doctor's office, where its contents can be explained and medical advice given. In real estate transactions, a lawyer should advise the client of the availability of title insurance to protect the client's interest in the property; however, the lawyer should explain that this is one option, and it is not a substitute for the lawyer diligently investigating the title and advising the client. If acting for a large organization, a lawyer who becomes aware of wrongdoing or criminal conduct has a duty to "report up" to the person who instructs him or her, and if that person does not respond, to report to progressively higher officials. In the end, if no responsible employee of the organization acts, the lawyer should withdraw his or her services.

3.3 CONFIDENTIALITY: A lawyer owes a duty of confidentiality to every client, even after the relationship ends, unless disclosure is authorized by law or required by a court, or where the lawyer believes there is imminent risk of harm to others by the client. A lawyer may also make disclosure to defend himself or herself or his or her employees in criminal or civil proceedings. Where a lawyer has a corporate client, and becomes aware of wrongdoing within the corporation, he or she is obliged to draw it to the attention of senior officers of the corporation or members of the board. In the wake of the passage of federal legislation on money laundering, the rule has been amended to require lawyers to keep detailed records when receiving large amounts of cash from a client, and to disclose those records to authorities under certain conditions, notwithstanding that such reporting would otherwise violate confidentiality requirements. A lawyer may disclose confidential information in order to obtain legal advice about a proposed course of conduct.

3.4 AVOIDANCE OF CONFLICT OF INTEREST: A lawyer must avoid any involvement in any activity that would likely affect the lawyer's judgment or loyalty to a client, and there is now a specific prohibition against acting where there is a conflict. This includes situations where there is now substantial risk of material adverse impact on a client. Specifically, a lawyer can only act for one side in a dispute, unless the client, adequately informed, agrees to the lawyer continuing to act. A lawyer may not act against a former client unless the matter is completely unconnected to the former matter. A lawyer's partner or associate may act in a new matter against a former client, where confidential information relevant to the former client is in issue, provided the former client consents and that measures are take to ensure that no disclosure of the confidential information takes place. Where a lawyer is retained by several clients, he or she must ensure there is no conflict between them, and if a conflict arises, he or she must withdraw from representing them. A lawyer may no longer act for a lender and borrower at the same time, except in a narrow range of situations (amount below $50,000 or the lender is a financial institution, or relatives or friends who are not at arm's length). In a real estate transaction, the transferor and transferee must be represented by different lawyers, although the lawyers may be in the same firm, provided they observe general conflict rules. Lawyers who prepare wills for spouses who have a shared and common intention about disposing of their property are jointly retained by both spouses; if one spouse later gives new instructions, that is a new retainer and the lawyer may not notify the other spouse of the request, but must also decline the retainer because it creates a potential conflict of interest. Lawyers who act for corporations and organizations must keep in mind that the interest of the organization or corporation may be different from that of those who direct and control it, and that the organization or corporation is the client that the lawyer is to serve if there is a conflict. The same duty applies if the lawyer is a director of an organization or corporation. There may be an obligation to report wrongdoing of corporate and organizational officers in this context. Where a lawyer is affiliated with others who are not lawyers in offering legal services, as in a multi-disciplinary practice, the lawyer must clearly disclose to clients possible loss of solicitor–client privilege due to (i) involvement of non-lawyers working with the lawyer, and (ii) any financial arrangement between the lawyer and affiliated entity that may affect the lawyer's professional judgment.

EXHIBIT 10.1 (continued)

**Rules of Professional Conduct for Lawyers,
The Law Society of Upper Canada**

EFFECTIVE OCTOBER 2014

After making disclosure to the client on all aspects of the affiliation, the lawyer must obtain the client's explicit consent to accept the retainer. The lawyer must also have a system to search for conflict of interest of the affiliation. The lawyer shall take all steps to ensure that non-lawyers in a multi-disciplinary practice observe confidentiality. Generally all law firms are required to have systems set up to prevent disclosure of confidential information. To prevent mortgage fraud, a lawyer is obliged to assure himself or herself of the identity of a client and to take special care when acting on behalf of a borrower and a lender. The Law Society now requires that lawyers and paralegals take specific steps to verify a new client's identity. In certain limited circumstances, a lawyer may act for the transferor and transferee of real property: for examples, when the parties are related, or when the lawyer is providing service in a remote location where there are no other lawyers.

3.4-17–3.4-26   CONFLICTS FROM TRANSFER BETWEEN LAW FIRMS: When a lawyer leaves a firm that acted for a client, and moves to a firm that is acting against that client, and the transferring lawyer possesses actual knowledge of matters harmful to the client, the firm to which the lawyer has transferred shall cease to act in a matter in which the client's interests may be harmed unless the client consents. This rule also applies to transferring employees, in that lawyers are expected to exercise due diligence and make inquiries of new employees to ensure the rule is not violated. Where a law firm is a multi-jurisdiction firm, it is treated as if it is one firm for the purpose of this rule. The rule also applies to transfers to and from corporations, as in-house counsel, and to transfers involving government departments as transferring firm or transferee firm.

3.4-37–3.4-41   DOING BUSINESS WITH A CLIENT: A lawyer who enters into business transactions with clients put himself or herself in a conflict of interest situation. The lawyer is obliged to disclose and explain the potential conflict, must require independent legal representation in the transaction, and recommend that the client receive independent legal advice. If the client wishes the lawyer to continue to act, then the lawyer must obtain the client's written consent. A lawyer shall not borrow from a client, unless the client is a lending institution or a related person. A lawyer shall not invest in mortgages from which the client is borrowing or lending money, subject to some exceptions. Nor shall a lawyer give a guarantee on a loan transaction where the client is a borrower or lender. Lawyers who draft wills in which they are to be retained as counsel to estate trustee must inform the trustee that this arrangement is not binding. Nor are lawyers permitted to draft wills in which they receive bequests or intersts, unless they are family members. Lawyers are now limited in their right to act as surety or to put up bail for a client being considered for judicial interim release on pending criminal charges.

3.5   PRESERVATION OF CLIENT'S PROPERTY: A lawyer shall care for a client's property in a careful and prudent manner and observe all relevant rules in safeguarding the client's property and interests in property.

3.6   FEES AND DISBURSEMENTS: Fees shall be reasonable, and interest on overdue accounts shall be in accordance with the *Solicitors Act*. The lawyer shall not acquire an interest in the subject matter of litigation. Contingency fees may now be charged except in criminal and family law matters. Any contingency agreement must be clear as to how the fee is calculated, and indicate that it may be reviewed by the court. In rendering accounts the lawyer shall separate fees from disbursements, and shall divide fees fairly when acting for several clients. A lawyer who refers a matter to another lawyer or paralegal may accept a referral fee if it is reasonable and the client consents. A paralegal may also refer a matter to a lawyer and accept a referral fee. Where a client consents, fees may be divided between licencees in different firms, provided the fee is divided in proportion to the work done by each licencee. Lawyers shall not split fees with non-licencees or pay a referral fee to anyone who is not a licencee. However, in multi-disciplinary firms, lawyers may split fees with non-licencees in the firm, or share with non-licencees the general revenue and cash flow of a multi-disciplinary firm. If a lawyer's account is assessed by the court and he or she is ordered to return fees and disbursements to the client, this must be done promptly.

3.7   WITHDRAWAL FROM REPRESENTATION: A lawyer may not withdraw services except where there is a serious loss of confidence between the parties, the lawyer cannot obtain instructions, or the client has not paid fees. The lawyer must give the client reasonable notice. In a criminal matter, and in some other situations, the right to withdraw may be subject to court review and supervision. A lawyer must withdraw if fired by the client, if told by the client to do something that conflicts with the lawyer's duty as officer of the court, if the client is engaged in dishonesty in the proceeding, or if the lawyer is not competent to handle the matter. On withdrawal, the lawyer is responsible for minimizing hardship to the client. This includes returning all client property, providing the client with necessary information, accounting for all funds, promptly rendering an account, and co-operating with the lawyer the client retains. When giving reasons to a court for withdrawing, the lawyer must not breach the obligation to the client to maintain confidentiality.

CHAPTER 4: THE PRACTICE OF LAW

4.1   MAKING LEGAL SERVICES AVAILABLE: A lawyer shall make services available to the public in an effective and convenient way; a lawyer may decline to take on a particular client, but the right to do so should be exercised prudently.

4.2 and *4.3*   MARKETING and ADVERTISING: This is permitted if it is "tasteful" and does not compare rates charged by other firms. Fees may be advertised but the advertisement shall contain an accurate statement of amounts, including disbursements and taxes, and service at that price must be made available to all clients. A lawyer may advertise that he or she is a certified specialist if that is true, and a lawyer may advertise that he or she restricts the practice of law to specific areas of law. If the firm is multi-disciplinary (containing accountants, for example) that fact may be advertised. Offering professional services may be done by any means in a reasonable way that does not exploit or take advantage of clients who are vulnerable due to traumatic events that affect their physical or mental state.

CHAPTER 5: RELATIONSHIP TO THE ADMINISTRATION OF JUSTICE

5.1   THE LAWYER AS ADVOCATE: Generally, the lawyer shall resolutely defend the client's interest, but shall not permit the client to mislead the court or engage in dishonest conduct in connection with the proceeding; nor shall the lawyer behave discourteously to opponents, witnesses, or the court. Nor shall a lawyer appear in court while under the influence of alcohol or drugs. In civil matters, the lawyer shall ensure that the client makes full disclosure on discovery, and that errors and omissions are corrected, and that undertakings to provide information are honoured. The lawyer shall act prudently in arranging and negotiating a plea bargain with a prosecutor in a criminal matter. The lawyer shall scrupulously honour all undertakings given to a party or to the court.

5.2   THE LAWYER AS WITNESS: A lawyer who is appearing as advocate shall not submit his own affidavit in evidence or give oral evidence unless otherwise required by law to do so or the evidence is of a non-controversial nature.

5.3   INTERVIEWING WITNESSES: A lawyer may interview anyone as a witness; however, a lawyer must not approach a person represented by another lawyer or a corporation where there is in-house counsel, except by going through the lawyer for the person or corporation, or where a client is seeking a second opinion of a lawyer or paralegal.

5.4   COMMUNICATING WITH WITNESSES GIVING EVIDENCE: A lawyer may not engage in conversations with a witness, particularly one favourable to his or her cause, where the conversation might influence or direct the witness as to what evidence the witness should give. This rule now specifically identifies the circumstances where a lawyer may or may not discuss a witness's evidence. The rule distinguishes between talking to "friendly" and opposing witnesses, and is generally designed to prevent a lawyer from tampering with a witness's evidence. When there is any doubt, a lawyer wishing to speak to a witness should get the consent of opposing counsel or of the court.

5.5   RELATIONS WITH JURORS: A lawyer shall not communicate with anyone he or she knows to be a member of a jury panel.

5.6   THE LAWYER AND THE ADMINISTRATION OF JUSTICE: The lawyer shall encourage public respect for the administration of justice.

5.7 LAWYERS AS MEDIATORS: A lawyer who acts as a mediator shall tell participants that he or she is not acting in his or her capacity as a lawyer, and that the mediation is not protected by solicitor–client privilege.

CHAPTER 6: RELATIONSHIP TO STUDENTS, EMPLOYEES AND OTHERS

6.1 SUPERVISION: The lawyer is responsible for ensuring that diskettes used to access the provincial online land registration system are kept secure and that the lawyer supervises the use of diskettes assigned to non-lawyer employees, and in general assumes complete responsibility for all work on the file. A lawyer shall not permit a non-lawyer to advise a client on title insurance, and a lawyer must take full responsibility for electronically signing documents.

6.2 STUDENTS: Lawyers shall observe procedures of the Law Society in recruiting students, and provide them with a meaningful articling experience. A student shall carry out in good faith all duties required by the articling principal. The lawyer is responsible for actions of students acting under his or her direction.

6.3 SEXUAL HARASSMENT: Lawyers shall not harass colleagues, staff, students, clients or any other person.

6.3.1 DISCRIMINATION: Lawyers have special responsibility not to discriminate in providing services and offering employment. A detailed commentary sets out the grounds for discrimination. There is a further provision imposing requirements on lawyers to take steps to ensure that there is no discrimination in employment within a firm, with a particular focus on accommodation of disabilities.

CHAPTER 7: RELATIONSHIP TO THE SOCIETY AND OTHER LAWYERS

7.1 RESPONSIBILITY TO THE PROFESSION GENERALLY: The lawyer shall conduct himself with integrity, and promptly meet financial obligations, including financial obligations incurred on behalf of clients. The lawyer has a duty to report misconduct by other lawyers, including criminal charges, and encourage clients who have claims against dishonest lawyers to report the claims. This duty also requires reporting a licencee in other circumstances, including mental disability that appears likely to harm a client's interests.

7.2 RESPONSIBILITY TO LAWYERS AND OTHERS: A lawyer is responsible for behaving with courtesy and good faith in his or her professional dealings, and is not to engage in sharp practice. In particular, the lawyer shall not record a conversation with another lawyer, or a client, without giving notice of the intention to do so. If a lawyer receives an inadvertent communication not intended for him or her, he or she must notify the sender. A lawyer shall not communicate with a represented person unless that person's legal representative consents. However, a lawyer may communicate with a person who is represented on a limited scope retainer, unless the lawyer so retained has identified matters or issues on which the opposing lawyer must communicate with the lawyer retained on a limited scope retainer. A lawyer must also clarify his or her role when dealing with an unrepresented person and, in particular, make clear that he or she cannot offer advice to the unrepresented litigant. A lawyer, who is not otherwise interested in a matter, may give a second opinion if retained to do so by the client's legal representative. The rule has been refined to indicate certain persons within an organization or entity, such as a corporation, with whom an opposing lawyer may not communicate. It, therefore, follows that other persons within the organization may be approached. The rule tries to strike a balance between protecting privileged information and requiring an entity to produce relevant information.

7.3 OUTSIDE INTERESTS AND THE PRACTICE OF LAW: A lawyer who engages in another business besides his or her law practice shall not allow participation in the other business to jeopardize professional integrity.

7.4 THE LAWYER IN PUBLIC OFFICE: A lawyer in public office shall carry out official duties adhering to standards as high as those that govern him or her professionally. Where a lawyer or an associate is a member of a public body, the lawyer shall not appear before that body unless its

---

**Rules of Professional Conduct for Lawyers,
The Law Society of Upper Canada**
EFFECTIVE OCTOBER 2014

EXHIBIT 10.1 (continued)

rules permit. When a lawyer leaves public office, he or she shall not act for a client in any matter for which the lawyer has responsibility before leaving public office.

7.5 PUBLIC APPEARANCES AND PUBLIC STATEMENTS: A lawyer is free to make public statements subject to obligations to clients, the profession and the courts. In particular, the lawyer shall not make statements about a matter before a tribunal that would detrimentally affect the right to a fair hearing.

7.6 PREVENTING UNAUTHORIZED PRACTICE: The lawyer shall assist in preventing the unauthorized practice of law, and shall not associate in his or her practice with anyone who has been disbarred or suspended by the Law Society from the practice of law. Obligations that must be observed by suspended lawyers are set out.

7.7 RETIRED JUDGES RETURNING TO PRACTICE: Appellate judges shall not return to practice without the express consent of Convocation. Judges of lower courts may not appear before their former judicial colleagues or before lower courts for a period of three years. A committee of convocation must know, review, and approve a retired judge's application to be re-admitted as a licencee to practice law.

7.8 ERRORS AND OMISSIONS: Where a lawyer discovers possible errors and omissions in his or her own work for a client, the lawyer must inform the client, advise the client to get separate legal advice, and must advise the insurer. A commentary to this rule now sets out a step-by-step protocol that a lawyer must follow with a client when a possible error or omission has occurred.

7.8.1 RESPONSIBILITY IN MULTI-DISCIPLINE PRACTICES: A lawyer in a multi-discipline practice must ensure that non-lawyers comply with these rules.

7.8.2 DISCIPLINE: A lawyer is subject to discipline by the Society no matter where the conduct occurs, and the lawyer can be disciplined for professional misconduct or for conduct unbecoming a lawyer.

The lofty notion of equal justice under law only applied if those seeking justice had the money to pay for it. As a judge once observed, "The law is like the Ritz Hotel. Anyone who can pay for a room is welcome to stay there."

In order to ensure that there was equal access to the judicial process, the provinces, starting in the 1960s, brought in programs to pay for legal services for those who could not afford a lawyer. The Ontario Legal Aid Plan, introduced in 1967, was typical of these plans.

Before 1998, the Ontario Legal Aid Plan was funded in part by the government and in part from interest paid on money held in trust by private law firms for their clients. In effect, private clients provided a subsidy to legal aid clients. The legal aid plan was administered by the Law Society, not by the government. This gave the legal profession more control over the plan than it otherwise might have. When the plan was first introduced, there was some resistance from the private Bar, where some feared they would lose business to the plan. Administrative control by the Law Society helped allay some of those fears, especially as the government supplied most of the funding for the plan's operation.

In 1998, the Law Society agreed to transfer its control and administration of the Legal Aid Plan to a public corporation set up by the Ontario government. The primary reason for this was the Law Society's disinclination to administer a system over which it had lost control due to government funding cutbacks. The funding cutbacks caused disagreements on how the plan should be run among several factions among the benchers and members. It also appeared that the Law Society might not be able to run the plan in the public interest without alienating many participating members of the Bar or the general public.

The new public corporation is funded primarily by the government, and its activities are much more likely to be affected by government control and fiscal considerations. Some benchers have voiced fears that the Legal Aid Plan will be influenced by political considerations that will override the objective task of providing equal access for clients of modest means to the justice system. There is also a fear that the corporation will abandon the certificate system (see next section) in its search for cheaper, more impersonal, assembly line justice, where client needs come second to operating an inexpensive legal aid system, and where the independent judgment of lawyers in serving their clients will be compromised.

The Certificate System

There are two payment schemes under the Ontario plan. The first scheme requires clients with a legal problem who cannot afford to hire a lawyer to prove to the legal aid plan that they qualify for legal aid; upon doing so, the plan will issue them a legal aid certificate. This is like a modified blank cheque — it provides payment for services to any lawyer prepared to accept the person with the certificate.

A client may then take the certificate to any lawyer who will accept their case by accepting the certificate. When a lawyer accepts the certificate, the lawyer agrees to be paid by legal aid at the legal aid rate, which is often much less than the fee paid to that lawyer by a non-legal aid client. The lawyer and client will then have a lawyer–client relationship that is the same as it would be for a non-legal aid client, except that legal aid will pay the legal fees.

The certificate system has some shortcomings. First, the cuts in government funding have caused legal aid to greatly reduce the number of certificates issued. Those involved in civil matters, including some family law matters, and those charged with less serious criminal offences rarely have certificates granted to them. Second, even where a certificate is issued, it arguably provides second-class service to clients on legal aid. There are often limits on what services a private lawyer is allowed to provide to a legally aided client on a certificate. For some legal problems, legal aid pays so far below market rates that many lawyers have refused to take legally aided clients. For example, many lawyers refuse to take family law cases of any complexity on legal aid, which means that many individuals in need of legal services for divorce and other family law matters cannot find adequate legal representation. Last, while many young lawyers do legal aid, as they obtain more experience and fee-paying clients, they cut down on or stop taking legal aid cases. The result is that relatively few experienced lawyers provide legal aid service, except in serious criminal matters. There is a sliding scale of legal aid fees based on experience, but the top of the scale is much below what an experienced lawyer would be paid by a private client. Therefore, there is little financial incentive for an experienced lawyer to participate in the legal aid system.

On the other hand, the certificate system virtually created the criminal defence Bar. Prior to legal aid, most of those accused of crimes who could not afford counsel represented themselves, often with dire results. Under legal aid, anyone who could not afford a lawyer when charged with an offence was likely to have a choice of criminal lawyers who would act under a legal aid certificate. Once lawyers were assured that someone would pay on behalf of accused criminals, it became feasible to practise criminal law on a regular basis, with the result that a growing number of lawyers developed expertise in this area. Now, however, the number and range of certificates in criminal matters has been greatly restricted.

The Clinic System

The second scheme under the legal aid plan is the legal aid clinic system. Here, instead of hiring a member of the private Bar at legal aid's expense, the client attends a legal aid clinic and receives legal services from clinic lawyers and staff. The clinics are funded by legal aid, and focus their attention on those whose legal problems or income preclude them from having access to the private Bar. For example, much of the legal activity in the poverty law area (public assistance, government-sponsored benefits, landlord and tenant) has been done by legal aid clinics that specialize in these kinds of legal problems, and often have staff with more expertise than most private law firms. It has been argued, with some justification, that legal aid clinics have done more to advance the legal interests of the poor and less powerful members of society than the private Bar has, simply because the clinics have been mandated to advance the law in this area and have developed the expertise to do it. By contrast, the private Bar has paid little or no attention to poverty law because people with problems in this area did not use lawyers for the obvious reason that they could not afford the services of a lawyer.

As the cost of running the legal aid system increases, it is likely that efforts will be made to increase the use of clinical services at the expense of the certificate system, because clinics are thought to deliver services in a less expensive way. There is a counter-argument, however, that the quality of service may not be as high in the clinics, because the caseload may be too high; as a result, clients get a more bureaucratized form of service than they would receive from a private lawyer retained on a certificate. At present, Ontario Legal Aid is examining a number of new clinic pilot projects and expanded use of duty counsel. Duty counsel are present in some courts to give parties general advice and help in representing themselves, but duty counsel cannot act for clients.

Access to justice continues to be a major problem in our system, particularly in civil matters, including family law. Lawyers and judges have noted increased numbers of litigants representing themselves in a court system designed by and for trained experts. The result here is less than satisfactory for the litigants and the system. Another recent alternative is the use of limited scope retainers, where instead of doing all of the usual legal work on a case, the lawyer undertakes to do only some of the work, such as speaking for the client in court, leaving the client to take the responsibility for doing other work related to the case. This may reduce overall costs for clients but may result in less effective representation for the client.

The Professional Role of Lawyers

Many people retain and use lawyers without really understanding the nature of the relationship a client has with a professional such as a lawyer. Professional values often make the relationship a client has with a lawyer different from what a relationship would be with those offering other types of goods or services. Some of the important differences are discussed below.

Officer of the Court

Although a lawyer's primary duty is to his client, he also owes a duty to the court as an officer of the court. This means that where the client's interest conflicts with the lawyer's duty to the court, the client's interest must give way.

As an officer of the court, the lawyer has a duty not to deceive or mislead the court in pursuit of the client's interest, or to otherwise contribute to perverting the course of justice.

So, while a lawyer, as an officer of the court, has a duty to fearlessly raise every issue, advance every argument, and ask every question, no matter how distasteful, a lawyer may not resort to illegal, discourteous, disrespectful, dishonest, or unfair behaviour. For example, a lawyer is expected not to advance evidence that is known to be untrue and that would have the effect of deceiving the court. If a client insists, the lawyer is caught in a peculiar conflict: on the one hand, the lawyer cannot assist the client with the deception; on the other hand, as we will see later in this chapter, the lawyer cannot inform the court the client is going to give false testimony, nor can the lawyer abandon the client. While there is some difference of opinion as to how a lawyer resolves this conflict, the general answer is that the lawyer must stop acting for the client, and then assist the client in finding a new lawyer. Although no longer acting for the client, the lawyer is obliged to keep silent and to not reveal the client's information to anyone.

The Contractual Relationship between a Lawyer and a Client

Lawyers are expected to make themselves available to any member of the public who wishes to retain their services, provided that their skills or competency meet the client's needs and that the client can pay their fees. Once **retained** by a client, lawyers are obliged to complete the work for which they were retained. Lawyers may not "fire" their client, unless the client has asked them to do something improper or illegal or refuses to pay fees or give instructions. No lawyer may refuse to act for a client merely because the client is unsavoury, unpleasant, or disreputable.

The lawyer also owes the client a duty of competence, and is obliged to keep the client informed as to the progress of work being done, answer the client's questions and, generally, provide the client with necessary information.

In general, the rule is that the lawyer advises the client, and the client gives the lawyer instructions after being advised. For example, if a lawyer receives an offer to settle a case, the lawyer is obliged to candidly discuss the offer with the client, even if it is unreasonable and not worthy of serious consideration. If a lawyer is given particular instructions by a client, the lawyer is obliged to carry them out unless it would be unlawful to do so. When a lawyer believes instructions from a client are ill-advised, the lawyer should tell the client so, and obtain the instructions in writing. A lawyer who acts on the instructions of a client, where the client claims no such instructions were given, will be found to have acted without instructions, unless the lawyer can prove otherwise. In this situation, the presumption is that the client's version of events is correct, unless the lawyer has the instructions in writing, in which case the lawyer will be able to rebut the presumption.

Unlike other contracts for service, a client is not obliged to simply pay any bill presented by a lawyer. A lawyer has an obligation to charge fairly for work done, based on the complexity of the work, the importance of the matter to the client, the degree of skill and experience of the lawyer, and the ultimate result for the client. If a client feels he or she has been overcharged, he or she may have his or her bill reviewed by an **assessment officer**. The assessment officer has the power to reduce a bill if there is overcharging. On occasion, the assessment officers have been known to reduce a bill to zero.

Confidentiality and Privilege

At the core of the lawyer–client relationship is the idea that whatever a client tells a lawyer, in the context of a lawyer–client relationship, is confidential and cannot be revealed by the lawyer to anyone without the client's consent. This is sometimes referred to as the **solicitor–client privilege**. We say that information given by a client to a lawyer is privileged. This means that third parties cannot compel either the lawyer or the client to reveal the content of communications between them. It is important to remember that the privilege is the client's, not the lawyer's. It is up to the client to decide if the privilege can be waived. The information a client gives a lawyer is privileged, even where the client admits breaking the law. As noted earlier, while a lawyer cannot assist the authorities by revealing this information, the lawyer also should not continue to act on behalf of the client, knowing the client intends to deceive the court.

Why does lawyer–client communication carry a legal privilege that is not available between doctor and patient, or priest and penitent? While doctors and priests are professionally required to not reveal things told to them in confidence, they can be compelled by a court to reveal what they were told. Lawyers cannot be compelled to reveal what their clients have told them. The usual reason given for lawyer–client privilege is that, in order to have perfect trust between a lawyer and client, and perfect frankness in their dealings, a client must be able to level with his lawyer and tell his lawyer the whole story so that the lawyer can give accurate and useful advice. If a client holds back information, the lawyer is prevented from effectively serving the client. Of course, similar arguments could be made in favour of doctors and priests, but they do not seem to have been taken as seriously by the courts as have the arguments for lawyer–client privilege.

LAW CLERKS

Many of the functions traditionally performed by lawyers can be performed by trained laypersons, working under a lawyer's supervision. Individuals who do this kind of work are called law clerks or legal assistants. Over the past 20 years, the number of persons employed as law clerks has increased dramatically, and this occupation continues to expand, as lawyers in both the private and public sectors discover that their operations can be more cost effective if some of their work is delegated to others.

Nature of the Work

Law clerks are employed in private law firms, government, corporations, banks, and insurance companies. In large firms or specialized operations, law clerks, like lawyers, specialize — a law clerk may do only corporate work, litigation, real estate, or wills and estates. In smaller, general practice firms, they may do a bit of everything. While a law clerk is supervised by lawyers, he or she is expected to use analytic skills, creativity and imagination; to work independently; to be a good problem solver, and to communicate well with other staff and clients, both orally and in writing. Numeracy skills are also important.

There are some changes in the nature of the work indicated by some emerging trends. Where a law firm has a large and complex case, it may hire law clerks, on a contract basis, with some of the work being administrative. Foreign-language skills are also becoming important as law firms go international. Those who have a computer background may find themselves working in the expanding area involved with the searching for and finding documentary evidence in electronic formats.

| **A Typical Day for a Law Clerk** | **EXHIBIT 10.2** |

A typical day for a generalist law clerk in a small general practice firm might begin at 9:00 a.m. The clerk opens and reviews mail, dictating answers to some letters. Next, the clerk may interview a client to obtain information to draft a statement of claim, and then draft the statement of claim for the lawyer's approval. In the afternoon, the clerk may complete a house purchase using the electronic registration system. The clerk may go the courthouse to file documents and check the trial list, and then meet with the supervising lawyer to discuss matters to be dealt with the next day.

Training and Qualifications

There are two career routes to becoming a law clerk. Some people start as legal secretaries, and advance into a legal assistant's position by learning the skills on the job. In some places, there are part-time courses in the evenings that provide some academic content in support of work experience. The other route to a law clerk's position is to attend a community college program, usually two years in length (full-time), where a student is taught law and procedure. Such programs usually have a work-experience component. Because language is the basic tool of law, law clerks must have excellent language skills, whichever way they train.

Ethics and Licensing

Because a law clerk works under the supervision of a lawyer as a lawyer's agent, the law clerk is bound by many of the ethical rules that bind a lawyer. For example, as a lawyer must keep a client's business confidential, so must that lawyer's law clerk.

While a law clerk is not a licensed occupation, law societies have expressed concerns about the scope of activity allowed to law clerks and other non-lawyers engaged by a lawyer to assist in the provision of legal services. With the licensing of paralegals, the boundaries of permissible activities have been further defined to ensure that non-lawyers are not performing functions that may only be performed by lawyers and licensed paralegals. By-Law 7.1 sets out the rules governing permissible and impermissible conduct (impermissible conduct was formerly set out in the Rules of Professional Conduct for lawyers). In general, By-Law 7.1 requires that lawyers closely supervise the work of their non-lawyer staff. Specifically, law clerks and other non-licencees are prohibited from the following:

- Taking instructions from clients or giving undertakings on behalf of a lawyer, unless the lawyer is closely supervising the work

- Giving legal advice to clients

- Negotiating with third parties without the client's specific approval and without the lawyer's supervising the process

- Signing or sending correspondence, other than on routine or administrative matters, unless it is reviewed by a lawyer

- Using the lawyer's personalized diskette to access the online real property registration system

- Appearing as advocates (the Law Society now requires non-lawyers employed by lawyers who appear before tribunals and lower courts to be licensed paralegals, unless the appearance is limited to routine or administrative matters, such as setting dates for trial in criminal courts)

- Sending collection letters on behalf of a client, unless reviewed by a lawyer

In general, these rules do not so much limit what a law clerk may do as impose a great deal of responsibility on a lawyer to closely oversee and supervise the work done by unlicensed non-lawyer employees.

With paralegals now recognized as a licensed professional group and with the restriction on advocacy work for law clerks, the Institute of Law Clerks, a voluntary association representing the interests of law clerks, has been clamouring for recognition and similar treatment. It is not hard to understand why. Professional standing will likely raise occupational status and income. It might also help to safeguard the scope of permissible activity for law clerks — as noted, the right to appear as advocates in lower courts and tribunals has been curtailed for law clerks in favour of paralegals.

Notwithstanding the limits on the activity of law clerks set out in By-Law 7.1, there is much that law clerks can do, depending on the nature of the law practice.

In a general practice, the work of law clerks will mirror the range of work done by lawyers in general practice. Here, law clerks may do legal research, write legal and factual memoranda for the supervising lawyer, and draft routine court documents, contracts, agreements, wills, and other legal documents in accordance with a lawyer's directions. Clerks may also interview clients and witnesses, attend to routine correspondence, and carry out land-title searches and other types of searches using public electronic and paper registration systems. In addition, law clerks may also do some secretarial work, the law firm's bookkeeping and routine collection work for the law firm's unpaid fees.

In large firms or in smaller "law boutiques" where lawyers are specialized, law clerks also tend to be specialized. In a real estate practice, law clerks handle routine matters involving transactions for the purchase and sale of land, prepare transfers and other title documents, search public records to verify the seller's right to sell, and complete purchase and sale transactions.

Corporate and commercial law clerks prepare and draft documents to incorporate businesses, keep corporate records up-to-date, handle routine correspondence, draft contracts and financial documents, and attend to the purchase and sale of businesses.

Law clerks working in the probate and estate law areas are concerned with the administration of the estates of deceased persons. Clerks may collect information, inventory property, prepare estate taxation documents and estate accounts, draft wills from instructions, and generally attend to routine estate administration.

Law clerks working with litigation lawyers collect information from clients, interview witnesses, draft court documents and some correspondence, research legal questions, and sometimes appear in the lower courts on routine or administrative matters.

THE LEGAL PROFESSION — PARALEGALS

Unlike law clerks, paralegals are non-lawyers who are licensed by the Law Society to offer advocacy services directly to the public without supervision by a lawyer. Historically, paralegals developed as an occupational group to appear in courts where non-lawyer agents could appear. As the number of paralegals increased and their scope of practice expanded, the Law Society tried to restrict paralegal activity. From the 1980s until 2005, there were a series of legal actions, task forces, and commissions examining whether or not paralegals should be given recognition, and if so how they should be regulated.[11]

The Law Society report, which finally accepted the legal existence of paralegals and their regulation by the Law Society, set the stage for government action to licensed paralegals. In 2005, the government introduced the *Access to Justice Act, 2005*. Schedule C of the Act amends *The Law Society Act* to give the Law Society the power to regulate all aspects of the provision of legal services by paralegals in 2007. Ontario is the first jurisdiction in North America to recognize independent paralegals as a legal professional group. As of 2013, British Columbia is looking at limited reconition of paralegals but will require them to work under the supervision of lawyers.

As a result of its recognition of paralegals as an independent profession, there are changes to the Law Society's governing structure. Two paralegal benchers have been added to Convocation (consisting of 40 lawyers and 8 non-lawyer benchers), which is the main governing body of the profession. Convocation also has a permanent standing committee on paralegals that will consist of five paralegals, five lawyer benchers and three lay benchers. The Law Society will appoint the benchers, but the paralegals elect their own members to this committee and to Convocation, as lawyers do.

All paralegals now have to be licensed. Licencees have to complete an approved college training program, pass a licensing exam, and be of "good character".

Scope of Practice

Paralegals are advocates and may appear in Small Claims Court, the Ontario Court of Justice under the *Provincial Offences Act*, and on summary conviction criminal offences where the maximum term of imprisonment is no more than six months. They may also appear before administrative tribunals, including the Financial Services Commission of Ontario in respect of no-fault auto insurance claims. Federal tribunals may regulate who appears before them and may permit those who are not licensed paralegals to appear or prevent paralegals from appearing. For example, the Law Society discovered in 2009 that the Federal Immigration and Refugee Board was refusing paralegals the right to appear. The Law Society made submissions to the federal government as a result of which the *Immigration and Refugee Protection Act* was amended in 2011 to permit paralegals to appear. There are other Acts, both federal and provincial, which may bar paralegals from appearing, and the Law Society will be working, over time, to eliminate those restrictions so that paralegals can appear before all administrative tribunals in Ontario, both federal and provincial.

As part of being advocates, paralegals may perform many of the related functions that are part of advocacy work. They may give legal advice, draft documents and negotiate settlements in connection to any proceeding in any forum where they are entitled to appear. Paralegals may not, however, offer non-advocacy services; they are not permitted to do traditional solicitor's work, such as preparing wills, administering estates, incorporating companies, preparing partnership agreements or separation agreements, or doing uncontested divorces.

---

[11] See *R. v. Lawrie and POINTTS* (1987) 59 O.R. (2d) 161 (Ont. C.A.); Ontario Task Force On Paralegals, *Report of the Task Force on Paralegals* prepared for the Ontario Ministry of the Attorney General (Toronto: Queen's Printer, 1990) [The Ianni Commission Report]; Hon. P. de C. Cory, "A framework for Regulating Paralegal Practice" (31 May 2000); *A Consultation Document on a Proposed Regulatory Framework*, Law Society Report to Convocation, 25 April 2002.

Licensing

The Law Society now has the authority to issue paralegal licences and has determined what standards an individual must meet to obtain a licence. Not everyone who offers advocacy services will require a licence. The following fall outside of the licensing provisions of the *Law Society Act* and do not require a licence:

- In-house employees preparing documents for their employer
- Persons who represent themselves, or appear occasionally to assist a friend or family member without charge
- Persons who carry on a business where they are governed by an Act of Parliament or the Legislature that specifically regulates their activities as professionals where they appear as advocates in the course of their work
- An employee or volunteer representative of a trade union who appears in connection with members' trade union matters

There are also individuals who are exempted by Law Society by-law:

- In-house legal service employees employed by a single employer
- Employees of legal aid clinics, including students working in clinics
- Aboriginal court workers
- Labour union staff representing members in compensation matters or representing retirees who were union members, and those representing families at Coroner's Inquests
- Certain members of regulated professions, such as architects, real property appraisers, and human resources officers who, as part of their duties, appear as advocates from time to time before provincial tribunals

Aside from these exceptions, the Law Society's position appears to be that other professionals who appear in courts and tribunals that are within the scope of a paralegal's permitted area of practice will have to be licensed.[12]

The Law Society has also indicated that it intends to reduce the categories of persons currently exempted by the Law Society By-Law 4, ss. 28–30.[13] It has already provided a simplified route for those in these categories to obtain paralegal licences, and many who are eligible have applied.

Two Paralegal Licensing Streams

An existing professional group facing licensing for the first time encounters a unique problem. Existing practitioners are already out there doing the work; they have learned the skills in a variety of ways and have varying levels of expertise. Licensing them involves verifying their paralegal skills and good character so that the licensing body is satisfied that they are competent to practise as paralegals. After the pre-licensing paralegals have been accounted for, new entrants to the profession without previous professional experience will be subjected to a different licensing regime, one that prescribes a detailed educational program prior to licensing.

Here is how the Law Society's licensing regime works:

- *Grandparented applicants*: Those who had been working as paralegals for at least three years in the last five years at the time the licensing

---

[12] This is a general description of exempt classes. A more detailed description is in By-Law 4 and on the Law Society website. As there are likely to be further changes in who or who is not exempt in the next few years, it is advisable to refer to the website for a detailed update (<www.lsu.org>; follow the link to "paralegals" and "licensing").

[13] *Report to the Attorney General Pursuant to s. 63.1 of the* Law Society Act [The 5-year Paralegal Review 2007–12] <http://www.lawsocietygazette.ca/wp-content/uploads/2012/07/Paralegal-5-year-Review.pdf>.

regime was established in May 2007 are considered to be **grandparented**. This means that they are licensed without the formal education and training that will be required of later applicants. Grandparented applicants had to apply for a licence by October 31, 2007, and if of "good character" their names were registered as paralegal candidates. They then had to write a qualifying exam before May 2008. If the grandparented applicants completed this process and showed evidence that they were insured for malpractice, they were licensed.

- *Transitional applicants*: Those who at the time of the establishment of the licensing process were not eligible to be grandfathered and who applied between November 1, 2007, and June 30, 2010, were licensed if they graduated from a Ministry of Training, Colleges and Universities-approved paralegal college diploma program within three years of making application, met the good character requirements, passed the licensing exam, and showed evidence of having necessary malpractice insurance.

- *Post-transitional applicants:* Those who apply after July 1, 2010, must have graduated from a Law Society certified college paralegal program, provide evidence of good character, pass the licensing exam, and show evidence of having malpractice insurance. Ministry-approved paralegal programs will now have to be certified by the Law Society; Seneca and Algonquin Colleges were the first to be certified in June 2008, and others have since followed.

Discipline and Ethical Standards

Paralegals now have a regulatory regime much like that for lawyers. This should not be a surprise, because the professions are similar, as are the regulatory issues regarding protection of the public and maintenance of professional standards. Paralegals have to be insured, maintain trust accounts for retainers and client's other funds, restrict themselves to the permitted areas of practice, and, generally, adhere to the Paralegal Rules of Professional Conduct, a summary of which is set out in Exhibit 10.3. You will note how similar these rules are to the professional conduct rules for lawyers in Exhibit 10.1.

In June 2012, as required by the s. 63.1 of the *Law Society Act*, a detailed consultation and review was carried out to assess the regulation of paralegals by the Law Society. The Law Society's view is that paralegal regulation has been a success, both for the profession and the public, by making the justice system more accessible and ensuring proper regulation and oversight of the paralegal profession. Some paralegals have argued, however, that they do not have the same rights to participate in the governance of the Law Society and the paralegal profession as lawyers do and that the Law Society continues to restrict and hamper them in the practice of their profession by limiting the kind of work paralegals do. It is reasonable to expect that paralegals, as a regulated profession, is still a work in progress.

COURT ADMINISTRATION STAFF

Nature of the Work

Court administration staff work in courts and administrative tribunals. Their primary duties are to provide services in courtrooms as clerk-recorders, court monitors and court reporters. They also staff court offices, overseeing the management of court files, ensuring procedural steps are properly followed and, in general, managing case files and the pre-trial process. In addition, some staff are employed in institutional maintenance roles, dealing with court employees, budget, physical resources, and planning. Staff must have

EXHIBIT 10.3

RULE 1: CITATION AND INTERPRETATION

1.01 and 1.02   DEFINES TERMS, RECOGNIZES TWO CLASSES OF LICENCES: Lawyers and paralegals. Paralegals recognized as being able to operate as sole proprietorships, partnerships, or limited liability corporations, as lawyers do.

RULE 2: PROFESSIONALISM

2.01   INTEGRITY AND CIVILITY: Paralegals shall conduct themselves so as to maintain the integrity of the profession and make legal services available in an efficient and convenient way compatible with the integrity and independence of the profession. They are also expected to uphold the standards of the legal profession and to assist in advancing its goals, organizations, and institutions. This includes acting in good faith and with civility. A paralegal who engages in other activities or holds public office must not allow those activities to compromise or impair the integrity or standards of the profession. A paralegal who acts as a mediator must make clear that he or she cannot act as a representative of either party.

2.02   UNDERTAKINGS AND TRUST CONDITIONS: An undertaking is a personal promise from a paralegal; it should be given and confirmed in writing where possible, and must be honoured. Undertakings that cannot be honoured should not be given. Paralegals are expected to honour whatever terms or conditions under which they hold property or documents in trust.

2.03   HARASSMENT AND DISCRIMINATION: The *Human Rights Code* applies to these rules and the profession. A paralegal shall not engage in sexual harassment or harassment under any of the prohibited grounds in the Code with respect to clients, other paralegals, their clients or other members of the public. A paralegal shall not discriminate against others under any of the provisions of the Code with respect to employment or the provision of services to the public.

RULE 3: DUTY TO CLIENTS

3.01   COMPETENCE: A paralegal shall not offer services to the public that he or she is not competent to perform. Generally, a paralegal is expected to provide thorough, competent, timely, conscientious, diligent, efficient, and civil service to clients. If a paralegal discovers that work for a client is beyond his or her competence, he or she must inform the client promptly and obtain the client's consent to obtain the advice and assistance of a licencee (another paralegal or a lawyer) who is competent to do the work. A competent paralegal is one who knows general legal principles and the law and procedure in the area where the paralegal provides services. The competent paralegal is able to investigate facts, identify issues, determine client objectives and, on that basis, advise clients as to their options; the competent paralegal implements the client's instructions. In this connection, the paralegal will know how to do legal research, analyze the issues, apply the law to the facts, write and draft appropriate documents, negotiate and know alternate dispute resolution (ADR) techniques, and possess the necessary advocacy skills. In addition, the paralegal is expected to work diligently and in a cost effective way on behalf of the client, meet all deadlines, respond promptly to client questions, manage the practice effectively, and meet changing standards, and changes in the law. In this connection a paralegal is expected to engage in continuing legal education as part of keeping up with the demands of his or her practice.

3.02   ADVISING CLIENTS: A paralegal shall give honest and candid advice and shall not knowingly assist in dishonesty, fraud or crime on behalf of clients, taking care not to become the dupe of a client of others. A paralegal's trust account is not to be used for any purpose other than with respect to legal services. If the paralegal discovers an institutional client engaging in dishonesty, fraud, or crime, the paralegal shall draw this to the attention of progressively senior officers of the organization; and if the impropriety is not corrected, the paralegal must withdraw under Rule 3.08. A paralegal shall not take on work outside the ordinary scope of his or her practice. A paralegal who accepts a limited scope retainer shall candidly and honestly outline the scope of the services to be rendered and confirm the nature of the limited scope retainer in writing. A paralegal shall try to settle a client's case and not litigate for the sake of litigating and will advise the client of ADR.

A paralegal is expected to not do anything for a client where he or she knew, or ought to have known, that he or she is being used by the client to facilitate fraud, illegality, or dishonesty.

If a client has a disability, the paralegal shall provide as normal a paralegal–client relationship as possible. If the client appears to be unable to manage his or her affairs, the paralegal shall take steps to see to the appointment of an appropriate representative. If a paralegal receives a medical-legal report on behalf of a client that contains a provision that it not be shown to a client, it is to be returned and no copy made, unless there are instructions from the client to receive a report on that basis. If a report contains information that might be harmful to the client, the paralegal shall attempt to dissuade the client from seeing the report, but it must be shown to the client if the latter insists, but the paralegal can insist the client attend at the doctor's office to see the report.

In the event the paralegal discovers an error or omission in the provision of legal services to a client, he or she must inform the client, advise the client to seek legal advice with respect to the consequences of the error and immediately inform the errors and omissions insurer. If a client speaks French, he or she must be advised of language rights under the *French Language Services Act*. If a paralegal acts on matters involving statutory automobile insurance benefits, in addition to complying with licence requirements, he or she must also comply with the regulations imposed under the *Insurance Act*.

A paralegal shall not threaten or advise a client to threaten criminal or quasi-criminal proceedings, including a complaint to a regulatory authority; but this does not bar a complaint to a regulatory authority made in good faith to which the client is entitled.

3.03 CONFIDENTIALITY: The paralegal shall keep strictly confidential anything told to him or her by a client and shall not reveal the information to anyone unless required by law. All client documents shall be kept safe and out of sight of anyone not entitled to see them. However, if a paralegal has information that indicates there may be serious harm to the health or safety of others, that may justify disclosure. A paralegal is also entitled to disclose client information in some circumstances where he or she is alleged to be criminally or civilly liable or guilty of professional misconduct as a result of a client's affairs or activity. A paralegal may also disclose client information in order to collect a debt for unpaid fees. However, no more information should be disclosed than is necessary in those circumstances. A paralegal may also disclose client information to the Law Society or under a court order. A paralegal is also permitted to make disclosure to seek legal advice about a proposed course of conduct.

3.04 CONFLICTS OF INTEREST — GENERAL: Paralegals are not to represent both sides in a dispute and may not act for a client where there is a conflict of interest with the paralegal unless the client is informed and consents. A conflict of interest involves a substantial risk that the paralegal's loyalty to the client's interest would be markedly and adversely affected in respect of the interests of other clients or third parties, but this must be more than a mere possibility. A paralegal may not act against a client a paralegal previously represented, if the paralegal has relevant knowledge from a previous retainer. However, a paralegal's partner may act against a former client of the paralegal, if the party consents, and if there are suitable safeguards to prevent the partner from obtaining information about the client from the other paralegal. Consent must be explicit and in writing, but may be inferred where the party is a government or large entity, or where there are in-house counsel. In these situations, the matters cannot be related; the paralegal cannot have relevant information about the other client; and the client has previously consented to such arrangements. Paralegals who act for more than one client on a matter must advise clients that information from one client is shared with all and that there is no confidentiality between the clients and the paralegal. If a paralegal has a continuing relationship with one joint client, the other must be advised of that fact. If a contentious matter arises between joint clients, the paralegal may have to transfer one or both of the clients to avoid a conflict of interest depending on the circumstances. The joint client rule is also more relaxed where the clients are deemed to be sophisticated. If the paralegal is in a multi-disciplinary practice or offers legal and other non-legal services through affiliated entities, confidentiality rules apply to non-licencees and with respect to affiliated, non-legal services in respect of a client.

3.05 CONFLICTS OF INTEREST — TRANSFERS: If a paralegal transfers from one firm to another, and has information about a former client which creates a conflict with a client in the new firm, the new firm must cease to act for its client, unless the client of the transferring paralegal consents, or unless the new firm can show that adequate safeguards will prevent confidential information about the client of the transferring paralegal reaching the new firm. A transferring paralegal may not disclose confidential information about a former client to the new firm, and no paralegal in the new firm can discuss its client's affairs with the transferring paralegal. If the confidential information is not relevant to a matter, the transferring paralegal must give notice to the former client and the new firm's client and swear an affidavit or declaration to that effect.

3.06 DOING BUSINESS WITH A CLIENT: If a paralegal's client enters into a business transaction with a paralegal, the latter has a duty prior to accepting any new retainer to inform the client of any potential or real conflicts of interest, and shall require the client to have independent legal advice, and if the client still wishes to have the paralegal act, the latter shall obtain an informed consent from the client. Generally, a business transaction with a client must be fair and reasonable to the client. If a paralegal is unable to disclose a conflicting interest to the client, because of other confidentiality concerns, the paralegal shall decline the retainer. A paralegal shall not borrow from clients unless the client is a financial institution or close relative. Nor shall a paralegal provide guarantees for a client who is a borrower, unless the lender is a financial institution providing a loan to a client who is a relative, or who is in a business venture with the paralegal, and the paralegal has disclosed potential conflicts of interest to the client and the lender, and both have had independent legal advice. A paralegal may not, with some exceptions, act as a surety for a client seeking judicial interim release (bail) using the paralegal's own funds or security to secure the accused client's release; nor may the paralegal act in a supervisory capacity on the accused client's release.

3.07 CLIENT PROPERTY: A paralegal shall exercise care and prudence with a client's property, inform the client of any property (including money) received on the client's behalf, and keep careful records to ensure the client's property is identifiable. A paralegal shall return a client's property on request.

3.08 WITHDRAWAL FROM REPRESENTATION: Having accepted a retainer, a paralegal shall not withdraw services from a client except as provided in these rules. Giving reasonable notice to the client is a precondition to withdrawing from the retainer; on discharge of the retainer, the paralegal is obliged to provide notice to the client in writing. A paralegal may withdraw, subject to a court or tribunal's approval if the client has lost confidence in the paralegal, or refuses to accept the paralegal's advice on an important point. A paralegal must withdraw if fired by the client, the client requires that the paralegal breach his or her duty to the court or tribunal, the client behaves dishonourably in the proceedings, or requires unethical and improper behaviour by the paralegal or the paralegal finds he or she is not competent to deal with the matter. Unless it would do serious harm to the client's interest a paralegal may withdraw if he or she has not been paid. In withdrawing from a case, if the matter is criminal and quasi-criminal, the client must have sufficient time to find a new representative, and the paralegal must account for monies received from the client, and notify the court of the withdrawal. If there is not sufficient time between withdrawal and the trial, the paralegal must try to obtain an adjournment and obtain the court's permission to withdraw. On withdrawal the paralegal must take steps not to prejudice the client's interests, must deliver to the client papers and property, provide necessary information, account for funds held and render a final account and co-operate with the successor for an orderly transfer of the case. A successor must also take steps to ensure that the former paralegal has in fact withdrawn.

RULE 4: ADVOCACY

4.01 THE PARALEGAL AS ADVOCATE: The paralegal shall represent the client resolutely and honourably, while treating the tribunal, opposing parties and their representatives with civility. The paralegal shall pursue all lawful claims, remedies and defences unless they have been waived by the client with an informed consent. The paralegal shall discourage the client from resorting to frivolous, vexatious, harassing and improper conduct. The paralegal shall not appear before a judicial officer with whom he or she has a conflict of interest. A paralegal shall not appear before a court while under the influence of alcohol or a drug. Nor shall a paralegal abuse the court process by misleading the court, manipulating witnesses or evidence, or harassing witnesses; a paralegal with a limited scope retainer shall disclose the nature of the retainer to the court. A paralegal shall not dissuade a witness from giving evidence. Where a client is required to disclose documents before trial, the paralegal shall ensure that full disclosure is made. If a paralegal does or omits to do what is required under this rule, he or she shall promptly disclose the error to the client. Where a charge has been or may be laid against a client, the paralegal may enter into plea bargaining negotiations with the prosecutor unless the client instructs otherwise provided the paralegal fully advises the client on the options available, the client is prepared to admit the charge, and the client voluntarily instructs the paralegal to enter a guilty plea. A paralegal who acts as a prosecutor shall act for the public good and treat the tribunal with candour and respect.

4.02   INTERVIEWING WITNESSES: There being no property in a witness, a paralegal may interview any witness or potential witness whether under subpoena or summons or not. However, if questioning a potential witness, the paralegal must disclose his or her interest and be careful not to subvert or suppress evidence, or try to discourage the witness from giving evidence. Where a person is represented by a licencee, that person may be questioned or approached only through the licencee who represents him or her, who can consent on behalf of his or her client.

4.03   COMMUNICATION WITH WITNESSES GIVING TESTIMONY: Generally, there are restrictions on discussions a paralegal may have with a favourable witness once the witness has begun to give evidence. Generally a paralegal may not discuss the witness's evidence with him or her until testimony has been concluded.

4.04   THE PARALEGAL AS WITNESS: A paralegal shall not submit his or her own affidavit in a proceeding where he or she is an advocate, subject to some exceptions. Similarly, the paralegal shall not give oral evidence in a proceeding in which he or she is also an advocate, unless the rules of the tribunal permit.

4.05   DEALING WITH UNREPRESENTED PERSONS: A paralegal should make clear that he or she cannot represent the person's interest, and that he or she must diligently act on behalf of the client who retained him or her.

RULE 5: FEES AND RETAINERS

5.01   FEES AND RETAINERS: Fees and retainers shall be fair and reasonable, reflecting the nature, complexity or difficulty of the work required, the amount involved, the importance of the issues at stake to the client, the results obtained, and the requirements of statutes that limit or control fees that may be charged. No fee paid on behalf of a client by someone else shall be accepted without informing the client. In sending out an account, a paralegal shall clearly set out fees and disbursements separately. If fees or disbursement charged to a client are reduced by court order, the paralegal must reimburse the client for the difference. Monies held in trust by a paralegal shall not be transferred to a paralegal's personal account unless an account is rendered to the client. A paralegal may enter into a contingency fee arrangement with a client in non-criminal or non–quasi-criminal matters. The client shall be informed of all of the factors determining the fee and when and how it is to be paid if the paralegal is successful, and there shall be clear evidence that the client consents to the arrangement. If there is a joint retainer, the fees must be fairly divided. A paralegal may not split fees with a non-licencee, but may split fees with another licencee in a different firm, provided the client consents, and the split is fair and reasonable. A paralegal may give and accept a referral fee from another licencee, provided it does not arise from a withdrawal of service, and further, provided the client gives an informed consent. This rule will permit paralegals and lawyers to split fees and to pay and receive referral fees. Paralegals, as well as lawyers, are now required to verify the identity of new clients.

EXHIBIT 10.3 (continued)

RULE 6: DUTY TO THE ADMINISTRATION OF JUSTICE

6.01   ENCOURAGING RESPECT FOR THE ADMINISTRATION OF JUSTICE: A paralegal shall foster respect for the administration of justice. If aware of a danger to the court or those in it, he or she shall inform the court of any dangerous situation. Provided it does not result in a conflict of interest or otherwise breach court orders or statutory rules, a paralegal may communicate with the media and make public statements provided the statements do not prejudice a party's right to a fair trial. A paralegal is required to report any unauthorized practice, and may not enter into partnership or other arrangements to offer legal services with any licencee who has been disbarred, struck off, or otherwise is not permitted to offer licensed services.

RULE 7: DUTY TO LICENSEES AND OTHERS

7.01   COURTESY AND GOOD FAITH: A paralegal shall not engage in sharp practice; he or she shall agree to reasonable requests for adjournments and waiver of procedural formalities where it does no harm to the client. A paralegal shall not engage in abusive or unprofessional behaviour, and should not engage in negative, disparaging comments about other licencees except in representing a client in a complaint against another licencee. A paralegal shall promptly respond to professional communications from other licencees, and be punctual in fulfilling commitments. A paralegal shall not record conversations with clients or licencees even if lawful, without informing the other person.

   A paralegal shall not use any device to record a conversation between the paralegal and a client or another licencee in any circumstances without first informing the other person of the intention to do so. A paralegal who receives an inadvertent communication not intended for the paralegal must notify the sender.

7.02   COMMUNICATION WITH A REPRESENTED PERSON, CORPORATION OR ORGANIZATION: If a person is represented by a legal practitioner in a matter, a paralegal shall not communicate with the person on the matter of the retainer, or attempt to settle the matter without the consent of the legal practitioner. There are two exceptions to this rule: (i) A paralegal may communicate with a person who has a limited scope retainer, provided the communication does not fall inside the boundaries of matters covered by the limited scope retainer. (ii) A paralegal not otherwise involved in the matter may give a second opinion to a person without notice to the legal practitioner. If a paralegal is retained to act in a matter involving a corporation or organization (including partnerships, unions, trusts, government departments and other artificial persons) that is represented by a legal practitioner, he or she shall not communicate about the matter (unless required to do so by law) with a person who is an officer, director, employee, or agent of the corporation with responsibility for providing information, advice, or who makes decisions for the company or organization dealing with the matter, without the legal practitioner's consent. If the person is separately represented in the matter, the legal practitioner may give consent for the paralegal to communicate with the person. These prohibitions apply to a paralegal who knows or ought to have known that the party he or she seeks to communicate with is legally represented.

RULE 8: PRACTICE MANAGEMENT

8.01   GENERAL OBLIGATIONS: A paralegal shall operate his or her practice in a responsible way, in particular, taking responsibility for the practice's finances, its professional operations, and for supervising staff, and pay any insurance deductible promptly as required. A paralegal shall supervise staff to whom tasks are delegated. In particular a paralegal may not permit non-licensed staff to provide legal services, to be held out as a licencee, to do things only paralegals may do, or do things paralegals are not permitted to do.

8.02   MAKING LEGAL SERVICES AVAILABLE: A paralegal shall make legal services available to the public in an efficient and convenient way. In offering legal services, a paralegal shall not make false, or misleading claims, use coercion or duress, or take advantage of a vulnerable person or one who has suffered trauma but not had a chance to recover. Nor shall a paralegal attempt to entice away a client from another licencee, unless the client initiates the change of retainer. A paralegal may not engage in communicating services in a way that brings the profession or the

Paralegal Rules of Conduct,
The Law Society of Upper Canada
EFFECTIVE OCTOBER 2014

EXHIBIT 10.3 (continued)

administration of justice into disrepute, nor shall he or she advertise services beyond the scope of permissible practice.

8.03 MARKETING: A paralegal may market legal services if the marketing is true, accurate, not misleading or deceptive and is in the best interest of the public, and consistent with the public interest and professional standards. A paralegal may advertise fees if the paralegal is precise as to services offered for the fee, discloses any extra charges, and the paralegal sticks to the fee quoted.

8.04 INSURANCE: All paralegals must obtain and maintain errors and omissions insurance as stipulated by the Law Society. Paralegals shall promptly report any claim for negligence, and shall assist the insurer in settling or defending the claim. If the insurer pays the claim, the paralegal must promptly pay the deductible.

RULE 9: RESPONSIBILITY TO THE LAW SOCIETY

9.01 RESPONSIBILITY TO THE LAW SOCIETY: A paralegal shall reply promptly and completely to any communication from the Law Society where a response is requested. The paralegal must report misconduct to the Law Society unless it would breach confidentiality or be unlawful. Reportable events include misappropriation of funds by a licensee, abandonment of a practice, criminal activity related to a licensee's practice, mental instability or other conduct prejudicial to the licensee's clients. With respect to reporting mental instability, it must be of such a serious nature that the licensee's clients are likely to be materially prejudiced. A paralegal is obliged to encourage a client to report dishonest conduct by another licensee. If the client refuses to report dishonest conduct, the licensee shall obtain the client's written direction not to report, while pursuing the client's other remedies. If the client makes a private deal with a dishonest licensee, the paralegal shall inform the client of the provisions of the criminal law with respect to the concealment of offences, and shall refuse to act for that client. If a paralegal is charged with an offence described in By-Law 8 he or she shall report the charge and its disposition to the Law Society. A paralegal may be disciplined by the Law Society for professional misconduct (conduct which violates the rules and practices governing paralegal practice) and conduct unbecoming a paralegal (conduct in the private life of a paralegal that would bring the profession into disrepute). The rule defines professional misconduct, and conduct unbecoming to a paralegal.

a detailed knowledge of court or tribunal operations and court or tribunal rules of procedure. In particular, they must be able to understand, interpret and apply procedural rules, and use court forms properly. They must develop language and numeracy skills to do problem solving and to provide advice to lawyers and the public. The work is usually done during normal business hours in court offices and courtrooms across the province. Court staff are a mix of full-time and contract workers, many of whom are part of a unionized civil service. Currently there are no professional or licensing requirements for this profession.

Training and Qualifications

Historically, staff were recruited from civil service applicants and trained on the job. However, some community colleges offer a court and tribunal administration diploma program in which students can acquire a background in law and procedure geared to court and tribunal administration settings, along with some of the generic literacy, numeracy and analytic skills essential to working in this area. Court reporters may also train in office administration programs, where they learn necessary word processing and dictation skills, although court staff operating recording equipment are replacing traditional court reporters. These individuals will only need transcription and word processing skills.

CHAPTER SUMMARY

Although this chapter is about the legal professions of lawyers and paralegals, it also examined the emerging legal services industry, in particular the increased role of individuals who are not lawyers but who perform a variety of specialized legal services.

The chapter presented a dynamic view of the legal profession of lawyers by comparing legal services offered by lawyers in the 1900s with those offered today. Important changes include the increasing size of law firms, additional specializations, changes in training of lawyers and other legal workers, more aggressive marketing of legal services, and the emergence of independent paralegals.

The legal profession was then examined in the context of the traditional model of professions: a self-regulating monopoly. The law society is the governing body of the profession, controlling who may enter the profession, governing the members' conduct, disciplining the members, and determining appropriate training for them. Detailed attention was paid to the rules governing professional conduct, as these have important implications for public acceptance of the profession's monopoly and for the guidance of others who provide legal services.

Duties and responsibilities of lawyers in their relationship with their own clients and the courts were examined, focusing on the tension that can arise in the face of conflicting duties owed to clients and to the courts.

The legal aid system was discussed in terms of the certificate and clinic systems, with a focus on emerging trends in offering legal aid services, as government and the law societies attempt to contain rising costs of the system.

Finally, three emerging occupational groups offering legal services were examined: law clerks/legal assistants, who perform legal services under the supervision of lawyers; specialized court and tribunal staff; and the newest legal profession, paralegals, who legitimately may offer a limited range of services directly to the public, either in competition with lawyers or in areas of the legal services market unserviced or underserviced by lawyers.

GLOSSARY OF NEW TERMS AND KEY CONCEPTS

articling clerk
Also called a **clerk under articles** or, more simply, an articling student. This is the title for a law student who has completed law school, and then works in a law firm under supervision for one year to acquire practice skills.

assessment officer
An officer of the court with the power to review a lawyer's bill if it is disputed by the client, and to determine costs payable by one party to another as a result of a court order for costs.

barrister and solicitor
The professional title of lawyers in Canada. For further discussions, see note 8 on page 206.

bencher
A lawyer elected by other lawyers to the **convocation**, the governing body of the law society. There are also a number of *lay benchers*, who are not lawyers but are appointed by the government to represent the interests of the general public.

call to the bar
A ceremony in which a law student, after completing the required legal education, officially becomes a lawyer and a member of the legal profession in a province.

convocation	The governing body of the Law Society of Upper Canada, which is composed of **benchers.**
disbarment	A process whereby a lawyer who has committed a serious infraction of the rules of professional conduct is made to leave the legal profession after a disciplinary hearing.
grandparented	A gender-neutral term referring to a class of persons existing prior to the imposition of a new system of rules, who are permitted to adhere to the system that existed prior to the establishment of the new system of rules.
mega-firm	A colloquial expression used to describe very large, often transprovincial or transnational, law firms.
peer review	A system used in the professions to assess the quality of a professional's work by having other skilled professionals review and comment on the quality of that work.
pro bono publico	A Latin expression that means "for the public good". It describes a situation where the client cannot afford to pay fees, so a lawyer takes on a worthy legal cause for no fee in order to see justice done.
retained	A client who has hired a lawyer has *retained* the lawyer's services by paying a deposit for legal services called a **retainer.**
retainer	Has several meanings, depending on the context. It describes the contract between a lawyer and client for services to be performed by the lawyer. Also, it can be used to describe the money deposit made by the client to the lawyer as advance payment on services to be performed by the lawyer. Last, it may refer to a contractual relationship in which the client pays the lawyer a fee for being available to provide whatever services the client requires during a stipulated time period. Here, the lawyer will also charge further amounts for the actual work done while he or she acts as retainer to the client. This kind of retainer is often used by corporate clients that need to have a lawyer on call.
solicitor–client privilege	A privilege, which belongs to the client, that requires that anything said to a lawyer by a client dealing with an issue for which the lawyer has been retained cannot be revealed to anyone without the client's consent.
systemic discrimination	An unintentional inequitable treatment of a minority that arises as a result of the negative impact on a minority of institutions or existing ways of doing things. For example, the requirement of long hours by large firms may give rise to systemic discrimination against women lawyers, who are primarily responsible for child care.

REVIEW QUESTIONS

1. What are the major differences between the law offices in 1900 and those of today with respect to the following:
   • women and minorities in the legal profession?
   • size of law firms?
   • specialization?
   • education and training of lawyers?
   • ways legal services are marketed to the public?

2. Discuss the chief characteristics of a profession, generally.

3. How does lawyering as a profession
   • govern itself?
   • train its members?
   • determine who may enter the profession?
   • control misbehaviour among its members?

4. How does the paralegal profession
   • govern itself?
   • train its members?

- determine who may enter the profession?
- control misbehaviour among its members?

5. While paralegals are licenced to appear in some of the lower courts, may others do so who are not licenced?

6. How does the legal aid plan deliver legal services to less qualified legal aid clients?

7. How is the legal aid plan funded?

8. What are the criticisms towards the legal aid plan with respect to the quality of legal service provided to clients?

9. What trends appear to emerge with respect to changes in the delivery of legal aid services?

10. What is a limited scope retainer?

11. Cite an example of the disciplinary offence, "professional misconduct". How is professional misconduct different from the offence of "conduct unbecoming to a barrister and solicitor"?

12. Describe the duty of a lawyer or a paralegal as an "officer of the court".

13. What are the characteristics of the contractual relationship between a lawyer or a paralegal and his or her client?

14. How are law clerks regulated?

15. May law clerks employed by and supervised by lawyers appear in lower courts where agents may appear?

16. In what courts and tribunals do licensed paralegals have the right to appear?

17. What requirements will a paralegal have to meet in order to be licensed?

DISCUSSION QUESTIONS

1. The Law Society has been described by some as well designed to protect the interests of the public; others have described it as the oldest monopoly in the province, protecting only the interests of its members. Discuss.

2. If you are asked to group the rules of professional conduct for lawyers into categories, what categories would you create? Which rules would you place in each category?

3. As a law clerk working for a lawyer, your firm's client tells you that to make sure she wins in her upcoming court case, she plans to give a version of relevant events that she knows is untrue. What should you do? What action should the lawyer responsible for this case take?

4. You are a paralegal. A husband and wife who have agreed to separate approach you. They ask you to draw up a separation agreement for them. Should you do this work? Discuss, assuming that there is no regulation of paralegals.

5. You are investing some money in a business venture with someone who happens to be a lawyer. The relationship you have with him is a business relationship, but it is not a lawyer–client relationship (you have not hired him or her as your lawyer). He asks for some money in cash as part of the venture, and without furnishing a receipt. You are reluctant to do this, but he persuades you, saying, "You can trust me, I'm a lawyer." Later, you discover that he has stolen your money. Is this professional misconduct? Discuss.

6. "The Law Society's regulatory issues for paralegals are virtually the same as they are for lawyers." Examining the Rules of Professional Conduct for both groups of licencees, comment on the accuracy of this statement.

7. You are a licensed paralegal who appears regularly in the Small Claims Court. What should you do if you encounter the following person as an opponent on the other side of a case you are doing?

   (i) The granny of the party is representing that party in court.
   (ii) A trade union local president is acting on behalf of a member defending a debt collection case where you act for the creditor.
   (iii) Someone who occasionally appears in court representing people and who charges a fee.
   (iv) A currently licensed paralegal who is currently under suspension by the Law Society.

SUGGESTED READING AND OTHER RESOURCES

Arthurs, H.W. "Paradoxes of Canadian Legal Education" (1977) 3 Dal. L.J. 639.

Eisen, L. *Technology in Practice*, 2d ed. (Toronto: Carswell, 1991).

Gold, N. (ed.) and Centre for Studies in Canadian Legal Education. *Essays on Legal Education* (Toronto: Butterworths, 1982).

Law Society of Upper Canada. *Transitions in the Legal Profession* (Toronto: The Law Society of Upper Canada, May 1991).

————. *Report to the Attorney General of Ontario Pursuant to Section 63.1 of the Law Society Act* (Toronto: The Law Society of Upper Canada, June 2012). Available online: <http://www.lawsocietygazette.ca/wp-content/uploads/2012/07/Paralegal-5-year-Review.pd>f

Ministry of the Attorney General (Ontario). *Task Force on Paralegals* (Toronto: The Queen's Printer, 1990) [The Ianni Commission Report].

Ontario, Working Group on Paralegals. "A Consultation Document on a Proposed Regulatory Framework" Report to Convocation, Government Relations Committee (25 April 2002).

Oughtred, Wendy. *Going it Alone: A Start Up Guide for the Sole Practitioner* (Toronto: Canada Law Book, 1995).

Plant, Albert. *Making Money: the Business of Law* (Toronto: Canada Law Book, 1993).

The Law Society of Upper Canada. *Report to the Attorney General of Ontario Pursuant to Section 63.1 of the* Law Society Act [The 5-year Paralegal Review 2007–12], June 2012. Available online: <http://www.lawsocietygazette.ca/wp-content/uploads/2012/07/Paralegal-5-year-Review.pdf>.

Towler, Patricia. *Articling in Canada: A Survival Guide 1996* (Toronto: Carswell, 1995).

Waddams, S.M. *Introduction to the Study of Law*, 7th ed. (Toronto: Carswell, 2010).

WEBSITES

Canadian Bar Association: <http://www.cba.org>

Law Society of Upper Canada: <http://www.lsuc.on.ca>

Law Society of Upper Canada *Gazette*: <http://www.lawsocietygazette.ca/>

Institute of Law Clerks of Ontario (ILCO): <http://www.ilco.on.ca/>

Paralegal Society of Ontario: <http://www.paralegalsociety.on.ca/flashpage.html>

Criminal Law

Mary Ann Kelly
BARRISTER AND SOLICITOR

Learning Objectives

After reading this chapter, the reader should be able to:

➢ understand the policy and legal issues in relation to criminal law
➢ understand the different elements of an offence
➢ understand the distinction between complete and incomplete offences
➢ understand who may be party to an offence
➢ understand and describe various criminal offences
➢ understand and describe various criminal defences

TABLE OF CONTENTS

INTRODUCTION

In Canadian law, a crime is not simply an offence committed against the particular victims. It is regarded as a wrong against society as a whole. Crime is seen as a potential breakdown in the social order and the safety and security of all Canadians. It is for this reason that criminal offences are not, for the most part, prosecuted by the actual victim of a particular offence. Rather, they are prosecuted by the state. In Canada, prosecutions are carried out in the name of the Queen, who is still the legal head of the Canadian state. The police investigate the offence, gather evidence and lay charges. Government lawyers, often referred to as Crown prosecutors, or Crown attorneys, prosecute the case before the courts.

Criminal law is an area of public law because it regulates the interaction of persons with the government, as opposed to private law, which regulates persons' relationships with each other. Under the Canadian Constitution, the power to make criminal law is assigned to the federal government.

Criminal law is contained in the *Criminal Code* of Canada, but it is not the only federal statute that deals with criminal offences. The *Controlled Drug and Substances Act*,[1] the *Food and Drugs Act*,[2] the *Income Tax Act*,[3] and the *Youth Criminal Justice Act*,[4] among other federal statutes, all contain criminal offences.

The provinces, while they have no criminal law-making authority under the Constitution, have the power to make laws regulating conduct in areas that fall within provincial law-making jurisdiction. Clearly, it would be very difficult to successfully regulate conduct if there were no consequences for failing to follow the provincial regulation. For instance, the power to regulate speed on highways in the province is a provincial responsibility. If there were no penalties attached to speeding, the provinces would have major difficulties enforcing speed limits. The provinces therefore have the jurisdiction to create provincial offences. Although these offences are sometimes referred to as quasi-criminal offences, they attract no criminal consequences and do not result in a criminal record.

The question of what causes crime has plagued sociologists and criminologists for many years. No one factor has been pinpointed as the primary cause of crime, but it is suggested that a host of biological, psychological and other social factors could predispose an individual to commit a crime. Some of these factors include poverty and the general distribution of wealth in society, heredity, physical defects, mental imbalance, emotional difficulties, lack of education and association with criminals.

Crime is not static but evolves as society evolves. While the nature of a particular act may not change, society's perception of it may. For example, the majority of Canadians have come to view the simple possession of marijuana for personal use as no longer deserving of a criminal penalty. Periodically, there are proposals made by various political parties to amend the criminal law to **decriminalize** or legalize simple possession for personal use. Decriminalization does not mean that marijuana possession would then be legal. It would still be illegal but would no longer attract criminal punishment, such as a potential jail term. Rather, a conviction would result in a fine, and there would be no criminal record for the convicted person. Clearly, this kind

---

[1] S.C. 1996, c. 19.
[2] R.S.C. 1985, c. F-27.
[3] R.S.C. 1985, c. 1.
[4] S.C. 2002, c. 1.

of change reflects a change in attitude about what kinds of wrongs are deserving of criminal consequences.

THE ELEMENTS OF AN OFFENCE

A criminal offence is made up of two separate elements: the **actus reus** and the **mens rea**. The *actus reus* are the elements of the offence that describe the wrongful conduct or actions, and the *mens rea* consists of the mental elements that are required for proving the offence. The Crown must prove every single element of the offence beyond a reasonable doubt, or the accused person will be acquitted of the charge. Moreover, the *Charter of Rights and Freedoms*, s. 11(d), provides that a person charged with a criminal offence is to be presumed innocent until proved guilty beyond a reasonable doubt.

Actus Reus

Actus reus is a Latin term that means "an action involving guilt". Before an accused person can be convicted, the Crown must prove that the accused committed the *actus reus* of the offence. The *actus reus* of each offence can be determined by carefully reading the provisions that create the offence. For instance, the elements for the offence of assault are laid out in section 265 of the *Criminal Code*:

> (1) A person commits an assault when
> > (*a*) without the consent of another person, he applies force intentionally to that other person, directly or indirectly ...

In order to establish the *actus reus* of this offence, the Crown must prove that the accused person applied force, directly or indirectly, to the victim and that the force was applied without the victim's consent. It is not sufficient merely to prove that the accused applied force. The Crown must also prove that the force was applied without the victim's consent. If the victim engaged in some voluntary activity with the accused, such as willingly stepping outside a bar to fight with the accused, that may be enough to imply that the victim was consenting to the force being applied. If that were the case, the Crown would not be successful in proving all the elements beyond a reasonable doubt.

In most offences, the accused must actually take some action in order to meet the *actus reus* of the offence. However, some offences involve a failure to act, or an omission. In order for the *actus reus* of an offence to involve an omission, there must be a positive legal duty upon the accused to take some action so that his failure to do so amounts to a wrongful action. For instance, failure to provide the necessaries of life to a dependant under 16 years old may amount to a guilty action.

Besides an *actus reus* that involves an action or an omission to do something that the accused has a legal duty to do, there are also other offences in which the *actus reus* does not require either. Rather, the *actus reus* of these latter offences requires that the accused be found in certain circumstances. For example, section 201(2)(a) of the *Criminal Code* makes it an offence to be "found, without lawful excuse, in a common gaming or common betting house". If the police arrive and find the accused in the room where the illegal gambling is taking place, he or she may be charged with and convicted of this offence. The accused does not have to actually be gambling. Being there without a lawful excuse may be enough.

Offences that involve "possession", e.g., of stolen goods or drugs, are other examples of this type of *actus reus*. Section 354 of the *Criminal Code* creates the offence of being in possession of property obtained by crime. The *actus reus* is being in possession, which is not an action but, rather, being in certain proscribed circumstances.

Mens Rea

Mens rea is another Latin term, and it means "a guilty mind". It is not sufficient for someone to merely commit a prohibited act. Generally speaking, at the same time that the accused is committing the wrongful action, he or she must have the necessary intent to accompany the action. In addition to proving that the accused committed the *actus reus* of a particular offence, the Crown must also prove beyond a reasonable doubt that the accused had a willing mind and was capable of making a choice to act. For example, if a person falls against another on a crowded bus when the bus stops suddenly, there has been an application of force, but the person applying the force did not mean it to happen and is, therefore, unlikely to be charged with a criminal offence. The *mens rea* of an offence is what makes the *actus reus* blameworthy, and it is therefore central to the commission of any true criminal offence.

In order to determine the particular mental element, or *mens rea*, necessary for a specific offence, one must read the statutory provision creating the offence. There are several categories of *mens rea*: knowledge or intent, recklessness or wilful blindness.

Knowledge or Intent

"Intent" means that a person intends or means to commit the offence and can foresee the wrongful results. Offences that require this level of *mens rea* often contain words like "intentionally", or "knowingly", or "wilfully". The Crown must prove beyond a reasonable doubt that the accused "intentionally", "knowingly", or "wilfully" committed the *actus reus* of the offence.

It is important to distinguish motive from intent. Intention is quite different from motive, but the two are sometimes confused. Motive explains the reason why a person may have acted the way that he or she did. It is often irrelevant to a finding of guilt in a criminal case. If a mother steals a loaf of bread to feed her starving children, she may have an unselfish motive, but she is intentionally stealing the bread. The reason she was stealing the bread is irrelevant in establishing her guilt. However, once she is convicted, the judge may take the reasons for committing the offence into consideration in determining her sentence.

Recklessness or Wilful Blindness

Some offences do not involve intention in the true sense. Instead, the accused deliberately takes a risk, knowing that certain wrongful consequences can flow from that risk-taking. For example, a person who aims and shoots an arrow at someone has performed an intentional act. However, an archer who takes her archery set to the local park and starts shooting arrows at a target near where children are playing and hits a child is committing a reckless act. Even though the archer does not hit the child on purpose, she has taken an unjustifiable risk; if it is proven that she could foresee the possibility that she could have hit a child, she may be found guilty of the offence based on being **reckless**.

Wilful blindness is closing one's mind to the consequences of one's actions. For example, a convenience store owner buys 100 cartons of cigarettes from someone selling them from the back of his SUV, at a quarter of their regular price. He asks no questions. It turns out the cigarettes are stolen goods. The store owner is unlikely to be able to escape criminal responsibility by simply claiming that he did not know the goods were stolen. A reasonable person would be highly suspicious of the circumstances of this purchase, and, if he did not know, it is likely due to the fact that he didn't want to know.

Strict and Absolute Liability Offences

In the Supreme Court of Canada decision in *R. v. Sault Ste. Marie*,[5] the Court examined the various types of *mens rea* that may be involved in both criminal and non-criminal provincial offences. In analyzing the issue, the Court determined that offences fall into three categories:

1. Offences in which *mens rea*, or a mental element, must be proven by the prosecution. Most criminal offences fall into this category. The prosecution must prove intention, recklessness or wilful blindness, according to whichever wording is contained in the provision that creates the offence.

2. **Strict liability offences**, in which the prosecution is only required to prove the *actus reus* of the offence. There is no requirement to prove a mental element. However, the defendant may raise a defence of due diligence. Due diligence requires a person to take all reasonable precautions to avoid the offence. If the defendant can establish this on the balance of probabilities, he or she will be acquitted of the charge.

3. **Absolute liability offences**, in which the prosecution need only prove the *actus reus* beyond a reasonable doubt. There is no requirement to establish a mental element to the offence. The defendant may not raise any defence related to *mens rea*. That the defendant took reasonable care to avoid committing the offence is irrelevant. He or she will be convicted if the *actus reus* has been proven and there is no defence established that is related to the commission of the *actus reus*.

Strict and absolute liability are not, for the most part, involved in criminal offences. They are primarily related to provincial or regulatory offences. We are discussing them here only to show the examination of the issue of *mens rea* in the *Sault St. Marie* case.

INCOMPLETE OFFENCES

Generally speaking, Canadian law does not hold people criminally responsible for a guilty mind if there is no accompanying guilty action. However, if there were no exceptions to this principle, it would be possible for people to plan criminal offences and for the police to be unable to intervene to stop the offence and charge the perpetrators before the *actus reus* of the offence was complete. Also, a criminal mastermind could direct the planning of a major offence, send other people in his gang to commit it, and avoid criminal responsibility because he did not participate in the *actus reus* of the offence. Clearly, both these scenarios are unacceptable.

Therefore, in criminal law there is the concept of incomplete offences. There are two types of incomplete offences: (i) attempts to commit a criminal offence, and (ii) conspiracy to commit a criminal offence.

Attempts

The fact that a person was unable to carry out an offence because "something went wrong" does not mean that an offence has not been committed. It is unlawful to **attempt** to commit an offence, as stated in section 24(1) of the *Criminal Code*:

> Every one who, having an intent to commit an offence, does or omits to do anything for the purpose of carrying out the intention is guilty of an attempt

---

[5] (1978), 40 C.C.C. (2d) 353.

to commit the offence whether or not it was possible under the circumstances to commit the offence.

The Crown must prove beyond a reasonable doubt that the accused had the intention to commit the offence. It need not, however, prove that the *actus reus* was complete, because it was not. The accused must only have taken steps towards the commission of the offence that went beyond mere preparation and have the necessary intent or *mens rea* to commit the offence in order to be found guilty of an attempt.

It also does not matter if the offence was impossible to commit. For instance, the robber intends to rob the bank and goes to the bank armed with a weapon. As he approaches the building he sees a police car outside the doughnut shop next door and turns around and walks away, he may still be charged with and convicted of an attempted robbery if he is caught by the police. The fact that he changed his mind just before committing the offence will not be a sufficient defence, because he has likely gone beyond mere preparation by arming himself and going to the bank. Likewise, if the robber went to the bank and it was unexpectedly closed due to a flood in basement, he can still be convicted of an attempted robbery even though it was impossible to rob the bank that day.

Conspiracy

Conspiracy is another example of an incomplete offence. A conspiracy is an agreement between two or more people to carry out a criminal offence. In order to prove a conspiracy, the Crown must prove that the people involved had a serious intention to carry out the proposed act. They need not prove that the *actus reus* was carried out by anyone. However, if the *actus reus* was actually completed by some members of the planning group and not others, the planners who took no part in the completion of the *actus reus* can still be convicted of conspiracy. Conspiracy is often used in drug offences and in charges laid against organized crime.

The penalty imposed upon a conviction for conspiracy is the same penalty one would have received if the offence had been fully carried out.

PERSONS WHO MAY BE CHARGED WITH AN OFFENCE

A person who actually commits the offence is the principal offender. In addition, people who assist the principal offender in some way to commit an offence may also be held criminally responsible for the offence and may be liable to the same punishment as the principal offender. The assistance may have been given before, during or after the commission of the main offence. Moreover, the persons who assist the principal offender may be convicted even if the principal offender is not.

Aiding and Abetting, s. 21

To be found guilty of **aiding** in the commission of an offence, the accused must have offered the principal offender some help in carrying out the offence. **Abetting** is encouraging the principal offender to commit the offence. The Crown must prove that the accused knew that the principal was committing or intended to commit an offence, and that the accused aided or assisted or helped the offender. Merely being present at the scene of a crime is not sufficient for a conviction. The accused must have known that a criminal offence was being committed and actually have intended to help or encourage the principal offender in some way.

If the accused was tricked or duped into helping the offender, he will not be held responsible for aiding or abetting. Rather, he will be regarded as an innocent agent.

For example, John brings prohibited drugs into Canada concealed in a box of chocolate with a false bottom that he was asked by his cousin to take to his sister as a gift. The fact that he is saying he did not know that the drugs were in the box could be raised as a defence. Of course, he will only be successful if he can raise a reasonable probability that he truly did not know.

Counselling, s. 22

A person who advises or solicits another person to commit an offence may be found guilty of the offence, even if the offence was committed in a different way than what was suggested. In fact, even if no offence is actually committed by the person who was counselled to commit it, the person who did the counselling may be convicted.

Accessory after the Fact, s. 23

One may also be held criminally liable for an offence if one knew that an offence has been committed and offered assistance to the offender for the purpose of helping him to escape detention or capture. Providing food, shelter or clothing to the offender after the commission of the offence are all considered sufficient for a conviction as an **accessory after the fact** as long as the aid was given to help the offender escape the police.

At one time, a spouse who offered assistance to an offender, even if it was to assist in escaping detection, could not be convicted as an accessory after the fact. However, section 23 of the *Criminal Code* has been amended, and a spouse is no longer excluded from criminal responsibility when acting as an accessory.

SPECIFIC OFFENCES

Violent Offences

Homicide

Under section 222(1) of the *Criminal Code*, homicide is an act that directly or indirectly causes the death of another person. Homicide can be culpable or non-culpable or, in simpler terms, blameworthy or non-blameworthy. Non-culpable homicide is not a criminal offence. The person who causes the death is not held criminally responsible. For example, if a death resulted from a traffic accident where the victim, the person who died, drove through a red light, the offence is non-culpable homicide. Culpable homicide, on the other hand, is an offence, and the person causing death is held criminally accountable for the death. The *Criminal Code* recognizes three forms of culpable homicide: murder, manslaughter and infanticide.

☐ MURDER

Murder is considered the most serious violent crime that one person can commit against another because the judicial system obviously cannot provide any remedy for the victim.

Murder is committed under the following circumstances stated in section 229 of the *Criminal Code*:

• If the person who causes the death means to do so.
• If the person who causes the death means to cause bodily harm and knows the act is likely to cause death.
• If the person who causes the death does so while committing a criminal act, whether the death is caused accidentally or not.

In other words, for a murder offence, both *actus reus* (the physical act) and *mens rea* (the mental intent) must be present (except under s. 231(4), where the victim is a law enforcement agent — e.g., a police officer).

There are two types of murder under the *Criminal Code*: first-degree and second-degree. Murders that are not first-degree murder are considered second-degree murder. Murder is first-degree when the death is caused on purpose (s. 231(2): "when it is planned and deliberate"). Moreover, if the victim is a police officer or any other law enforcement agent listed in section 231(4), or if the death occurs during the perpetration of, or an attempt to perpetrate, any of the offences listed in section 231(5), including a hijacking of a plane, a sexual assault, or a kidnapping, then the offence is automatically first-degree murder.

Sentencing for murder is mandatory. Murderers in Canada receive a sentence of life imprisonment. The only issue is when they may be eligible for parole. The minimum penalty for first-degree murder is life imprisonment without eligibility for parole for 25 years. For second-degree murder, the minimum time to be served in prison without parole eligibility can vary from 10 up to 25 years. The sentencing principles that judges consider in the length of sentence and parole are laid out in sections 718 to 718.21 and 745 of the *Criminal Code*.

□ MANSLAUGHTER

Manslaughter is a culpable homicide that does not fall under murder or infanticide, and it is further categorized as voluntary manslaughter and involuntary manslaughter.

Manslaughter is considered involuntary manslaughter if the killer lacks the mental intent to cause death. Involuntary manslaughter generally occurs in two situations: first, when the death is caused by criminal negligence, and second, when the death occurs during the commission of another crime, where there is no intent to cause bodily injury or death.

Voluntary manslaughter occurs when the intent exists but only after "adequate provocation" — that is, the accused has been sufficiently provoked to the extent that a "reasonable or ordinary person" would be incited to lose self-control. It should be noted that the time between provocation and the killing should not be enough to allow the passion to cool off or consider their actions.

Anyone who commits manslaughter, whether it is voluntary or involuntary, is guilty of an indictable offence and is liable to life in prison. There is also no minimum punishment or minimum time of ineligibility for parole. As a result, the sentences can vary greatly, depending on the circumstances of the death and the intent. A longer sentence may be given if the accused has been convicted of other offences.

□ INFANTICIDE

Infanticide, the final type of culpable homicide, is defined under the *Criminal Code*, section 233. It occurs when a mother, suffering from the side effects of giving birth so that her mind is disturbed, by a wilful act or omission, causes the death of her newborn child. Infanticide is the only culpable homicide that does not have a minimum or maximum sentence of life in prison. Under section 237 of the *Criminal Code*, the sentence for infanticide is imprisonment for a term not exceeding five years.

Property Offences

Offences involving property make up the vast majority of offences in the *Criminal Code*. In this discussion of the topic, we will focus on the offences of theft and break and enter as examples of property offences.

Theft

Theft is the most basic property offence. The *actus reus* of the offence requires taking or converting someone else's property. Converting property involves using property for one's own purposes as though one were the true legal owner, thereby depriving the rightful owner of his use of the property. An example of converting, or conversion, would be borrowing a friend's stereo while the friend was away on holiday, setting it up and then refusing to return it to the friend at the end of the loan period.

The *actus reus* must be accompanied by an intention to fraudulently deprive another person of her property. Moreover, the person taking or converting the property to his own use must do so without colour of right. The term **colour of right** refers to a situation in which a person honestly believes that they have a legal right to the property. To be convicted of theft, the Crown must prove the accused knew, or should have known, that he had no legal right to the property in question. For instance, if the accused found an old leather chair on the side of the road, he might believe that the chair had been abandoned and might take it home to use in his family room. He would be acting under "colour of right" if it was reasonable to believe that the chair actually had been abandoned, even if it had not but, instead, it had fallen off the back of a moving van and the true owner was searching for it.

The *Criminal Code* provides different penalties and modes of trial, depending on whether the value of the property taken or converted exceeds the value of $5,000. Theft of property valued at over $5,000 is an indictable offence, liable for punishment for a term of up to 10 years. Theft of property valued at less than $5,000 is a hybrid offence, subject to Crown election to be prosecuted as either an indictable offence or a summary conviction offence. The types of offences are discussed in more detail in Chapter 12, dealing with criminal procedure.

Break and Enter

A break and enter occurs if premises are illegally entered by a person who intends to commit an indictable offence once inside. The illegal entry does not necessarily have to involve the breaking of a window or a lock, or any other type of forced entry. Simply opening an unlocked door and going inside is sufficient to complete the *actus reus* of the offence.

The *mens rea* of the offence is the specific intent to commit an indictable offence inside the premises. The most common indictable offence that the accused intends to commit inside would be theft. The Crown is required to show that the accused entered with the intent of committing an indictable offence. However, evidence that the accused illegally entered the premises will normally be enough, absent evidence to the contrary, to prove that the accused was intending to commit an offence inside.

The penalty for break and enter is quite severe and includes a maximum penalty of life imprisonment where the offence involved a dwelling house, and a maximum of 10 years for any premises other than a dwelling house.

Controversial Offences

Abortion

Abortion is an extremely controversial issue that involves differing religious, moral and social viewpoints. "Pro-choice" groups believe that a decision to have an abortion should be between a woman and her doctor and that the Government of Canada and criminal law should not be involved at all. "Pro-life" groups take the anti-abortion position and believe that abortion should result in a criminal conviction.

Until 1988, a legal abortion could only be obtained if the woman received permission from a "therapeutic abortion committee" set up by an "approved hospital". The committee considered the applicant's medical information and the recommendations of her doctor and decided whether an abortion would be performed based on a finding that continuing the pregnancy would endanger the woman's health and well-being. However, not all hospitals had these committees and, in some areas of the country, abortions were unavailable because there was no hospital with a committee.

In 1988, in the case of *R. v Morgentaler, Smoling and Scott*,[6] the Supreme Court of Canada ruled that section 287 of the *Criminal Code* was unconstitutional in that it restricted approval of abortion to these hospital committees. The three accused were medical doctors who were charged with performing abortions in clinics without committee approval. The Supreme Court examined a number of *Charter* issues and, among other things, determined that "security of the person" within the meaning of section 7 of the *Charter* must include a right of access to medical treatment for a condition representing a danger to life or health without fear of criminal sanction. The Court then deemed section 287 of the *Criminal Code* to be of no force and effect because of its unconstitutionality.

As a result, although section 287 remains in the *Criminal Code*, it cannot be enforced; therefore, there is no enforceable law in Canada that prohibits abortions.

Obscenity

Obscenity is another offence that may generate public concern. Section 2 of the *Charter* guarantees freedom of expression, including freedom of the press. The issue then becomes, What kind of writing, photographs, films, etc., constitute obscenity, and how does freedom of expression interact with the *Criminal Code* provisions? In other words, just how involved should the criminal law be in prohibiting material, given freedom of expression, and when does material cross the line into "undue exploitation of sex"? Can some material be art in the eyes of some individuals while being obscene in the view of others? These are the questions courts are asked to examine when deliberating on obscenity offences.

Section 163 of the *Criminal Code* states the following:

(1) Every one commits an offence who
 (a) makes, prints, publishes, distributes, circulates, or has in his possession for the purpose of publication, distribution or circulation any obscene written matter, picture, model, phonograph record or other thing whatever ...

(8) For the purposes of this Act, any publication a dominant characteristic of which is the undue exploitation of sex, or of sex and any one or more of the following subjects, namely, crime, horror, cruelty and violence, shall be deemed to be obscene.

Pursuant to the above section and section 164, a judge may issue a warrant, allowing the police to seize any material deemed to be obscene. The person found with the material will be charged and, if convicted, will be liable for up to two years imprisonment.

The defences that accused persons usually bring forward to such a charge include challenging the allegation that the "dominant characteristic" of the materials is sexual, or that it there is an "undue exploitation of sex". In deciding these issues, the courts will generally look to accepted community standards of tolerance at the time the material was seized. For instance, the

---

[6] [1988] 1 S.C.R. 30.

standard of tolerance in a big city may be significantly higher than in a small town or villiage.

Prostitution

Prostitution itself is not a criminal offence in Canada. However, section 213 makes it an offence to communicate for the purpose of prostitution. The offence involves stopping, or attempting to stop, another person, in a public place, for the purpose of asking them to engage in prostitution. Both the prostitute and/or the client may be charged with this offence. It is a summary conviction offence.

In addition to section 213, there are several other sections of the *Criminal Code* that create prostitution-related offences. Section 210 makes it an offence to keep or be found in a common bawdy house (a place where prostitution occurs); section 211 makes it an offence to knowingly transport a person to a bawdy house; section 212 makes it an offence to procure a person into prostitution or to live off the avails of prostitution, i.e., live off the money that a prostitute makes, although it is not an offence for a prostitute to live off the money he or she makes.

There are many people in the community who believe that prostitution is not being properly controlled by the *Criminal Code*, and that it would be better to set up "red light" districts, where prostitutes are licensed and regulated by the government. Those who take this particular approach say that rounding up prostitutes and taking them to jail overnight does little to stop them, and that the next night they will be out on the same streets again. Instead, some propose that the sex trade be confined to a particular district where residents of neighbourhoods are not exposed to it, and where prostitutes can be protected from pimps through government licensing.

Those opposed to this approach argue that licensing prostitutes is not a proper activity for governments and that prostitution is very closely linked with other offences, such as the drug trade. These people believe that decriminalizing prostitution would create an opportunity for organized crime. In addition, there are concerns about the trafficking in women from poorer countries, who may be enticed into prostitution unwittingly.

In late 2013, the Supreme Court of Canada, in the case of *Canada (Attorney General) v. Bedford*, determined that sections 210, 212(1)(j), and 213(1), violate the right of the sex workers to security of the person under section 7 of the *Charter of Rights and Freedoms*.[7]

The **Charter challenge** case was brought by several sex workers. They were arguing that certain sections of the *Criminal Code* violated their right to security of the person under section 7 of the *Charter*, as they were forced to work in total privacy, without any protection from a driver or bodyguard or even the protection found in being on a public street, with others around. The Court agreed that the challenged sections, specifically sections 210, 212(1)(j), and 213(1)(c), did breach section 7 of the *Charter* as it created controls that placed prostitutes in danger even though they were engaged in an activity that was, in itself, not illegal. The Court delayed the declaration of invalidity of the sections for one year to allow the government to pass new legislation that would not violate *Charter* rights. At the time of publication, the government is working on drafting new legislation. Only time will tell if they have succeeded in creating law imposes limitations on prostitution-related activity that are not inconsistent with the *Charter*.

---

[7] *Canada (Attorney General) v. Bedford*, 2013 SCC 72, [2013] 3 SCR 1101.

Possession of Marijuana for Personal Use

For well over a decade, there has been serious discussion about the decriminalization or legalization of possession of small amounts of marijuana for personal use. Decriminalization would mean that possession for personal use would not be legal but, instead of being dealt with as a criminal law matter, which would lead to a criminal record upon a finding of guilt, the offence would be dealt with as a regulatory offence that would result in a fine, like a speeding ticket. No criminal record would result from a conviction.

Legalization, on the other hand, would remove any type of offence, criminal or regulatory, and there would be no legal consequences attached to possession of small amounts. Some lawmakers, proposing legalization, suggest that the government take over the sale of marijuana and sell it for personal use in licensed stores.

Whether it is decriminalization or legalization being proposed, it would still be a criminal offence to possess large amounts or to traffic in marijuana.

People in support of this change to the legislation take the position that the use of marijuana is not addictive and that there is no evidence that it leads to the use of harder drugs. It is recognized that large numbers of people in Canada have used or experimented with marijuana, and it is, to many, unfair that people who are caught with a small amount should be followed throughout their lives by a criminal record.

However, there is another group opposed to decriminalization. This group is concerned that marijuana use can lead to involvement with more serious drugs and that decriminalization does not give police a range of escalating options for dealing with the offence.

DEFENCES

Canadian criminal law developed from British common law. However, for well over a hundred years Canada has had a criminal law statute. There are no common law offences left in Canada. The only offences of which a person may be charged and convicted are prescribed by the *Criminal Code* or another federal statute that contains criminal offences, such as the *Controlled Drugs and Substances Act*. However, the *Criminal Code* specifically preserved common law defences.[8] Therefore, common law defences are still available under Canadian criminal law. This means that there are defences that are not in a statute but are, rather, based in the common law; there are defences that are in statutes, primarily the *Criminal Code*; and there are defences that are both common law and statute-based.

Some defences are raised in relation to whether the accused actually committed the *actus reus* of the offence, and other defences go to the *mens rea* elements — i.e., the defence is claiming that the accused did not have the intent required to commit a criminal offence.

In order to meet the requisite elements of the *actus reus*, it is essential that the accused person performed the wrongful actions voluntarily. If he did not have control over his actions, he may be able to raise a successful defence that negates one or more elements of the *actus reus*.

Automatism

Automatism is a common law defence. The term refers to behaviour that a person performs while in a state of impaired consciousness. The most com-

---

[8] *Criminal Code*, R.S.C. 1985. Chap. C-46, s. 8(3).

248 / CHAPTER 11

mon example of a state of automatism is a person who is sleepwalking. There are two types of automatism recognized in Canadian criminal law:

1. Automatism caused by a mental disorder or extreme intoxication. This type of automatism is treated the same way as the defence of mental disorder, discussed below. It is sometimes referred to as "insane automatism".

2. Automatism caused by something other than a mental disorder or extreme intoxication. This is usually caused by some sort of physiological or neurological disorder. The most common example of this type of automatism is a person who is sleepwalking.

The defence may be raised in relation to any offence and, if successful, would result in the complete acquittal of the accused. Automatism is, therefore, a complete defence to the charge. However, such a defence is very difficult to establish.

Provocation

Provocation is a defence created by the *Criminal Code*, s. 232. It can only be used as a defence to a charge of murder; it is not applicable to any other offence. If the defence is accepted, the conviction for murder will be reduced to the lesser and included offence of manslaughter. Provocation is, therefore, only a partial defence, not a complete defence, because the accused is not acquitted.

Provocation may involve blows, words, or gestures that cause a person to lose the power of self-control. It must be sudden, and the reaction of the accused must be immediate. The accused must not have had any time at all to consider the consequences of his actions.

The standard for establishing provocation is an objective one. The provocation must have been of such magnitude that it would have caused the average person to lose control. If an accused has little self-control and is liable to fly off the handle at minor slights, he will likely have considerable difficulty establishing this defence.

Duress

Duress is a very complicated defence, with both a statutory and a common law aspect.

Section 17 of the *Criminal Code* provides the statutory defence.

> A person who commits an offence under compulsion by threats of immediate death or bodily harm from a person who is present when the offence is committed is excused for committing the offence if the person believes that the threats will be carried out and if the person is not a party to a conspiracy or association whereby the person is subject to compulsion, but this section does not apply where the offence that is committed is high treason or treason, murder, piracy, attempted murder, sexual assault, sexual assault with a weapon, threats to a third party or causing bodily harm, aggravated sexual assault, forcible abduction, hostage taking, robbery, assault with a weapon or causing bodily harm, aggravated assault, unlawfully causing bodily harm, arson or an offence under sections 280 to 283 (abduction and detention of young persons).

The statute requires that, in order for this defence to be established, the accused must act under the threat of imminent bodily harm or death to herself or members of her family. Second, the person making the threats must be present when the offence is committed; and finally, the defence is not available for the offences excluded by section 17, which includes most of the serious offences, such as murder, assault causing bodily harm, arson, and sexual assault.

In 2001 the Supreme Court of Canada found section 17 to be in violation of section 7 of the *Charter* to the extent that it allows individuals who acted involuntarily to be found guilty of a criminal offence. The requirement in the section that the person issuing the threat be present at the commission of the offence, coupled with the necessity of the threat being immediate, created the constitutional issue. There are circumstances where the threat may not be immediate from a person present at the scene, and yet the act may still be involuntary in the sense that the person had no realistic choice other than breaking the law to avoid the threat being carried out. An example might be a situation in which a loved one or family member of the accused is being threatened with death, a death that the accused believes will be carried out, unless the accused commits the crime that the person doing the threatening is demanding be committed. Thus, said the Supreme Court, section 17 is too restrictive and is a violation of the *Charter*. As a result, the requirement in section 17 that the person doing the threatening be present at the commission of the offence was struck down and is of no force and effect.

The common law version of the defence of duress never included the statutory requirement that the person doing the threatening be present for the commission of the offence or that the threat be immediate. Thus, the Supreme Court found that it created no constitutional violations in that regard. The court restated the elements that must be established for the common law defence to succeed:

1. The accused must have acted solely as a result of threats of death or serious bodily harm to herself or another person.

2. The threats must have been of such gravity or seriousness that the accused believed that the threats would be carried out. However, a threat that is too far in the future may be found not to be a real threat.

3. The threats must have been of such gravity that they might well have caused a reasonable person placed in the same situation as the accused to act in the same manner as she did. To put that another way: Would a person of reasonable firmness, sharing the characteristics of the accused, such as her age and her background, have responded to the threats?

4. Finally, the accused must not have had an obvious safe avenue of escape.

Necessity

Necessity is similar to duress in that the accused is arguing that he or she had no other option but to commit the offence; it is, however, different in that duress is caused by a person making a threat of harm to the accused or his or her loved ones, while necessity deals with circumstances that forced the accused to break the law.

In raising the defence of necessity, the accused is saying that some sort of urgent or exigent circumstances or a situation of great danger required him or her to commit the offence. In other words, he or she broke the law in order to prevent the infliction of a greater harm.

In addition, the defence of necessity requires that the following two conditions be met:

1. There must be no other reasonable legal alternative available to the accused. If there is a legal alternative available, then the accused must take the legal avenue.

2. The harm caused by the commission of the offence must be weighed against the harm avoided by the commission of the offence. This is called a proportionality test.

Necessity is a common law defence.

Self-Defence

Self-defence is a statutory defence contained in sections 34 and 35 of the *Criminal Code*. It is a complete defence in that, if successful, it will lead to the acquittal of the accused.

A person is permitted to use reasonable force to protect themselves, and those under their protection, from an unprovoked assault by another. However, the defence will only be successful when the force used was not intended to cause death or grievous bodily harm and when the force was no more than what was necessary to repel the attack. The criteria the court must consider in applying self-defence are laid out in section 34 of the *Criminal ode*.

Section 35 deals with defence of property and the amount of force that a person may use to defend that property. The amount of force that may be used is much less than in circumstances in which a person is defending himself or herself or someone else from an assault or attack of some nature.

Mental Disorder

The defence of mental disorder has replaced the defence of insanity in Canadian law. The defence is laid out in section 16 of the *Criminal Code*:

> (1) No person is criminally responsible for an act committed or an omission made while suffering from a mental disorder that rendered the person incapable of appreciating the nature and quality of the act or omission or of knowing that it was wrong.

In order to establish the defence, several elements must be proved. First, an accused must be suffering from a mental disorder. A mental disorder is defined in section 2 of the *Criminal Code* as a "disease of the mind". In determining what constitutes a disease of the mind, courts apply a legal test, not simply a medical test. A psychiatrist or psychologist may give evidence as to the accused's mental health, but it is up to the judge to determine whether the legal definition has been met.

Second, once the disease of the mind has been established, one of two tests must be met. It must be proved that the disease of the mind is such that the accused is incapable

1. of appreciating the nature or quality of his act, or
2. of knowing it is wrong.

Courts have drawn a distinction between "knowing" and "appreciating". To "know" means to merely be aware of one's physical actions. To "appreciate" involves a higher awareness and understanding of the consequences of one's actions. The courts have interpreted "knowing it is wrong" to mean that in addition to knowing it was legally wrong, the accused must also know his or her actions were morally wrong.

A person found not criminally responsible by reason of a mental disorder is not automatically set free into the community. There must be a disposition hearing at which the accused faces court-ordered detention in a mental health facility for an indeterminate period of time. There are built-in periodic reviews to determine whether or not the person has recovered from the mental disorder to such a degree that he or she poses no further danger to the public.

Intoxication

Intoxication is another defence that has both common law and statutory elements.

We will look at the common law elements first in our discussion.

Offences in the *Criminal Code* can be divided into specific intent offences and general intent offences. The defence of intoxication is available for specific intent offences only.

For most offences, the Crown must prove only that the accused committed the *actus reus* intentionally, knowingly or recklessly, etc., as the case may be. These offences are general intent offences. The vast majority of offences in the *Criminal Code* are general intent offences, and a defence of intoxication is not available for these offences.

Specific intent offences are sometimes referred to as offences requiring an ulterior or additional level of intent. In other words, the Crown must prove what amounts to two levels of intent. For example, the offence of break and enter is a specific intent offence. The Crown must prove not only that the accused intended to break and enter the premises but also — and this is the second level of intent — that the accused intended to commit an indictable offence once inside. Other examples of specific intent offences are murder, theft, and assault with a weapon.

The defence of intoxication may be used to establish that the accused was too impaired to form the necessary second level of intent for specific intent offences.

In 1994, in the case of *R. v. Daviault*, the Supreme Court of Canada ruled that intoxication could be a defence to a general intent offence if the level of intoxication was so extreme that it produced a state in the accused akin to a mental disorder or automatism. This case was widely criticized in the media, particularly as it involved a violent sexual assault. In response to the public outcry, the federal government added section 33.1 to the *Criminal Code*. The section statutorily overrides the case law in *Daviault* and precludes the use of self-induced, voluntary intoxication as a defence to a general intent offence involving an element of assault or interference with the bodily integrity of another.

Mistake of Fact

This defence involves the accused establishing that although she committed the *mens rea*, she did so based on an honest belief in a set of facts that made her believe she was not committing an offence — for instance, if the accused truly believed that her husband had died while on a geological expedition in a remote area and she then entered into a marriage with another man even while, unbeknownst to her, her first husband was still alive. Certainly the *actus reus* of the offence of bigamy would be complete. She entered into a marriage with a second husband while the first husband was still alive and while she was still married to him. However, if she could prove that she honestly believed her first husband was dead, she could successfully raise a *mens rea* defence. She did not intend to break the law.[9]

CHAPTER SUMMARY

This chapter provided a brief introduction to substantive criminal law in Canada. Criminal law is a type of public law that involves the Crown as one of the parties. The person accused of the offence is the other party. The purpose

---

[9] *Tolson*, (1889) 23 Q.B.D. 168.

of criminal law is to prosecute and punish an accused on behalf of society as a whole, and not necessarily on behalf of the alleged victim of the offence.

In a criminal prosecution, the Crown has the burden of proving each of the elements of the offence, beyond a reasonable doubt. The elements of an offence may be divided into the wrongful act — the *actus reus* — and the wrongful intent — the *mens rea*.

A number of offences were discussed, dealing with both offences against persons and offences against property. A number of controversial offences were presented to illustrate that as Canadian society changes, public opinion about what constitutes criminal behaviour may change. Further, as a barometer of change, the *Charter of Rights and Freedoms* has also been used to test whether criminal law complies with the constitutional rights and freedoms guaranteed to Canadians.

The chapter then reviewed some selected common law and statutory defences.

GLOSSARY OF NEW TERMS AND KEY CONCEPTS

abetting	To encourage, incite, or set another on to commit a crime.
absolute liability offence	A type of offence where the Crown could obtain a conviction by simply proving that the accused committed the prohibited act.
accessory after the fact	Someone who assists or protects another after the other person has committed a crime.
actus reus	This is a Latin term that means "a guilty act". The *actus reus*, along with *mens rea*, is one of the two essential elements of a crime.
aiding	To help, assist, or facilitate the commission of a crime.
attempt	Any act done with intent to commit a criminal offence.
automatism	An unconscious, involuntary act, where the mind does not go with what is being done.
***Charter* challenge**	A case brought to court by a person or persons who believe their *Charter* rights have been violated by a law and who want the court to determine if this is so.
colour of right	the genuine appearance or presumption that there is an existing legal right when, in fact, no such right exists.
conspiracy	An agreement between two or more people to carry out a crime.
decriminalize	The act of removing a particular offence from criminal liability while not making the actions legal. Actions that were once regarded as criminal offences remain offences but no longer attract a criminal record.
mens rea	This is a Latin term that means "a guilty mind". *Mens rea*, along with *actus reus*, is one of the two essential elements of a crime.
recklessness	A state of mind that pays no regard to the possible injurious consequences of an act.
strict liability offence	An offence for which the Crown need only prove that the accused committed the actions required to complete the offence. There is no need to prove the intention or *mens rea* of the offence, but the accused may raise the defence of due diligence, meaning that the accused took all due care to try to prevent the commission of the offence.
wilful blindness	A conscious closing of one's mind to the consequences of one's acts.

REVIEW QUESTIONS

1. What is the difference between *actus reus* and *mens rea*?

2. Describe two different levels of intent in criminal law.

3. What is an incomplete crime? Give two examples.

4. Describe three forms of culpable homicide.

5. Give two circumstances where a charge of assault could be successfully defended by the accused.

6. What is the present law in Canada regarding abortion (or procuring a miscarriage)?

7. Why should an accused have more than "tactical defence" reasons for advocating the defence of "not guilty by reason of mental defect"?

8. What elements must be established to effectively raise the defence of necessity?

9. What is the difference between a specific intent offence and a general intent offence? Why is it important to be able to make this distinction in establishing a defence such as drunkenness?

10. Who may be convicted of an offence?

DISCUSSION QUESTIONS

1. Recent political campaigns have stressed the need to focus on crime prevention as a means of making our communities safer and more secure. One argument is that we can prevent crime by addressing the causes of crime. What, in your view, are the causes of crime?

2. Do you think some crimes — for example, prostitution — should be decriminalized and regulated or legalized rather than prohibited? What should be the criteria for determining which of the crimes in the *Criminal Code* could be repealed?

3. *Mens rea* is a necessary component in assessing guilt in a criminal proceeding. If John has taken drugs or consumed alcohol to the point where he is so impaired that he does not know what he is doing, should he be able to successfully argue that he did not have the necessary *mens rea* at the time of the offence?

4. In the *Criminal Code*, compare the sections relating to the crimes of (i) impaired driving causing death, (ii) criminal negligence causing death, (iii) manslaughter, (iv) second-degree murder, and (iv) first-degree murder, and answer the following:

   (a) Briefly, what are the levels of intent required to convict an accused on each of those charges?
   (b) Briefly, explain the rationale for the differences in punishment.

5. Discuss the following statement: "The defence of not guilty by reason of mental disorder is an easy way to avoid responsibility for criminal liability."

SUGGESTED READING AND OTHER RESOURCES

Barnhorst, Sherrie, & Richard Barnhorst. *Criminal Law and the Canadian Criminal Code*, 5th ed. (Toronto: McGraw-Hill Ryerson, 2009).

Greenspan, E., & M. Rosenberg, eds. *Martin's Annual Criminal Code* (Aurora, Ont.: Canada Law Book, 2013 [updated annually]).

Gulycz, Michael, & Mary Ann Kelly, *Criminal Law for Legal Professionals* (Toronto: Emond Montgomery Publications, 2013).

Pink, Joel E., Q.C., & David Perrier. *From Crime to Punishment: An Introduction to the Criminal System*, 7th ed. (Toronto: Thomson Carswell, 2010).

Verdun-Jones, Simon N. *Criminal Law in Canada, Cases, Questions and the Code*, 5th ed. (Toronto: Nelson Education, 2011).

WEBSITES

CanLII: <http://www.canlii.org/en/index.html>

Canadian Bar Association: <http://www.cbabc.org/For-the-Public/Dial-A-Law/Scripts/Criminal-Law>

Justice Laws Website, *Criminal Code*: <http://laws-lois.justice.gc.ca/eng/acts/c-46/> (See also federal and provincial ministries of attorney general websites.)

The Law Dictionary: <http://thelawdictionary.org/>

Criminal Procedure

Mary Ann Kelly
BARRISTER AND SOLICITOR

Learning Objectives

After reading this chapter, the reader should be able to:

➢ identify the role of criminal procedure in the justice system in general and the criminal law system in particular

➢ understand the various types of jurisdiction involved when dealing with criminal offences

➢ describe the various classifications of criminal offences and the procedure for prosecuting each type of offence

➢ demonstrate an understanding of the procedure for bringing the accused before the court, including powers of arrest and purpose of a bail hearing

➢ describe the various investigatory powers available to the police and the role the *Charter of Rights and Freedoms* plays in relation to police investigatory powers

➢ outline the various steps in a criminal trial

➢ describe the various sentencing principles applied by the court and the sentencing options available to the court in relation to different types of offences

➢ provide an overview of the procedure for dealing with young persons in the criminal justice system

TABLE OF CONTENTS

INTRODUCTION

This chapter provides an overview of procedural criminal law. Procedural criminal law deals with the power of the police to investigate offences and the methods of bringing the accused before the court, the jurisdiction of the court to hear the case, and the process for prosecuting different kinds of offences. It is different from substantive criminal law in that unlike substantive law it is not the area of law that creates offences or defences.

Criminal procedure is more than just a "technicality". Since it is the government or state that is prosecuting the offence, it is essential that proper procedure be followed in order to ensure a fair process. The state has multiple resources available to it: police who investigate alleged offences; government forensic specialists and laboratories that process crime scenes and examine physical evidence; Crown attorneys/counsel who prosecute the cases. All of these resources are directed at the prosecution of individuals; and, in order that individuals who normally are not able to avail themselves of similar resources have a fair opportunity to defend themselves, the prosecution will be held to strict procedural standards. This has always been the case in Canadian law but is even more crucial since the enactment of the *Charter of Rights and Freedoms*.

CLASSIFICATION OF OFFENCES

All offences in the *Criminal Code*, R.S.C. 1985, c. C-46, may be classified into one of three categories:

- **Indictable offences** are the most serious offences and include murder, robbery, arson, serious assaults.
- **Summary conviction offences** are the least serious forms of criminal offence.
- **Hybrid offences**, or "Crown option" offences, are those offences that may be prosecuted as an indictable offence or a summary conviction offence on the election or choice of the Crown.

The classification of an offence determines the procedure to be followed in arresting the accused and in charging him. It also determines which level of court will hear the case and the route to be followed through the court system in the event of an appeal.

In addition to the offences in the *Criminal Code* and a number of other federal statutes, there are also offences created by provincial statutes. These offences are not criminal offences but are, rather, regulatory offences anacted and governed by a provincial statute, like the offence of speeding in the *Highway Traffic Act*. In some provinces, including Ontario, these provincial offences are prosecuted under a provincial statute. In other provinces, however, these provincial offences are prosecuted under the procedure for the prosecution of summary conviction offences provided in the *Criminal Code*. The manner in which these provincial offences are prosecuted may differ, but no matter how they are prosecuted, they do not lead to a criminal record. A discussion of provincial offences is outside the scope of this chapter.

Summary Conviction Offences

These offences are the most minor in the *Criminal Code*. The procedure for dealing with them is contained in Part XXVII of the *Code*.

Trials for summary conviction offences are held in the provincial court before a judge alone; there is no provision for a jury trial for these offences, and penalties are much lower than for other offences. Pursuant to section 787 of the *Criminal Code*, the general penalty on conviction for a summary conviction offence is a maximum fine of $5,000 and/or a maximum jail term of six months, although some summary offences do provide for a long maximum penalty than that prescribed by the general penalty. Both a fine and a jail sentence can be imposed: for instance, an offender may be sentenced to 30 days in jail and a fine of $200.

A document called an **Information** commences the court proceeding against the accused and contains the charges for which the accused is being prosecuted. As indicated, both Informations are discussed later in this chapter.

Indictable Offences These offences are the most serious in the *Criminal Code*. The procedure for prosecution of indictable offences is more complex. Indictable offences fall into one of three categories according to their seriousness. Each of this group has a different mode of trial.

The first group of offences is listed in section 469 of the *Criminal Code*, and they are the most serious indictable offences. They include murder and treason. Trials of these matters must be heard before a judge of the superior court and a jury, unless both the Crown and the accused consent to proceed without a jury.

The second category of indictable offences is listed in section 553 of the *Code*. Generally speaking, these offences are the least serious indictable offences. They are more serious than summary conviction offences but considerably less serious than the offences listed in section 469. This group of offences includes driving while disqualified and keeping a gaming and betting house. Trials of these matters must be heard in the provincial court by a judge sitting alone without a jury. There is no provision for trial by jury for offences listed in section 553.

All indictable offences not listed in sections 469 or 553 fall into the final group. When charged with one of these offences, the accused is permitted to choose or elect the mode of trial according to the procedure outlined in section 536. The options are as follows:

* Trial by a provincial court judge without a jury and without preliminary hearing
* Trial by a superior court judge alone
* Trial by a superior court judge and a jury

Failure of the accused to elect one of these options will result in the accused being deemed to have elected a trial by a judge and a jury in the superior court.

The election as to the mode of trial must be made before a judge of the lower court or court of first instance, such as the provincial court. In Ontario, the accused is given the choice to be tried by a judge alone at the Superior Court of Justice or by a provincial judge in the Ontario Court of Justice. If the accused elects a trial in the superior court and requests a preliminary inquiry, the preliminary inquiry will be held in the provincial court. Preliminary inquiries are discussed later in this chapter.

The legal document upon which the accused is prosecuted varies, depending upon the level of court in which his trial is held. If he is tried in the provincial court, either because that is his election or because it is an offence listed in section 553, he will be tried on a document called an Information. If he is tried before the superior court, he will be tried on the basis of a legal document called an **Indictment**. Both of these documents are discussed in detail later in this chapter.

Hybrid or Crown Option Offences

Many offences in the *Criminal Code* are neither summary conviction offences nor indictable offences. They may be tried as either, depending upon the manner in which the Crown wishes to prosecute. These offences are commonly referred to as hybrid offences, although that term itself is not used in the *Code*. Until the Crown elects to proceed by summary conviction, the offence is deemed to be an indictable offence and proceeds in that manner. If the Crown then chooses to prosecute as a summary conviction offence, the summary conviction procedures kick in at that point. The Crown normally makes this election at the time the accused is arraigned. The arraignment, the process of being arraigned, occurs when the accused appears before a judge to hear the details of the charge(s) laid against him or her and to enter a plea of guilty or not guilty.

If the Crown elects to prosecute by Indictment, the accused will then be given an election as to the mode of trial: either by a judge in the provincial court or by a judge in the superior court with or without a jury. If the accused elects a superior court trial, there will then be a preliminary inquiry if the Crown or accused requests it; otherwise, it goes straight to trial. It is important to distinguish between the election that the accused makes and the election the Crown makes on how to proceed on a hybrid offence.

If the Crown elects to proceed summarily, the matter will be set over for trial in the provincial court, and the penalties available for a conviction will be those available for any summary conviction offence. The accused will have no election available in the same way as if he were charged from the beginning with a summary conviction offence.

You can determine whether an offence is hybrid by its wording. For instance, section 267, assault with a weapon or causing bodily harm, is a hybrid offence:

> Every one who, in committing an assault,
>
> (*a*) carries, uses or threatens to use a weapon or an imitation thereof, or
> (*b*) causes bodily harm to the complainant,
>
> *is guilty of an indictable offence and liable to imprisonment for a term not exceeding ten years or an offence punishable on summary conviction and liable to imprisonment for a term not exceeding eighteen months.* [italics added]

TRIAL JURISDICTION

When we say that a court has jurisdiction, we mean that it has the power or authority to deal with a matter. A court that has jurisdiction over a criminal matter has the power to try a case. There are two types of jurisdiction that we will discuss here. A court must have a general jurisdiction over the offence, which means the power to hear that type of offence. It must also have the territorial jurisdiction or authority in the geographical area in which the offence is alleged to have occurred.

Jurisdiction over the Offence

The *Criminal Code* sets up a relatively complex structure for determining which courts have jurisdiction to hear which offences. If a court has absolute jurisdiction to hear an offence, it is the only court that may deal with that type of offence. The following is a simplified overview of the structure within the Ontario court system:

1. Summary conviction offences are heard in the Ontario Court of Justice.

2. The most serious indictable offences listed in section 469 of the *Code*, which include murder, treason and piracy, are in the absolute jurisdiction of the Superior Court of Justice.

3. The least serious indictable offences, listed in section 553, are in the absolute jurisdiction of the Ontario Court of Justice.

4. Indictable offences not listed in sections 469 or 553 may be heard by either the Ontario Court of Justice or the Superior Court of Justice, depending on the election of the accused, as discussed above, in relation to indictable offences.

Territorial Jurisdiction

In order for a court to have territorial jurisdiction over an offence — i.e., the power to hear that case — the offence and/or the accused must have some connection with that province. The general rule is that a court in a province cannot deal with a criminal case unless the offence is alleged to have been committed, in whole or in part, in that province. However, if the accused is found, arrested, or is in custody in a province that was not where the offence was committed, although a court in that province may not try him, but may, with the consent of the Attorney General, accept a guilty plea even though the offence was not committed there.[1]

The courts in Canada normally only have jurisdiction to try criminal matters where the offence was allegedly committed, in whole or in part, in Canada. However, there are some exceptions to the rule. The *Code* provides that some offences, including piracy, hostage-taking, hijacking, treason and conspiracy, among others, may be tried in Canada if the offence has some real and substantial connection with Canada, even though it was not committed in Canada. In addition, there are special provisions for the prosecution of offences committed elsewhere, including those committed at sea and in an aircraft, and for war crimes and crimes against humanity.

Limits upon Jurisdiction

There is generally no time limit for the prosecution of indictable offences. Normally an accused may be tried for an indictable offence at any time, and the court never loses jurisdiction to hear the matter. Practically, however, the longer the time between the commission of the offence and the trial, the more difficult it becomes for the Crown to obtain a conviction. With the passage of time, witnesses' memories fade and evidence may become weaker.

In relation to summary conviction offences, or for a hybrid offence where the Crown elects to proceed summarily, the Information must be laid within six months of the commission of the offence. After that time, the court will have no jurisdiction to hear the matter.

Section 11(b) of the *Charter of Rights and Freedoms*

One of the legal rights guaranteed by the *Charter of Rights and Freedoms*[2] is the right, under section 11(b), to be tried within a reasonable time. There is, however, no strict definition of what amount of time is "reasonable". In deciding whether the amount of time between the laying of the charge and the trial is reasonable, the court will look at the reason for the delay; any waiver of any time periods by the Crown or the defence; the resulting prejudice to the accused, if any; and the length of the delay. Should the court find that the rights of the accused have been infringed on, the court would grant a stay or a dismissal of proceedings under section 24(1) of the *Charter*.

---

[1] *Criminal Code*, s. 470.
[2] Schedule B to the *Constitution Act, 1982*, R.S.C. 1985, Appendix II, No. 44.

INVESTIGATORY POWERS

The role of the police in the criminal justice system is to investigate offences and to charge and, possibly, arrest the people accused of committing them. The *Criminal Code* provides the procedural law regarding search and seizure, questioning of suspects and the powers of arrest.

Because the police powers to search, question an accused are some of the most intrusive powers available in our legal system, they must be exercised in accordance with the *Charter of Rights and Freedoms*. Failure of police to honour an individual's rights may result in evidence being found to be inadmissible or, even, in a charge being dismissed or stayed.

Search and Seizure

All searches conducted by the police must follow the common law and statutory rules for exercising these powers. The *Criminal Code* and the *Controlled Drug and Substances Act*[3] and the *Food and Drugs Act*[4], among other statutes, all provide procedure for conducting searches. The Supreme Court of Canada has ruled that in most instances police must obtain a warrant in order to legally conduct a search and seizure. Some powers to search without a warrant are authorized by the common law in some limited circumstances. For instance, an accused may be searched as part of a lawful arrest during an investigatory detention, or on consent.

Charter Issues

Section 8 of the *Charter* guarantees everyone the right to be "secure against unreasonable search and seizure". The question then becomes whether a search meets the requirement of being "reasonable". In the case of *R. v. Collins*,[5] the Supreme Court of Canada set out the test for determining whether or not a search is reasonable:

- The search must be authorized by either the common law or statute law.
- The law authorizing the search must be reasonable.
- The search itself must be conducted in a reasonable manner.

In addition, to be found reasonable, a search cannot be arbitrary and must be based on reasonable and probable grounds that an offence has been committed and that evidence relating to that offence is likely to be found at the place to be searched. Any evidence gathered as a result of an "unreasonable" search — i.e., one not meeting these criteria — may become inadmissible in court, by virtue of section 24 of the *Charter*. That section provides that evidence that brings the administration of justice into disrepute shall be excluded.

In the case of *R. v. Grant*, the Supreme Court of Canada set out a three-part test to be applied by all courts in determining whether to admit or exclude evidence obtained in violation of the accused's *Charter* rights:

1. **The Seriousness of the *Charter* Breach**
   Was the breach a major one in which the police intentionally and knowingly violated the person's rights, or was it a more minor breach, conducted in good faith by the police? In the first case the evidence may very well be excluded, but in the latter case it is possible that the evidence will be admitted.

---

[3] S.C. 1996, c. 19.
[4] R.S.C. 1985, c. F-27.
[5] (1987), 33 C.C.C. (3d) 1 (S.C.C.).

2. **Impact of the *Charter* Breach on the Interests of the Accused**
   This criterion focuses on (i) whether the *Charter* infringement had the effect of being profoundly intrusive on the accused's rights or (ii) whether it was more, in the words of the court, "fleeting or technical" in nature. If the impact on the accused was more fleeting and technical, the *Charter* infringement will not necessarily bring the administration of justice into disrepute. An example of a profoundly intrusive violation of rights might be an illegal strip-search of the accused.

3. **Society's Interest in a Trial on the Merits**
   The Canadian public has a strong interest in ensuring that those who may have committed a criminal offence are given a fair and just trial, based on reliable findings of the truth. Therefore, if the court finds that the accused's *Charter* rights have been violated, the court must determine whether the breach compromised the reliability of the evidence and affected its ability to help find the truth. Admitting unreliable evidence would undermine the truth-finding function expected of the courts and would bring the administration of justice into disrepute. For instance, if the accused was held by the police in oppressive circumstances that bordered on torture, was not advised of his/her right to counsel, and confessed to a crime simply to end the torture-like conditions, such a confession would not likely be regarded as reliable. The person may have said anything in the hopes of having the oppressive circumstances end.

The Search Warrant

Other than in exceptional circumstances, such as in cases in which a warrant cannot be obtained because it would be impractical to obtain it by reason of urgent or exigent circumstances, the police must obtain a warrant to conduct a search and seizure. A search with a properly obtained warrant is constitutional as long as there is nothing in the manner in which the search is conducted that is unreasonable. Section 487 of the *Criminal Code* provides a justice with the authority to issue a **search warrant** to search a place.

In order to obtain a warrant, a police officer must swear an Information before a justice of the peace. An Information is a legal document similar to an Information for laying a charge, which is discussed later in the chapter. The justice must be satisfied that there are reasonable and probable grounds to believe there is physical evidence relevant to an offence that has been committed or is suspected of having been committed to be found in the place to be searched. If so satisfied, the justice may issue a warrant authorizing a search.

The warrant must contain the following:

- Sufficient detail to identify the offence that was committed or is suspected of having been committed — i.e., the section number of the offence, the date and time of the offence, the name of the victim and the manner in which the offence was committed.

- A list of the items to be seized, described sufficiently that they can be identified.

- A clear identification of the place or receptacle to be searched; for instance, if it is a building, the address must be provided.

Section 487(2.1) and (2.2) provides that the person authorized under the warrant to search for data may use a computer system in the place searched to locate or reproduce data stored on a computer at the premises.

Section 487.05 provides authority to a provincial judge to issue a warrant to seize bodily substances for DNA analysis, and section 487.091 provides similar authority to obtain handprints, fingerprints, footprints, teeth impressions, or other bodily impressions.

Although the normal procedure for obtaining a warrant would involve the attendance of the person seeking the warrant before a justice of the peace, the police may also obtain a warrant over the telephone. However, this warrant, called a telewarrant, will be granted only in circumstances where the offence being investigated is an indictable offence and there is no time to obtain a warrant by way of the normal procedure. For instance, if the police had reasonable or probable grounds to believe that the time involved in obtaining a warrant through the regular procedure would result in the destruction of evidence or danger to a person or the public, they would seek a telewarrant.

Execution of the Search Warrant

Even if the search is authorized by law, the search must be conducted reasonably. The police officer must normally have the warrant in his or her possession and must present it if asked to do so by the occupants of the premises. Only reasonable force may be used in the execution of the warrant. Unless the police have reasonable grounds for believing that evidence will be destroyed unless they enter the premises without warning, they must make a demand to open before making a forcible entry. Finally, a warrant may be executed only during the day, unless the warrant specifically permits a night execution.

Search and Seizure without a Warrant

In some limited circumstances, the common law permits a police officer to conduct a search without a warrant. The person may be searched as an incident to a lawful arrest, during an investigative detention, or upon consent. This means that when the police arrest or detain a person for the purpose of investigating an offence, they may search him if they have a valid reason, related to the arrest, for conducting the search, such as protecting themselves, protecting the evidence, or discovering evidence. The search must still meet the test of being a reasonable search.

In addition to the common law rules authorizing some limited power to search without a warrant, section 487.11 of the *Criminal Code* gives a police officer the authority to conduct a warrantless search in exigent or urgent circumstances. The circumstances must be such that it would be impracticable for the police to obtain a warrant. For instance, if the police were in hot pursuit of a suspect who ran into his house to escape arrest and to immediately destroy evidence, they may conduct a search without a warrant.

Investigation and Questioning of Suspects

Questioning suspects is another manner in which the police may intrude upon the privacy of individuals and, as such, the law requires that certain limits be placed on the police power of interrogation.

When a Person Is Not Detained

Police may question a person with regard to a criminal offence, but the person is under no obligation to answer the questions. The person may exercise his or her right to remain silent. The police must let a person walk away if the person wishes to remain silent and if the police have no grounds for making an arrest. However, if a person wishes to speak, he or she may not intentionally mislead the police, or he or she may be charged with several offences, such as obstructing a police officer or public mischief. In addition, anything the person does say may be used as evidence in court against him or her if the police later decide to charge him or her with an offence.

When a Person Is Detained and Arrested

Section 9 of the *Charter of Rights and Freedoms* grants everyone the right not to be arbitrarily detained or imprisoned. This means that the police do not have the power to arbitrarily stop and question a person without reasonable grounds to believe the person may be connected to a criminal offence. The power of the police to arrest and detain individuals deprives these individuals of their freedom. Therefore, when a person is put under arrest or detention, additional rights are accorded the arrested person under the *Charter*, and certain limitations and duties are imposed upon the police.

Upon arrest or detention, section 10 of the *Charter* requires that the police promptly inform the accused of the reason for his arrest, advise him of his right to retain counsel and his right to retain counsel without delay. The accused must also be given a reasonable opportunity to consult a lawyer if he indicates a wish to do so.

In addition to being advised of his specific rights afforded under section 10 of the *Charter*, he must be told of his right to remain silent and that, if he chooses to speak, anything he says may be used against him in court. This is commonly referred to as the police obligation to read the person his rights. Failure of the police to do so may prohibit anything the accused says from being admitted into evidence, and this violation of his rights may even result in the entire case against the accused being dismissed.

Section 10 talks about both arrest and detention. A person may be detained but not necessarily arrested. Clearly, when a person is arrested he is being detained, but if he is detained prior to an arrest, he is entitled to be advised of his rights at that point. Failure of the police to advise the accused is a direct violation of his rights and can result in a stay or dismissal of any charges laid against him. Sometimes, the police and the courts take a different view of what amounts to a "detention", that would trigger the detainee's rights.

In the case of *R. v. Grant*,[6] the Supreme Court of Canada ruled that a detention occurs when a person reasonably believes that they must comply with the police and remain under police control. The police need not use any physical restraint or words to detain the person. The test is whether the person believed he was unable to leave.

Once the person indicates a wish to remain silent until he has consulted a lawyer, the police must stop questioning him until he has been given an opportunity to speak to counsel. Once the person has consulted a lawyer, the police may resume questioning, but the person being detained has no obligation to answer. If the person is advised of his/her rights and chooses not to contact a lawyer or wants to answer questions when his/her lawyer has advised him/her not to do so, that is up to him/her; and the police may continue to question him/her.

Other Investigative Tests

The police may ask the accused to participate in other investigative procedures in addition to an interrogation.

Lineups

A suspect in a police investigation may be asked to participate in a lineup. There is no obligation upon a person to do so, and the person may

---

[6] 2009 SCC 32, [2009] 2 S.C.R. 353.

refuse. However, if the suspect refuses to participate in person, the police may still use a photo lineup in which the victim or other witnesses will be shown a set of photographs of different people and asked if they recognize anyone. To be admitted as evidence against the accused, the lineup must have involved people of somewhat similar age and physical appearance as the suspect.

Breath and Sobriety Tests

If a police officer has reasonable grounds to believe that an individual has been driving while impaired by alcohol, section 254 of the *Criminal Code* permits that officer to require the driver to take a Breathalyzer test. The driver must comply with the request, or she will be charged with the criminal offence of failing to comply with a breath demand. This offence carries penalties as serious as the charge of driving while impaired, so there is no advantage to the suspect in refusing to comply.

Polygraph Tests

Polygraph or lie detector tests are not admissible as evidence in any court of law. The technology is not regarded as reliable enough to meet evidentiary requirements. Nevertheless, the police use the test fairly regularly as an investigative tool. A suspect is never obligated to consent to take a test of this kind.

BRINGING THE ACCUSED BEFORE THE COURT

It is the role of the police to investigate crime, gather evidence and lay appropriate charges against particular accused persons. The next step in the process is bringing the accused before the court to be prosecuted, so her guilt can be legally tested according to Canadian law. The way to best ensure that an accused is brought before the court would be for the police to arrest her and detain her until her court date. However, this is neither practical nor feasible. It would mean that we would have many people detained for extremely minor offences, at considerable public expense, while awaiting their day in court. In addition, and more importantly, such a process would be open to constitutional challenge on a number of levels. Remember that the *Charter* guarantees that everyone charged with an offence the right to be presumed innocent until proven guilty beyond a reasonable doubt. Therefore, there are a number of procedures available for bringing the accused before the court, some that involve arrest and some that do not. If arrested, it is the court that ultimately must decide if the accused must remain incarcerated while awaiting trial.

Process One: Summons or Arrest Warrant

A criminal prosecution formally begins with the laying of a document called an **Information**. A person called an informant, who is usually a police officer, appears before a justice of the peace and provides sworn allegations that the accused has committed an offence. The Information will not be laid unless the justice of the peace is satisfied that there are reasonable grounds to believe an offence has been committed by the accused.

If the justice is properly satisfied, she may do one of two things:

1. Issue a **summons** requiring the accused to appear before the court on a specified day, at a specified time, to answer the charge. The summons is then delivered personally to the accused. This personal delivery is called service. Failure of the accused to appear as required will result

in the accused's being charged with the additional criminal offence of failing to appear. A warrant will be issued for the accused's arrest, and the accused will be detained and brought before the court to answer both the original charge and the additional charges resulting from the accused's initial failure to obey the summons.

2. Issue a warrant for the arrest of the accused. A warrant for arrest is a court order directing the police in a particular location to take the accused into custody and deliver the accused to the court.

There is a positive duty, under the *Code*, on the justice to issue a summons rather than an arrest warrant, unless the evidence of the informant establishes, on reasonable and probable grounds, that it is in the public interest to arrest the accused. This usually means that an arrest warrant will be issued for more serious offences when there is concern that an accused may destroy evidence or when it appears that the accused may try to escape justice by fleeing the jurisdiction and not attending court for his/her trial.

Process Two: Appearance Notice or Arrest without a Warrant

Process One is followed when the police have been investigating a crime, and they believe they have found the perpetrator whom they wish to now charge with the offence. However, a great deal of crime comes to the attention of the police before they have an opportunity to lay the Information. For instance, the police receive a telephone call to come to the scene of an alleged offence. When they arrive, they conduct an investigation on the spot; as a result of their investigation, they have reasonable grounds to charge a person who is present at the scene. Obviously, it is impractical for the police to ask the accused to wait while they head off to find a justice and swear out an Information. The *Criminal Code*, therefore, provides another procedure for starting the process to bring the accused before the court prior to the Information being laid.

A police officer may arrest a person without a warrant in the following circumstances:

1. The police officer has reasonable grounds to believe the person has committed, or is about to commit, an indictable offence.
2. The police officer finds the person committing an offence, either indictable or summary conviction.
3. The police officer has reasonable grounds to believe there is an executable warrant out for the arrest of the person.[7]

However, the *Code* prohibits the officer from arresting a person without a warrant for less serious indictable offences, hybrid offences, and summary conviction offences unless the officer has reasonable grounds to believe that it is in the public interest to do so or that the person may not appear in court.

Where the police officer has no reasonable grounds to arrest the accused without a warrant, the officer may issue an appearance notice to the accused. The appearance notice is a document requiring the accused to attend in court on a specified day and time to answer the criminal charge. If the accused fails to appear, he faces the same consequences as an accused who fails to honour a summons — i.e., arrest and further criminal charges for failing to appear.

[7] *Criminal Code*, s. 495.

The officer must swear the Information before a justice as soon as is practicable after the accused has been arrested without a warrant or issued an appearance notice.

RELEASE OF THE ACCUSED PRIOR TO TRIAL

Usually, if the accused has been arrested with a warrant, he/she will be held in custody; the police will have no power to release him/her without a court order unless the justice who issued the arrest warrant specifically gives them written permission at the time the warrant was issued.

If the accused has been arrested, with or without a warrant, it does not automatically mean that the accused will remain incarcerated right up until trial. There are several procedural steps that permit the accused to be released even after an arrest has been made.

Release by the Arresting Officer

If a police officer finds it necessary to arrest a person without a warrant — because the officer has reason to believe the accused will not attend court or for some other reason such as to establish the accused's identity, prevent the repetition of the offence, secure evidence, or protect any victims or witnesses — the arresting officer may release the person without holding him or her for a bail hearing if the reason why that person was arrested no longer applies. For example, if John is charged with committing a minor offence and refuses to identify himself, the officer has no choice but to arrest him. If the officer does not know the accused's name, the officer cannot issue an appearance notice. However, if John has a change of heart after he is taken to the police station and he decides the best course of action is to now identify himself, the reason for his being arrested no longer exists. The arresting officer may then release John by way of a summons or an appearance notice. The officer may only exercise this option for minor indictable offences, hybrid offences or any summary conviction offences.

If the officer decides not to arrest the accused, the accused will then be handed over to be dealt with by the officer in charge of the police station.

Release by the Officer in Charge

The officer in charge will review the circumstances of the arrest and then has several options. The first is to release the accused on a summons or a promise to appear (in court). The officer in charge may also have the accused enter into a recognizance. A recognizance is a promise that the accused or someone who agrees to do so will pay a certain amount of money, most often $500, if he or she fails to appear in court.

Finally, the officer in charge may also release the accused on an undertaking. In an undertaking, the accused person must agree, or undertake, to abide by certain specified conditions that the *Criminal Code* authorizes the officer in charge to place on him. These conditions are things like remaining in the jurisdiction of the court, depositing their passport, refraining from contacting the victim or witnesses, refraining from alcohol use, etc.[8]

The accused will only be released by the officer in charge if the offence charged is a minor indictable offence, a hybrid offence, or a summary conviction offence. The authority of the officer in charge to release an accused is broader than that of the arresting officer in that he can release an accused

---

[8] See *Criminal Code*, s. 503(2.1), for more conditions.

charged with any indictable offence carrying a potential jail sentence of five years or less.

If the accused has been charged with a serious indictable offence and if the offence is one that grants an automatic bail hearing, he/she will, in most instances, be held in custody for a bail hearing. See below for examples of offences where there is no automatic right to such a hearing.

Judicial Interim Release

The officer in charge may decide that the appropriate course of action is to detain the accused, pending a bail hearing. The formal name for bail is judicial interim release. This option is used (i) when the accused has been charged with a serious indictable offence or has a prior record for failing to appear in court, or (ii) when the police believe the accused should be released only under rigorous conditions placed upon him or her by a judge or a justice of the peace as a term of the release or not released at all until trial.

In these situations, the accused must appear in court for a "show cause hearing", often referred to as a bail hearing. Normally, the hearing must take place within 24 hours of the arrest. The purpose of a bail hearing is for a justice of the peace or a judge to determine whether the accused should be released while awaiting trial, and if so, what conditions should be placed upon him or her in the meantime.

The justice may order the release of the accused in several ways and must use the least restrictive method possible for that particular accused.

The least restrictive method is an undertaking with conditions, then a recognizance without sureties, then a recognizance with sureties without a deposit of money, then a recognizance with a deposit of money.

The purposes of any conditions are to ensure, as much as is possible, that the accused appears in court for trial and is not a danger to the public if released. Common conditions to ensure public safety include prohibitions from drinking alcohol, being in the presence of certain persons, possessing firearms and other weapons, or contacting the victim. In addition, the accused may be required to report to the police any change of address or employment and to surrender his passport.

The court may require the accused to enter into a recognizance, with or without sureties. In a recognizance without sureties, the accused will forfeit an amount of money or valuable property should he or she fail to appear for trial or breach any of the conditions placed upon release. In a recognizance with sureties, someone other than the accused promises to pay money or surrender valuables in the event that the accused does not appear at trial or breaches release conditions.

There are three types of bail provided for under the *Criminal Code*:

1. Regular bail situations.
2. Reverse-onus situations.
3. Bail for offences listed in section 469.

Regular Bail Hearings

In regular bail situations, the Crown bears the onus of proving why the accused should not be released on bail while awaiting trial.[9] Generally speaking, the justice of the peace is required to release the accused without conditions, pending trial, unless the Crown is able to prove, on the balance of probabilities, that (i) the accused is unlikely to appear for trial; (ii) the accused poses a risk to public safety if released; or (iii) the accused's detention is necessary in order to maintain confidence in the administration of justice.

---

[9] *Criminal Code*, s. 515.

If the Crown is able to establish the primary ground — that is, there is a risk that the accused will not appear for trial — there is no need to move on to the second or third ground. However, if the Crown cannot prove the primary ground, the Crown can then attempt to prove the secondary — that is, there is a risk to public safety if the accused is released.

In evaluating the risk to public safety, the court is required by section 515(10)(b) of the *Code* to consider "all circumstances", such as the seriousness of the alleged offence, the criminal record of the accused, the strength of the case against the accused, the likelihood of the accused committing a further offence, any danger the accused may pose to witnesses or victims, and the accused's employment and living situation.

Even if the court is satisfied that bail should be denied on the primary or secondary grounds, it must also consider under section 515(10)(c) whether the release of the accused would undermine the public's confidence in the justice system. This tertiary ground for detention is rarely used, and if the accused is to remain in custody awaiting trial, the accused is usually held under one of the other grounds.

Reverse-Onus Situations

Although in most bail situations the onus is on the Crown to prove, on the balance of probabilities, that the accused should not be released on bail, the onus to prove that they should be released awaiting trial shifts to the accused in the following situations:

1. The accused is charged with an indictable offence committed while he or she is out on bail awaiting trial for another indictable offence.
2. The accused is charged with an indictable offence and is not a Canadian resident.
3. The accused is charged with the offence of failing to appear at a court hearing or with a breach of condition of a bail order.
4. The accused is charged with committing an offence under the *Controlled Drug and Substances Act*, which carries a potential sentence of life imprisonment.
5. The accused is charged with an offence involving organized crime, a terrorist offence, or certain offences related to terrorism.

If an accused is successful in showing cause why he or she should be released on bail, the judge or justice of the peace may order his or her release pursuant to a recognizance or other conditions.

The grounds for release are the same as in a regular bail situation, i.e., the likelihood that the accused will appear for trial, the risk to public safety, and the public's confidence in the justice system if the accused is released.

Bail for Offences in s. 469

Section 469 contains some of the most serious offences in the *Criminal Code*, including murder and major offences against the state, such as treason. There is no automatic entitlement to a bail hearing for these offences. An accused must apply for release under section 522, and if a bail hearing is granted, it must take place before a judge of the Superior Court.

Bail Review

There is a provision in section 520 of the *Criminal Code* for the accused to challenge a denial of bail or the imposition of specific conditions that the accused believes are unfair or improper. This process is called a bail review. The accused applies to a judge of the superior court. The Crown must be given at least two days' notice of the request for a review. At the hearing, the judge will hear any evidence, review the transcripts of the bail hearing, and either dismiss the application or vacate the original bail order and make a new order granting bail or altering the conditions of release.

THE ARRAIGNMENT

The arraignment is the reading of the charge against the accused in open court, and it marks the commencement of the trial process. The court clerk reads out the charges, and the accused is asked how he or she wishes to plead. The arraignment takes place before a provincial court judge.

If the plea is guilty, the accused will be sentenced or the court may ask for a pre-sentence report to assist it in determining the most appropriate punishment for the accused.

If the accused pleads not guilty, what happens next will depend on the charge against the accused. If the charge is a summary conviction offence or one of the less serious indictable offences listed in section 553, or if the accused chooses trial by a provincial court judge, the accused will go to trial in the provincial court (e.g., Ontario Court of Justice). The trial does not normally proceed immediately after the arraignment due to court scheduling problems, but it could take place right away. Usually a future date is set for trial, and the accused must return.

If the offence is an indictable offence that is to be heard in the superior court either because the accused has elected to be tried in that court or because the provincial court has no jurisdiction to hear that type of offence, the accused may request a preliminary hearing or preliminary inquiry.

THE PRELIMINARY INQUIRY

The purpose of the **preliminary inquiry** is for a provincial court judge to determine whether the Crown has sufficient evidence to warrant sending the accused to trial. A preliminary inquiry is available in the following circumstances:

1. The accused has been charged with an offence listed in section 469 of the *Criminal Code* — for example, murder or treason.

2. The accused has been charged with an indictable offence that permits an election by the accused of the mode of trial, and the accused has elected trial before a judge of the Superior Court, sitting with or without a jury.

3. A provincial court judge has declined jurisdiction to try the case and has decided to hold a preliminary inquiry instead of a trial.

The accused is not entitled to a preliminary inquiry for a summary conviction offence or for an offence on which the accused has elected to be tried before a provincial court judge and the judge does not decline jurisdiction to hear the trial.

A right to have a preliminary inquiry can be waived by the defence; however, it is normally not waived because the inquiry gives the defence an opportunity to test some of the Crown's witnesses through cross-examination and to assess the strength of the Crown's case. Although the defence is entitled to call evidence at the inquiry, it is not required and it is rarely, if ever, done. Calling defence evidence would alert the Crown to the defences raised by the accused and give the Crown an opportunity to mend any evidentiary holes in its case.

Under the *Criminal Code*, the Attorney General of the province may send the accused to trial without a preliminary inquiry, even if the accused would normally be entitled to one, based on the three criteria listed above. This is called preferring an Indictment. The provincial Attorney General rarely uses this process.[10]

A preliminary inquiry is always held before a provincial court judge. In Ontario, that would be a judge of the Ontario Court of Justice. The Crown must satisfy the judge that there is sufficient evidence that, if believed, would result in a reasonable, properly instructed jury finding the accused guilty. The provincial court judge does not, at this point, assess or weigh the evidence on its credibility. The judge merely determines whether there is enough evidence against the accused to warrant a trial. At the end of the inquiry, the judge will either commit the accused for trial or dismiss the charges. In the vast majority of cases, the accused is committed for trial. It is then up to the trial judge in the Superior Court — and the jury, if there is one — to determine the strength, weight, and credibility of the Crown's evidence and to hear and assess the defences raised by the accused.

INFORMATIONS AND INDICTMENTS

Informations and Indictments are legal documents prescribed by the *Criminal Code* that contain the charges against an accused. The documents must provide enough detail so that the accused can fully appreciate the charge and be able to prepare a full answer and defence to the charge. The documents form part of the court file related to the prosecution of the offence.

The Information

All criminal prosecutions formally commence with the laying of an Information. As discussed above, the informant, who is usually a police officer, must appear before a justice and provide sworn evidence that the accused committed an offence or that the officer believes, on reasonable and probable grounds, that the accused has committed an offence. The justice must be satisfied that there are, indeed, reasonable grounds for believing that the accused committed an offence.

If the accused is tried in the provincial court (e.g., the Ontario Court of Justice), either because the accused has been charged with a summary conviction offence or because the accused has elected trial by a provincial court judge, then the accused will be tried on the basis of the written allegation in the Information. The Information will be the only written allegation of the offence charged.

The Indictment

If the accused is to be tried in the superior court, then the Information that commenced the prosecution will be replaced with an Indictment. This replacement takes place after the preliminary inquiry or, if there is no preliminary inquiry, after the accused has been committed to trial on consent or on a **preferred Indictment**. The Indictment is not a sworn document, but the Crown Attorney signs it. Like an Information, it sets out the allegations against the accused.

---

[10] See the Ontario case against Paul Bernardo.

Rules Respecting the Wording of Counts

The Information or the Indictment may contain a number of counts against the accused. A count, in this context, means the allegations against the accused. Numerous counts may be included in one Information or Indictment, but there are rules about how they must be presented.[11]

Each count must contain a "single transaction". This means that each count can contain only one alleged offence. If the accused is charged, for instance, with committing a sexual assault against a number of victims, the allegations against the accused, in relation to each victim, must be contained in a separate count in the Information or Indictment.

In addition, the "single transaction" rule requires that if the accused is charged with more than one type of offence involving the same victim — for instance, fraud and theft — each offence must be contained in a separate count of the Information or Indictment. If a count contains more than one transaction, it is said to be duplicitous and may be challenged on that basis.

Finally, there is a requirement that each count must disclose an "offence known to law". If an Information is not properly drafted, it may be unclear or leave out important aspects of the charge such that the document does not disclose an actual offence. The accused must know with what offence he or she is being charged in order to mount a proper defence.

Informations or Indictments that contain errors of a more minor nature, such as contravening the rules of practice, are normally simply amended to comply. However, if the defect is more serious and causes an injustice or prejudice to the accused, an amendment will not be granted, and the charges against the accused will be quashed.

THE TRIAL

At trial, the onus or burden is upon the Crown to prove each element of the offence beyond a reasonable doubt. Failure of the Crown to meet this burden of proof on any aspect of the charge will result in the acquittal of the accused.

The Crown presents its case first. The prosecution calls all of its witnesses to give evidence, one after another. Witnesses are normally served with a subpoena requiring them to attend at court to give evidence at a certain date and time. Failure of a witness to obey a subpoena has legal consequences, and the witness may even be apprehended and brought to court under a warrant to testify.

The Crown attorney conducts an examination-in-chief or direct examination of each of the witnesses it calls. This means that the Crown asks non-leading questions of the witness, who has taken an oath or affirmation to tell the truth. Non-leading questions are those that do not suggest the answer. For instance, "It was raining that night, was it not?" is a leading question. The question itself implies that it was, indeed, raining. Asking the witness what the weather was that night is a not a leading question. There is no answer suggested by the person asking the question.

After the Crown has examined each of its witnesses, the lawyer for the defence may ask questions. This is called cross-examination. There is no rule in cross-examination that prohibits leading questions, and the cross-examiner may ask all the leading questions he or she likes. The purpose of cross-examination is to test the credibility of the witnesses — that is, to see if their story holds up under pointed questioning. When the defence has finished its cross-examination of the witness, the Crown may be given a chance to re-

---

[11] See s. 581 of the *Criminal Code*.

| | **EXHIBIT 12.1** |

Aspects of Trial Procedure

First Court Appearance
The first date scheduled for a court appearance on the matter is normally not the date on which the case will be heard. This is often referred to as the "set date". The accused often does not have a lawyer at this point and requires an adjournment to retain counsel.

Pre-trial Conference
The major purpose of the pre-trial conference is to ensure the efficient use of court time by narrowing the issues and addressing any pre-trial procedural matters, such as the plea to be entered, which motions will be argued, and whether any *Charter* issues will be raised. Section 625.1 of the *Code* provides that pre-trial conferences are mandatory in any Superior Court trial before a judge and a jury, and they may be ordered for a non-jury trial. However, in some Ontario jurisdictions, including Toronto, pre-trials are required by judges in all Superior Court criminal trials.

Pre-trials are informal meetings that involve a judge and the Crown and the accused. However, the judge hearing the pre-trial will not be the same judge who hears the trial. This is done to ensure that the judge hearing the trial is not influenced by anything said in the informal setting of a pre-trial.

Voire Dires
A *voire dire* is a mini hearing that takes place to determine whether a certain piece of evidence is admissible in a trial. A *voire dire* is often referred to as "a trial within a trial". It may take place either before the trial begins or during a trial if an issue arises about the admissibility of a piece of evidence. If the *voire dire* is held during the course of a jury trial, the jury is required to leave the courtroom for the duration of the *voire dire*.

The Arraignment
The arraignment is the reading of the charges to the accused in the courtroom and the request from the court for the accused to enter a plea to the charges. It marks the formal commencement of the trial.

Plea of Guilty
If the accused pleads guilty at the arraignment, the court will either proceed with sentencing or request that a pre-sentence report be prepared to supply the court with further information about the background, character and general circumstances of the accused. The pre-sentence report is prepared by a probation officer, and its purpose is to aid the court in determining which sentence is most appropriate for the accused.

Charge to the Jury
In a jury trial, the judge must prepare the jury to deliberate on the case after counsel have made their closing arguments. This is called the judge's charge to the jury. The purpose of the charge to the jury is for the judge to summarize the Crown and the defence's cases, to draw the jury's attention to any major pieces or points of evidence, and to advise jury members on how the law relates to the offence that the accused has been charged with. Following the charge, the jury is sequestered or closed away to determine the guilt or non-guilt of the accused.

---

examine the witness to clarify answers given by the witness during cross-examination.

When the Crown has called all its witnesses, the defence has to decide if it believes the Crown has met the burden of proving the case beyond a reasonable doubt. If the defence believes that the Crown has not done this, the defence will bring a motion for a directed verdict. This means that the defence lawyer will ask the judge to find the accused not guilty on the basis that the Crown has not proved the case against the accused.

If the motion for a directed verdict is unsuccessful, the Crown and counsel for the defence will then make legal arguments that support their position to the court. These legal arguments are called submissions.

At the end of submissions, if there is a jury, the jury will retire to determine the facts of the case; and if there is no jury, the judge alone will determine whether the accused is guilty or not guilty.

SENTENCING

Principles of Sentencing

For most offences there are a number of options available to the court in imposing a sentence on the accused who has been found guilty at the end of a trial or who has pleaded guilty without a trial. The basic principles of sentencing in Canadian law, set out in s. 718 of the *Criminal Code*, include denunciation, deterrence, rehabilitation, separation of the offender from society where necessary, reparation of harm done to victims or the community, and promoting a sense of responsibility in offenders.

Denunciation

The purpose of denunciation is to convey the fact that society condemns the offender's actions. Any sentence imposed must be sufficient to demonstrate this condemnation for breaking the legal rules that govern society. Through the principle of denunciation, society is demonstrating to each of its members that failure to respect the rules and abide by them will result in a proper penalty. This is not about revenge. It is about disapproval.

Deterrence

The purpose of **deterrence** is to discourage continued criminal behaviour. Specific deterrence attempts to ensure that this specific offender will receive a significant enough sentence that he or she will not be prone to committing further offences. It is the principle of specific deterrence that results in more serious sentences for repeat offenders who are not getting the message.

General deterrence works to discourage the general public from committing the offence, since they know that it will attract a particular legal consequence.

When focusing on general deterrence, courts look at the gravity of the offence, the actual harm caused by the offence, and the public attitude towards the offence. If the court, on the other hand, chooses to focus on specific deterrence, greater consideration will be given to the individual, the individual's criminal record and attitude, and the possibility of rehabilitation.

Rehabilitation

Rehabilitation works to address any underlying issues that have contributed to the offender committing the offence, such as addiction, mental disorder, social conditions, lack of education, etc. It is hoped that with sufficient rehabilitation programs the offender, once released, will not be subjected to the same factors and will, therefore, be less likely to re-offend.

Separation of the Offender from Society

In some instances, the offender must be incarcerated or jailed in order to protect society. Also, if the offence was committed because the offender has some addiction or mental health problem, a period of incarceration so that the offender may get some treatement may be appropriate.

Reparation of Harm

The primary purpose of criminal law is not to compensate the victim of an offence. That is the function of tort law, and the victim may sue the offender for any losses or damages caused by the criminal behaviour of the offender. However, the *Code* does contain provisions for a sentence involving a restitution order. The offender is required to pay a specified sum of money to the victim, but a restitution order is not appropriate in many instances, including those in which the offender has no ability to pay such restitution.

Promote a Sense of Responsibility in the Offender

It is believed that offenders who acknowledge their criminal activity and take responsibility for their actions are less likely to re-offend.

Gladue Principle

In the 1999 case of *R. v. Gladue*, the Supreme Court of Canada ruled that in sentencing Aborniginal offenders the courts must take into account the often disadvantageous circumstances of Aboriginal people in Canada. Incarceration should be avoided in as many situations as possible, and principles of Aboriginal cultural options, such as healing circles set up by the Aboriginal community, should be applied where appropriate.

Aggravating and Mitigating Factors in Sentencing

Aggravating factors are circumstances that increase the seriousness of the offender's actions, while mitigating factors are circumstances that decrease the seriousness of the offender's actions. Section 718.2 of the *Code* requires the court to consider these factors in determining an appropriate sentence for the offender.

Aggravating factors include offences committed on the basis of hatred of the victim's race, ethnicity, sexual orientation, etc.; offences involving spousal or child abuse; offences involving breach of trust or authority; offences involving firearms; offences involving terrorism; and offences committed as part of a criminal organization.

Mitigating factors may include the age of the offender; the mental or physical disability of the offender; the fact that the offender eventually cooperated with the authorities and pleaded guilty, thus avoiding forcing the victim to testify and saving the government the cost of a trial; and the fact that the offence is a first offence.

The Sentencing Process

Once the accused has been found guilty at trial, or if the accused pleads guilty, the sentencing process begins. The offender may be sentenced immediately following the finding or the plea, but in many instances, particularly with first offenders, the court may ask for a **pre-sentence report**. This report is prepared by a probation officer, who looks into the background of the accused and provides the court with information as to the accused's character apart from the offence, the accused's residential circumstances and employment, the accused's chances of being rehabilitated, the accused's remorse, etc. The judge will use this report to assist in determining the most appropriate sentence for the offender.

Another type of report that may be presented to the court is a **victim impact statement**. People who have suffered emotional or physical damage as a result of an offence, or the relatives of a deceased victim, may provide a written statement to the court that outlines the effect of the offence on their lives. In addition, during the sentencing process the Crown may wish to call evidence from the victims or other relevant people who will provide the court with information on the impact of the offence on the victim.

Before sentencing, both the Crown and the defence may make submissions to the court on the appropriate sentence. Sometimes, the Crown and the defence will agree beforehand on the appropriate sentence, and this proposed sentence will be presented to the judge. This is called a joint submission. The court is under no obligation to accept such a sentencing recommendation, but normally it does.

Types of Sentences

Once the accused has pleaded guilty or is found guilty at the conclusion of a trial, the judge can impose the following sentencing alternatives as set out in the *Criminal Code*. These sentencing alternatives may be imposed separately, or some of them may be combined. When applying the sentence, as well as the sentencing principles in the *Criminal Code* discussed above, the judge will take into consideration a number of factors, including the nature of the offence, any aggravating or mitigating evidence, the circumstances of the accused and the need for public safety.

Absolute or Conditional Discharge

The judge may grant an absolute or conditional **discharge** where the accused is a first-time offender and the offence is minor. The authority to impose these sentences is found in section 730(1) of the *Criminal Code*. These sentences may not be imposed where an accused is convicted of an offence for which a minimum penalty is prescribed by the *Code* or where a maximum penalty of 14 years or life is prescribed.

With either type of discharge, there is no conviction registered against the accused. This means that the accused will not have a criminal record.

An absolute discharge is effective immediately, and the accused will have no further obligation to deal with the criminal justice system in relation to that offence. Courts will apply this sentence only in the most unusual of circumstances. The absolute discharge disappears after one year without the convicted person taking any further action.

A conditional discharge requires the accused to abide by certain conditions for a specified period of time, usually one year, but it can be up to three years. For instance, the accused may be required to keep the peace and be of good behaviour, or be required to abstain from alcohol. The conditions are placed in the form of a probation order. If the accused abides by the conditions for the requisite period, the accused will have no conviction registered. The conditional discharge will appear on the accused's record for three years, which will be removed after that time. If the accused fails to obey the conditions, the accused may be charged with the further offence of failure to comply and may be sentenced for the original offence.

Before deciding to grant a discharge, a court must be satisfied that it would be in the best interests of the accused and not contrary to the public interest.

Fines

Section 734 of the *Code* provides that the court can order the offender to pay money as a penalty. This sentencing option is available only where there is no minimum sentence of imprisonment prescribed for that particular offence. In addition, the court may impose a fine only after it is satisfied that the offender has the ability to pay, or that the offender is eligible for the fine option program established under section 738. The fine option program permits the offender to discharge a fine by performing certain work over a period of two years. These programs have not been established in every jurisdiction.

At the time the fine is imposed, the court will usually provide an alternate jail sentence in the event the fine is not paid. For example, the court may order a fine of $250 or 30 days in jail. If the offender requires more time to pay the fine, the court may grant an extension of the time period for making payment.

Fines will be used for only fairly minor criminal offences and for provincial offences. The maximum fine for a summary conviction offence is $5,000 for individuals and $100,000 for an organization, such as a corporation. There is no maximum fine for an indictable offence.

Restitution

An offender may be required to pay money directly to a victim to help cover the victim's losses or for damage to property caused by the crime. This type of payment is called a restitution order. The purposes of restitution are to provide victims with some financial compensation for the crime committed against them or their property and to promote a sense of responsibility in the offenders through acknowledging the harm they have caused.

Victim Surcharge

Major changes were made to the victim surcharge by the federal government in late 2013. Each offence carries with it a victim surcharge, which is an amount of money the offender must pay upon conviction for any offence. The money is paid to the provincial and territorial governments to develop and provide programs, services, and assistance to victims of crime. The amount of the victim surcharge is 30 percent of any fine that is imposed on an offender or, if no fine is imposed, $100 for a summary conviction offence or $200 for an indictable offence.

The victim surcharge is mandatory in that judges are required to apply it. However, there has been considerable displeasure expressed by judges on the mandatory nature of the surcharge. Some judges are refusing to apply it or are finding creative ways around it, such as giving an offender 99 years to pay. These judges are of the view that making minor offenders, many of whom are totally impoverished or mentally ill, pay money is cruel and unusual punishment. The Crown is appealing a number of these cases but, as of the date of publication, none of the appeals have yet been heard.

Suspended Sentence and Probation

Probation may be ordered following a jail term, or the jail term may be suspended as long as the offender abides by the conditions of his probation.

Probation may be attached to and follow any jail sentence of two years or less. Once released from custody, the accused must follow the conditions set out in the probation order.

These conditions may require the offender to do certain things or to refrain from certain behaviour. For example, in addition to the mandatory conditions of being required to report to a probation officer at a particular time and place, keep the peace and be of good behaviour, and appear before the court as required, the offender also may be required to perform community service, provide "restitution" to the victim, live in a certain location, and refrain from using alcohol or drugs and from owning firearms, etc. The conditions are normally set in such a way as to fit the particular offence involved and to ensure, as much as possible, that they avoid the circumstances in which they found themselves when they committed the offence.

If the offender breaches any of the terms or conditions of the order, he or she can be charged with the further criminal offence of breach of probation. A probation order may last for up to three years. It is important to remember that even though the offender is not placed in custody if the probation terms are kept, this type of sentence still results in a criminal record.

The court may decide to delay or suspend passing a sentence and release the offender on probation for a specified period of time. This sentencing option is provided in section 731 of the *Code*. Suspended sentences are available only for offences that do not carry a minimum sentence.

An offender on probation with a suspended sentence remains out of custody but is supervised by a probation officer and must follow any conditions included in the probation order.

Conditional Sentence of Imprisonment

If an offender is convicted and the court imposes a sentence of less than two years' imprisonment, section 742.1 of the *Code* provides that the court may order that the sentence be served in the community, with certain conditions, instead of in jail. The court must be satisfied that serving the sentence in the community will not endanger the safety of the public. The offender must live at a specific location, usually the offender's own home, under very detailed and quite restrictive conditions; normally, they can't leave the house unless it is to go to work, school, or a medical appointment. If the conditions are not met, the offender may, after a hearing, be required to serve the rest of the sentence in jail.

The use of conditional sentences has become progressively restricted in recent years. Parliament has passed amendments to the *Criminal Code* limiting the courts' ability to apply this type of sentence. A judge can only impose a conditional sentence in the following circumstances:

• The sentence of imprisonment is less than two years.
• The offence does not carry a minimum amount of time in jail (this is called a mandatory minimum sentence).
• The offence does not involve serious personal injury, terrorism, or participation in a criminal organization prosecuted by way of Indictment for which the maximum term of imprisonment is 10 years or more.
• The judge is satisfied that letting the offender serve the sentence in the community would not threaten the safety of the community.
• The judge is satisfied that having the offender serve the sentence in the community is consistent with the sentencing principles of the *Criminal Code*.

Imprisonment

Imprisonment is the most serious sentence available, and it is used for the more serious offences or for repeat offences. The general maximum period of imprisonment available for a summary conviction offence is six months, although for some specific offences it may be longer. For indictable offences, the maximum period of imprisonment varies according to the offence, and for some offences it ranges as high as life imprisonment.

An offender who receives a sentence of less than two years serves the sentence in a provincial correctional institution. In most instances, this means that the offender is closer to his or her family and support network while serving the sentence. Maintaining these connections may be very important for the offender's rehabilitation and reintegration into the community at the end of the imprisonment. An offender sentenced to two years or more usually serves the sentence in a federal penitentiary.

If the sentence imposed is 90 days or less, the court may order that the sentence be served intermittently. Offenders serving intermittent sentences are allowed to leave the institution for blocks of time for a specific purpose, such as attending school or work, or caring for a family member who needs help. Usually, they are released during the week but must report back to the institution on weekends until they have served the time set out in the sentence. An intermittent sentence must be accompanied by a probation order, which sets out the conditions the offender must follow while he or she is not in jail. If the offender breaches any condition, the offender can be charged with the additional offence of breach of probation and may face being imprisoned full-time.

Indeterminate Sentence for Dangerous Offenders

Normally, a sentence of imprisonment sets out the specific amount of time that the offender must serve. However, an offender convicted of a violent offence may be declared to be a dangerous offender and sentenced to an *indeterminate* period of detention. *Indeterminate* means that the court does not specify a time period that the offender must serve. The Crown must make a special application to have a person declared a dangerous offender. This type of application is normally made only when an offender has a long series of violent or serious sexually based offences (see s. 752 for the list of offences). A person declared a dangerous offender is kept in jail with no fixed date for release. The Parole Board of Canada reviews the case after seven years, and every two years after that.

YOUNG PERSONS IN CONFLICT WITH THE LAW

Under British common law, the age of criminal responsibility was 7. In Canada, historically, children who committed criminal offences and were 14 years of age or older were tried in adult courts, as were those between 7 and 13 if it could be proven that they had the ability to form a criminal intent. By the latter part of the 19th century, however, Canadian society had begun to recognize that children had special needs and should, therefore, be tried separately from adult offenders. In 1908, the federal government passed the *Juvenile Delinquents Act*. It was amended in 1929. Under this statute, the age of criminal responsibility ranged from 7 to 16 years.

By the early 1980s, the *Juvenile Delinquents Act* had attracted some severe criticism from both legal and social welfare quarters. It was viewed as paternalistic, and the legal rights of children were often ignored in that they were rarely represented by counsel in court, and judges, police and probation officers were given too much control over the offender. In 1984, the *Juvenile Delinquents Act* was repealed, and the *Young Offenders Act* came into force. It raised the age of criminal responsibility to 12 and extended the definition of *youth* to include those up to 18 years of age. However, an application could be made under the statute for any youth over 14 years of age to be tried as an adult. Normally it was the Crown who would make this application for some young people who were charged with serious violent offences, such as murder, manslaughter, or sexual assault.

By the late 1990s, significant problems had been identified in the youth justice system. These included the overuse of incarceration as a sentence (Canada has the highest youth incarceration rate in the Western world); the lack of a coherent process to ensure the effective reintegration of the young person being released from custody; the failure to make a distinction between serious, violent offences and less serious offences; the complicated and time-consuming procedure for applying for transfer to adult court; the inconsistency in sentencing; and the insufficient recognition of the concerns of victims.

In an effort to address these issues, Parliament enacted the *Youth Criminal Justice Act* (YCJA).

The *Youth Criminal Justice Act*

The *Youth Criminal Justice Act* came into force on April 1, 2003. The YCJA, like the legislation preceding it, does not, for the most part, create offences; rather, it is primarily a procedural statute setting out the process for young persons to be tried for criminal offences. In order to determine the substantive law — that is, the elements of offences and the various defences available, reference must be made to the *Criminal Code*.

The following are the principles of the YCJA:

- The youth justice system must protect society.

- Youth must be treated separately from adults in the criminal justice system, given their differing needs and maturity levels, and the youth justice system must provide due process to young persons, as well as rehabilitation, and reintegration into society.

- Measures to address youth crime must
  - hold the offender accountable;
  - address the offending behaviour of the youth;
  - reinforce respect for social values;
  - encourage repair of the harm done to victims and the community;
  - respect gender, ethnic, cultural and linguistic differences;
  - involve the family, community and other agencies; and
  - be responsive to the circumstances of youth with special requirements.

- The parents and victims both have a role in the system and should be encouraged to participate.

In order to achieve these goals, the statute sets up a new procedural framework for dealing with sentencing, publication of records, custody, and reintegration into the community.

Sentencing Options

There are a number of different options for sentencing available in the *YCJA*, some of which are similar to or the same as sentencing options for adults and others that are quite different. Very often, given the age of the young offender, rehabilitation or redirection may be the primary principle of sentencing in many instances, although certainly the court will have to take into account all the principles required by the Act.

Types of Sentences

Reprimand

For minor offences, the judge may issue a reprimand. This is a severe warning or scolding of an offender by a judge in open court. It is most commonly used with first offenders where it appears that a warning may be sufficient to deter the offender from further criminal behaviour.

Discharge

This option is basically the same as that available under the *Criminal Code* for adult offenders. A discharge can be granted absolutely or with any conditions that the young person must follow for a specified period of time before the discharge takes effect.

Fine

Young persons can also be subjected to a fine of not more than $1,000, and the court may provide that the fine be paid over time.

Restitution

The *YCJA* provides for different types of restitution. An offender may be required to pay money to the victim for personal injury or damage to property; he or she may be ordered to compensate the victim by providing personal services — e.g., a young person found guilty of shoplifting in a store may be required to go and stack boxes in the store for a specified period of time.

Community Service

A community service order requires the young person to report to a probation officer on dates and times fixed by the court to provide work service to a charity or community organization. The order will specify the number of hours of work required, but they can be no more than 240 hours in total and cannot extend beyond a 12-month period.

Prohibition Order

A youth justice court has the power to make any prohibition, seizure, or forfeiture order that can be imposed under any federal statute, including the *Criminal Code*. For example, the young person may be prohibited from owning or possessing firearms, and the police will be given the power to seize the weapons, which will then be forfeited by the offender.

Probation

As with an adult, a young person may be placed on probation and be required to follow specified conditions, but the length of a probation order cannot be longer than two years.

Intensive Support and Supervision

This option is essentially an intensive probation order that requires the offender to have more intensive contact with his or her probation officer. The theory behind this type of order is that the young person will benefit from the closer contact with a positive role model and guide.

Attendance Order

The offender can be ordered to attend a specified program for up to 240 hours for a period not exceeding six months. This type of program may include something like an anger management course if such a course would be applicable to the young person's offence.

Deferred Custody and Supervision

This option is essentially a conditional sentence of imprisonment for young offenders. If the offence does not involve serious violence, a young person may be permitted to serve his or her sentence in the community. As with an adult offender, conditions will be applied that must be followed. Any breach of the conditions may result in the young person being required to serve the balance of the sentence in custody.

Custody and Supervision

In relation to custodial sentences, for most offences the young person can be incarcerated for up to two years. For offences, other than murder, for which an adult may be sentenced to life imprisonment, a young person may be given a sentence of up to three years. For first-degree murder the sentence is up to 10 years, with no more than six years spent in custody and the balance on conditional supervision. Finally, for second-degree murder, the young offender may be sentenced to up to seven years, with no more than four years in custody and the balance on conditional supervision.

Under the sentencing principles of the YCJA, custody is to be reserved primarily for violent offenders and serious repeat offenders.

One major change to sentencing in the YCJA is that adult sentences are available for any youth over 14 years of age who is convicted of an offence that carries a sentence of more than two years. There is no requirement for an application to transfer the trial to adult court in order for an adult sentence. Rather, once the young person has been found guilty of a serious offence, the youth justice court judge may apply an adult sentence. If an adult sentence were applied, the young person would be held not in an adult prison but in a youth facility, unless it would not be in the best interests of the young person or would endanger the safety of others.

Intensive Rehabilitative Custody and Supervision Order

It is an option available for serious, violent offenders. This order is available if

- the young person has been found guilty of murder or attempted murder.
- the young person has been found guilty of aggravated sexual assault or is a repeat offender of violent offences.
- the young person is suffering from a mental or psychological disorder or emotional disturbance.
- a treatment plan has been developed for the young person and there is an appropriate program available.

Custody and Reintegration

One of the general principles of the YCJA is that young persons in conflict with the law are more easily rehabilitated than are adults in similar situations. Therefore, every sentence involving custody must consider the eventual reintegration of the young person into the community with supports to help prevent the young person from re-offending. Every period of custody must be followed by a mandatory period of supervision in the community, and the supervision period must be equal to half the period of custody imposed. This means that if a young person receives a custodial sentence of two years, the young person must be supervised in the community for one year. During this time, the young person is to be monitored and controlled in order to ensure that he or she receives the necessary treatment and programs to return successfully to the community.

All periods of supervision must contain mandatory conditions prescribed by the legislation, such as keeping the peace and reporting to authorities. In addition, specific conditions, tailored to meet a particular young person's circumstances, may be applied, such as attending school, keeping a curfew, and attending designated treatment programs.

If the young person does not abide by any of the conditions while on supervision, the young person may be returned to custody. However, if the breach was minor, the court may apply additional conditions or vary the existing conditions rather than re-incarcerate the young person.

All young persons held in custody must be separated from adult offenders. If the young person is being held past his 18th birthday on a youth justice court sentence, it is presumed under the YCJA that he will be moved to an adult facility upon reaching the age of 20. However, the statute also provides that the young person may be held in a youth facility past his 20th birthday if provincial authorities determine it is appropriate to do so.

Measures outside the Formal Court Process

Almost half the matters brought to youth justice court are minor offences, such as shoplifting, possession of stolen property, failure to appear, and breach of a probation condition. Often these matters may be better dealt with outside the formal court process. The YCJA provides a number of options that may result in the young person never being prosecuted for the offence. The Act requires the police, in every case, to consider all options, including informal alternatives to the court process, before laying charges. In addition, each province may determine whether it is appropriate to require Crown counsel to pre-screen charges before they are laid against a youth. These measures help to ensure that the more expensive and formal court process is reserved for youth crimes that warrant it.

Jurisdiction of the Youth Justice Court

Young persons charged with offences are brought before special courts, separate from adults. These courts are all called youth justice courts. Each province may designate whether it wishes to appoint provincially or federally appointed judges to deal with criminal matters involving young persons. In Ontario, judges of the Ontario Court of Justice who deal with adult criminal matters are the provincially designated judges to sit in youth justice court, which is, very often, simply a separate courtroom in a courthouse dealing with adult criminal prosecutions.

Publication and Records

Contrary to what many members of the public believe, records of young persons are not destroyed at age 18. Evidence of prior findings of guilt is often used against adults in court at bail hearings and sentencing. However, a record may be made unavailable under certain circumstances after certain periods of time. Sentences other than alternative measures and discharges will not be purged, however, if there is an intervening offence within the specified time period. Fingerprints of a young person may be kept for an additional period of time.

Under the *Young Offenders Act*, in most circumstances it was an offence to publish the name of a young person, whether it is before or after a finding of guilt, unless the young offender had been transferred to adult court. A special order had to be obtained if the police wished to publish the name and photograph of a young person who was wanted for a specific offence. Such orders were rarely granted. The rationale for this was that the publication of the young person's name would interfere with the person's rehabilitation.

It is still a core principle of the YCJA that the identity of the young person be protected. However, the procedure will permit publication of the names of all youth convicted of a crime who receive an adult sentence. In addition, the names of 14- to 17-year-olds given a youth sentence for murder, attempted murder, manslaughter, aggravated sexual assault, or repeat violent offences may be allowed. Publication would also be allowed if a youth were at large and considered by a judge to be dangerous. The court may decide that publication is not appropriate in a particular case. Finally, the records of youth who receive adult sentences are treated the same as the records of adult offenders.

CHAPTER SUMMARY

This chapter provided an outline of procedural law in the Canadian criminal justice system. Procedural law is central to the system in that it provides the crucial balance between the interests and the power of the state in apprehending and prosecuting offenders and the rights of the individual who has been drawn into the system.

The different classifications of criminal offences were examined first because the type of offence charged dictates the procedure to be followed. Whether the offence is a summary conviction offence, an indictable offence, or a hybrid offence will determine the powers of arrest, the appropriate court to which the accused will be brought, and the process the case will take through the court system.

The chapter then examined the jurisdiction of courts to hear criminal cases. There are two bases for jurisdiction: jurisdiction over the offence and territorial jurisdiction. Some cases must be heard in the superior court, and others in the provincial court.

The first step in any criminal case is the police investigation and the laying of the charge. Police powers to investigate were outlined. Police investigatory powers are limited by the rights of the individual under the *Charter of Rights and Freedoms*. An improperly conducted investigation that violates a suspect's rights can result in the case being tossed out of the system. Police must, therefore, follow the rules laid out in the *Criminal Code* for conducting searches and seizures, questioning suspects, and holding lineups and other investigatory tests.

The procedure for bringing the accused before the court was then discussed. It is a principle of our criminal justice system that the accused must not be held in detention awaiting trial unless the Crown can establish on the balance of probabilities that there is sufficient reason for holding the accused in custody. The chapter summarized the various procedural requirements for arrest and detention and the different types of bail hearings that may be conducted, depending upon the offence charged.

We then looked at the different charging documents, Informations and Indictments, and then followed a criminal case through the court, from the preliminary inquiry through to sentencing. The principles of sentencing were discussed, and then the available sentencing options were examined.

Finally, the chapter presented an overview of the youth criminal justice system that is governed by the federal *Youth Criminal Justice Act*. We discussed the special provisions, policies, and procedures for prosecuting young persons between the ages of 12 and 18 years of age.

GLOSSARY OF NEW TERMS AND KEY CONCEPTS

deterrence
A principle of sentencing directed at discouraging an offender from re-offending or dissuading a member of the public from committing a similar offence.

discharge
A sentence whereby there is no conviction registered against the accused, even though the charge was proved.

hybrid offence
An offence for which the *Criminal Code* permits the Crown to elect whether to proceed by Indictment or by way of summary conviction.

indictable offence
The more serious offences in the *Criminal Code*.

Information
The sworn legal document that formally starts the prosecution of the accused by alleging that there are reasonable and probable grounds to believe that the accused committed the specific offence charged.

Indictment
The legal document setting out the allegations against the accused, which replaces the Information when the matter is to be tried in the superior court.

preliminary inquiry
A hearing prior to the trial of an indictable offence, at which the Crown must establish that there is enough evidence against the accused to justify placing the accused on trial.

preferred Indictment	The process whereby the Attorney General of a province has the authority under the *Criminal Code*, in certain circumstances, to commit the accused person to trial in the superior court, without a preliminary inquiry.
pre-sentence report	A report prepared by a probation officer with information as to the character, residential circumstances, employment, chances of being rehabilitated, and remorse, etc. of the offender, which a judge will use to assist in determining the most appropriate sentence.
search warrant	A court order that permits the police to enter and search specified premises to look for specified evidence that the police have satisfied the court they have reasonable grounds for believing is located at or in those premises.
summary conviction offence	A less serious criminal offence that is tried in the provincial court or before a provincial court judge.
summons	A court order requiring an accused to appear in court to answer a criminal charge.
victim impact statement	A type of report or written statement presented to the court, outlining the effect of the offence on their lives, by people who have suffered emotional or physical damage as a result of an offence or by the relatives of a deceased victim.

REVIEW QUESTIONS

1. What are the differences between an indictable offence, a summary conviction offence and a hybrid offence?

2. Under what circumstances will an accused be able to elect the level of court at which he or she wishes to be tried?

3. What is jurisdiction, and how does it affect criminal proceedings in Canada?

4. When may the police conduct a search without a warrant?

5. Constable Sharma is a police officer. While on patrol in the police car, he is called into Shepherd's Drug Mart in Wacco Mall. There he finds Bertha, who is being held by the store detectives. She has apparently stolen nail polish valued at $27.00. He decides to charge her with theft. Do you think he should arrest her?

6. Under what circumstances may the police arrest a person without a warrant?

7. What is the difference between a regular bail hearing and a reverse onus bail hearing?

8. What is the difference between specific deterrence and general deterrence?

9. What would you consider to be the major difference in procedure between the adult criminal system and the system under the *Youth Criminal Justice Act*?

10. Describe the three classifications of offences in the *Criminal Code*.

DISCUSSION QUESTIONS

1. In regard to the three principles of sentencing — denunciation, deterrence and rehabilitation — which do you think should be the most important, and why? Based on what you hear or read in the media, discuss whether or not you believe the Canadian criminal courts

are appropriately applying the principle that you believe is the most important.

2. "Since the introduction of the *Charter of Rights and Freedoms*, courts have become more concerned with the rights of the criminals than they are with the rights of the victims."

   Discuss this statement in the context of the following:
   (i) The right of the police to search and to seize evidence
   (ii) The power of the police to arrest the accused
   (iii) The procedure on bail hearings

3. In the following scenarios, discuss the procedural steps that a police officer wishing to charge the accused should follow.
   (i) After an investigation, there is sufficient evidence for Martin to be charged with murder in the death of his business partner.
   (ii) The police officer received a 911 call about an assault and, upon arriving at the club, he found Desmond kicking a smaller man, who was down on the ground. The officer is going to charge Desmond with assault under section 265 of the *Criminal Code*. He looks in the *Criminal Code* and determines that this is a hybrid offence.

4. "Youth crime will continue to be a problem in Canada because the *Youth Criminal Justice Act* isn't taken seriously by youth."

   Do you think this is a valid statement? Discuss your views.

5. The Government of Canada has relatively recently amended the *Criminal Code* to provide that reverse-onus bail provisions will apply to persons who are charged with serious gun offences. Do you think these provisions will reduce gun-related offences?

SUGGESTED READING AND OTHER RESOURCES

Bala, Nicolas. *Youth Criminal Justice Law*, 3d ed. (Toronto: Irwin Law, 2012).

Greenspan, E., & M. Rosenberg, eds. *Martin's Annual Criminal Code* (Aurora, Ont.: Canada Law Book, 2013).

Gulycz, Michael, & Mary Ann Kelly, *Criminal Law for Legal Professionals* (Toronto: Emond Montgomery Publications, 2013).

Pink, Joel E., Q.C., & David Perrier. *From Crime to Punishment: An Introduction to the Criminal System*, 6th ed. (Toronto: Thomson Carswell, 2010).

WEBSITES

CanLII: <http://www.canlii.org/en/index.html>

Justice Canada: <http://www.justice.gc.ca/eng/cjjp/yj-jj/ycja-lsjpa/back-hist.html>
   (See also provincial ministries of attorney general websites.)

The Law Dictionary: <http://thelawdictionary.org/>

The Law of Torts

JoAnn Kurtz
SENECA COLLEGE

Learning Objectives

After reading this chapter, the reader should be able to:

➢ identify and understand the elements of a tort
➢ identify and understand the different levels of guilty
   mentality in the commission of an act
➢ identify and understand variously named intentional
   torts
➢ identify and understand the main defences to
   intentional torts
➢ analyze and apply to fact situations the law as it
   relates to intentional torts and the defences to
   intentional torts
➢ identify and understand the elements of negligence
➢ analyze and apply to fact situations the elements of
   negligence
➢ understand the law of occupiers' liability
➢ understand the law as it relates to strict liability torts
➢ identify and understand the different kinds of damages
   awarded in tort actions

TABLE OF CONTENTS

INTRODUCTION

Torts is the area of law that deals with compensation of individuals for harm done to them by others in a non-contractual relationship. Together with actions for breach of contract, tort law is the basis for the vast majority of civil litigation.

Tort law includes matters as diverse as the following:

- Assault and battery
- Trespass to property
- Medical malpractice
- Nuisance
- Fraud
- Product liability
- Defamation
- Motor vehicle accidents

A discussion of torts is a discussion of civil wrongs, although the conduct involved may or may not also constitute a criminal wrong. In tort law, the victim of the wrongful act sues the wrongdoer for damages, and the major focus is on compensation of the victim. In criminal law, the state prosecutes the wrongdoer, and the major focus is on punishment of the wrongdoer.

What Are Torts?

Tort law dates from the time of the Norman Conquest of England in 1066. The word **tort** means "wrong" and comes from the old Norman-French language, which was used by the English courts until after the Middle Ages.

The law of torts, which has evolved over time, deals with certain types of wrongful and/or harmful conduct that cause certain types of harm or damage to another person. There are three elements in this definition of a tort:

1. Wrongful conduct
2. Harm
3. Cause

Each element must be examined.

What Types of Wrongful Conduct Constitute a Tort?

The answer to this question is rather unsatisfying, at least initially. The types of conduct that constitute a tort are those the courts have, over time, recognized as being redressable by some appropriate legal action. The range of categories has expanded since 1066, and is still growing today.

What Is Meant by Harm?

For there to be a tort, it is not enough to have a wrongful conduct; that wrongful conduct must have harmed the victim, and the type of harm must be one that is recognized by the courts.

Example
John decided to have a party. He invited all of his neighbours to the party except Jane, as a result of which her feelings were terribly hurt.

Unfortunately for Jane, hurt feelings is not a type of harm recognized by the courts.

The kinds of harm recognized by the courts have expanded over the years. In the 19th century, emotional or nervous shock was not a recognized category of harm, but now it is.

What Is Meant by Cause?

As stated earlier, the wrongful conduct must cause harm to the plaintiff. At the simplest level, there must be a physical connection between the act of the wrongdoer and the harm suffered by the victim. However, the legal definition of cause is not limited to simply establishing a causal connection between the wrongful conduct and the harm. Questions of remoteness of harm also arise, as will be discussed later in this chapter.

LEVELS OF GUILTY MENTALITY

Tort law looks at the wrongdoer as well as the victim. In particular, tort law examines the wrongdoer's state of mind while committing the wrongful act or conduct. This examination takes place because for different types of torts, different levels of blameworthiness or guilty mentality are required by the courts before a wrongdoer will be found liable in law to his victim.

Intentional Acts

An act is **intentionally** committed if the person committing the act wishes to produce the results that follow from her act. If a woman swings her fist at a man, wishing to strike that man in the nose and does, in fact, hit him in the nose, she is said to have intentionally hit his nose. The focus here is on the act itself, and not on the consequences of the act. In the situation just described, what is relevant is that the wrongdoer hit the victim's nose intentionally. The fact that she may or may not have intended to break his nose by doing so is irrelevant.

Intentional conduct is considered to carry the highest level of blameworthiness. This chapter will discuss classes of torts that must be intentionally caused to be actionable.

Recklessness

When an act is **recklessly** committed, the person undertaking a course of action has no specific intention or wish to cause harm, but has specific knowledge that the course of action might cause harm, and the course of action is undertaken in any event.

> *Example*
> A young man drives his car at high speed through a crowded schoolyard. The driver knows that by doing so he may well strike a child with his car. While he does not intend to hit any particular child in that he does not aim his car at any particular child, he nonetheless hits a young child with his car. In this instance, it would be said that the driver recklessly struck the child with his car. While he had no specific intention to strike the particular child with his car, he did know that he would likely strike some child, and undertook the activity in any event. Note that the focus here is on the striking of the child with the car. That is the act that is said to be recklessly committed.

Reckless conduct carries the next highest level of blameworthiness, and is more relevant to criminal law than to civil law. In tort law, the next level of guilty mentality after intention is negligence, the definition of which is broad enough to encompass reckless conduct.

Negligence

As with recklessness, when an act is **negligently** committed, the person undertaking a course of action has no specific intention or wish to cause harm. However, unlike recklessness, there is no requirement that the wrongdoer have specific knowledge that the course of action might cause harm. It does not matter what the wrongdoer knows or thinks. The test is whether a reasonable person in the position of the wrongdoer would know that harm might occur. If the answer is yes, the wrongdoer is held responsible on the basis that she ought to have known that her course of action would or could cause harm.

Example
Anne is driving her car at an excessive rate of speed. She is a skilled driver who always speeds and is confident that she is capable of handling her car and avoiding any accidents. Suddenly, the car in front of Anne stops, and Anne collides with the stopped car. If she had been driving at the posted speed limit, she would have been able to stop.

In this example, Anne did not intentionally collide with the car. She did not recklessly collide with the car (because she had no specific knowledge that this collision might occur). She was, however, negligent, because a reasonable person would have known that this collision might occur. Accordingly, the law states that Anne ought to have known.

This chapter will discuss classes of torts that must be negligently caused to be actionable.

Strict Liability

In all of the previous categories of guilty mentality, there is some element of blameworthiness on the part of the wrongdoer. What if a person's act causes harm to another, but the act is not intentionally, recklessly or negligently committed; in other words, the person is blameless? Generally, in such circumstances, the person will not be liable in law to the person harmed.

There are, however, some circumstances in which a blameless person causing harm may be held liable to the victim. The circumstances where this occurs are called **strict liability** torts. This category of torts will be discussed later in this chapter.

INTENTIONAL TORTS

It is to be remembered that a tort is comprised of three elements: wrongful conduct + harm + cause. This section discusses those kinds of conduct recognized by the courts to be wrongful when committed intentionally — in other words, when the level of guilty mentality required by the wrongdoer is that of intention.

In examining the definitions of the various intentional torts, it is to be noted that the elements of harm and the causal connection between the wrongful conduct and the harm are included in each definition.

What follows is a brief discussion of the most common intentional torts. There are other torts — such as malicious prosecution, abuse of process, maintenance and champerty, the intentional infliction of mental suffering, deceit and interference with contractual relations — that are not discussed.[1]

---

[1] Readers interested in obtaining more information about these other named torts should consult the torts texts listed under the heading "Suggested Readings".

Battery

Battery is the intentional infliction of a harmful or offensive contact with another person, including something that the person is wearing or carrying. That contact can be made by a part of the wrongdoer's body, by something the wrongdoer is carrying, or by something the wrongdoer has thrown.

The contact does not have to harm the victim to constitute battery; it must merely be offensive or unwanted (e.g., spitting). If the contact is unwanted by the victim, it does not matter that the wrongdoer did not intend it to be offensive (e.g., an unwanted kiss). However, jostling in a crowd or tapping someone on the shoulder to get the person's attention do not constitute battery because a certain amount of unwanted contact is considered by the courts to be inevitable in everyday life.

Contact with a person, if unwanted and offensive to that person, will constitute battery, even if the purpose of the contact is meant to benefit the victim. So, for example, surgery, even if beneficial to a patient, is considered battery if performed without that person's consent.

Unwanted or offensive contact constitutes battery even if the victim is unaware of the contact at the time it is made (e.g., sexual touching of a patient by a dentist when the patient is anaesthetized). The cause of action arises when the victim discovers the wrongdoing.

Assault

In tort law, **assault** is the intentional creation in the victim of a reasonable apprehension of imminent harmful or offensive contact. Keeping in mind that battery is defined as harmful or offensive contact, it can be said that assault is the creation of a reasonable apprehension of imminent battery.

Usually the victim's apprehension of imminent harmful or offensive contact is followed rapidly by that contact, and so battery usually follows quickly upon the heels of assault. But it is possible for each one to occur without the other.

> *Example 1*
> Lucy and Ethel are facing each other. Lucy takes a punch at Ethel's head but does not hit Ethel because Ethel ducks.

In this situation, Lucy has intentionally created in Ethel a reasonable fear of being punched in the head — a quite offensive contact. However, the contact does not occur. In other words, Lucy has committed the tort of assault but not battery.

> *Example 2*
> Ethel sneaks up behind Lucy, who remains totally unaware of Ethel's presence, and hits her in the head with a fry pan.

In this case, Ethel has committed the tort of battery but not assault. There was a very offensive contact, but because Lucy had no idea it was about to occur, there was no creation of fear of that contact.

Assault includes actions such as shaking a fist at another person or pointing a gun at another person.

The victim must reasonably fear that the offensive contact is imminent. So if a wrongdoer phones a victim from across town and tells the victim the wrongdoer will be coming over in two hours to beat the victim, that conduct, while wrong and perhaps even criminal, does not constitute the tort of assault. If, however, the wrongdoer tells the victim that a bomb has been planted in the victim's apartment that will be detonated by the wrongdoer over the phone, the tort of assault has been committed.

False Imprisonment

False imprisonment occurs when a person intentionally and without lawful justification confines another person within fixed boundaries.

The word "false" means wrongful. The word "imprisonment" does not mean that confinement in a prison is required. A person can be confined anywhere, such as a home, a car, or a boat. The victim must be totally confined within definite boundaries. There is no false imprisonment if there is a reasonable means of escape from the area of confinement. So, for example, there can be no false imprisonment in a room with two doors, if only one is blocked. However, the means of escape must be reasonable — in other words, available to the victim without danger. So, for example, there would be false imprisonment if, in order to escape, the victim would have to jump from a window, out of a moving car or out of a boat into the ocean.

There is no false imprisonment where a person voluntarily submits to confinement — for example, on a bus or plane trip. However, it is false imprisonment if a victim "voluntarily" goes into a confined area to avoid embarrassment, for example, if detained without justification on suspicion of shoplifting.

Trespass to Chattels

Historically, there were three torts to deal with chattels: trespass to chattels, detinue and conversion. While there are differences in both the definition of each tort and the remedy available in each case, they all involve the intentional interference with chattels owned by or in the lawful possession of another person. Because the distinctions among the three torts are quite subtle, for the purpose of this discussion all three will be referred to as **trespass to chattels**.

This tort covers the unjustified touching of chattels owned by or in the lawful possession of another, whether or not damage is caused to the chattel. For example, a teenager who scratches a neighbour's car with his keys has committed the tort of trespass to chattels.

It would also constitute trespass to chattels to take possession of a chattel contrary to the wishes of the person who owns or is in lawful possession of the chattel. For example, a teenager who takes his neighbour's car without permission has committed the tort of trespass to chattels.

Trespass to chattels not only covers the unlawful taking of a chattel but also the unlawful keeping of a chattel that has been obtained lawfully.

Example
George is a mechanic. Jerry gives his car to George to repair and return to him later that day. George does not do the repairs but instead takes the car on a one-week trip to Florida.

George's actions in this situation constitute a trespass to chattels. While George obtained possession of Jerry's car lawfully, the possession became unlawful when the car was used for a different purpose than authorized by Jerry, and also when the car was kept by George longer than authorized by Jerry.

Trespass to Land

Trespass to land involves the intentional interference with land owned by or in the lawful possession of another person. The tort of trespass to land is committed when the wrongdoer enters, without consent, the lands owned by or in the lawful possession of another person. It is also trespass to lands to refuse to leave the property when ordered to do so by the owner or person in lawful possession, even if the initial entry onto the property was lawful.

This action is used primarily as a means of asserting a right of ownership to real property so as to prevent the trespasser from obtaining a possessory title to the property.

Nuisance

Nuisance is interference with a landowner's use and enjoyment of his lands as a result of actions or conduct on neighbouring lands. Put another way, it is the intentional use of land in a way that interferes with a neighbour's use and enjoyment of her land.

This tort must be compared with the tort of trespass to lands, which protects the rights of landowners from interference by the actions of wrongdoers on the landowner's property. The tort of nuisance protects these rights by restricting behaviour on neighbouring land.

The tort of nuisance has been used to try to prevent or obtain damages for such matters as noise, odours, damage by a neighbour's tree roots and pollution from neighbouring factories.

In determining cases involving nuisance, the courts must balance the competing interests of neighbouring landowners: one owner's right to use his land as desired as opposed to the other owner's right not to be disturbed.

Defamation

Defamation is the publication of a statement that a reasonable person would see as damaging to one's reputation; or that holds the person up to contempt, hatred, scorn, or ridicule; or that causes the person to be discredited or shunned.[2]

Defamation is comprised of two torts: slander and libel. Slander involves spoken words or gestures. Libel involves more permanent statements, such as those in writing, in movies or on television.

Defamation law is a very complex area with its own defences, the best known of which is that the statement made is true. A more complete discussion of this area of law is beyond the ambit of this chapter.[3]

Conclusion

All of the intentional torts contain the three elements discussed earlier: wrongful conduct + harm + cause.

All of the intentional torts are examples of conduct that the courts consider to be wrongful when the acts are committed intentionally. The elements of harm and the causal connection between the wrongful conduct and the harm are included in the definition of each tort.

DEFENCES TO THE INTENTIONAL TORTS

A plaintiff may succeed in proving that a defendant has committed an intentional tort. However, if the defendant can successfully establish one of the recognized defences to the intentional torts, the defendant will not be liable to the plaintiff.

What follows is a brief discussion of the most common defences to the intentional torts. There are other defences, such as legal authority and necessity, that are not discussed.[4]

---

[2] *Murphy v. LaMarsh* (1970), 73 W.W.R. 114 (B.C.S.C.).

[3] Readers interested in the subject of defamation should consult the torts texts listed under the heading "Suggested Readings".

[4] Readers interested in these additional defences should consult the torts texts listed under the heading "Suggested Readings".

Consent

If the victim consents to the commission of an act that would otherwise constitute a tort, the wrongdoer is not liable. The consent may be express (i.e., stated) or implied (i.e., by conduct).

Consent is invalid if obtained by fraud, under duress, or from someone who is legally incapable of consenting — for example, under a mental disability.

The defence of consent is especially significant in tort actions arising from medical treatment or sports-related injuries. Where a person voluntarily participates in a sport, that person is taken to have consented to all contact within the rules, and probably to contact not intended to cause injury resulting from common infractions of the rules.

Self-Defence/ Provocation

A person may, without liability, harm another in order to protect himself from an actual or threatened attack. To constitute **self-defence**, the purpose of the action must be to prevent future or continued aggression, not to retaliate for a past attack. The degree of force used must be only that necessary to prevent the attack. For the defence to succeed, the use of force itself must be reasonably necessary, and the amount of force used must be reasonable.

Example 1
Frasier and Niles are having a heated discussion when, all of a sudden, Frasier punches Niles in the jaw. Niles, seeing that Frasier is preparing to punch him a second time, punches Frasier in the stomach to prevent him from doing so.

In this example, Niles can clearly sue Frasier for the torts of assault and battery. Frasier might, however, also sue Niles for assault and battery, in which case Niles could rely on the defence of self-defence.

Self-defence should not be confused with **provocation**, which is not a defence but a mitigating factor. Provocation is conduct on the part of the victim that causes the wrongdoer to lose her power of self-control and occurs at the time of, or shortly before, the wrongdoer's wrongful conduct.

Example 2
Frasier and Niles are having a heated discussion. Niles taunts Frasier by repeatedly insulting Frasier's mother. Frasier finally loses his self-control and punches Niles in the mouth.

In this example, Frasier cannot rely upon the defence of self-defence because he was not seeking to protect himself from physical attack. However, Frasier could rely upon Niles's provocation as a mitigating factor.

If the mitigating factor of provocation is successfully invoked, the damages otherwise payable to the victim will be reduced, but the wrongdoer will not totally avoid liability, as would be the case with the successful invocation of the defence of self-defence.

Defence of Others

This defence would arise where a person harms another person in order to protect a third person. The same principles apply to this defence as to the defence of self-defence. There are very few cases where this defence has been raised.

Defence of Property

A person is permitted to defend his property against wrongful interference by the use of reasonable force.

This defence is most commonly raised where a property owner takes steps to physically eject a trespasser. The force used must be only sufficient to expel the trespasser and must not cause unnecessary injury. If the trespasser initially entered the land lawfully, force cannot be used to eject the trespasser until she has first been asked to leave and has not done so.

NEGLIGENCE

Once again, it is important to remember the three elements of a tort: wrongful conduct + harm + cause. Under the heading "Intentional Torts", it was shown that wrongful conduct includes those acts intentionally committed that fall within the recognized and named intentional tort categories. Those categories cover injury to the person, both emotional and physical (e.g., assault, battery, false imprisonment, and emotional infliction of mental suffering); injury to property (e.g., trespass to lands and trespass to chattels); and economic injury (e.g., deceit).

In examining the law of negligence, the focus is still on the element of wrongful conduct. However, the definition of *wrongful conduct* will now be expanded to include acts committed negligently, as opposed to intentionally. As with intentional torts, the conduct examined causes injury to the person, injury to property or economic injury.

Wrongful Conduct — Duty of Care

The level of guilty mentality called negligence has previously been defined. Harm is said to be negligently caused if the wrongdoer ought to have known that his conduct was likely to cause harm. The question to be asked, then, is, harm to whom?

According to the law of negligence, a person undertaking an act is not required to know about the world at large. In deciding what actions to undertake, people are not required to think about everybody all the time; they are only required to think about some people. The question is, who?

This question is answered through the legal concept of **duty of care**. A person is responsible in law to (that is, ought to know about) those to whom the law says she owes a duty of care. To whom is a duty of care owed? A duty of care is owed to those

who are so closely and directly affected by my act that I ought reasonably to have them in contemplation as being so affected when I am directing my mind to the acts or omissions ... in question.

Duty of Care: Definition

EXHIBIT 13.1

The plaintiff's friend bought her a bottle of ginger beer at a store in Scotland. The ginger beer was manufactured by the defendant. The plaintiff could not examine the contents of the glass bottle prior to opening it because the bottle was opaque. After drinking part of the ginger beer, the plaintiff discovered that the bottle had contained the remains of a decomposed snail. This discovery caused the plaintiff to become ill.

The House of Lords held that the defendant manufacturer, in manufacturing its ginger beer, ought to have the ultimate consumers of the product in contemplation, and therefore owed a duty of care to the plaintiff.

Source: *Donoghue v. Stevenson*, [1932] A.C. 562.

EXHIBIT 13.2	Is there a Duty of Care Owed?

The plaintiff was a passenger on a bus. As she was getting off the bus, the defendant, who was on a motorcycle, speeded by the other side of the bus and collided with a car approximately 50 feet past the bus. The defendant was killed in the collision. The plaintiff heard the noise of the impact but saw nothing of the accident other than the blood left on the street after the defendant's body had been taken away. The plaintiff suffered nervous shock in reaction to the event. The plaintiff sued the defendant's estate.

The House of Lords held that the defendant owed the plaintiff no duty of care because he could not reasonably have expected a person in the position of the plaintiff to have been affected by his conduct. The defendant certainly owed a duty of care to the owner of the car with which he collided, but he was not liable to the plaintiff because no duty of care was owed to her.

Source: *Bourhill v. Young*, [1943] A.C. 92.

This definition of duty of care comes from a decision of the House of Lords called *Donoghue v. Stevenson* (see Exhibit 13.1).

It should be noted from the definition of *duty of care* that the identity of those to whom a duty of care is owed depends on the activity being undertaken (acts) or the activity being refrained from (omissions). Responsibility can flow both from positive acts and from omissions (refraining from acting).

Before a defendant can be held liable to a particular plaintiff, the plaintiff must demonstrate that the defendant owed a duty of care to him. This principle is illustrated in another decision of the House of Lords, *Bourhill v. Young* (see Exhibit 13.2). As can be seen in this case, it is not enough for a defendant merely to owe and breach a duty of care; the duty of care must be owed to the plaintiff in question.

In determining whether a duty of care is owed, one should ask whether a reasonable person in the position of the defendant could anticipate the possibility of harm occurring to the plaintiff if the defendant acted carelessly in the circumstances. If the answer to the question is yes, a duty of care is owed by the defendant to the plaintiff.

Wrongful Conduct — Breach of Duty of Care/ Standard of Care

Once it is established that a person owes a duty of care to another, it is necessary to ask two questions:

- What standard of care is required of that person?
- Has that person breached that standard?

The standard of care owed by one person to another is a duty to exercise reasonable care and skill towards the other person so as to avoid causing harm to that person. The standard is measured by reference to the reasonable person. A person is required to behave as a reasonable person would have done to prevent harm to the ultimate victim. What is reasonable will vary with the circumstances, so the specific standard of care will vary with the circumstances. But the general rule is always the same.

The circumstances that will affect the specific standard of care include

- the inherent danger of the activity in question, including
  - the likelihood or chance that injury of some kind can occur as a result of the activity in question;
  - the seriousness of the injury that might occur;

- the importance to the community at large of the activity in question; and
- the position, profession, or occupation of the defendant.

Inherent Danger of the Activity

The more inherently dangerous an activity is, the higher the standard of care to which the person undertaking the activity will be held. The courts examine both the likelihood of injury occurring and the seriousness of the injury that might occur. So, for example, a person delivering explosives is held to a higher standard of care than a person delivering groceries, both because it is more likely that some injury can occur as a result of the first activity and because any injury that might result would be far more serious.

Importance to the Community

A person engaged in an activity for personal gain is held to a higher standard of care than a person engaged in an activity that is of importance to the community. So, a person transporting passengers in a taxi would be held to a higher standard of care with respect to his driving than would be the driver of a municipal ambulance transporting an injured person to the hospital.

Profession or Occupation of the Defendant

If the defendant is a member of a profession that involves the employment of particular skills, she is required to behave in accordance with the standards of the reasonable practitioner in that profession. A nurse carrying out an emergency operation at a remote location, therefore, would not be held to as high a standard of care as a surgeon carrying out the same operation in a hospital.

To summarize, wrongful conduct includes acts committed negligently. A defendant is negligent vis-à-vis a particular plaintiff if the defendant owes that plaintiff a duty of care, and the duty of care has been breached.

Harm

For a defendant to be liable to a plaintiff in negligence, in addition to wrongful conduct, there must be actual loss or harm to the plaintiff, and the loss or harm must be to a legally recognized interest.

Example

Murphy is driving her car, and Miles is driving his car directly behind her. They are both travelling quite slowly, but Miles is following Murphy's car too closely. When Murphy stops her car, Miles's car is so close as to strike Murphy's car. However, because of the slow speed at which he was driving, no damage is done to Murphy's car, and she suffers no physical injuries or emotional harm.

In this case, there is wrongful conduct. Miles owed Murphy a duty of care, and he breached that duty of care by driving too closely behind her car. However, Murphy suffered no loss or harm. Accordingly, Murphy would not succeed in an action in negligence against Miles.

Legally recognized interests include the following:

- Damage to person
- Damage to property
- Nervous shock or emotional trauma
- Economic loss
- Damage to reputation

Cause

It is not enough for a plaintiff to prove wrongful conduct on the part of the defendant and harm suffered by the plaintiff. As previously stated, the wrongful conduct of the defendant must have caused the harm to the plaintiff.

At the simplest level, there must be some physical connection between the act of the wrongdoer and the harm suffered by the victim. One way to determine whether or not this physical connection exists is to use the "but for" test. Can you say that the harm to the plaintiff would not have happened but for the conduct of the defendant? If so, it can be said that the defendant's conduct was the cause of the harm to the plaintiff.

> *Example 1*
> Alex is standing at the curb with his back to Fred. Fred swings a baseball bat at Alex's head. Alex, totally unaware of Fred's conduct, steps off the curb, walks into the path of an oncoming car and is injured.

In this instance, there is wrongful conduct — Fred's swinging the baseball bat at Alex's head. There is also harm — the injuries suffered by Alex when he is struck by the car. There is, however, no causal connection between the two: Fred's conduct did not cause Alex's injury.

If the facts of Example 1 are changed slightly, the result is different.

> *Example 2*
> Alex is standing at the curb with his back to Fred. Fred swings a baseball bat at Alex's head. As Fred is doing so, Alex sees Fred's reflection in a nearby store window and, in attempting to escape Fred's attack, runs into the path of an oncoming car and is injured.

Again, there is wrongful conduct, and there is also harm. This time, however, there is a causal connection: Fred's conduct caused Alex's injury.

These two examples serve to illustrate factual causation, or causation in fact. However, the legal definition of *cause* is not limited to simply establishing a physical, causal connection between the wrongful conduct and the harm. Once that connection is established, the courts will examine the connection to ensure that the connection is **proximate** and not too remote.

While the term "proximate" means close, and the term "remote" means far, the terms do not address issues of physical closeness. Rather, the issue is one of reasonable foreseeability: Was it reasonable to foresee that the harm to the victim was a likely result of the conduct of the wrongdoer?

This issue is well illustrated by the New York State Court of Appeals decision of *Palsgraf v. Long Island Railroad Co.* (see Exhibit 13.3). In this case, there was causation in fact, but not causation in law because the conduct was not the proximate cause of the harm to the plaintiff. Causation in fact is physical causation, while causation in law is proximate causation.

Conclusion

When all three factors — wrongful conduct + harm + causation — are present, the plaintiff will have a cause of action in tort against the defendant. In negligence the element of wrongful conduct is present if the defendant owes a duty of care to the plaintiff and the defendant breaches that duty, and so the required elements may be summarized as follows:

- A duty of care owed by the defendant to the plaintiff
- Breach of that duty by the defendant
- Harm to a legally recognized interest of the plaintiff
- Causation that is proximate

| **Negligence and Proximate Cause** | **EXHIBIT 13.3** |

The plaintiff was standing at the defendant's railway station platform. As a train bound for another destination began to pull away from the station, two men ran to catch the train. One man reached the train without incident. The second man, who was carrying a package, made it aboard the train but looked as if he were about to fall. A guard on the train reached forward to help him in, while a guard on the platform pushed him from behind, and the package was dislodged and fell onto the tracks. The package, which was quite small and ordinary looking, in fact contained fireworks, which exploded when they fell. The force of the explosion knocked over some scales at the other end of the platform, many feet away, where the plaintiff was standing. The plaintiff was injured. The plaintiff sued the Long Island Railroad Co. for the negligence of its employees.

The court held that, while the conduct of the guards started a chain of events that resulted in the plaintiff's injury, it was not reasonably foreseeable that the conduct of the guards could cause any injury to the plaintiff.

Source: *Palsgraf v. Long Island Railroad Co.* (1928), 248 N.Y. 339; 162 N.E. 99.

EFFECT OF THE CONDUCT OF THE PLAINTIFF IN NEGLIGENCE

Even if all of the elements of a cause of action in negligence are proved, the plaintiff's right to recover damages from the defendant may be limited or eliminated as a result of certain kinds of conduct by him.

Voluntary Assumption of Risk

This defence to a negligence action is very closely related to the defence of consent in intentional torts. When consent is used as a defence to an intentional tort, the argument made is that the plaintiff consented to the commission of the specific act that forms the basis of the tort. The basis of the defence of voluntary assumption of risk, also known by the Latin phrase *volenti non fit injuria*, is not that the plaintiff consented to being injured, but that she consented to accept the risk of being injured by participation in a particular activity.

In order to establish this defence, the defendant must prove that

* the plaintiff had knowledge of the risk of injury involved in the activity; and
* the plaintiff consented to, or assumed, the risk involved.

This agreement to assume the risk may be expressed, or it may be implied from the conduct of the plaintiff.

Because this defence is based on consent, as with the defence of consent, the plaintiff must be legally capable of giving consent for the defence to apply. It will not apply if the plaintiff was incapable of consenting because of, for example, fraud, duress, or mental disability.

This defence has been successfully applied with respect to sports-related injuries, voluntary participation in fights and injuries suffered by willing passengers in cars driven by drunk drivers. The courts have declined to apply the defence, on public policy grounds, to risks of danger assumed by a person rescuing someone from a situation caused by someone else's negligence (e.g., someone running into a burning building to rescue a person trapped there).

Illegality

The defence of illegality is also known by the Latin phrase *ex turpi causa non oritur actio*. This defence, in some cases, prevents a plaintiff who was participating in criminal conduct at the time of his injury from successfully suing the defendant who caused the injury. It is considered contrary to public policy to permit wrongdoers to profit from their wrongdoing. It has also been said that there is no duty of care owed to a person involved in a crime.

> *Example*
> Fred and Barney are engaged in the armed robbery of a bank. Fred fires his gun negligently, and Barney is injured.

In this case, Barney would not succeed in an action for damages in negligence against Fred.

PROOF OF NEGLIGENCE

Burden of Proof

In the usual case, the burden of proof is on the plaintiff to prove all of the required elements of negligence — that is, a duty of care owed by the defendant to the plaintiff, a breach of that duty, harm to the plaintiff, and proximate causation. The plaintiff must present evidence that will satisfy the court on the balance of probabilities that all of these elements are present and that the plaintiff's cause of action has, therefore, been established.

Res Ipsa Loquitur

The plaintiff will not be able to provide evidence proving all elements of an action in negligence if he does not know how the accident was caused. In such a case, the plaintiff may be able to rely on the maxim *res ipsa loquitur*, which means, "The thing speaks for itself." *Res ipsa loquitur* is a rule of evidence by which the plaintiff, because he cannot explain how the accident happened, asks the court to make a *prima facie* finding of negligence, which the defendant then has an opportunity to rebut.

Where the maxim applies, once the plaintiff proves that the particular accident occurred, the court presumes, or makes a prima facie finding of, negligence on the part of the defendant. It is then up to the defendant to try to rebut that presumption.

> *When the Maxim Applies*
> The maxim will apply only where three conditions are met:

- The thing that caused the damage must have been in the sole control of the defendant.
- The accident was of the kind that would not ordinarily have happened without negligence.
- There must be no explanation as to how the accident happened.

Some examples of cases where the maxim has been applied are as follows:

- A case where a barrel fell out of a window
- Cases of foreign objects found in consumer products
- A case where swabs were left inside a surgical patient
- A case where a glass door shattered after being opened in a normal way

> *Effect of the Maxim on the Defendant's Case*
> As stated earlier, where the maxim applies, once the plaintiff proves that the accident occurred, negligence on the part of the defendant is presumed,

and it is up to the defendant to rebut that presumption. In order to do so, the defendant may prove how the accident took place, and that it took place without negligence on her part: in other words, that she, in fact, took reasonable care. Alternatively, the defendant may simply provide a reasonable explanation, consistent with the evidence, as to how the accident might have occurred without negligence on her part.

CONTRIBUTORY NEGLIGENCE

This topic addresses how the courts handle the situation where more than one party is negligent. Perhaps the plaintiff was negligent. Perhaps there are two defendants, whose negligence both contributed to the plaintiff's injury. The term "contributory negligence" applies to both of these situations.

Contributory Negligence of the Plaintiff

What It Is
Where there has been contributory negligence on the part of the plaintiff, it means that the plaintiff has failed to act carefully in protecting his own safety; it does *not* mean that the plaintiff has necessarily breached any duty owed to the defendant.

Example
Burt is running through a crowded corridor. Ernie is reading a book while walking through the corridor in the opposite direction. Burt runs into Ernie. Had Ernie been looking where he was going, he could have gotten out of Burt's way.

In this situation, Ernie did not cause the collision; Burt did. But had Ernie been adequately looking after his own safety, the collision could have been avoided. Ernie is not liable in negligence to Burt for any injuries Burt might have suffered but is contributorily negligent with respect to his own injuries.

Effect of Plaintiff's Contributory Negligence
Historically, any negligence on the part of the plaintiff totally prevented her from recovering any damages from the defendant. Over time, this rule was revised by the courts and was ultimately replaced by statutory provisions that state that the plaintiff will not be totally disentitled to damages; rather, the plaintiff's damages will be reduced proportionally to the extent to which she was at fault. In Ontario, the statute dealing with contributory negligence is the *Negligence Act*.

Damages in tort actions are discussed later in this chapter. It should be noted now, however, that the court will put a dollar value on the plaintiff's injuries and then reduce that amount by the percentage to which the plaintiff was at fault. So, in the example above, if Ernie's damages were assessed initially at $10,000, and Ernie were found to be 15 percent at fault in the accident, Burt would be ordered to pay Ernie only $8,500.

Joint Tortfeasors

The word "tortfeasor" means someone who commits a tort. The term "joint tortfeasors" is used when more than one person is responsible in tort for the injuries caused to a plaintiff. Under the provisions of the Ontario *Negligence Act*, the court determines the extent of responsibility of each of the tortfeasors and then apportions liability for damages accordingly. How this apportionment takes place will depend on the circumstances of the accident.

Example 1

A pedestrian is struck by a car driven by Thelma, as a result of which the pedestrian's leg is broken. The pedestrian is then struck by a car driven by Louise, as a result of which the pedestrian's arm is broken.

In this case, two accidents happen in rapid succession, and while only one plaintiff is involved, each accident results in clearly separate injuries to the plaintiff. In such a case, which is unusual, the court would be able to ascertain the damages appropriate to each injury. Thelma would be responsible for the damages calculated for the broken leg, and Louise would be responsible for the damages calculated for the broken arm.

In the more typical contributory negligence situation, one set of injuries to the plaintiff is caused by the negligence of two or more defendants.

Example 2

The plaintiff is a passenger in Thelma's car. Thelma is speeding. Louise is driving her car in the other direction and makes an improper left hand turn into the path of Thelma's car. As a result, Thelma's car broadsides Louise's car. The plaintiff is injured in the collision.

In this case, the plaintiff has suffered one set of injuries, for which both Thelma and Louise are at fault. The court would first set a monetary value on the plaintiff's injuries. Then the court would determine the degree to which Thelma and Louise were respectively at fault for the accident, and would apportion responsibility for the plaintiff's damages accordingly.

The Ontario legislation states that each of the joint tortfeasors is jointly and severally liable to the plaintiff for the entire amount of the damages awarded, but as between themselves, each is liable to contribute and indemnify each other to the degree to which each is at fault. So, in Example 2, if the plaintiff's damages are $10,000, and Thelma is 40 percent at fault and Louise is 60 percent at fault, the plaintiff can obtain payment of the $10,000 from either of the defendants or from both in any combination (so long as the total amount of the damages collected does not exceed $10,000). However, as between Thelma and Louise, Thelma is only responsible for $4,000 and Louise, for $6,000. If the plaintiff collects more than $4,000 from Thelma, Thelma can force Louise to repay her the amount in excess of $4,000.

Usually, the plaintiff will sue all parties responsible for the accident that causes his injuries. However, if the plaintiff fails to do so, the other tortfeasor can, by a proceeding called a **third party proceeding**, have the omitted tortfeasor made a party to the action.

OCCUPIERS' LIABILITY

This is an area of negligence law dealing with the liability of occupiers of property to those injured on their property. It is an area in which a statute defines the parties who owe a duty of care, the parties to whom the duty of care is owed, and what the standard of care is. A plaintiff would have to establish that a duty of care was owed to her by the defendant, in accordance with the statute, and that the standard of care established by the statute was breached. As with any other tort, the plaintiff would also have to establish harm and causation.

The Common Law   The common law in this area was very confusing. Persons entering onto the property of others were classified into categories according to whether or not they had the permission of the owner and the nature of that permission. Different standards of care were owed by owners of property to each category of entrant.

Legislation   In Ontario, this area of law is now governed by a statute called the *Occupiers' Liability Act*, which replaces the common law. In Ontario, the *Trespass to Property Act* also has some relevance to this area.

Definition of Occupier

An occupier is the person who is in physical possession of the premises or who has responsibility for and control over the condition of the premises, the activities conducted on the premises, or the persons allowed to enter the premises. All occupiers owe a duty of care to those persons specified in the legislation.

If a landlord has a contractual duty to maintain or repair the premises, and is in default of that duty, he is considered to be an occupier and can then be sued by an entrant. In this circumstance, the tenant would be an occupier as well.

To Whom Duty of Care Is Owed

An occupier owes a duty of care to persons entering on the premises.

General Standard of Care

The standard of care required by an occupier is to take reasonable care to see that persons entering the premises and the property they bring with them are reasonably safe while on the premises.

Contract

The general standard of care can be restricted or modified by contract.

Assumption of Risks

The standard of care owed by the occupier is lower where the person entering the premises willingly assumes, expressly or impliedly, the risks of entering the premises. Whether or not the entrant has assumed those risks is determined in the same way as with the doctrine of voluntary assumption of risk elsewhere in negligence law. However, unlike elsewhere in negligence law, if there has been an assumption of risk, it does not act as a complete defence against liability; it merely results in a lower standard of care being applied.

In such cases, the occupier's standard of care is not to create a danger with the deliberate intent of doing harm or damage to the person entering the premises or her property, and not to act with reckless disregard of the presence of that person or her property.

In the Ontario statute, the classes of persons who are deemed to have willingly assumed all risks are stated to include

- those who enter the premises intending to commit criminal acts;

- those who trespass on rural, agricultural premises, vacant premises, wilderness premises, closed golf courses, utility rights of way, unopened road allowances, private roads, and recreational trails, or who enter on such premises for free recreational purposes.

STRICT LIABILITY

Strict liability torts are those where a defendant is held responsible for harm done to the plaintiff even though the conduct involved was neither intentional nor negligent. The circumstances in which a blameless person is held responsible are quite limited. In those limited circumstances, the conduct is considered "wrongful" even though committed without intention or negligence. The additional elements of harm to the plaintiff and causation also have to be proved.

Rylands v. Fletcher

The decision of the House of Lords in *Rylands v. Fletcher*, (1868) L.R. 3 H.L 330, is the basis of strict liability in contemporary tort law. The case relates to the escape of a dangerous substance:

> The defendant built a reservoir on his land to supply water to his mill. There were unused mine shafts under the land that, unknown to the defendant, were connected to the plaintiff's mine. When the reservoir was filled, water flowed through the unused mine shafts and flooded the plaintiff's mine.
>
> The trial judge held the defendant to be liable to the plaintiff even though the harm was neither intentionally nor negligently caused. He stated, "the person who for his own purposes brings on his lands and collects and keeps there anything likely to do mischief if it escapes, must keep it in at his peril, and, if he does not do so, is prima facie answerable for all the damage which is the natural consequence of its escape."
>
> The House of Lords added an additional requirement for liability: that the defendant must have put his land to a non-natural use.

The requirements for liability under the rule in *Rylands v. Fletcher* are as follows:

- The thing that escapes must have been brought onto the land. There is no liability, under this rule, for the escape of things naturally on the land.

- The thing that escapes must be either inherently dangerous or something that, while ordinarily safe, may become dangerous if it escapes.

- The thing must escape from land over which the defendant has control, to a place outside his control.

- The defendant must have put his land to a non-natural use — that is, a use that introduces special dangers to the neighbourhood.

Defences

There are several defences available under *Rylands v. Fletcher*. The defendant is relieved of liability if the escape is the result of an act of God — that is, an extraordinary, natural event that could not be foreseen or protected against. It is also a defence if the escape of the object was the result of the unforeseeable intentional or negligent act of the plaintiff or of a third party. If the act was foreseeable, the defence will not apply on the basis that it should have been protected against. The express or implied consent of the plaintiff to the presence of the dangerous thing is also a defence.

Vicarious Liability

A person's liability is said to be **vicarious** when it is not based on the person's own wrongdoing but on someone else's wrongdoing. Vicarious liability is a form of strict liability in that the level of guilty mentality of the person is irrelevant: a person who is totally blameless can be held liable for damages. The most common example of vicarious liability is that of an employer for torts committed by his employee during the course of employment. If an employee commits a tort in the course of her employment, the employer is vicariously liable, even if totally innocent of any individual wrongdoing. Another example of vicarious liability is the liability of the owner of a motor vehicle for any torts committed by a person who drives the motor vehicle with the owner's consent.

DAMAGES IN TORTS

As stated at the outset of this chapter, the major purpose of tort law is the compensation of victims, rather than the punishment of wrongdoers. Victims of torts are compensated by being awarded an amount of money called *damages*, and the courts are called upon to put a dollar value on the injuries inflicted on them. It must be remembered that no damages will be awarded unless the plaintiff succeeds in establishing all of the required elements of a tort.

Damages awarded for the purpose of compensating the plaintiff are called **compensatory damages**. In addition, in unusual circumstances the court may also award the plaintiff **punitive damages**, the purpose of which is to punish the defendant.

Compensatory Damages

There are two categories of compensatory damages: special damages and general damages.

Special Damages

Special damages, also called specific damages, compensate the plaintiff for actual monetary losses and out-of-pocket expenses incurred prior to judgment (e.g., medical expenses, the cost of repair of damaged property and lost income).

To be awarded special damages, it is necessary to specifically ask for them in the statement of claim. It is also necessary to prove each and every item requested.

General Damages

There are two types of general damages. The first type compensates the plaintiff for items of non-pecuniary loss — that is, loss not easily measurable in dollar terms, such as pain and suffering and loss of enjoyment of life.

In order to be awarded this type of damages, the plaintiff must present evidence in court as to pain she has endured and the impact that the injuries suffered have had on her life. Based on this evidence, the court will assess her damages by placing a dollar value on her loss.

The second type of general damages compensates the plaintiff for anticipated out-of-pocket expenses, such as future medical expenses and future loss of wages. The court will estimate the amount of these expenses.

Punitive Damages

If the court considers the conduct of the defendant to be particularly outrageous, it has the jurisdiction to award *punitive damages*, also called **exemplary damages**. The purpose of these damages is to punish the defendant and, by making an example of him, to deter others from behaving in a similar fashion. This category of damages is not commonly awarded.

LIMITATION PERIODS IN TORT LAW

In all the provinces, there are statutes that limit the period of time in which lawsuits for various causes of action must be commenced. In the area of tort law, there are many different limitation periods, depending on the manner in which the injury arose and the identity of the defendant. So, for example, there are special limitation periods that apply to motor vehicle accident cases, to medical malpractice cases and to actions against government bodies.

CHAPTER SUMMARY

In this chapter, the reader was introduced to the history and nature of torts, and to the three elements required of a cause of action in tort — namely, wrongful conduct + harm + cause. The chapter then discussed the different levels of guilty mentality with which an act may be committed.

The circumstances in which a conduct is considered wrongful when committed with the different levels of guilty mentality were examined. Various specifically named intentional torts and the most common defences to the intentional torts were studied. The chapter also presented the elements of negligence, proof of negligence, defences to negligence and contributory negligence. Specific areas of occupiers' liability and strict liability torts were covered as well. In addition to wrongful conduct, there was a discussion of the requirement of harm to a legally recognized interest of the plaintiff, and a discussion of causation, including the distinction between causation in fact and causation in law.

The chapter concluded with a description of the different types of damages in tort actions and a brief review of limitation periods in tort actions.

GLOSSARY OF NEW TERMS AND KEY CONCEPTS

assault	The intentional creation in the victim of a reasonable apprehension of imminent harmful or offensive conduct.
battery	The intentional infliction of a harmful or offensive contact with another person.
compensatory damages	A monetary award made to a successful plaintiff to compensate the plaintiff for the injuries and losses the plaintiff suffered because of the acts of the defendant.
defamation	The publication of a statement that tends to tarnish a person's reputation in the estimation of right-thinking members of society or holds that person up to hatred, ridicule, or contempt.
duty of care	A duty owed by all persons contemplating an act or omission to all persons who might reasonably be affected by the act or omission.
exemplary damages	See **punitive damages**.
ex turpi causa non oritur actio	A defence that prevents another from making a successful tort claim, on the basis that the claimant was engaged in illegal behaviour.
false imprisonment	When a person intentionally and without lawful justification confines another person within fixed boundaries.
intentional act	An act that is committed with the wish to produce the results that follow from the act.
negligent act	One in which there is no intention to cause harm, or even any knowledge that harm might be caused, but in which a "reasonable person" would know that harm might be caused by the act.

nuisance	Interference with a landowner's use and enjoyment of her lands as a result of action or conduct on neighbouring lands.
provocation	Conduct on the part of a victim that causes the wrongdoer to lose self-control. The conduct by the wrongdoer must be a near-immediate response to the victim's provocative conduct. Provocation is a mitigating factor, but not a defence.
proximate cause	The connection between an act and its effect. An act is a proximate cause of an effect if the effect is reasonably foreseeable by a reasonable person doing the act.
punitive damages	Damages paid to a plaintiff not as compensation for a loss, but to punish exceptionally outrageous or wrongful conduct by a defendant.
reckless act	One acts recklessly when one knows that one's actions might cause harm, even where there is no intention to produce harmful results.
res ipsa loquitur	A situation where negligence is apparent from what has happened and from the surrounding circumstances so that the plaintiff need not prove specifically how the defendant was negligent.
self-defence	Acts that are designed to prevent or stop physical aggression by another, not including revenge or retaliation.
strict liability	Situations where an actor is liable for harm resulting from an act, whether or not the actor is blameworthy.
third party proceeding	A procedure in a lawsuit where, if *P* sues *D* and *D* claims the damage was done by *X*, *D* can have *X* added as a third party in the lawsuit.
tort	A legal wrong for which a person can sue to recover money damages.
trespass to chattels	The wrongful interference with things owned by or in lawful possession of another person.
trespass to land	The intentional interference with rights in land owned or in the lawful possession of another person.
vicarious liability	A situation where one is liable to someone not for one's own acts but for the acts of another for whom one is legally responsible in some way.
volenti non fit injuria	A situation where a person cannot claim against another, where the person agreed to undertake a risky activity that might cause the harm that occurred.

REVIEW QUESTIONS

1. What is the major purpose of tort law?

2. Name three elements of a tort.

3. (a) What is the level of guilty mentality required in an intentional act?
   (b) What is the level of guilty mentality required in a reckless act?
   (c) What is the level of guilty mentality required in a negligent act?
   (d) What is the level of guilty mentality required in a strict liability tort?

4. In what types of actions is the defence of consent especially significant?

5. What must be proved to establish the defence of self-defence?

6. Discuss the major differences between self-defence and provocation.

7. To whom does one owe a duty of care?

8. What factors are taken into account in determining the standard of care owed by one party to another?

9. Give some examples of legally recognized harm.

10. What is the difference between causation in fact and causation in law?

11. What must the defendant prove to establish the defence of *volenti non fit injuria*?

12. Explain the defence of *ex turpi causa non oritur actio*.

13. (a) What is *res ipsa loquitur*?
    (b) In what circumstances does it apply?
    (c) What is its effect?

14. What is the effect on the plaintiff's case if the plaintiff is found to be contributorily negligent?

15. (a) Define "an occupier".
    (b) To whom does an occupier owe a duty of care?
    (c) What is the general standard of care required by an occupier?

16. Provide two examples of strict liability.

17. (a) What are special damages, and how are they calculated?
    (b) What are general damages, and how are they calculated?
    (c) What are punitive damages?

18. Define "joint liability" in tort.

19. If two persons are found to have injured another, how are damages apportioned?

DISCUSSION QUESTIONS

1. Eric and James were friends. Eric lent James his car for a period of one week, to be returned on Monday at 8:00 a.m. James did not return Eric's car until Wednesday at 10:00 a.m. Eric was very angry and told James so. Rather than apologizing, James punched Eric in the nose and then turned around and walked away. Eric was so stunned that he did nothing for several minutes. When James was about 10 feet away, Eric threw his car keys at James, striking him in the back.

    Discuss all possible causes of action between the parties and all possible defences or other mitigating factors.

2. Alfred spilled a cup of coffee on the tiled floor of the corridor outside his office. He went to get some paper towels to clean the spill, but he got into a conversation with a fellow office worker and forgot all about it. Gus was walking down the hall carrying a box of ball bearings. He slipped on the spilled coffee and dropped the box, which broke, causing the ball bearings to roll down the length of the corridor. At the same time, a pizza delivery man was just turning into Harrison's office, at the far end of the corridor from Alfred's office. He slipped on several of the ball bearings and fell into Harrison's office, dropping the pizza box on Harrison. The pizza box opened and the hot cheese from the pizza burned Harrison.

    Discuss whether or not Alfred's conduct caused Harrison's injury in fact and in law.

3. As a result of the facts in Question 2, Harrison suffered very painful injuries that prevented him from working for an entire year. He had no income for that period. Serious burns to Harrison's hands prevented him from participating in two of his favourite activities, bowling and knitting, for a period of one year. In addition, Harrison had medical and other expenses related to his recovery.

If Harrison successfully sued Alfred, what kind(s) of damages might he be awarded, what is the purpose of those damages, and how would they be calculated?

4. Eberhardt was walking through a fairground when someone threw a lit firecracker at him. Instinctively, he grabbed it and pitched it away from himself. The firecracker landed under a car and went off. Unbeknownst to Eberhardt, the car was full of a very sensitive explosive. The shaking of the car from the firecracker caused the explosives in the car to go off, injuring Florinda. If Florinda sued Eberhardt, discuss the defences he might use.

SUGGESTED READINGS

Fridman, G.H.L. *The Law of Torts in Canada*, 2d ed. (Toronto, Ont.: Carswell, 2002).

Kerr, M., J. Kurtz & L.M. Olivo. *Canadian Tort Law in a Nutshell*, 2d ed. (Toronto, Ont.: Carswell, 2005).

Klar, L. *Tort Law*, 3d ed. (Toronto, Ont.: Carswell, 2003).

The Law of Contract

JoAnn Kurtz
SENECA COLLEGE

Learning Objectives

After reading this chapter, the reader should be able to:

➢ describe the nature of a contract and its use and value in society
➢ identify the essential components of a contract
➢ describe the formal requirements necessary to create a valid contract
➢ identify the grounds upon which a contract may be attacked
➢ understand how contracts are interpreted
➢ understand how contracts are discharged
➢ understand how a contract is breached
➢ understand the remedies for breach of contract

TABLE OF CONTENTS

INTRODUCTION

Contracts in Everyday Life

Despite their popular image, **contracts** are not just long, incomprehensible documents with tiny print. Contracts are an everyday part of everyone's life, and can be oral or in writing. Leases, credit cards, the purchase of a car, membership in a health club and the purchase of groceries all involve contracts.

As varied as these examples of contracts are, they all have elements in common.

Elements of a Contract

A contract is an agreement between two or more parties that is enforceable at law.

All contracts contain the following elements:

- The parties must have reached an *agreement*, as evidenced by the fact that there has been *offer* and *acceptance*.
- The parties must *intend to be legally bound*.
- Both parties must have given *valuable consideration*, such as payment or an act, or a promise to pay or act.
- The parties must have the *legal capacity* to contract.
- In some cases, certain *legal formalities* must be complied with (e.g., some contracts must be in writing).

Classification of Contracts

Contracts may be classified in a number of ways:

Deeds are written contracts that have been signed, witnessed, sealed and delivered. As will be seen later in this chapter, the seal takes the place of consideration.

Simple contracts are all contracts that are not deeds. They may be oral or written.

Bilateral contracts are contracts in which a promise by one party is exchanged for a promise by the other party (e.g., the promise to do something in return for a promise of payment).

Unilateral contracts are contracts where one party promises to do something if the other party does something first — for example, a promise to pay a reward if someone finds your lost dog. Only the person promising to pay the reward is bound to do anything by such a contract.

CONTRACT FORMATION: OFFER AND ACCEPTANCE

In order to determine whether or not a contract has been formed, the courts ask whether an agreement has been arrived at. This issue is addressed by asking whether one party, called the **offeror**, has made an offer that has been accepted by the other party, called the **offeree**.

Offer

An **offer** is an expression of willingness to enter into a contract on the terms specified in the offer. It is made with the intention that the offer will become a binding contract if it is accepted.

An offer may be express (i.e., stated) or implied (by conduct), and it may be made to one particular person or to a group of people. It may also be made to the world at large, which is the case when a person offers a reward.

Invitation to Treat

An offer must be distinguished from an *invitation to treat*, which is a request for offers that can then be accepted or rejected.

When a store advertises merchandise for sale, the advertisement is not an offer to sell the goods, but merely a request for shoppers to make an offer to purchase the goods at the advertised price. Likewise, when a store displays merchandise for sale, the store is requesting that shoppers make an offer to purchase the goods at the display price. In both cases, under contract law, the store is not legally bound to actually sell the goods at the advertised price (although it would be poor business not to do so, and contrary to certain consumer protection legislation).

Acceptance

Acceptance is the unconditional agreement to, and acceptance of the terms of, the offer. Acceptance must be communicated to the offeror.

Acceptance must be *unconditional*. There can be no changes made to the terms of the offer. If any changes are made, the result is a *counter-offer*, the effect of which is to end the original offer.

> *Example 1*
> Fred offers to sell Barney his car for $2,000. Barney agrees to buy the car but says he will only pay $1,750. Fred says no. Barney then tells Fred that he will pay $2,000.

In this example, Fred is not obligated to sell the car to Barney for $2,000. When Barney changed the price, he made a counter-offer that Fred was free to accept or reject. When Fred rejected the counter-offer, Barney could no longer accept Fred's original offer because his counter-offer had terminated it.

Acceptance must be made in the manner requested in the offer. If no specific manner is stated, it must be made in a reasonable manner. An offer cannot be worded in such a way that if the offeree says nothing it constitutes acceptance — some act of acceptance is required.

Acceptance must be made within the time stated in the offer. If no time limit is set, acceptance must be made within a reasonable time.

Acceptance must be communicated to the offeror. The only exception is for unilateral contracts, where performance constitutes acceptance, and there is no need to notify the offeror in advance of one's intention to accept.

Acceptance is effective when it is communicated to the offeror. When it is reasonable or required that acceptance be made by mail, acceptance becomes effective when it is mailed, even though the offeror is unaware that the offer has been accepted. This rule, called the **postal acceptance rule**, applies even if the letter is delayed, destroyed, or lost.

> *Example 2*
> Thelma mails a letter to Louise on September 1, offering to buy Louise's computer for $500. Louise receives the letter on September 7. On September 10, Louise mails a letter to Thelma accepting her offer. The letter is not received by Thelma until September 17. On September 15, Thelma telephones Louise to tell her she no longer wants to buy the computer and so is withdrawing her offer.

In this example, the offer was accepted on September 10, when Louise mailed her letter of acceptance to Thelma. After this date, Thelma could no longer withdraw her offer.

In Ontario, the *Electronic Commerce Act*[1] governs the time of receipt of acceptance by electronic means such as e-mail, fax, voice messaging and interactive websites. If the offeror designates an electronic method of acceptance, acceptance becomes effective when the message enters the designated electronic system and is able to be retrieved.

Termination of Offer

An offer can be terminated in a number of ways. An offer is terminated if the offeree makes a counter-offer, or if the offeree rejects the offer.

An offer can be terminated by **revocation**. An offeror can revoke or withdraw the offer any time before it is accepted by the offeree.

An offer can also terminate by **lapse**. If an offer is stated to be open for acceptance for a fixed period of time, at the expiry of that time period it will lapse. If the offer does not state a period of time, the offer lapses after a reasonable time.

An offer also terminates on the death of the offeror.

CONTRACT FORMATION: INTENTION TO BE LEGALLY BOUND

For there to be a binding contract, the parties must intend to create a legally enforceable agreement. If this intention is lacking, even though all the other elements of a contract are met, no contract will be formed.

In contract law, exaggerated advertising claims are not treated as forming the basis of a binding contract but are considered "mere puff". There is now, however, consumer protection legislation that limits this principle.

No contract will result from an offer made as a joke — for example, if a mother jokingly offers to pay $500 to any woman who will marry her son. In addition, no contract will result from social arrangements.

Example
Elaine invites Jerry over for dinner, and Jerry accepts. Elaine spends a great deal of time and money on the dinner, and then Jerry forgets to show up.

Even though Elaine prepared the dinner on Jerry's promise to show up, it is a well established principle of contract law, as noted by the authors of a leading contracts text, that "to offer a friend a meal is not to invite litigation."[2]

CONTRACT FORMATION: CONSIDERATION

In contracts, no one does anything for nothing. A contract is not enforceable unless something of value is given by each party to the other. That something of value is called **consideration**. Without consideration, there is only a **gratuitous promise**, which the courts will not enforce. Consideration may be an act, a promise to act, or a promise to refrain from acting (**forbearance**).

---

[1] S.O. 2000, c. 17.
[2] G.C. Cheshire, C.H.S. Fifoot & M.P. Furmston, *The Law of Contract* (London, U.K.: Butterworths, 1972).

Rules Relating to Consideration

Past Consideration

In contract law, *past consideration* is no consideration at all. Consideration, to be valid, must be a present or future act. Past consideration is a past act, or services rendered, or a benefit conferred in the past.

Example

Niles, a not-too-bright budding entrepreneur, decides to go into the lawn maintenance business. He arrives at Frasier's home when Frasier is at work. His plan is to mow and fertilize Frasier's lawn and then present him with a bill on his return from work. When Frasier returns from work, Niles proudly shows him the work he has done and presents Frasier with a bill for $50. In order to get Niles to leave, Frasier promises to pay him the $50 the next week. The next day, Frasier delivers a letter to Niles telling him that he won't pay the bill.

Niles cannot enforce Frasier's promise to pay him $50. Frasier's promise was given in exchange for work already completed. This is a promise given in exchange for past consideration, which is no consideration at all. Therefore the promise to pay is considered a gratuitous promise and is unenforceable.

Adequacy of Consideration

Consideration must be valuable — that is, it must have monetary value — but the courts will not generally examine whether or not the value of the consideration is adequate. In the absence of fraud or misrepresentation, it is considered to be up to the parties to negotiate their deal, not the courts.

Performance of an Existing Duty

Performance of an existing duty or a promise to perform an existing duty is not good consideration. The existing duty can be a public duty or a contractual duty. So, for example, a policeman, who has a public duty to protect the public, cannot charge a citizen money to protect her. If the citizen agreed to pay the policeman, the promise would be gratuitous and unenforceable.

Example

Laverne agreed to build a bookcase for Shirley to be completed on June 15. Shirley agreed to pay Laverne $250. On June 10, Laverne told Shirley she would not be able to complete the job on time. Shirley offered her an additional $50 to complete the bookcase by June 15. Laverne agreed, and the bookcase was completed on time.

Laverne cannot enforce Shirley's promise to pay her the extra $50. Laverne was already under a contractual duty to complete the bookcase by June 15. Her renewed promise to do so did not constitute valid consideration, and so Shirley's promise is a gratuitous promise and, therefore, unenforceable.

Part Payment of Debts

The principle that performance of an existing duty does not constitute valid consideration causes a problem for debtors who wish to settle their debts for an amount less than the original amount owing.

Example

George owes Jerry $10,000 but cannot afford to pay him. George approaches Jerry to try to settle the debt for a lesser amount. Jerry agrees to accept $5,000 in full settlement of the debt.

Under the common law of contract, Jerry's agreement to accept $5,000 is not enforceable because George is not giving him any valid consideration; he is already contractually obliged to pay the $5,000.

In Ontario, the common law position has been changed by a statute called the *Mercantile Law Amendment Act*. According to the provisions of that statute, Jerry's acceptance of the lesser sum of $5,000 would act as a full discharge of the debt. If Jerry agrees to accept $5,000, he can change his mind at any point before payment is received by him.

Promissory Estoppel

While a person cannot sue to enforce a gratuitous promise, sometimes a gratuitous promise can be used as a defence against a lawsuit that contradicts the promise. The equitable principle that allows a defendant to do this is called **promissory estoppel**.

Assume in the above example that George told Jerry he had no money of his own to repay the loan but would borrow $5,000 to do so. If he borrowed the money in reliance upon Jerry's promise not to sue for the balance, Jerry would be *estopped* from suing George for the balance. This principle could be used by George in addition to the provisions of the *Mercantile Law Amendment Act*.

There are three elements required before promissory estoppel can be relied upon:

- The other party must make a clear and unambiguous promise not to enforce his legal rights.
- The party seeking to invoke the principle must have acted in reliance on that promise to his detriment.
- It would be inequitable for the other party to go back on his word.

Exceptions to Requirement for Consideration

Deeds — in other words, contracts under seal — do not require consideration to be enforceable. The seal takes the place of consideration. In medieval times, sealing a deed involved impressing a coat of arms into a pool of hot wax poured on the document. Today, the usual practice is to attach a round red sticker on the document.

A gratuitous *promise to make a gift to a charity* will be enforced if

- the charity has made a legal commitment based on the pledge (e.g., the hiring of a contractor or the purchase of materials); or
- other donors have also pledged money; because if one donor fails to pay, it undermines the gift of the others.

CONTRACT FORMATION: CAPACITY

A contract cannot be enforced against a person not mentally competent to enter into it.

Corporations

Corporations are recognized as persons and can enter into contracts. The document by which a particular company is created sets out the corporation's objects. The contract must be within those objects. Most incorporating documents define the corporate objects very broadly.

Mentally Impaired Persons

This topic covers persons impaired by disability, drugs, or drunkenness. Mentally impaired persons are liable for contracts they enter into for **neces-**

saries: that is, essentials of life, such as food, clothing, shelter, medical care, education, tools to earn a living, and transportation to work.

For non-necessaries, the contract is valid unless

- the mentally impaired person was incapable of understanding the nature of the transaction; and
- the other party was aware of the incapacity.

In such a case, the contract is voidable at the option of the mentally impaired person. The impaired person must

- repudiate (i.e., end) the contract as soon as her impairment disappears; and
- be able to return all the benefits she received under the contract.

Minors

Minors are also called infants. In Ontario, both terms refer to persons under the age of 18.

Because minors are considered to need protection from their lack of knowledge and experience, the law provides that most contracts entered into by minors are *voidable* by the minor; in other words, the minor can choose to end the contract. The adult party is bound by the contract even though the minor is not. The result is that, for most contracts, a minor can sue to enforce his rights under a contract, but the adult party cannot.

Whether or not a contract is voidable depends on the subject matter of the contract.

Contracts for Necessaries

If a contract for necessaries (defined above) has been *partly executed* (i.e., partly performed), in that the adult party has sold and delivered the goods to the minor, the minor is bound by the contract and must pay for the goods. The minor is only required, however, to pay a reasonable price.

If a contract for necessaries is *executory* (i.e., both parties have exchanged only promises and no performance has yet taken place), the minor is not bound. An example of an executory contract is one where the minor has ordered books, but they have neither been delivered nor paid for.

If a contract for necessaries is *fully executed* (i.e., fully performed), the contract will not be set aside. A fully executed contract is one where the goods have been delivered and paid for.

If *money is lent* to a minor for the purchase of necessaries, and the money is, in fact, used that way, the minor is contractually bound to repay the money.

A minor is bound by a *beneficial contract of service* — for example, a contract of apprenticeship — if the contract is not exploitative.

Contracts for Non-necessaries

The adult party to a contract with a minor for non-necessaries is bound by the contract; the contract is enforceable against the adult party. The minor may have the contract declared void, but if the minor repudiates the contract, she must, if she is the buyer of goods, return the goods, whatever state they are in; if she is the seller, she must be able to return the money paid to her.

If the contract has been fully executed — that is, the goods sold and fully paid for — the contract will not be set aside, but the court may order the adult party to refund any excessive amount charged to the minor.

If the contract is an ongoing one — for example, a book-of-the-month club — and the minor has received some benefit under the contract, the minor cannot recover money he has paid for benefits already received but can repudiate the contract with respect to future liability.

When the Minor Reaches the Age of Majority

Where the contract in question is for necessaries, the minor's liability to pay continues after he reaches the age of majority.

Where the contract is for non-necessaries and benefits the minor on one occasion only, the minor must ratify the contract in writing after she becomes 18 years old, or the contract automatically ends.

Example

Mark Minor orders a stereo on June 15, to be delivered on June 30. Mark's 18th birthday is June 25.

In this example, Mark must ratify the contract in writing after he becomes 18, or the contract automatically terminates, and any deposit he might have paid would have to be refunded.

Where the contract confers a continuous benefit on the minor, such as a partnership agreement or the purchase of a car on instalments, the minor must repudiate the contract upon becoming 18 in order to end it. If he does nothing or continues to use the item or make payments, he will be bound.

CONTRACT FORMATION: FORMALITIES

Contracts can be oral, written without a seal (a simple contract), or written and under seal (a formal contract or deed). They are all equally valid. There are, however, certain contracts that must be in writing to be enforceable.

The Statute of Frauds

The original *Statute of Frauds* was passed in England in 1677, and there is still a Statute of Frauds in Ontario. By its provisions, contracts dealing with certain subjects are not enforceable unless the agreement, or some note or memorandum of the agreement, is in writing and is signed by the person being sued. These contracts include the following:

- a *promise of an executor* by which the executor agrees to pay the debts of the estate personally;

- *guarantees*. A **guarantee** is a promise by one person to pay the debt of another person if he defaults. A guarantor's liability arises only if the principal debtor defaults. Therefore, the guarantor's liability is said to be a secondary, not primary, liability. An agreement to pay, whether or not the other debtor first defaults, is called an **indemnity** and does not need to be in writing;

- *contracts relating to land*, except for leases of less than three years.

To satisfy the requirement of the statute, the contract itself may be in writing, or there may be some memorandum or note of the agreement in writing. Such things as letters, receipts, telegrams, and notes will satisfy this requirement as long as the documents contain all the essential terms of the agreement. Only the person who is being sued must have signed the document.

The Doctrine of Part Performance

If strictly applied, the requirements of the *Statute of Frauds* could be used to allow a party to avoid responsibility under an otherwise valid contract.

> *Example*
> Woody agrees to work for Mia for a period of five years. Mia agrees to transfer a one-half interest in her house to Woody at the end of the five-year period. Woody works for Mia for five years and then asks Mia to transfer the one-half interest in her house to him. Mia says, "Contract? What contract?"

If the provisions of the *Statute of Frauds* were strictly applied, Mia would be able to take advantage of the statute to, in effect, perpetrate a fraud on Woody.

The *doctrine of part performance* was developed to protect against such a situation. According to the doctrine, the *Statute of Frauds* does not apply where

- there has been part performance of the contract alleged;
- the acts that constitute the part performance are clearly referable to the contract being alleged and tend to prove the existence of the contract;
- it would be a fraud to allow the party who is trying to avoid her obligations to take advantage of the fact that the contract is not in writing; and
- except for the requirement of writing, there is a valid and enforceable contract.

Other Statutes

There are other statutes that require that certain formalities be complied with for specific types of contracts. Some examples follow.

> *Sale of Goods Act*
> A contract for the sale of goods of a value exceeding $40 must be in writing to be enforceable unless the buyer accepts all or part of the goods, gives something in earnest to bind the contract, or makes partial payment on the contract.

> *Consumer Protection Act*
> An executory contract for goods or services of a value exceeding $50 is not binding on the buyer unless the contract is signed by the parties and each party has received a duplicate copy of the original contract.

> *Family Law Act*
> Marriage contracts, paternity agreements, cohabitation agreements, and separation agreements are unenforceable unless made in writing, signed by the parties and witnessed.

GROUNDS ON WHICH A CONTRACT MAY BE ATTACKED

Mistake

An implicit element of any contract is that the parties have truly and freely agreed or consented to the terms of the contract. The requirement that the parties have mental capacity to enter into the agreement is one way that this issue of consent is addressed. In addition, a party to a contract can avoid contractual responsibility in some instances where the consent was obtained by *mistake*. It must be kept in mind that the legal meaning of *mistake* is far more restrictive than the ordinary meaning of the word.

Common Mistake

It is possible for both parties to enter into a contract on the basis of a false assumption. If both parties make the same mistake, it is called an identical or **common mistake.**

If the parties enter into a contract and are both mistaken as to the existence of the subject matter of the contract, the contract will be void.

Example 1

Alan and Sandy enter into a contract for the sale of Alan's book collection. Neither of them knows that the warehouse where Alan's books are stored has burned down, thus destroying the books.

Both parties mistakenly believed the subject matter of the contract to exist. The contract would be void.

However, where the parties are both mistaken as to the value or quality of the subject matter, the contract will be valid.

Example 2

Max sells Jacob a painting. They both believe that the painting was painted by a famous artist and is very valuable. It is later discovered that the painting was painted by someone else and is worth a lot less than either of them thought.

This contract will be valid.

Mutual Mistake

This term is used to describe the situation where both parties are mistaken, but the mistakes are different. An example of a **mutual mistake** is the English case of *Raffles v. Wichelhaus* (see Exhibit 14.1). As can be seen, in a case such as this, the position of the defendant is favoured, because the court will not enforce such an ambiguous contract.

Unilateral Mistake

This term is used to describe the situation where only one party is mistaken, and the other party is aware of the mistake. If the mistake relates to the terms of the contract itself, as opposed to a mere error in judgment as to the quality of the subject matter of the contract, the contract will be void.

Mutual Mistake   **EXHIBIT 14.1**

The defendant agreed to buy cotton from the plaintiff to be shipped from Bombay aboard a ship called *Peerless*. Neither party was aware of the fact that there were two ships by that name scheduled to leave Bombay: one in October and another in December. The plaintiff was referring to the ship leaving in December, while the defendant was referring to the ship leaving in October. The plaintiff's shipment arrived two months later than the defendant had anticipated. As a result of price fluctuations in that period, the defendant refused to accept and pay for the shipment. The plaintiff sued for payment. The defendant pleaded mistake as a defence.

The court held that the contract was totally ambiguous, and a reasonable person could not tell whose interpretation to choose. Accordingly, the plaintiff's claim was dismissed.

Source: *Raffles v. Wichelhaus* (1864), 159 E.R. 375.

Example

Lisa offers to sell to Michael her French landscape painting for $500. Michael agrees, believing it to be the painting hanging in her living room. In fact, Lisa owns two French landscape paintings, and she is offering for sale her less valuable painting that hangs in her den. Lisa is aware of Michael's mistake.

In this case, the contract would be void. However, if Michael knows that Lisa is offering to sell the painting in her den and accepts the offer in the mistaken belief that it is worth more than it actually is, the contract will not be void.

Mistake as to the Identity of One of the Contracting Parties

Where one person is mistaken as to the identity of the other contracting party, the contract will be void if

- the identity of the other party is of crucial importance to the contract;
- the mistaken party had an identifiable person in mind with whom he intended to contract; and
- the other party was aware of the mistake.

Clerical Mistake

If a party can show that the parties were in complete agreement on the terms of their contract, but by an error wrote down these terms incorrectly, the court can correct the error. This remedy is called *rectification*.

Non Est Factum

The general rule is that a person is bound by the contracts she signs, even if the person has not read or understood the document. An exception to this rule is where the person, through no carelessness of her own, is totally mistaken as to the nature and effect of the document signed.

In this case the person would plead **non est factum**. Generally, the party relying upon this defence is either illiterate or prevented by some disability from reading the document and is, therefore, forced to rely upon someone else's representation as to the nature and effect of the document signed.

Misrepresentation

A **misrepresentation** is a *false statement of fact* that *induces* the other party to enter into the contract. The misrepresentation may be either fraudulently or innocently made.

Where a misrepresentation is made, the other party may be entitled to have the contract terminated.

False Statement of Fact

The false statement must be with respect to a specific existing fact or a past event. Even if false, the following do not constitute misrepresentation in law:

- A statement of future conduct or intention
- A statement of opinion or belief
- A statement as to what the law is

To be a misrepresentation, a statement must exist. Generally, silence or non-disclosure does not constitute misrepresentation.

Meaning of Inducement

The other party must have relied upon the false statement in deciding whether or not to enter into the contract, and the false statement must have been a major factor — although not necessarily the only factor — in her deciding to enter into the contract. There is no inducement if the other party used his own judgment, or if he did not rely on the statement.

Remedies for Misrepresentation

The main remedy for misrepresentation is the equitable remedy of **rescission**. In other words, the innocent party may seek to have the contract set aside, and have the parties put back in the position they would have been in if the contract had never been made. In order to obtain this remedy, the innocent party must act promptly, and it must be possible to substantially restore the parties to their original position.

If the misrepresentation was negligently or fraudulently made, the innocent party may, in addition to rescission, also seek damages in tort for deceit (fraudulent misrepresentation) or for negligent misrepresentation. If the misrepresentation was innocent, there is no right to claim damages.

Undue Influence and Duress

Where a contract is entered into as a result of one party's having exerted improper pressure over the other party, the contract may be set aside.

The term **undue influence** describes a situation where a party enters into a contract as a result of improper pressure being brought to bear on her so as to render her "morally unable" to resist the will of the other party. As a result of this pressure, the party enters into a contract that is not to her advantage but is to the advantage of the other party.

In most cases, the innocent party must prove that undue influence was applied. However, in some relationships the court presumes that some degree of influence exists, such as the influence of parent over child or solicitor over client.

The term **duress** applies to the situation where a party entered into a contract as a result of actual or threatened violence, against him or his family, or as a result of a threat of criminal prosecution or libel. The threat must have been made by the other party to the contract.

Illegality

The courts will not enforce contracts whose purpose is illegal. The purpose of the contract may be illegal because it contravenes the provisions of a statute or because it contravenes public policy. If the purpose of a contract is illegal, the contract will be considered void. In some situations, the contract will also be considered illegal.

Different Treatment of Void and Illegal Contracts

A contract that is considered *void* because of an illegal purpose will be void only in so far as it contravenes the particular statute or public policy. If only a term is considered illegal, the void term may be severed, and the remainder of the contract enforced, if it is possible to do so without substantially altering the contract. If a contract is merely void for illegal purpose, the courts will assist the parties in disengaging from the void contract. Either party may sue to recover any money paid or property transferred pursuant to the contract.

If the contract is not only void but *illegal*, the effect on the parties will depend on whether or not the contract is illegal as formed. Contracts to commit a crime or contracts expressly forbidden by statute are contracts illegal as formed. In these contracts, generally, neither party will be able to sue or acquire rights under the contract, or recover money paid or property transferred under the contract. If the contract was legal as formed, but one party (and not the other) performs or intends to perform the contract in an illegal manner, the "guilty" party cannot sue on the contract for damages or recover money paid or property transferred under the contract, but the innocent party may be able to sue on the contract.

Illegal Contracts

A contract may be illegal by virtue of a provision in a statute, or it may be illegal at common law. A contract is *illegal by statute* if the statute expressly or implicitly forbids the making of the contract. Where a statute requires that a member of a trade or profession be licensed, the failure of the person to have a licence will be a good defence to an action by that person to collect fees for work performed. If, however, the person to whom the services were performed wishes to sue, the unlicensed individual cannot rely on her own lack of a licence as a defence.

The following are examples of contracts considered *illegal at common law*:

- Contracts to commit a crime or a tort
- Contracts encouraging sexual immorality
- Contracts prejudicial to public safety
- Contracts prejudicial to the administration of justice
- Contracts encouraging public corruption

Void Contracts

Contracts may be *void by statute* or *void at common law*. An example is found in the *Workplace Safety and Insurance Act*, which states that any provision in any employment contract that purports to deprive an employee of the protection of the legislation is void. Another example is the *Gaming Control Act* of Ontario. While it is not necessarily illegal to bet, a winner of a bet cannot use the courts to collect on the bet, and a loser of a bet cannot use the courts to recover what he paid.

The most common example of a contract void at common law is a contract in restraint of trade.

Contracts in Restraint of Trade

Contracts to lessen competition are considered contrary to public policy and are void, unless they are reasonable as between the parties and with respect to the public interest. There are three types of contracts in restraint of trade:

- Agreements between manufacturers to fix prices or to limit production
- Agreements between an employer and an employee regarding subsequent employment of the employee
- Agreements between the buyer and seller of a business

Agreements between manufacturers to fix prices or to limit production are void not only at common law, but under the federal *Competition Act*.

Courts look very carefully at contractual provisions by the employer that attempt to restrict the employee's right to work after the employment is terminated. Such provisions are considered to be reasonable only if the employee has knowledge of trade secrets or secret processes or is in a position of influence to entice away customers. Even if the circumstances make it reasonable for restrictions to be placed, the nature of the restrictions must be no wider than reasonably necessary, and they must be reasonable as to geographic area and duration.

Agreements by a seller of a business not to subsequently compete are looked upon more favourably by the courts. Again, however, the person seeking to uphold the restrictions must show that they are reasonable in view of the nature of the business being sold. The restrictions must again be reasonable in scope, duration, and geographic area.

In both employment and business sale situations, if the restrictions as drafted are found to be unreasonable, they will be void in total; the courts will not redraft the provisions for the parties.

INTERPRETATION OF CONTRACTS

The statements, promises, and provisions of a contract are called the **terms of the contract.** It is the terms of the contract that determine the rights and obligations of the parties. A term of a contract may be express or implied. If a term is broken, the importance of the term determines the remedies available to the wronged party.

Before the court can enforce a contract, the court must determine what the term or terms in question mean. In doing so, the court tries to ascertain the true intention of the parties as expressed in the language of the contract. This exercise will involve a balance between interpreting the language of the contract in accordance with its plain meaning and interpreting the contract in the context of the circumstances surrounding it.

The Requirement of Certainty

For a contract to be enforced by the court, its terms must be reasonably certain. If the terms of the contract are too vague, the court will not know what to enforce, and the contract will, therefore, be unenforceable or void.

The Parol Evidence Rule

The *parol evidence rule* is a rule used in the interpretation of written contracts. The rule limits the use of extrinsic evidence, whether written or oral, in interpreting the written language of the contract. Such evidence is not admissible to add to, subtract from, change or contradict the terms of the contract as written. This rule flows from the presumption that, when a contract is reduced to writing, the written document is meant to include all of the terms of the contract. The rule could be used to exclude oral statements, draft contracts, or correspondence.

As with any rule, there are exceptions to the parol evidence rule. The main exceptions are as follows:

- Evidence of the customs of an area or of trade usage of a particular term may be admitted to add to, but not contradict, a written agreement (e.g., a baker's dozen is 13, not 12).

- Evidence is admissible that the contract has not yet come into operation or has ceased to operate.

- The presumption that the written document is meant to include all of the terms of the contract may be rebutted by evidence proving that the contract was partly written and partly oral. The additional oral terms must not vary or contradict the written terms; they may only complete the written terms.

- Evidence is admissible if it relates to the validity of the contract. Accordingly, the court will hear evidence on issues such as mistake, misrepresentation, lack of capacity, or lack of consideration.

- The court will admit evidence of clerical error in recording the terms of the agreement, leading to the remedy of rectification.

- The court will admit extrinsic evidence to explain ambiguous terms in the contract.

- The court will admit evidence as to the existence of a **collateral contract.** In such a case, the argument would be that external evidence is not being offered to contradict the written terms of the contract; instead, it is evidence of a separate and additional contract between the parties, which may contradict the written contract. For such evidence to be admitted, the collateral contract must itself have all of the elements of a valid contract, including separate consideration.

Classification of Terms

Not all terms of a contract are of equal importance. Contract law categorizes terms based on their importance. Breaches of different categories of terms have different effects.

Condition

This expression is used to describe an important term of the contract. Breach of a **condition** entitles the wronged party to sue for damages and to treat the contract as over, relieving her of any obligation to perform under the contract.

Warranty

This expression is used to describe a less important term of the contract. Put another way, any terms that are not conditions are **warranties.** When a warranty is breached, the wronged party has the right to sue for damages, but he cannot treat the contract as over and must still perform his obligations under the contract.

Implied Terms

Certain contract terms may be implied into a contract, even though not expressed by the parties. There are three ways this can occur: by statute, by custom and by the court.

Terms Implied by Statute

There are certain statutes that imply terms into particular types of contracts. For example, the *Residential Tenancies Act* states that certain provisions with respect to the termination of a residential tenancy are included in all residential leases, whether or not expressly stated in the contract between the landlord and the tenant.

Terms Implied by Custom

Where the contract is silent on a particular matter, the court may imply terms based on evidence of local custom or trade usage.

Terms Implied by the Court

The court may imply a term not expressly stated by the parties, where the court's opinion is that the parties must have intended to include the term in order to give effect to the contract. For the court to do so, the term must be so obvious as to go without saying. In implying such terms, the court is attempting to give effect to what must have been the intention of the parties.

Exculpatory Clauses

Exculpatory clauses are clauses by which a party attempts to limit her liability for breach of contract, misrepresentation, or negligence. These clauses are also called disclaimer clauses or exclusion clauses.

Before a court will give effect to such a clause, the court must be satisfied that the clause has been incorporated into — in other words, is part of — the contract and that, as a matter of interpretation, it covers the situation in question.

Incorporation

If the contract containing the exculpatory clause is written and signed, the other party is bound by the clause even if he has not read the document, and whether or not he understands the clause. The clause can, however, be rendered ineffective if there has been a misrepresentation as to its effect. (See Exhibit 14.2.)

If the contract containing the exculpatory clause is not signed, reasonable and sufficient notice of the exclusion clause must be given to the other party. To satisfy this notice requirement, the following must occur:

- The clause must be in a document that the other party would assume to contain contractual terms and not in a document that merely acknowledges payment, such as a receipt.

- The existence of the clause must be brought to the notice of the other party before or at the time the contract is entered into, not after.

Interpretation

Once the court finds that the exculpatory clause is, in fact, part of the agreement, the court must interpret the clause to determine whether or not it covers the situation in question. In doing so, the court interprets the entire contract. The courts have held that liability can be excluded only by clear words.

The court applies certain rules of construction in interpreting exculpatory clauses. The main rules of construction are as follows:

- Under the *contra preferentem rule*, an exculpatory clause is construed strictly against the party who drafted the clause. Any ambiguity in the language of the clause will be construed as narrowly as possible. Especially clear words are required to exclude liability for negligence.

- There is a presumption of construction that an exculpatory clause is not intended to defeat the main purpose of the contract.

An Example of the Effect of Misrepresentation

EXHIBIT 14.2

The plaintiff took a dress to the defendants to be cleaned. She signed a receipt after being told it excluded the defendant's liability for damage to sequins. In fact, the clause excluded the defendants from liability for damage of any kind. The dress was returned with a stain.

The court held that, because the defendants misrepresented to the plaintiff the effect of the clause, the exemption clause would in this instance protect the defendants only for damage done to sequins.

Source: *Curtis v. Chemical Cleaning & Dyeing Co. Ltd.*, [1951] K.B. 805.

- An exculpatory clause can protect the party relying upon the clause against liability for a **fundamental breach** of contract only if the language of the clause specifically and clearly covers the breach in question. A fundamental breach of contract is a serious breach of the contract.

PRIVITY OF CONTRACT AND ASSIGNMENT OF CONTRACT RIGHTS

Privity of Contract

The general rule at common law is that a contract does not confer any rights or impose any obligations on a person who is not a party to the contract. A person who is not a party to a contract is said not to be *privy to the contract* and is called a third party or a *stranger to the contract*. To succeed in an action in contract, the plaintiff must prove **privity of contract** between her and the defendant. In other words, the plaintiff must prove that they were both parties to the same contract.

> *Example 1*
> Alice buys a tuna salad sandwich from a takeout delicatessen. The mayonnaise in the tuna salad has gone bad. Alice gives the sandwich to Ralph, who develops food poisoning.

In this example, Ralph would have no cause of action in contract against the delicatessen because he was not a party to the contract with the delicatessen for the purchase of the sandwich. Put another way, there was no privity of contract between Ralph and the delicatessen.

> *Example 2*
> Bob owes Carol $200. Bob offers to repair Ted's car if Ted will pay Carol $200. Bob does the repairs on Ted's car. Ted does not pay Carol.

In this example, Carol cannot sue Ted. There is no privity of contract between them. Carol can sue only Bob, and only Bob can sue Ted.

> *Example 3*
> The facts are the same as in Example 2, except Carol is also made a party to the contract with Bob and Ted.

Carol is still unable to sue Ted. While there is privity of contract and consideration flowing between Bob and Ted, there is no consideration flowing from Carol to Ted. For a person to be able to sue on a contract, there must be not only privity of contract between the parties but also consideration for the promise given by the person who is suing to enforce the promise.

> *Example 4*
> A landlord rents a store to a tenant. Under the contract between them, the landlord agrees to make the store available to the tenant, and the tenant agrees to pay the rent. The tenant in turn sublets the store. The subtenant agrees to pay the rent directly to the landlord. The subtenant fails to pay the rent.

In this example, the landlord would be unable to sue the subtenant directly for the rent. The landlord would have to sue the tenant, with whom she had privity of contract. The tenant in turn can sue the sub-tenant.

Assignment of Contractual Rights and Obligations

This subject is related to privity of contract. Most contracts confer rights and impose obligations on both parties. For example, in a lease, the landlord has the obligation to make the premises available to the tenant and has the right to receive rent; the tenant has the right to occupy the premises and the obligation to pay rent.

Contractual Obligations

A party to a contract cannot assign or transfer his obligations under the contract to a third party without the consent of the promisee (the person to whom the obligation is owed under the contract).

Where the contract involves the provision of a unique service — for example, that of an entertainer or a portrait painter — the obligation must be personally performed.

Where the contract does not involve the provision of a unique service, the **promisor** (the person who owes the obligation under the contract) may arrange for someone else to carry out the obligation on her behalf. However, the promisor remains responsible to the **promisee** for the proper performance of the contract obligation. This is known as *vicarious performance*. The promisor assumes the role of an employer and, in essence, hires someone to do his work for him. However, the contract work is being done on the promisor's behalf and, if it is not done properly, the promisee sues the promisor, not the person who did the work on her behalf.

Example

Burt hires Ernie to wash the windows of his house. Ernie hires Elmo to wash the windows for him. Elmo breaks one of Burt's windows.

In this example, Burt cannot sue Elmo in contract because there is no privity of contract between them. However, Burt can sue Ernie because Burt remains responsible under the contract to see that his contractual obligations are properly performed.

Contractual Rights

A party to a contract may assign his rights under a contract to a third party without the consent of the promisor. The person who assigns contract rights to another is called the **assignor**. The person to whom the contract rights are assigned is called the **assignee**.

Once the contract rights have been assigned, if the promisor does not fulfill her obligation, the assignee may sue the promisor on the original contract without having to join the assignor (who was the original promisee) as a party to the action, provided that the following conditions are met:

- the assignment was absolute — in other words, unconditional and complete;
- the assignment was in writing; and
- the promisor was given notice in writing of the assignment.

Example

Gaugin lends Picasso $12,000. Picasso agrees to repay the loan in instalments of $1,000 per month plus 10 percent interest. Gaugin decides to move to Tahiti and needs the money immediately. He agrees to sell his right to receive the loan payments to Monet. Monet pays him $10,000. Gaugin is willing to accept this lesser amount in return for getting the money immediately. Gaugin and Monet draft and sign a written agreement in which Gaugin unconditionally assigns to Monet his right to receive the loan payments from Picasso. Gaugin notifies Picasso in writing of the assignment.

Upon receipt of the notice of the assignment, Picasso is obligated to make all future payments to Monet. If Picasso does not make the payments, Monet can sue Picasso directly, without having to add Gaugin as a party, even though there is no privity of contract between Picasso and Monet. If Monet were to sue Picasso, Picasso would be able to rely upon any defences he could have raised against Gaugin.

DISCHARGE OF CONTRACTS

When a contract is discharged, it means that the obligations under the contract are cancelled and that the contract is no longer operative. A contract may be discharged by performance, by agreement, by frustration, by operation of law, or by breach.

Discharge by Performance

When parties enter into a contract, they expect that the obligations under the contract will be performed by both parties and, when performance is completed, that the contract will come to an end. In fact, this is what occurs in the majority of contracts.

Before a contract can be said to be discharged by performance, both parties must have fulfilled their obligations under the contract.

The general rule is that performance under the contract must be exactly in compliance with the contract provisions. There is, however, an exception in the case of *substantial performance*. Where a party has substantially performed his obligations under the contract, he may enforce performance of the other party's obligations. The court may, however, reduce the other party's obligations because of the incomplete performance. (See Exhibit 14.3.)

Tender of Performance

Sometimes a party's attempt to perform her contractual obligation will be refused by the other party. An attempt to perform is called a **tender of performance.**

EXHIBIT 14.3

The Principle of Substantial Performance

The plaintiff and defendant entered into a contract for the plaintiff to carry out repairs to the defendant's house. The work as completed by the plaintiffs differed from the contract in three minor respects that could be corrected at a relatively small cost to the defendants. The defendant refused to pay the plaintiff on the grounds that the contract had not been performed as required.

The court held that the defendant was not relieved of his obligation to pay because of a trivial failure of performance. The defendant was ordered to fulfill his obligation under the contract, which was to pay the contract price, subject to a deduction equal to the cost of correcting the defects in the plaintiff's work.

Source: *Dakin & Co. Ltd. v. Lee*, [1916] 1 K.B. 566.

Example
Alex, who owns a dress shop, agrees to buy 50 dresses from Kim for $75 each. Delivery is to take place on April 1. Prior to the scheduled delivery date, Alex finds similar dresses from another supplier for $60 each, and buys from that supplier instead. When Kim attempts to deliver the dresses on April 1, Alex refuses to accept delivery, thinking that, as a result, he will not have to pay the contract price.

In this case, Kim's tender of performance relieves her of any further obligation under the contract. Her tender of performance is the equivalent of performance, and she can sue Alex for the contract price.

Tender of Payment
A tender of payment is treated somewhat differently than a tender of performance. If a party is under a contractual obligation to pay money, and the other party, for some strange reason, refuses to accept payment, the party is not relieved of his obligation to pay under the contract. However, he will not have to pay any interest on the money or any costs in any subsequent court action to collect the money.

When money is to be paid under a contract, unless the contract provides otherwise, payment is to be made in cash.

Discharge by Agreement

The parties to a contract may, by subsequent agreement, agree that the contract is at an end.

Waiver
A **waiver** is an agreement between parties to an existing contract that the contract is not to be performed. A waiver is itself a contract and must be supported by consideration. If the contract being terminated is one under which neither party has performed, the consideration flowing from each party is a release of the other party's obligation to perform under the contract. If one party has performed under the contract and the other party has not, the waiver must either be supported by its own consideration or be under seal.

Material Alteration of the Contract Terms
Sometimes the parties to an agreement wish to change the terms of the agreement. If the agreed-upon change results in a material alteration of the terms of the original contract, the effect is to discharge the original contract and replace it with a new one.

Accord and Satisfaction
This term describes the situation where a promisor who cannot perform her obligation under the contract offers the promisee money or some other substitute if the promisee will release her from her original obligation.

Example
Elizabeth enters into a contract to buy carpeting from Hugh, to be delivered on June 30. Hugh is unable to obtain the carpeting from his supplier in time for delivery and so offers a different style of carpeting to Elizabeth at a reduced price. Elizabeth accepts.

Discharge by Frustration

Sometimes, without the fault of either party, it becomes impossible to perform under the contract as required. In some of those situations, the doctrine of frustration provides that the contract is discharged.

The following are the situations where the doctrine has been held to apply:

- The doctrine applies where performance becomes *impossible* — for example, a contract to rent a concert hall for a piano recital where the concert hall burns down before the concert date.

- A contract is frustrated where a change in law, while the contract is in effect, renders further performance under the contract *illegal*.

- The contract may be considered frustrated where performance, though possible, would be something radically different than what the parties originally intended. For example, a person rents a hotel room for the express purpose of watching a parade, which is then cancelled.

The doctrine of frustration does not apply in cases where performance of the contractual obligations is possible but will cause hardship. The fact that a party's contractual obligations prove to be more onerous than expected does not constitute sufficient grounds for frustration. The doctrine will also not apply to a situation where a party wilfully disables himself from performing.

In Ontario, the *Frustrated Contracts Act* sets out what happens if a contract is frustrated:

- If a party started to perform her obligations before the contract was frustrated (whether or not the other party has received any benefit from the performance) and that party has received any payments from the other party, the party can keep the money already paid to the extent that she has incurred expenses. Any excess over expenses must be returned.

- If a party started to perform his obligations before the contract was frustrated (whether or not the other party has received any benefit from the performance) and payments were due from the other party but unpaid at the time of frustration, the party can sue to recover his expenses up to the amount of money that was due to be paid.

- If a party started to perform her obligations before the contract was frustrated, and the other party has received benefits under the contract, the party receiving the benefits must pay for the benefits received.

Under these rules, a party who performed part of a contract would have to bear the entire loss if he incurred expenses but the other party received no benefit and was not liable to pay any money at that time. Accordingly, it is prudent when drafting a contract to arrange for payments by instalments sufficient to cover expenses as they are incurred.

Discharge by Operation of Law

When a person who files for, or is petitioned into, bankruptcy is subsequently discharged from bankruptcy, she is discharged from most contractual liabilities.

A person who wishes to sue upon a contract must do so within the time limits specified by the *Statute of Limitations* or other relevant legislation. If no action is taken within the specified time, the cause of action expires.

BREACH OF CONTRACT

A breach of contract occurs when a party does not fulfill his obligations under the contract as promised. Some breaches of contract will relieve the other party of her responsibility under the contract; others will not.

Only breach of a condition (i.e., an essential term) will give the other party the right to treat the contract as being at an end and to sue for damages. A breach of warranty (i.e., a less important term) will give the innocent party the right to sue for damages, but he will still be required to perform his obligations under the contract.

Express Repudiation

A party may breach a contract by **express repudiation**. In such a case, one party tells the other party that she does not intend to perform her contractual obligation as promised. In such a case, the innocent party does not have to sit and wait for the appointed date of performance to come and go before suing for damages. Instead, if the term in question is a condition, the innocent party can treat the contract as being immediately at an end by notifying the promisor of this fact and stating his intention to sue for damages.

Alternatively, the innocent party can choose to insist on performance and wait until non-performance on the appointed date, and then sue for damages. There is a risk, if this option is chosen, that the contract will be frustrated before the date set for performance.

When a contract is expressly repudiated before the time fixed for performance, it is called an **anticipatory breach**. Repudiation can also occur after performance has begun.

Performance Rendered Impossible by One Party

A breach of contract occurs if a party wilfully or negligently renders her performance impossible.

> *Example*
> Fred agrees to sell Barney his car for $5,000, with the car to be delivered in two weeks. The next day, Fred is offered $7,500 for the car and sells it to Wilma.

In this example, Fred cannot rely on his inability to perform as a defence, since he made himself unable to perform.

Failure to Perform

This term describes the situation where, without advance warning, a party does not fulfill his contractual obligations. This failure to perform can take the form of a total failure to perform, or significantly inadequate performance, or performance that fails to comply with the contract in a minor way. The extent of the failure affects the remedy available to the other party.

The major question for the innocent party is whether or not the party is relieved of her obligations under the contract. As stated earlier, the innocent party can treat the contract as at an end only where there has been a breach of a significant term (condition) of the contract.

Determining whether or not such a breach has taken place is particularly tricky with respect to contracts intended to be performed in instalments. In such a case, the innocent party will be relieved of his duty to perform only where

- there is good reason to believe that future performance will be equally deficient; or
- the deficiency is significant in relation to the whole performance promised.

Example
Dave owns a flower store. He enters into a contract with Beth to
supply him with 10 dozen roses each week for a period of one year.
During the first week, Beth supplies Dave with only 2 dozen roses.

In this example, Dave would be free to find himself another supplier. He
would not be obliged to continue to accept deliveries from Beth.

As stated previously, where a party substantially performs her obligations
under a contract, the other party cannot rely on trivial breaches to relieve him
of the obligation to perform. Rather, that party, while entitled to damages
for the defective performance, is bound to perform his obligations under the
contract.

REMEDIES FOR BREACH OF CONTRACT

Types of Remedies

The remedies available to the innocent party following a breach of contract
depend on the nature and seriousness of the breach in question. If the breach
is significant enough, the innocent party may be able to *repudiate* the contract.
In other words, the innocent party can treat the contract as being at an end,
and will be relieved of her obligation to perform under the contract. Both in
cases where the breach is significant enough to give rise to the right of repudiation, and in cases of less significant breaches, the innocent party may have
the right to sue for *damages*. In some cases, the innocent party may be entitled to the *equitable remedies of rescission* — **specific performance**, *injunction*,
or *quantum meruit*.

Damages

Purpose of Damages
Generally, in contract law, the purpose of damages is to place the innocent party in the same position he would have been in if the contract had
been performed. However, the plaintiff in an action for breach of contract may
not be awarded damages for all of his losses if some of the losses suffered are
too *remote* a consequence of the defendant's breach. In other words, the court
will not force the defendant to compensate the plaintiff if the losses suffered
by the plaintiff are too far removed from, or are not reasonably foreseeable
consequences of, the defendant's breach.

Remoteness of Damages
To establish that the plaintiff's damages are not too remote, the plaintiff
must be able to prove either of the following:

- The loss in question flows naturally from the breach. In other words, the
  nature of the loss is such that a reasonable party to the contract would
  have expected it to result from the breach in question.

- If the loss is special or unusual, it is reasonable to believe, given the circumstances of the particular contract, that at the time the contract was
  made, the parties would have been aware that the loss in question would
  be a probable result of the breach. (See Exhibit 14.4.)

Measure of Damages
Once it is determined that a certain type of loss is not too remote, the
court must determine how the damages for the loss are to be calculated.
Since the purpose of contract damages is to put the innocent party in the
position she would have been in had the contract been performed, the damage
award will include an amount equal to the profits she might reasonably have

EXHIBIT 14.4

The Principles of Remoteness of Damage

These principles are illustrated in the following two English cases.

Hadley v. Baxendale

The plaintiffs, who owned a mill, ordered a new mill shaft from the defendants. They gave the defendants their broken mill shaft to use as a pattern for a new shaft. The defendants promised to deliver the new mill shaft within a day but did not deliver it until a week later. Unknown to the defendants, the plaintiffs did not own a spare mill shaft, and the mill was out of operation for the week. The plaintiffs sued for damages for their loss of profits for the period of the delay.

The court held that the damages were too remote. The damages did not arise naturally from the breach because the plaintiffs might well have owned a spare mill shaft. The damages were not reasonable in contemplation of the parties when the contract was entered into because the defendants did not know that they had been given the plaintiffs' only mill shaft.

Source: *Hadley v. Baxendale* (1854), E.R. 145.

Victoria Laundry (Windsor) Ltd. v. Newman Industries Ltd.

The plaintiffs owned a laundry and dyeing company. They decided to purchase an additional boiler so that they could expand their business. They would also then be in a position to obtain certain profitable dyeing contracts. The plaintiffs contracted with the defendants for the purchase of a boiler. The defendants were aware that the plaintiffs required the boiler immediately. The defendants were five months late in delivering the boiler. The plaintiffs sued the defendants for loss of profits of two kinds: the loss of normal profits from the additional business that could have been handled with the additional boiler; and the loss of profits from the profitable dyeing contracts they were unable to obtain because they did not have the additional boiler.

The court held the defendants liable for the loss of normal profits but not for the loss of profits from the dyeing contracts. The loss of profits from the dyeing contracts did not flow naturally from the breach, and the defendants did not and could not have known about them.

Source: *Victoria Laundry (Windsor) Ltd. v. Newman Industries Ltd.*, [1949] 2 K.B. 528.

expected to make if the contract had been performed. It is not enough to simply compensate the wronged party for her out-of-pocket expenses, which would have the effect of putting her in the position she would have been in if the contract had never been made. Damages for loss of anticipated profits are called **expectation damages.**

Example
Esther owned a swimsuit manufacturing company. She purchased fabric from Ben. The fabric was to be dyed with water-resistant colours. Esther used the fabric to manufacture a line of swimsuits. It was then discovered that the dye used to colour the fabric ran when the fabric was placed in water, and the swimsuits had to be destroyed.

In this example, Esther would be entitled to damages based on the profit she would have made on the sale of the swimsuits to her customers. The damages would not be calculated to simply compensate her for the purchase price of the fabric and the cost of manufacturing the swimsuits because this approach would not provide her with her lost profits.

There are unusual cases in which the courts have held that the more appropriate approach would be to simply compensate the plaintiff for expenses incurred in reliance on the contract, which have been wasted by the defendant's breach. This approach puts the plaintiff in the position he would have been in if the contract had never been made. An example of such a case is the English decision of *Anglia T.V. v. Reed*, [1971] 3 All E.R. 690, summarized below:

> The plaintiff hired the defendant, an actor, to appear in a movie. The plaintiff hired a director and a designer. The defendant then repudiated the contract. It was held that the plaintiff could recover its wasted expenditure on the director and the designer.

Generally, the nature of damages in a contract case is limited to economic damages. There are, however, some unusual cases in which damages have been awarded for *mental anguish* arising out of a breach of contract.

Damages for mental anguish have been awarded in a contract for a vacation that did not turn out as promised. Because there is no loss of profits for the vacationer, damages would otherwise be limited to a return of the money paid.

The courts have also, although rarely, awarded damages for mental anguish in wrongful dismissal cases.

Mitigation of Damages

While a plaintiff is entitled to be compensated by an award of damages for all reasonably foreseeable losses caused by the wrongdoer's breach of contract, the plaintiff is under a duty to take all reasonable steps to **mitigate** her **damages**. In other words, the plaintiff must take all reasonable steps to reduce the amount of loss caused by the breach of contract. The plaintiff will not be awarded damages for any part of the loss that she could have mitigated.

Example

Theresa rents a store from Lawrence for $1,000 per month for a period of one year. After two months, she decides to close down her business. She vacates the premises and stops paying her rent. Lawrence tries to find another tenant, but nobody is willing to pay $1,000 per month for the store. One prospective tenant offers to pay him $800 per month, but he refuses. The store remains vacant for the remaining 10 months of the lease.

In this example, Lawrence will not be able to recover the full 10 months' lost rent of $10,000 from Theresa because he could have reduced his losses by re-renting the store for $800 per month. Had he done so, his losses under the lease would have been only $2,000 instead of $10,000. Lawrence will, therefore, be awarded only $2,000 in damages.

Liquidated Damages and Penalties

Some contracts contain a clause setting out what a party will pay if he breaches the contract. The court will allow the other party to recover this amount from the wrongdoer, without requiring her to prove her actual loss, if the amount specified in the contract represents a genuine attempt to pre-estimate the loss that would be caused by such a breach. This type of provision is called a **liquidated damages clause**. If, on the other hand, the amount is not a pre-estimate of damages but is, instead, designed to be used as a threat to compel performance by the other party, the clause is called a **penalty clause** and will not be enforced. Instead, the innocent party will be able to recover only the damages she can prove.

Equitable Remedies

There are a number of equitable remedies that may be granted in breach of contract cases. These remedies are available only at the discretion of the court where the remedy of damages would be inappropriate or inadequate.

Rescission

Under this remedy, the courts declare that a contract is void. It is as if the contract had never been made, and the parties are put in the position they would have been in if the contract had never been made. The purpose of rescission is totally different from that of damages, which is to put the parties in the position they would have been in if the contract had been performed. Accordingly, a party cannot both seek rescission *and* sue for damages.

This remedy is available, at the option of the wronged party, in cases of misrepresentation, duress, undue influence, and for some kinds of mistake.

Specific Performance

Under this remedy, the breaching party is ordered to perform his obligations under the contract. Specific performance will be ordered only where damages would be an inadequate remedy (e.g., in a contract for the sale of a unique item). This remedy is most commonly granted with respect to contracts for the sale of land because each parcel of land is considered to be unique.

Specific performance will not be ordered with respect to a contract for personal services.

Injunction

Under this remedy, a party to a contract is ordered to refrain from conduct that constitutes a breach of the contract. For example, a manufacturer may have a contract to supply goods to a wholesaler in which she agrees not to sell the goods to any other wholesaler. If the manufacturer were to attempt to sell the goods to someone else, the wholesaler may be able to obtain an injunction to prevent her from doing so.

Quantum Meruit

A claim in quantum meruit is a claim for reasonable remuneration. This remedy is sought where it is found that there is no contract between the parties or where there was a contract but it ends.

Example

Alice hires Robert to renovate her kitchen. Halfway through the job, Alice refuses to let Robert in to complete his work and then refuses to pay him on the basis that the contract provided for payment upon completion, and the contract was not completed.

In this example, the contract does not set out how to calculate payment for a partial job. Robert would be entitled to reasonable compensation for the work done.

CHAPTER SUMMARY

In this chapter, the reader was introduced to the basics of contract law and the fact that all contracts contain the same elements: offer and acceptance; the intention to be legally bound; valuable consideration; legal capacity of the parties to the contract; and, in some cases, compliance with certain legal formalities. The chapter explored these elements in a discussion of the manner in which contracts are formed.

The chapter then analyzed the grounds on which a contract, once formed, may be attacked. Mistake, misrepresentation, undue influence, duress, and illegality were discussed.

There was also a discussion of the way in which contracts are interpreted by the courts, including the approach taken to express terms and implied terms.

The requirement of privity of contract was explored, as was the manner and extent to which contractual rights and responsibilities may be assigned by the parties to a contract.

The chapter proceeded with a discussion of the ways in which a contract can be discharged: by performance, by agreement, by frustration, by operation of law, and by breach. Different forms of breach of contract were identified and discussed.

The chapter concluded with a discussion of the different remedies for breach of contract. Both damages and the equitable remedies of rescission, specific performance, injunction, and *quantum meruit* were explored.

GLOSSARY OF NEW TERMS AND KEY CONCEPTS

anticipatory breach	When a contract is expressly repudiated before the time fixed for performance, it is called an anticipatory breach.
assignee	The assignee is the person to whom the contract rights are assigned.
assignor	A person who assigns her rights under a contract to a third party.
bilateral contracts	Contracts in which a promise by one party is exchanged for a promise by the other party.
collateral contract	A separate, additional contract between parties to a contract in writing. A collateral contract must have all of the elements of a valid contract.
common mistake	It is possible for both parties to enter into a contract on the basis of a false assumption. If both parties make the same mistake, it is called a common or identical mistake.
condition	An important term of the contract.
consideration	Something of value given by each party of a contract to the other.
contract	An agreement between two or more parties that is enforceable at law.
deeds	Contracts that are written, signed, witnessed, sealed, and delivered.
duress	A situation where a party enters into a contract as a result of actual or threatened violence against the party or the party's family, or as a result of a threat of criminal prosecution or libel. The threat must have been made by the other party to the contract.
exculpatory clause	A clause by which a party attempts to limit his liability for breach of contract, misrepresentation, or negligence.
expectation damages	The award of damages in an amount equal to the profits the innocent party might reasonably have expected to make if the contract had been performed.
express repudiation	The situation where one party tells the other party that she does not intend to perform her contractual obligation as promised.

forbearance	Refraining from action; giving up a right.
fundamental breach	A serious breach of the contract.
gratuitous promise	A promise to do something for which no consideration is given and which is, therefore, unenforceable.
guarantee	A promise by one person to pay the debt of another person if that person defaults.
indemnity	A promise by one person to pay the debt of another person, whether or not the other debtor first defaults.
lapse	The expiry of an offer, either at its stated expiry date or, in no stated expiry date, after a reasonable time.
liquidated damages clause	A clause in a contract that states the amount of damages to be paid in the event of a breach of the contract, where the amount specified represents a genuine pre-estimate of the damages that would be caused by such a breach.
misrepresentation	A false statement of fact that induces the other party to enter into the contract.
mitigation of damages	The plaintiff is under a duty to mitigate his damages. In other words, he must take all reasonable steps to reduce the amount of the loss caused by the breach of contract.
mutual mistake	The situation where both parties to a contract are mistaken, but the mistakes are different.
necessaries	Essentials of life, such as food, clothing, shelter, medical care, education, tools to earn a living, and transportation to work.
non est factum	A defence pleaded by a person who, through no fault or carelessness of her own, is mistaken as to the nature and effect of a contract signed.
offer	An expression of willingness to enter into a contract on the specified terms, made with the intention of it becoming a binding contract if accepted.
offeree	The person to whom the offer is made.
offeror	The person who makes an offer.
penalty clause	A clause that specifies the amount of damages to be paid in the event of a breach of contract, where the amount is not a genuine pre-estimate of the damages that would actually be caused by such a breach but is, instead, an amount sufficient to be used as a threat to compel performance of the contract.
postal acceptance rule	When it is reasonable or required that acceptance be made by mail, acceptance becomes effective when it is mailed, even though the offeror is unaware that the offer has been accepted. This rule applies even if the letter is delayed, destroyed, or lost.
privity of contract	The relationship between two persons who are parties to the same contract.
promisee	The person to whom the promise is made; the person to whom the obligation is owed.
promisor	The person who makes a promise under a contract; the person who owes the obligation.
promissory estoppel	An equitable principle that allows a defendant, in some circumstances, to use a gratuitous promise made to him as a defence to a lawsuit that contradicts the promise.
rectification	The equitable remedy whereby a court corrects the clerical mistake made by the parties in reducing their agreement to writing.
rescission	An equitable remedy whereby the court is asked to set aside a contract and restore the parties to the position they would have been in if the contract had never been made.
revocation of offer	The withdrawal of the offer by the offeror. It may be done at any time before acceptance by the offeree.
simple contracts	Any contracts that are not deeds. They may be oral or written.
specific performance	Under this equitable remedy, the breaching party is ordered to perform her obligations under the contract.

tender of performance	An attempt by a party to a contract to perform his obligations under the contract.
terms of the contract	The statements, promises, and provisions of a contract are called the terms of the contract. These terms of the contract determine the rights and obligations of the parties. A term of a contract may be expressed or implied.
undue influence	Where a party enters into a contract as a result of improper pressure being brought to bear on her so as to render her "morally unable" to resist the will of the other party. As a result of this pressure, the party enters into a contract that is not to her advantage but is to the advantage of the other party.
unilateral contracts	One party promises to do something if the other party does something.
waiver	An agreement between parties to an existing contract that the contract is not to be performed.
warranty	A less important term of the contract. Put another way, any terms that are not conditions are warranties.

REVIEW QUESTIONS

1. How is an invitation to treat different from an offer?

2. What is the postal acceptance rule?

3. Name five ways an offer can be terminated.

4. (a) What is past consideration?
   (b) Is it valid consideration?

5. What is promissory estoppel?

6. What are a minor's rights and responsibilities on a contract for necessaries?

7. What are a minor's rights and responsibilities on a contract for non-necessaries?

8. What is the doctrine of part performance?

9. (a) What is a common mistake?
   (b) What is a mutual mistake?
   (c) What is a unilateral mistake?

10. (a) What is a misrepresentation?
    (b) What is the remedy for misrepresentation?

11. What is undue influence?

12. What is duress?

13. How are void contracts and illegal contracts treated differently by the courts?

14. What is the parol evidence rule?

15. (a) What is a condition?
    (b) What is a warranty?

16. Can an exculpatory clause protect a party from liability for fundamental breach of contract and, if so, in what circumstances?

17. What is vicarious performance?

18. (a) What does it mean when a contract is discharged?
    (b) Name five ways a contract may be discharged.

19. (a) What is an anticipatory breach?
    (b) What may the innocent party do in the event of an anticipatory breach?

20. What is the purpose of damages in contract?

21. How can a plaintiff establish that his damages are not too remote?

22. What is meant by the statement that the plaintiff is under a duty to mitigate her damages?

23. What is rescission, and when is it available?

24. What is specific performance, and when is it available?

25. What is an injunction?

26. What is *quantum meruit*?

27. What is the difference between tender by performance and tender by payment?

28. What is a frustrated contract?

DISCUSSION QUESTIONS

1. Larry wrote to Joyce, offering to buy her car for $3,000, and asked for a reply by mail. Joyce received Larry's offer on January 3. At 10:00 a.m. on January 4, Joyce mailed a letter to Larry in which she accepted his offer. Larry did not receive the letter until January 11. On January 5, he saw another car he liked better and telephoned Joyce to revoke his offer. Can he do so? Why or why not? Would the answer be different if Joyce's letter was lost in the mail and never received by Larry? Why or why not?

2. Marlene bought a shirt from Tom Taylor's Shirt Shop and gave it to her husband Robert as a birthday present. When Robert wore the shirt, he developed a terrible skin rash. It was discovered that the shirt fabric had been dipped in an acid-like substance as part of the manufacturing process and that the acid had not been rinsed out. What rights in contract, if any, does Robert have against Tom Taylor's Shirt Shop?

3. Elizabeth owns a factory that manufactures casual shirts and sweatshirts. In January, the heating system of the factory broke down, and she had to shut down the factory. She hired Tony's Plumbing and Heating to repair the heating system. It was a term of the contract that Tony's would finish the repairs within a week. Tony's had some trouble getting supplies, which delayed completion of the work as promised. The repairs took two months and, as a result, Elizabeth lost her regular monthly profits of $1,000 per month. In addition, Elizabeth lost a valuable contract to make sweatshirts for a Rolling Stones concert tour on which she would have made a profit of $10,000. Elizabeth sues Tony's. What is Tony's liability for damages to Elizabeth?

4. Morris wants to sell his ratty old sofa for $100. He walks into a bar and meets his friend Victoria. He offers to buy her a drink or two. She accepts but becomes drunk. When she is drunk, Morris tells her he has a sofa that she could use, and he will sell it to her for only $100. He also tells her that it is a collector's item and worth far more than the price he is asking. He then hands her what he says is a purchase

agreement, but in fact it is a two-month lease of the sofa for $400. She agrees to buy it for the price he is asking. She wakes up the next morning, realizes she bought a sofa she didn't need, calls Morris and tells him she won't pay him and doesn't want the sofa. If Morris sues, what defence(s) can she raise?

SUGGESTED READINGS

Fridman, G.H.L. *The Law of Contract in Canada*, 5th ed. (Toronto, Ont.: Carswell, 2006).

Waddams, S.M. *The Law of Contract*, 5th ed. (Toronto, Ont.: Canada Law Book, 2006).

Real Property Law

Judy Wolf
Seneca College

Learning Objectives

After reading this chapter, the reader should be able to:

- ➢ understand the difference between real property and personal property
- ➢ differentiate between the various estates and interests in land
- ➢ understand the concept of adverse possession and interests created by prescription
- ➢ explain how co-owners of a property hold title to land and the right of survivorship
- ➢ understand the advantages of title insurance
- ➢ explain basic mortgage terminology
- ➢ explain the obligations of a mortgagor
- ➢ identify the priority of mortgages
- ➢ differentiate between the various mortgage remedies available to a mortgagee

TABLE OF CONTENTS

INTRODUCTION TO REAL PROPERTY LAW

Real property is the legal term used to describe land and includes everything that is attached to land, such as buildings, fences, and decks. Real property also includes anything that is attached to or in the buildings, such as countertops in a kitchen and light fixtures attached to the ceiling. Any of these items that are permanently attached to the land are called **fixtures**.

Real property can be contrasted with personal property, or **chattels**, which are movable and not fixed to the land or to buildings on the land. Examples of chattels are a desk, a table, or a floor lamp which is not permanently attached to the floor. If, however, a chattel becomes permanently fixed to the land or to the building on the land, it becomes a fixture. For example, a book shelf is a chattel until it is attached to the floor or wall, at which point it becomes a fixture.

Identifying an item either as a chattel or fixture is important because the law treats chattels and fixtures differently. For example, when someone purchases real property, fixtures — such as bathroom cabinets and doors — are deemed to be included, while chattels — such as a couch and piano — are deemed to be excluded. This general rule can be altered by putting a clause into the Agreement of Purchase and Sale (discussed below) stating that either a fixture is excluded or a chattel is included. For example, if a purchaser wants the couch included or the seller wants to keep the bathroom cabinets, this could be negotiated and agreed to by both parties in the Agreement of Purchase and Sale.

Real property law dates back to feudal times in England, during which time the King of England owned all land, and granted rights to use the land while maintaining the ultimate ownership.

Our laws surrounding real property are premised on the English law; even though people have **estates** and **interests** in land, the Crown is still the ultimate landowner. For example, the government has the right to **expropriate** land if it requires the land, such as, for example, to widen a road or build a new road. Another example of the Crown's ultimate ownership is the **doctrine of escheat**, which provides that if a landowner dies without a will and without any heirs (anyone entitled to inherit the landowner's property), the land **escheats**, or reverts back, to the ultimate owner, the Crown.

Because the Crown is the ultimate owner of all land, while landowners have possession of land, the landowners are not owners of real property in the same way as they are with personal property. Land ownership is described as an estate or interest in land, and the extent of the rights to the land that the landowner has depends on the type of estate or interest.

ESTATES IN LAND

An estate in land is a right to land that includes the right to **exclusive possession** of the land. The extent of the right depends on the type of estate. The three types of estates in land to be discussed are (i) Fee Simple Estate, (ii) Life Estate, and (iii) Leasehold Estate.

Fee Simple Estate

The **fee simple estate** is the highest possible form of ownership in land and gives the owner in fee simple the right to exclusive possession of his or her land. Even though this is the highest form of ownership, and owners in fee simple believe that they are the absolute owners of their land, there are limitations to the landowner's ownership. These limits include the right of the Crown to expropriate, the doctrine of escheat, as well as restrictions and limitations imposed by **municipal by-laws**. For example, each municipality has the right to pass by-laws that limit the use of land. These limits can include any of the following:

- Limits on the use of the property, called **zoning**. For example, if the zoning is for residential use, a landowner cannot use the property for commercial use.

- Limits on the right to build structures on the property. For example, if a landowner wants to build an addition to the house, he or she would require consent from the municipality, which is called a **building permit**.

- Limits on the actual location of structures on the property. For example, structures must be a minimum distance from the lot lines of the property as stipulated in the municipal by-law. These are called **set-back requirements**.

Life Estate

A **life estate** provides the owner of this estate, called the **life tenant**, the right to exclusive possession of the property for the length of his or her lifetime. When the life tenant dies, the life estate ends, and the right to possession of the property reverts to the owner of the fee simple estate. The owner in fee simple of a life estate is called the **remainderman**.

An owner in fee simple has the right to convey his or her interest in land and can create a life estate by granting exclusive possession to a life tenant and conveying the fee simple to the remainderman. For example, a man can transfer a life estate in his house to his mother, and the fee simple estate to his son. Although the son will now be the owner in fee simple, he will not have any right to possession of the house until his grandmother dies. And during the grandmother's lifetime, she will have the right to exclusive possession. The grandmother, as a life tenant, has the responsibility to preserve the property for owner in fee simple, which would involve maintaining the property and paying the expenses associated with the property during her lifetime.

The owner of a life estate in land may grant a **leasehold estate** (discussed below) to someone else, but that right to possession will end when the life tenant dies. In other words, the right to possession cannot extend beyond the lifetime of the life tenant. For example, if Danny granted a life estate to his daughter Daniella and a fee simple estate to his son David, Daniella would have exclusive possession during her lifetime. If Daniella chose to rent the property to her friend Susanna and then died, the lease to Susanna would end upon Daniella's death, and David would then get exclusive possession of the property.

It should be noted that life estates are very uncommon today. The most common estate by far is the fee simple estate.

Leasehold Estate

A leasehold estate grants the right to exclusive possession of the property to a **tenant** while the owner, the **landlord**, retains the fee simple ownership without having exclusive possession. Both the tenant and the landlord have legal rights to the property. For example, if Lenny rents his house to Alice, Alice has exclusive possession during the term of the lease. Lenny still owns the property in fee simple but does not have possession of the property until the lease agreement has ended. When the lease agreement has terminated, Alice no longer has any rights in the property, and Lenny regains exclusive possession of the property.

CONDOMINIUMS

Condominium ownership is a type of fee simple ownership for the unit(s) to which the owner has actual title. In addition, the owner of a condominium unit shares ownership of all the common areas of the building — for example, the hallways, lobby, elevator, recreational facilities, etc. — with the other owners of the condominium units.

A person can have title to a dwelling unit (where he or she lives) as well as a parking unit (a parking space) and a locker unit (a storage locker). The owner has exclusive possession of any and all of the units that he or she owns. In other words, the owner is the only person who has the legal right to use the dwelling unit, park in the parking space, and use the storage locker to store his or her possessions. As an owner in fee simple of any of these units, the owner of a condominium unit also has the right to borrow money against the unit(s) by putting a **mortgage** on the unit (to be discussed later) and to sell the unit(s) to someone else.

Sometimes, there are parts of the common areas that an owner does not own in fee simple but still has exclusive possession. That would be called "exclusive use" common areas. For example, parking units in some condominiums are not transferred as separate units. Instead, they are designated to be used exclusively by specific unit owners. To illustrate, let's say the owner of Suite 1105 has exclusive use of parking Unit 61 on Level B. If Jeremiah is the owner of Suite 1105, he is the only person who has the legal right to park in Unit 61 Level B, just as he would if Unit 61 Level B was separately **deeded** to him. But since the parking unit is not separately deeded, Jeremiah cannot sell the parking unit separately from the dwelling unit. He could only sell the parking unit as part of the dwelling unit.

Dwelling units are always separately deeded. Whether other units, such as parking units and storage units, are separately deeded or designated as "exclusive use" depends on the particular condominium and how it was created.

INTERESTS IN LAND

An interest in land is the right to use land by someone other than the actual owner, and is not an exclusive right to use the property. The three types of interests discussed are easements, encroachments and restrictive covenants.

Easements

An **easement** is a **right of way,** or a right of passage, over a portion of someone else's property for a specific purpose. An example of an easement would be a mutual driveway, as illustrated Exhibit 15.1.

In Exhibit 15.1, assume that Arnold owns property A and Bertha owns property B. The mutual driveway comprises Parts 1 and 2 and allows both Arnold and Bertha to drive on a portion of each other's land for the purpose of accessing their respective garages at the back of their properties. Arnold is allowed to travel over, or has right of way over, Part 2, even though Part 2 is owned by Bertha, and Bertha has the right to travel over Part 1, even though Part 1 is owned by Arnold. This is an example of a mutual easement, where there are actually two separate easements that together form a mutual driveway.

Every easement must have a **dominant tenement** and a **servient tenement.** The dominant tenement is the land that benefits from the easement, and the servient tenement is the land that is subject to the easement. In the above example, Arnold's land is the dominant tenement of easement #2 and

EXHIBIT 15.1

What Is an Easement?

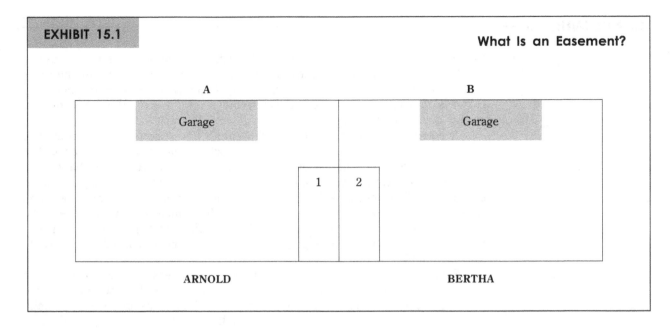

is the servient tenement for easement #1, while Bertha's land is the dominant tenement for easement #1 and is the servient tenement for easement #2.

Easement interests attach to the land, not the owner. In other words, if Arnold sells his property to Calvin, Calvin has the right to use easement #2 and cannot be prevented from doing so by Bertha. Similarly, Daniella would have the same right to Easement #1 if she bought the land from Bertha. Arnold cannot stop Daniella from using the easement. It is the landowner of property B that has the right to use the easement, regardless of who that landowner is.

Easements do not have to be mutual, as in a mutual drive, in order to be considered valid easements. If an easement is not mutual, there will only be one dominant tenement and one servient tenement. For example, an easement right in favour of Bell Canada or a utility company typically exists over the rear four feet of many properties in Ontario. This easement permits Bell Canada or the utility company to use someone's land in order to access wiring or utility poles, as necessary. In that situation, Bell Canada is the dominant tenement, and the land on which the easement is situated is the servient tenement.

These types of easement, both the mutual drive and the utility easement, are easements that are created by **express grant**, or by agreement between the owner of the servient tenement and the owner of the dominant tenement. Easements can also be created by **prescription**, which means that the easement is created merely by the dominant tenement using the property for a period of time and not by express grant. Easements by prescription are discussed below under the heading Adverse Interests in Land.

The owner of the servient tenement cannot do anything to obstruct the easement. For example, Arnold cannot park his car on the mutual driveway and thereby prevent Bertha from using the driveway to get to her garage. Nor can the owner of the property that contains the utility easement build a permanent structure, such as a shed, on the easement if that would have the effect of obstructing the dominant tenement from using the property. If a landowner does anything to obstruct the right of passage of the dominant tenement, the landowner would be said to be in breach of the easement.

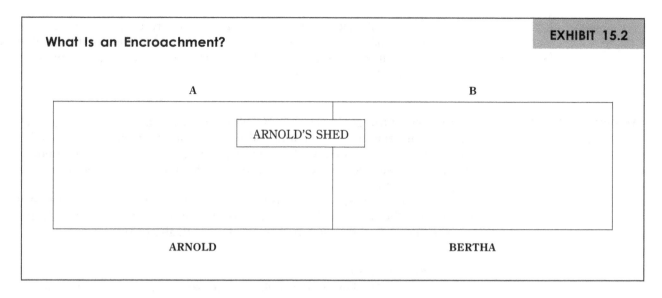

EXHIBIT 15.2

What Is an Encroachment?

A   B

ARNOLD'S SHED

ARNOLD   BERTHA

Encroachments

An **encroachment** is any building or structure that extends on to a neighbour's property. For example, a shed that is partially sitting on the neighbour's property is said to encroach, and the neighbour can insist that the shed be removed or moved over since it is sitting on his or her property. An example of an encroachment can be seen in Exhibit 15.2.

In Exhibit 15.2, Bertha can compel Arnold to remove the portion of the shed that is sitting on her property because it is an encroachment.

In some situations, however, an owner of land may lose the right to insist that the encroachment be removed. This only happens if the property is registered in the Registry System (discussed below) and after the encroachment has existed for a certain period of time. This right to have an encroachment remain and not have to remove it would be called an **encroachment by prescription** and is discussed below under the heading Adverse Interests in Land.

Restrictive Covenants

A **restrictive covenant** imposes restrictions on the use of the property by the landowner. Because it is registered on title, a restrictive covenant is binding on all subsequent owners. For example, if Brian bought a piece of land that had a restrictive covenant registered on title and Brian then sold the property to Arnoldo, Arnoldo would be bound to the restrictive covenant, just as Brian was.

A restrictive covenant is a promise to refrain from doing something, as opposed to a promise to do something. For example, "front doors cannot be painted green" is a restrictive covenant because it imposes an obligation on landowners to not paint their doors green. However, "front doors must be painted red" is not a valid restrictive covenant because it imposes an obligation to do something and is not *negative in nature*.

The restriction must also be reasonable in nature and cannot be contrary to public interest in order to be enforceable. Saying that front doors cannot be painted at all may not be reasonable, and saying that front doors must have religious symbols painted on them would be contrary to public interest. These restrictive covenants would not be enforceable.

Builders often use restrictive covenants in subdivision developments to maintain uniformity in the appearance of homes, and the covenants will be binding on the original owners as well as all subsequent owners. A common restrictive covenant that was used in the past was a restrictive covenant prohibiting the use of large satellite dishes on the front of houses as the satellite dishes were deemed to be unsightly. This is typically not an issue anymore as those large satellite dishes are no longer used.

Adverse Interests in Land

An **adverse interest in land** is acquired by using another person's land, without permission, for a certain period of time, and will result in the creation of a permanent right to use the land. The three types of adverse interests discussed are adverse possession, easements by prescription, and encroachments by prescription.

There are two systems of land registration in Ontario — the Registry System and the Land Titles System, which are discussed below. Adverse interests only exist for land registered in the Registry System.

Adverse Possession

Adverse possession is the right to fee simple ownership in someone else's land, which is acquired simply by using the other person's land for a period of time. This would occur if a person uses another person's property exclusively (to the exclusion of the owner) and adversely (without the owner's permission, but with the owner's knowledge), for a period of 10 years of uninterrupted use. Once the adverse possession right is created, the right of the registered owner to title to the piece of land that is being used will be extinguished.

For example, assume that Amanda takes care of a flower garden on land that is owned by her neighbour, Bosco. Although Bosco knows about the garden on his land, he does not consent, nor does he do anything to stop Amanda. After 10 years, Amanda will acquire a valid claim to the land by adverse possession, and Bosco will lose the right to regain possession of the land. If at any time during the 10 years Bosco is concerned about losing his right of ownership to his land, all he has to do is to stop the 10 years from running by using the land himself, even for a short time; because in order for adverse possession to be created, Amanda must not only have exclusive use, but it must be continuous for 10 years.

Adverse possession rights attach to the land, not the owner. For example, if Amanda sells her property to Carlos after using the garden on Bosco's property for eight years, Carlos would only have to continue to use the land to Bosco's exclusion for a further two years, after which time Carlos would have adverse possession over that portion of Bosco's property.

Easement by Prescription

An easement by prescription is a right of way that has not been expressly granted, as discussed above, but rather is created by a dominant tenement using the property of the servient tenement for a period of 20 years openly and continuously, without the consent of the servient tenement but with the knowledge of the servient tenement. If the servient tenement wants to prevent the easement by prescription from being created, he or she can do so by stopping the dominant tenement from using the property, even for a short period of time. For example, if Rachel has been walking across a path over Samson's property for 20 years, Rachel will obtain an easement by prescription, or a right of way, over that path after 20 years. If Samson wanted to be sure that the legal right was not created, he could prevent Rachel from using the path for a short time during the 20-year period, in order to stop the 20 years from being continuous.

Encroachment by Prescription

If an owner of land permits an encroachment to exist for at least 20 years, the right to object to the encroachment is lost and the landowner can no longer demand its removal.

For example, if Arnold's shed has been partially situated on Bertha's property for 20 years, Bertha can no longer insist that Arnold remove it. Arnold is said to have an encroachment by prescription, which is a legal right to leave his shed on Bertha's property.

It should be noted that adverse possession, easements by prescription, and encroachments by prescription only exist in the Land Registry System and not in the Land Titles System. In the Land Titles System, no rights are created solely by virtue of the passage of time.

TITLE TO LAND

Ownership in land is called *title to land*, and a person who owns the fee simple in land is said to have title to the land. Title can be held by one person or by more than one person.

When two or more people own property together, they can hold title together either as **joint tenants** or as **tenants in common**.

Joint Tenants

When two or more people hold title to property as joint tenants, each person has an undivided interest in the entire property. They do not each own a certain percentage; instead, they jointly own 100 percent of the property. If one joint tenant dies, the property automatically goes to the other joint tenant(s) by virtue of a **right of survivorship**. The property will not pass to the estate of the deceased person, but it will go to the remaining joint tenants. For example, if Douglas and Everett own property as joint tenants and Everett dies, Douglas will automatically become the sole owner of the property.

A joint tenancy can be between more than two people. For example, assume that Douglas, Everett, and Franklin own a property as joint tenants. If Everett dies, his interest will automatically pass to Douglas and Franklin, who will then own the property together as joint tenants. Married couples who own property usually hold title as joint tenants. A wife will likely want her husband to inherit her property when she dies, and similarly, a husband will typically want his wife to inherit the property when he dies. If, however, the intent is for the share of each owner to pass to their estate, the owners would take title as tenants in common.

Tenants in Common

When two or more people hold title as tenants in common, there is no right of survivorship, and the interests do not have to be equal. For example, one tenant in common can own 60 percent of the property, while the other tenant in common owns 40 percent. Because the interest is divisible, each tenant in common may transfer his or her individual interest either during his or her lifetime or in his or her will, in which case his or her share of the property will go to his or her estate.

Using the above Douglas and Everett example, but instead of owning the property as joint tenants, they own the property as tenants in common. In this case, if Everett dies, his share of the property will go to his estate and pass pursuant to his wishes in his will.

Tenants in common are deemed to have an equal, divisible ownership, unless the title document states otherwise. For example, if there are two owners as tenants in common with no specified percentage, they are deemed to each own 50 percent. If the intention, however, is not to have an equal interest, that would be stated. Using the example of Douglas and Everett, without specified percentage they each own 50 percent. If the intent was that Douglas own 80 percent, the title document would state that Douglas owns 80 percent and Everett owns 20 percent. When Everett dies, his estate will receive 20 percent of the property.

LAND REGISTRATION SYSTEMS

Documents creating an interest in land and other title-related information are recorded in a public system called a land registration system. Because it is a public system, once a document is registered, there is deemed notice that the document exists (even without actual notice) and the registration establishes **priority** between competing interests in land. For example, if Gertrude is buying a property from Henry and there are two existing mortgages on the property — one in favour of Bank A, registered January 5th; and the second in favour of Bank B, registered January 10th — Gertrude is deemed to have knowledge of the two mortgages, whether or not she is told about the mortgages. Furthermore, Bank A is said to be in priority to Bank B because its mortgage was registered before the mortgage in favour of Bank B.

There are two land registration systems in Ontario — the Registry System and the Land Titles System. All land, when developed, was assigned to one of these two systems.

Registry System

The **Registry System** was the first land registration system in Ontario. Under the Registry System, registration simply provides notice that a document has been registered; it does not guarantee that the document is legally valid or effective. A title search is the only way to determine whether the documents registered in the Registry System have the legal effect they claim to have.

Title searching in the Registry System is complicated because it involves examining all registered documents affecting title to ensure their legal effectiveness. The system provides notice of the documents registered against title, but it does not guarantee the legal effectiveness of any of those documents — nor does it certify the current owner's title. Because title is not guaranteed in the Registry System (this will be contrasted to the Land Titles System, below), a Registry System title search involves examining the history of ownership of the property for the last 40 years prior to the date on which the title search is conducted, and the start date would be the most recent deed that is prior to the 40 years. This deed is usually referred to as the **root deed**. For example, if a title search is being conducted on January 10, 2014, the person searching title would have to start with the deed that was registered prior to January 10, 1974. If there was a deed registered in 1980 and one, prior to that, in 1972, the 1972 deed would be the root deed. To determine good title, the title search would involve two steps: (i) obtaining a copy of all the documents registered since the 1972 deed; and (ii) examining each document to ensure that it is legally valid and effective. The understanding is that if there is a claim against the property that has not been raised for 40 years, it is no longer valid.

In conjunction with a title search, the person searching title must do an execution search to determine if any **executions** against owners in the chain of title have attached to the property. For example, in the above search, the title searcher would have to conduct an execution search against everyone on title from 1972 to the current day. It should be noted, however, that if title insurance is obtained (discussed below), executions need only to be searched against the current owner, since title insurance insures the buyer against any executions that may have been filed against prior owners.

Land Titles System

The **Land Titles System** is the newer system of land registration and is a much better system in that title in the Land Titles System is guaranteed. Unlike the Registry System, which simply provides a record of documents affecting title, this system provides a statement of title as a fact. Because title is guaranteed by the government, a title search in the Land Titles System only involves searching back to the current owner, which is clearly simpler than searching back 40 years or more to the root deed, as required in the Land Registry System. In addition, executions only have to be searched against the current owner in the Land Titles System. This is not only simpler, but also less costly.

Adverse interests do not exist in Land Titles System because title in the Land Titles System is guaranteed. The government could not guarantee title to property if there were possible adverse claims that the government was not aware of.

Ontario is currently in the process of converting all Registry System properties to the Land Titles System. According to the *Toronto Star* (December 13, 2013), 99 percent of the land in Ontario has been registered in the Land Titles System.

Electronic Registration

In 1985 Ontario began a major reform to the land registration systems with a project called **POLARIS** (Province of Ontario Land Registration Information System), which involves not only converting all properties from the Registry System to the Land Titles System, but also making the land registration system an electronic system. The electronic system of registration (known as e-reg) is called Teraview, which enables lawyers to register documents on title from their office without having to physically attend the land registration office. This makes the process of completing a real estate closing much simpler and more efficient. Although E-reg is available only for properties in the Land Titles System, it will eventually accommodate all properties in Ontario when all properties are converted to the Land Titles System.

PURCHASE AND SALE OF LAND

The contract between a buyer and a seller of real property is called an **Agreement of Purchase and Sale**. An Agreement of Purchase and Sale is used when buying and selling any type of real property, including vacant land, land with a house on it, and a condominium.

The buyer and seller will negotiate the terms of the contract. These terms will include the price to be paid, the **deposit** to be paid, the chattels to be included, and the fixtures to be excluded. The general rule is that fixtures are included unless they are specifically excluded in the agreement, and chattels are excluded unless they are specifically included in the agreement. For example, if Edna is purchasing a property and she really wants the kitchen table and chairs, which are chattels, she can negotiate in the agreement to have it included. Similarly, if Sam the seller wants to keep his dining room chandelier, which is a fixture, he would exclude the dining room chandelier in the Agreement of Purchase and Sale.

The **closing date** will also be negotiated, and it is the date that the seller will have to give possession and title to the buyer and the buyer will have to pay to the seller the balance of the purchase price.

Once the agreement has been negotiated by the buyer and the seller, the lawyer acting for the purchaser will have to start the search process in order to make sure that the purchaser will be obtaining good title on closing. There is the title search as well as *off-title searches*, which include writing to the property tax department, the building department, and various utility companies. The title search will either be a 40-year search, if the property is in the Registry System, or just be a search of the current owner, if the property is in the Land Titles System. Either way, executions against the current owner (Land Titles System) or all owners in the **chain of title** (Registry System) will have to be searched. Any problems arising out of the searches (both the title search and the off-title searches) must be presented to the lawyer for the seller in a letter called a **requisition letter**, and this must be done by the **requisition date** set out in the agreement. The lawyer for the seller will then have the onus of resolving the issues raised in the requisition letter.

TITLE INSURANCE

In the past, a client, being a purchaser or mortgagee, was protected against title problems by having the assurance of a lawyer's legal opinion. While this is still an option today, there is also the option of title insurance. Title insurance has become increasingly prevalent in real estate transactions. In fact, mortgagees often insist on title insurance to ensure that any future problems with title are easily corrected.

Unlike other types of insurance, title insurance can only be ordered by a lawyer on behalf of the client — the buyer, the lender, or both the buyer and the lender. The reason that the title insurance must be ordered through a lawyer is the lawyer still has to do the title search and advise the title insurance company if there are any problems with title. The lawyer does not, however, have to do many of the off-title searches, and this ultimately saves the client money. Therefore, because of the cost savings, obtaining title insurance may actually be the less expensive option than choosing to rely on a lawyer's opinion on title.

For example, most purchasers will be borrowing money from the bank to finance the purchase of real property. The bank will require a **survey** of the property being purchased to ensure that the structures on the property are actually in the proper location. Surveys are expensive and are often misplaced, or become outdated over time if changes have occurred in the location of the structures. With title insurance, however, a survey is not required because one of the assurances provided by the insurer is that the property complies with the set-back requirements of the relevant by-law, and the insurer will take whatever measures are necessary to correct the problem if it doesn't. Also, when title insurance is obtained, an execution search is conducted against the current owner only, even in the Registry System, and this can save the purchaser a lot of money.

An owner's title insurance policy is paid for only once and remains in effect as long as the insured has title to the property. If a problem arises with title — for example, realty taxes that the seller did not pay before closing — the purchaser just contacts the insurance company to correct the problem, which the insurance company will do by paying the taxes owing. The purchaser does not have to sue the lawyer and establish negligence on the lawyer's part, which is what a purchaser has to do if he/she chooses to rely on the lawyer's title opinion. Similarly, a lender's policy remains in effect as long as the lender has a registered mortgage on the property.

One problem with relying on the lawyer's title opinion is that a lawyer's title opinion cannot protect the client in the event of fraud. Title insurance, however, does protect the client in the event of fraud. For example, if there is a charge fraudulently registered against title to a property, or a property is fraudulently conveyed, title insurance will protect the insured and provide compensation.

For these reasons, title insurance is the option most often used today. All a purchaser has to do is prove that a problem exists that is covered by the policy, and the purchaser is then covered for damages or the cost of clearing title.

Lawyers typically arrange title insurance on behalf of a client who is purchasing property. However, title insurance can also be arranged by lawyers for existing property owners, who may be concerned about potential fraud.

The introduction of title insurance in Ontario has greatly expedited and simplified real estate transactions.

MORTGAGES

A mortgage or charge is a loan that is secured by real property. When a person buys property and he or she does not have enough money to pay for the property in full, he or she will borrow money from a lender. In order to secure the loan, the lender will have a mortgage registered against the property. Similarly, when a person owns real property and wants to borrow money from a lender, he or she can use the property as **collateral**, known as a mortgage, for the loan.

Mortgage Terminology

The borrower is called a **chargor** or **mortgagor**, and the lender is called a **chargee** or **mortgagee**. A chargor or mortgagor can be one or more persons or a corporation. A chargee or mortgagee can be an **institutional lender**, such as a bank or trust company, or can be a **private lender**. A private lender is either an individual or a corporation that is not a lending institution.

If the lender requires another person to guarantee the mortgage payments, that person is known as a **guarantor**. A guarantor would be responsible for the mortgage payments, just as the mortgagors are responsible, but the guarantor is not an actual owner of the property. For example, if Pedro and Ramona are borrowing money from the bank and the bank is concerned that Pedro and Ramona may not be able to afford the mortgage payments, the bank may insist that an additional person, such as Pedro's father, sign the mortgage as a guarantor. That way, the bank has more comfort that the payments will be made.

Money that is borrowed pursuant to a mortgage is called the **principal** and will be paid off during the **term** of the mortgage, together with **interest**, and any amount remaining at the end of the term will have to be paid at that time. The term of the mortgage is the length of the contract between the mortgagee and the mortgagor. A term is usually between one and five years.

Payments are usually **blended payments**, made up of both principal and interest. When the total blended payment is the same each month, the mortgage is said to be **amortized**. That means the portion of the total payment that is being allocated to the principal increases each month, while the portion of the total payment that is being allocated to the interest decreases each month. The **amortization period** is the length of time that it will take to pay off a mortgage in full, using a constant blended payment of principal and interest. A typical amortization period is 25 years; if it is shorter, the payments will be larger, and the mortgage will therefore be paid off sooner.

At the end of the term, the borrower will still owe money. For example, if the term is 5 years and the payments are amortized over 25 years, there will still be a significant amount owing at the end of the term. This amount is called a **balloon payment**. The borrower can either pay this amount in full (if he or she has the money), renew the term of the charge at the current interest rate, or refinance with a different lender. Renewing the term of the mortgage and/or refinancing the amount outstanding requires the mortgagor to negotiate with the existing mortgagee or a different mortgagee to obtain the best interest rate possible.

A mortgage can be either an **open mortgage** or a **closed mortgage**. A mortgage is said to be open if the mortgagor has the right to pay off any amount prior to maturity of the mortgage without incurring any **prepayment penalty**. A mortgage is closed if the mortgagor does not have the right to prepay the mortgage, and if the mortgagor does pay off the mortgage prior to maturity because, for example, the mortgagor sells the property, the mortgagor will have to pay a penalty to the mortgagee for paying off the mortgage prior to maturity. Whether a mortgage is open or closed will depend on what was negotiated when the mortgage was arranged. An open mortgage is more beneficial to the mortgagor, and therefore will likely have a higher interest rate than a closed mortgage.

How a Mortgage Is Created

A mortgage can be created (i) by the property owner or buyer of a property arranging a mortgage; (ii) by the buyer of the property assuming a mortgage; or (iii) by the seller of a property lending money to the buyer, which is known as a vendor take-back mortgage.

Arranged Mortgage

An **arranged mortgage** is used when an owner of real property or purchaser of real property goes to a lender, for example a bank, and arranges to borrow money. The bank will provide mortgage instructions to the lawyer who will be representing the bank. The lawyer will ensure that the bank is given security for the loan by preparing and registering a mortgage against title to the property; once that has been done, the lawyer will give the money to the borrower.

For example, assume that Harold is buying a property from Gerald for $350,000. Harold has savings of $200,000 and needs to borrow $150,000 from Friendly Bank. Title to the real property will show Harold as the owner, and a charge in favour of the Friendly Bank in the amount of $150,000. See Exhibit 15.3.

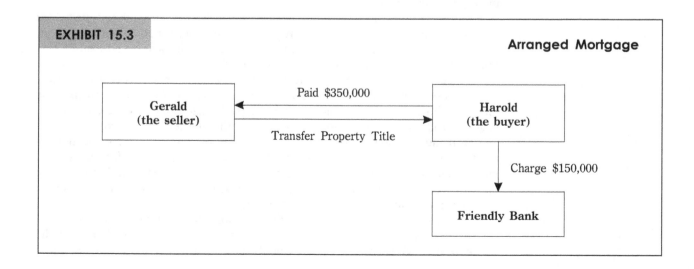

| EXHIBIT 15.3 | Arranged Mortgage |

Gerald (the seller) ← Paid $350,000 / Transfer Property Title → Harold (the buyer)

Harold (the buyer) → Charge $150,000 → Friendly Bank

Assumed Mortgage

EXHIBIT 15.4

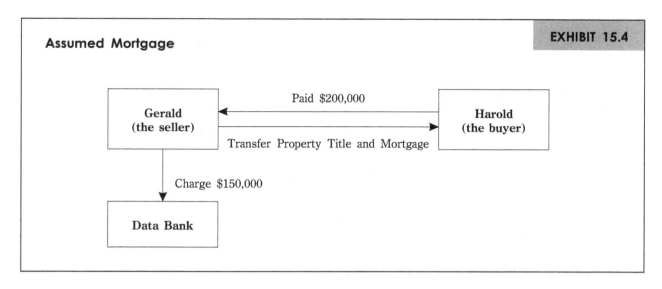

Gerald
(the seller)

Paid $200,000

Harold
(the buyer)

Transfer Property Title and Mortgage

Charge $150,000

Data Bank

Assumed Mortgage

If a purchaser of real property wants to take over an existing mortgage on the property he/she is buying, the purchaser is said to be **assuming** the mortgage.

A purchaser may agree to assume an existing mortgage registered against title to the property he or she is buying when the existing mortgage has favourable terms. In this situation, the purchaser will pay the vendor the purchase price, less the amount of the outstanding mortgage.

To illustrate, let's revisit the example of Harold buying Gerald's property for $350,000. Rather than arranging his own mortgage, Harold has the option of taking over Gerald's mortgage with Data Bank. If the interest rate on the mortgage with Data Bank is lower than Harold could arrange with a new mortgage, it would be beneficial for Harold to assume the existing mortgage in favour of Data Bank. Gerald also benefits from his mortgage being assumed. If Gerald were to pay the amount owing on a mortgage before the end of the agreed upon time for doing so (the term), the lender will likely charge a prepayment penalty for breaking the contract early. If Harold assumes Gerald's mortgage, Gerald will not have to pay the penalty, because he will not be paying off the mortgage early.

In this situation, title to the property will show Harold as owner and Data Bank as the chargee. As you can see, the charge will be registered before Harold takes title; but because Harold bought the property with the mortgage registered to Data Bank, Harold is assuming the mortgage. See Exhibit 15.4.

Vendor Take-Back Mortgage

Sometimes a purchaser is unable to raise enough money to purchase the property. For example, if the purchaser has a bad credit history or does not have enough income, the purchaser may be unable to borrow money from a bank or another lender. In this situation, a purchaser may ask the seller (vendor) to lend him or her part of the money needed to purchase the property. If the vendor secures the loan as a mortgage registered on the title to the property being sold, this mortgage is called a **vendor take-back mortgage**.

To show how this work, let's use the example of Gerald and Harold again. In the example, Gerald is selling the property for $350,000, but Harold only has $200,000. If Gerald really wants to complete the deal with Harold, he

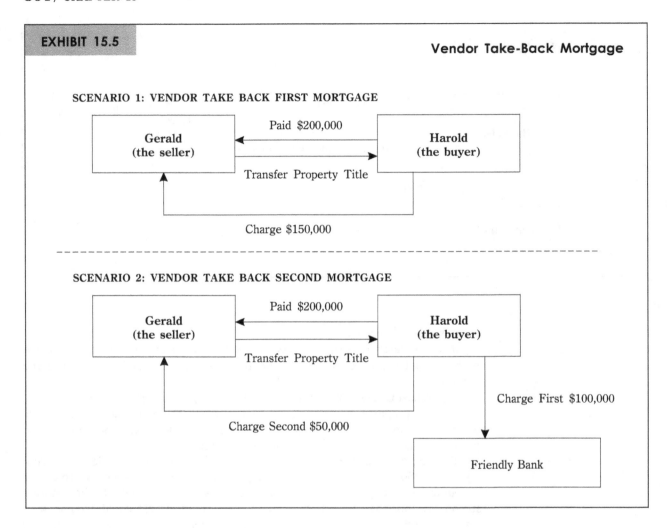

EXHIBIT 15.5   Vendor Take-Back Mortgage

SCENARIO 1: VENDOR TAKE BACK FIRST MORTGAGE

Gerald (the seller) ← Paid $200,000 ← Harold (the buyer)

Transfer Property Title →

Charge $150,000

SCENARIO 2: VENDOR TAKE BACK SECOND MORTGAGE

Gerald (the seller) ← Paid $200,000 ← Harold (the buyer)

Transfer Property Title →

Charge Second $50,000

Charge First $100,000

Friendly Bank

can accept the $200,000 and give Harold a loan for the difference by taking back a charge on the property in the amount of $150,000.

In this situation, title to the property will show Harold as the owner and Gerald as the chargee. See Exhibit 15.5.

A vendor take-back mortgage may also be negotiated between a purchaser and a vendor when the purchaser is able to get a mortgage from a lender, such as a bank, but is unable to get enough money. For example, if Harold is able to borrow only $100,000 from the bank in addition to his own $200,000, he may ask Gerald to take back a charge in the amount of $50,000 so that he is able to complete the transaction. In this example, Harold would have a first mortgage with the bank and a second mortgage with Gerald.

Priorities of Mortgages

A mortgagor can have more than one mortgage registered against his or her property. The **priority** of a mortgage is determined by the date and time of registration of the mortgage. For example, if Waneda has a mortgage with Friendly Bank that was registered on January 2nd and a mortgage with Data Bank that was registered on January 4th, the Friendly Bank mortgage is a first mortgage and the Data Bank mortgage is a second mortgage. The priority of a mortgage is very important because it determines which lender would receive its money first in the event of default by the mortgagor (discussed below). In other words, a first mortgagee is in a safer position because its money will be paid out in priority to the second mortgage. For this reason, a second mortgage is riskier from the perspective of the mortgagee. To mitigate the higher risk, the second mortgagee will likely ask for a higher interest rate to be paid by the mortgagor.

Rights and Obligations

When a borrower signs a mortgage, he or she is also bound by a document called the mortgagee's **Standard Charge Terms**.

Standard Charge Terms set out the obligations of the mortgagor and the rights of the mortgagee. It is important that a borrower understand his or her obligations to the lender as well as the consequences of breaching those obligations. In addition to the obligation to make regular mortgage payments, the mortgagor has other obligations, such as making payment to prior mortgagees, paying realty taxes, maintaining the property and insuring the property against fire.

- The borrower is obligated to make payments to prior mortgagees because a lender with a prior interest would be paid out first in the event that the mortgagor is in default. The same logic applies to realty taxes (also known as property taxes). Realty taxes are always a first priority on land, which means that realty taxes that are in arrears will be paid out before any mortgage, in the event that the mortgagor is in default. Any time there is an interest that will take priority over the mortgage, the mortgagor must make those payments as well. For example, if Alan has a first mortgage with Friendly Bank and a second mortgage with Data Bank of Canada, Alan's obligations to Data Bank of Canada include making payments to the realty tax department and to Friendly Bank.

- The mortgagor also has an obligation to maintain the property because the property's value may decrease if it is not maintained. If the property value goes down when the mortgage goes in to default, the lender might lose money.

- The mortgagor has the obligation to insure the property against fire to protect the mortgagee from losing its money if the property burns down.

Discharge of a Mortgage

When a charge has been paid in full, a document called a **discharge** must be registered on title. Paying off the mortgage is not enough. Because the land registration system is a public system, proof that the mortgage has been paid off must be made public by registering a discharge on title to the property.

Default Remedies

Default of a mortgage occurs when the chargor breaches one or more of the obligations contained in the charge. The most obvious and most common default is the failure to make the principal and interest payments. Other breaches that can be classified as default include failing to have adequate fire insurance on the property, failing to pay property taxes and failing to keep the premises in a reasonable state of repair.

Power of Sale

A power of sale is by far the most common mortgage remedy because it is relatively quick, inexpensive and simple. A power of sale permits the chargee to sell the property to a third party in order for the chargee to get back its money. The chargee has an obligation to sell the property for its **fair market value**, and it is fully accountable to subsequent encumbrancers and to the mortgagor for the proceeds of the sale. Once the property is sold, the chargee is required to apply the proceeds to pay off the outstanding debt, including all costs incurred in the sale. Any **surplus** will be paid to the subsequent encumbrancers in order of priority, and the balance, if any, will be paid to the chargor. If the proceeds of sale are less than the debt, the chargee can sue the chargor for the **deficiency**.

For example, if $250,000, including principal, interests and costs, is owing to the first mortgagee and the property is sold under power of sale for $300,000, the surplus (or $50,000) will be paid to the mortgagor, assuming that there are no subsequent encumbrances. If there is a second mortgage in the amount of $40,000, that amount of $40,000 will be paid to the second mortgagee; the mortgagor will be paid with the remaining balance, in this case $10,000.

If, on the other hand, the property is sold for $230,000, the mortgagee can sue the mortgagor for $20,000, being the deficiency incurred upon the sale of the property.

The person who buys the property under power of sale acquires good title to the property, provided that the sale was properly conducted and that all appropriate parties were duly served with the notice of sale.

Foreclosure

The mortgagee can commence a court action for a judgment for **foreclosure**, which gives legal title of the property to the mortgagee. Once the mortgagee becomes the registered owner of the property, he/she is no longer accountable to the mortgagor or other subsequent encumbrancers. Their rights will have been extinguished by the final order for foreclosure. This means that if the mortgagee eventually sells the mortgaged property and the proceeds are more than the amount of the debt, the mortgagee can keep the surplus. The mortgagee does not have to pay the surplus to any subsequent encumbrancers or the mortgagor.

Similarly, the mortgagor is no longer accountable to the mortgagee in the event that the proceeds from a subsequent sale of the property are less than the amount of the debt. The mortgagee cannot sue the mortgagor for a deficiency, as is the case in a power of sale.

The mortgagor can defend the foreclosure action or request time to bring the charge back into good standing. The mortgagor can also request that the property be sold instead. The foreclosure would then become a **judicial sale** (discussed below). A mortgagor would defend a foreclosure action and request a sale if there is a lot of **equity** in the property and the mortgagor does not want the mortgagee to gain a windfall when the mortgagee sells the property. For example, if the mortgagor owes $200,000 to the mortgagee and the property is worth $300,000, the mortgagor would object to a foreclosure action because the mortgagor would end up losing the entire $300,000. If the property was sold, the mortgagor would be entitled to receive the surplus of $100,000.

Judicial Sale

In a judicial sale, the court orders the sale of the property and oversees all matters related to the sale. A mortgagee might prefer this route if the mortgagee is concerned about a potential lawsuit from the mortgagor or even from a subsequent encumbrancer. By having the court supervise and condone every step of the sale process, the mortgagee who is selling the property is protected from the potential of a lawsuit because the mortgagee's actions cannot be challenged.

A mortgagee can start an action for a judicial sale; but, more commonly, a judicial sale takes place when a mortgagor asks that a foreclosure action be converted to a sale.

The proceeds from a judicial sale are applied first against the mortgage debt and any expenses of the sale. Any surplus will then be applied against the amount outstanding on any subsequent mortgages, and the balance, if any, will go to the mortgagor. As with a power of sale, the mortgagee selling the property in a judicial sale can only recover what is owing on the mortgage and expenses incurred, but not any additional amount.

It should be noted that a power of sale is, by far, the most common remedy used in the case of a mortgage default.

CHAPTER SUMMARY

This chapter provides a basic understanding of real property law and mortgage law and shows how these areas of law are related.

We examined the various estates in land and the resulting rights of the owners of the land. We also looked at interests in land and how those interests have an impact on the actual owners. Adverse interests, that exist in the Registry System, were also examined. In order to understand adverse interests, we looked at the land registration systems and the changes that have occurred in land registration. We went on to examine the ways in which owners can own land, including the right of survivorship.

We then went on to discuss the process of buying land, including the relevance of title insurance on a purchase transaction.

Last, we examined an overview of mortgage law. We discussed basic mortgage terminology and how mortgage relationships are created. We looked at the rights and obligations of the parties to a mortgage, including the rights of a mortgagee when a mortgage goes into default.

GLOSSARY OF NEW TERMS AND KEY CONCEPTS

adverse interest in land	An interest in someone else's land that is acquired by using that person's land, without permission, for a certain period of time.
adverse possession	Valid title to land acquired through open, visible, and uninterrupted possession of that property, without the owner's permission for a period of at least 10 years.
Agreement of Purchase and Sale	The contract between a buyer (purchaser) and seller (vendor) of real property.
amortized	The term used to describe a mortgage with constant blended payments that will pay itself off over a period of time.
amortization period	The length of time it takes to repay a loan in full based on constant blended payments.
arranged mortgage	A new mortgage that is negotiated between a borrower and a lender.
assumed mortgage	A mortgage that is taken over from an existing mortgagor.
balloon payment	Final payment for the amount of principal that remains owing at the end of the term of a charge (loan or mortgage).
blended payment	A mortgage payment that combines principal and interest.
building permit	Written permission to build from the municipality.
chain of title	The period of time throughout which title is examined in order to establish good title; used in the Registry System.
chargee/mortgagee	The lender in a mortgage transaction.
chargor/mortgagor	The borrower in a mortgage transaction.

chattels	Possessions that can be moved and are not attached to a real property Agreement of Purchase and Sale.
closed mortgage	A mortgage that cannot be paid off prior to maturity without the mortgagor having to pay a prepayment penalty.
closing date	The date in the Agreement of Purchase and Sale when title will be transferred from the seller to the buyer.
collateral	Something that is given as security until repayment of a loan.
condominium	A type of ownership of real property that combines fee simple ownership and shared ownership.
deeded	The process of obtaining title.
deficiency	The shortfall of money that remains owing in a power of sale after the principal, interest and costs have been paid in full.
deposit	What is paid by the buyer to the seller when an Agreement of Purchase and Sale is negotiated.
discharge	Document registered on title when a mortgage is paid off.
doctrine of escheat	A common law doctrine providing that if a land owner dies without a will and without heirs to inherit his or her land, the land will revert to the Crown.
dominant tenement	Land that benefits from an easement.
easement	Right to use a portion of someone else's land for a specific purpose.
easement by prescription	A right of way over someone else's land that is acquired after a period of open and uninterrupted use.
encroachment	A building or structure that intrudes on someone else's land.
encroachment by prescription	Right to keep an encroaching building or structure on someone else's land after it has existed for 20 years.
equity	The net value of property after deducting the value of encumbrances.
escheats	Property reverts to the Crown.
estates	Interests in land that also provide the right to exclusive possession.
exclusive possession	The right to use land exclusively and to prevent others from using the land.
execution	Judicial order addressed to the sheriff requiring the enforcement of a judgment.
express grant	Creation of an easement that is explicitly granted in writing.
expropriate	Reacquire land, with compensation, by the Crown for public purposes.
fair market value	The amount that property would sell for in the open market.
fee simple estate	The right to exclusive possession and the right to sell land; the highest form of ownership.
fixtures	Possessions that have become attached or affixed to real property.
foreclosure	Court action whereby the chargee obtains legal title to the property after default by the chargor.
guarantor	A person who is not an owner of property and who is responsible for the mortgage.
institutional lender	A bank, trust company, credit union or insurance company that is in the business of lending money.
interest	The amount added to the principal amount of a loan, and which must be paid in addition to the principal amount.
interests	Rights to use someone else's land that are not estates and do not give a right to exclusive possession.

joint tenants	Two or more people owning property where on the death of one, the survivor(s) inherit the deceased's share.
judicial sale	Sale of charged property ordered and administered by a court after default by the mortgagor.
land titles system	Land registration system in Ontario governed by the *Land Titles Act*.
landlord	A person or corporation who rents property to another.
leasehold estate	Right to exclusive possession of the property for a specified period of time in return for the payment of rent.
life estate	Right to exclusive possession of the property for the duration of someone's lifetime.
life tenant	The owner of a life estate.
mortgage/charge	A loan secured by real property.
municipal by-laws	Laws that are passed by municipalities.
open mortgage	A mortgage that can be paid off prior to maturity without the mortgagor having to pay a prepayment penalty.
POLARIS	Province of Ontario Land Registration Information System — a project to simplify land registration in Ontario.
power of sale	Power to exercise the remedy of sale in case of default under a charge whereby the mortgagee sells the property to a third party.
prepayment penalty	An amount that a borrower may have to pay when ending a mortgage contract prior to the end of the term.
principal	The sum of money borrowed from a mortgagee.
priority	The right that is in preference to another by virtue of having been registered first.
private lender	An individual or business that lends money, but is not a bank, trust company, credit union or insurance company.
real property	Land and everything that is attached to the land.
registry system	Land registration system in Ontario governed by the *Registry Act*.
remainderman	The owner in fee simple, when there is a life tenant, who must wait until a life estate ends before acquiring possession.
requisition letter	The letter sent by the buyer's lawyer to the seller's lawyer requesting that all title and off-title matters be resolved.
requisition date	The deadline for the requisition letter.
restrictive covenant	Promise by an owner of land to refrain from doing something on the property.
right of survivorship	Automatic vesting of an interest in the surviving joint tenant or tenants when one joint tenant dies.
right-of-way	Right to use a portion of another's land for access purposes.
root deed	First conveyance of the fee simple estate (a deed, grant, or transfer) registered before the commencement date of a title search.
servient tenement	Land over which an easement runs.
set-back requirements	The minimum amount of distance required between structures and lot lines, as determined by the municipality.
standard charge terms	Mortgage terms that set out the obligations of the mortgagor and the rights of the mortgagee.
surplus	The amount of money that is left in a power of sale after the principal, interest and costs have been paid in full.
survey	A diagram prepared by a surveyor showing the dimensions of a property and the location of structures on the property.

tenant	A person or corporation who rents property from another.
tenants in common	Two or more people owning property where, on the death of one, the deceased's share passes to his or her heirs rather than the other owners; no right of survivorship.
Teraview	The software system used for electronic registration.
term	The length of time that the borrower and lender are bound by the mortgage contract.
title	Ownership to real property.
title insurance	A type of optional insurance that insures a buyer and/or mortgagee against certain title issues and is used in lieu of a lawyer's opinion on title.
vendor take-back mortgage	A charge created when a seller agrees to lend the buyer money towards the purchase price and the buyer gives the seller a charge on the property as security for the loan.
zoning	The designated usage of land, as determined by the municipality.

REVIEW QUESTIONS

1. Explain the difference between a joint tenancy and a tenancy in common.

2. Name two mortgage remedies that are available to a mortgagee when a mortgage is in default.

3. What document gets registered on title after a mortgage has been paid off in full?

4. What can a life tenant do with property that he/she does not want to use?

5. Is title insurance mandatory?

6. What are the two land registration systems in Ontario?

7. In which land registration system are documents registered electronically in Ontario?

8. If someone takes over someone else's mortgage, what is this called?

9. Edward has a mortgage with Data Bank that was registered in January and a mortgage with ABC Bank that was registered in March of the same year. Which mortgage is the first mortgage, and which mortgage is the second mortgage?

DISCUSSION QUESTIONS

1. In the Land Titles System, adverse interests are not possible. How is this advantageous to the property owner?

2. Bonnie Builder is developing a subdivision and wants to register the following restrictive covenants. State whether each restrictive covenant will be valid or not.
    (i) Front doors must be painted dark brown.
    (ii) There shall not be more than three vehicles parked on each driveway.
    (iii) Front doors cannot be painted green.

3. Larry Landlord rented out his house to Rosa Renter.

   (a) Who is the owner of the property?
   (b) Who has the right to exclusive possession?

4. Brian lives next door to Avis. Avis has been doing the gardening in Brian's garden for the past nine years. Brian is aware that Avis has been taking care of his garden; he doesn't mind because he doesn't like to garden, and Avis is very good at what she does. Brian never even goes near the garden.

   (a) What right may Avis acquire in Brian's land where the garden is located?
   (b) What might you suggest to Brian in order for him to protect his land? Explain.

5. Bernard has a mortgage with ABC Bank that has a five-year term and a 25-year amortization. What will happen at the end of the five years? What options will Bernard have at that time?

6. Victoria sold her house to Velma for $250,000, and part of the transaction involved Victoria lending Velma $100,000. How should Victoria secure this loan to Velma? Explain.

7. George is buying a house and is debating getting title insurance.

   (a) Does he need his lawyer to be involved in the process of obtaining title insurance?
   (b) Name one advantage of obtaining title insurance.

SUGGESTED READING AND OTHER RESOURCES

Kurtz J., J. Emmans & A. Blatt, *Residential Real Estate Transactions*, 3d ed. (Toronto: Emond Montgomery Publications, 2009).

McCallum M., & the late Alan M. Sinclair, *An Introduction to Real Property Law*, 6th ed. (LexisNexis Canada, 2012).

Walma, M. *Advanced Residential Real Estate Transactions*, 2d ed. (Toronto: Emond Montgomery Publications, 2003).

WEBSITES
Bora Laskin Law Library, Research Guides: <http://guides.library.utoronto.ca/content.php?pid=221715&sid=3590910>
CanLII: <http://www.canlii.ca/en/index.html>
The Law Dictionary: <http://thelawdictionary.org/>
Law of the Land Blog: <http://lawoftheland.blogs.com/>
Lay of the Land Blog: <http://www.canadianrealpropertylawblog.com/>
Legaltree.ca: <http://www.legaltree.ca/node/315>
Ontario Real Estate Source: <http://ontariorealestatesource.blogspot.ca/>
Western Libraries: <http://www.lib.uwo.ca/law/realpropertylaw.html>

Business Organizations

Ginevra M. Saylor

DENTONS CANADA LLP

Learning Objectives

After reading this chapter, the reader should be able to:

➢ understand the main sources of law regulating business organizations in Canada

➢ recognize the main factors to consider when choosing the best way to organize a business and how the method chosen allocates responsibility for the business's liabilities

➢ identify several kinds of business organizations and understand how the main types are created, owned, operated, and ended

➢ identify the advantages and disadvantages associated with each kind of business organization

➢ recognize the main documents that must be filed and understand the requirements that must be met to operate a corporation

© 2014 by Captus Press Inc. The author acknowledges, with gratitude, the research and editorial assistance of Kirran Iveson.

TABLE OF CONTENTS

INTRODUCTION

Imagine you would like to start your own business selling goods or providing a service. How would you run your business? Would you want complete control, or would you rather share responsibility for making important decisions with others whose skills complement your own? Where would you get the money to start your business? Would you feel comfortable shouldering all of the risks, knowing that you might be personally liable for all of the debts your business incurs? Would you be willing to follow formal requirements for starting and running the business, which might mean having to hire a lawyer? Every entrepreneur who decides to go into any business — from offering to clean houses, to manufacturing and selling highly technical medical equipment worldwide — must consider these and a host of other questions when choosing the best way to organize the business enterprise.

Businesses can be organized in many ways, and each way has advantages and disadvantages. In every instance, the advantages and disadvantages must be weighed against the backdrop of the particular market, industry, and economy, as well as the entrepreneur's goals, desires, personality, and appetite for risk.

Business organizations provide substantial benefits that Canadian law recognizes and encourages. They provide structures that allow for orderly, efficient business organizations that benefit consumers and business owners. Business organizations offer options for financing a commercial venture that allocate both the risk of loss and profit, introducing predictability and order for those who invest in them.

SOURCE OF LAW

Federal and provincial legislation address aspects of establishing and operating partnerships and corporations. Many also govern how sole proprietorships, franchises, and other business organizations must behave. Much of contract and tort (the law of injury) law is governed by common law, which also establishes many of the remedies available to those who suffer loss or are wronged.

Some laws, like corporate, partnership, and contract law, directly regulate commercial activity. Other, equally important, laws affect only distinct activities or aspects of a business. The latter include, for example, employment standards and labour legislation, securities regulations, and tax law. Combined, these establish the framework within which modern business organizations operate in Canada.

SOLE PROPRIETORSHIPS

Of the many ways to operate a business, the **sole proprietorship** is the easiest and quickest to get going. Any time individuals start running a business for their own benefit without forming a corporation, partnership or other kind of organization, they have created a sole proprietorship. Establishing and operating a sole proprietorship involves very few formal requirements. Far less preparation is required, apart from that related to the business itself, making the sole proprietorship very attractive to first-time business people embarking on a small-scale enterprise.

Starting the Business

Depending on the type of business and jurisdiction, the entrepreneur may need do no more than simply begin operating. However, certain businesses in some locations may require a bit more. Some jurisdictions require sole proprietors to register their businesses to ensure that creditors can easily find information on exactly who owns the businesses. In Ontario, for example, all those operating a business under any name other than their own must register under the *Business Names Act*. Failing to register can result in fines and other significant penalties.

Many provinces regulate certain professions, requiring specific education, degrees, and licences, as well as membership in a regulatory body. Common examples include lawyers, doctors, dentists, and engineers. Before a sole proprietorship begins delivering any of these services, the owner would need to have the appropriate provincial licence and membership in the qualifying organization. Additionally, many municipalities require licences to operate certain businesses, such as restaurants and taxi services.

Another requirement sole proprietors need to consider is taxes that might apply to all businesses, regardless of how they are organized. Many Canadian provinces require business people to charge customers and pay the government tax on goods and services. In some provinces, this requirement kicks in only after the business earns a threshold amount of money in a tax year. If the business employs others, other tax and withholding requirements also may apply.

Who Runs the Show?

As the only owner and operator, the sole proprietor has complete control, setting strategy and planning the course the business will take. Any profits the business reaps go to the sole proprietor and, because the business and owner are the same, the owner may use business profits to satisfy purely personal debts in no way related to the business or its activities. But, the reverse is also true: the fact that the business and owner are the same makes the owner fully responsible for all debts the business incurs. So, the business's creditors are free to collect from not only the business's accounts and assets, but from the owner's personal bank accounts and property. The owner's house, car, and any other personal assets all are equally at risk as any property associated with or used in the business. Depending on the nature and size of the business, the owner's exposure to potential liability could be quite extensive. Along with any money the business owes suppliers, landlords, customers and others, the sole proprietor could also become responsible for unanticipated liabilities, like, for instance, personal injuries someone suffers while at the place of business or injuries employees negligently cause to others on the job. Although sole proprietors can limit their exposure to some of these potential liabilities by purchasing insurance and carefully negotiating contracts with those they do business with, doing this can quickly become costly and addresses only a portion of the risk.

Employing Others

Although sole proprietors must run their business alone, they are free to hire employees to work for them. However, because owners have no separate identity from their business, they may not treat themselves as an employee. Employees may in no way be involved in running the business and making major decisions; otherwise, the law at some point may consider the business a partnership, regardless of how the owner and employee see their working relationship. Employees are paid wages, vacation, and bonuses, rather than sharing in a portion of the profits. Likewise, employees are not liable for the business's debts.

Growing and Changing

Given that sole proprietors are personally liable for all of their business's debts when businesses start to grow, take on a broader clientele, enter into more contracts, and expand to more locations, they confront greater risk. At some point, the dollar value of the potential personal liability becomes just too great for one person to bear, and many decide to abandon sole proprietorship for another type of business organization. Additionally, as a business becomes larger, it may diversify and become increasingly complex, making it prudent to involve others with different skills and expertise. Finally, a business with potential for huge expansion and growth could require financial backing from more investors to reach its full potential. All of these reasons could signal the end of the sole proprietorship and the birth of a new business organization.

Closing Shop

Sometimes sole proprietors choose to end their businesses entirely, rather than transforming to another business form. As the only owner and decision maker, the sole proprietor may end the business at any time, whether failing or succeeding. Of course, the sole proprietor remains personally responsible for paying all of the business's debts, including taxes, and, after doing so, is entitled to any remaining assets.

Advantages and Disadvantages

A great deal can be said for the sole proprietorship, including having complete control over how the business is run. Because so few formalities are required, starting the business can be quick and relatively inexpensive. And, naturally, being able to keep all profits is a substantial reward for the time, money and effort invested in a business. On the other hand, raising all of the money needed to start a business can be extremely difficult, if not impossible, and could require borrowing heavily. Once the business is started, establishing goodwill, name recognition, and steady customers can take more time than some small businesses can afford to stay afloat and compete. Finally, and most significantly, being responsible for all debts and other liabilities the business incurs to the full extent of one's personal assets poses a formidable downside for sole proprietors.

PARTNERSHIPS

We have just learned that the hallmark of sole proprietorships is one person's owning and operating a business alone. For many reasons, some people prefer to involve others. Although this does mean sharing the profits and giving up some measure of control, it also spreads among others the financial burden and responsibility for future liabilities. Better still, the business may benefit from the diverse skills, expertise and strengths others bring to the organization.

A **partnership** exists whenever two or more people carry on business together with a view to profit. But not all commercial arrangements involving more than one person are partnerships. Because the parties' activities must be taken with a view to profit, a purely charitable or strictly social enterprise probably would not be a partnership. Likewise, passively co-owning property with others might not be a partnership, even if the property generates some income for the co-owners. Even though sharing profits strongly suggests that a partnership exists, profit-sharing alone is not conclusive. For instance, under Ontario's *Partnership Act*, a creditor who is repaid fixed amounts from the profits of a debtor's business is not in partnership with the debtor. Similarly, employees taking part in a profit sharing plan at work are not in partnership with their employer.

Governing Law

Although recognized at common law, today partnerships in Canada are governed extensively by statute as all of the provinces have enacted partnership legislation. Generally speaking, these partnership laws serve two functions. First, they provide a set of mandatory rules governing the relationship between partnerships and third parties they deal with, such as customers and suppliers. Second, the laws supply rules for a partnership's internal operations and the partners' relationship. Unlike the former, the latter rules apply only if the partners themselves have entered into no partnership agreement establishing their internal relations.

Starting a Partnership

As soon as two or more individuals start carrying out an activity that brings them within the definition of partnership, a partnership exists. In fact, a partnership may exist without the partners' knowledge or intent to operate as a partnership, and people may be deemed to be in partnership where they have entered into no oral or written agreement and have expressly stated their intention not to be partners. Even so, as with sole proprietorships, partnerships may need to obtain provincial or municipal licences to engage in specific businesses, register their business names in certain jurisdictions, and comply with other similar requirements. Although not required, many partners also enter a partnership agreement when forming their business.

Partnership Agreements

A partnership agreement helps a business operate more harmoniously by addressing in advance such issues as how decisions will be made, who will be responsible for which aspects of the business, how and when profits will be distributed, how the partnership will admit new members, and how it may be dissolved. As observed, in the absence of a partnership agreement, the relevant provincial statute determines these and other issues regarding the partnerships' internal operations. Where the partnership agreement addresses any of these internal issues differently than the applicable statute, the terms of the partnership agreement will prevail. However, if the partnership agreement tries to change the relationship between the partnership and external third parties in a way that contradicts the statute, the statutory requirements prevail.

If no partnership agreement exists, provincial statutes generally provide that partners share equally in partnership profits and losses and that all may participate in managing the business. While most decisions may be made by a majority of the partners, admitting new partners and changing the fundamental nature of the business requires unanimous agreement.

Concept of the Firm

As observed, a partnership creates no new legal entity separate from the partners. Commonly called firms, partnerships may employ others but may not employ the partners themselves. The partnership is not taxed as an entity. Instead, partnership profits are included as income of the partners, who are taxed as individuals. By statute, the partnership's net profit is allocated equally among all partners, unless a partnership agreement provides otherwise. The partnership's losses are allocated to the partners in the same way.

Partners' Rights and Duties

Historically, partnerships are founded on mutual trust and confidence. Partners owe each other a fiduciary duty, meaning they must deal with each other and their business in utmost good faith and never put their personal interest ahead of the partnership's. Developed at common law, partners' fiduciary relationship to each other has been expressly incorporated into some provinces' partnership statutes — British Columbia's, for instance. Other provincial statutes, like Ontario's, make no express reference to the fiduciary duty; however, the duty is evidenced throughout the statutory provisions addressing partners' specific duties to each other. For example, Ontario's *Partnership Act* requires partners to provide the partnership with true accounts and full information regarding the partnership; to disclose all benefits derived from transactions involving the partnership and from using the partnership's name, property or business connections; and to reveal any profits made from competing with the partnership's business. Partners may choose to modify some of these responsibilities to each other through a partnership agreement.

Like sole proprietors, partners directly operate their business. Although provincial partnership statutes give all partners the right to take part in managing the partnership, the particular role each plays often is defined more particularly in a partnership agreement. In this way, partners may allocate responsibility among themselves according to their strengths, expertise, education, and interests.

. The law considers each partner to be an agent of the partnership, meaning each alone can bind the partnership to contracts and other obligations without the other partners' consent as long as the partner is acting in the ordinary course of the partnership's normal business. This fundamental principle of **agency** means that partners who neither consented to, authorized, nor later ratified another partner's actions may become obligated to perform contracts, be liable for the individual partner's torts, and be vicariously liable for employees' acts done in the ordinary course of business. Because the partnership is not bound by a partner's action falling outside the scope of its normal business, what constitutes the partnership's normal business has been the subject of court cases. Exceptions to this principle do exist, however, particularly concerning third parties who contract with the partnership under circumstances that are not quite so innocent. For instance, a partnership might not be bound by a contract one partner entered into with a third party who knew that the partner had no authority to enter into the contract.

Partnership statutes also treat certain property as partnership property, regardless of whether title to the property remains in the name of an individual partner. Ontario's statute includes as partnership property all property each partner contributed to the partnership and all property acquired on the partnership's behalf during its course of business. Additionally, property regularly used in the business may become partnership property even if the partner who individually owned it never expressly gave it to the business. When property becomes partnership property, partners lose their individual rights to it. Again, partners can modify their rights to partnership property through a partnership agreement.

Responsibility for Partnership Liabilities

Given that partnerships have no separate existence from their partners, every partner faces unlimited personal liability for partnership liabilities. This means each partner's personal property is at risk along with the partnership property should the partnership have insufficient assets to cover its debts. Partners may try to mitigate this harsh result through their partnership agreement by requiring themselves to reimburse any partner who individually covers partnership debts or allocating more responsibility for partnership debts to certain partners than others. However, these agreements bind only the partners and have no effect on third parties dealing with the partnership. So, regardless of the partnership agreement's terms, an aggrieved third party has recourse against all partners, and a partner who pays out more than stated in the partnership agreement has recourse against only the other partners.

Timing is important in determining a partner's liability for partnership debt as partners generally are liable for obligations that arose only while they were a partner. Note, however, that liability for obligations that arose during a partner's tenure remains after the partner leaves and even dies, with the debt passing to the deceased partner's estate.

Even though partners generally face no liability for obligations arising after they leave the partnership, they must take care to ensure that they do not inadvertently become liable. In most provinces, this involves notifying the public of the partner's retirement and not allowing the firm to give the appearance that the partner remains.

Types of Partnerships

The partnerships discussed so far, where all partners are liable for the partnership's acts and debts, are called **general partnerships**. However, other types of partnerships may be permitted by statute depending on the jurisdiction.

Limited Partnerships

Another type of partnership is the **limited partnership**. Unlike general partnerships, limited partnerships are a creature of statute and come into existence only if those involved take certain steps in compliance with the jurisdiction's governing law. In other words, they are not formed by simply starting to operate as a partnership; rather, a document must be filed and, in some jurisdictions, periodically renewed with the appropriate ministry or department. In many provinces, such as Ontario, limited partnerships are governed by a separate statute, called the *Limited Partnership Act*.

In a limited partnership, one or more general partners are personally liable for the partnership liabilities, while one or more limited partners are liable only to the extent of their individual investment in the limited partnership. In this way, general partners have the opportunity to involve others in the business as somewhat passive investors. The general partners manage and operate the business on their own with little or no input from the limited partners. In fact, a limited partner who takes too active a role in managing the business runs the risk of being deemed to be a general partner and losing the protection of limited liability. In return for their investment, the limited partners share in the partnership's profits and have other rights, including, for instance, having their contribution returned, dissolving the partnership, and reviewing the partnership's books and accounts.

Limited Liability Partnerships

The fact that many professions may not incorporate in jurisdictions throughout Canada has generated another type of special partnership, the **limited liability partnership** (or LLP). In some provinces, professionals, including lawyers and accountants, for example, may form limited liability partnerships to limit individual partners' liability for their employees' and fellow partners' negligence. Although the individual partners' liability is somewhat limited, they remain personally liable for all other partnership liabilities, their own negligence, and the negligence of others that they personally supervise. Additionally, the partnership remains fully responsible for all liabilities, including individual partners' and employees' negligence.

In most jurisdictions, partnerships must meet certain requirements to become a limited liability partnership. For instance, Ontario's *Partnership Act* requires the partners to enter an agreement to operate as a limited liability partnership, be part of a profession whose governing statute permits operating as a limited liability partnership, register under the *Business Names Act*, and include LLP in the partnership's name.

**Dissolving
the Partnership**

Partnerships may voluntarily choose to go out of business or be forced to close shop. Partnerships might involuntarily be stopped from continuing with their business if their activities become illegal or if operating the type of business as a partnership becomes illegal. Sometimes courts have discretion to terminate a partnership, for example, where a partner becomes mentally incompetent or incapacitated.

Provincial statutes typically codify when and how partnerships end. For instance, under Ontario's *Partnership Act*, a partnership ends when (i) a fixed term for which it was created expires, (ii) the single undertaking it was created for is accomplished, (iii) any partner dies or becomes insolvent (unable to meet debts as they come due), or (iv) any partner notifies the others of an intent to end the partnership. However, partners can change some of the circumstances that will trigger the partnership's end through their partnership agreement.

Whatever the reason, when a partnership dissolves, debts to all third parties are paid first. Next, money the partnership might owe to individual partners is repaid, and capital contributed to the partnership is then returned to the partners. Finally, any net assets remaining are divided among the partners equally or according to the partnership agreement.

**Advantages and
Disadvantages**

The main advantages of a partnership are sharing the cost of financing a new business among more than one individual and having the opportunity to involve people with a broader range of skills, expertise, business connections, and experience. The possibility of entering into a partnership agreement gives the partners flexibility in structuring their relationship and dividing responsibility for different aspects of the business according to skills and interests.

The major and very serious drawback is the partners' unlimited personal liability for the partnerships' obligations and each other's actions in the ordinary course of business. Additionally, becoming obligated to perform contracts and being liable for other partners' actions without consent presents a serious disadvantage, as does the possibility of remaining liable after retiring from the partnership unless certain steps are taken.

CORPORATIONS

The business organizations discussed so far have shared one crucial element: the owners' personal liability for their business's liabilities. Although participants may be able to reduce their exposure or limit the extent of their personal liability, the very real risk of losing more than one's investment in the business generally remains. The risk to one's personal assets exists because fundamentally the business and its owners are as one.

Many people entering business are unwilling to take on such far-reaching risk and expose their personal assets, given how many unknowns come with any business and how much of that risk falls completely outside of the owners' control. What is more, as a business succeeds, it often grows and with growth comes even greater exposure to increasingly substantial liability. For these and other reasons, many entrepreneurs choose to incorporate.

**Corporation:
A Separate Legal
Entity**

The **corporation**'s appeal as a business organization primarily stems from the legal fiction that grants corporations a separate legal identity. So, unlike partnerships and sole proprietorships, corporations are distinct from their owners. As recognized legal persons in their own right, corporations enjoy many of the Constitutional and other entitlements any other person in Canada enjoys, including the right to own property, enter contracts, take legal action against others, and form partnerships. In fact, even some of the rights under Canada's *Charter of Rights and Freedoms* apply to corporations. But, along with rights, corporations have responsibilities that may subject them to contract, tort, and even criminal liability.

The distinguishing feature of corporations is this separation of ownership from liability. In a corporation, one or more people purchase **shares** in the corporation, with the percentage of shares held equalling the portion of the corporation the shareholder owns. Each shareholder's liability is limited to the amount invested in purchasing the corporation's shares and, absent extraordinary circumstances, the shareholder has no personal liability for the corporation's obligations. Although shareholders may take some part in managing and running the business, in many corporations the day-to-day operations are left entirely to others.

Origin of the Law of Corporations

The law has recognized corporations for hundreds of years, although how they are formed and operated has changed over time. A watershed event in the history of corporations happened in 1897 when the British House of Lords crystallized the concept of the corporation as a separate legal entity in the seminal case, *Salomon v. Salomon & Co.*[1]

In this case, Mr. Salomon had operated for many years as a sole proprietor before incorporating his business. After incorporating, Mr. Salomon held a significant majority of the company's shares and continued to run the business; a half-dozen members of Mr. Salomon's family owned the remaining shares. The company also owed a secured debt to Mr. Salomon. Unfortunately, some time after incorporation, the business fell on hard times, and a liquidator was appointed to settle the company's debts and distribute to the shareholders what (if anything) remained. The case arose when the liquidator resisted paying Mr. Salomon the secured debt the company owed him before paying other creditors whose debts were not secured, even though the law requires that secured creditors be paid first.

In ruling in Mr. Salomon's favour, the court fully embraced the notion of separate legal existence, even where a very closely held corporation is, in essence, run by a single majority shareholder. As a secured creditor of the corporation, Mr. Salomon was entitled to recover because he had complied with all legal requirements for incorporation. However, since Salomon, courts have had many opportunities to re-examine this legal fiction and have been willing to "pierce the corporate veil" of limited liability and hold shareholders personally liable, albeit in very rare circumstances involving fraud, a sham company, or other egregious wrongdoing.

Creating a corporation is a far more formal process than starting up a sole proprietorship or partnership. Formal registration, fees, and other requirements must be followed to create, operate, change, sell, and ultimately end a corporation. The law comes from a number of sources.

Modern corporations are governed primarily by statute, with most incorporating either federally or provincially. Generally speaking, businesses incorporate federally if their enterprise falls within a federally regulated sphere, such as telecommunications, or will operate in more than one province. The *Canada Business Corporations Act* (the CBCA) establishes the rules for incorporating and operating a federal corporation. On the other hand, businesses incorporate under the laws of a Canadian province or territory if they intend to operate within one province or territory. In the past several decades, most

---

[1] [1897] A.C. 22, 66 L.J. Ch. 35 (H.L.).

of the provinces and territories have adopted corporate law statutes similar to the federal CBCA, making the incorporation process fairly uniform across much of the country.

A company incorporated in one province wishing to operate in another province must obtain permission under that province's extra-provincial licensing laws. The requirements for operating extra-provincially vary somewhat across the jurisdictions. Although federal corporations need no extra-provincial licence to operate in any of Canada's provinces or territories, they generally must file information similar to that required for an extra-provincial licence before starting to operate in most provinces.

Federal and Provincial Incorporation by Certificate

Under the federal and most provincial statutes, businesses incorporate by registering with a designated government authority. Once the required documentation is filed along with a fee, a **certificate of incorporation** is issued, and the corporation is born. In these jurisdictions, the certificate of incorporation must be issued once all registration requirements have been met if the registration appears to be correct on its face. In fact, a certificate may be refused only for failing to meet the registration requirements and for no other reason.

The registration process is fairly straightforward, streamlined and fast. In fact, businesses that will involve few shareholders and complexities can be incorporated without a lawyer's help as many commercial incorporation packages containing the needed forms and instructions are available for purchase. Even so, a lawyer's advice is prudent for more complex incorporations involving, for example, more than one class of shares with different rights attached or property that will be transferred to the new corporation. Additionally, nearly all new corporations would benefit from a tax lawyer's advice.

Incorporation Process

The incorporation process typically involves three steps.

Step One. The first step in incorporating under federal and comparable provincial systems is preparing the **articles of incorporation** for the proposed company. The statute and associated regulations establish the required content and form of the articles. The articles must include the corporation's name if it will operate under a corporate name. Instead, a corporation may decide to operate as a number company, either initially or perpetually. In this case, Corporations Canada (or comparable provincial authority if filed provincially) assigns a number that becomes the corporation's name. (For more information on corporate names, see Exhibit 16.1.) The articles also must name the city or town and province where the corporation will have its head office in Canada; the full address may be provided later on a separate form.

Next, the articles must state a fixed number of **directors** the corporation will maintain on its board of directors or the minimum and maximum number of directors the corporation must have at any given time. The articles must also indicate the classes and maximum number of shares the corporation will be authorized to issue. Although corporations are free to impose no restrictions on their shares, if they wish to impose restrictions they must do so in the articles of incorporation. A corporation planning to have two or more classes of shares must specify the rights, privileges, restrictions, and any conditions attached to each class. Similarly, if the corporation will issue shares in series, the articles must give the directors authority to fix the number of shares in each series and determine the rights, privileges, restrictions, and conditions attached to each series.

Corporations may, but need not, restrict the business they may conduct. If they choose to restrict the business, they must do so in the articles.

Naming the Corporation

EXHIBIT 16.1

Federal and provincial statutes and their associated regulations require all corporations to have a name and specify restrictions and requirements the name must meet. These requirements are intended to make it easy for the public to distinguish one company from the next and ensure that corporations' names in no way mislead or deceive the public. Although requirements vary across jurisdictions, generally corporate names must be unique and distinct from other corporations' names and may not exceed a specified maximum number of characters or be too general, nondescript, or obscene. The name must include one of the words that designate the legal status as a limited liability corporation, such as Incorporated, Inc., or Limited.

In Ontario, corporations may use a trade name in conjunction with, and in some circumstances instead of, their official name. However, the trade name must be registered under the *Business Names Act*, and the proper corporate name must be used on contracts, invoices, negotiable instruments, and orders for goods and services.

Because a corporation's name may not be confusingly similar to other corporations' names, the proposed name should be carefully researched before submitting the articles of incorporation. For example, in Ontario, corporations planning to operate under a name other than a number name must submit evidence that the proposed name most likely is safe to use. The evidence is a report of a search for the name in the computerized name search system. The report must reveal that the proposed name conflicts with no existing or proposed corporate name. Private search firms perform these searches and provide the reports for a fee.

To avoid the cost and time associated with the name search, some corporations opt for a number name. If the corporation later wants to adopt a proper name, it may obtain a search and change its name by filing amended articles of incorporation.

In the absence of business restrictions in the articles of incorporation, a corporation has the capacity to carry on any business. The articles may also include any other provisions that the applicable statute allows corporations to include in their **by-laws** or a **unanimous shareholder agreement** (both discussed below). If the company will be a private (or **non-offering**) **corporation**, meaning that its shares will not be sold to the public (as opposed to a public or **offering corporation** whose shares are sold to the public), the articles must restrict the number of shareholders the corporation may have and prohibit offering shares to the public.

Finally, the articles of incorporation must list the names, addresses, and signatures of the incorporators. Simply stated, incorporators are the people asking for incorporation. Although the incorporators may be, and often are, the people actually interested in starting the corporation, they need not be. Frequently, the incorporators signing the articles are the lawyers handling the incorporation.

Step Two. The next step in incorporation includes filing the articles of incorporation, filing fee, and completing the Initial Registered Office and First Board of Directors form, which states the full address of the head office and lists the names of the corporation's first directors. The first directors set up the corporation and serve only until the shareholders elect actual directors at their first shareholders' meeting. Although the incorporators sometimes take on the role of first directors, they need not.

Step Three. In the final step in incorporation, the federal or comparable provincial authority signs and issues the certificate of incorporation. The corporation exists as of the date on the certificate of incorporation.

Other Methods of Incorporation

Throughout Canada, the certificate system outlined above is by far the most common way businesses are incorporated. However, two other methods bear mention: incorporation by **letters patent** and by **memorandum of association**. In the letters patent system, incorporation is a sovereign act, meaning the Crown or province issues a charter to the corporation in the form of letters patent granting the corporation's existence. This older system remains for specific types of corporations across the country.

Under the other system, registration by memorandum of association, a corporation comes into existence on registration of a memorandum of association. The main difference between this and the certificate system is that the memorandum of association creates a contractual relationship among a company's members, with their rights and duties emanating from the contract. By contrast, corporations given existence through a certificate of incorporation are statutory constructs, with all rights and duties emanating from the governing statute.

How Corporations Run

As observed, a great deal of activity takes place before a corporation exists. The people involved in setting up the corporation are called **promoters**. The promoters sometimes are the same people who end up preparing, signing, and filing the articles of incorporation; often, however, they are not. Commonly, promoters prepare for the corporation's management, perform several initial administrative functions, float securities, and may set up contracts for the corporation. When promoters arrange pre-incorporation contracts, they must take care not to become personally liable on the contracts, which the corporation must ratify on coming into existence to become party to them. Promoters have a fiduciary relationship with the corporation they promote, meaning they must deal fairly and act in the corporation's best interests. Although promoters may choose to, they are required to neither subscribe for the corporation's shares nor become first directors.

After the corporation comes into existence, still more must be done to get the business up and running, and the federal and provincial statutes provide some structure. The first order of business is the first directors' meeting, which any incorporator or first director may call. At this organizational meeting, the first directors may adopt the form of the new corporation's shares and corporate records, authorize shares to be issued, appoint **officers**, appoint an auditor to hold office until the first annual shareholders' meeting is held, make banking arrangements, make by-laws, and transact any other business.

By-laws are permanent and continuing rules that commonly address the corporation's administration and how it will conduct business and define the members' rights and duties among themselves. Neither the Ontario nor the federal *Business Corporations Act* insists that corporations have any by-laws, while some other jurisdictions require every corporation to pass by-laws or the equivalent. In some provinces, the by-laws also must be publicly filed with the articles of incorporation. Aspects of a corporation's affairs that by-laws commonly cover include the following:

- How the corporation's shares will be subscribed for, allotted, and recorded
- The books and records the corporation will keep and who will maintain them
- Who has signing authority
- The time, place, notice, procedural, and **quorum** requirements for directors and shareholders' meetings
- The appointment, pay, duties, and removal of directors, officers, agents and employees
- Banking arrangements

To be valid, by-laws must be made in good faith, in the corporation's best interests, and for a proper purpose; they may not be discriminatory, unreasonable, oppressive, illegal, or contrary to public policy.

Ownership

Corporations are owned through shareholdings. One or more persons own an interest in the corporation by exchanging property or money for shares of the corporation. So, the amount of shares an individual holds represents that person's capital investment in the corporation.

Historically and under modern statutes, corporations typically have one or both of two major types or classes of shares: common and preferred. Common shares generally give holders the right to participate in the corporation through, for instance, unrestricted rights to periodic payments from the corporation's profits (called **dividends**) and distribution of whatever property remains after all creditors are paid when the company goes out of business. When a corporation establishes only one class of shares with no differentiation among them, the shares are common shares. By contrast, preferred shares generally are special shares with some type of priority or other preferential treatment attached to them. Typical preferences include a priority right to receive dividends, special voting rights, and the right to be repaid one's capital investment if the company dissolves.

Within these two broad classifications exist a number of possibilities, and large companies offering their shares to the public may have several classes and series of shares with different rights, restrictions, and preferences attached to them. In addition to being governed by the federal or provincial business corporations statutes, public — or offering — companies' share classes and restrictions, as well as their dealings with shareholders, are highly regulated by securities legislation and a Securities Commission, which regulates stock markets.

Some shareholders investing in a corporation wish to retain a certain percentage ownership interest in the corporation. To accomplish this, some corporations will attach pre-emptive rights to certain preferred shares. Pre-emptive rights give the holders of that class of shares the first opportunity to buy a sufficient number of any new shares issued to retain their proportionate ownership interest in the corporation. If these shareholders decline the shares, the corporation is free to sell to others.

Shareholders acquire their shares in any number of ways, with the two most frequent being buying shares from existing holders and subscribing for newly issued shares. "Subscribing" simply means offering to buy shares through a written application to the corporation. Because the subscription is an offer, the corporation is not bound to sell the shares until it accepts the offer.

Shareholder Powers, Rights and Remedies

Particularly in companies with many shareholders and absent special arrangements, shareholders generally take no part in a corporation's day-to-day management and affairs. However, this does not mean shareholders wield no power. In fact, Canadian corporate law statutes grant shareholders specific powers, rights, and remedies.

The first major power shareholders have is to elect and remove the corporation's directors, a power they exercise through annual shareholder meetings. The CBCA requires the directors of new corporations to call the first annual shareholders' meeting within 18 months of incorporation and annually from then on. Provincial statutes have similar requirements. At the annual shareholders' meeting, shareholders take care of three matters. First, the shareholders elect new directors as needed; because directors' terms often are staggered, the shareholders typically are filling vacancies on the board as individual terms end. Second, they review the corporation's financial statement for the year and the auditor's report. Finally, they either reappoint the auditor or waive appointment. These three are the only business matters conducted at the annual meeting. However, shareholders may also hold special meetings to discuss other business; should they wish to combine a special with the annual meeting, they may do so in a combined Annual and Special Meeting of the Shareholders.

Under the federal and provincial statutes, a minimum percentage of all shareholders — called a quorum — must be present at the meeting, either in person or by proxy. Attending by proxy means appointing in writing any other person to vote one's shares. In large companies with publicly sold and traded shares, federal and provincial *Securities Acts* apply stringent rules to soliciting proxies.

Unless the corporation's by-laws state otherwise, one share carries one vote, and **resolutions** are passed by a simple majority. However, special resolutions dealing with a fundamental change in the corporation (like amending the by-laws or articles of incorporation, or deciding to end the corporation) generally require two-thirds of the shareholders' votes to pass.

Shareholders also have the right to obtain access to certain information and put forward shareholder proposals at their meetings. Additionally, shareholders may augment their powers through a unanimous shareholder agreement. Signed by all shareholders, the agreement reserves some or all of the powers of directors — essentially the company's management and operations — for the shareholders. When shareholders take on all or part of the directors' powers, they also assume a commensurate degree of responsibility and potential liability associated with being a director. So, instead of their liability being limited to the amount invested in the company, the shareholders may open themselves to greater risk and potential personal liability by entering into a unanimous shareholder agreement.

Federal and provincial legislation governing corporations also gives shareholders a number of remedies when they are dissatisfied with how the corporation is managed or how they are treated. Although a detailed look at the available remedies is beyond this chapter's scope, a few bear mention. The federal and Ontario statutes both provide an **oppression remedy**, which allows shareholders, creditors, directors, or officers to apply to the court for relief if they believe that any actual or threatened act or failure to act by the corporation or any use of the directors' powers is oppressive or unfairly prejudicial.

Another shareholder remedy — the **derivative action** — allows an individual to bring or intervene in (become a party to) a court action in the name, or on behalf, of the corporation. In this class action, the individual acts as a representative for others in asserting or defending the corporation's rights. The court's decision then binds all other shareholders as though they themselves participated. In addition to current and former shareholders, current and former directors and officers, and anyone else a court considers proper, may bring a derivative action.

Available both federally and provincially, depending on the province, is an application for an inspection or investigative order. Here, the shareholder asks the court for an order directing an investigation into the corporation.

Directors

At common law and under Canadian federal and provincial legislation, a corporation's directors manage the corporation's affairs and plan its strategy in line with its articles of incorporation. Although a unanimous shareholders agreement may modify this, most corporations — particularly widely held companies with many shareholders — operate under this model. The CBCA requires directors to be an individual person (not a legal entity, like a corporation) 18 years or older, who is of sound mind and not an undischarged bankrupt. The federal and provincial statutes also have Canadian residency requirements for boards of Canadian corporations. For instance, the federal act requires at least 25 percent of the directors on a corporation's board to be Canadian residents. Corporations with four or fewer directors (including those with one director) must have at least one Canadian resident director.

The first directors listed in the articles of incorporation hold power until the first annual shareholders' meeting, at which time the shareholders elect the first true board. Directors must consent to be a director and, once elected, remain in office either until their term expires (without re-election), the shareholders remove them, or they die or resign. Each year, the shareholders elect, by a simple majority vote, new directors to fill any vacancies. The legislation the business is incorporated under sets out a code for directors' meetings, which must be followed unless the corporation's articles or by-laws provide otherwise. As with shareholder meetings, a quorum of directors, defined by statute or established in the company's articles or by-laws, must be present to conduct business.

At their meetings, the directors may conduct any of the corporation's business, deciding issues and taking action through resolutions. At a minimum, directors must call an annual shareholders' meeting and approve the corporation's financial statements each year. Directors present at any meeting are deemed to consent to any resolution passed, unless they require their dissent to be recorded in the minutes, send a written dissent to the board secretary before the meeting is adjourned, or send by registered mail or deliver to the corporate office their dissent immediately after the meeting is adjourned. Directors absent from the meeting also are deemed to consent to all action taken at the meeting, unless they send their written dissent or require their dissent to be recorded in the minutes within seven days of learning about a resolution. Each director has one vote, which may not be assigned to a proxy. In one-director corporations, the sole director may act through written resolutions instead of meetings.

Directors' Duties and Liabilities

The directors of any corporation have two broad responsibilities, commonly called the **fiduciary duty** and the duty of care. The fiduciary duty requires directors to act honestly and in good faith with a view to the best interests of the corporation, putting the corporation's interests ahead of their own and avoiding conflicts of interest. Typical conflicts arise when a director holds a personal interest in a material contract with the corporation or gains an opportunity because of information learned in the course of being a director. Directors must disclose all conflicts and refrain from voting on any related resolution. Failure to disclose a conflict may make a director liable for any gain earned from the conflicting interest. Directors also generally are prohibited from taking advantage of a business opportunity the corporation had or sought; personal liability can attach even where the director resigns before taking the opportunity and the corporation suffers no real loss. The second duty requires directors to exercise a minimum standard of care in carrying out their duties, often described as the care, diligence, and skill a reasonably prudent person would exercise in similar circumstances.

Holding directors liable for certain actions taken in their corporate capacity helps keep them accountable to shareholders and responsible for the corporation's failure to meet its legal obligations. Traditionally, director obligations extended only to shareholders, but Canadian courts have extended directors' duties to employees, creditors, and other stakeholders.

Along with the two broad duties discussed above, some corporate law statutes impose liability on directors for specific actions, such as voting to issue shares for insufficient value, declaring dividends when the corporation is unable to pay its liabilities, improperly using confidential information, and allowing employee wages and vacation to go unpaid. Directors who do not comply with statutory duties may be forced to account for any benefit, reimburse the corporation for improper expenditures, and disgorge their profits, and — in some cases — may be fined or imprisoned. In addition to specific duties that corporate law statutes impose, a number of other federal and provincial statutes impose duties on directors that expose them to potential personal liability, including liability for failure to withhold and remit certain taxes and pension contributions, environmental offences and damages, and failure to take reasonable measures to ensure employee health and safety.

To fully understand the scope of potential liability, however, one must also look at whom the law considers to be a director or officer. In some cases, directors' liabilities may attach to individuals who have been neither elected nor appointed to office. So individuals who assume some or all of a director's duties, or actively and directly guide a corporation's affairs, could be deemed to be de facto directors and face personal liability.

Of course, some of the potential liability can be reduced through directors' and officers' insurance. Directors also may raise several defences that could eliminate or reduce their liability. Defences include that the director exercised reasonable due diligence, skill, and care in taking the action; was not a director at the time an action was taken or liability arose; and reasonably relied on another professional as permitted by statute.

Officers

The board of directors often delegates some of its powers to one or more of their number, designated as the managing director or management committee. Federal and provincial legislation also allows directors to delegate some of their powers to a number of officers that they appoint. Directors may serve as officers and may even hold more than one office in the same corporation. Typical offices include chairman of the board, secretary, treasurer, president, vice-president, chief executive officer, general manager, and comptroller. Generally, officers owe the corporation the same duties and face some of the same potential liabilities as directors.

Funding the Corporation

The money corporations bring in from their business activities often is augmented by equity and debt capital. The investment owners make in the corporation through buying shares constitutes equity capital. But corporations also are funded through debt. Just like any other legal person, most corporations finance themselves, at least in part, by borrowing money and buying on credit. Along with borrowing from financial lending institutions, corporations sometimes borrow from their own shareholders, and nothing in the law prohibits being an owner and creditor of the same corporation. Corporations frequently issue bonds and debentures in exchange for money lent, with the holders of bonds and debentures repaid the amount loaned with interest.

Corporate Records and Corporate Governance

To ensure accountability, federal and provincial statutes require corporations to keep certain corporate records in a specified form and make them available to specific people involved in the corporation, including shareholders, directors, and creditors. Although the specifics vary among jurisdictions, some common principles prevail. Generally, corporations must keep a register of the articles of incorporation, by-laws, and any unanimous shareholder agreement; a register of the corporation's directors; and registers of all minutes and resolutions

	EXHIBIT 16.2
Unlimited Liability Corporations	

Even though one of incorporation's primary attractions is the limited liability the owners enjoy, a few Canadian provinces — Nova Scotia and Alberta, for instance — provide an alternative option called the **unlimited liability corporation** (ULC). Nova Scotia was the first Canadian province to allow ULCs. Under Nova Scotia's statute, a business may incorporate a company whose members have unlimited liability to the corporation's creditors, while in every other respect the corporation is a full corporation with separate status as a legal person and the associated powers and rights.

Although for many years the option was rarely used, the use of ULCs has increased dramatically, mainly as a tax planning strategy in cross-border matters. Differences in how the United States and Canada treat corporations for income tax purposes triggered the ULC's increased popularity. Under Canadian tax law, parent corporations cannot flow their profits and losses through to their United States subsidiaries, or the reverse, to reduce the taxable amount by offsetting one company's profits with the other's losses. Although this applies equally to ULCs, ULCs do derive the positive tax treatment that corporations receive. Conversely, because of their unlimited liability, ULCs are excluded from the definition of corporation for United States tax purposes. So, United States tax law treats ULCs as flow-through entities, meaning a Canadian parent or subsidiary corporation can apply its United States subsidiary's or parent's losses to offset the related Canadian corporation's profits.

Nova Scotia's law provides some measures for limiting the liability of certain members of a ULC. For instance, members generally are liable only for debts that existed up to the time they stopped being a member, and former members are not required to contribute unless the current members cannot satisfy the debts. Liability may also be limited by contract as some creditors are willing to agree to enter into arrangements where only specified members will be held liable to satisfy the debt if unpaid.

of every shareholders', directors', and committee meetings. Corporations must also keep a register of all shareholders, including their names, addresses, number of shares held, and the date and details of the shares' issuance and transfer. Finally, corporations must keep accounting records consisting of, for example, documents supporting their financial statements, contracts, invoices, and bank statements.

Large public corporations have come under pressure to improve their corporate governance and become more accountable. With several highly publicized scandals on both sides of the border and the stunning collapse of corporate giants, both the government and investors seek ways to ensure corporations keep a tight rein on their management. The United States' passage of the *Sarbanes Oxley Act*, which imposd tighter regulations on such corporate matters as financial reporting, disclosure, and conflicts, had an impact on Canadian corporations as well, given the number that issue shares in the United States and have parent or subsidiary corporations there.

Amalgamating Companies

Corporations often decide to join with another business to expand geographically, in size, or both. Under the federal and many provincial statutes, when two or more corporations choose to consolidate into a single new corporation, an **amalgamation** occurs. These statutes provide a specific process that must be followed to amalgamate. The federal statute allows three methods for amalgamating, depending on the relationship the companies involved had going into the process.

The first method is a long-form amalgamation. This method must be followed when neither of the amalgamating companies is a wholly-owned subsidiary of the other, and both are not wholly-owned subsidiaries of the same parent company. If, instead, one of the corporations is a wholly-owned subsidiary of the other, the vertical short-form procedure may be followed. Finally, the horizontal short-form procedure applies where both amalgamating companies are wholly-owned subsidiaries of the same parent corporation.

In the long-form procedure, an amalgamation agreement is approved by the shareholders of each corporation, **articles of amalgamation** are filed, and a Certificate of Amalgamation is issued. The short-form procedures are the same, except no amalgamation agreement or shareholder approval is needed.

Winding Up and Dissolving a Corporation

Like the other forms of business organizations, corporations sometimes choose or are forced to go out of business. The provincial and federal corporate law statutes provide a procedure for voluntarily and involuntarily settling a corporation's affairs and ending its existence if the corporation is solvent. If the corporation is insolvent, it instead falls within the federal *Bankruptcy and Insolvency Act*'s jurisdiction and that Act's procedures apply. In the case of solvent corporations, whether voluntary or involuntary, the process involves two distinct steps.

The first step involves **winding up** the corporation's affairs and liquidating the company. Basically, all of the corporation's property and assets are called in and converted to money to pay the corporation's debts. After the debts are paid and any remaining assets are distributed to the shareholders, the second step is to dissolve the company. A consent to **dissolution** is obtained from the Minister of Finance, and the consent and Articles of Dissolution are filed. At this point, a certificate of dissolution is issued, and the corporation no longer exists.

Advantages and Disadvantages of Incorporation

The primary and very substantial advantage of incorporation is the limited liability conferred on the owners by virtue of the corporation's separate legal identity. The owners of shares are not personally liable for the debts or wrongful acts of the corporation, which is a separate legal entity from the individual shareholders. At most, shareholders will lose the value of their shares. However, in some cases, a major or controlling shareholder may be held personally liable for a corporation's liabilities if they were the controlling or directing mind of the corporation and used the corporation to engage in fraud or illegal acts, or to benefit the shareholder at the expense of the corporation. In these situations, the court may invoke the **doctrine of the corporate alter ego**, "lifting the corporate veil" to fix liability on individual shareholders who improperly used and manipulated the corporation. Additionally, corporations have greater flexibility in financing their operations and raising capital and may involve hundreds and even thousands in owning, managing, and operating the business. Other than the formalities that must be followed, incorporation really carries very few disadvantages and has become perhaps the most prevalent way of carrying on even small businesses involving few or even one person.

FRANCHISES

Many people intrigued by the possibility of operating their own business lack the money, know-how, and skills to take on full responsibility for all aspects of establishing and operating a business. Considering all the elements that go into building a profitable business — from scoping out a good location, to developing attractive advertising and marketing, to knowing what to charge customers and pay suppliers — the many hurdles, uncertainties, and risks can be daunting. Enter the **franchise**, which for many first-time entrepreneurs appears to offer a more balanced and secure middle-ground. A franchise agreement is a contract between the owner of an established business (called the franchisor) and another party (called the franchisee), giving the franchisee the right to operate a business using the franchisor's business, name, and approach at an agreed-upon location. The franchise agreement generally indicates that the parties' relationship is neither a partnership nor a joint venture (see below). Perhaps the most prominent examples include fast-food restaurants.

Because these relationships carry a very real potential for abuse, given the imbalance of power that often characterizes them at the outset, many provinces have enacted laws governing franchises, typically requiring such safeguards as obliging the franchisor to deal fairly with and disclose specified information to franchisees and entitling franchisees to withdraw from an agreement within a specified number of days after entering into it.

Franchise Agreements

Although franchise agreements vary significantly depending on the business, parties, and other circumstances, certain terms are fairly common to most. Generally, the agreement gives the franchisee a licence to use the franchisor's trademarks and other intellectual property related to the enterprise. The franchisor often agrees to help find a good location, possibly design or build the business premises, and provide some training in the business approach. The franchisee typically agrees to operate the business under the franchisor's established standards and pay a fee, often related to the volume of business. Sometimes the franchisee also must purchase supplies from only the franchisor and promote the business using only the franchisor's approved advertising.

Advantages and Disadvantages for the Franchisor

Franchising a business allows the owner to move into new locations and grow its name recognition without the burden of financing and running a business at each location. While giving up some control, the owner often retains substantial say over the business's standards, quality, look, promotion, and other elements comprising its goodwill and value. The owner also earns fees from each franchise agreement.

On the other hand, regardless of the standards and other rules the franchise agreement requires of the franchisee, the franchisor loses some measure of control over its name and goodwill, courting the risk that any one of its franchisees may operate the business poorly and tarnish the business's reputation. Additionally, ending the franchise relationship can be difficult, stressful, and problematic at times.

Advantages and Disadvantages for the Franchisee

For many, the franchise represents an opportunity to start one's own business that might otherwise not exist. Opening a new business under an established name, with business processes known to work well, and training and other support available greatly enhances the first-time businessperson's likelihood of succeeding. In many cases, the franchisor has already identified good locations for franchises, sells the franchisor the product and other supplies needed to operate, and even supplies promotional items and advertising.

But being tightly associated with the franchisor also has drawbacks. Many people who decide to go into business for themselves are attracted by the thought of calling the shots and operating as they think best. Depending on the franchise agreement's terms, the franchisee may feel limited by the standards and other rules restricting how the business may be run. Additionally, while being required to purchase supplies from the franchisor often brings the franchisee lower cost on some products because of the franchisor's bulk purchases at discounted prices, some franchisees find themselves unable to take advantage of lower local prices and at the franchisor's mercy when requests for supplies are filled too slowly. Depending on the volume of sales and agreement made, the franchisee may be disappointed in the amount of profits realized at the end of the day.

OTHER FORMS OF BUSINESS ARRANGEMENT

Licences

Licence arrangements arise purely from contract. Typically, the owner of intellectual property, like a trademark or copyright, gives another permission to use the intellectual property in connection with a business in return for a fee or royalty. Common examples include a movie company's licensing clothing manufacturers and toy companies to use its characters and name on their goods.

Distributorships

Distributorships occur under a variety of arrangements where one business agrees to sell another business's products. In some cases, the agreement grants the business the exclusive right to distribute the other's products in a particular location or region. Sometimes the distributor agrees to assume responsibility for warranty services along with distributing the manufacturer's products. In any case, the arrangement brings the manufacturer yet another opportunity to get its product out to more customers.

Joint Ventures

The joint venture can take many forms, including that of partnership or corporation. A joint venture typically refers to any situation where two or more parties — which themselves may be individuals, partnerships or corporations — agree to combine their resources for a common enterprise. **Joint ventures** commonly arise where the stakes and risks are high and the likelihood of success is low, but the anticipated payoff on success is substantial. Common examples include exploration and scientific research.

Strategic Alliances

Similar to joint ventures, **strategic alliances** are arrangements where two or more businesses agree to work together on a specific project or towards a common goal. Examples include agreements to combine research and development activities or refer business to one another in the other's jurisdiction.

CHAPTER SUMMARY

In this chapter, we learned to distinguish among the three primary and a few additional methods for organizing and operating a business in Canada. We also examined the major advantages and disadvantages associated with each of these business structures, paying particular attention to the extent to which each shifts the owners' and operators' personal responsibility for the business enterprise's liabilities. Finally, we took a closer look at how corporations are formed, owned, operated, financed, changed and, ultimately, dissolved under both federal and provincial laws.

GLOSSARY OF NEW TERMS AND KEY CONCEPTS

agency	An arrangement where one party, the agent, is given authority to act on behalf of the other party, the principal, and create binding obligations between the principal and third parties.
amalgamation	A process where two or more corporations combine to form a new corporation.
articles of amalgamation	Under federal and some provincial corporate law statutes, the document that sets out the name and structure of a new corporation made up of two combined or amalgamated corporations.
articles of incorporation	Under federal and some provincial corporate law statutes in Canada, the document that sets out a corporation's name and basic structure.
by-laws	The relatively permanent rules establishing how a corporation will be managed and operated.
certificate of incorporation	In many Canadian jurisdictions, the document that signifies the corporation's existence as a separate legal entity and the date when it came into existence.
corporation	A business entity created by the federal or provincial government.
derivative action	A court action that a representative initiates or intervenes in to assert a right or defence on a corporation's behalf.
director	An individual named in the articles of incorporation or elected by a corporation's shareholders to manage a corporation.
dissolution	The way a corporation's or partnership's business is terminated.
distributorship	An arrangement where one business agrees to sell another business's products and may take on the business's warranty services as well.
dividend	A payment to shareholders from the corporation's profits, representing the shareholder's proportional interest in the profits.
doctrine of the corporate alter ego	A legal doctrine that permits the courts, in cases of fraud or other wrongs that might not be remedied, to ignore the corporate structure and fix liability on individual controlling shareholders of the corporation.
fiduciary duty	A duty one party owes to another to act in utmost good faith and in the other's best interest.
franchise	An arrangement where the owner of an established business contracts with another, giving the other party the right to operate a business using the owner's business's name and process or approach at an agreed-on location.
general partnership	A form of business where two or more people carry on a business with a view to profit, with each partner acting as agent for the partnership and other partners and having unlimited personal liability.
joint venture	An arrangement where two or more individuals, partnerships, corporations, or other entities agree to pool resources for a common enterprise.
letters patent	A sovereign grant of corporate existence from the Crown.
licence	A business arrangement where the owner of intellectual property allows another to use property in connection with another business in return for a fee or royalty.
limited partnership	A partnership made up of one or more general partners with unlimited personal liability and responsibility for running the business and one or more limited partners whose liability is limited generally to the extent of their investment in the business and who take no part in running it.
limited liability partnership	A form of partnership some jurisdictions permit for certain professionals who may not otherwise limit their liability through incorporation; the limited liability partnership generally limits individual professionals' liability for their employees' and other partners' negligence.

memorandum of association	In some jurisdictions, a document that establishes a corporation's basic structure.
non-offering corporation	A corporation whose shares are not offered to the public; also called a private company or corporation.
offering corporation	A corporation whose shares are offered to the public; also called a public company or corporation.
officer	An individual appointed by the directors of a corporation to perform certain of the directors' duties that are delegated to the officer.
oppression remedy	Relief a court grants to one or more shareholders whom a corporation has treated unfairly or with prejudice.
partnership	A business organization where two or more people carry on business together with a view to profit.
promoter	A person interested in creating a corporation who takes on the preliminary tasks required to file for incorporation and prepare the business for operation as a corporation.
quorum	The number of shareholders or directors that must be present at a meeting to conduct business.
resolution	A decision a corporation's directors have made authorizing the corporation to do a specific action or transaction.
shares	The portion of a limited liability corporation that an individual owns.
sole proprietorship	A business owned and operated by a single individual without creating another form of business organization.
strategic alliance	An arrangement where two or more businesses agree to work together on a specific project or towards a common outcome.
unanimous shareholder agreement	An agreement that some or all of a corporation's shareholders enter into, often to preserve some or all power to manage the corporation themselves instead of the officers and directors.
unlimited liability corporation	A special kind of corporation some Canadian provinces permit, where the owners remain personally liable for the corporation's actions and debts; because one of the primary advantages of incorporation is lost, this form of business organization is used for very limited and strategic purposes, typically related to obtaining favourable tax consequences for a number of related companies or transactions.
winding up	The process of calling all of a corporation's property in to be liquidated and first paid to all creditors and then distributed to owners before dissolving the corporation.

REVIEW QUESTIONS

1. In the context of business organizations, what does "limited liability" mean, and why is it important?

2. Describe the main steps involved in incorporating a federal corporation.

3. What is the difference between an incorporator and a promoter of a corporation?

4. What business must be conducted at the annual shareholders' meeting?

5. In general, what is the difference between a common share and a preferred share?

6. How does a corporation acquire directors, and what do the directors do?

7. Who appoints officers, and from where do they derive their powers?

8. What is the difference between share capital and debt capital?

9. What is a joint venture, and who may participate in one?

10. What is the difference between a general partnership and a limited partnership?

11. Explain the legality and potential consequences of each of these actions:

    (a) Xavier owns a sole proprietorship and has three employees. By Christmas, his company has made a gross profit of $900. Instead of giving everyone a bonus of $300, he spends $600 of the company's profits on a personal computer, $150 on a date, and gives $50 bonuses to his employees.
    (b) Gareth, a sole proprietor, is having trouble paying his debts to a bank. The bank has begun telling him that he must sell his Mercedes Benz to pay off his loans.
    (c) Bullseye, a major corporation, is struggling to pay its liabilities. However, it declares dividends to its loyal investors. To compensate for this, Bullseye takes out another loan.

12. Compare and contrast the following:

    (a) limited vs. unlimited liability
        (i) In what business organizations does each exist?
        (ii) Why is the difference important within a business context?
        (iii) Create a situation in which not knowing the difference could be costly to a business owner in a partnership.
    (b) equity vs. debt capital
        (i) Who contributes to each type of capital?
        (ii) What legal obligations are present from the receiver of the capital?
        (iii) What are the benefits and failings of each type of capital?
    (c) general vs. limited partnership
        (i) What role does liability play in the differentiation?
        (ii) What does the leadership of each partnership look like?
        (iii) Describe a situation where a Limited Partnership would be more appropriate than a General Partnership.

DISCUSSION QUESTIONS

1. What are the major advantages and disadvantages associated with operating a sole proprietorship?

2. What are the major advantages and disadvantages of operating a partnership?

3. What does "piercing the corporate veil" mean? Do you think the concept is fair? Under what circumstances do you think a court should consider applying this concept?

4. Under what circumstances might the directors of a corporation become personally liable?

5. Describe some of the powers shareholders have, and some ways shareholders maintain control over a corporation.

6. Why might a businessperson choose to operate a franchise?

7. For each of the following, create a scenario where the owner or owners would be most benefitted by pursuing that form of business arrangement:

   (a) sole proprietorship
   (b) general partnership
   (c) limited partnership
   (d) limited liability partnership
   (e) corporation
   (f) franchise
   (g) licence
   (h) distributorship
   (i) joint venture
   (j) strategic alliance

SUGGESTED READING AND OTHER RESOURCES

Business Corporations Act (Ontario), R.S.O. 1990, c. B.16.

Canada Business Corporations Act, R.S.C. 1985, c. C-44.

Companies Act (Nova Scotia), R.S.N.S. 1989, c. 81.

Martel, P. *Business Corporations in Canada: Legal and Practical Aspects* (Toronto: Thomson Canada Ltd., 2007).

McGuiness, K.P. *Canadian Business Corporations Law*, 2d ed. (Markham, Ont.: LexisNexis Canada Inc., 2007).

VanDuzer, J.A. *The Law of Partnerships and Corporations*, 3d ed. (Toronto: Irwin Law, 2009).

WEBSITES

CanLII: <http://www.canlii.org/en/index.html>

Justice Law Website: <http://laws-lois.justice.gc.ca/eng/> (See also provincial ministries of attorney general websites.)

The Law Dictionary: <http://thelawdictionary.org/>

Debtors' Rights and Creditors' Remedies

Ginevra M. Saylor
DENTONS CANADA LLP

Learning Objectives

After reading this chapter, the reader should be able to:

➤ understand the relationship between debtors and creditors

➤ describe security and the concept of secured transactions

➤ describe the various remedies available to the creditor for the collection of overdue debts

➤ identify the principal steps involved in the litigation of collections actions in court

➤ describe the major methods available for the enforcement of judgments obtained through litigation

➤ understand the purpose, procedure, and effect of bankruptcy proceedings

➤ identify the protection provided to the debtor, and explain the role of consumer protection legislation

© 2014 by Captus Press Inc. The author acknowledges, with gratitude, the research and editorial assistance of Kirran Iveson.

TABLE OF CONTENTS

INTRODUCTION

> He solemnly conjured me, I remember, to take warning by his fate; and to observe that if a man had twenty pounds a year for his income, and spent nineteen pounds nineteen shillings and six pence, he would be happy, but that if he spent twenty pounds one he would be miserable.
>
> —*David Copperfield* by Charles Dickens

So goes the advice of Mr. Micawber, a veteran of England's 19th century debtors' prison, to young David Copperfield on approaching the responsibilities of adulthood. The formula seems simple enough: never spend more money than you have. Yet Mr. Micawber, and most members of modern society, do find themselves in debt at one time or another. Some also find themselves unable to meet those debts as they come due. And so begins the relationship of the debtor and creditor and the debt collection process.

Creation of a Debt

In a simple commercial transaction, one party offers goods or services for sale and the other accepts by paying for them. However, in our complex society, a variety of arrangements permit consumers to receive the benefit of the transaction before paying.

For example, many people buying a car do not pay the entire amount in one payment. Rather, the buyer pays a small portion of the total sale price as a down payment and agrees to pay the remaining balance in the future under terms agreed on by the buyer and seller. The arrangement benefits both parties. Clearly, far fewer would be able to buy a big ticket item like a car were such arrangements not available. The seller, in turn, would not sell as many cars and could not command as high a price.

Similarly, people often need cash that they do not currently have. Suppose an individual wishes to buy items from a seller who is unwilling to extend the buyer credit. That individual may contact a financial lending institution, such as a bank, to borrow money. The bank may agree to lend an amount of money on the borrower's promise to repay the sum within a specific time and in a mutually acceptable way. The borrower also generally agrees to pay an additional sum, in the nature of **interest**, as a fee for using the lender's money. The interest typically is an amount calculated in terms of the sum originally borrowed (the **principal**).

In each of the above examples, one party receives the benefit of a transaction and, in return, promises to fully repay the other at some future date, creating a debt. A **debt** is an amount of money one person owes to another. Our economic system not only encourages but also relies on credit and the creation of debt. It is only when problems arise that the legal system may be called in to intervene. For example, suppose the borrower has agreed to repay the bank a certain amount each month and fails to pay for three months. Or, an automobile buyer claims the car was defective and refuses to pay the balance owed. In each case, the person who extended the credit will attempt to recover the unpaid amount.

Types of Debtors

Any person who owes money to another is a **debtor**. However, not all debtors — or their debts — are alike. The way a creditor chooses to pursue collection is largely determined by the type of debtor and debt involved.

Consumer debtors are individuals who have acquired debt purchasing goods and services or borrowing money for use in their personal life. Two common examples of consumer debt are credit card purchases and residential mortgages.

People who owe money may fail to honour their debts on time for many reasons. Often, the consumer faces an unexpected and innocent financial setback. Consumers may suddenly lose their job or come down with a debilitating illness that prevents them from earning an income for an extended period of time. Marital breakdown leading up to separation or divorce often causes financial uncertainty for many. Consumer debtors in these circumstances may want to meet their financial obligations but honestly lack the means to do so. In these circumstances, some creditors may be inclined to take a lenient approach to collection and try to work with the debtor, operating under the theory that "you cannot get blood from a stone." The amount of leniency the creditor extends often depends on the debtor's own conduct. Debtors who communicate with their creditors and act in good faith are more likely to receive sympathetic treatment.

However, not all debtors fall into their financial difficulties innocently. Some recklessly or irresponsibly manage their affairs, with little regard for whether they will be able to pay their debts when due. Still others intentionally avoid paying their debts, ignoring overdue notices, raising unfounded claims against creditors, and leaving the jurisdiction. In these cases, a creditor may take more aggressive steps to collect the debt. The creditor may seek help from others, such as a **collection agency**, an investigator, or a lawyer. If necessary, the creditor may pursue the matter in court through a civil action against the delinquent debtor.

Another kind of debtor is the commercial debtor. Commercial debt is created when a business owes money for expenses incidental to operating the business. This debt may come from buying materials used to manufacture a product, leasing equipment, hiring services, or acquiring inventory.

As with consumer debtors, many factors may lead commercial debtors to stop paying their debts on time. A major societal event, such as an economic recession, a crisis in the company's industry, or a political controversy may cause a business to face an unexpected sales or production reduction. A company may experience a protracted strike or lose key management personnel. Or the business may fail because of incompetence or mismanagement. Again, the reason for the debtor's failure to pay and the debtor's behaviour play a large part in how creditors decide to pursue the debts.

Debts do not die with the debtor. When people die owing money to others, those debts become their estate's debts. An estate consists of all property and assets the deceased owned at the time of death. An individual or group of individuals appointed by the court or the deceased through a will must administer the deceased's estate. Before distributing the estate's assets to the deceased's heirs or beneficiaries, the estate's personal representative must ensure all proper debts of the deceased are paid. In discharging this duty, the personal representative must advertise for creditors, advising them whom to contact to collect their debts. The personal representative's failure to satisfy the estate's debts before final distribution of the assets can result in personal liability for paying the creditors from the representative's own assets.

Secured and General Creditors

As observed, a **creditor** is a person or entity to whom something is owed. Creditors range from individuals who independently sell a friend their computer to major institutional lenders making commercial loans of several million dollars to large corporations. Not all creditors, however, start from the same position when collecting their debts.

Many creditors at the inception of the debtor-creditor relationship take steps to enhance their likelihood of ultimately recovering the amount owed. Creditors may structure their agreement with a debtor to provide direct recourse against some of the debtor's property. Additionally, arrangements might provide creditors with priority in collecting their debt before some or all of the debtor's other creditors. Such advantages are obtained by requiring **security**. A creditor who has taken some form of security is called a **secured creditor**.

Security comes in many forms, such as real estate, personal goods, stocks, bonds, or the equipment a business uses. Security often is referred to as collateral.

A common secured transaction is buying a home with a mortgage. Quite often, a home buyer will obtain the bulk of the money needed to complete the transaction from a bank through a special type of loan arrangement known as a mortgage or charge. Through the agreement, the lender obtains not only the borrower's promise to repay the debt but also a claim against the land itself. Consequently, should the borrower fail to repay the debt according to the agreement's terms, the lender may enforce its claim against the property by taking possession of and ultimately selling it to satisfy the debt. Assuming all statutory requirements for protecting the secured interest have been met, the lender has access to the property used as collateral before any of the debtor's other creditors, even those whose claims arose before the lender's.

Whatever the form of security, the essential features of secured transactions are that the secured creditor obtains special rights against one or more assets of the debtor, and those rights stand in priority to the claims of the debtor's other creditors. However, to ensure their preferred status over other creditors, secured creditors generally must meet two requirements. First, the agreement or contract creating the secured interest must be in writing and describe the property in sufficient detail to accurately identify it. Second, secured creditors must comply with all statutory requirements for registering a secured interest with the proper public office. For example, a secured interest in land must be registered against title to the land in the appropriate Land Registry Office. Likewise, an interest in personal property must be filed with the designated ministry under provincial *Personal Property Security Acts*.

Not all secured interests arise from a contract between parties. Sometimes a creditor receives a preferred or special interest in a debtor's property by statute or under common law (as discussed in the next section).

By contrast, a creditor who takes no security and obtains no preferred claim over specific assets is called an unsecured or **general creditor**. A general creditor may have no option but to bring a court action against a debtor who does not satisfy a debt. Making matters worse, the general creditor ranks behind the debtor's secured creditors, at least with respect to the assets used as collateral.

METHODS OF COLLECTION

Demand for Payment

Creditors want to be paid as quickly and inexpensively as possible. Sometimes, though, creditors also want to preserve their relationship with the debtor so that they may conduct more business together in the future. This arises where the debtor is the creditor's ongoing commercial client, experiencing a temporary setback in business. Finally, creditors have an underlying interest in preserving their reputation and goodwill.

The collection process typically begins with one or more notices to the debtor, advising that the account is overdue and demanding payment. The demand states the total amount due, including interest or late fees, the date when the amount must be fully paid, and the possible consequences of failing to pay or contact the creditor. The creditor might also telephone the debtor to demand payment and find out the debtor's intentions. If the debtor is co-operative and communicative at this point, many creditors are willing to agree to partial or periodic payments. A creditor may even agree to reduce the debt in exchange for an immediate lump-sum payment. The more reasonable the debtor's behaviour, the more likely early and amicable settlement becomes. Creditors know all too well the expense and difficulty involved in the collection process and generally would rather receive a certain, albeit lesser, amount than face the uncertainties and delay inherent in later stages of the process.

Many creditors involve others in the collection process. Where a debtor cannot be found, the creditor may hire an investigator to help find the debtor. Using information the creditor provides, investigators search public records and other sources to trace debtors.

Creditors are also known to turn delinquent accounts over to a collection agency. A collection agency is an independent company whose business is obtaining debt repayment for its clients. Given the nature of the service and the potential for abusing and harassing debtors, these agencies are regulated by the government and generally must be registered.

Enforcing a Lien

As observed, creditors may enhance their likelihood of collecting by requiring security in return for an extension of credit. The common law and modern statutes have developed similar rights for individuals performing certain kinds of labour and services by operation of law through the creation of a **lien**. While some liens entitle one person to retain property belonging to another until the property's owner satisfies specific demands, other liens are non-possessory and operate more like a charge.

Consider an individual who takes an automobile to a garage for repairs. Suppose the mechanic and the car owner agree that repairs will be made for a specific amount to be paid when the repairs are completed. If the owner fails to pay when notified that the work is done, the mechanic may keep the car until the owner pays in full. The mechanic creates a lien on the automobile by improving the property with the owner's permission.

Common Law

At common law, the right to a lien was restricted to (i) those who performed services in the nature of repairs or improvements to goods; (ii) innkeepers, over the property of their guests; and (iii) common carriers (those engaged in shipping and transportation), over goods shipped. Some professionals, such as lawyers and bankers, have a common law lien over documents prepared by them or left in their possession. To enforce their rights over the debtor's property, lien claimants must have already performed the services, and payment must be due. At common law, the lien provided only the right to withhold the goods and did not include a right to sell those goods to satisfy the debt.

Extension by Statute

Statutory law extends the protection of liens to more professions and businesses and adds the right to sell the goods in some circumstances. For example, in many jurisdictions the lien obtained by one who performs work on an item of personal property (called chattel) includes the right to sell the property and use the proceeds to cover the debt after a designated period of time and notice to the debtor. Similarly, under innkeeper statutes, hoteliers may sell guests' property on the premises, after the bills remain unpaid for a specified period and after providing proper notice to the guest. These laws also extend the entitlement to operators of boarding and lodging houses. Notably, however, the right to sell the property has not been

---

Lien for Storage   **EXHIBIT 17.1**

Suppose Frank buys furniture from Furno-rama in Ottawa and asks the store to ship the goods to Toronto, where he lives. The store agrees to ship the furniture to a storage facility in Toronto, and Frank agrees to pay the storage fee and arrange for final transport to his residence when notified that the goods have arrived. When the goods arrive, the warehouse notifies Frank, but he makes no arrangement for transport to his home and tenders no payment for storage. After four months, the warehouse decides to sell the furniture.

Under Ontario's statutory scheme, the warehouse must notify both Frank and the furniture store of its intention to sell the goods unless the charges are paid in full by a specific date. The notice must state that the goods will be advertised for sale at a public auction and must include the proposed sale's time, date, and location. The notice must be sent to any other person the warehouse knows to have an interest in the goods.

---

extended to common carriers, although nothing prevents individual common carriers from securing this right by including an express term in their contracts with consumers.

Although the details vary among the provinces, statutes authorizing the right to sale generally require the following:

- A specific number of months to pass after payment comes due
- Advance notice to the owner of the creditor's intent to sell the property if the debt is not paid
- Advertisement of the time, date, and place of the sale
- Sale by public auction
- The proceeds be used first to cover costs of the sale and, next, to pay the overdue debt, with any surplus going to the debtor

The statutes provide strict guidelines regarding the sale's advertisement and conduct.

Warehouse and other storage operators are one class of labourers who had no lien at common law but now have a lien by statutes, like Ontario's *Repair and Storage Liens Act*.[1] Under this Act, warehouse operators may hold goods stored at their facility for the amount of the charges due and sell the goods to cover the unpaid debt.

Construction Liens

Another industry that benefited from statutory extension of liens is the building and construction trade. Under such provincial legislation, all tradespeople supplying labour or materials to improve a piece of land may obtain a lien, or charge, against the land to secure payment for the work or supplies provided. The construction lien gives the lien claimant the right to ultimately sell the land to satisfy the debt if it remains unpaid and the lien is not discharged.

A large-scale construction project involves a series of contracts and subcontracts. Generally, the owner enters into an agreement with a general contractor, who assumes responsibility for the entire project. The general contractor then engages electricians, carpenters, roofers, plumbers and other tradespeople through a series of subcontracts. Each of the subcontractors in

---

[1] R.S.O. 1990, c. R-25.

turn may enter into subsidiary contracts for goods or services to be supplied at the construction site. Under this scheme, the only individual who has a direct contractual relationship with the landowner is the general contractor. To sue in contract under common law, the aggrieved person — called the plaintiff — must have privity of contract with the defendant, meaning that the plaintiff and defendant both are parties to the contract. So, at common law, no subcontractor could sue the owner for failing to pay for services rendered, even though the owner received the benefit of those services. Rather, the subcontractors needed to commence action against the party with whom they directly dealt.

Legislation, such as Ontario's *Construction Lien Act*,[2] removes the obstruction to recovery that privity of contract imposes. The Act outlines the steps subcontractors must take to generate (preserve) and enforce (perfect) a lien against the land. The Act also establishes a less formal and faster procedure for enforcing the lien and recovering the debt through the courts. Finally, the statute creates a system of holdbacks to amass a fund from which all unpaid contractors on the project could be paid. Each time the owner pays the general contractor or one subcontractor pays another, a certain percentage is held back to ensure the remaining unpaid contractors are paid.

Landlord's Right of Distraint

Provincial landlord and tenant legislation generally gives landlords a right to seize (distrain) a tenant's property located in the leased premises and sell it to recover unpaid rent. However, the landlord's right of **distraint** is limited. First, the landlord has rights only over property to which the tenant holds title. Second, the right to distrain depends entirely on the existence of a lease. So, if the landlord decides to terminate the lease and evict the tenant, the right to distrain the tenant's property is lost. Finally, should the tenant fall into bankruptcy, the landlord's right to distrain becomes a preferred claim for three months' back and three months' accelerated rent, which ranks ahead of most other creditors under the *Bankruptcy and Insolvency Act*.

Other Statutory Liens

Various statutes create liens against a landowner's property for arrears in payments related to the land, such as real estate taxes, government loans for improvements to land, and utility services. Statutes create similar rights in employees against their employers for wages, vacation time, and other employee benefits accrued.

Conditional Sales Contracts and Repossession

Many sellers of expensive durable goods use a special form of contract called **conditional sales contracts**. These contracts give sellers a direct remedy against defaulting purchasers through the very goods sold.

In the standard conditional sales contract — say, for the purchase of a car — the buyer makes an initial down payment and agrees to pay the remaining balance with interest in monthly instalments for a set time. The buyer obtains immediate possession, while the seller retains title until the balance owed is paid in full. The buyer also might agree to insure the car and keep it in good condition. These agreements typically give sellers the right to repossess and resell the car if the buyer fails to make the monthly payments. The seller may exercise these rights in priority to other creditors with claims against the purchaser. In many provinces, however, sellers need to register under a pro-

---

[2] R.S.O. 1990, c. C-30.

vincial *Personal Property Security Act* (for instance, Ontario's R.S.O. 1990, c. P.10).

Like other sales contracts involving credit, the essential feature of conditional sales contracts is the creation of a debt. So, the creditor has the ordinary contract remedy for breach — namely, the right to sue to recover the debt. The right to repossession is another avenue available.

Repossession and sale is a powerful remedy, with much potential for abuse by the creditor and serious hardship to the debtor. The provinces have instituted legislation to mitigate the harm to the buyer and curtail creditors' reckless use of the right. Although provincial statutes vary, they share some common features.

Most jurisdictions prohibit sellers from using force to regain possession of the goods sold. Although sellers are free to either enlist the services of the local sheriff or repossess the goods themselves, if they choose to do it themselves, they must employ no unlawful or abusive means. If the seller enters the buyer's property without permission or responds to the buyer's resistance with physical force, the buyer may assert civil claims against the seller for trespass and assault. The seller's proper response to a buyer's resistance is to obtain a court order authorizing steps to repossess. If the buyer continues to resist after a court order is issued, the buyer risks being held in contempt of court.

As observed, following repossession the seller may resell to a new purchaser. Many statutes protect buyers before resale. The buyer generally has the right to regain possession if he pays the entire balance due plus any costs the seller incurred repossessing and initiating collection procedures. Notice must be given that the buyer's default in payment accelerates the deadline for payment of the full balance, meaning the buyer must now pay all remaining payments and not just the missed back payments to regain possession. Some provincial legislation defeats the seller's right to repossess after the buyer has completed a substantial portion of the contract, such as paying two-thirds of the contract price. These statutes protect buyers who have made timely payments for an extended period from losing the goods for simply missing one payment near the end of the contract. Were the law otherwise, the seller would receive a significant windfall for a buyer's minor breach.

Statutes also regulate the required notice, conduct, and distribution of proceeds from the sale. Generally, sellers may first reimburse themselves for costs associated with the resale, then apply the proceeds to satisfy the debt. In some jurisdictions, if the proceeds are insufficient to cover the debt, the seller retains the right to sue for the balance. Although rare, the situation may arise where the proceeds of the sale are greater than needed to clear the debt, resulting in a surplus. Under Ontario law, any surplus realized on repossession and resale, beyond that needed to pay the debt and all attendant costs, must be released to the debtor.

Some conditional sales contracts are further complicated by third parties. In practice, merchants often do not finance conditional sales arrangements themselves. Rather, the contract is turned over, or assigned, to a finance company for collection. If the debtor defaults, the seller is liable to the finance company. The finance company taking the contract is called the **assignee**. Under contract law, a contract's assignee takes the contract subject to any personal defences the buyer has against the seller. For example, if the goods are defective, the buyer may raise this as a defence against paying the finance company, in the same way the defence could have been raised directly against the seller.

Bank Loans

Bank loans are regulated by the federal government, through the *Bank Act*.[3] One major feature of the Act is the inclusion of more kinds of assets permitted as collateral. The Act also identifies criteria as to who may qualify for a bank loan.

An important section of the Act, section 427, empowers chartered banks to lend to a wide range of businesses and tradespeople, including wholesale and retail purchasers of goods, manufacturers, farmers, and fisherpeople. Under section 427, borrowers may use as collateral the inventory, equipment, or future products of the business or trade. For example, a farmer may borrow money to finance the purchase of farm machinery, seeds, and other material needed to grow crops. In return, the farmer may use future crops that will be grown using the purchases made with the borrowed funds as collateral. Note that banks may take other types of security as well.

Borrowers are expected to use the money they earn through sale of the goods produced to reduce the outstanding loan. Should the borrower fail to do so, the Act provides the bank with a remedy against the goods or equipment used to secure the debt. Thus, the bank may take possession of the goods, sell them and apply the proceeds to reduce the debt and cover any incidental costs. If the sale yields a surplus, it goes to the borrower. If the sale does not raise enough to satisfy the debt, the bank may sue for the deficiency.

Foreclosure and Power of Sale

As noted above, in most transactions involving real property (land), the land itself secures the debt. In transactions involving a mortgage, or charge, borrowers deliver a charge of their land to their lender, creating a legal interest in the land. In the event of default, the lender may enforce this interest in the land, using one of two main methods: foreclosure and power of sale.

In the power of sale, creditors have the right to seize and sell the charged property, following non-payment for a set number of months. For instance, under Ontario's *Mortgages Act*,[4] the right to sell arises on three months' default. Creditors must follow statutory requirements for giving all interested parties notice and conducting the sale. In a power of sale, creditors retain the right to sue the debtor for any deficiency but must relinquish any surplus to the debtor. Note that creditors need not first invoke the powers of the court to enforce their interest through a power of sale.

Conversely, foreclosure is a court action. In response to an action in foreclosure, a debtor may choose to file a response and defend against the action or try to cure the default. Creditors who succeed in their action become owners of the property and may do as they please with it. If they decide to sell the property and realize an amount greater than the debt owed, they may keep the surplus. However, if the proceeds of the sale do not fully satisfy the debt, they may not sue the debtor for the deficiency.

Enforcement of Security

Many different types of secured transactions and forms of collateral exist. Even so, steps generally must be followed whenever creditors choose to enforce a secured interest.

Creditors must demand payment before enforcing their interest against a debtor's assets. The demand must provide the debtor with reasonable notice of the time within which the debtor must pay the amount demanded.

Secured creditors next must choose an appropriate way to take control of the asset, either by themselves or with help. Alternatively, where the asset is

---

[3] S.C. 1991, c. 46.
[4] R.S.O. 1990, c. M-40.

an operating business, creditors may ask the court to appoint a **receiver** to manage the business and collect the income.

Before the asset may be sold, notice must be given to the debtor and any others who may also have an interest in the asset. The law clearly sets out the requirements for the amount, manner, and method of notice to give debtors a full and fair opportunity to cure the default and preserve their asset.

Finally, the law requires that the creditor act in good faith and in a commercially reasonable manner when selling the asset. Creditors who fail to meet the legal standards at any stage of the process could be liable for damages to the debtor or others injured as a consequence.

LITIGATION

Deciding whether to collect a debt through court action is not easy. The basic question that creditors must consider is the likelihood of being able to enforce a court judgment if successful. Some debtors simply have no assets or income from which a judgment could be collected. Because we no longer punish individuals who cannot meet their debts, the creditor's judgment may be worthless.

Given the expense and time involved in litigation, most creditors would not want to invest in obtaining a judgment that may never pay off. Similarly, creditors may decide that pursuing a court judgment against a business that has gone under due to extreme financial loss is not worth the effort. Before initiating court proceedings, creditors should carefully address the following questions:

- Is collecting this debt crucial to my financial position?
- Does the debtor have assets or income from which enforcement is likely?
- Is pursuing this debt worth possibly damaging my business relationship with this debtor?
- Are less expensive means available for minimizing the impact on my business of not collecting this debt?

After weighing the costs and benefits, creditors who decide to pursue collection through litigation initiate an action by filing a claim with the appropriate court.

Generally, two levels of court hear these claims, depending on the amount of the debt and kind of relief the creditor seeks. In Ontario, the two courts are the Superior Court of Justice and the Ontario Small Claims Court. Using Ontario as an example, we will look at the major steps involved in the court process.

Small Claims Court Small Claims Court offers a faster, cheaper, and relatively informal forum to litigate claims falling within its limited jurisdiction. Although the court applies settled principles of law, it operates extensively on good conscience and fairness. Many rules of evidence and trial procedure are relaxed, and the court helps litigants navigate the proceedings.

Small Claims Court jurisdiction is subject to the following restrictions:

- The claim must be to recover property or money.
- The amount of money or value of property must be below a specified amount.
- The action must be commenced in the territorial division where either the matter arose or the debtor lives or conducts business.

Although parties may have lawyers, many claims are successfully litigated in Small Claims Court without a lawyer's help. So, many choose to either represent themselves or be represented by a paralegal.

Before filing a Small Claims action, creditors send debtors a written demand letter, outlining the facts supporting the claim and the exact amount due. Next, creditors complete a pre-printed claim form, obtained from the Small Claims Court clerk. If asked, the clerk may help creditors — now plaintiffs — complete and file the form. The claim indicates all parties' names and addresses, a concise statement of facts in the case, and the exact amount claimed, including interest. Relevant documents, like invoices, are attached to the claim, which the plaintiff files along with a fee. The document is served on the debtor, now the defendant, usually by a private process server.

Defendants must complete and file a defence within 20 days of being served with the claim if they wish to contest the matter. The defence form includes a concise statement of the defendant's reasons for disputing the claim. Both the claim and defence are drafted in plain language and focus on the facts.

A defendant with a claim against the plaintiff may raise it in the same action as a **counterclaim**, which is called a defendant's claim in Small Claims Court. If the counterclaim is for an amount exceeding the monetary threshold, a motion may be made to transfer the matter to a higher court. Similarly, if the plaintiff has sued more than one defendant, any defendant may file a **cross-claim** arising from the same transaction against a co-defendant. Finally, the defendant may bring an entirely new party into the matter, by filing a **third-party claim** against an individual also involved in the transaction that gave rise to the original claim. All of these are initiated through a defendant's claim. The plaintiff, and any others against whom claims are filed, may file responses.

At this point, many debtors acknowledge the debt and file no response to the claim. Under such circumstances, the creditor may obtain a **default judgment** against the debtor, by following the procedures set out in the rules of practice. If the claim is for a specific amount, the default judgment is issued administratively with no need for hearing. If an unspecified amount is demanded, the defendant is noted in default; a damages hearing is held, where a judge receives evidence and ascertains the amount of damages.

If the defendant disputes the claim, the parties are assigned a date for trial. Before the trial, the parties may exchange documents related to the case and typically engage in at least one pre-trial conference with a judge to try to settle the dispute and streamline the hearing.

The Small Claims Court trial is far less formal than a regular court proceeding, with judges taking an active role in drawing forth evidence and helping unrepresented parties present their cases. If a judgment is entered against the defendant debtor for an amount beyond a set limit, the debtor may file an appeal. If no appeal is taken, the plaintiff may take steps to enforce the judgment.

Formal Court Proceedings

Debts exceeding the Small Claims Court's monetary limits must be commenced in a formal court of record with strict rules of practice. As a result, most litigants in formal court proceedings are represented by a lawyer.

The plaintiff creditor commences an action by filing a formal **pleading**, called the statement of claim. The claim identifies the parties, states the precise relief requested, and sets forth all material facts giving rise to the plaintiff's claim. The plaintiff may also request pre- and post-judgment interest, as well as costs of the litigation. The claim is filed along with the mandatory filing fee.

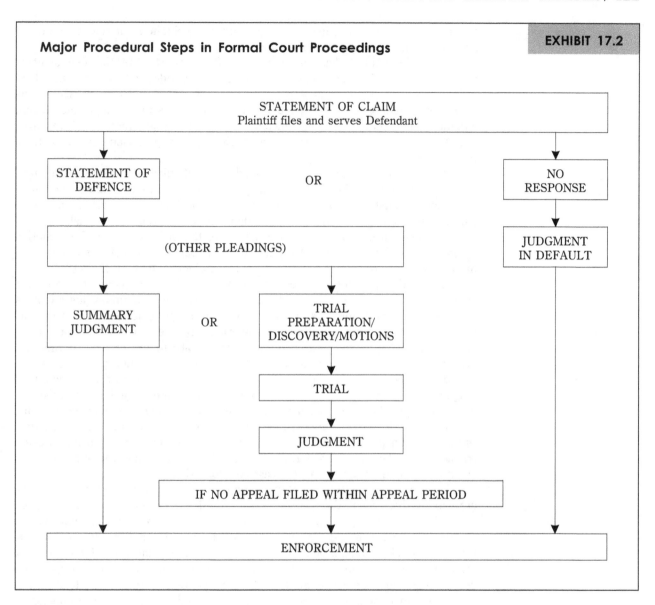

Major Procedural Steps in Formal Court Proceedings

EXHIBIT 17.2

The plaintiff must deliver the statement of claim to the defendant. **Service** must be made on the defendant within six months of filing, although the court may grant an extension of this time if need can be established.

Once served, defendants must file a statement of defence within 20 days if they are within Canada, 40 days if in the United States, and 60 days if in another country. In their defence, defendants must specifically outline all of the plaintiff's allegations that they admit, all those that they deny, and those of which they have no knowledge. Furthermore, they must plead their own version of the facts and clearly assert all defences they have against the claim. Defendants may raise any counterclaim, cross-claim, or third-party claim in addition to their defence. In turn, the plaintiff may file a reply to the defence and a defence to the counterclaim. Parties on a cross-claim or third-party claim may also file responsive pleadings.

Defendants who do not respond to a statement of claim may face serious consequences. First, they are deemed to have admitted to all allegations that the plaintiff made in the statement of claim. Second, the plaintiff may have them noted in default. Finally, the plaintiff may obtain a judgment in default against them, avoiding the need for trial.

After the plaintiff has the registrar of the court note the defendant in default, the plaintiff may obtain the actual default judgment. Where the plaintiff's demand is for a liquidated amount or for property to be returned, the plaintiff's lawyer may file a requisition for the registrar to sign the default judgment. The requisition must include a copy of the statement of claim, proof that the claim was served on the defendant, and a proposed bill of costs of the proceeding.

If, instead, the plaintiff demanded an unliquidated amount, the final judgment cannot be obtained by simply filing a requisition. Rather, the plaintiff's lawyer must file a formal motion before the court. At hearing, the judge will either grant judgment or order that the case proceed to trial.

Whenever a default judgment is awarded, the defendant may file a motion to have the order set aside. To succeed, defendants must establish at a minimum that they received either no or insufficient notice of the claim.

Either the plaintiff or the defendant may obtain a judgment from the court without the need for trial by filing a motion for **summary judgment**. A summary judgment may be obtained only after the statement of claim and defence and any other pleadings in the case have been filed. Summary judgment is available where one party can demonstrate to the court that the case presents no genuine issue for trial. Rather, the case either presents only a question of law or no issue at all, and the party is, therefore, entitled to a judgment as a matter of law. The motion for summary judgment must set forth the grounds for entitlement and must include any affidavits, documents, transcripts, or other evidence supporting the request. To counter the motion, the responding party must present evidence that the case does, in fact, raise a triable issue. The judge will then decide whether to grant the moving party summary judgment or send the case on for trial.

In contested matters, parties attempt to settle the matter by mutual agreement throughout the entire process, until a judgment is entered. Before trial, the parties also engage in various forms of **discovery**, or information sharing, including producing all relevant documents and orally questioning parties through examinations for discovery. An important part of the process, discovery helps define the real issues in the case, helps lawyers prepare for court, helps advance settlement, and helps prevent surprises at trial.

If no settlement is reached, the case is listed for trial. At the conclusion of the trial, a judgment is issued. The unsuccessful party has the right to file an appeal within a prescribed period of time. If no appeal is filed, the judgment becomes final. Creditors who have succeeded in obtaining judgment in their favour, from which no appeal is taken, must then begin the process of collecting or enforcing the judgment.

ENFORCEMENT OF ORDERS

Following the entry of an order in court, the debt becomes a judgment debt, and the parties are designated "judgment creditor" and "judgment debtor". At this point, assuming a judgment debtor has the means available, he or she may pay the entire judgment. Instead, the judgment debtor may make arrangements with the judgment creditors or through the court to pay the judgment over time. Some judgment debtors simply do nothing. In the face of no payment or arrangements, some judgment creditors choose to enforce their judgment through one or more available mechanisms.

Protection of the Debtor

Debtor's Rights

All of the enforcement mechanisms impose strict requirements for giving judgment debtors adequate notice of action planned against them. For instance, debtors must have an opportunity to contest the action or to prepare for the hardship that may follow. Notice also gives debtors one more chance to pay and stop the proposed action.

Assets Exempt from Enforcement

At early common law, sheriffs could seize nearly all debtors' assets except the clothes on their back. Both federal and provincial legislation greatly expand the protection afforded judgment debtor, by exempting certain property to ensure that debtors are left with some food, clothing, shelter, and means to earn a living. Even so, some exemptions are not available for debtors owing spousal or child support.

Federal exemptions include federal government benefits, such as Canada Pension Plan benefits, government annuities, and veteran's allowance benefits. The major common law exemption protects damages orders for pain and suffering awarded to the debtors in a lawsuit.

Provincial statutes supplement the federal and common law with a range of exemptions. Depending on the jurisdiction, these may include the following:

- Provincial welfare payments
- Pensions (except to satisfy an order for support and maintenance)
- Worker's compensation benefits
- Necessary and ordinary clothing, up to a certain value
- Household furniture and utensils, up to a certain value
- Tools of trade, livestock, equipment, feed and similar items of values specified in amounts
- A percentage of one's wages

Major Methods of Enforcement

Writ of Seizure and Sale

Under this procedure, the sheriff is empowered to take possession of the debtor's assets and sell them. The money realized is distributed to judgment creditors who have filed writs with the sheriff. To initiate this procedure, creditors obtain a writ from the registrar of the court after filing a requisition stating the date and amount of the judgment, the amount and dates of any payments the debtor made, and the amount remaining.

The creditor files the writ with the sheriff, along with a direction to enforce the writ. The writ remains in effect for six years from the date it is filed and may be renewed for an indefinite number of periods.

In response to the writ and direction, the sheriff seizes all of the debtor's property within the sheriff's jurisdiction. Creditors should file a writ in each district where they believe the debtor owns property. Where personal property (as opposed to real estate) is seized, the sheriff must give the debtor an inventory of the seized items if the debtor asks.

Before selling the debtor's real and personal property, the sheriff must give the debtor notice, by both mail and newspaper publication. Even after a sale is held, courts will void any transaction if the debtor satisfies the debt before purchasers have paid for and received title to the debtor's property.

Finally, proceeds of the sale are distributed to the debtor's creditors, in the way the statute prescribes. Some provincial statutes require sheriffs to distribute the proceeds to all of the debtor's judgment creditors who have filed a writ (called execution creditors).

Garnishment

A second enforcement method is income **garnishment**, which allows creditors to collect directly from third parties (garnishees) who owe money to the judgment debtor. For example, subject to an exemption of a certain percentage, the judgment debtor's employer could be required to pay a portion of the debtor's pay each pay period to the sheriff for the garnishor's benefit.

The judgment creditor starts the garnishment process by filing a requisition with the court registrar, including a copy of the judgment, an affidavit stating the amount owed, and the names of the proposed garnishees. The notice of garnishment is sent to the named garnishees, the sheriff of the county where the proceeding began, and the judgment debtor.

Once notified, the garnishee must pay the specified amount to the sheriff; failing to do so can result in an order against the garnishee and in favour of the garnishor. However, the rules do provide garnishees with a mechanism for contesting a garnishment by disputing the underlying debt to the judgment debtor. To dispute the underlying debt, the garnishee submits a garnishee's statement describing the grounds for dispute to the garnishor, the judgment debtor, and the court. The garnishor, garnishee, judgment debtor, and any other interested party may file a motion for a garnishment hearing to address any issues.

Examination in Aid of Execution

Many creditors do not ask for a significant amount of information regarding the debtor when entering into commercial relationships. So when collection problems arise, judgment creditors often have insufficient information to make adequate use of the available enforcement measures. Likewise, the judgment debtor's circumstances may change over the course of the time required to fully satisfy a debt. The rules entitle judgment creditors to orally question debtors about their assets, liabilities, and resources for paying a judgment in an "examination in aid of execution".

At the examination, the debtors must disclose under oath all such information regarding the nature and location of all non-exempt property they own, all sources of income, any property they disposed of before or since entry of the judgment, and their intentions with regard to satisfying the judgment. In certain circumstances, such as situations involving debtors whose whereabouts are not known or who are entirely uncooperative, the court may permit the creditor to orally examine others with information about the debtors, their income, or their assets.

Writs of Possession, Delivery, and Sequestration

Not all judgments are for a sum of money. For instance, the judgment may instead permit the plaintiff to recover from the defendant a parcel of land or an item of personal property. Such judgments are enforced through a writ of possession for land and a writ of delivery for personal property. Each writ directs the property to be delivered to the judgment holder. If a writ of delivery is ignored, the aggrieved party may file a motion for a writ of sequestration, directing the sheriff to take possession of and hold the property until the party complies with the order.

Other Assistance

The court may provide other help to judgment creditors having difficulty enforcing judgments. Courts may issue contempt orders against judgment debtors for non-compliance and other obstructive behaviour, such as hiding or transferring property to others to defraud their creditors. Additionally, specific statutes provide creditors with relief from such wilful behaviour.

Tracing the Proceeds	EXHIBIT 17.3

Suppose Joe owes Moe $100,000. Joe owns a cottage, valued at approximately $200,000, which he transfers to his wife, Roe. Roe sells the cottage to Beau for $200,000 and places the proceeds in her own bank account. If Moe obtains a judgment against Joe in court, provincial legislation allows Moe to unravel the transaction and trace the proceeds of the cottage's sale, originally owned by Joe, to Roe's individual bank account to enforce his judgment against Joe.

Other provincial statutes provide remedies for specific behaviour, such as transferring property to another to defeat creditors' rights. These statutes allow creditors to bring suit against the third party the property was transferred to and recover the asset. A common example is where debtors sell their property to friends or family for very little or no money. Similar relief may permit creditors to trace the proceeds of a fraudulent sale of a debtor's property into the hands of others for recovery. (For an example, see Exhibit 17.3.) Some provincial laws also provide creditors with relief from debtors with insufficient assets to cover all of their debts who choose to pay some creditors and ignore others.

Finally, courts may appoint one or more individuals, called receivers, to help collect and distribute a debtor's assets. The receiver may, for example, collect rent from the tenants in a building the debtor owns or revenue the debtor's business generates.

BANKRUPTCY

Individuals whose income and other assets are not enough to pay their financial obligations as they come due are **insolvent**. At some point following their insolvency, debtors may become **bankrupt** by voluntarily entering or being forced into the process governed by the federal *Bankruptcy and Insolvency Act*.[5] The Act provides a uniform procedure throughout Canada to address both creditors' and debtors' rights. The Act performs three essential functions for society:

- Protects creditors through a framework for fairly distributing a debtor's assets to all creditors.
- Gives debtors a chance to clear their debts and begin with a clean slate.
- Helps debtors and creditors compromise by restructuring all of the debts under court supervision.

Commencing the Proceedings

Consumer bankruptcy proceedings are initiated in one of three ways. First, the debtor may file an assignment in bankruptcy. Here, debtors recognizing the poor state of their financial affairs voluntarily assign their assets to a **trustee** for ultimate distribution to their creditors. The debtor files the assignment and a sworn statement of affairs. Depending on the size of the debtor's estate, the matter may be eligible for summary administration of the estate.

In the second method, an insolvent debtor starts a proceeding in the hope of avoiding bankruptcy by making a proposal to the creditors. Debtors, through

---

[5] R.S.C. 1985, c. B-3 as am. by S.C. 1992, c. 27.

a proposal trustee, offer their creditors a compromise plan for paying their debts. The creditors vote in classes to accept or reject the proposal. If the proposal is accepted by the creditors, it must be approved and supervised by the court. The debtor's later failure to meet the plan's terms may change the matter into a full bankruptcy proceeding. Likewise, the creditors' rejection or the court's disapproval of the plan generally leads to a declaration of bankruptcy.

The third method for commencing consumer bankruptcy proceedings is involuntary. Any of the debtor's creditors with a claim of $1,000 or more, or any group of creditors whose aggregate claims exceed $1,000, may file an application for a bankruptcy order against the debtor. The applicant must demonstrate that the debtor's creditors are not being paid and that the debtor has committed an act of bankruptcy under the Act within the past six months. Acts of bankruptcy cover a wide range of behaviour, including failure to meet liabilities as they come due, attempting to remove or hide property, and defaulting in a proposal to creditors. The debtor is served with notice, and a hearing is scheduled. Debtors wishing to dispute the application may file a response before the hearing date. If the creditors succeed, a bankruptcy order is issued and a trustee takes control of the debtor's assets and administers the bankruptcy.

Administering the Bankruptcy

Whether started voluntarily or involuntarily, proceedings follow a similar course. Immediately, other proceedings that unsecured creditors may have initiated to assert their individual claims against the debtor are frozen (stayed). These creditors must now file and prove their claims with the debtor's trustee instead. Secured creditors, however, generally retain their right to enforce their interest in secured property against the trustee. Debtors immediately lose the capacity to enter into contracts, engage in commercial activity, and deal with their property.

Within a specified number of days, the trustee calls the first meeting of the bankrupt's creditors to address preliminary matters, typically including the creditors' approval of the trustee's appointment, a review of the debtor's sworn statement of assets and liabilities, and the report summarizing the debtor's oral examination, and other matters related to administering the bankrupt's estate. The trustee must collect and sell the debtor's assets, through tender, public auction, or private contract. Strict guidelines mandate how assets are sold. Following disposition of the assets, the trustee distributes the proceeds to the creditors according to a scheme detailed in the Act. Under the scheme, subject to rights of secured creditors, proceeds are distributed in the following order:

1. Cover costs of administering the bankrupt's estate (including any legal fees).
2. Pay preferred creditors, as defined in the Act.
3. Pay ordinary unsecured creditors their *pro rata* shares equally.

The underlying principle appears to treat all unsecured creditors equally. Absent bankruptcy, some of the debtor's creditors may be fully compensated, while others receive nothing. Through bankruptcy, all creditors who have proven their claims with the trustee receive a proportionate share of the available assets. Thus, no general creditor receives full payment, but neither is any left unpaid.

Discharging the Bankrupt

The final phase of the typical consumer bankruptcy is **discharging the bankrupt**, which gives the bankrupt a chance to start fresh, unencumbered by the burden of insurmountable debt. A discharge releases the debtor from liability for most debts remaining after distribution of the assets. In other words, the debts are treated as though paid in full.

Individuals facing a consumer bankruptcy for the first time are entitled to an automatic discharge from bankruptcy within nine months of the proceeding's start. Where no one objects, the discharge is entered either absolutely or with conditions imposed on the debtor.

Sometimes, one or more creditors or the trustee objects to the discharge. In that case, a hearing regarding the circumstances and the bankrupt's behaviour before and throughout the proceedings is held. Hearings also are required for bankrupts not initially entitled to an automatic discharge.

One circumstance that raises the need for a hearing is where the debtor's assets are too low to pay the creditors at least 50 cents on each dollar of debt. At hearing, bankrupts must satisfy the court that they cannot justly be held responsible for this result. Usually misconduct — such as refusing to co-operate during the process, hiding or transferring assets, or engaging in commercial transactions after insolvency — can jeopardize entitlement to a discharge.

Even absolute discharge does not release a bankrupt from certain debts. For example, family obligations, such as alimony and support arrears, remain following discharge. Once discharged, the debtor is neither insolvent nor bankrupt, and regains the capacity to enter into contracts and own and deal with property.

CONSUMER PROTECTION LEGISLATION

To satisfy principles of justice and fairness, the law demonstrates an equal concern for the problems and rights of both debtors and creditors. Faced with the frustration inherent in collecting delinquent debts, creditors sometimes are tempted to use means beyond the bounds of what society considers appropriate. When creditors use legitimate methods excessively or use entirely impermissible approaches, both common and statutory law step in to protect debtors.

Creditors who exert undue pressure on debtors through constant harassment, threats of harm, and other offensive behaviour or who publicly malign debtors could find themselves liable under tort or criminal law. Debtors have successfully sued overzealous creditors for torts, including assault, trespass, defamation, and false imprisonment. Creditors have also faced prosecution for such criminal offences as threats, harassment, extortion, and conspiracy. So, even though creditors may at times need to exert some pressure to inspire payment, they must take care to never cross the line into tortious or criminal misconduct.

In addition to debtors' traditional remedies, Canadian provinces have enacted legislation to protect consumers from unfair business practices and unconscionable collection methods. Generally, these laws are designed to

- ensure that consumers freely enter into contracts they truly intend to be bound by;
- protect consumers from defective, dangerous, and useless products;
- make consumers fully aware of the total costs of their contracts; and
- stop creditors from harassing, threatening, or injuring consumers in the collection process.

Most consumer protection legislation tries to balance consumers' and entrepreneurs' interests along with society's interest in encouraging the continued commercial activity a thriving economy needs. Although a detailed survey of the varied consumer protection laws Canadian provinces have enacted is beyond this chapter's scope, the following highlights a few key concepts.

Recognizing that many consumers might be induced to enter contracts for goods or services based on sellers' inflated representations only to find that their purchases fall disappointingly short, consumer protection laws typically prohibit unfair practices. For example, Ontario's *Consumer Protection Act* considers making any false, misleading, deceptive, or unconscionable representation to be an unfair practice. Below are some examples of false, misleading, or deceptive representations:

- Representing that goods are of a particular standard, quality, grade, style, or model that they do not meet
- Representing that goods will be available or can be delivered at a specific time when it is known or ought to be known that they cannot
- Representing that goods are new or unused if they are not

Representations may be unconscionable when a seller knows or ought to know that, for instance,

- the consumer is not reasonably able to protect himself or herself because of disability, ignorance, illiteracy, or inability to understand the language an agreement is in;
- the price grossly exceeds the price that similar goods and services are available for;
- the transaction is excessively one-sided in favour of the party dealing with the consumer; and
- the consumer is subjected to undue pressure to enter the transaction.

Depending on the jurisdiction, consumers induced to enter a contract as the result of an unfair practice may be able to rescind the contract and pursue any remedy available at law, including monetary damages. If the contract cannot be rescinded under the circumstances, the consumer may be able to recover the amount by which the consumer's payment exceeded the true value of the goods or services delivered, the damages, or both.

Consumer protection legislation also typically regulates specific kinds of sales and contracts where consumers could be susceptible to pressure or caught off guard. For this reason, many provincial consumer protection statutes regulate agreements (i) that are entered into over the telephone or Internet or at locations other than the seller's place of business, or (ii) that involve credit or instalment payments. Additionally, some provincial statutes regulate what may be charged for repairs (to an automobile, for example) after a mechanic or other service provider has given the consumer an estimate of what the job will cost.

A third area provincial legislation regulates is the registration and practices of collection agencies. As noted above, creditors often hire collection agencies to contact their debtors to arrange or obtain payment. Along with licensing and registration requirements, these statutes may create a general regulatory scheme, providing for investigations, hearings, sanctions, fines and even imprisonment. These provincial statutes also regulate collection agencies' operations and conduct. The wide range of behaviour these statutes prohibit includes, for instance,

- using threatening, intimidating, coercive, or profane language;
- calling debtors on holidays and other specified days or times of day (such as early morning or late at night);

- giving false or misleading information to others that might harm the debtor or debtor's family;

- continuing to contact a debtor who has given the name and contact information of the debtor's lawyer and asked that the lawyer be contacted instead; and

- contacting the debtor's employer more than once to obtain employment information, unless the employer guaranteed the debt, the consumer has given written authorization, or a court order or wage assignment has been entered.

Additionally, these laws often establish how frequently collection agencies may contact debtors.

CHAPTER SUMMARY

In this chapter, the reader was introduced to the concept of debt, significant elements in the relationship between debtors and creditors, and the wide range of methods used to collect debts. The chapter described different ways to secure debt and other ways creditors may obtain an advantage in collecting their debts over other creditors' claims.

The reader was introduced to the procedure involved in litigating a creditor's claim against a debtor and the many devices available for enforcing a judgment obtained in court.

The chapter discussed the purpose and effect of bankruptcy proceedings and how the law of bankruptcy seeks to protect the interests of both creditors and debtors. A survey of the main steps involved in the typical consumer bankruptcy was reviewed.

The discussion concluded with a brief look at legislation designed to protect consumers against unfair business practices and unconscionable collection activities.

GLOSSARY OF NEW TERMS AND KEY CONCEPTS

assignee	A person who has been granted a benefit by someone; usually a person granted contract benefits by one of the original contracting parties.
bankrupt	An insolvent person against whom or by whom bankruptcy proceedings are instituted under the federal *Bankruptcy and Insolvency Act*.
collection agency	A business engaged in obtaining and arranging the payment of money owed to another.
conditional sales contracts	A contract where the purchaser obtains delivery of the goods, but does not obtain legal ownership until some or all of the purchase price is paid.
counterclaim	A claim asserted by the defendant against the plaintiff in a legal proceeding.
creditor	A person to whom a debt is owed.
cross-claim	In a legal proceeding by a plaintiff against two or more defendants, a claim by one defendant against a co-defendant.
debt	A sum of money one person owes to another.
debtor	A person who owes a sum of money to another.
default judgment	A court order entered against a defendant who has failed to defend or respond to a legal action instituted in court.

discharge (of a bankrupt)	The release of a person from the legal status of bankruptcy. The person regains the legal capacity to enter into contracts and deal with his or her own property. The discharge may include forgiving unpaid debts.
discovery	The process of gathering and exchanging information relevant to a legal proceeding in preparation for trial. Discovery may include the production of documents and questioning parties orally.
distraint	A landlord's right to take possession and sell a tenant's property found within the leased premises to compensate the landlord for unpaid rent.
garnishment	The process that allows a creditor to collect money from a third party who owes money to the debtor to enforce a court judgment the creditor obtained against the debtor.
general creditor	An unsecured creditor with no priority or special rights; a creditor who has neither taken nor otherwise acquired an interest in the debtors' assets to ensure payment of the debt.
insolvent	In general, one whose income and assets are insufficient to pay obligations as they become due.
interest	The compensation paid to another for the use of borrowed money.
lien	A right to retain possession of property belonging to another to compel payment of a debt. A legal interest in property titled to another.
pleading	A document filed with the court, setting out a party's claim or defence in a legal proceeding.
principal	With respect to lending money, the amount the borrower originally borrowed and actually received.
receiver	A person appointed by a secured creditor or court to collect and hold income generated by assets owned by a party in a legal proceeding.
repossession	An action by the seller on a conditional sale contract or by the lender on a secured loan, where the seller/lender seizes the property that was sold under a conditional sale contract, or given as collateral for a loan.
secured creditor	A creditor who has required the debtor to give collateral in return for extending credit or has otherwise acquired an interest in a debtor's property concerning a debt.
security	A legal interest in real or personal property that a debtor gives to a creditor to ensure payment of the debt. Also known as collateral, the security gives the creditor access to the property if the debt is not paid and priority over other creditors regarding the asset used as collateral.
service	Delivery of a court document to a party in legal proceedings in the manner specified by the Rules of Civil Practice.
summary judgment	An order of the court in favour of a party who can satisfy the court that the case presents no issue of fact for trial or no issue at all.
third-party claim	In legal proceedings, a claim a defendant makes against a person not already a party to the proceedings, regarding the same event or transaction as the plaintiff's main action.
trustee	The individual responsible for administration of a bankrupt's estate, including disposing the bankrupt's assets and distributing the proceeds to the bankrupt's creditors.

REVIEW QUESTIONS

1. Explain some of the reasons a creditor might prefer out-of-court collection methods rather than commencing a court action against a debtor.

2. What is the difference between a secured creditor and a general creditor, and how do their rights differ?

3. What is a construction lien? In response to what dilemma was legislation providing for the construction lien passed?

4. Over what claims does a Small Claims Court have jurisdiction? Outline some of the major differences between litigation of a claim in Small Claims Court and in a formal court.

5. Define "garnishment", and identify the garnishor and the garnishee in these proceedings.

6. What are the main forms of protection provided to the debtor by law with respect to a judgment creditor's enforcement of a court judgment against the debtor?

7. Describe the main purposes and functions of the federal *Bankruptcy and Insolvency Act.*

8. Describe the likely legal obligations of the debtor and creditor in the following cases:

   (a) Lorna brought her watch to Donald's Watch Repairs and asked him to replace the watch strap. Donald told her that a standard watch strap replacement would cost her $25, and Lorna agreed to pay the cost when the repairs were completed. While Donald was repairing the strap, the watch battery died, having run its normal course. So, Donald decided to replace the battery, at an additional cost of $10. Also observing that the watch face was badly scratched to the point that the time could no longer be read easily, he replaced the watch face for an additional $5. When Lorna returned to collect the watch, Donald explained the additional work he had performed and asked for $40.

   (b) Butch bought an ornate and quite expensive pink lawn flamingo from Just Because Designs. Not having sufficient cash on hand to cover the cost, he agreed to pay for the flamingo in 12 monthly instalments. He paid the instalments for a couple of months then fell on hard times. After failing to pay for three months, Butch started to receive repeated letters from Why Not, a collection agency acting on Just Because's behalf. The letters outlined the total amount due and the deadline for payment. When Butch still failed to pay, a representative from Why Not went onto Butch's lawn and seized the flamingo.

   (c) PiggyBank, a very small financial institution, legally repossesses a house from Kermit. Kermit has accrued $100,000 in debt but has regularly paid his mortgage, which was amounting to approximately $45,000, up until the repossession. To repossess the house, PiggyBank spends $10,000. The bank sells the house for $125,000 and spends the $15,000 profit on floor maintenance.

9. Describe the main issues that might arise for creditors in the following situations:

   (a) A landlord wants to take possession of a leased property because the tenant has stopped paying the rent.

   (b) An unsecured creditor's debtor goes bankrupt.

DISCUSSION QUESTIONS

1. Billy Bob sues Buster in court for non-payment of a debt and obtains a judgment of $5,000. After the expiration of the appeal period, Billy Bob decides to enforce the judgment against Buster. Buster owns a fully paid boat, a stereo system, a valuable coin collection, and a cottage, all in the same location. He is currently employed by the Big Bang Balloon Company. How might Billy Bob go about enforcing his judgment?

2. Allard purchases an automobile from Zoey's Autorama for $7,000. He gives Zoey a down payment of $5,000, and agrees to pay the remaining balance in monthly instalments of $100. Allard and Zoey sign a standard conditional sale contract, which includes a clause permitting Zoey to repossess and sell the automobile in the event of Allard's default in payment. With three instalments remaining, Allard misses one monthly payment. In response, Zoey goes to Allard's home at 4:00 a.m. to repossess the automobile, which is parked in Allard's garage. The garage door is open, so Zoey enters. However, Allard, hearing a noise, goes to the garage and shouts, "Stop! Thief!" Zoey shoves him aside, jumps into the car, and drives away. Discuss the issues raised by the above and the likely outcome of those issues.

3. Chet takes his motorcycle to Freda's garage for repairs. Freda makes the needed repairs, then calls Chet to tell him that the motorcycle is ready to be picked up and that he owes her $600. Chet arrives at the shop and says, "I'm here to pick up my bike, but I can't pay you for a couple of months because I just got fired." What may Freda do?

4. Penny rents an apartment from Bill under a one-year lease. Penny fails to pay the rent for four months. Frustrated, Bill notifies Penny that he is terminating the lease and commences the process of evicting Penny. In the meantime, Bill takes possession of the property in Penny's apartment, including a stereo system and table Penny borrowed from her friend Guy. When Penny and Guy ask Bill to return the seized items, Bill states that he will return the property as soon as Penny pays the four months' back rent she owes. Discuss the issues raised by the problem.

5. Given that a secured creditor has far greater rights than a general creditor, why would a creditor ever choose to enter into an unsecured transaction?

6. Analyze the following situations and discuss whether bankruptcy is appropriate and, if not, what other options the creditor may consider pursui.ng

   (a) Amanda has accrued $900 in debt through various transactions. It has been over a year since her creditors have received payments, and they are tiring of her excuses. In the past year, Amanda has contracted an illness that has kept her from working, and her medical costs are mounting.

   (b) Aneesh, a freelance writer, is having a hard time paying all of his debts. He creates a proposal to repay the $1500 he owes over an extended period of time, which the creditors accept without assistance from the courts. After six months, he defaults on one of these payments. The creditors then demand he file for bankruptcy.

SUGGESTED READING AND OTHER RESOURCES

Bankruptcy and Insolvency Act, R.S.C. 1985, c. B-3, as am. 1985 (1st Supp.), c. 27.

Bennett, Frank. *Bennett on Bankruptcy*, 14th ed. (Toronto: CCH Canada Ltd. 2012).

———. *Bennett on Collections*, 5th ed. (Toronto: Carswell, 2003).

Collection Agencies Act, R.S.O. 1990, c. C-14.

Consumer Protection Act, 2002, S.O. 2002, c. 30, Sched. A.

Olivo, L.M., and DeeAnn Gonsalves, *Debtor-Creditor Law and Procedure*, 4th ed. (Toronto: Emond Montgomery Publications, 2011).

Olivo, L.M., and DeeAnn Gonsalves, *Small Claims Court Practice and Procedure in Ontario* (Concord, Ont.: Captus Press Inc., 2011).

WEBSITES

CanLII: <http://www.canlii.org/en/index.html>

Credit Institute of Canada: <http://www.creditedu.org/RESOURCES/newsletters/news-letter_summer_12/index.html>

Justice Law Website: <http://laws-lois.justice.gc.ca/eng/> (See also provincial ministries of attorney general websites.)

The Law Dictionary: <http://thelawdictionary.org/>

Office of the Superintendent of Bankruptcy Canada: <http://www.ic.gc.ca/eic/site/bsf-osb.nsf/eng/home>

Employment Law

Michael Mac Neil
CARLETON UNIVERSITY

Learning Objectives

After reading this chapter, the reader should be able to:

➢ identify different legal devices regulating the employer–employee relationship

➢ compare some of the advantages and disadvantages of each of the regulating devices

➢ identify rights of workers and employers in the employment relationship

➢ understand the interaction between contracts, statutes, and collective bargaining in defining employment rights and obligations

➢ know some of the institutions from which a worker can obtain assistance in claiming their rights

TABLE OF CONTENTS

GOVERNING THE WORKPLACE

Every society organizes systems for producing the goods and services it needs. In many non-industrialized societies, individuals or families are responsible for looking after most of their own needs, including the growing or hunting of food, the building of shelter, and the supplying of other necessities. In more complex societies, a division of labour occurs. People specialize in specific tasks, and sell their products or services to others, using either a barter or a money-payment system. This allows the specialists to acquire the necessities or luxury goods that they are not able to produce for themselves. In modern industrial societies, even more specialization occurs, and many goods or services are produced by large corporate or governmental entities, who hire workers to provide their labour for a wage payment and to work under the direction of persons responsible for the management of the workplace. This sale of labour for wages is the central feature of an **employment relationship**, and is the primary means by which most people in our society can expect to provide for their wants and needs.

A 2012 report of the Law Commission of Ontario notes that, for many, the nature of employment is evolving. We are moving from a standard employment model, in which workers are employed full-time in continuous employment with access to good wages and benefits, to more precarious forms of employment with vulnerable workers "whose work is characterized by low wages or insufficient hours of work, few or no benefits, little job security and minimal control over their work conditions. They are disproportionately women, immigrants (both newcomers and those established in Canada) or racialized persons."

Given the extent and importance of employment relationships in our society, it is not surprising that they are regulated by law. There are three main sources of regulation: contract, statute, and collective bargaining.

The Contract of Employment

The employment relationship is regarded as a contractual one. Individuals are not forced to work against their will. To do so would be to impose a form of slavery upon them. The law assumes that people voluntarily agree to work for others, and the voluntariness is not undermined by the fact that people have to work to acquire the wages they need to pay for wants and necessities. Thinking of the employment relationship as a contractual one has a number of consequences.

Formalities
In order to determine if there is an employment contract, one must ensure that the formalities for entering a contract have been complied with:

- offer of employment
- acceptance
- **consideration** moving forward from both parties
- sufficient certainty

Contracts in Writing
The contract need not be in writing, unless it is for a period of more than one year. In many employment contracts, no definite period of employment is expressed, and such contracts need not be in writing.

Enforcement of Contracts
The general rules of contract law apply with respect to the interpretation and enforcement of the employment contract, although the courts also

acknowledge the special nature of the employment relationship given the importance of work and the inequality of bargaining power that typically exists between employers and employees. This means, for instance, that a worker who claims that the employer has wrongfully terminated the contract by firing her is not normally entitled to reinstatement as a remedy, but is only entitled to damages for the wrongful dismissal.

Implied Terms

Where the contract is silent on an issue, as informal and even written contracts of employment sometimes are, the court will nevertheless find that certain rights and obligations are implied terms of the contract. For instance, there is an implied duty of loyalty placed on employees, and an implied duty on an employer to give reasonable notice before dismissing an employee, if the contract is of indefinite duration and does not explicitly set out the notice period. However, an express term in the contract will override a term that would otherwise have been implied, as long as it does not contravene a statutory standard.

One of the problems with thinking of the employment relationship as contractual is that one tends to lose sight of the fact that the contracting parties are not equal. In many situations, the employee does not bargain about the terms of the employment relationship, but instead takes or leaves the package that the employer offers. Thus, the employer sets the wage rate, and may include a variety of express terms in the contract that may limit the rights that employees might otherwise expect to obtain, such as the length of notice to which they are entitled before being laid off, or restrictions on taking a job with a competitor of the present employer.

Statutes

For many reasons, legislatures have enacted statutes that regulate the employment relationship. One reason is a concern that the inequality of bargaining power that exists between employers and employees often leads to contracts that are unfair. Hence, these statutes set out rights and obligations that apply, despite what a contract may say. These statutory interventions deal with many aspects of the employment relationship, including minimum terms and conditions of employment, occupational health and safety, discrimination in employment, workers' compensation for job-related illnesses and injury, unemployment insurance, and pension plans. More details on many of these statutes are provided in the discussion of employer and employee obligations.

Collective Bargaining

In Canada, **freedom of association** is regarded as a fundamental right. This means, in the context of employment, that employees in most workplaces have the right to form a union, and to demand that the union represent them in bargaining with the employer. Workers often decide to join together in such a fashion, at least in part, because they believe they are more likely to make a better deal with the employer through collective action than by having each worker enter into individual employment contracts. Legislation has been enacted by each province and by the federal government that provides a mechanism by which a trade union can obtain **certification** as the bargaining representative of employees.

Once a union has been certified, the employer is required to **bargain in good faith** with the union, and no longer to bargain individually with employees. The legislation protects workers who engage in union activity by prohibiting employers from discriminating against or firing workers because they are engaged in such activity. As well, employers are prohibited from interfering with the activities of the trade union. These **unfair labour practices** give meaning to the concept of freedom of association.

If the union and the employer are successful in making a collective agreement, that agreement is binding for all employees in the bargaining unit, whether they agree with it or not. Some people have described the effect of a collective agreement as being similar to legislation, in that it sets out the rules to which the citizens (i.e., the workers) of the workplace are bound. The collective agreement typically deals with such issues as wages, job classifications, promotions, seniority, fringe benefits, etc. The agreement often contains a union security clause, which ensures financial security for the union, and may even make it a condition of employment that employees be members of the union. The collective agreement also must contain a clause providing that disagreements about the interpretation and application of the collective agreement shall be settled by **grievance or rights arbitration.**

If the parties are not successful in making a collective agreement, then the general approach of labour legislation in Canada, especially in the private sector, is to allow the parties to engage in strikes or lockouts as means of trying to force the other side to capitulate. A variety of conditions must be met before a strike can occur, but once those conditions are met, workers are free to withdraw their labour and to set up picket lines seeking support. The government, however, does seek to help prevent such strikes, or to bring them to an end, by providing conciliation and mediation services. Furthermore, picketing is stringently regulated. For many public-sector workers, although certainly not all, striking is prohibited, and the parties are required to submit their dispute to **interest arbitration**. As well, the government sometimes will decide that a strike, which is permitted by the statutes, is nevertheless causing too much harm to the public interest, and will enact an ad hoc statute requiring the strike to end, and usually providing for binding arbitration.

It is important to understand the interrelationship between collective bargaining and the other modes of regulating the employment relationship. A collective agreement displaces individual contracts of employment so that in a unionized workplace, an individual employee is not entitled to enter into an individual contract of employment. If such an employee is fired, for example, he would not be able to commence an action for wrongful dismissal in court, but must rely on the grievance/arbitration mechanism set out in the collective agreement to obtain a remedy. However, many statutory provisions regulating the workplace also apply to unionized workers. Hence, individual workers, or the union acting on their behalf, can make complaints that a statute has been violated. Some statutes, such as occupational health and safety laws and employment equity laws, actually provide a role for the union, where one exists, on committees and in other aspects of the enforcement of the statutes.

THE EMPLOYMENT RELATIONSHIP

Forming the Employment Relationship

Although employment is a dominant means of organizing the performance of work in our society, it is not the only means. Roughly 15 percent of Ontario workers are self-employed and regarded at law as **independent contractors** rather than employees, selling their services to others. It is often necessary to distinguish between employees and independent contractors because many statutes apply only to employees, not to independent contractors. For instance, an independent contractor is not entitled to minimum protection guaranteed by the *Employment Standards Act*, nor must deductions be made from his/her pay

---

Who Is an Employee?

The manager of a convenience store makes a claim under the *Employment Standards Act*. To do so, she must establish that she is an employee for the purposes of the Act. The contract signed by the manager specifically states that the manager is not an employee but, rather, an independent contractor. The evidence establishes the following:

1. All stock handled by the manager remains the property of the company. A daily allowance is made for breakage or pilferage of the inventory, but any shrinkage beyond this amount is the responsibility of the manager. However, if a break-in occurred, the manager would not be responsible for what was stolen.

2. The manager is required to put up a performance bond, and any default in the contract by the manager, including quitting without notice, will allow the store to recover the full amount of the bond as liquidated damages for loss of profits and goodwill.

3. The company maintains ownership of the premises, all fixtures and merchandise. It holds the insurance policy on all assets. It supplies the shirts and aprons worn by the manager and provides laundering at its expense.

4. The manager has discretion to determine hours of work, is free to hire others to assist her, and has discretion in the ordering of goods. However, the manager is required to devote her whole time to the business, and is not permitted to engage in another. Any wages paid to the assistants are made by the company, but are deducted from the amounts otherwise payable to the manager. The company regularly monitors these additional employees, provides them with uniforms, and pays for laundry. The manager can only order inventory from suppliers designated by the company.

5. A clause in the contract allows the contract to be terminated at any time, with or without cause.

On the basis of these factors, an adjudicator concluded that the store manager was, indeed, an employee for the purposes of the *Employment Standards Act*, rather than an independent contractor. Do you agree?

---

for unemployment insurance. This may be a particular problem for precarious workers whose earnings are low, who have little job security and few benefits.

At common law, there were a number of terms used to describe the employment relationship. It was once common to call it a master–servant relationship, and even today one can find the use of such language. Another term used to distinguish an employment contract from one made with an independent contractor is to call the former a contract of service, and the latter a contract for services. There is no single test for determining whether a person is an employee or an independent contractor. The most important factor that the courts will examine is the extent to which the employer is able to control the work being done. If the employer can specify the work and how it is to be done, it is more likely that the person performing the work is an employee.

However, the issue of control does not always determine the issue. For example, a doctor may be employed by a hospital or clinic, but when it comes to the treating of patients, very little control would be exerted by the employer. Hence, it is necessary to look at other factors as well, such as who owns the tools, who bears the risk of making a profit or loss, and where the work is being performed. Another way of thinking about it is to ask, "Whose business is it?" Is the person carrying on business for himself, or is he working for somebody else? Another way of attempting to answer the question is to ask whether the worker is part of the employer's business — i.e., whether she is functionally integrated into the employer's operations. Still another test looks at the economic realities of the relationship.

In all of these tests, it is often a matter of weighing conflicting elements in order to determine the outcome. Even where a contract explicitly states that a person is not an employee, when one looks at all the elements of the relationship, it may still be possible to conclude that it really is an employment one.

The issue is becoming more problematic these days because employers are often seeking the greater flexibility and, sometimes, lesser costs that can be achieved by using contractors. With the growing emphasis on knowledge-based jobs, with less need for production-line work, and with the use of computers and modems at home, the issue of what constitutes an employee is a challenging one.

Employers' Obligations

In the individual employment relationship, the obligations owed by the employer to the employee arise from three sources. First are the express contractual provisions. For example, the duty to pay wages for work done is normally a contractual one, although employment standards legislation now typically stipulates that at least a minimum wage must be paid. The second major source of obligations is the various statutes described above. They impose a wide variety of obligations on employers and create rights for employees, as well as creating institutional mechanisms by which those rights can be enforced. A third source of obligations arises from terms in the employment contract implied by the courts. These terms are sometimes meant to fill in gaps where the parties have failed to specify necessary terms, and are sometimes a means of incorporating customary practices into the legal framework. A discussion of some of the employer's most important obligations follows.

Payment of Wages

All Canadian provinces and territories impose a minimum wage requirement. As of July 2014, Ontario and Nunavut have a general minimum wage of $11.00 per hour. The remaining provinces and territories have general minimum wages set between $10.00 and $10.72 per hour. There are a number of reasons governments have introduced minimum wages: to help combat poverty, prevent exploitation of workers, and further equality goals. However, minimum wages have been criticized as distorting labour markets and causing employers to invest more in labour-saving devices, thus causing higher levels of unemployment. In practice, minimum wage levels are rarely high enough to ensure that a family would be able to live above the poverty level on the minimum wages of a single wage earner. As well, minimum wage schedules often provide for a lower minimum wage level for youths, and for employees who receive tips, such as waiters and bartenders.

Some employees believe that it is unfair that employers may make deductions from their wages. In Ontario, a regulation pursuant to the *Employment Standards Act* stipulates that no deductions may be made from wages unless required by statute or a court order, or if a written authorization by the employee so permits. Even with a written authorization, the employer may not make deductions for faulty workmanship, loss of property, or cash shortages if another person, other than the employee, has access to the cash or property.

The biggest pay-related problem for workers arises from the fact that the employee is, in effect, a creditor of the employer. An employee does not typically get paid until after the work has been done. For a variety of reasons, an employer may refuse, or be unable to pay, the wages owed. As a creditor, the employee has a number of avenues that can be followed, such as bringing an action in court; but typically, these are unsatisfactory because of the expense and delay involved. For that reason, it is common for employment standards legislation to create special mechanisms for the collection of wages owed. Where the employer has become insolvent or bankrupt, in the absence of statutory protection, workers would merely rank as unsecured creditors. This means that, after all the secured creditors have seized all the assets, they would not be very likely to recover any or a substantial portion of the payments owed to them. Some employment standards Acts seek to alleviate this problem to some extent by treating the claims of employees as if they were secured interests, thereby allowing employees to rank ahead of unsecured creditors. Another means of increasing the likelihood of employees receiving their wages is to make the directors of a company personally liable for wages in the event that the company fails to pay. However, even this protection is not likely to guarantee the payment of all wages owed. For that reason, the federal government has established a wage earner protection program that will pay a portion of wages owing to eligible employees, up to a maximum of four weeks of insurable Employment Insurance earnings ($3,738 in 2014), where the employer has become insolvent.

Employment Standards

Employment standards legislation typically covers a wide variety of issues. As already mentioned, it provides for minimum wages and mechanisms for the collection of wages owed. It also provides for minimum standards for such issues as vacations, overtime work and pay, fringe benefits, notice of termination, parental leave, etc. The exact details of these statutory provisions vary from province to province; but normally these standards are minimums, which means that the parties to the employment contract may negotiate terms that are better for the employee, but may not include contract terms that provide for less than these minimums. Any contractual term that provided for lesser benefits would not be enforced. In some jurisdictions, a union can agree in a collective agreement to provisions that may not be as good as certain statutory standards, and some statutory provisions may not apply at all to any employee covered by a collective agreement. Moreover, there any many categories of employees exempted from specific standards, making the scheme complex and inconsistent.

Not only do the statutes provide substantive rights, they also often create special mechanisms for the enforcement of these rights. Rather than requiring employees to go to court to collect wages owed or to obtain other remedies for violation of the statute, a special process will be established for receiving and dealing with employee complaints. In Ontario, for example, a complaint may be made to the Ministry of Labour. An employment standards officer is typically appointed to investigate the complaint, and if she finds that it is warranted, she may make an order requiring the employer to comply with the Act. An order, or the refusal to make an order, can be reviewed by the Labour Relations Board, whose decision can be reviewed by a court. Employees covered by collective agreements, however, must file a grievance and use the dispute resolution process created by the collective agreement. They are not entitled to file a complaint with the Ministry of Labour.

One of the problems with employment standards legislation is that it often fails to provide swift relief to employees. There may be insufficient resources allocated to the enforcement of the statute, so there may be considerable delays in obtaining any sums that are owed. The emphasis on individual complaints has been criticized as a sub-optimal means of enforcement, with critics suggesting that proactive inspections are likely to be more effective.

Healthy and Safe Working Environment

One of the ongoing problems facing workers is the hazards to which they are exposed in the workplace. Every year, thousands of workers are injured on the job, many are affected by illnesses that can be linked to workplace conditions, and many die. The law has a role to play both in attempting to reduce the level of workplace injuries and illnesses, and in providing compensation to those who would otherwise lose income as a result of these illnesses and accidents.

At common law, employers were required to provide workers with safe tools, a safe system of work, and fellow workers who did not carelessly endanger them. However, the common law duty has largely been made irrelevant by the introduction of statutory regimes imposing a wide range of requirements on employers to ensure that workplaces are healthy and safe. As well, workers' compensation statutes provide a means of ensuring income security to injured workers, while simultaneously providing incentives for employers to make investments that will ensure a safer workplace.

Occupational health and safety statutes use a number of devices to protect workers:

1. *General performance standards.* These impose obligations on employers and employees alike, similar to those that existed at common law, to take reasonable steps to ensure the health and safety of the workplace. These provisions are enforced by inspectors, and by the possibility of prosecution, which normally takes place only if a serious accident has occurred.

2. *Set specific standards.* These may include the wearing of protective equipment, the guarding of dangerous equipment, the reduction of toxic substances in the workplace, etc. These standards can be enforced by inspectors who have the authority to order an employer to comply, failing which fines may be imposed, or the employer's operations shut down until compliance is achieved.

3. *Joint responsibility.* Employers and employees are required to co-operate on committees that investigate and come up with plans for making the workplace safer.

4. *Right to refuse unsafe work.* Employees are given the right to look after their own interests by refusing to perform work that they believe is unsafe. There may be disagreements about whether work is actually unsafe, so processes are normally established by which an inspector can be called in to assess the situation. To make the right effective, an employee who reasonably refuses unsafe work must be protected from discipline or dismissal by the employer.

5. *Providing information.* One means of ensuring that workers act in a safe manner and take steps to protect themselves is to ensure that they are informed about the hazards in the workplace, and the best means of dealing with those hazards. Occupational health and safety statutes now provide for a system called **WHMIS (Workplace Hazardous Materials Information System)**, in which manufacturers of hazardous products are required to label their products and provide information about the hazards. Employers, in turn, are required to train workers in the identification and handling of hazardous products.

6. *Requiring employers to implement specific policies.* Employers in Ontario have been required to implement specific programs or policies designed to prevent workplace harassment and violence. Employers are expected

to identify risks and establish measures to control risks, as well as provide mechanisms for investigating complaints.

None of these measures ensures that workers will not be injured on the job, and they have often been criticized for their inadequacies. For instance, prosecution is often not an effective deterrent, in part because few contraventions of the Act are prosecuted, convictions are difficult to obtain, and the level of fines in the past has not been large enough to be a major deterrent. The inspection system has been criticized because of low levels of staffing, a traditional reluctance of inspectors to be confrontational, and because of the difficulty of having an outsider impose the best solutions on a particular workplace. The setting of standards has been problematic, with standards set at such levels that workers continue to be exposed to risks, and to bear the uncertainties where scientific evidence has not yet established clear causal links between toxic substances and workplace diseases. Internal responsibility systems have not been as effective as they may have been, in part because of the failure to actually establish them as required in some workplaces, as well as the lack of training for committee members, inadequate communication in the workplace, and failure to give the health and safety committee any real powers to make changes in the workplace.

Workers' Compensation

Given that workers continue to be injured, some system must be in place to provide compensation for injured workers. **Workers' compensation** statutes were introduced early in the 20th century in recognition of the inadequacies of the common law system. At common law, an employee had to prove that an employer was negligent in order to establish a claim, and a variety of defences were available to employers that made it difficult for workers to succeed. Under the workers' compensation Acts, the right of workers to sue their employer in court was taken away, in exchange for a guarantee of a right to compensation for a workplace-related illness or accident, without having to prove that the employer was at fault. Over the years, the levels of benefits have changed, but the system has remained relatively stable.

The payments to workers are funded by premiums paid by the employer. These premiums reflect the level of claims made by workers in that particular industry and may also include a factor that measures the safety record of the individual employer (**experience rating**). The use of individualized experience rating is designed to encourage employers to invest more in safety. The danger is that it may cause an employer to pressure workers not to report compensable injuries.

There are several aspects of workers' compensation schemes worth mentioning:

1. *Not all employees are covered by the legislation.* Typical exclusions include homework, funeral work, taxidermy, veterinary work, education, photography, etc. One must consult the legislation and regulations in each province to determine who is and who is not covered.

2. *No compensation will be paid unless the disease or accident arises out of and in the course of employment.* It will often be difficult to pinpoint the cause of a worker's illness, and there is often considerable litigation about whether a worker's absence is caused by an injury or disease that arose out of, and in the course of, employment. This is particularly problematic with respect to diseases that may have long incubation periods, and the best one can demonstrate is a probability that there is a connection between workplace exposure to a toxic substance and the disease.

3. *The heads and quantum of compensation are determined by the legislation.* There are four main categories of benefits: death, total disability, permanent partial disability, and temporary. As well, medical expenses and costs of rehabilitation are normally covered. Workers usually obtain only a percentage of lost wages, ranging from 75 to 90 percent, with an upper cap on the wages that will be covered. This is, in part, designed to discourage workers who are able to work from malingering.

4. *A complex administrative system is established to administer workers' compensation statutes.* In Ontario, the Workplace Safety and Insurance Board and its employees make decisions about whether an injury is compensable, the level of compensation, the level of premiums to be levied, etc. There is typically some process by which initial decisions can be appealed.

Anti-Discrimination Legislation

Discrimination in employment is generally prohibited by human rights statutes. This means that employers are generally prohibited from discriminating on named grounds, both in making decisions about whom to employ, and with respect to terms and conditions of employment. The grounds of prohibited discrimination have increased over the years. Ontario, for example, now prohibits discrimination on the following grounds: race, ancestry, place of origin, colour, ethnic origin, citizenship, creed, sex, sexual orientation, age, record of offences, marital status, family status, and handicap. In 2012, it added gender identity and gender expression as prohibited grounds of discrimination.

Human rights norms clearly evolve over time. For example, many jurisdictions commonly defined "age" in their human rights statutes so as to allow employers to engage in a policy of mandatory retirement at the age of 65. The Supreme Court of Canada held that defining "age" in this way did not violate the equality guarantee in section 15 of the *Charter of Rights and Freedoms*, at least as applied to university professors. However, with changing demographics, many governments now wish to encourage workers to work for longer periods, and so many provinces, such as Ontario and British Columbia that used to permit mandatory retirement no longer do so.

Another example of emerging human rights norms can be found in relation to the prohibition of discrimination on the basis of family and marital status. Again, because of changing demographics, as well as due to increased participation of women in the workforce, and because of greater commitment of fathers to family responsibilities, employers are being asked to accommodate family responsibilities, especially child care arrangements. Courts, arbitrators and human rights tribunals are struggling to determine the extent of employers' duties in this area.

The prohibition on discrimination means that an employer may not ask certain kinds of questions when hiring people. For instance, questions about race, marital status, ethnic origin, etc. would normally not be permitted, unless the employer can demonstrate that questions relate to a ground of discrimination that is not prohibited by the statute.

Proving that discrimination in hiring has occurred is often very difficult. In the absence of a direct statement made by the employer, the most that the individual can do is establish a *prima facie* case by showing that they applied for the job, were qualified for the job, did not get the job, and either that the job has not been filled or that it has been filled by someone who is not a member of the same class listed in the statute. In that event, the onus would then be placed on the employer to provide a credible explanation of how the decision was made without any discriminatory intent.

EXHIBIT 18.2

Firefighters, Aerobic Capacity and Indirect Discrimination

In 1994, the government of British Columbia introduced a set of standards to ensure the ability of their employees engaged in fighting forest fires to perform their jobs safely and efficiently. Meiorin, a female, had been hired three years earlier, and had been found to be a satisfactory employee. However, of the four tests she was required to complete, she was unable to meet the standard for one designed to test aerobic capacity. She took 11 minutes, 49.4 seconds to run a designated distance — the standard required that she be able to do it in 11 minutes. As a result of her failure to meet the standard, she was dismissed. Her union filed a grievance on her behalf, arguing that the standard was discriminatory.

The Supreme Court of Canada accepted evidence that, owing to physiological differences, most women have lower aerobic capacity than men, and that most women, even with training, could not increase their aerobic capacity to the level required by the standard. This meant that the standard, on its face, had a discriminatory impact, with the consequence that the employer had to demonstrate that it was a b.f.o.r. The Court accepted that the standard was adopted for a purpose rationally connected to the performance of the job — namely, to ensure safety and efficiency. It also accepted that the standard was adopted in good faith. However, it rejected the claim that the standard was reasonably necessary to ensure safe and efficient performance of the job. Part of the problem was that the employer was not able to show that the process by which the standard was developed took sufficient account of the differing aerobic capacities of men and women and, therefore, was unable to show that the standard did not discriminate unnecessarily on the basis of sex. Furthermore, the employer failed to demonstrate that it could not accommodate Meiorin without undue hardship, given the evidence that she had been performing the job satisfactorily for three years without imposing any safety risks on herself, her colleagues or the general public.

As a result, the employer was ordered to reinstate Meiorin to her position as a firefighter, and to compensate her for her losses flowing from her dismissal.

Source: *British Columbia (Public Service Employee Relations Commission) v. BCGSEU (Meiorin)*, [1999] 3 S.C.R. 3.

It is not, however, necessary to demonstrate that an employer had the intention to discriminate, if it can be shown that the effect of an employer's policy is to discriminate. For an employer to demonstrate the acceptability of a rule or standard that either directly discriminates or has an adverse impact on a identifiable group, it can show that the rule is a *bona fide* **occupational requirement (b.f.o.r.)**. The Supreme Court of Canada has held that the employer must show: "1) that the employer adopted the standard for a purpose rationally connected to the performance of the job; 2) that the employer adopted the particular standard in an honest and good faith belief that it was necessary for that legitimate work-related purpose; and 3) that the standard is reasonably necessary to the accomplishment of that legitimate work-related purpose." To demonstrate the last point, the employer must show "that it is impossible to accommodate individual employees sharing the characteristic of the employee without imposing undue hardship on the employer" (**reasonable accommodation**).

Another discrimination issue of which both employers and employees should be aware is **harassment**. Harassment can occur on any of the prohibited grounds of discrimination, but the one that has received the most attention is harassment on the basis of sex and race. Harassment can take several forms. One form, sometimes referred to as **poisoned environment** harassment, involves a course of vexatious conduct or comment that is known, or that ought reasonably to be known, to be unwelcome. This might involve sexual or racial slurs, propositioning, etc. A second form, applicable primarily to sexual harassment, is sometimes called **quid pro quo harassment**. It involves a sexual solicitation or advance made by a person in a position to confer or deny a benefit or advancement, where it is known or ought reasonably to be known that the solicitation or advance is unwelcome. It also includes reprisals, or threats of reprisals, where such a solicitation or advance is rejected.

Harassment can be engaged in by managers towards the workers for whom they are responsible or by co-workers, or it can arise between customers and employees. The employer has an affirmative duty to prevent such harassment, and there is a growing trend towards requiring the establishment of sexual harassment policies, through which workers are clearly informed about prohibited conduct, and that provide mechanisms through which complaints about such conduct can be adequately investigated and remedied if it is found that there has been harassment.

If a person is unable to obtain a satisfactory resolution of a complaint of discrimination or harassment through the employer, a formal complaint can be made to a human rights commission or directly to a human rights tribunal. In jurisdictions where the complaint is to a commission, it will normally investigate the complaint and will often try to mediate a settlement. If that is not successful, the commission then can refer the complaint to a board of inquiry or tribunal, which will conduct a hearing and make a binding decision. In some jurisdictions, like Ontario or British Columbia, the complainant brings the matter directly to the tribunal without any investigation or vetting of the complaint by a human rights commission. In some jurisdictions, the commission may represent the complainant at a hearing, thus relieving the individual of the expense of self-representation; although in practice, complainants sometimes choose to have their own independent representation. However, complainants in Ontario and British Columbia are responsible for their own representation, perhaps assisted by a publicly funded law clinic. An alternative avenue of redress is open to employees covered by a collective agreement. They can file a grievance, and arbitrators in many jurisdictions have been granted the authority to interpret and enforce human rights statutes.

There are many criticisms of the human rights system. In particular, it has been noted that despite the existence of human rights commissions for some time, there is substantial evidence of under-representation of women, visible minorities, and the disabled in many workplaces. As well, there is considerable evidence demonstrating that women's work is under-valued in terms of remuneration. The traditional human rights statutes have not adequately addressed systemic forms of discrimination, and this is now leading, in some jurisdictions, to new forms of legislation that attempt to address problems of pay and employment equity.

Pay Equity

There is considerable evidence to demonstrate that women are under-paid compared to men. There are a number of reasons why this might occur, including lower educational attainment of women, their frequent absences from the workforce because of parental and familial obligations, working shorter hours, etc. However, even when these factors are taken into account, studies show there is a significant portion of the differences in pay that can only be accounted for by discrimination. This discrimination may take the form of segregating women in lower-paying jobs, and under-valuing the worth of their work.

There have been several traditional legal responses to this form of discrimination in employment standards and human rights statutes. The first was to impose a requirement of **equal pay for equal work**. This required that if a man and a woman, working for the same employer, were doing the same job, they should be paid the same. The requirement of equal work meant that the two jobs had to be substantially the same before they could be compared. For instance, a nurse's aide and a nurse's orderly have been held to be performing the same work. A comparison of this kind allows protection against the most overt forms of discrimination, but it does little to deal with the problems of occupational segregation and under-valuing of women's work.

The second response was to require **equal pay for work of equal value**. Under this standard, rather than comparing two jobs, one compares the value of the jobs being performed. Value is normally determined by looking at a composite of skill, effort, responsibility, and the conditions under which the job is being performed. This allows for the comparison of jobs, say that of a gardener and a secretary, even though the two jobs are not the same. However, the mechanisms for the implementation of equal pay for equal value have often been inadequate, relying on individual complaints, which for various reasons are often not made.

Pay equity statutes have been the most recent attempt in some jurisdictions to deal with the problem of pay inequality. The organizing concept continues to be equal pay for work of equal value, but the process by which it is achieved is substantially different. A positive obligation is placed on employers to achieve pay equity by preparing a pay equity plan. To do so, the employer must systematically compare female and male job classes to determine whether pay equity exists. This requires a classification of jobs into male and female classes, an evaluation of the value of those job classes, and a comparison of pay rates for those classes. If this process of evaluation demonstrates that pay inequities exist, the employer is required to rectify the pay inequities within a specified time period. The pay equity statutes in most jurisdictions apply only to public sector workers, except in Ontario, where private sector employers with more than 100 employees are required to develop a pay equity plan.

Despite these developments, a number of questions must be asked. One is how one deals with the problem when there is no male job class to which a female job class can be compared. Another is to ask whether one should concentrate on only the wage element of discrimination, or whether one should also focus on the factors that cause occupational segregation. This might involve emphasizing the education of women for jobs that have not been traditionally regarded as women's work, and the use of affirmative action strategies to overcome job segregation.

Employment Equity

It is widely acknowledged that discrimination is sometimes systemic in nature, and many argue that systemic remedies and more proactive strategies are required to eliminate these forms of discrimination. Systemic discrimination is often identified by the under-representation of certain groups of employees in particular workplaces or particular occupations. For example, if there is evidence that five per cent of all job applicants have disabilities, but evidence shows that less than one per cent of workers in a particular workplace have a disability, then one might want to look more closely to determine if this under-representation is the result of systemic forms of discrimination. There have been several human rights cases where employers have been ordered to engage in a thorough review of their hiring and promotion policies in order to identify and eliminate barriers to employment of women and visible minorities. In addition, the federal government has enacted **employment equity** legislation, imposing obligations on federally regulated employers to take steps to achieve more equitable representation of certain designated, traditionally under-represented groups — namely, women, Aboriginal people, visible minorities and disabled workers. Ontario had a similar statute in effect for several years, but it was repealed in 1996. A much more limited statute, applying to public sector employers and confined to removing access barriers for persons with disabilities, was enacted in Ontario in 2001.

Under the federal *Employment Equity Act*, the employer is required to collect workforce data that will enable it to determine the representation of the designated groups in various occupations. The employer is then expected to assess the extent to which designated groups are under-represented in all occupational categories. Next, the employer is expected to review its employment systems to determine what barriers, if any, might be contributing to the under-representation of designated groups. The employer should then, in consultation with employees and any unions representing its employees, develop plans to eliminate these barriers, and to accommodate members of under-represented designated groups. Normally, the employer will be required to establish hiring and promotion targets, as well as representation targets, and to put in place positive programs that will help to achieve these targets.

The *Employment Equity Act* is a controversial statute. While there may be a fairly general consensus about the goal of eliminating discrimination in our society, there is considerable disagreement about the means by which it should be achieved. Proponents of the statute argue that previous attempts to deal with the problem through human rights statutes have failed, as is evidenced by the continuing under-representation of the designated groups in many workplaces, occupational categories and levels. Opponents of the statute claim that the imposition of numerical goals amounts to a form of reverse discrimination and is antithetical to the norms of equality before the law and equal opportunity, which they claim are part of our socio-legal heritage. They argue that more qualified members of non-designated groups will end up not being hired. These people end up being innocent victims who bear the burden of eliminating discriminatory activities in which they did not engage. Proponents, however, argue that while these individuals may not be responsible for the discrimination, they are often the beneficiaries of past discriminatory activities, and that individuals have no claim of right to particular jobs: a society can take measures to distribute employment opportunities in order to alleviate the consequences of past discriminatory conduct and to produce a more just distribution of employment opportunities.

Employees' Obligations

Employee obligations arise from the same three sources as those of employers: express terms, statutory regulation, and implied terms. However, as you may have noted from the analysis of employer obligations, the use of statutory regulation is very important in determining the rights of employees and the obligations of employers. An analysis of employer rights and employee obligations tends to demonstrate, however, that express, and especially implied, contractual terms play a much more important role. This may be a reflection of the power relations that exist between employers and unions, and the tendency of the judiciary to regulate the employment relationship in such a way as to fortify property rights and status concepts.

An employee's express obligations tend to take the form of an agreement to perform the job specified in accordance with the rules and regulations of the employer. There may be details about the hours to be worked, breaks, vacation periods, etc. One problematic issue that sometimes arises is the extent to which an employer is entitled to modify those obligations, for example, by transferring the employee to a new location or by changing job duties. The employer's right to do so may arise as an implied term of the contract or as a result of mutual agreement between the parties. An employee who refuses to accept such changes may be entitled to quit and to bring an action for **constructive dismissal**, arguing that the employer's unilateral attempt to modify the obligations of the employee is a breach of the contract

---

EXHIBIT 18.3	Employees' Obligation — Loyalty and Whistleblowing

Employees are expected to be loyal to their employers. The Supreme Court of Canada has held, for example, in a case involving a federal government employee, that the employee must not engage in a "sustained and highly visible attack on major Government policies" as that displays a lack of loyalty to the employer that is "inconsistent with his duties as an employee": *Fraser v. PSSRB*, [1985] 2 S.C.R. 455. However, there are also situations where there may be a public interest in encouraging employees to act as whistleblowers, to report illegal action or wrongdoing, an obligation that may conflict with the obligation of loyalty. The Supreme Court has indicated that such whistleblowing may be justified where the employer is engaged in illegal acts or policies that jeopardize the life, health, or safety of the employee or of others. Nevertheless, it is clear that the duty of loyalty may act as a limit on the free expression rights of employees, especially government employees. A number of cases have emphasized the especially high loyalty expectations of employees such as police officers, the breach of which can easily justify dismissal.

More recently, various statutes have been enacted designed to protect whistleblowing employees, whether public servants or private sector employees, from discipline or dismissal. The federal Public Servants' Disclosure Protection Act, for example, prohibits reprisals against a public servant who has made a disclosure pursuant to the Act, and provides that a complaint about a reprisal may be made to the Public Sector Integrity Commissioner. The Saskatchewan Labour Standards Act prohibits reprisals against employees who have reported unlawful activities to a lawful authority. The Supreme Court of Canada has held that this provision protects an employee who has reported financial misconduct by her immediate supervisors to supervisors further up the ladder within the employer organization: *Merk v. International Association of Bridge, Structural, Ornamental and Reinforcing Iron Workers, Local 771*, 2005 SCC 70.

---

of employment. Constructive dismissals are discussed in more detail later in this chapter.

Another express obligation to which many employees are subject arises from restrictive covenants contained in the contract of employment. A **restrictive covenant** is a promise by the employee not to do certain things that might harm an employer's goodwill, data, trade secrets, or expertise. A restrictive covenant will often limit the right of an employee to go to work for a competitor or to set up a business in competition with that of the employer. The law has traditionally been somewhat suspicious about restrictive covenants, because they limit the rights of individuals to engage in economic activity. Hence, before a court will enforce a restrictive covenant, it must be satisfied that the covenant is reasonable, and needed to protect a legitimate proprietary interest of the employer. Hence, restrictive covenants often specifically refer to a geographical location, a specified time limit, and a precise occupation in which the employee is limited in competing with the employer. An employer is not entitled to merely prevent competition, but is entitled to protect legitimate assets such as goodwill, trade secrets, and confidential information. If employees have been wrongfully dismissed, they would not be bound by the terms of a restrictive covenant.

Most of the important obligations owed by an employee to the employer arise as the result of implied terms. These include obligations to be loyal and work in furtherance of an employer's interest, to obey lawful orders, to avoid misconduct, to work in a competent manner, to serve honestly and faithfully, and to indemnify the employer for economic losses arising from the employee's negligence. Upper-level managerial employees and directors of a company also owe **fiduciary duties** to the employer, in addition to the obligation of fidelity. This, in effect, means that such an employee is not entitled to try and capture for herself a business advantage or opportunity that rightfully belongs to the company.

These obligations have their genesis in the historical master–servant relationship, which depended on notions of status. In other words, they do not arise out of express agreement by the employee, but out of the idea that certain obligations arise from your status in life. The status of servant makes one subject to the rule of the master, and the servant is expected to act in accordance with the master's wishes and interests. While modern courts no longer use the language of master and servant, they have adapted the law so that the employer–employee relationship continues to be one in which the employee is expected to act in ways that further the interests of the employer. The content of these obligations most often arises in the context of a wrongful dismissal suit, in which the employer is claiming that the employee's actions provided cause for dismissal, and the employee is claiming not to have done anything that warranted summary dismissal.

TERMINATION OF EMPLOYMENT

The ending of an employment relationship can have severe consequences for employees. Not only are they left without a source of income, they are left without the opportunity to engage in a meaningful, productive activity. Studies have shown that communities affected by plant closings and high rates of unemployment typically have greater levels of both physical and mental diseases, as well as higher levels of crime. While the impact of job termination on individuals is likely to vary widely, there is no doubt that for many it causes considerable stress. Nevertheless, in a globally based, competitive economy, employers seek to maximize flexibility in the deployment of workers, including the ability to lay off employees with minimal cost.

The legal framework regulating the termination of employees is quite complex. It is influenced by the contractual nature of the employment relationship, as well as by statutory protections, and any additional protection that may be gained by workers through collective bargaining.

The contract of employment may be for a specified period of time, in which case the relationship comes to an end automatically at the time specified.

Retirement

The employment relationship may also come to an end when an employee retires. Until recently, many workplaces had a mandatory retirement age, unilaterally imposed by the employer or established in a collective agreement. Many argue that this is a form of discrimination on the basis of age, and in most provinces, mandatory retirement is now prohibited. In the case of *McKinney v. University of Guelph*, the Supreme Court of Canada held that it was not a violation of the Charter of Rights for a university to have a mandatory retirement policy, nor was it a violation for the provincial legislature to enact a statute permitting an employer to impose a mandatory retirement policy.

Firing

The general principle is that a worker may be terminated at any time for cause. An employer has cause for dismissal when an employee has violated the employment contract in a sufficiently serious manner that the employer is justified in terminating it immediately. In most instances, cause is associated with misconduct by an employee. This may take the form of theft, insubordination, or conduct that is detrimental to the employer's interests. Not all forms of misconduct will constitute cause. Courts must determine whether the employee's conduct "gives rise to a breakdown in the employment relationship". Incompetence can be cause for dismissal; however, the employer must demonstrate that the incompetence was serious, and that the employee was warned about it and was given an opportunity to improve performance. Where the employer acts because of economic circumstances, lack of work, or for other reasons not associated with the employee's conduct, there is no cause for dismissal.

In the absence of cause, an employer can end the employment relationship by giving appropriate notice. Employment standards statutes typically provide minimal periods of notice that must be provided in the absence of cause. In Ontario, the minimum period of notice varies between one and eight weeks, depending on the length of the employment relationship. These are only minimums, and an employee may be entitled to more notice as the result of either an express or implied term of the contract.

If the contract provides for notice greater than that of the statute, then that defines the notice that must be given. If the contract is of indefinite duration and is silent with respect to notice, courts typically read into the contract of employment the requirement of **reasonable notice**. What is reasonable will depend on a variety of factors, with the most important being the length of time served by the employee, as well as age, level of responsibility, and availability of similar employment. The employee is entitled to whichever is the greater, reasonable notice or the minimum notice provided for in the employment standards legislation. In practice, an employer will often make a payment in lieu of notice, rather than expecting an employee to continue working during the notice period.

If the employer dismisses an employee without cause, and without giving reasonable notice or payment in lieu, the employee may commence an action for **wrongful dismissal**. In a wrongful dismissal action, the employer has the onus to show that there was cause for dismissal. If the employer does not show cause, then the employee is entitled to damages measured on the basis of wages and other benefits that would have been received during the period of reasonable notice. Additional damages can be awarded where an employer's unfair or bad faith conduct during the course of dismissal leads to damages beyond the loss of wages caused by the failure to give reasonable notice, for example, where such conduct causes psychological trauma for the dismissed employee. A court may award punitive damages where employer conduct is particularly high-handed or outrageous, and merits special sanction, if that conduct constitutes a separate actionable harm. Reinstatement is not a remedy that is available in a wrongful dismissal action. However, for employees covered by a collective agreement that prohibits dismissal except for **just cause**, reinstatement is a remedy that is commonly used if the employer is unable to show just cause for dismissal. A unionized employee, rather than bringing an action for wrongful dismissal, would file a grievance that, if not settled between the union and the employer, would go to grievance or rights arbitration. It is the arbitrator, rather than the court, that would decide whether there was cause for dismissal, and whether the employee should be reinstated.

A dismissed employee who is seeking damages may be under an obligation of **mitigation** in order to reduce the amount of damages arising from the dismissal. The employer is required to demonstrate that the employee has failed to make a reasonable effort to find alternative employment and that such alternate employment was available. A recent Supreme Court of Canada decision has concluded that the dismissed employee may, in some circumstances, be required to mitigate damages by accepting an offer of employment from the employer that has dismissed him or her.

Wrongful Dismissal — Reasonable Notice

EXHIBIT 18.4

When Edna Cronk was dismissed from her job with Canadian General Insurance Co. at the age of 55, she had been working for the company and its predecessor full-time for a period of 28 years, with a six-year break when she stayed home to look after children. Even then, she worked on a part-time basis for the company. She was terminated as a result of an internal reorganization by the employer. She claimed that she should be entitled to 20 months' notice of dismissal.

The court was required to address two issues. In determining the amount of notice that should be provided where there is no cause for dismissal, it is normal to consider both the length of time the employee has been working for the employer, and the level of responsibility of the job. Employees with longer service and more responsible, especially managerial, positions, are normally entitled to more notice.

The Court decided that Cronk's notice period should be calculated using the full length of time that she had worked for the employer and its predecessor, given that she had left full-time employment to raise a family, continued to work part-time while doing so, and returned to full-time employment at the request of the employer. However, the Court of Appeal reversed the trial judge's ruling that she should be entitled to the same length of notice as a senior managerial employee. The court held that the well-established rule that senior managerial and specialized employees are entitled to a longer period of notice should be followed. It was important to adhere to precedent to promote reasonable certainty and predictability. As a result, the Court of Appeal reduced the notice period from 20 months to 12 months.

More recently, the Ontario Court of Appeal refused to reduce the 22-month notice that a trial court found was reasonable for Antonio Di Tomaso, who was dismissed at the age of 63 after working for 33 years as an unskilled worker in a non-managerial position. The Court held that the character of employment is a factor of declining relative importance in determining the period of reasonable notice, especially in the face of empirical evidence showing that it is not any easier for persons in such positions to find alternative employment.

Source: *Cronk v. Canadian General Insurance Co.* (1995), 25 O.R. (3d) 505 (C.A.); *Di Tomaso v. Crown Metal Packaging Canada*, 2011 ONCA 469 (CanLII).

Sometimes an employer, rather than dismissing an employee, will change the working conditions in such a way that the employee will quit. In such circumstances, the employee may still be able to claim that the change in working conditions amounts to a *constructive dismissal* and, therefore, damages should be awarded in the same manner as if a wrongful dismissal had taken place. It is not always easy to know whether changes in working conditions or breaches of the employment contract justify an employee's resignation and treating it as a dismissal. An employer must have some flexibility in being able to modify work assignments. On the other hand, from the employee's perspective, there must be some core of employment conditions that the employer cannot be entitled to unilaterally modify or, at least, not to modify without giving due notice. Hence, courts are called upon to balance the conflicting interests, which they do by determining what the terms of the contract are, whether they have been breached, and whether those breaches are fundamental.

Quitting

Just as there is a duty on an employer to provide reasonable notice in terminating a contract of indefinite duration, there is a corresponding duty on an employee if he wishes to terminate the contract by quitting. Some, but not

---

EXHIBIT 18.5

Wrongful Dismissal — Damages

Kevin Keays worked for Honda Canada. After working for several years, he developed Chronic Fatigue Syndrome, which his doctor reported was likely to cause him to be absent from work about four days per month. The employer initially accommodated these absences. However, the employer changed its position, telling Keays that their doctors, in reviewing Keays's files, had concluded that he did not have a disability justifying regular absences from work. This was despite clear documentation in Keays' files confirming the Chronic Fatigue Syndrome diagnosis. Honda then demanded that Keays meet with Honda's occupational health specialist. When Keays asked for clarification of the purpose of the meeting, the methodology to be used by the doctor, and the parameters for his assessment, he was told by the employer that no further explanation would be given. As a result, Keays refused to meet with the doctor, and Honda fired him for insubordination.

The trial judge found that the dismissal was wrongful because the order for Keays to meet with the company doctor was not reasonable, given the employer's refusal to respond to Keays' questions. An employer has no just cause to dismiss an employee for refusing to follow an unreasonable employer order. Moreover, in this case, the trial judge concluded that the employer was acting in bad faith in making the order because it was using the order as a prelude to dismissing Keays so that it would not have to accommodate his disability.

In determining damages, the trial judge concluded that Keays was entitled to reasonable notice of 15 months. Moreover, because he found the employer had acted in bad faith in the manner in which it dismissed Keays, leading to significant medical consequences for him, aggravated damages were awarded by increasing the notice period to 24 months. The trial judge also concluded that punitive damages in the amount of $500,000 were warranted, given that Honda's actions were discriminatory, high handed and outrageous.

On appeal, the Supreme Court of Canada upheld the finding that Keays was wrongfully dismissed and entitled to 15 months' notice, but found that the employer was not acting in bad faith nor in discriminatory fashion. As a result, Keays was neither entitled to aggravated damages through an extended notice nor to punitive damages. The decision makes it difficult for an employee to claim damages for mental distress arising from a dismissal and to claim that an employer is acting in bad faith.

Sources: *Keays v. Honda Canada Inc.*, 2008 SCC 39, [2008] 2 SCR 36 aff'g in part 2 (2006), 82 O.R. (3d) 161 (C.A); aff'g, in part, (2005), 40 C.C.E.L. (3d) 258 (Ont. S.C.J.)

---

all, provinces provide for a minimum period of notice in their employment standards legislation. In practice, there have been very few cases in which courts have been asked to provide a remedy to an employer for the failure of an employee to provide reasonable notice of an intention to quit. This is probably because the level of damages likely to be obtained in a successful action is sufficiently low that it does not justify the expenses involved in bringing an action.

Plant Closings

One form of termination that merits special legislative treatment arises where there is a full or partial closing of the employer's operations. Where this results in a large number of employees being let go at one time, there may be special difficulties for the employees in adjusting to the layoffs. For that reason, many provinces specify longer than usual notice periods. For instance, in Ontario, if 50–199 persons are laid off, eight weeks' notice must be given; 200–499 employees, 12 weeks; 500 or more employees, 16 weeks. In addition, an employer can be required to participate in actions to consider alternatives to the terminations and to facilitate the adjustment process by, for example, providing job placement (sometimes called "outplacement") counselling to terminated employees. The government does not actually prevent an employer from laying off employees; it merely seeks to cushion the impact on employees by providing longer notice periods and by seeking ways of helping employees to adjust to the changed circumstances.

Severance Pay

Another measure that has been taken in some jurisdictions, including Ontario, and for employees that are governed by the *Canada Labour Code*, is to require an employer to pay **severance pay** when an employee is terminated. In Ontario, an employer is required to pay severance pay where 50 or more employees are terminated as a result of the permanent discontinuance of all or part of the employer's business. As well, if the employer has a payroll of more than $2.5 million per annum, severance pay must be paid even in the case of individual terminations. Only employees who have been employed for five or more years are so entitled. The severance pay is in addition to any amount that the employee may be entitled to as pay in lieu of statutory notice. Several justifications are offered for requiring severance payments. They are an additional cushion to help employees adjust to being laid off. They recognize that even employees who find alternative employment immediately lose tangible benefits, such as seniority. As well, it is a way of forcing an employer to internalize some of the costs of a layoff so that in some situations, an employer may decide that the costs of laying off exceed the costs of maintaining employment at the usual level.

CHAPTER SUMMARY

This chapter has described three regimes by which the legal system regulates the rights and obligations of employees. The contract of employment, legislation, and collective bargaining are each used, sometimes in overlapping fashion, to determine the rules by which employees and employers come together in order to engage in productive activity. Legislation and collective bargaining can both be seen as responses to the inadequacy of individual employment contracts to ensure justice in the workplace. Nevertheless, for many workers, individual contracts continue to be a very important determinant of their rights.

The rights under an individual contract are primarily enforced by courts, especially in the context of wrongful dismissal cases. Unionized workers rely primarily on the grievance/arbitration system. Both groups of employees, however, may be able to turn to a number of different statutory agencies to protect rights created by legislation. Human rights commissions, workers' compensation boards, safety inspectors, employment standards officers, and other public officials and institutions are responsible for ensuring that statutory rights are fulfilled.

The law recognizes an expanse of rights and obligations possessed by employers and employees. These range from employee obligations of fidelity and obedience to employer obligations to maintain a workplace that is safe, free from discrimination, and that meets minimum employment standards. However one assesses these forms of regulation, difficult issues of fairness and efficiency inevitably must be taken into account.

GLOSSARY OF NEW TERMS AND KEY CONCEPTS

bargain in good faith (duty to)   A statutory duty placed on unions and employers when negotiating a collective agreement.

bona fide occupational requirement (b.f.o.r.)	A defence available to employers whose rules have an adverse discriminatory impact on particular groups; the employer must show that the rules are necessary and adopted in good faith.
certification	A process by which a union, enjoying the support of the majority of employees in a bargaining unit, obtains the right to bargain exclusively with the employer on behalf of those employees.
consideration	Before a contractual promise is enforceable, the person seeking to enforce it must give something in exchange for the promise: consideration, which can be money payment, provision of goods or services, or a promise to do something in the future.
constructive dismissal	A situation in which an employee who has quit is entitled to bring an action for wrongful dismissal on the basis that the employer has caused the dismissal by breaching the employment contract.
employment equity	A policy that has the goal of eliminating barriers to equality in employment and ensuring the proportional representation of all groups in the workplace.
employment relationship	A legal relationship, based in a contract that is sometimes referred to as a contract of service, and that is distinguished from independent contracting or a contract for services.
employment standards	Minimum legislative standards are set out in legislation to which employers and employees are bound, dealing with such issues as minimum wages, vacation pay, holidays, notice of termination, etc.
experience rating	A means by which the premium paid by an employer for workers' compensation reflects that employer's record with respect to compensable injuries.
equal pay for equal work	A principle that requires an employer to pay a man and a woman the same wages if they are doing substantially the same job. (*See also* **equal pay for work of equal value** and **pay equity**.)
equal pay for work of equal value	A principle which requires an employer to pay a man and a woman the same wages if their jobs are of equal value; the jobs themselves may be different. (*See also* **equal pay for equal work** and **pay equity**.)
fiduciary duties	Obligations owed by upper-level managerial employees to place the employer's interest ahead of their own when it comes to business opportunities.
freedom of association	A general principle of international law that is recognized by the *Charter of Rights* and by collective bargaining statutes, whereby workers are free to join a union and participate in its lawful activities free from employer interference.
grievance or rights arbitration	A process by which grievances under a collective agreement are settled by a neutral third party, whose decision is binding on the union, the employer, and the employees. Grievance, or rights arbitration, differs from interest arbitration in that a rights arbitrator decides what rights have already been created by the collective agreement, while an interest arbitrator actually creates the rights that are then inserted into the collective agreement.
harassment	A form of prohibited discrimination in which a person either seeks to use coercion to solicit sexual favours, or engages in a course of vexatious comment or conduct that the person knows, or ought reasonably to know, is unwelcome.
independent contractor	Workers who are not considered at common law to be employees, but rather in business for themselves or self-employed, such as a truck owner who transports goods for a company. Independent contractors may sometimes, however, be treated as employees for purposes of regulatory statutes.
interest arbitration	A process by which collective bargaining disputes are settled by a neutral third party, rather than through the use of strikes or lockouts. The arbitrator's decision is binding on the union and the employer for the duration of the collective agreement.
just cause	A requirement under collective agreements that prohibits an employer from dismissing an employee unless it can be shown that there is a good, reasonable, or just cause for the dismissal.

mitigation	Obligation on a dismissed employee to seek reasonable alternative employment, in order to reduce the amount of damages arising from a wrongful dismissal. The onus is on the employer to demonstrate that an employee has failed to make reasonable efforts, and to show that if reasonable efforts were made, the employee likely could have obtained reasonable alternate employment.
pay equity	A principle that requires equal pay for work of equal value (see above), and that requires an employer to implement a review of pay practices to determine if such inequities exist, and to take measures to end them.
poisoned environment	A form of harassment in which a person's course of conduct or vexatious comment, especially of a sexual or racial nature, makes it very unpleasant for other workers.
quid pro quo harassment	A form of harassment in which a person who exercises managerial or supervisory control seeks to solicit sexual favours by making threats or promises.
reasonable accommodation	An employer who has a rule that adversely discriminates against members of a group must demonstrate that it has made reasonable efforts to accommodate the needs of that group.
reasonable notice	In a contract of employment, where no express term provides otherwise, there is an implied term that an employee must receive reasonable notice before being laid off or dismissed. The reasonableness of notice depends on a variety of factors, such as the length of time the employee has worked, age, and the availability of similar employment.
restrictive covenant	An express term of an employment contract in which the employee agrees not to engage in employment, or start a business that would interfere with the employer's proprietary rights, such as goodwill, trade secrets, and confidential information.
severance pay	An entitlement of workers, under some employment standards legislation, to a payment when their jobs are terminated, usually based on a formula that multiplies weekly or daily wages by the number of years worked.
unfair labour practices	Limits, contained in collective-bargaining statutes, on the conduct in which an employer or a union can engage, designed to protect the freedom of association of workers and the autonomy of unions.
WHMIS (Workplace Hazardous Materials Information System)	A system required by occupational health and safety statutes to label toxic substances in the workplace, and to educate workers about how to properly handle such substances.
workers' compensation	An employer-funded statutory scheme by which workers are entitled to be compensated for wages lost as a result of workplace accidents or disease, without having to demonstrate negligence or fault by the employer.
wrongful dismissal	A dismissal in which the employer has violated the contract of employment by firing an employee without cause and without giving reasonable notice.

REVIEW QUESTIONS

1. What are the three major systems for regulating the employment relationship?

2. What is the difference between an employee and an independent contractor?

3. What are three requirements for a valid employment contract?

4. What remedies are available to an employee who has not received wages owed by an employer?

5. Describe some employment standards and how they interact with a collective-bargaining regime.

6. Describe four ways in which occupational health and safety statutes attempt to ensure a safer and healthier workplace.

7. What is the difference between equal pay for equal work, equal pay for work of equal value, and pay equity?

8. Name at least three objectives required by employment equity principles.

9. For employees not covered by collective agreements, name the three primary sources of employee obligations.

10. In a successful wrongful dismissal action, what is the primary remedy given by the courts?

11. What are some of the problems with thinking of the employment relationship as contractual?

12. Why have legislatures enacted statutes to regulate the employment relationship?

DISCUSSION QUESTIONS

1. When should employees have a right to strike, and when are governments justified in prohibiting employees from striking?

2. In a globalizing world, is it more important for employment standards legislation to provide robust minimum standards, or is it more important to have flexible standards so that employers will be able to compete against companies based in other countries?

3. Canada has relatively high levels of deaths and injuries on the job. How can we improve the legal regulation of occupational health and safety so as to make the workplace safer?

4. What steps, if any, should Canada be taking to ensure pay equity and to deal with under-representation of women, minorities and the disabled in the workplace?

5. Should there be a law that prohibits employers from firing workers unless they can show that there is just cause for doing so?

6. What are some of the pros and cons of governments enacting collective bargaining statutes?

SUGGESTED READING AND OTHER RESOURCES

Adams, George W. *Canadian Labour Law*, 2d ed. with annual supplements (Aurora, Ont.: Canada Law Book, 1993).

Aggarwal, Arjun, & Madhu M. Gupta. *Sexual Harassment in the Workplace*, 3d ed. (Toronto: Butterworths, 2000).

Barnetson, Bob. *The Political Economy of Workplace Injury in Canada* (Edmonton, Alta.: Athabasca University Press, 2010).

Carter, Donald D., et al. *Labour Law in Canada*, 5th ed. (The Hague: Kluwer Law International, 2002).

Dee, Garth. *Ontario Workplace Safety and Insurance Act and Commentary* (Markham, Ont.: LexisNexis Butterworths, 2004).

Echlin, Randall S., *For Better or Worse: A Practical Guide to Canadian Employment Law* (Aurora, Ont.: Aurora Professional Press, 2003).

England, Geoffrey. *Individual Employment Law*, 2d ed. (Toronto: Irwin Law, 2008).

England, G., *Employment Law in Canada*, 4th ed. (Markham, Ont.: LexisNexis Canada, 2005).

Fudge, Judy, & Eric Tucker, *Work on Trial, Canadian Labour Law Struggles* (Toronto: Irwin Law for the Osgoode Society for Canadian Legal History, 2010).

Fudge, Judy, & Patricia McDermott, eds. *Just Wages: A Feminist Assessment of Pay Equity* (Toronto: University of Toronto Press, 1991).

Gilbert, Douglas G., & L.A. Liversidge. *Workers Compensation in Ontario, A Guide to the Workplace Safety and Insurance Act*, 3d ed. (Aurora, Ont.: Canada Law Book, 2001).

Grossman, Michael. *The Law of Occupational Health and Safety in Ontario*, 2d ed. (Toronto: Butterworths, 1994).

Labour Law Casebook Group, *Labour and Employment Law: Cases, Material and Commentary*, 8th ed. (Toronto: Irwin Law, 2011).

Law Commission of Ontario, *Vulnerable Workers and Precarious Work*, Final Report, (Toronto: Law Commission of Ontario, December 2012).

Law Society of Upper Canada, *Employment Law* (Toronto: Irwin Law, 2007).

Levitt, Howard A., *The Law of Dismissal for Human Resource Professionals* (Aurora, Ont.: Canada Law Book, 2007).

MacKillop, Malcolm, *Employment Law Solutions* (Markham, Ont.: LexisNexis, 2010).

Neumann, Peter, & Jeffrey Sack, *eText on Wrongful Dismissal and Employment Law*, 1st ed., Lancaster House (CanLII) <http://canlii.org/en/commentary/wrongfuldismissal/>

Pay Equity Task Force. *Pay Equity: A New Approach to a Fundamental Right* (Ottawa, Pay Equity Task Force, 2004).

Rayside, David. *Equity, Diversity and Canadian Labour* (Toronto: University of Toronto Press, 2007).

Rootham, Christopher. *Labour and Employment Law in the Federal Public Service* (Toronto: Irwin Law, 2007).

Sproat, John R. *The Wrongful Dismissal Handbook*, 2d ed. (Toronto: Butterworths, 2002).

Thomas, Mark P., *Regulating Flexibility: The Political Economy of Employment Standards* (Montreal, Que.: McGill-Queens University Press, 2009).

Weiner, Nan. *Employment Equity: Making It Work* (Toronto: Butterworths, 1993).

Weiner, Nan, & Morley Gunderson. *Pay Equity: Issues, Options and Experiences* (Toronto: Butterworths, 1990).

Vosko, Leah, ed. *Precarious Employment: Understanding Labour Market Insecurity in Canada* (Montreal, Que.: McGill Queen's University Press, 2006).

WEBSITES

Canadian Employment Law Today: <http://www.employmentlawtoday.com/>

CanLII: <http://www.canlii.ca/en/index.html>

Hourly Minimum Wages in CANADA for Adult Workers: <http://srv116.services.gc.ca/dimt-wid/sm-mw/rpt2.aspx?lang=eng&dec=5>

Labour Program: <http://www.labour.gc.ca/eng/home.shtml>

The Law Dictionary: <http://thelawdictionary.org/>

Employment Law in the Unionized Workplace

Omar Ha-Redeye
BARRISTER AND SOLICITOR, TORONTO

Learning Objectives

After reading this chapter, the reader should be able to:

➤ understand the history and the tensions which led to the development of labour legislation in Canada

➤ learn how unions are formed, funded, and certified

➤ understand the duties of unions to their members and to employers

➤ understand how the contract bargaining process works and how it is regulated by government

➤ appreciate how labour law provides mechanisms for dispute resolution

➤ identify some of the strategic obstacles that unions face in today's economy

© 2014 by Captus Press Inc. With special acknowledgement to Anna Rolbin and Peter MacDonald of Fleet Street Law and Mayssia El-Ajami of the University of Sussex.

TABLE OF CONTENTS

INTRODUCTION

Public opinion of unions in Canada often goes hand in hand with the economic climate. In times of increasing unemployment, Canadians may wonder why unionized employees are entitled to strike and cause service disruptions that negatively impact the lives of other Canadians. When garbage pick-up is cancelled or teachers refuse to lead extracurricular activities, public frustration often mounts against unions. Some Canadians even go so far as to question whether unions are still necessary in the contemporary Canadian workplace. However, this outlook often ignores the advances that unions have made for both their own members and for workers in general.

Unionization has impacted Canadian society in many important ways. Unions were and are a major force in Canadian society because they ensure that workers are treated fairly. Many of the benefits of employment that Canadians now take for granted resulted from the efforts of unions to organize and represent the interests of workers. The creation of the five-day work week, the 35-hour week, workplace safety laws, and a middle class with large numbers of working people in it are largely the result of long term, concerted efforts by unions. Unions also work behind the scenes to prevent uncontrolled conflict in the labour market and to generally ensure a stable and healthy working class. Unions also play a role in helping to develop the workplace through job training, and by helping the labour force adapt to new challenges arising from globalization, technological development and social change.

When unions were established in Canada in the 1860s, their main purpose was to combat unfair wage levels, overly long working hours, and unsafe or inhumane working conditions. Unions focused on the unacceptable treatment of employees by their employer. By joining together and advocating for the interests of larger groups of workers, unions attempted to remedy the significant power imbalance that existed between employers and individual employees. The overarching idea behind unionization is "strength in numbers", the notion that cooperation in the interest of a common goal can lead to greater results than those which can be achieved on an individual level. This collaborative approach between employees helps offset the power imbalances between workers, especially when they are unskilled, and an employer who can often be far more powerful and resourceful.

The growth of unions came as a response to industrialization, which brought with it an increase in the incidence of abusive employment policies by the owners of mining companies and large factories. These abusive policies led to disputes between employers and workers. Disputes often erupted into violence, which in turn led in some instances to disruptions in production, or even the complete closure of companies. The violence and disruptions benefited neither the workers nor the owners and had a negative effect on the entire economy. The overall negative impact of labour disputes served as a catalyst for the development of labour relations regimes. These regimes provided an effective alternative for voicing workplace concerns and set out dispute resolution mechanisms that did not result in violence or business closures.

Today, the role of unions in Canada is changing. While the number of unions in the public sector hold steady, private sector unions are shrinking. Only 17% of the private sector workforce belongs to a union, down from 26% in 1984. This decline is largely attributable to changes in the economy, shifts to more service-based industries and the disappearance of unionized manufacturing jobs. While many of the life-threatening working conditions present in the workforce 150 years ago have been addressed through government regulation, unions still play an important role in ensuring an appropriate balance between the interests of employers and employees.

UNION ORGANIZATION

The Right to Form, Join and Participate in a Union

Prior to the enactment of labour laws in Canada, workers did not have the "legal right" to form unions, bargain collectively, or participate in strikes as means of changing unsatisfactory working conditions. Unions were considered illegal in Canada until the *Trade Unions Act*, introduced by Sir John A. MacDonald in 1872. The Act recognized unions as a legitimate way for workers to fight for their rights. Prior to that time the law viewed unionization as an illegal conspiracy to interfere with and restrain competition in a free market.

Today, all Canadian employees have the right to form unions, as long as they meet certain legal requirements. Unionization and collective bargaining rights were codified through the enactment of federal and provincial labour statutes across Canada, including the federal *Canada Labour Code* and Ontario's *Labour Relations Act*. In addition to protection under specific labour statutes, attempts have been made over the years to characterize unionization and collective bargaining rights as "fundamental rights" under the *Canadian Charter of Rights and Freedoms*. It remains unclear whether these rights are protected by the *Charter*, and the issue continues to be the subject of much debate in Canada's highest courts.[1]

The process of unionization starts when a group of employees in a particular workplace decide that they want to form a union. Employees who want to unionize may form a new union, or they can join an existing union as an offshoot or "**Local**" of that union. Some categories of employees are excluded from membership in a union for reasons relating to their jobs. For example, managerial employees with the powers to hire or fire other employees are typically excluded from membership. The rationale for this exclusion is that employees in positions of power and control over other employees are more akin to employers. Their interests align more closely with the interests of employers, and participation in a union with other employees may therefore result in conflicts of interest.

Unfair Labour Practices

Many employers today continue to be highly resistant to unionization, citing concerns that the formation of unions unduly limits their ability to conduct their businesses in a profitable manner. As a result of the continued struggle between employers and employees, Canadian labour statutes contain protective measures that are designed to prevent employers from engaging in union busting activities. One such protective measure is the prohibition against unfair labour practices.

An **unfair labour practice** (ULP) is any action that is prohibited by the laws of a jurisdiction which deal with unions and workers' rights to unionize. In Canada, the term "unfair labour practice" is not explicitly defined in legislation. Instead, the various federal, provincial, and territorial labour statutes set out categories of prohibited conduct and describe specific prohibited actions as ULPs. Broadly speaking, an action is characterized as a ULP if it interferes with a worker's right to form, join or participate in a union, or if it interferes with a union's ability to fully and properly represent its members.

Although it is possible for employers, unions, and even individuals to engage in ULPs, most statutes focus on prohibitions against employers.

---

[1] In the 2007 case of *Health Services and Support — Facilities Subsector Bargaining Assn. v. British Columbia*, 2007 SCC 27, [2007] 2 S.C.R. 391, the Supreme Court of Canada ruled that the right to bargain collectively forms part of the right to freedom of association under section 2(d) of the *Charter*. However, subsequently, in the 2011 case of *Ontario (Attorney General) v. Fraser*, 2011 SCC 20, [2011] 2 S.C.R. 3, the Supreme Court of Canada appeared to go back on its earlier decision and was divided as to whether collective bargaining is a *Charter* right.

	EXHIBIT 19.1

Union Busting

Employers historically opposed the creation and codification of employees' union rights. Their opposition to unions stemmed from a desire to have more freedom in how their business was administered. Employers were interested in retaining power and discretion to enter into contracts with employees on whatever terms they saw fit. The process of collective bargaining was perceived as a threat to profitability, as it tended to result in employment contracts mandating higher wages and better working conditions, which had the potential to increase operational costs. The long-term consequences of job instability for workers and the costs of workplace injury were often secondary considerations. Employers responded to unionization by blocking the formation of unions in their business or disassembling unions which had already formed. Their tactics included intimidation, restriction or termination of employees who tried to form unions in the workplace. These **"union busting"** activities were historically seen as a desirable method of increasing trade by legislators.

Employers can be guilty of engaging in ULPs if their actions fall into any of the following:

- Interfering in the formation or administration of a union.
- Preventing an employee from joining a union.
- Resulting in reprisals against union members or union officers for raising labour issues in the workplace.
- Stopping an employee from participating in a union's lawful activities.
- Interfering with a union's ability to represent its members.

Some labour statutes also provide non-exhaustive lists of specific prohibited actions. For example, an employer can be found guilty of engaging in ULPs for any of the following behaviours:

- Refusing to employ or to continue to employ a person who is a member of a union, becomes a member of a union while employed, or indicates that he/she would like to become a member of a union.
- Discriminating against an employee who is member of a union, or becomes a member of a union, or indicates that he/she would like to become a member of a union.
- Threatening, intimidating, or belittling an employee who files a grievance against the employer.
- Restricting or threatening to restrict an employee's rights in an attempt to coerce the employee to withdraw a grievance.
- Withdrawing job offers or assignments from an employee who indicates that he/she will file a grievance over a condition in that job or assignment.
- Threatening, restricting, terminating, or otherwise discriminating against an employee who becomes a union representative, or indicates that he/she would like to become a union representative.
- Threatening a union representative who is representing an employee or former employee.

Unions and union representatives can be found to engage in ULPs for any of the following:

- Attending at a place of employment during working hours without the employer's consent, and trying to persuade employees to become, refrain from becoming, continue to be, or cease to be members of a union.

- Denying or suspending an employee's membership in a union in a discriminatory manner.
- Disciplining or penalizing an employee in a discriminatory manner.
- Threatening, intimidating, or belittling an employee who files a complaint against the union.
- Restricting, penalizing, or terminating an employee's membership in an attempt to coerce the employee to withdraw a complaint filed against the union.
- Failing to meet their duties of fair representation.

A worker or union representative who believes that his/her employer or union has engaged in a ULP may file an **unfair labour practices complaint** (ULP complaint) with the **Labour Board** in his/her jurisdiction (for example, the Ontario Labour Relations Board). ULP Complaints are viewed as serious violations of labour rights. Accordingly, unions generally will not file such complaints unless there is a very serious interference with an employee's labour rights.

After a ULP Complaint is filed with the Labour Board, a dispute resolution process begins. The Board sets deadlines for the respondent to reply to the allegations made by the complainant. The Board also appoints a Board officer to assist the parties in settlement meeting(s). The goal of the settlement meeting(s) is to give the parties an opportunity to try and resolve the issues directly. If the dispute is not settled, the Board holds a hearing to decide on the outstanding issues. During the hearing, a Board Panel hears the allegations of the employee or union representative, and each side gets an opportunity to present evidence in support of his/her position. The burden of proof rests with the party that filed the complaint to show that the alleged actions took place. If it is demonstrated that the employer did commit a certain action (for example, disciplining or dismissing an employee), the burden shifts to the employer to show that his/her actions against the employee were not related to the employee's union-related activities.

If the Board finds that an employer's or a union's practices constitute a ULP, the Board can order the employer or union to terminate the illegal practice. The Board can also order an employer to **reinstate** and/or issue **back pay** to any employee who was suspended, terminated or otherwise restricted. Finally, in order to discourage employers from ULPs, the Board is also empowered to order **automatic certification**. This order allows a union to represent employees in a workplace without meeting procedural certification requirements. Automatic certification may be ordered in situations where an employer's actions make it likely that employees would not vote in favour of unionization for fear of retribution by the employer.

Certification

In order to legally represent a group of employees in a particular workplace, a union must receive **certification** from the Labour Board in the appropriate jurisdiction. Upon certification employees lose their right to enter into individual employment contracts and their right to personally negotiate with their employer. Once the union is certified, it gains the exclusive right to negotiate with the employer on behalf of the employees in the bargaining unit. (This is known as the **doctrine of exclusive representation**.) The loss of autonomy in independently negotiating employment terms is a significant change in the employment relationship, which is why certification must proceed before a Labour Board for examination. The Board will only issue certification in the following conditions:

- A majority of the employees support the formation of the union.
- The employees have a shared interest in bargaining.

	EXHIBIT 19.2
Unfair Labour Practice: Case Study	

By Linelle S. Mogado, Legal Counsel
The Professional Institute of the Public Service of Canada

Novotel Canada, Inc. v. UNITE-HERE, [2012] O.L.R.B. Rep. 836 [*Novotel*], illustrates the limits set on employer speech during union-organizing efforts. The Union was organizing at the Novotel Mississauga, in Ontario. A part-time server was very active in organizing her fellow workers, and met with them at their homes to discuss the union and to have certification cards signed. Some workers complained to management, which began to hold meetings with its workers. The hotel's messages included information regarding unionization later found to be false.

The hotel's messages included, "If the Union tells you they can give you job security it is [a] promise they cannot keep. Ask the president to sign and give you in writing that he will secure your job. Look around you and see the different companies and hotels that are unionized and when they have to lay off or close that still happens."[1]

As the part-time server became more vocal and active in the organizing campaign, she spoke at rallies and appeared in union flyers. She underwent performance appraisals at this time with negative results, and was also disciplined. When a full-time position became available, the employer did not offer it to her, and it gradually eliminated her from the shift schedule. The burden on the employer before the Ontario Labour Relations Board was to demonstrate that its actions in relation to the organizer were "not tainted by anti-union animus", and the arbitrator found that the hotel failed at this.[2]

The union filed its certification application, which triggered a vote, and the employer disseminated the following message: " 'In these hard economic times we have seen hotels and businesses closing and laying off ... we have not been in these situations of layoffs or closing down because we have taken some good decisions.' (emphasis added)." The arbitrator noted, "Then later the Hotel made clear that voting against the union was a 'good decision': 'Today, as we stand here on the brink of a decision making day, I ask you to make the time to make a good decision.' "[3]

The Board concluded:

> Here, the employer made a series of statements about job security which individually might constitute legitimate employer free speech. However, the cumulative effect of employees being repeatedly reminded that Unions cannot guarantee job security along with examples of unionized businesses (including hotels) forced to close down or lay off (particularly in the general economic context which existed at that time in Ontario) constituted coercion, undue influence and interference.
>
> In my view the only purpose of repeating the job security statements was to send a message which cannot have been missed by the average employee — that if the union were to get in, there would be a risk of job loss. This conclusion is enhanced by the Hotel's decision, once it learned that an application for certification had been filed, to reference the "hard economic times", "hotels and businesses closing and lay-offs" and then claiming that they had not been in that situation because they had made good decisions and that an equally good decision was to vote against the Union.[4]

Notes
1. *Novotel*, para. 13.
2. *Novotel*, para. 103.
3. *Novotel*, paras. 113 and 114.
4. *Novotel*, paras. 116–117.

Majority Support

Prior to filing a **certification application**, union representatives distribute membership cards to the employees of the workplace where the new union will potentially form. The employees are asked to sign and return the membership cards as evidence that they want to join the union. Employees fill out these membership cards confidentially. Employers do not have the right to know which of their employees signed cards. If an employer compels employees to disclose their position on unionization, or discriminates against employees who are known to support the creation of the union, the employer can be found guilty of engaging in a ULP. Unions file the signed membership cards with the Labour Board as part of the certification application in order to demonstrate majority support.

In most provincial jurisdictions (including Ontario), the collection of signed membership cards is only the first step, and majority support among the employees must be demonstrated through a mandatory **representation vote**. Labour Boards will order a representation vote only if a minimum threshold of employees have signed membership cards. This threshold is usually between 40% and 45%, depending on the jurisdiction, and if it is not met the Labour Board will reject the certification application. If a representation vote is ordered, employers are required to conspicuously post notices about the vote and allow all employees to cast a confidential vote, free of interference. If the majority of ballots indicate support for the union, the Board will issue the certification.

In a few jurisdictions (including at the federal level and in Quebec), the representation vote is not mandatory. Labour Boards in these jurisdictions will certify a union if a clear majority of employees (either 50% + 1 or 55%, depending on the jurisdiction) have signed union membership cards. Where there is no clear majority of signed cards, but a minimum percentage of employees did sign the cards (between 35% and 45%, depending on the jurisdiction), the Labour Board will order a representation vote. If the majority of ballots indicate support for the union, the Board will issue the certification.

Labour Boards generally proceed with caution when determining majority support and will try to ascertain the true wishes of the employees. In some jurisdictions, Boards can nullify a representation vote and/or order a second vote, if it appears that the original vote does not accurately reflect the position of the employees whose rights will be impacted. For example, at the federal level, a representation vote is void if fewer than 35% of employees cast ballots, and the Board cannot rely on such a vote. In British Columbia, the Labour Board has discretion to order a second vote if fewer than 55% of employees cast ballots.

Boards in several jurisdictions are also empowered, in limited circumstances, to order automatic certifications even when legislative requirements for majority support are not met. Such certifications are rare but can be ordered if a Board finds that

- the employer restricted the ability of employees to freely and truthfully express support for unionization and in doing so engaged in a ULP;
- the signed membership cards and/or the result of the representation vote do not reflect the true wishes of the employees;
- there would likely have been majority support for the union if the employer had not engaged in the ULP;
- other remedies under the legislation (such as ordering a second vote) will not be sufficient to counter the negative impact of the employer's actions.

Shared Interest in Bargaining

The next step after demonstrating majority support is for the union to demonstrate to the Labour Board that a clear and appropriate bargaining unit can be established. A **bargaining unit** is a group of employees who are represented by a union in collective bargaining and other interactions with their employer. In order to form an appropriate bargaining unit the members of the unit must share a "community of interest". A **community of interest** exists

EXHIBIT 19.3

The Rand Formula

Canadian law requires all employees in a bargaining unit to pay union dues irrespective of union membership. This requirement was developed by Justice Ivan Rand during his arbitration of the 100-day-long Windsor Strike at the Ford Motor Company in 1945 and is known as the **Rand Formula**. Justice Rand noted that unions work for the benefit of all workers within the bargaining unit, not just the union members, and therefore all workers within the unit should be responsible for financially supporting the union and ensuring its continued operation. Union dues are paid by way of a mandatory deduction from salary.

Due to the complex nature of many businesses, union members often work side by side with non-members. Although union membership is not mandatory, employees in a unionized workplace cannot opt out of union representation and the corollary financial obligations. An employee who falls within the parameters of a bargaining unit will be represented by the union and will be subject to the bargaining unit's collective agreement even if he/she does not wish to be a member of the union. Any infringement on individual rights is mitigated by the reality that large employers are generally unwilling to negotiate with individuals, and that collective bargaining generally results in a better deal for the individual than individual negotiation.

Some Canadian politicians have criticized unions in recent years for using the Rand Formula to collect union dues which are then used for political purposes, which they argue runs contrary to the intent of the structure. They argue that union dues are collected from all employees for the purpose of funding the bargaining and administration of the collective agreement. Unions have responded to these allegations by saying the political process, and the laws created by politicians, affect labour laws governing unions and social policies which affect the workplace.

Workers have tried to challenge the mandatory nature of union dues in the courts, but have not met with much success. In *Lavigne v. OPSEU*, an employee unsuccessfully argued that freedom of association included freedom of association *from* associations. The Supreme Court of Canada upheld the formula (i) as a necessary structure for effective union functioning and (ii) in the interests of a free and democratic society.

Sources:
Pierre Poilievre, "Unions ignore the Rand formula", *Financial Post* (February 5, 2013).
Sid Ryan, "Tories Attack Rand Formula to Silence Workers", *Huffington Post* (February 14, 2013).

when a group of employees have common concerns and common goals relevant to the terms of every group member's employment. The mere fact that employees have the same employer is not sufficient to give rise to a "community of interest". The union must demonstrate additional similarities, such as similarities in job functions, wages, benefits, work hours, qualification for promotions, etc. If groups of employees within a workplace have different "communities of interest", the union may divide the employees into separate bargaining units. In these situations each bargaining unit will need to be certified separately, since the Board will want to ensure that there is majority support for the union within each group of employees.

The composition of a bargaining unit is largely influenced by the relevant similarities of the employees. Consider a scenario where the nurses, administrative staff, and janitorial staff of a hospital all decide to unionize. While these employees can all be considered "supporting staff", they will likely not be able to form a proper bargaining unit due to significant differences in their respective job functions, wages and work hours. In this case, it would be difficult to argue that there is a "community of interest" among all three groups of employees.

The size and scope of a bargaining unit can affect the bargaining power of the union, and determine the terms that a union will try to include in the unit's collective agreement. Larger unions, often comprised of a larger number of bargaining units, potentially wield more leverage against an employer and generally have greater purchasing power for insurance and benefits. However, if the interests of the members of the bargaining unit are too diverse, a union may find it difficult to effectively address the concerns of all unit members. Too large a bargaining unit may result in a disproportionate emphasis on minority interests, or on positions that are not shared by the unit as a whole. On the other hand, too small a bargaining unit may have insufficient leverage when negotiating with an employer. For example, a labour disruption affecting only a small percentage of the employer's total workforce will not cause the degree of financial impact that a larger labour disruption might cause because it applies less pressure on an employer to make the changes that the bargaining unit is seeking.

The Duty of Fair Representation (DFR)

The responsibility of unions to the bargaining units they represent are described in section 37 of the *Canada Labour Code* as the **duty of fair representation**. This duty prohibits unions and their agents from acting in ways which are arbitrary, discriminatory or in bad faith towards members of the bargaining unit they have the exclusive right to represent. This pressures unions to demonstrate that they are treating all members of the bargaining unit equally, regardless of the member's standing in the union. If an employee feels they have been represented unfairly by their union they can apply to a Labour Board with a DFR application, although these typically have a success rate of less than 5–10%.

The history behind the DFR application is that unions were not always inclusive. At times they only accepted senior members of a workplace, and at other times they deliberately excluded racialized minorities. Unions also acted in retaliatory ways against employees who did not vote for the union, or who voiced their objections to union policies, by failing to pursue their grievances. Allowing these individuals to independently refer grievances to arbitration without union oversight would be too costly, so in law the union has express control over the grievance process and can decide for strategic reasons whether to take a grievance to arbitration. However, in exercising this discretion, the union must consider the merits or the effect of the grievance, or the likely arbitration decision, and not decide the matter in a way that discriminates against the member on personal grounds.

The Supreme Court of Canada has established that a union is free to pursue legitimate goals and protect its interest, and the right of pursuing a grievance is that of the union, and not the employee. Protecting the collective interests and rights of the union membership means unions make difficult decisions which may at times have a negative impact on individual members, but can ultimately create benefits for everyone. For example, a union may not decide to pursue every single claim of sexual harassment against a particular manager, and instead advance only those claims with the most convincing evidence, in order to retain credibility with the arbitrator. However, protecting the interests of the membership is not necessarily as simple as looking at the interests of the simple majority. Instead, the union is required to carefully contemplate and consider specific accommodation needs and the appropriate human rights legislation.

THE COLLECTIVE BARGAINING PROCESS

The collective bargaining process is intended to help resolve differences between employers and employees. It is a managed conflict process, which uses specific steps to bring about resolution. But conflicts in collective

	EXHIBIT 19.4
B.C. Nurses Union and the Health Employers Association of British Columbia	

As opposed to the decentralized collective agreements that make up the majority of collective agreements in Canada, some industries are so interdependent that they create large scale collective agreements between multiple employers and multiple bargaining units. The B.C. Nurses Union represents 40,000 different allied health employees, including Registered Nurses, Licensed Practical Nurses, and other support staff, and negotiates with the Health Employers Association of British Columbia, which coordinates labour interests and human resources for over 260 healthcare employers in the province. Having a single expiration date for a contract can provide greater certainty for the employer by limiting the number of concurrent collective agreements, which could each create their own risk of a strike. The downside to greater centralization is that it often fosters greater formality and limits flexibility.

bargaining can occur before an agreement is even in place. Once certification is complete the union will negotiate a **first collective agreement** on behalf of the employees.

Bargaining Structure

The structure bargaining takes is one of the formative features that shape outcomes. The most common structure for bargaining in Canada is to have a single union and employer work out collective agreements from workplace to workplace. While this level of bargaining can simplify negotiations, and help address regional interests, it is also considerably less effective, and increases the risk of labour disputes if bargaining results in agreements where some workplaces strike a better or worse deal than others.

At times a single employer will need to negotiate with many unions at once and create separate collective agreements that are agreed on by all parties involved. Air Canada negotiates with three unions that represent pilots, ground crews, and flight attendants, and it needs to negotiate with all three unions at once and to create separate collective agreements that are agreed on by all parties involved. This is common with large employers, such as airlines, automobile manufacturers and rail and communication companies.

The Duty to Bargain in Good Faith

All negotiations require parties to enter discussions with the interest and the intention to try and reach a reasonable compromise. The **duty to bargain in good faith** is legislated in the *Canada Labour Code* and requires parties to make every reasonable effort to enter into a collective agreement. Although Labour Boards will rarely attempt to assess how fair a proposal by either side is, they can look at the conduct of the parties and the communications between them. The duty itself does not impose specific terms of the collective agreement, but it does impose a requirement that the parties conduct themselves appropriately and behave in a genuine fashion instead of simply posturing. The conduct of the parties is often viewed subjectively, and their efforts to create a collective agreement assessed objectively. The Duty to Bargain in Good Faith, although highly fact-specific, acts as a principle which referees labour disputes through the potential threat of equitable remedies imposed by the Board.

Assessing this conduct can be quite difficult for Labour Boards, but they will often look to see whether or not a party refuses to budge, hear the argument of the other side, or meet them entirely. They may look to see if parties attend and participate in meetings at a reasonable time, whether they have disclosed relevant information in a timely fashion, and if any form of deception is present by either side. A Board may find it notable that a representative in negotiations is not empowered to make any concessions or provide any flexibility, which could be considered a form of **surface bargaining**, where offers are made simply for the sake of appearances. An employer can submit a package to an employee and term it a fair and firm offer and then accompany it with a public relations campaign to portray the union as being unreasonable and greedy. Alternatively, the lack of concessions during negotiations may simply be considered a form of **hard bargaining**, where one side is just making a case vigorously. There is also typically no requirement that a representative be provided the authority to make a binding agreement at the outset.

The Collective Agreement

The **collective agreement** spells out the rights and obligations between the parties, and is a distinguishing feature in labour law from other forms of employment. A valid collective agreement will be in writing, will be between the employer and an association of employees, and must contain terms and conditions of employment. A collective agreement automatically extinguishes all previous contracts of employment with individuals because all employees in the bargaining unit are automatically included under its provisions. A collective agreement enhances the rights of employees beyond that of non-unionized employees by providing the right to strike as well as providing new remedies to workplace grievances. The interpretation of collective agreements can come under dispute well after the parties have put it on paper. An arbitrator will try to determine what the true intentions of the parties were without looking at any outside information, but may refer to minutes from negotiations or previous agreements if the language is ambiguous.

Mandatory Terms

Collective agreements are ultimately contracts between two parties, and like any contract the parties are free to determine the majority of its contents. However, most jurisdictions have placed some requirements on collective agreements. Some are procedural; in Ontario, for instance, the minimum length of a collective agreement is set at 12 months. Another is that only one collective agreement can be in place at a time. Other requirements are more substantive, describing what a collective agreement must include. Some of the common requirements for a collective agreement are:

- **Recognition Provision**
  Recognition provisions specify the nature of the bargaining unit that is party to the collective agreement. This provision can simply mirror the decision of the Labour Board that certified the union, or it can include a formula for expanding the bargaining unit in the future.

- **No Strikes or Lockouts Provision**
  No Strikes or Lockouts provisions forbid strikes and lockouts for the duration of the collective agreement.

- **Grievance and Arbitration Procedure**
  All collective agreements must in some way describe their method of settling disputes around the nature of the agreement without resorting to work stoppages. These sections tend to vary greatly, and usually go far beyond the statutory requirements.

- **Term Provision**

  Collective agreements are required to have a set start and end date and generally have a minimum length. Term provisions are often expanded to include when bargaining for the next collective agreement is expected to begin.

  Other Terms

  While not legislatively required to be in a collective agreement, bargains between Unions and Employers tend to include most of the following:

- **Management's Rights Provision**

  Management's rights provisions are added to agreements as a catch-all for powers not defined by other sections of the agreement. They generally state that the employer has the exclusive rights to determine elements of the employer's business, like staffing levels or work scheduling, which are not described in the collective agreement. They are also used to give the employer control over technological changes which could radically transform the workplace.

- **Seniority Provision**

  Seniority provisions are negotiated into a collective agreement for the benefit of the employees with the longest length of service to the company. The nature of seniority provisions can vary greatly between employers. The goal of seniority provisions is to provide job security to long term employees, and to protect against capricious management with respect to promotion, and in particular, dismissal. The provision works to protect senior employees from layoffs, as well as providing a fair method of handling choice of shifts and vacations, the assignment of benefits, and access to overtime.

- **Discipline Provision**

  Discipline provisions seek to outline the ability of an employer to discipline or terminate an employee. The provisions usually center around the concept of what constitutes "just cause" for discipline. They outline specific grievance procedures for discipline, sometimes including specific penalties.

- **Union Security Provision**

  Union security provisions exist to limit the ability of the employer to hire non-union members. **Union shop** provisions make membership in the union a requirement for all new hires, whereas **closed shop** provisions are used for larger unions, often in trades like carpentry or plumbing, to prevent the employer from hiring workers who are not already members of the union. These provisions contrast with **agency shop** provisions, which allow the employer to hire non-unionized workers so long as they pay union dues, as described above in the Rand Formula.

DISPUTE RESOLUTION DURING COLLECTIVE BARGAINING

The purpose of labour legislation is to resolve disputes between an employer and the union in the most amicable manner possible. Both the union and the employer should recognize that they will continue to be working with each other after resolving isolated incidents, and the law seeks to control and limit the punitive and retaliatory actions that each side can take against the other. This is a particular problem when a contract expires and a new one is being negotiated, or where a union has been certified and is negotiating its first contract. Labour legislation clearly recognizes the collective bargaining process as being especially prone to conflict as each side attempts to strengthen its bargaining position. To keep collective bargaining from running amok, labour legislation often builds mediation and other conflict control processes into the dispute resolution processes to resolve disputes between employers and trade unions that arise in the course of collective bargaining.

Depending on the jurisdiction the parties are bargaining in, a number of dispute resolution paths are available to them during contract negotiation. The parties usually have access to **mediation** at all stages of negotiation. Some provinces feature mandatory mediation, known as **conciliation**, before strikes and lockouts can occur. In order to minimize harm from labour disputes, some jurisdictions even impose arbitration as a binding dispute resolution mechanism (usually referred to as binding arbitration).

Mediation and Conciliation

Mediation can be used by the parties at any time, including during an arbitration process they had previously agreed to. The mediators are typically found in the private sector, unless the mediation is done in the context of conciliation, during the bargaining process, where the mediator is provided by the government. Governments actively involve themselves in assisting employers and trade unions in creating collective agreements. If either party is dissatisfied with direct bargaining over terms in a collective agreement, they are entitled to strike or, in the case of the employer, have a lockout. Before reaching that point the parties may first be required by labour legislation to go through conciliation. The vast majority of collective bargaining disputes in the federally regulated sector are resolved without any work stoppages, largely due to conciliation support provided by the government.

The provinces offer conciliation services because they have an interest in avoiding work stoppages in order to foster more harmonious work relationships and promote greater economic growth. They may also offer free preventive mediation and grievance mediation services, as well as specialized training through workshops, to help improve the effectiveness of communications between employers and the unions.

The Conciliation Process

Provinces will typically offer a trained conciliation officer to the parties for free to help resolve any disputes, usually when the parties have reached an impasse or are deadlocked and negotiation is not progressing. A union may conduct a strike vote by secret ballot towards the end of a collective agreement expiring or any time after it, but if it is a first collective agreement the vote will usually take place after the conciliation officer is appointed. A conciliation officer cannot impose a decision on the parties, but can help identify alternative perspectives to problems and offer suggestions on potential solutions by acting as a neutral third party. A conciliation officer will not make judgments on the merits and positions of each side. Conciliation boards also exist across Canada, but their use is in decline.

The desired outcome of a conciliation is for the parties to agree on a proposed contract, which is then voted on by the union's members. If the parties are unable to reach an agreement, the conciliator so reports to the government and the Ministry of Labour may provide a **no-board report** to the parties, which terminates the conciliation process. After this report is issued the parties will typically continue to negotiate for a short period of time, although the union, if it has a strike vote in place, may strike, and the company may lock out employees. The terms and conditions of any previous employment agreement are usually frozen throughout this process to avoid affecting the rights of either side. In some jurisdictions, however, the employer may also impose terms that alter the current collective agreement, until such time as a new one is negotiated or imposed by binding arbitration.

Federally regulated industries, like airlines and banks, have the benefit of the Federal Mediation and Conciliation Service (FMCS) for dispute resolution and dispute prevention. Federal labour disputes are subject to the Minister of Labour intervening by appointing a mediator to help resolve differences. While a conciliator is a member of the FMCS, a mediator is often someone with subject matter expertise in a high profile dispute of significant public interest who isn't from the FMCS itself.

Interest-Based Arbitration

Interest arbitration, as previously noted, is used to resolve any issues that the employer and the union may have during the collective bargaining process. Interest arbitration usually happens when the parties are unable to negotiate the terms in a collective agreement. If the parties are unable to come to an agreement, they are often referred to a third party to perform this sort of arbitration.

Binding Interest Arbitration

Sometimes negotiations stagnate during labour disputes and fail to move forward while a significant public interest is adversely affected. In these situations an approach of **binding interest arbitration** may be used to delegate power to a third party to resolve the impasse. The parties in a binding interest arbitration will be compelled to abide by the decision of the third party.

The composition of the arbitration board is through a nomination process by the union and the employer. If the parties cannot agree on the arbitrators, it may be appointed for them by the Labour Board. Arbitration boards will consider a broad spectrum of evidence in making their decisions, similar to the factors referred to in conciliation and mediation. The decision of an arbitration is final and binding, and can be enforced through the court system. If a party fails to abide by an arbitration they may be found in contempt of court.

The approaches that arbitrators can use in a dispute has been described by A.V. Subbarao as follows:[2]

- Final Offer Selection: an award based on one of the parties' final offer
- Last Offer by Issue: an award based on one of the parties' final offers on each issue
- Open Award: an independent award which disregards the final positions of the parties
- Compromise Award: a split in the difference between the final positions of the parties

A common critique of interest-based arbitration today is that it often fails to produce fair results, and is typically what would be considered an open award that may fail to meet the interests of either of the parties. There are other problems — bargaining units often use sector benchmarks and other settlements to determine their negotiating positions, rather than looking at the employer's ability to pay, knowing that arbitrators look for consistency between decisions. The employer may take an inflexible position to gather public favour, and then blame the arbitrator for the result of the labour dispute. Often neither side actually attempts to find a middle ground when interest-based arbitration is looming on the horizon.

---

[2] A.V. Subbarao, "The Impact of Binding Interest Arbitration on Negotiation and Process Outcome: An Experimental Study", (March 1978) 22:1 *Journal of Conflict Resolution* 79–103.

First Agreement Arbitration

If the parties are unsuccessful in their negotiations of a first collective agreement, they can apply to a Labour Board to attempt to have the settlement decided for them. In federal and provincial jurisdictions (except in New Brunswick and PEI) a process known as **first contract arbitration** (FCA) exists to resolve disputes over collective agreements. FCA is particularly useful where there is significant resistance by the employer in recognizing a union, or where there is bad faith bargaining. Some employers view FCA unfavourably because it allows a third party, who may not know the intricate details of their business, to decide the terms of employment on their behalf.

There are four types of FCA regimes across Canada:

1. Automatic: occurs when time limits to reach agreement have been exceeded and there is no evidence of fault.
2. Some fault, with Ministry referral: the Minister has to refer the parties to the Labour Board, and the application must show evidence of bad faith bargaining or dysfunctional bargaining.
3. Some fault, with direct application: the application made directly to the Labour Board demonstrates evidence that both parties have failed to agree and no further progress is possible.
4. Mediation is supported: available when progress is not possible and a strike vote has occurred.

In Quebec and Newfoundland, and at the Federal level, FCA is considered an exceptional remedy when there is no reasonable prospect of settlement. In Manitoba, there is an automatic access FCA model as soon as the applicable deadlines expire, but any work stoppages must terminate as soon as the FCA application is filed. A no-fault FCA regime is present in Ontario and Saskatchewan, and is available where the relevant statutes specify specific circumstances. British Columbia views FCA as a process to support collective bargaining and not as a remedy.

Important factors that an arbitrator must consider when he or she is determining the term of a FCA include the following:

1. The collective agreement should not contain innovative clauses; nor should the collective agreement be an industry standard agreement.
2. Objective criteria for equal terms and conditions provided to similar employees performing the same work.
3. Equality among employees.
4. The financial state of the employer and their ability to pay employees.
5. Economic and market conditions of that specific sector or industry.

Strikes, Lockouts and Picketing

Strikes are broadly defined in section 1 of the *Labour Relations Act*, and generally include any cessation of work by employees. There is a common understanding that the term can also apply to work slowdowns or a restricting of work-related activities. While a strike could occur with a group as small as two employees, for it to be a legally recognized strike, a majority of the union must have voted to strike. Strikes and lockouts have a negative effect not only on the business they shut down, and the employees that are involved, but the community as a whole.

Lockouts are described under the *Canada Labour Code* as the closing of a place of employment, a suspension of work by an employer or a refusal by an employer to continue to employ a number of their employees. They are usually done to compel employees to agree to terms or conditions of employment. While the lockout is ongoing, the employer is still required to bargain in good faith.

For a strike or lockout to be legal, a number of steps must be satisfied. Generally, there needs to have been at least one meeting during the course of negotiating a contract between the parties prior to the strike, and it must be clear that negotiations have broken down. Strikes prior to the expiry of a collective agreement are generally prohibited under most Canadian labour legislation. In most jurisdictions there is usually a form of non-binding mediation/conciliation offered by the government. If the mediation fails, lock-outs and strikes become legal after a brief period (two weeks in Ontario, but other jurisdictions vary).

An employer is able to discipline participants in an illegal strike, but participating in an illegal strike isn't usually sufficient by itself to sever an employment relationship. An example of an illegal strike is a **sympathy strike**, when a bargaining unit strikes on behalf of and in solidarity with another bargaining unit. These employees can also be disciplined, unless sympathy strikes are explicitly permitted in the collective agreement.

Picketing is a form of protest that often accompanies but is separate from a strike. Some workers who do not have the legal right to strike still picket, and some strikes occur without picketing. Picketing can also be a response to a lockout. Protesters will stand outside a location and either attempt to dissuade people from entering (in the case of a business) or share information about their grievances (in the case of a public service). Pickets are generally legal, so long as they are part of a legal strike and do not physically prevent entrance to a business. Picketing can even be a right protected under the *Charter* as a form of free expression, provided that it is conducted in a lawful manner.[3]

Picketing can be illegal if it encourages other workers to engage in an unlawful strike. The picketers cannot engage in criminal conduct, such as assaulting others or damaging property, and also cannot engage in civil wrongs, such as trespass or nuisance. When picketing occurs at the workplace where the dispute occurs, it is called **primary picketing**. If picketers target a business that is owned by their employer, but not the location of their labour, this is called **allied picketing**, and it occurs generally to make a strike even more visible and to place more pressure on an employer. **Secondary picketing** is a protest that targets a third party, normally a client of the business. If the picketers abide by the rules given above and do not engage in illegal behaviour, Secondary Picketing can be considered a valid form of protest.

Striking and picketing are both tactics used by unions to pressure employers during bargaining, but they aren't the only tools available to unions. Other tactics include slowing the pace of work and refusing overtime, co-ordinating the use of sick days, or completing tasks more slowly than usual. Unions can also start boycotts of their employers. Employers have the ability to pressure unions through lockouts, waiting out strikes, and continuing operations through use of supervisory personnel, replacement workers, or members that cross picket lines.

The ability of employers to strike and for employers to lock out is an important step in the collective bargaining agreement because they can break deadlocks. The restrictions placed on picketing and lockouts help achieve an appropriate balance between maintaining the freedoms of association and the interest in preventing industrial conflicts from getting out of control. The use of strikes and lockouts can frequently be a necessary step before the parties are ready to submit their disputes to binding arbitration.

---

[3] *R.W.D.S.U., Local 558 v. Pepsi-Cola Canada Beverages (West) Ltd.*, 2002 SCC 8, [2002] 1 S.C.R. 156.

THE GRIEVANCE AND ARBITRATION PROCESS

The sweeping labour reforms made in Canada during and following World War II forced employers to negotiate directly with unions. Before this time a collective agreement was not considered enforceable as a union did not have legal status and could not enter a contract, so courts would refuse to address any disputes around the collective agreement. The new labour law system allowed for enforcement of the collective agreement through a grievance system, which includes mandatory **rights arbitration**. A **grievance** is the claim by an employee that a violation of the collective agreement affecting the grievor's rights has occurred.

Steps in the Grievance Procedure

Each union will have a slightly different process for dealing with grievances, usually detailed in their collective agreements. Complaints about violations over the collective agreement are typically passed on to a **union steward**, who is a working representative of the union within the workplace. The steward will then meet the worker's supervisor, with the worker, in an informal meeting, and then send this complaint to the employer in writing within a certain timeframe. If the time limits are missed it is possible that the grievance may be dismissed entirely. The time limits are usually shorter earlier on in the procedure, and are longer the closer they get to arbitration.

The supervisor usually has the option of resolving the situation or providing a written response detailing why they believe the collective agreement has not been violated. If the grievance is not resolved at this point, it proceeds to more senior individuals, in both the union and the employer's structures, to resolve it at that level. If the conflict is still not resolved at these higher levels the collective agreement will state that the matter should be referred to binding arbitration.

Although grievances are intended to focus on violations of the collective agreement, the vast majority of grievances involve complaints over what could be considered implicit terms of the agreement, rather than explicit clauses. However, if an issue has not been addressed by the collective agreement at all, both sides may be reluctant to refer the matter to arbitration because it puts the decision making entirely in the hands of other individuals.

Unions have been known to use grievances strategically in labour relations. They can file specific grievances immediately prior to the negotiation of a new collective agreement to highlight the importance of an issue. They can use grievances as a means of protesting unilateral decisions by the employer, by filing large numbers of grievances in response. The grievance process can enhance union solidarity internally, but it can also benefit management by helping to highlight issues that are of priority to their workers, especially as these selectively move up the grievance process.

The Arbitration Hearing

Administrative tribunals developed in the Canadian legal system to allow for a quicker way to resolve conflicts than in the courts, and for the greater specialization of a tribunal to focus on a particular area of law. Labour tribunals provide a similar function, and recent decisions by the Supreme Court of Canada have conferred exclusive jurisdiction on them for resolving workplace disputes where the central issue emerges from the collective agreement.[4] However, what is a dispute emerging from the collective agreement and what

---

[4] *Weber v. Ontario Hydro* (1995), 125 D.L.R. (4th) 583 (S.C.C.).

EXHIBIT 19.5

Grievance Arbitration: Case Study

—————————————————————————— By Lisa Feinberg of Watson Burns LLP

Unions have been instrumental in advancing the rights of individuals who have historically faced discrimination. Through the collection of union dues, unions ensure that there are resources to litigate such instances of discrimination. Instances of discrimination are often complex and subtle, and as a result, the union and employer will seek the expertise of a private arbitrator to make a just decision.

The case of *National Grocers Co. v. United Food and Commercial Workers Unions, Local 1000A (Brown Grievance)* (2010), 198 L.A.C. (4th) 367 (Armstrong), illustrates how these issues can be resolved in the workplace.

The employer, National Grocers, had an obligation under the *Human Rights Code* to accommodate workers with disabilities up to the point of undue hardship. Over a five-year period, the employee Mr. Brown experienced injuries to his feet and hands at work. For the most part, the employer had accommodated him for these injuries by transferring him to do modified work. In 2005, Mr. Brown experienced a recurrence of a previous foot injury and his performance worsened. The employer's physician examined Mr. Brown and recommended that the employer send him for an independent medical examination. Instead, the employer summarily terminated Mr. Brown for inadequate performance. The union then filed a grievance on Mr. Brown's behalf. This grievance was eventually referred to arbitration.

In argument before the arbitrator, the employer claimed that Mr. Brown was either unwilling to perform his duties or to provide sufficient medical documentation to establish that he could not do so. The employer therefore argued that it had met its duty under the *Human Rights Code* and had given Mr. Brown an opportunity to provide information to prove that he needed accommodation. The union in turn argued that Mr. Brown had documented disabilities, and he was not properly accommodated for these disabilities. Beyond that, the union argued that the employer had not met its own policies for administering discipline progressively, that is, in stages.

The arbitrator found that the employer had not met its duty to accommodate Mr. Brown and was not justified in terminating him. The arbitrator emphasized the legitimate interests of the employer to ensure productive work, at para. 89:

> That the Employer was troubled, even frustrated, is understandable. The grievor had suffered and claimed incapacity during five of the seven calendar years of his employment. His productivity was at an unacceptably low level. Nonetheless, the WSIB had recognized that he was genuinely disabled [...]

However, on balance, the arbitrator found that the employer's ultimately illegal decision to terminate Mr. Brown was detrimental to his health, at para. 93:

> In the result, I find that by failing to pursue the disability dispute in the manner recommended by [the company doctor] and instead deciding to terminate the grievor's employment without conducting an independent evaluation, the Employer has failed to meet the onus of establishing that there was just cause for the grievor's discharge on March 7, 2006. I also find that his wrongful termination was the culminating event in the Employer's unsympathetic and disputative responses to the grievor's assertions of disability over an extended period, and that as a result the grievor has suffered and continues to suffer from anxiety, stress and general psychological trauma, the cumulative effect of which has had a seriously negative impact, both on his personal life and on his capacity to engage in productive employment.

When considering a suitable remedy, all parties agreed that Mr. Brown's reinstatement was not appropriate due to his troubled relationship with the employer. Instead, the arbitrator awarded Mr. Brown $25,000 in general damages and $20,000 in compensatory damages, in hopes that this sum would assist him in his efforts to return to the workplace.

is not continues to be debated by both employers and unions. Human rights disputes may also be heard by an arbitrator, except for issues of pay equity.

The arbitration process varies across Canada depending on the jurisdiction. In some provinces it is possible for the arbitrator to have mediated an issue before arbitrating on it. The parties will normally choose an arbitrator, or arbitral panel, based on their past experiences with the arbitrator and familiarity with their decisions. A panel will typically consist of a member selected by the union and the employer. The union and the employer decide on the chairperson together. If parties are unable to agree on a single arbitrator, or a single arbitrator is required in the circumstances, the arbitrator may be appointed for the parties by the Minister of Labour.

One of the challenges with parties selecting arbitrators is that they are more likely to agree on individuals who have a history of creating compromises. If an arbitrator is known for being too favourable to either the union or the employer, the other side is likely to object. However, not every labour dispute necessarily requires a compromise, and sometimes one side is clearly more in the wrong than the other. This leads to the critique of the process that arbitration will water down the merits of a dispute even where there is a strong case present.

In preparation for an arbitration, the parties will exchange lists of witnesses. The parties are required to produce all the relevant documents prior to the arbitration, but as a practical matter this rarely occurs in time or to the satisfaction of both parties.

Arbitration hearings are rather informal affairs. The proceedings do not resemble the judicial process in courts, which can often be a surprise to employees who appear before an arbitrator for the first time. A typical arbitration may also include numerous breaks to allow the parties the opportunity to discuss and independently resolve issues, but they can create an appearance of inefficiency for a grievor who believes that the matter is urgent.

The onus for proving a case lies with the party who is filing a grievance, and decisions are made on the evidence based on a **balance of probabilities**.[5] The exception to this rule is with discipline or dismissal cases, because it is assumed that only the employer would know the reasons for the decision and is best positioned to provide information and material to make that case. In making their submissions at arbitration, the employer will typically go first in discipline cases, and the union will go first for all other grievances. The parties will present their evidence and have their witnesses cross-examined to test their credibility. If an arbitrator is hearing a case on discipline or dismissal, they will usually look at the **William Scott factors**:

- Whether there has been "just and reasonable cause for some kind of discipline by the Employer"
- Was the discipline imposed "excessive in all the circumstances"
- The seriousness of the offence
- Whether the conduct was pre-meditated or repetitive, or whether it was an isolated incident
- The employee's history of service with the employer and history of discipline
- Whether the employer unsuccessfully attempted more moderate forms of discipline
- Whether the treatment is consistent with treatment to other employees in the same situation

[5] *F.H. v. McDougall*, 2008 SCC 53, [2008] 3 S.C.R. 41.

When interpreting collective agreements, arbitrators will only use precedent from other cases for persuasive value. Previously decided cases are not binding, as they would be in court. The purpose of tribunals is to avoid legal formalism and rigidity in order to meet the needs of the parties and to adapt to changing market conditions in a timely fashion. They will often look to negotiating history and past practices for interpretation. If there are any conflicts between the collective agreement and labour law statutes, the statute prevails. Some cases have even indicated that arbitrators have an obligation to apply statutes to collective agreements even if they are not incorporated into them.

The current arbitration system has some shortcomings around costs and delays. Arbitrators are appointed by the parties instead of by the state, which can give rise to its own disputes. An average arbitration often costs each side of the dispute between $8,000–$10,000 when accounting for legal costs, and it can take up to two years from the time of filing a grievance to the time when an arbitrator issues an award. The use of expedited arbitration procedures, where the parties exchange information in advance and put time limits on oral arguments, holds some promise in returning the arbitration process to its originally intended role of speedy and cost-effective dispute resolution.

THE FUTURE OF UNIONS IN CANADA

With changes to the Canadian economy unions in Canada are finding themselves facing different challenges than the industrial and mining dominated industries of the previous century. Some are finding that emerging issues like privacy law are of considerable importance and concern to their membership, as employers have increasing access to data about their workers and personal information about them outside the workforce. Other unions are finding new frontiers in fighting and combating workplace harassment, or promoting greater inclusion for vulnerable minorities.

Canadian unions are also finding fresh opportunities in the new economy. The service industry is the fastest growing part of the economy, and cannot be outsourced overseas the way many of the industrial jobs have been. Union drives at the Toronto area hotels in recent years have resulted in a union 75% density rate, which is extremely high for any sector. The UNITE HERE union has a membership in 47 hotels in the Greater Toronto Area (GTA) alone. Their involvement with these hotels has led in higher pay and better jobs for hotel workers, especially when contrasted to the hotel industry in Alberta, where there is considerably higher turnover and less unionization.

Regardless of whether they belong to a union, the entire Canadian workforce benefits from the changes and the protections unions secure as the improvements ripple through the workforce. If an employer in a non-union workplace is too heavy-handed or unreasonable in their approach to their employees, they risk a union organizing drive and potential certification. The protections in place surrounding the unionization process ensure that employers cannot threaten or intimidate employees from asserting their rights in a collective fashion. Rather than deal with the complications of unionization and the potentially higher administrative burden in labour relations, many employers proactively provide better working conditions so that employees don't believe there is a necessity in unionizing their workplace.

The decline of union membership in Canada should not then necessarily speak to the ultimate usefulness of unions in the new economy, but rather that working conditions are better than they have been in previous years. Polls by the Canadian Labour Congress show that 80% of its members are satisfied with the performance of their union. Despite these successes, Canada needs to maintain unions as part of its labour regime to ensure that working conditions do not deteriorate in the future, and to provide an alternative dispute mechanism to allow workplace conflicts to be effectively and efficiently resolved. Unions are a reminder of the horrendous workplace conditions that workers endured in the past; they are also a reminder and a reassurance that Canada has developed a system to prevent these practices from occurring again in the future.

CHAPTER SUMMARY

This chapter began by examining misconceptions about the role of unions. It then briefly described the background of labour disputes and the negative impacts on everyone involved and on the larger society, as part of the historical backdrop which led to the creation of our labour law regimes in Canada.

The next section covered the concept of union organizing, including the right to join and participate in a union, as well as illegal efforts employers make to prevent workers from doing so. The creation of the union through certification was described, as well as the unique labour structure in Canada where employees can benefit from the union, pay mandatory union dues, and still not be a member of that union. A union is required to represent all workers in their bargaining unit equally, even if that worker is not a union member or has anti-union views.

The chapter then discussed the collective bargaining process, with consideration of the particular bargaining structure in a workplace, and how different structures can reflect a shared "community of interest". The collective bargaining process was expanded on by touching on the requirement to bargain in good faith, and concluded with discussing where disputes could arise in this bargaining and when it may be necessary to use dispute resolution mechanisms such as mediation, conciliation, and arbitration. The chapter discussed the main types of disputes that were over the specific terms of a contract and their interpretation, although most disputes center around what parties claim are implied terms to a collective agreement.

The chapter moved on to examine what happens when negotiations break down, and what pressures the parties can apply to each other through strikes, lockouts, and picketing. Each of these measures has significant restrictions attached to it to ensure that there is no abuse, it does not get out of control, and the relationship between the parties is preserved as much as possible. The chapter examined the procedures that are in place for complaints of an individual nature through a grievance process and the mandatory mediation that is required in the absence of any resolution for these grievances. The chapter closed with a discussion of the role of unions in the future.

GLOSSARY OF NEW TERMS AND KEY CONCEPTS

agency shop A union security provision in a collective agreement that allows an employer to hire non-unionized employees, as long as these employees pay union membership dues.

allied picketing A form of picketing where employees picket a business that is owned by their employer, but not the location of their labour.

arbitration An extra-judicial dispute resolution process wherein a neutral third party conducts a hearing and makes a determination with respect to a dispute between the parties.

automatic certification A rarely used form of certification where the Labour Board certifies a union notwithstanding that the union was unable to demonstrate majority support on a vote in accordance with legislative requirements. Generally ordered as a remedy for unfair labour practices (where a Labour Board finds that majority support for unionization would have been demonstrated but for illegal actions of an employer).

back pay
A remedial measure used in the context of ULP Complaints and Grievances. Back pay requires an employer to pay an employee any missed wages, bonuses, and commissions retroactively to the date on which these payments were not made as a result of the employer's illegal conduct.

balance of probabilities
A standard of proof that requires the decision maker (judge, arbitrator) to find that, based on the available evidence, one party's version of the facts is more likely to be true than the other party's version of the facts. This standard of proof is generally used in civil matters, and can be contracted with the criminal standard of proof "beyond a reasonable doubt".

bargaining unit
A group of employees who share a "community of interest" and who are represented by a union in collective bargaining and other interactions with their employer.

binding interest arbitration
A dispute resolution arrangement wherein the parties agree in advance that they will submit their dispute to arbitration in the event that they are unable to agree, and agree they will abide by the decision of the third party.

certification
The process by which a union receives the legal right to represent a bargaining unit in a workplace.

certification application
The application a potential union files to its Labour Board to seek certification. It must include signed membership cards from employees from the workplace. The amount required can vary by jurisdiction.

closed shop provision
A union security provision in a collective agreement that prohibits employers from hiring any workers who are not already part of the union that exists in the workplace. This provision is often used in collective agreements of larger trade unions.

collective agreement
The employment contract between a bargaining unit and an employer that governs the employment terms of all members of the bargaining unit. Upon entering into a collective agreement, all previous employment contracts between the employer and individual members of the bargaining unit are extinguished.

community of interest
A group of employees who have common concerns and common goals relevant to the terms of every group member's employment.

conciliation
A form of legislatively required mediation, conducted with the assistance of a government appointed conciliator. Some provinces require employers and unions to attend conciliation before strikes and lockouts can occur.

doctrine of exclusive representation
The notion that, upon receiving certification, a union gains the exclusive right to bargain with an employer on behalf of all the members of a bargaining unit (including non-union members of the bargaining unit).

duty of fair representation
A duty that requires unions and their agents to treat every member of a bargaining unit equally, irrespective of that member's membership status or standing within the union.

duty to bargain in good faith
A legislated duty that requires parties to make every reasonable effort to enter into a collective agreement. The duty itself doesn't impose specific terms of the collective agreement, but does mandate that the parties conduct themselves appropriately and try to reach an agreement instead of posturing.

first collective agreement
The first agreement that is negotiated by the union on behalf of a bargaining unit following the certification of a union. The first collective agreement extinguishes all previous individual employment contracts between members of the bargaining unit and the employer.

first contract arbitration (FCA)
A form of interest arbitration that takes place when a union and employer are not able to agree on the terms of the first collective agreement. There are four types of FCA regimes across Canada: Automatic, fault-based with ministry referral, fault-based with direct application, and mediation supported FCA.

grievance
A claim by an employee that a violation of the collective agreement has occurred.

grievance arbitration	A form of rights-based arbitration, in which an arbitrator decides whether or not a contract violation has occurred.
hard bargaining	Taking a firm stance on an issue in bargaining, and being resistant to compromise.
interest arbitration	A form of arbitration wherein a neutral third party adjudicates the parties' interest-based disputes.
Labour Board	A regulatory body established by the labour statutes of each jurisdiction, whose mandate is to ensure that employers, unions, and employees comply with the applicable labour laws of the jurisdiction.
local	An offshoot of an existing union that represents a bargaining unit within a particular workplace. For example, CUPE is a nation-wide union that represents a large number of bargaining units across Canada; CUPE Local 79 represents a bargaining unit composed of civic employees in the City of Toronto.
lockout	The closing of a place of employment, a suspension of work by an employer or a refusal by an employer to continue to employ a number of their employees. Lockouts are designed to compel their employees to agree to terms or conditions of employment. While the lockout is ongoing, the employer is still required to bargain in good faith.
management's rights provision	A provision in the collective agreement that delineates the rights and powers of the employer which are not covered elsewhere in the collective agreement. The provision generally states that the employer has the exclusive rights to determine elements of his business that are not addressed in the agreement, and can also be used to account for changes that may radically transform the workplace (e.g., technological changes).
mediation	A dispute resolution process wherein a neutral third party (the mediator) attempts to facilitate a resolution between disputing parties. The mediator may make recommendations, but he/she is not empowered to make binding decisions without agreement from both parties.
no-board report	A report provided by the conciliator to the parties that terminates the conciliation process. A no-board report is generally issued where the parties are unable to resolve their dispute and further negotiation is unlikely to be fruitful.
picketing	A form of protest where protesters stand outside a location, and either attempt to dissuade people from entering in the case of a business, or share information about their grievances. Picketing often accompanies, but is separate from, a strike.
primary picketing	Picketing that occurs at the workplace location where the dispute occurs.
Rand formula	The legal requirement that mandates all members of a bargaining unit to pay union membership dues, irrespective of actual membership in the union.
reinstatement	A remedial measure used in the context of unfair labour practice complaints and grievances. Reinstatement requires an employer to give an employee his/her job back on the same terms as existed prior to the wrongful restriction or termination of employment.
representation vote	A vote taken by employees in a workplace to determine whether there is majority support for the formation of a union in that workplace. Depending on the jurisdiction, a representation vote may be a mandatory or an optional component of the certification process.
rights arbitration	A form of arbitration wherein a neutral third party adjudicates the parties' rights-based disputes. Grievance arbitration is a form of rights arbitration.
secondary picketing	Picketing that targets a third party other than the employer, normally a client of the employer.
seniority provision	Provisions that are negotiated into a collective agreement for the benefit of employees with the longest length of service in the workplace. The goal of seniority provisions is to provide job security and delineate perquisites to long term employees (e.g., sick days and other benefits that are tied to length of service).

strike	A labour disruption, which is generally characterized by a cessation of work by employees but can also include work slowdowns or a restricting of work-related activities by employees. Striking is a method that enables employees to put pressure on employers in the context of collective bargaining.
surface bargaining	A form of bad faith bargaining in collective bargaining where a party merely goes through the motions with no intention of reaching an agreement.
sympathy strike	Occurs when one bargaining unit strikes on behalf of and in solidarity with another bargaining unit.
unfair labour practice (ULP)	Any action that is prohibited by the labour laws of a jurisdiction. An action is characterized as a ULP if it interferes with a worker's right to form, join or participate in a union, or if it interferes with a union's ability to fully and properly represent its members.
ULP complaint	A remedial process designed to address unfair labour practices. If an employee or union representative believes that an employer or union is engaging in an unfair labour practice, a ULP complaint can be filed with the Labour Board.
union busting	Activities or measures taken by employers (or governments) that have the goal and/or effect of restricting or interfering with the formation and effective operation of unions in the workplace.
union shop	A union security provision that makes membership in the union mandatory for all new employees that are hired into a unionized workplace.
union steward	A working representative of the union within the workplace.
William Scott factors	A list of factors that will be considered by the arbitrator in a hearing involving discipline or dismissal.

REVIEW QUESTIONS

1. What are unfair labour practices (ULP)? Give an example of an unfair labour practice by an employer, and discuss how such a practice could be addressed and remedied.

2. Describe the three methods by which a union can become certified in Canada.

3. What is a bargaining unit? Who forms part of the bargaining unit?

4. What is the duty of fair representation, and what are the sources of this duty?

5. Describe the different bargaining structures that are legally possible in Canada. Which is the most widely used?

6. What are the differences between "interest arbitrations" and "rights arbitrations"?

7. Describe how the conciliation process works.

8. What is the Duty to Bargain in Good Faith, and what are its elements?

DISCUSSION QUESTIONS

1. What functions do unions serve in Canada today? What is the importance of these functions?

2. What are some current obstacles that unions in Canada are facing? What impact, if any, do these obstacles have on unionized workers and on workers seeking union representation?

3. Why is the duty to bargain in good faith important? What might be the ramifications if the duty to bargain in good faith was not part of federal and provincial labour legislation?

4. Discuss the importance of the duty of fair representation. What are the benefits and limitations of the duty of fair representation? Give an example of a situation where the duty of fair representation may result in tensions within the bargaining unit.

5. Discuss the importance of the right to strike, and in particular, the competing interests of employees, employers, and the general public. Consider the following issues:

   (i) Should the right to strike be limited? If so, under what circumstances should it be permitted?
   (ii) What types of limitations might be appropriate?
   (iii) Should employers be allowed to hire replacement employees during a strike?

SUGGESTED READING AND OTHER RESOURCES

B.W. Burkett, D.G. Gilbert, J.D.R. Craig, & M. Gavins, *Federal Labour Law and Practice* (Toronto: Canada Law Book, 2013).

D.D. Carter, *Labour Law in Canada* (London, U.K.: Kluwer Law International, 2002).

H.J. Glasbeek & H.W. Arthurs, *Labour Law & Industrial Relations in Canada* (Markham, Ont.: Lexis Law Pub., 1994).

WEBSITES

CanLII: <http://www.canlii.ca/en/index.html>

The International Labour Organization [I.L.O.] — A United Nations agency: <www.ilo.org>

The Law Dictionary: <http://thelawdictionary.org/>

LawofWork website: <http://lawofwork.ca/>

Listing of Federal and Provincial Labour Boards across Canada including URLs for board websites: <http://lancasterhouse.com/labourMinBoardsTribunals/boards>

UFCW (United Food and Commercial Workers Union) website: <http://www.ufcw.ca>

Index

For ease of use, this index appears in both volume 1 and volume 2.
The page numbers span across both volumes.